East Asian Social Science Monographs

The Demographic Dimension in Indonesian Development

The Demographic Dimension in Indonesian Development

Graeme J. Hugo
Terence H. Hull
Valerie J. Hull
Gavin W. Jones

SINGAPORE
OXFORD UNIVERSITY PRESS
OXFORD NEW YORK
1987

Oxford University Press

Oxford New York Toronto
Petaling Jaya Singapore Hong Kong Tokyo
Delhi Bombay Calcutta Madras Karachi
Nairobi Dar es Salaam Cape Town
Melbourne Auckland

and associates in
Beirut Berlin Ibadan Nicosia

British Library Cataloguing in Publication Data

The Demographic dimension in Indonesian
   development.—(East Asian social science
   monographs).
   1. Indonesia—Population
   I. Hugo, Graeme J.   II. Series
   304.6'09598   HB3647
   ISBN 0-19-582699-X

Library of Congress Cataloging-in-Publication Data

The Demographic dimension in Indonesian development.

   (East Asian social science monographs)
   Bibliography: p.
   Includes index.
   1. Indonesia—Population. I. Hugo, Graeme.
II. Series.
HB3647.D45 1987   304.6'09598   87-11021
ISBN 0-19-582699-X

Printed in Singapore by Kim Hup Lee Printing Co. Pte. Ltd.
Published by Oxford University Press Pte. Ltd.,
Unit 221, Ubi Avenue 4, Singapore 1440

Sekedar sumbangsih untuk rekan-rekan di Indonesia yang sedang giat membangun untuk nusa dan bangsa.

(A small contribution for friends in Indonesia who are working tirelessly to develop their nation.)

Preface

BY any yardstick, Indonesia must be ranked as one of the world's major countries, though it clearly ranks much higher in terms of its population (fifth) than in terms of its GDP (twenty-second). It straddles vital sea links between Asia and Europe, is one of the world's major oil producers, and scored impressive achievements in economic and social development during the 1970s and early 1980s. It also faces daunting problems in bringing prosperity to its vast population, problems which have been underscored by the drastic fall in the price of oil in 1986.

The four authors have each been undertaking demographic analysis of Indonesia since the early 1970s, and have developed an affection for the country and its people. Our efforts to put together this volume began in the late 1970s in the belief that our collective experience of Indonesia and a pooling of our different specialities would result in a richer and more authoritative volume than any of us could have hoped to produce individually. We have listed our names alphabetically as authors in recognition of the truly collaborative nature of the book, with no one author playing a dominant role.

The definitive work on population history in Indonesia by Professor Widjojo Nitisastro, though published more than a quarter of a century ago, remains the most important starting point for any serious student of the subject. This volume is intended to extend and update that text. A great deal of information has emerged since the earlier work, and a new generation of Indonesian demographers has carried out important basic research, not all of which could be reviewed here.

One of the strongest motivations underlying our work is the belief that demographic trends are intimately bound up in the process of economic development and improvement of welfare. The demographic trends themselves therefore need to be carefully analysed and their complex interactions with economic and social development explored. Too often today, policy-makers and the public at large talk of solving 'the population problem'. We hope that this book will demonstrate the shortsightedness of such an attitude. There are many population problems, not one, and they are never finally solved. Each generation must adapt to a changing set of circumstances. Individuals and families must face the challenges of family formation, decisions about education, work and migration, and—finally—

death, seeking their own personal accommodation to these basic life events; the State, in representing the public interest, must determine whether the sum of these individual accommodations is consistent with agreed goals of the society.

We hope this book will ring true to our Indonesian friends and help explain to the world at large the diversity of Indonesia, its tremendous achievements, and the great challenges it still faces.

Canberra   GRAEME J. HUGO
November 1986   TERENCE H. HULL
                                                      VALERIE J. HULL
                                                      GAVIN W. JONES

Acknowledgements

WE would like to thank many people and organizations who have contributed to the completion of this book. Each of us has benefited immeasurably from working with colleagues in Indonesia over the last fifteen years. Indeed, what is in this volume is shaped not only by our own research, but also by extended periods of field-work and living in Indonesia and by our interaction with Indonesian friends to whom we are extremely grateful. Within Indonesia, we have gained many types of assistance and encouragement from the Central Bureau of Statistics (BPS), the National Family Planning Co-ordinating Board (BKKBN) and the State Ministry for Population and Environment (KLH), and we wish to record our heartfelt appreciation to each of these organizations, their leaders and staff. Similarly, the two institutions in Australia with which we have been associated over the period of writing this book, the Australian National University and the Flinders University of South Australia, have generously made facilities and resources available which have assisted us greatly in bringing this book to completion, and we acknowledge their important assistance. We would also like to thank the many people who have worked with us on the various chapters. In particular, to Pat Quiggin, Nancy Kuskie, Marian Obenchain, Patricia Pyne, Deborah Faulkner, Margaret Young and Janet Matta, who have been our research assistants at various stages of the project, we owe a considerable debt of thanks. The index was compiled by Pat Quiggin and we would especially like to thank her for the skill and enthusiasm which she brought to this task. Similarly, to Mrs Patricia Mooney and Mrs Jean Lange who typed the various drafts of chapters and to Andrew Little and Jens Smith who drafted many of the maps and diagrams. To these people, and to many colleagues in both Indonesia and Australia who have commented on earlier drafts of the material included in the book, we owe a considerable debt of gratitude.

Contents

Appendices

Tables

Figures

Abbreviations and Glossary

abangan	Muslims still strongly influenced by pre-Islamic Javanese belief
adat	customary law
anak buah	client (as in patron–client relationships)
ASEAN	Association of South-East Asian Nations
ASMEN IV KLH	(*Asisten Menteri, Kependudukan dan Lingkungan Hidup*) Assistant Minister for Population in the State Ministry for Population and Environment
Bahasa Indonesia	Indonesian language
Balita	0–4 year olds
bangsawan	nobility
bapak	lit. 'father'; patron (as in patron–client relationships)
Bappeda	(*Badan Perencanaan Pembangunan Daerah*) Provincial Level Development Planning Board
Bappenas	(*Badan Perencanaan Pembangunan Nasional*) National Development Planning Board
becak	pedicab
BKIA	(*Badan Kesehatan Ibu dan Anak*) maternal and child health centres
BKKBN	(*Badan Koordinasi Keluarga Berencana Nasional*) National Family Planning Co-ordinating Board
BPS	(*Biro Pusat Statistik*) Central Bureau of Statistics
Butsi	development volunteer
cacah	household units used in population counts in Java in colonial times
camat, bupati	appointed officials at head of *kecamatan* and *kabupaten* administrations respectively
Candak Kulak	credit-providing agency
CBR	Crude Birth Rate
CDR	Crude Death Rate
dana sehat	community health insurance scheme
desa halaman	village of origin
doktor djawa	native medical practitioner (colonial period)
DPR	(*Dewan Perwakilan Rakyat*) House of People's Representatives (national and provincial parliaments)

EKUIN	(*Ekonomi, Keuangan dan Industri*) group of ministers dealing with economic matters, industry and finance
E_0^o	life expectancy at birth
FELDA	Federal Land Development Authority (Malaysia)
GBHN	(*Garis-garis Besar Haluan Negara*) Broad Outlines of State Policy
GDP	Gross Domestic Product
GNP	Gross National Product
gotong royong	mutual self-help
GRR	Gross Reproduction Rate
hygiene mantri	paramedical officer/health officer
IKIP	(*Institut Keguruan Ilmu Pendidikan*) Teachers' College
IMF	International Monetary Fund
IMR	Infant Mortality Rate
Index of Dissimilarity	Measures the extent of non-overlap between two percentage distributions. It can range in value from 0 to 100 and may be interpreted as showing the proportion of one distribution that would need to be reorganized to fit the other
Inpres	(*Instruksi Presiden*) presidential instruction
IUD	intrauterine device
Jabotabek	Jakarta, Bogor, Tangerang and Bekasi
jamu	traditional herbal tonics
kabupaten	regency, or sub-provincial administrative district
kader gizi	nutrition cadres
kader kesehatan	health cadres
KDI	Korean Development Institute
kecamatan	subdistrict of the *kabupaten* or *kotamadya*
kelurahan	administrative village, village complex, below the *kecamatan*
KESRA	(*Kesejahteraan Rakyat*) group of ministers dealing with issues related to the people's welfare
KIK	(*Kredit Investasi Kecil*) small investment credit
KKN	(*Kuliah Kerja Nyata*) university student work experience
KLH	(*Kependudukan dan Lingkungan Hidup*) State Ministry for Population and Environment
kotamadya	municipality, having the same administrative status as a *kabupaten*
Leknas	(*Lembaga Ekonomi dan Sosial Nasional*) National Institute of Economic and Social Research
LKBN	(*Lembaga Keluarga Berencana Nasional*) National Family Planning Institute
lurah	elected village official
madam	to leave one's natural area and cross the sea with the aim of increasing one's wealth

madrasah	Islamic schools
membendung	dam up
mencari pengalaman	to seek experience
merantau	to travel away from community of origin for lengthy periods
mondok	to stay in one place for several months
MPR	(*Majlis Perwakilan Rakyat*) People's Consultative/ Deliberative/Representative Assembly
mufakat	consensus decision-making
musjawarah	mutual deliberation
nginep	to stay in a place several days before returning home
nglaju	travel to a place but return home in same day
NUDSP	National Urban Development Strategy Project
Padat Karya	labour intensive project
palawidja	non-rice food crops
pasang surut	tidal irrigation
pax Neerlandica	end of internecine wars in Java in the early nineteenth century
penghijauan	'greening' (reforestation) programme
pindah	migrate to another place
PKBI	(*Perkumpulan Keluarga Berencana Indonesia*) Indonesian Planned Parenthood Association
PKMD	(*Pembangunan Kesehatan Masyarakat Desa*) Village Community Health Development Programme
POLKAM	(*Polisi dan Keamanan*) group of ministers dealing with external and internal security
pondok or *pesantren*	a mosque-linked religious school
Posyandu	Integrated Service Post (for health services)
prau	traditional sailing boat
prokesa	(*promotor kesehatan*) village-level health workers
Puskesmas	(*Pusat Kesehatan Masyarakat*) community health centres
Repelita	(Rencana Pembangunan Lima Tahun) Five Year Development Plan
revolusi colt	transport revolution (especially minibuses)
RGDP	Regional Gross Domestic Product
Rho	Spearmans Rank Correlation Coefficient
romusha	forced labour (during Japanese Occupation)
Rp	Rupiah—Indonesian unit of currency
Sakernas	National Labour Force Survey
santri	a person consciously and exclusively Moslem
sawah	wet rice
Sensus Industri	Industrial Census
SLAR	side-looking air borne radar
Statistik Industri	Industrial Statistics (published by CBS)
sukubangsa	ethnicities
Supas	Intercensal Survey

surat keterangan	
lalu lintas	letter of permission to leave home place
Susenas	National Social and Economic Survey
SVRP	Sample Vital Registration Project
team penertiban	control team
tegal	dry land cultivation
TFR	Total Fertility Rate
transmigration	
swakarsa	partly sponsored transmigrant
umum	public, general
UN	United Nations
UNDP	United Nations Development Programme
UNFPA	United Nations Fund for Population Activities
UNICEF	United Nations Children's Fund
UPGK	(*Usaha Perbaikan Gizi Keluarga*) Family Nutrition Improvement Programme
USAID	United States Agency for International Development
UUD '45	(*Undang-Undang Dasar '45*) Indonesian Constitution
VCDC	Village Contraceptive Distribution Centre
VISTA	Volunteers in Service to America
Volkstelling 1930	1930 Census
wereng	brown leaf hopper which destroyed rice crops in the 1970s
WHO	World Health Organization
YIS	(*Yayasan Indonesia Sejahtera*) Indonesian Welfare Foundation

Notes on Contributors

GRAEME J. HUGO, Reader in Geography, School of Social Sciences, The Flinders University of South Australia, has been working on Indonesian population issues and problems (especially those associated with population movement, distribution and urbanization) since 1972. He has been especially involved in research and teaching at Pajajaran University in Bandung and Hasanuddin University in Ujung Pandang.

TERENCE H. HULL, Senior Research Fellow and Co-ordinator, International Population Dynamics Program, Department of Demography, Research School of Social Sciences, Australian National University. He worked for several years with the Population Studies Centre at Gadjah Mada University, Yogyakarta and conducted research and published widely in the areas of fertility, family planning, mortality and population policy in Indonesia.

VALERIE J. HULL, Director of Sectoral Studies, Australian Development Assistance Bureau, Canberra. She has held research fellow positions with the Department of Demography, Australian National University and the Population Studies Centre at Gadjah Mada University and is widely recognized for her work in Indonesia on fertility, family planning, the role of women and health.

GAVIN W. JONES, Professorial Fellow, Department of Demography, Research School of Social Sciences, Australian National University. He is the author of several books and many papers concerned with the demography of Asian countries and has had extensive research experience in several of those countries. He has held a number of advisory and consultancy positions in Indonesia, including extended periods with the Demographic Institute at the University of Indonesia and most recently with the Indonesian Ministry of Population and Environment.

1 Introduction: Unity in Diversity

Introduction

IN any consideration of the world's population, Indonesia must loom large. It is the fifth most populous nation after China, India, the USSR and the USA, and its 164 million people (1985) make up more than half of the total population living in the South-East Asian region (Figure 1.1). It is somewhat surprising then that no major comprehensive systematic study of

FIGURE 1.1

South-East Asia: Population of Countries, 1983

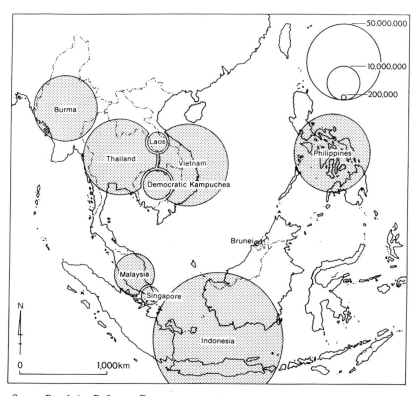

Source: Population Reference Bureau.

Indonesia's contemporary demography exists, especially as Indonesia has seen some of the world's largest-scale attempts to initiate policies and programmes with the explicit purpose of changing the rate of growth and patterns of distribution of its population. The aim of this book is to provide an overview of Indonesia's current demographic situation. The results of the 1980 Census of Indonesia make it possible to establish details of recent trends in population growth and its components, population composition and distribution. However, an understanding of these patterns is dependent upon how they are interrelated with, and have an impact on, wider social and economic change in Indonesia. Our objective here is not only to provide a systematic statistical analysis of demographic change in Indonesia but also to attempt to relate these trends to economic development and social change within Indonesia.

Indonesia's demography has much in common with other Third World nations. Table 1.1 shows that Indonesia has comparatively high fertility and mortality levels, although, as is explained in subsequent chapters, there have been significant reductions in these levels during the last decade. Hence Indonesia's current rate of population growth is somewhat lower than the average for the South-East Asian region and for less developed countries more generally. However, Indonesia's age structure as depicted in Figure 1.2 is the archetypical 'young' or 'expansive' distribution charac- teristic of many Third World countries, with each age cohort significantly larger than the cohort born before it. Such a structure means of course, in the short term, that enormous pressure is being (and will be) placed on the education system and other service delivery systems as well as upon the

FIGURE 1.2

Indonesia: Age–Sex Distribution at the 1961 and 1980 Censuses

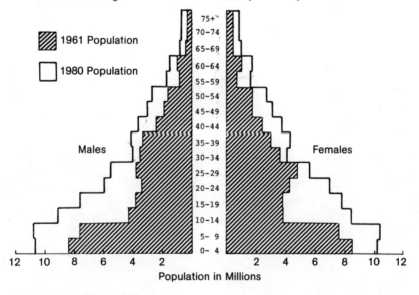

Source: Central Bureau of Statistics.

TABLE 1.1

Indonesia: Some Basic Demographic Indicators, 1984

Indicator	Indonesia	South-East Asia	Less Developed Countries		More Developed Countries
			Excluding China	*Including China*	
1. Total population (in millions)	161.6	393.0	2,561.0	3,596.0	1,166.0
2. Natural increase (annual per cent)	2.1	2.2	2.4	2.1	0.6
3. Doubling time in years (at current rate)	33.0	31.0	29.0	33.0	112.0
4. Projected population to year 2000 (in millions)	210.6	529.0	3,676.0	4,980.0	1,270.0
5. Infant mortality rate	92.0	85.0	107.0	94.0	19.0
6. Life expectancy at birth	49.0	56.0	55.0	58.0	73.0
7. Total fertility rate	4.4	4.5	5.1	4.4	2.0
8. Per cent population aged under 15 years	39.0	40.0	40.0	38.0	23.0
9. Per cent population aged 65 or more	3.0	3.0	4.0	4.0	12.0
10. Urban population (%)	22.0	24.0	36.0	32.0	71.0

Source: Population Reference Bureau, 1984.

labour market. However, in the longer term, the huge numbers of young women entering the fecund age categories over the next decade or so indicate that there is a tremendous momentum built in to the age structure which will ensure that rapid population growth will continue even if there is a reduction in intrinsic fertility.

Table 1.1 indicates that Indonesia's level of urbanization is below average for the South-East Asian region; however, it will be shown later that this figure is somewhat misleading and that population movement between rural and urban areas, as well as between rural areas, is more complex and on a greater scale than is shown in conventional demographic measures.

Before moving on to explore in detail Indonesia's major demographic trends and patterns, we need to establish the context in which demographic change is occurring. Such a setting of the scene is necessary if we are to approach an understanding not only of these population trends but also their major causes and effects. Hence the initial section of this book is devoted to briefly establishing some of the contextual elements which are most important to an understanding of Indonesia's contemporary demography. In particular, the historical and developmental context of population change are sketched in as necessary background to later chapters. In the present chapter, we will introduce some themes which occur throughout this study and which are basic to an understanding of Indonesian population trends.

Population Change and Development

The complex relationships between population change, economic development and social change remain little understood—perhaps due partly to a tendency for many demographers to eschew theory and concentrate upon the careful measurement of trends in situations in which available data is limited and/or of poor quality. Until the early 1970s, there was a general acceptance of the view that demographic change was very largely a function of economic development. As development proceeded, it was believed, there was a definite sequence of stages in the decline of fertility and mortality levels from the high levels obtaining in traditional societies following the well-known classical Demographic Transition model (Notestein, 1945). Similarly Zelinsky (1971: 221-2) put forward a 'Mobility Transition' which integrated the third basic demographic process of population movement into traditional Demographic Transition Theory and which stated that: 'There are definite patterned regularities in the growth of personal mobility through space-time during recent history, and these regularities comprise an essential component of the modernization process.' Hence demographic change was generally seen as a dependent variable, with predominantly economic processes associated with the growth of a modern urban industrial society being the fundamental explanatory forces. This view is perhaps best encapsulated in the catchcry which emerged from the 1974 World Population Conference in Bucharest that 'development is the best contraceptive'. It was also reflected in the attempt by the United Nations to apply a 'threshold hypothesis' that aimed 'to identify a relatively narrow range of values for a number of social and economic indicators which when reached would signal the onset of a downturn in fertility levels' (Jones, 1984a: 2).

During the 1970s, this slavish acceptance of an economic determinism in explaining demographic change crumbled as more demographers focused their research upon the development and testing of explanations of demographic change. Historical studies of the European demographic transition (for example, Coale, 1973; van de Walle and Knodel, 1980) suggested that cultural and linguistic differences were often more salient than differences in levels of development in explaining geographical variations in fertility at any given point in time. Caldwell (1976; 1982), drawing on contemporary Third World experience, reformulated Demographic Transition Theory by explaining stable high fertility in pre-transitional societies and the onset of fertility decline in terms of changes in the direction of net intergenerational flows of wealth. While recognizing that economic changes associated with 'modernization' are sufficient to initiate a reversal of this net flow, Caldwell maintains that they are not necessary and that the fundamental causes of the decline are social, involving changes in the pattern of interrelationships within families. Knodel (1977: 244–8) has stressed the importance of diffusion processes, with family limitation being viewed as innovative behaviour which may not only diffuse rapidly throughout a population but also itself serve as a catalyst to change fertility desires, especially if it occurs in a context of social and economic change. Hull (1978), among others, has shown that mass communication, along with more ready availability of improved birth control procedures, can facilitate rapid fertility declines even without much improvement in the traditional indicators of economic development. The importance of a modern communication system as well as the school system in the rapid transformation of family structure and aspirations has also been stressed by Caldwell (1976) and Freedman (1979).

It is clear therefore that explanation of fertility decline in pure economic-development deterministic terms is inappropriate. As Jones (1984a: 3) has concluded:

... social and economic forces impinge on fertility through changes in age at marriage, family structure, value of children, interspouse relationships, practice of contraception and abortion and other variables which differ widely among different cultures and can be expected to alter differently when exposed to the same kind of social and economic changes. Moreover diffusion of ideas might be just as important as changes in the underlying social and economic conditions in ushering in fertility decline.

Not only are the relationships between development and demographic changes much more complex than has generally been assumed, but also the causal linkages between them are not always one-way. There is a vast literature on the economic consequences of demographic trends, which highlights the wide range of possible causal linkages (Cassen, 1976; National Research Council, 1986; McNicoll, 1984).

In this book, we explore some of these interrelationships between population change and development; it is therefore necessary at the outset to establish Indonesia's present status with respect to economic and social development. A detailed examination of this complex topic is not possible here, but a few points need to be made. The World Bank (1983: 142) divides developing countries into low and middle-income economies (with 1981 GNP per person of US$410 being the threshold) and categorizes Indonesia as a 'middle-income, oil exporting' country. In 1978, Indonesia was classified as the best off of the thirty-eight countries classified as 'low income' (World Bank, 1980: 110) and, in the intervening period, made the transition to the lower levels of the middle-income countries. Hence, as far as the (albeit inadequate) macro-indicator of GNP per capita is concerned, Indonesia is in the middle group of the so-called developing countries and is upwardly mobile within that group. This improved position is largely due to greatly increased foreign exchange earnings from oil exports during the last decade. However, with the dramatic fall in oil prices during the mid-1980s, this situation was transformed, and Indonesian policy-makers and planners were presented with 'a daunting prospect of declining tax revenues and an expanded deficit in the balance of payments' (Glassburner, 1986: 1). This has put a brake on economic growth in the short term at least and, almost certainly, will have significant implications for longer-term economic development.

The improvement notwithstanding, however, Indonesia is squarely within that group of countries usually designated 'developing' or 'less developed'. The macro-indicators listed in Table 1.2 reflect this and, although such data should be interpreted with considerable caution, they also establish the broad national context of social and economic development in Indonesia. The table shows that GNP per capita for Indonesia in 1984 was double the average for developing countries, but still only a fraction of that for developed nations. The annual rate of growth in GNP per capita over the last two decades has been high, and there is agreement among most commentators that there has been a general improvement in living standards over the last decade, especially in rural areas.

However, the extent to which such figures as those in Table 1.2 are fully indicative of changes in the level of well-being of the majority of Indonesians is questionable, and many argue that much of the improvement has been absorbed by a relatively small wealthy élite. An examination of studies of income distribution in Indonesia presents a picture which Booth and Sundrum (1981: 214) describe as being a 'blurred and confused one'. Figure 1.3 presents income distribution data for 1976 and indicates a significant degree of inequality with the gini-coefficient being 33. Commentators such as Papanek (1980: 56) maintain that such a distribution can be regarded as relatively egalitarian when set against other comparable countries. The fact remains, however, that there are very large numbers of Indonesians living in poverty.

TABLE 1.2

Indonesia: Some Basic Social and Economic Indicators in the Early 1980s

Indicator	Indonesia	Less Developed Countries	More Developed Countries
1. GNP per capita			
US dollars 1982	580	280	11,070
average annual growth (%), 1960–82	4.2	3.0	3.3
2. Average annual growth (%) in GDP			
1960–70	3.9	4.5	5.1
1970–82	7.7	4.5	2.8
3. Volume of cereal imports 1974	1,919	22,774	65,494
(thousands of metric tons) 1982	1,912	29,260	66,103
4. Fertilizer consumption (per hectare of arable land)			
1970	119	184	985
1981	744	581	1,191
5. Average index of food production per capita (1969–71=100) 1980–2	117	110	114
6. Percentage of labour force in agriculture			
1960	75	77	18
1980	58	72	6
7. Average annual growth of labour force (%)			
1970–82	2.5	2.0	1.2
1980–2000	1.9	2.0	0.6
8. Population per physician, 1980	11,530	5,772	554
9. Daily per capita calorie supply, 1981	2,342	2,219	3,396
10. Number enrolled in primary school as percentage of age group, 1981	100	94	101
11. Number enrolled in secondary school as percentage of age group, 1981	30	34	90
12. Number enrolled in higher education as percentage of population aged 20–24, 1981	3	4	37
13. Adult literacy rate (%), 1980	62	52	99
14. Central government expenditure per capita (1975 US dollars), 1981			
defence	12.7	18.3	13.6
education	7.9	5.9	5.1
health	2.5	2.9	11.4

Source: World Bank, 1984.

Leiserson *et al.* (1980: 84) established a poverty line in Indonesia as being an average per capita monthly expenditure of Rp 3,000 and used data from the 1976 National Social and Economic Survey (*Susenas*) to show the incidence of poverty. Their data, presented in Table 1.3, show that half of the rural population and a fifth of urban dwellers had expenditure levels falling below the poverty line, although significant regional differentials are

FIGURE 1.3

Indonesia: Distribution of Income, 1976

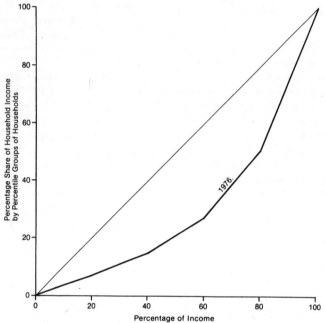

Source: Susenas.

TABLE 1.3

Incidence of Poverty in Urban and Rural Sectors of Indonesian
Regions, 1976

Region	Percentage of Population with Monthly Per Capita Consumption Below Rp 3,000		Rural : Urban Ratio
	Urban	*Rural*	
Sumatra	13.5	28.5	2.1
Java	20.7	58.7	2.8
Jakarta	7.5	—	—
West Java	24.8	40.7	1.6
Central Java	33.4	67.8	2.0
Yogyakarta	21.5	60.5	2.8
East Java	28.0	66.3	2.4
Bali–Nusa Tenggara	27.4	49.5	1.8
Kalimantan	13.9	17.3	1.2
Sulawesi	15.7	45.0	2.9
Maluku	31.2	61.9	2.0
Indonesia	18.7	50.2	2.7

Source: Leiserson *et al.*, 1980: 84.

in evidence. Several authors (for example, Arief, 1979; Dapice, 1980) have suggested that there was a deterioration in income distribution for much of the 1970s, especially in rural areas. This situation subsequently improved in the late 1970s and early 1980s. Collier *et al.* (1982: 86), for example, maintain: 'Not only did rural development accelerate during this period, but poor people were also able to participate in this advance.' These improvements notwithstanding, Table 1.4 shows that at the 1980 Census, of the 82 per cent of all households who rely on agriculture for their livelihood, 29 per cent own no land at all, and a further 46 per cent have less than half a hectare, or less than the area of wet rice land which Penny and Singarimbun (1973: 2) suggest is needed to support a family. The table shows that the incidence of such landlessness and insufficiency of land owned or operated to meet the family's needs is greater in Java than in the other islands.

Leaving aside questions of *distribution* of wealth, the social and economic indicators presented in Table 1.2 reflect to some degree the improvement in Indonesia's *aggregate* situation. The rates of increase during the 1970s in per capita GNP, GDP, food production and fertilizer use were not only greater than the average for all low income countries but greater than in developed countries. Levels of food imports have stabilized, and per capita calorie supply is above the average for developing countries. Moreover, in the early 1980s, Indonesia achieved self-sufficiency in rice—a goal which few commentators of the early 1970s would have thought possible. Clearly too, there are significant structural changes occurring with the rapid decline in the proportion of the work-force engaged in agriculture. On the other hand, there remains a high (albeit declining) proportion of the work-force engaged in agricultural occupations, and the increase in the size of the work-force is rapid by any standards.

The inequalities which exist in Indonesian society are only too starkly reflected in the limited access to, and availability of, basic social services. Hence the population per physician is double that of the average for Third World countries, only a quarter of the eligible population reach secondary school, less than 1 per cent are able to gain access to higher education, and more than a third of adults are illiterate.

One of the key structural characteristics of Indonesia's population which has critical planning and developmental implications is its age structure. Indonesia's population is a very young one by any standards, with some 41 per cent being below the age of 15 years and only 3 per cent 65 years or older. This compares to equivalent figures of 39 and 4 per cent for all less developed countries and 23 and 12 per cent for all more developed countries (Population Reference Bureau, 1985). The youthfulness evident in the current age structure (Figure 1.2) means that there is a built-in momentum to population growth which will ensure that Indonesia's population will continue to increase substantially for some time to come. As noted earlier, even if intrinsic fertility falls, the number of births is likely to increase because of the passage of the large cohorts currently aged less than 15 years into the childbearing age groups. However, it should be

TABLE 1.4

Indonesia: Households According to Whether or Not They Work at All in Agriculture in Earning Their Livelihood, 1980

	Java/Bali		Other Islands		Indonesia	
	Number of Households	Per Cent	Number of Households	Per Cent	Number of Households	Per Cent
Operate less than 0.25 ha of agricultural land	4,499,671	22	1,464,683	14	5,964,354	20
Operate 0.25–0.49 ha of agricultural land	3,202,553	16	1,860,746	18	5,063,299	18
Operate more than 0.5 ha of agricultural land	2,976,873	15	3,464,034	34	6,440,907	22
Total operating agricultural land	10,679,097	53	6,789,463	67	17,468,560	58
Total landless agricultural households	6,080,587	30	1,150,154	11	7,230,741	24
Total non-agricultural households	3,347,775	17	2,216,197	22	5,563,972	18
Total	20,107,459	100	10,155,814	100	39,263,273	100

Source: 1980 Indonesian Census.

noted in Figure 1.2 that there is some slight undercutting at the base of the pyramid suggesting that reduced fertility is starting to have an impact on age structure.

In Figure 1.2, the 1980 age–sex structure of the population is super-imposed over the 1961 pyramid. It will be noticed that the latter has substantial deficits in the 10–19 age groups. During the 1960s, this was a subject of some controversy (Keyfitz, 1965; van de Walle, 1966). There was little disagreement that there was an underenumeration of these age groups, although it was considered also that the excess mortality and reduced fertility of the war and independence struggle years also was partly responsible. The main debate, however, was between those who argued that the underenumeration of 10–19 year olds was due to age misstatement and others who suggested that many in this group were missed in the census count since they are the most mobile age group. The two sub-sequent censuses have suggested that there was truth in both arguments.

Indonesia then is squarely within the middle echelons of that group of nations usually referred to as 'developing'. By any criteria, Indonesia must be regarded as a poor country with a significant number of its citizens living in poverty. The aggregate measures used here do not however reveal the inequalities which exist between groups and regions, between city and country, between different sectors of the economy, and between the core areas of the country and the periphery—all of which are of relevance to Indonesia's demography and which are taken up in subsequent chapters. Indeed, the issues of the complex interrelationships between development and population change and of the influence of social and spatial inequal-ities are recurring themes in this book. Some of the other themes which are taken up in several subsequent chapters and which we consider to be fundamental to understanding Indonesia's demography are briefly in-troduced below.

The Geographical Setting

Indonesia's national motto of 'unity in diversity' is an unusually apt one. Its people are distributed between more than 300 distinct ethnolinguistic groups and live in an archipelago of over 13,000 islands extending over some 40 degrees of longitude (Figure 1.4). This aspect of diversity is one of the major themes which needs to be appreciated in studying Indonesia. The most frequently drawn contrast is that between 'inner' (Java, Madura, and Bali) and 'outer' (Sumatra, Kalimantan, Sulawesi and the other islands) Indonesia. The 'inner–outer' dichotomy usually presented is based upon the 'uneven' distribution of Indonesia's population. In 1980, Java, Madura and Bali supported 63.6 per cent of Indonesia's population on 6.9 per cent of the nation's land area. Figure 1.5 shows the great disparity in population densities. In inner Indonesia, *rural* population densities exceed 500 persons per square kilometre, more than five times the density in the most closely populated of the outer island provinces. Fisher (1967) has clearly established that these wide disparities are largely a reflection of the

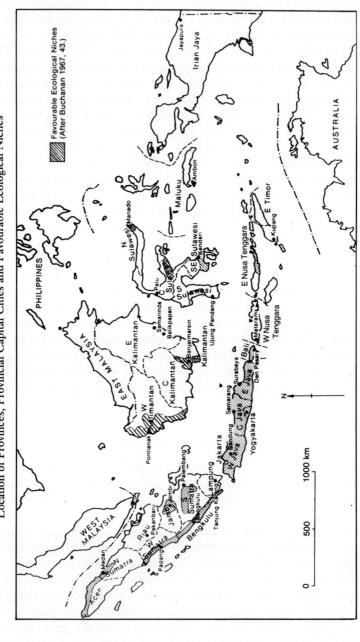

FIGURE 1.4

Location of Provinces, Provincial Capital Cities and Favourable Ecological Niches

Source: Buchanan, 1967.

FIGURE 1.5

Indonesia: Population Density, 1980

Source: Central Bureau of Statistics, 1980 Census.

reality of major ecological differences (especially in soil) between the regions and their relative capacities for sustained intensive cultivation of food. The inner–outer contrast thus extends to the dominant agricultural systems as Geertz (1963: 13) explains:

Estate agriculture aside, of the minute part of the Outer Islands which is cultivated, about 90 per cent is farmed by ... swidden agriculture ... in which fields are cleared, farmed for one or more years and allowed to return to bush for fallowing.... On Java ... field land is in wet rice terraces, about half of them double cropped....

Some commentators suggest that there is also a political–economic contrast to be drawn between Java and the other islands along the lines of the core–periphery model. Java is not only the location of two-thirds of the national population, the dominant ethnic group, and the nation's capital but also the seat of national political and economic power and decision-making.

Population numbers and density are only one dimension of the demographic differences between Java and the other islands. Table 1.5 shows that there are substantial contrasts in population growth rates, especially between Java and Sumatra. It is clear that lower fertility in Java has produced somewhat lower growth rates and that this, together with net out-migration from Java–Bali, is slowly reducing the magnitude of the inner–outer Indonesia contrast with respect to population distribution. While the inner–outer Indonesia dichotomy remains significant in any consideration of the nation's population, it is a gross over-simplification which masks important variations within these broad regions. Some of these variations in context are explored in Chapter 3 and are referred to in subsequent chapters.

It is not our intention here to present a detailed description of Indonesia's physical environment, but a few features of major significance need to be pointed out. The fact that Indonesia is an archipelago—indeed is the world's largest island complex (Pelzer, 1963: 1)—is influential in shaping patterns of human activity and regional demographic variations. Indonesia's physical structure is complex (Fisher, 1964; Pelzer, 1963), but its major features are shown in Figure 1.6 and can be outlined briefly. The main physical limiting factors to settlement in Indonesia are relief, soils and climate.

The alignment of the islands of Indonesia is dictated by a series of arcs of geological activity and 'in most cases their relief is dominated, virtually from end to end, by rugged mountain backbones, capped in the volcanic zone by numerous majestic cones, many of which rise to well over 10,000 feet above sea level' (Fisher, 1964: 17). Most settlement has been concentrated in the lowland areas, especially the well drained, fertile alluvial plains of East and Central Java and, to a lesser extent, North Sumatra and parts of Nusa Tenggara. On the other hand, the low-lying coastal plains of eastern Sumatra, West and South Kalimantan, and south-western Irian are swampy and less attractive to settlement.

TABLE 1.5

Main Regions of Indonesia: Basic Demographic Parameters, 1980

Region	1930		1980		Density (Persons/km²)	Average Annual Growth 1971–80	Annual Average 1971–80		
	Population (m)	Per Cent	Population (m)	Per Cent			CBR	CDR	Rate of Natural Increase (%)
Java–Madura	41.7	68.7	91.3	61.9	690	2.0	35	15	2.0
Sumatra	8.2	13.5	28.0	19.0	59	3.3	40	13	2.7
Kalimantan	2.2	3.6	6.7	4.5	12	2.8	40	15	2.5
Sulawesi	4.2	6.9	10.4	7.1	55	2.2	41	15	2.6
Other Islands	4.4	7.3	11.1	7.5	19	2.8	45	17	2.8
Indonesia	60.7	100.0	147.5	100.0	77	2.3	38	15	2.3

Sources: Central Bureau of Statistics, 1980 Indonesian Census; McNicoll and Singarimbun, 1983: 9.

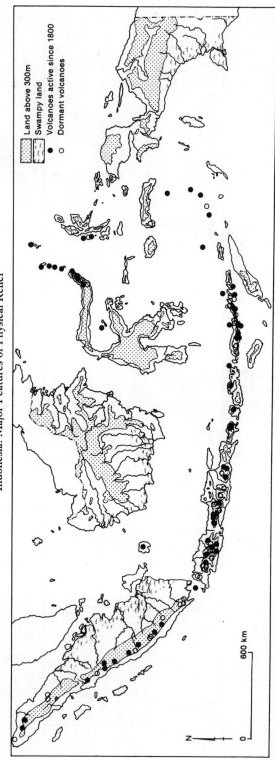

FIGURE 1.6

Indonesia: Major Features of Physical Relief

Land above 300m
Swampy land
Volcanoes active since 1800
Dormant volcanoes

600 km

Source: After Missen, 1972: 24–5.

Soil fertility varies enormously and is the major determinant of variations in rural population density. In common with most tropical areas, the bulk of Indonesia's soils are poor due to leaching. There are exceptions, however, and those of most significance are the extensive sections of East and Central Java, Bali and Lombok, and smaller areas of West Java, Sumatra and Sulawesi with neutral or basic soils derived from recent volcanic ejecta, which are exceptionally rich and support some of the highest densities of agricultural population in the world. The other major exceptions lie in river valleys and well-drained coastal areas where recently deposited alluvium is conducive to intensive agriculture. However, in places where acidic volcanic or heavily leached lateritic soils predominate, agricultural potential is limited.

Indonesia has a tropical climate, with mean monthly temperatures invariably above 18 °C (Fisher, 1964: 21) and with little seasonal or regional variation. There are, however, significant declines in average temperature with altitude, and these have a major influence upon the types of agriculture practised in particular areas. Rainfall is generally high and not as limiting an influence on agriculture as are soils, drainage and temperature conditions. The west coasts of the main islands receive the heaviest rainfall (more than 254 cm per annum) under the influence of the south-west monsoon. There are, however, areas in which rainfall is not only lower (below 102 cm) but, more importantly, unreliable. These areas are predominantly in the eastern part of the archipelago (especially in the Nusa Tenggara islands stretching from Lombok to Timor), and these are the major areas in which crop failure, food crises and famines have been reported in recent years. Rainfall failure also occurs, albeit much less frequently, in the southern part of Sulawesi, the eastern part of Java and the north-western coast of Java.

We can summarize this brief consideration of Indonesia's geographical background with reference to what Buchanan (1967: 43) identifies as 'favourable ecological niches'. These are areas in which the conjunction of the nature of the soils, the amount and distribution of rainfall and the drainage conditions are such that the area lends itself most favourably to intensive agricultural activity. Such areas identified by Buchanan in Indonesia are shown in Figure 1.4, and they include the following types:

1. Coastal plains except on the eastern coasts where swampy conditions prevail;

2. Alluvial valleys and plains (often terraced) except where there are drainage problems;

3. Volcanic slopes of neutral or basic materials—over much of Java.

It is interesting to note that Buchanan classified virtually all of Java as a favourable ecological niche.

We should also note the areas which are difficult environments for intensive agricultural production:

1. Coastal swamp environments (for example, east coast of Sumatra);

2. Forested steep inland hills;

3. Dry zones (for example, Nusa Tenggara; southern South Sulawesi);

4. Very wet zones of heavy erosion and soil leaching (for example, parts of Kalimantan and Sulawesi).

These broadly then are the main characteristics of Indonesia's physical environment. What of the people who inhabit it?

Indonesia's Ethnolinguistic Mosaic

Indonesia's strategic maritime location has opened it over the centuries to various waves of migrations and the spread of ideas, beliefs, goods and technology from both the north (China) and west (India, the Arab world and finally Europe). As a result, it is probably the most ethnically and culturally heterogeneous of the world's largest nations. Hildred Geertz (1963: 24) summarizes this diversity as follows: 'There are over three hundred different ethnic groups in Indonesia, each with its own cultural identity, and more than two hundred and fifty distinct languages are spoken ... nearly all the important world religions are represented, in addition to a wide range of indigenous ones.' Within ethnic groups, too, Indonesians have loyalties to kinship and regional and local groupings, and frequently their behaviour is influenced by group norms formalized into a body of customary law (*adat*). Such groupings, of course, are of significance in the study of demographic behaviour.

The potential divisiveness of ethnic identity in Indonesia is such that no post-Independence government has allowed the inclusion of an ethnicity question in a census, the immense cultural, social and economic significance of ethnicity in the country notwithstanding. Hence the most complete set of ethnicity information is from the last colonial census, conducted in 1930, and this has been used here to construct an ethnic map of Indonesia at that time. The cultural diversity of Indonesia is reflected in the complexity of this map; indeed, it has been necessary to construct two maps to indicate the distribution of the major ethnolinguistic groups by province. In the maps, the dark circle represents the size of the total population and the shaded wedges indicate the proportions of that population made up of particular ethnic groups. The problems of vast differences in total numbers has meant that, in provinces with comparatively small populations, a light, larger, standard-sized circle was superimposed to effectively show the proportional representation of each ethnic group.

The first map (Figure 1.7) shows the distribution of the dominant Java-origin groups. In 1930, 47 per cent of the indigenous population were ethnic Javanese. Figure 1.7 shows their dominance in their central Java heartland and in East Java. Significant numbers have moved into the eastern and northern parts of West Java, to the plantation areas on the north-east coast of Sumatra as 'contract coolies' in the first three decades of this century, and in the land settlement areas of southern Sumatra. Post-Independence transmigration programmes and transfer of government employees have increased the representation of Javanese outside Java and in Jakarta, but the broad pattern depicted in the map still generally holds.

In fact, we can get an impression of the extent of post-Independence

FIGURE 1.7

Indonesia: Distribution of Java-Origin and Foreign Ethnic Groups, 1930

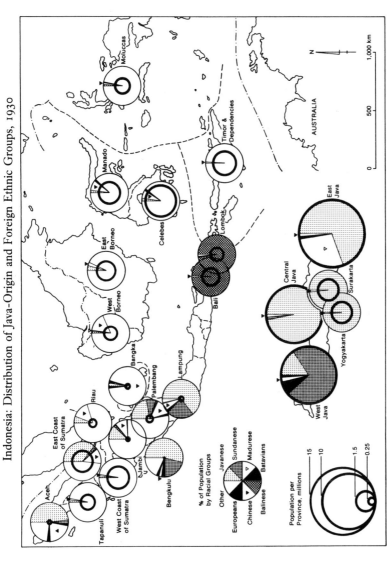

Source: Volkstelling, 1933–6.

Note: In this map the dark circles are proportional to the size of the population of provinces. Where these are very small, a standard-sized light-edged circle has been superimposed and this circle has been divided up to show the proportional representation of the various ethnic groups.

Javanese penetration of the other islands from 1980 census data relating to language spoken in the home (Table 1.6). Clearly these data will under-estimate the size of ethnic groups since some Javanese will use the Indonesian language in the home while others will be in the 'not stated' category. Nevertheless, the Javanese dominance is apparent with their language being used daily in the homes of 40 per cent of Indonesians and 58 per cent of those living in Java. However, it may come as something of a surprise to find that Javanese is the most common single language used at home in Sumatra where more than a fifth of residents use it. As is shown in Chapter 6, this is due to the substantial migrations of Javanese people into Sumatra during the colonial period as 'contract coolies' and, more recently (and more importantly), under the transmigration programme which has sought to resettle large numbers of people from Java and Bali in outer island agricultural settlements.

The second largest ethnolinguistic group are the Sundanese (14.5 per cent in 1930 and 15.1 per cent in 1980) who are largely confined to their West Java heartland with small numbers in Central Java and South Sumatra. Again it is striking that more than half a million Sumatran residents use the Sundanese language in the home. The third largest ethnic group, the Madurese (7.3 per cent), have spread out from their small island home area to settle in East Java. The 1980 language data indicate that 4.7 per cent of Indonesians use the Madurese language in the home (7.4 per cent of Javan residents). The migration of Madurese to Kalimantan is reflected in the fact that 2.7 per cent of residents of Kalimantan speak their language. In 1930, some 11.7 per cent of indigen-ous residents were reported as being 'Batavians'. This group, now referred to as the 'Jakarta Asli' or 'Betawi', emerged as a distinct ethnolinguistic group during the colonial period through the intermarriage in Jakarta (then called Batavia) of indigenous groups (especially Balinese) with Chinese, Arabs and Europeans. They are confined mainly to Java (in and near Jakarta) and, in the 1980 data, are subsumed in the Indonesian-speaking group. The Balinese in 1930 were concentrated almost entirely on Bali and Lombok (in Figure 1.7, Sasaks from Lombok are included with the Balinese). Although their recent participation in the transmigration pro-gramme (especially movements to Sulawesi) is in evidence, in the 1980 language data they remain predominantly localized.

Figure 1.7 also shows the distribution of non-indigenous groups in 1930, of which the Chinese were, and still are, the most significant. Ethnic Chinese make up around 2–3 per cent of Indonesia's population (Coppel, 1980: 792), although their dominance in some sectors of the economy is perceived by some to give them a significance out of proportion to their numbers. The formal and informal sensitivity regarding the Chinese is reflected in the fact that no separate language category was allocated to them at the 1980 Census. The map shows that, in 1930, the Chinese were significantly represented in most areas, mainly in the urban sectors of those provinces. However, they were especially strong proportionately in areas where they had been brought in by the Dutch to work as coolies on

TABLE 1.6
Indonesia: Population by Major Region by Language Used at Home, 1980

Language		Sumatra	Java	Kalimantan	Sulawesi	Other Islands	Total
Indonesian	No.	4,150,279	9,704,896	654,501	1,448,490	1,547,137	17,505,303
	%	14.82	10.64	9.74	13.93	14.81	11.93
Javanese	No.	5,994,242	52,869,890	299,417	136,210	57,281	59,357,040
	%	21.41	57.96	4.46	1.31	0.55	40.44
Sundanese	No.	578,933	21,500,563	18,046	9,911	2,950	22,110,403
	%	2.07	23.57	0.27	0.10	0.03	15.06
Madurese	No.	11,502	6,709,337	180,677	568	11,893	6,913,977
	%	0.04	7.36	2.69	0.01	0.11	4.71
Batak	No.	3,064,232	31,237	3,697	5,529	2,275	3,106,970
	%	10.94	0.03	0.06	0.05	0.02	2.12
Minang	No.	3,509,471	34,569	1,243	273	372	3,545,928
	%	12.54	0.04	0.02	0.00	0.00	2.42
Balinese	No.	30,326	3,283	4,358	55,761	2,387,521	2,481,249
	%	0.11	0.00	0.06	0.54	22.86	1.69
Buginese	No.	113,788	9,711	138,655	3,050,777	9,261	3,322,192
	%	0.41	0.01	2.06	29.33	0.09	2.26
Banjarese	No.	77,974	5,739	1,576,127	1,255	700	1,661,795
	%	0.28	0.01	23.47	0.01	0.01	1.13
Not stated	No.	303,411	13,782	138,025	445,594	217,426	1,118,235
	%	1.08	0.01	2.05	4.28	2.08	0.76
Others	No.	10,161,769	333,963	3,702,150	5,246,180	6,209,316	25,653,378
	%	36.30	0.37	55.12	50.44	59.44	17.48
Total	No.	27,995,927	91,216,970	6,716,896	10,400,548	10,446,132	146,776,470
	%	100.00	100.00	100.00	100.00	100.00	100.00

Source: Central Bureau of Statistics, 1983a.

plantations and in mines (northern and eastern Sumatra and West Kalimantan).

Figure 1.8 shows the distribution of the major outer island-origin groups recognized at the 1930 Census. The situation here is much more complex than in Java since there are many small groups which have their own distinctive language and culture. In 1930, 71 per cent of Indonesians belonged to Java-origin groups. The largest single outer island group was the Minangkabau (3.4 per cent of all indigenous people) whose heartland is West Sumatra, but whose peripatetic nature has ensured that they have spread widely throughout the archipelago. The 1980 language data indicate that 2.4 per cent of Indonesians use Minangkabau in the home, although the language's closeness to Indonesian undoubtedly has meant that there was leakage of ethnic Minangkabau persons into that category, especially in Java. The Minangkabau have spread widely through Sumatra and make up the largest single Sumatran-origin group. The Bataks comprise a number of distinct groups which together, in 1930, accounted for 2 per cent of the native population, a share that Table 1.6 suggests they have maintained. Their concentration in North Sumatra is readily apparent in Figure 1.8. Another significant group are the 'coastal Malays' who made up 7.5 per cent of the total indigenous population in 1930, but who comprise a number of subgroups and, in 1980, are absorbed in the 'Indonesian' and 'other' language-speaking categories. However, their distribution along the east coast of Sumatra and the Kalimantan coast is evident.

Unfortunately, in 1980, little breakdown was made of the dominant groups in the other islands, and the residual category in Table 1.6 is hence large for them. Figure 1.8 shows that, in Kalimantan in 1930, three indigenous groups dominated—the coastal Malays referred to above, the Dayaks (1.1 per cent of the total) who lived in the interior, and the Banjarese of the southern coastal area. The Banjarese made up 1.5 per cent of the total indigenous population in 1930, and 1.1 per cent of the population reported in 1980 that they used the Banjarese language (which is also similar to Indonesian) in the home. In Sulawesi, the southern half is dominated by the Bugis who made up 2.6 per cent of the total Indonesian indigenous population in 1930 while, in 1980, 2.3 per cent of Indonesians used the Bugis language in the home. In South Sulawesi, however, there are also other distinct and significant ethnic groups like the Makassarese (1.1 per cent in 1930), Torajanese (0.9 per cent in 1930) and Mandarese (0.3 per cent), but these—together with the Minahassans who dominate the northern part of the island (0.9 per cent in 1930)—were not distinguished separately at the 1980 Census. Figure 1.8 shows that, in the remaining islands, the largest groups are the Moluccans, Timorese and Papuans, although a host of other (albeit smaller) distinct ethnic groups live in those areas. In eastern Indonesia, there are groups who are ethnically and culturally much more similar to the Melanesian groups further east than to the Malay groups in the rest of Indonesia.

It is important to appreciate the enormous ethnic and cultural complexity of Indonesia, since it does impinge upon several aspects of the nation's

23

Indonesia: Distribution of Outer Island-Origin Ethnic Groups, 1930

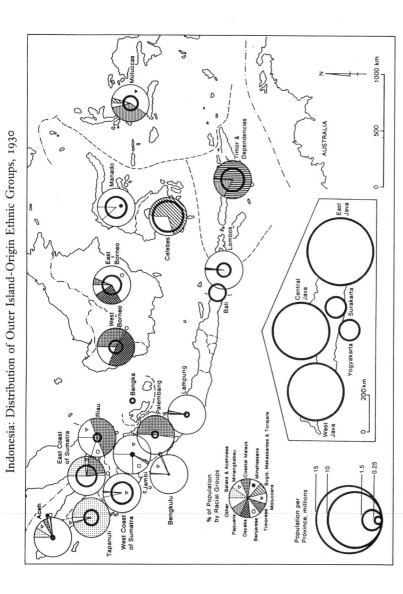

Source: Volkstelling, 1933–6.

Note: In this map the dark circles are proportional to the size of the population of provinces. Where these are very small, a standard-sized light-edged circle has been superimposed and this circle has been divided up to show the proportional representation of the various ethnic groups.

demography. Moreover, this heterogeneity is reflected in other areas. At the 1980 Census, 87 per cent of the population were reported to be Muslim, 9 per cent Christian, 2 per cent Hindu and 1 per cent Buddhist. These data do not give a true picture, however, since there is an enormous interregional variation in the strength with which Islam is embraced, which Muslim practices are followed, and the extent to which the religion is infused with local traditional religious ideas and practices. In the light of this manifest heterogeneity, it may be legitimately asked wherein Indonesia's unity lies, beyond the contiguity of the nation's islands. A major common element lies in Indonesia's politico-economic history. Although some pre-European kingdoms succeeded in bringing large parts of present-day Indonesia within their control, it was not until the nineteenth century that the islands were welded into a single political unit, then known as the Netherlands East Indies. Indeed, Dutch colonial heritage was the primary common unifying element among the various disparate groups when Indonesia was declared an independent nation in 1945. However, with the 1975 annexation of the former Portuguese territory of East Timor, the universality of this common colonial background was broken.

The Historical Dimension in Indonesia's Demography

Current patterns of demographic behaviour are obviously strongly influenced by contemporary cultural circumstances. However, as McNicoll and Singarimbun (1983: 15) have pointed out, demographic change in any society is not only influenced by current socio-economic and cultural circumstances, but is also 'a consequence of behavioural patterns formed over past generations'. This brings us to another theme which is taken up in this study—the importance of the historical dimension in understanding contemporary demographic change. The next chapter will trace population growth in Indonesia up to the contemporary period, but it is necessary to stress here that current demographic processes are shaped, not only by contemporary conditions and events, but also by those of the past. It is important, for example, to establish that Indonesia's recent history has been characterized by forces of change which are intrinsically different from those experienced in Western societies as their mortality and fertility levels began the transition from the high levels characteristic of traditional or pre-transitional societies. The critical independent variable which has intervened in the evolution of Indonesia's economy and society in recent centuries has been colonialism. This powerful influence, involving the pre-eminence of the goals and needs of the colonial rather than the colonized peoples, has no counterpart in Western societies.

Our knowledge of Indonesia's demography in pre-colonial times and for much of the colonial period is extremely limited, and thus there is little research into the demographic impact and implications of colonial rule. Clearly, there were policy measures taken by the colonial regime which impinged directly upon population growth and distribution. More importantly, however, are the implicit demographic policies—the demographic spin-offs of policies and practices designed to achieve the politico-economic goals of the colonial power.

European influence and control gradually increased during the sixteenth, seventeenth and eighteenth centuries until it reached its florescence during the late nineteenth and early twentieth centuries. As will be shown later, it is clear that this had a range of direct and indirect effects upon mortality and fertility levels, thus influencing levels of population growth. Equally, their impact on population distribution and composition was profound. The fundamentally exploitative colonial system was designed to control the local population and to expedite the extraction of raw materials in the most cost-efficient way: in so doing, it shaped patterns of population which have yet to be significantly altered. The influence of colonialism is reflected, for example, in Indonesia's significant Chinese minority, the bulk of whom are the ancestors of immigrant workers brought into the Netherlands East Indies by the colonial administration.

The last half-century has witnessed enormous political, social and economic change in Indonesia. The disruptions of the Great Depression of the 1930s, the ending of the colonial era, the Japanese Occupation of the Second World War, and the post-war struggle for Independence all left their mark on Indonesia's present-day demography. The subsequent period has been divided almost equally between the Soekarno era, which ended in the 1960s, and the 'New Order' government of Suharto. The former was a period of great nationalist fervour and, in its latter years, of economic decline. Arndt (1975: 85) has described the pattern of development during this period thus:

From 1950 until 1958, successive governments struggled to promote economic development in conditions of chronic inflation, balance-of-payments difficulties and increasing political instability. From 1958 until 1965 under Guided Democracy, as orderly processes of government, including the capacity to tax, gradually disintegrated and inflation turned into hyperinflation, as everchanging and multiplying regulations superimposed new direct controls on unenforceable older ones, as output nationalized estates and industrial plants declined and smuggling further dissipated the country's dwindling foreign exchange earnings, as Sukarno's diminishing capacity to raise further foreign credits prompted him to tell the world to 'go to hell' with its foreign aid, economic activity continued despite rather than because of the government.

This situation culminated in an attempted coup in 1965 which was followed by several months of violent reprisals against suspected Communist Party cadres. From this President Suharto's 'New Order' government emerged. As McNicoll and Singarimbun (1983: 25) have pointed out, it is important to have some understanding of the first fifteen years of Indonesia's independence since 'some of the roots of recent demographic change are to be found in these earlier years and in the traumatic period of the middle 1960s'.

The Suharto era has been one in which the dominant technocratic approach to development has seen the initiation of a series of five-year plans, large foreign exchange gains from oil revenues, and rapid aggregate economic growth as discussed earlier in this chapter. President Soekarno espoused a pro-natalist policy, stating for example in 1964 (quoted in Hull, Hull and Singarimbun, 1977: 5): 'My solution is exploit more land— because if you exploit all the land in Indonesia you can feed 250 million, and I have only 103 million.... In my country, the more (children) the better.' The Suharto regime on the other hand has given family planning a high priority and, at the time of writing, it is reported that more than half of Indonesian women in the childbearing age groups are practising family planning. Such differences in explicit population policy, however, are only the visible tip of the iceberg of a multitude of changes which have impinged upon the growth, structure and distribution of Indonesia's population since Independence. By adopting in this book an approach which has a historical dimension and hence takes account of these changes, it is hoped to enhance our understanding of current demographic processes and patterns.

There can be no doubt that Indonesia has undergone major social and economic changes since the late 1960s. Some of these changes are captured in the aggregate data presented earlier in the chapter but are also reflected in community level studies where individual villages or small regions have been resurveyed (Singarimbun, 1976; Edmundson, 1977; Collier et al., 1982; Keyfitz, 1985). There have been enormous changes wrought by the greatly increased spatial mobility (see Chapter 6) of most Indonesians and the penetration by modern mass media of the most remote areas of the archipelago. A satellite telecommunications system, programmes to place public television sets in each village, the fact that 36 per cent of all rural households have radios and 4 per cent have television sets while the comparable percentages in urban areas in 1980 were 57 and 29 per cent respectively, all mean that even hitherto-remote areas are now subject to intense penetration of Western ideas and values, consumerism and commercialization, as well as increased government influence. These pressures have undoubtedly challenged and changed traditional authority structures and local family and kinship loyalties.

Conclusion

This chapter, together with the two that follow, was designed to establish the setting within which contemporary demographic change is taking place. Each of the succeeding chapters then takes up in some depth one aspect of Indonesia's contemporary demography. Before proceeding, however, a general note of caution must be sounded regarding the quality of Indonesian demographic data. As in most Third World countries, the quantity and quality of data available to demographers is limited. This especially applies to the period prior to the 1971 Census. Little systematic time-series analysis covering the entire post-Independence period, let alone earlier years, is therefore possible. Although Indonesia has a vital registration system, it is not usable on a national scale. Much has to be gleaned from small-scale studies and national sample surveys. There has been an exponential improvement in both the quality and quantity of data available, beginning with the 1971 Population Census. Data issues are not dealt with here, but each of the chapters that follow points out the nature, strengths and limitations of the data which they employ.

2 Historical Population Growth in Indonesia

Introduction

THE population of Indonesia has increased thirteen-fold over the past two centuries. From perhaps 10 million in 1700, it grew to about 13 million in 1800, 40 million in 1900 and to 164 million in 1985. As we will show in this chapter, both the exact pace, and the reasons for, this growth have been the subjects of intense discussion and argument, and the disagreements are by no means fully resolved. What can be agreed on, however, is that there has been an extraordinary increase in population density and an intensification of agricultural production to support this increased population over the past two centuries, both in Java and in many areas of the other islands (for example, Bali, Lombok, West Sumatra and Lampung, and parts of South and North Sulawesi).

The explanation of this multiplication of population size in Indonesia, and especially Java, was one of the major preoccupations of colonial writers. Allegedly unprecedented rates of population growth were said to have been the result of beneficial effects of the introduction of plantation agriculture, social order and new systems of transportation (Cabaton, 1911: 19–21). It also spawned many theories, some focusing exclusively on the Indonesian situation and others purporting to provide universal explanations of the processes of agricultural intensification. Boeke (1953) and Geertz's 'agricultural involution' (1963) are examples of the former, while Boserup (1965) drew on the Java case in developing her theories that increased population pressure was the major force behind the expansion of cultivated area and the shortening of fallowing periods associated with increased production. Myrdal (1968: 1395–8) and Wittfogel (1957) are other prominent theorists who have given attention to the case of Java in their attempts to explain population–resources links.

Like the rest of South-East Asia, and in contrast with neighbouring China and India, Indonesia was sparsely populated in 1600. Indonesia's overall density of about 5 persons per square kilometre contrasted with densities for South Asia of about 32 persons per square kilometre and for China (excluding Tibet) of about 37. Europe at the same time had about double the Indonesian population density. Within Indonesia, the population was heavily concentrated in pockets of intensively irrigated wet-rice cultivation in Central and East Java, Bali and South Sulawesi. By contrast, the mountainous province of West Java, which today (including Jakarta) contains well over one-third of Java's population, in the 1700s probably had only one-eighth of the island's total. In such regions, inhabitants were largely restricted to various types of shifting cultivation and gathering forest products.

The Early Size and Growth of Indonesia's Population

Remarkably little attention has been given to the pre-nineteenth century population in Java, and even less to that of the outer islands. McDonald (1980: 82–4) has argued that the population of Java at that time may well have been substantially larger than commonly believed—perhaps more than five million at the end of the first Mataram dynasty in the tenth century. After all, under Mataram and Shailendra rule from the eighth to the tenth centuries, to a lesser extent under the succeeding kingdoms and again under the Majapahit Kingdom in the fourteenth and fifteenth centuries, Java had most of the characteristics of Wittfogel's 'hydraulic society'— advanced agricultural technology, political stability over an extensive area, trade based on large towns, and bureaucratic control over land and irrigation (see van Setten van der Meer, 1979)—and, therefore it is not unrealistic to expect that it also had the other main characteristic of such societies—a substantial, growing and densely settled population, albeit one that was concentrated in pockets of wet-rice cultivation with much sur- rounding forest. Certainly, the population was large enough and sufficiently concentrated to generate both the agricultural surplus and organizational ability to allow the construction of the majestic eighth-century edifices of Central Java (Borobodur, Prambanan, and the many temples so widespread throughout the region), although it must be admitted that the great cathedrals of England were built by a population of three million or less on a comparable-sized island. Marvellous works are not necessarily a good indication of population size.

During the millennium following AD 800, there were periods when the kingdoms were in a state of decline, social control was reduced or eliminated, and the land was ravaged by wars, famines, epidemics, floods and volcanic eruptions. At such times, long periods of stagnation of population growth, and indeed of population decline, undoubtedly occurred. But at various times before the nineteenth century, it seems quite possible that Java's population exceeded five million.

Reid (1983b: 13) concurs that there were probably quite sharp fluctu- ations in population size in pre-colonial South-East Asia:

When conditions of reasonable stability prevailed, the combination of early marriage, abundant food and relative health probably gave rise to quite rapid population growth, at least among the wet-rice cultivators and urban traders of the lowland and coast. Population must have declined equally sharply when these areas were laid waste by the movement of armies, however. Java probably underwent several such periods of population decline in the three turbulent centuries before 1755, and certainly did so in 1675–1755.

The latter eighty-year period was a time of almost constant warfare between rival claimants to the throne of Mataram. Populations of some areas were reduced to half or a quarter of their previous size (Reid, 1983b: 14):

In densely settled wet-rice areas much of the loss of population was caused by destruction of food crops—either as a tactic of war or as a result of the passage of thousands of troops. In Sultan Agung's campaigns against the coastal regions of East Java and Madura in 1620–1625, 80,000 troops beseiged Surabaya and its nearby towns off and on for 5 years, devastating all the rice crops, and even poisoning and damming up the river water of the city.

The net effect of such population losses on the population of Java as a whole would depend on the extent to which local population losses were due to deaths or births postponed, and the extent to which they were due to movement of people away to other regions. However, figures for Central and East Java based on official counts of *cacah*, or taxable households, suggest a substantial population decline between 1642 and 1755.

Outside Java, the Palembang-centred Sriwijaya Empire may have been based on a fairly large population in the surrounding areas of South Sumatra, but the densest population concentrations before the nineteenth century appear to have been in Bali and South Sulawesi. In these areas, not only was agriculture elaborately developed, but the ongoing export of slaves suggests a condition of labour surplus (Reid, 1983a: 30–3). West Sumatra and Aceh were probably the other main concentrations of population in Sumatra. Reliable figures for the pre-nineteenth century population of the outer islands are lacking. Even the *Kolonial Verslag* estimates in the nineteenth century show declines from 10.4 million in 1849 to 3.0 million in 1860, 2.9 million in 1865 and up to 4.3 million in 1870, despite the absence of any devastating events to lend credence to such fluctuations. Not surprisingly, such data were evaluated by Widjojo (1970: 62) to be 'insufficiently reliable to be of any use'.

What is clear is that there was great regional variation in population density and growth. Aside from warfare, factors such as royal polygamy, the extremely heavy work-load of women in swidden cultivation and venereal disease were important in keeping population growth rates down in some regions. Sultan Iskandar Muda of Aceh kept in his palace three thousand women who were forbidden to talk to any man except himself and the eunuchs of court, though from all of them he was able to produce no male heir (Beaulieu, 1666: 102, cited in Reid, 1983b: 7). The ruler of tiny Tidore had four hundred secluded women in his harem, but only twenty-six children. The demographic significance of such royal polygamy would depend partly on the degree to which it was replicated by lesser nobles and courtiers. As for the heavy work-load of women in shifting cultivation areas, this has long been noted by analysts, and the 1930 Census reported exceptionally low birth rates among largely swidden cultivators such as animists of the Batu and Mentawai islands off Sumatra, East Sumba, numerous Dayak groups of Borneo, and the Torajans of Central Sulawesi. By contrast, recently Christianized peoples such as the Toba Batak and South Nias people had exceptionally high birth rates. Reid (1983b: 9) notes that '... if changes similar to those associated with Christianization for animist swidden cultivators (which may involve physical security, hygiene and agricultural practice as well as belief systems) were occurring on a wider scale with the gradual movement into Islam and Buddhism, then profound demographic consequences may be expected'.

Table 2.1 presents a set of estimates of population of different regions of Indonesia between 1600 and 1930. The estimates for the early years are very uncertain. For example, it is possible that Java's population was as large as 5 or 6 million in 1600 rather than the 3.4 million estimated by Reid, especially if we accept (1) a higher figure (approaching 10 million?) for 1800 as Peper and others suggest (see p. 32), and (2) that Java's population in the period 1700–50 may well have been smaller than it was in 1600 due to the wars of succession. In any case, a figure as low as 3.4 million for 1600—implying a figure of, say, 3 million in 1750—would imply an impossibly high rate of growth to reach 10 million in 1800. Alternatively, a population of 5 million in 1600, falling to say 4.5 million in 1700, would not be consistent with an estimate as low as 5.2 million in 1800. The plausibility of each sequence of estimates rests largely on the construction of consistent scenarios which fit the sketchy data at our disposal.

TABLE 2.1

Estimates of Population Size: Java and Other Islands, 1600–1930
(in Thousands)

Region	1600	1800	1900	1920	1930
All Indonesia	9,145–10,745	13,500–18,300	40,150	49,155	60,727
Java	3,400–5,000	5,200–10,000	29,000	34,984	41,718
Other Islands	5,745	8,300	11,150	14,171	19,009
Bali	600	700	800	947	1,101
Sumatra	2,400	3,500	4,500	6,298	8,255
Sulawesi	1,200	1,800	2,500	3,108	4,232
Kalimantan	670	1,000	1,300	1,626	2,169
Lesser Sundas	600	900	1,400	1,764	2,359
Maluku	275	400	500	427	893
Percentage in Java	37–47	38–55	72	71	69

Sources: 1600 and 1800: Reid, 1983b and alternative estimates for Java as implied by Peper and others; 1900: Authors' estimates adjusting 1900 'census' figures upwards to ensure that 1900–30 growth rate was below 2 per cent per annum; 1920 and 1930: Census figures.
Note: Excluding New Guinea, for which data is extremely problematic. Total population, including both native-born and foreign. Columns may not sum due to rounding errors.

Population Growth in the Nineteenth Century

Whatever figures we finally use for the period prior to 1800, it is clear that nineteenth-century population growth in Indonesia was the story of Java's population growth outstripping that of the other islands. It is likely that in both 1600 and 1800, the total population in the other islands exceeded that of Java. There is even less doubt that by 1900, Java's population was more than double that of the other islands. It is important, then, to understand how this tremendous growth in Java's population came about.

Colonial writers considered that population growth in Java in the nineteenth century was unique in international terms. According to population estimates generated by the population counts conducted by Raffles in 1815 and the census conducted in 1900, Java's population had grown at an average annual rate of 2.2 per cent throughout the intervening period. Using even Bleeker's population estimate for 1802 and ignoring the Raffles census, the rate over the century was 2.1 per cent. No other Asian or even European country had experienced so rapid a population growth rate over so long a period. Dutch administrators expressed some degree of pride in this high rate of population growth, seeming as it did to vindicate their policies, but, as time went by, the pride became mixed with apprehension at the declining welfare of the native people. It was common to attribute the rapid population growth to:

1. the pax Neerlandica, or the end of internecine wars and the establishment of peace that came with Dutch control;

2. medical advances, particularly smallpox vaccination and, later, the introduction of elementary sanitation and hygiene;

3. improvement in living standards and nutrition brought about by Dutch agricultural policies.

More recently, however, many have questioned the accuracy of the nineteenth century population estimates (Breman, 1971; Wander, 1965; Widjojo, 1970; Peper, 1970; McDonald, 1980), and a number of writers have reconsidered the three above-mentioned explanations of high population growth (White, 1973 and 1974; Geertz, 1973; van de Walle, 1973; Boomgaard, 1980; Alexander, 1984). There is general agreement that the Bleeker and Raffles population estimates were too low. After all, neither used a census in the modern-day understanding of that term. Raffles' data were compiled from information supplied to local officers by village heads, and contained arithmetic errors and obvious omissions. The degree of unintentional and deliberate underreporting was probably very high, especially because of the direct relation between the collection of population data and the administration of the taxation system. Furthermore, the coverage of a number of regions was far from adequate (Widjojo, 1970: 18–26).

The difficulty lies in deciding just how much Raffles underestimated the true population. We have a wide range of estimates of the actual population of Java in 1815 to choose from: 10 to 15 million are the estimates favoured by Keyfitz (1972) and McDonald (1980); 8 to 10 million are those favoured by Peper; Reid, however, arguing that these estimates are overly weighted by 'demographic' considerations (the need to lower the implausibly high nineteenth-century growth rate to make it fit demographic principles), favours a figure of 5.2 million in Java in 1800, implying around 6.5 million in 1815. Reid's suggestion is roughly consistent with Wander's (1965) estimate of 7.0 million and Breman's (1963) estimate of 6.3 million for 1815.

In deciding what is a plausible figure for 1815, we need to examine not only the procedures for carrying out the 1815 count, but also the maximum likely sustainable population growth rate in the nineteenth century, given the economic and security conditions in Java at the time and what we know about growth in comparable populations elsewhere at the same time. The difficulty with such reconstructions over long periods of time is that, to make them tractable, there is a need to assume average trends in growth rates over fairly long periods, thus 'smoothing over' the considerable fluctuations which undoubtedly occurred in reality and left their imprint on the age structure, thereby influencing population growth in later years. Such 'averaging' is acceptable provided that it is possible to estimate the net outcome of the many fluctuations in fertility and mortality arising from wars, harvest failures and other upsets. To do this, however, requires a large element of judgement.

As far as the early part of the century is concerned, commentators— including Widjojo (1970), Peper (1970) and White (1973)—have provided trenchant critiques of the case made for rapid population growth. The Java Wars of 1825–30 killed more than 200,000 people, and thousands of hectares were laid waste through Central and East Java. (It must be borne in mind, however, that 200,000 deaths over a five-year period, of which 'hardly one-tenth' occurred in actual fighting (see Vlekke, 1965: 287; or 1943: 268), implies a rise of only about four per thousand persons in the death rate (representing less than a 15 per cent increase), and therefore would not have caused a major fall in population growth rates unless associated with substantially lowered fertility due to separation of spouses and other causes. The early 1840s were also a time of famine and epidemics. The contention that the spread of medical facilities lowered the death rate of the native population is questioned by Widjojo on the grounds that the vaccination campaigns were very limited until late in the century. High rates of mortality among the European population, who had the most ready access to available medical facilities, are also taken as evidence that the native population could not have had low mortality.

One reason for overestimates of growth rates in the official figures is that the swidden cultivators and pioneers (whose numbers were probably decreasing over time as settled agriculture gradually covered more and more of Java) were more likely to be undercounted in early periods than the settled agriculturalists. Even among rice-cultivating populations in East Java, there is some cause for concern over estimates based on *cacah* since such enumerations focused on landowners and people with ties to established families, while there was a substantial number of 'floating' workers who migrated almost nomadically in search of employment, or away from difficulties. As systems of recordkeeping were improved and extended to the fringe areas, and as the frontier and floating populations came under the ambit of government control, those formerly excluded would have been counted as part of the population increase.

Reconstructions of population history of the nineteenth century, based on the more reliable end-of-century estimates, have to involve judgements about the relative impact of these various factors, along with a judgement about the likely degree of undercount in the various official population estimates.

One of the most ambitious attempts to re-estimate the population at various times is that of Peper (1970: 83–4). Accepting Breman's estimate of the population in 1900 as 29.5 million, thus correcting for the inevitable undercounting, Peper corrected the estimate for 1865 on the basis of a cadastral (land ownership and use) and statistical survey held in that year. That survey indicated a 15 per cent underenumeration in the population registers. Application of this figure to the population recorded at the time raised it to 16.513 million, implying a rate of growth of more than 1.6 per cent per annum between 1865 and 1900. Peper then assumed that the same rate of growth would have prevailed between 1850 and 1865, with the implication that the 1850 population was 13.106 million. Assuming that the growth rate between 1800 and 1900 must have been significantly less than that of the last half of the century (representing growth rates for the 1800–50 period of, say, between 0.5 and 1.0 per cent) due to the disruptions mentioned above, Peper produced two population estimates for 1800: 7.987 and 10.175 million. He regarded the former, which implied a 0.5 per cent growth rate on average from 1800 to 1850, as an absolute minimum estimate.

Once the population estimate for the early part of the nineteenth century is suitably inflated, nineteenth century Java ceases to be unique in demographic history. However, this does not mean that there is then nothing left to explain in respect of nineteenth century population growth in Java. Even with the data corrections, the population of the island increased from between 7 and 10 million in 1800 to around 30 million in 1900. This represented a dramatic break from the pattern of fairly rapid growth followed by periods of stagnation or depopulation which characterized pre-nineteenth century Java. At least 20 million people were added to Java's population in a century despite the crises of the Java War in the 1820s and the famine of the 1840s. In addition, late nineteenth-century Java would have been subjected to disease mortality crises of a lesser magnitude, and it seems fair to conclude that the Pax Neerlandica resulted in less warfare and disruption over the course of the nineteenth century as a whole, than had been the case in earlier times, especially over the 1675–1755 period.

If these arguments are accepted, attention turns to the conditions in agriculture and whether food production and work opportunities were expanding rapidly enough to sustain the population increase which appears to have taken place. There is no need to contend that Dutch rule had widespread or deeply beneficial effects on the living conditions of the Javanese in order to argue that colonialism laid the conditions for rapid population growth to take place. The changes could have been quite narrow, and could have taken place within a system which seriously exploited Javanese farmers and deprived them of many important elements of overall welfare. The evidence is strong that population grew more rapidly in West Java and East Java than in Central Java and that, within West Java, the highest growth took place in the Priangan region and, in East Java, in the peninsula area. In both areas, a considerable amount of land not formerly utilized for settled agriculture was colonized over the period—and this included the establishment of estates. Thus higher population growth was centred in the areas of greater Dutch activity.

Geertz's *Agricultural Involution* (Geertz, 1963) describes most of the agricultural changes sustaining population growth through the nineteenth century and into the twentieth century. Based on this and other sources, McDonald (1980: 87–8) isolated certain key factors, the first five of which were important at least from 1830 onwards, whereas the second five became important from about 1880 onwards:

1. A large number of work opportunities were generated on the upland estates, which did not exist previously. Again this change was particularly evident in West and East Java. The Culture System may also have generated a greater demand for labour in the more traditional farming areas (White, 1973).

2. There was a considerable expansion of the area under wet-rice cultivation. Some of this expansion, particularly in the areas near the estates, such as the intermontane basins of the Priangan, may well have been given stimulus by the need to provide a food supply to the estate workers. Hugo (1975: 90–108) has described the way in which Javanese *sawah* technology was transferred to areas in West Java mainly in the nineteenth century.

3. The estates were not so much established on unused land as upon land which had been previously used by *ladang* farmers. The *ladang* cultivators were, therefore, forced to change to shorter-fallow agriculture. As *ladang* farming was a particularly precarious lifestyle, the change to shorter-fallow sustained population growth.

4. The colonial administration built a network of roads which were, of course, primarily for the purpose of shifting export produce to coastal ports but which at the same time opened up more areas to the local movement of subsistence crops.

5. The roads would also have facilitated much greater mobility of the population, a necessary adjunct to the labour demands of the estates and the expansion of total land under cultivation. The movement of Madurese to estates in East Java is a good example of how increased mobility may have relieved population pressure.

6. Cultivation of the dry, upland areas for subsistence crops such as corn and cassava began to increase rapidly at the end of the nineteenth century (Booth, 1977: 39). This trend had started slowly and was even remarked upon by Raffles (1965 I: 121) as early as 1815.

7. There was a growth of towns and associated commercial activities which provided a broader diversity of opportunities.

8. From 1880 onwards the Dutch became heavily involved in the building and improvement of irrigation systems. The amount of land irrigated by running water increased by 60 per cent between 1880 and 1915. In the same period, however,

total land under cultivation increased by almost 100 per cent, reflecting the very large increase in dry-land farming (Booth, 1977: 39).

9. Agricultural involution became evident. *Sawah* was more intensively cultivated by more workers. Similar comments apply to the sugar industry and the rotation of sugar and rice cultivation on the same land may have been one of the factors stimulating more intensive *sawah* cultivation.

10. Vast changes were occurring in a range of socio-economic variables such as land tenure, credit, tax and land rent, social organization in the peasant sector and development of the commercial sector. These changes led to a more complex and diversified economy, the effects of which on population are very difficult to gauge.

In summary, the nineteenth century saw a dramatic increase in the area of land under cultivation in Java. While the statistics may be doubtful, Raffles (1965 I:108) claimed that in 1815 the soil was entirely neglected or only half-cultivated in seven-eighths of Java. In contrast, in 1905 the Dutch administration commenced the policy of moving people from the more densely settled areas of Java to farming settlements in south Sumatra.

These points do not directly address the question of what demographic mechanism generated more rapid population growth. We have mentioned the doubts cast on the role of reduced mortality; White (1973) put the alternative view that the heavy labour demands of the Culture System after 1830 provided an incentive for increased fertility to create a larger house-hold labour force. Alexander (forthcoming) has postulated a mechanism by which this increased childbearing could have been achieved: that women forced to undertake more arduous work found it increasingly difficult to fully breastfeed their children, thus average durations of breastfeeding and hence of postpartum abstinence fell, and fertility increased. This argument ignores the possible deleterious effects on fertility of arduous work and increasing mobility. Increasing levels of sub-fecundity due to nutritional deficiencies in a subsistence economy disrupted by commercialization, and increases in sterility caused by venereal disease and other infections also might have been expected. The lack of data on fertility rates and child-bearing behaviour for the period makes it difficult to evaluate Alexander's hypothesis. It could have been important for some women in some regions but it is unlikely that it was universally true.

In other islands, population growth in the nineteenth century was considerably slower than in Java, though if the estimates in Table 2.1 are near the mark, growth did occur more or less universally. In understanding why growth was less than in Java, emphasis would again need to be put on factors such as the degree of disruption due to warfare, famine and epidemics, and the degree to which agricultural systems remained un-changed. Dutch control was actually quite limited in most of the outer islands before the last third of the nineteenth century and, in others (notably Aceh, Bali, central Sulawesi, parts of Kalimantan and Irian Jaya), until into the twentieth century (see Figure 2.1). Swidden cultivation, with its tendency to support only slow population growth, maintained a much higher share of total agricultural activity in the outer islands than in Java. Although the estates of North Sumatra were developing rapidly towards the

37

FIGURE 2.1

Expansion of Dutch Colonial Control in Indonesia, 1619–1942

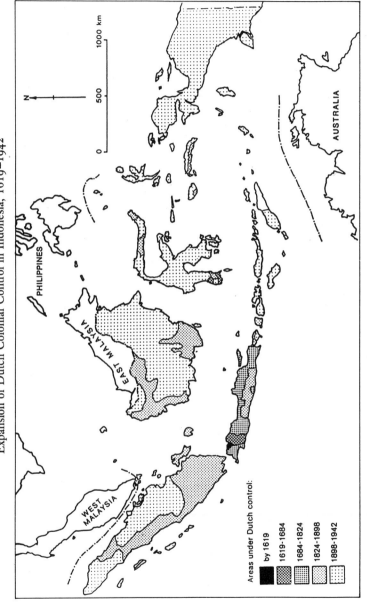

Source: After Soedjatmoko *et al.*, 1965: 358.

end of the century, commercial agriculture in the outer islands over most of the century was far behind that in Java. Attempts to control troublesome regions led the Dutch into armed conflict in the Bugis areas of South Sulawesi (1858–9), Bali (the 1840s and 1906–8), Aceh (from 1873 onwards) and elsewhere. In many other areas, local conflicts, piracy and other disorders prevailed. Therefore, it is not surprising that over the course of the nineteenth century, population growth appears to have been considerably slower in the outer islands than in Java. But there is little doubt that population growth in the outer islands was accelerating in the last decades of the century, due to declines in mortality as central administrative control strengthened and the pace of transport and commercial developments quickened, and possibly due as well to increases in fertility.

It must also be remembered that mortality trends are very sensitive to environmental factors, and there is a very thin line between survival and death for many weak members of society. A rough balance of population numbers can be maintained if infants, children and the very old are exposed to conditions of marginal nutrition, infection or social disruption such that otherwise-preventable illness occurs, and otherwise-preventable death takes its toll. To observers at the time, such a rise in mortality sufficient to reduce growth rates to zero might not have seemed a dramatic, or even a very significant affair since, by and large, active adult members of society were not carried off.

To summarize, the general picture of severe undercount in the first half of the 1800s and improved enumerations over time would seem to support the generalization that population in Java grew at less than 1 per cent per annum in the early 1800s, increasing to about 1.5 per cent by 1900, but only exceeding 2 per cent for any sustained period of time in the twentieth century. There is also broad agreement that mortality fell at an increasing rate over time, though there is controversy concerning the base levels and patterns of change. Much less is known about fertility, but it is possible that birth rates rose gradually during the nineteenth century. In the other islands, too, the evidence is that population growth accelerated towards the end of the nineteenth century, though over the course of the century population growth in Java well and truly outstripped that elsewhere.

The Twentieth Century

As early as 1827, Du Bus de Gisignies expressed the fear that, without policies designed to develop the agricultural sector, Java would eventually have:

... over its whole surface a population quite the same as that which now inhabits and cultivates a part of that surface: ... millions of tenants on whole, half, and quarter acres of land, each farming to obtain his food, each growing rice and nothing else, each farming for an income like that of the meanest day labourer (in Boeke, 1927, reprinted as 1966: 275).

Exactly a century later Boeke expanded this warning:

The more intensive agricultural production becomes under these circumstances, the more dangerous, for intensification means only that the existence of a constantly growing number of people is made dependent on a fixed amount of land, so that the vicissitudes of the yield affect ever larger numbers of people (Boeke, 1927, reprinted as 1966: 275).

Yet Java's population has nearly trebled since that time (see Figure 2.2), its mortality levels are very much lower than they were, and the socio-economic welfare of the people has certainly improved. Fundamental to this great increase in population has been a rise in productivity in Javanese agriculture such that the ability to supply most of the population's needs with locally produced foodstuffs has been maintained, and the diversification of non-agricultural employment opportunities has served to absorb a substantial portion of the work-force.

In terms of 'Java–other island' differences, the twentieth century has witnessed a reversal of the relative growth trends of the nineteenth century. Apparently since early in the century, a combination of higher rates of natural increase in the other islands and a net migration flow to them from Java has resulted in a slow but steady climb in their share of Indonesia's population, reaching 39 per cent in 1985. There is every prospect that this rise will continue throughout the foreseeable future, based on both higher rates of natural increase than in Java and a net migration transfer from Java. In the eight decades from 1900 to the present, the other islands have sustained at least a five-fold increase in their population, a remarkable growth by any standard. The notion of a small, sparse other-islands population is no longer sustainable: if Sumatra were a separate country, its population of 33 million would rank it twenty-sixth among the world's nations, and its density is higher than that of Malaysia and only 35 per cent lower than that of Thailand.

Though not as rapid as population growth in the other islands, Java's population growth this century has been very substantial. The rapid growth of Java's population in the twentieth century has not been a steady trend, and was interrupted on a number of occasions before 1950 (see Figure 2.2). Between 1950 and the late 1970s, however, Java's population growth averaged only slightly below 2 per cent per annum, enough to double the population in less than four decades. At the start of the century when the Ethical Policy was enunciated, the population of Java was somewhere around 30 million and growing at over 1 per cent per annum. Between 1900 and 1905, crop failures and a cholera epidemic probably dampened the growth rate and later, in 1918–19, the impact of the world-wide influenza epidemic probably produced a negative growth rate for a short time so that, by the time of the 1920 Census, the population of Java was around 35 million. The rate of population growth in the 1920s appears to have been uniformly higher than in the 1930s when the export sector of the Indonesian economy collapsed as a result of the Great Depression. Widjojo (1970: 100–3) believes that birth rates for the 1930s were probably above

FIGURE 2.2

Schematic Representation of Twentieth-Century Population
Growth in Java and Other Islands

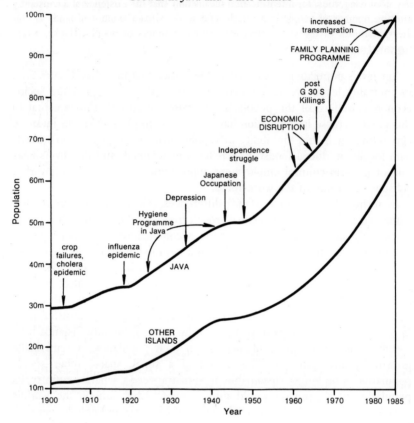

Sources: Adapted from data in Tables 2.1 and 2.2 and information on historical events which
affected population growth.

40 births per thousand population for the entire period and death rates
were probably constant or increasing slightly, but any absolute answer is
impossible in the absence of better data.

Had the economic depression passed from the scene as previous re-
cessions had done, it is likely that the rate of population growth would have
rebounded to levels higher than those experienced in the 1920s. The
colonial government's programmes of public health, education and native
welfare were reaching larger numbers of Javanese peasants and, despite the
economic pressures of the time, it was clear that the demographic conditions would respond quickly to a return to prosperity. In the event,
however, war, occupation by the Japanese, and the struggle for Independence followed hard on the heels of the Depression and, through the
1940s as a whole, Java's population barely increased at all (Keyfitz,
1953: 654). It was not until the 1950s, when a period of stability in
government and the implementation of massive programmes of social and

economic welfare, combined with the arrival in the childbearing ages of the relatively large cohorts of women born in the 1920s and early 1930s, that the potential for rapid population growth in Java was realized—in fact, to such an extent that Java's population grew by more than 80 per cent in the 1950–85 period. Even the slaughter following the abortive coup of 1965 (in which some 300,000 people or, according to some estimates, as many as half a million people were killed) produced no more than a slight wavering in the upward growth curve (see Figure 2.2). The underlying determinants of this growth will be discussed in detail in the following chapters.

The main point to be stressed here is the sharp increase in population densities in Java. This will be discussed in greater length in the next chapter where it is shown that *kabupaten* in Java with a population density of more than 600 persons per square kilometre rose from a tiny proportion of all *kabupaten* in 1920 and a scarcely larger proportion in 1930 to become almost a majority of all *kabupaten* in 1971 and a clear majority in 1980. By 1980, in fact, 12 per cent of all *kabupaten* in Java had population densities exceeding 1,000 persons per square kilometre.

At the beginning of the twentieth century there were still a few areas of frontier settlement in Java: southern parts of the 'east hook' of East Java, south-western Java and the upland mountain areas along the length of the island. But the area under cultivation was being pushed rapidly to its limits: *sawah* replacing *tegal* wherever irrigation systems could be developed, and *tegal* being pushed further up slopes and into less accessible areas. *Palawidja* (non-rice food crops) became increasingly important in the last decades of the nineteenth century and the early decades of the twentieth century, both as an off-season crop in *sawah* areas and as the main crop on *tegal*. By the mid-1930s, the proportion of total peasant-cropped land in Java had fallen to 45 per cent, much below the percentage in Thailand, Indochina, Burma and the Philippines (Geertz, 1963: 94). In Geertz's (1963: 95) colourful metaphor, the expansion of *palawidja* cultivations 'merely gave the multiplying Javanese a bigger pool in which more of them could tread water'. Nevertheless, the rapid post-war increase in Java's population showed that a population 'saturation point' had by no means been reached. Later chapters will discuss the dynamics of this renewed growth and the socio-economic changes that enabled it to be sustained.

Population Growth in Independent Indonesia

The period of rapid population growth in the 1950s was barely documented at all. There was no parallel in Indonesia to the Malayan censuses of 1947 and 1957. Since 1961, however, there have been three censuses and two intercensal population surveys, enabling us to trace the evolution of population in the different provinces fairly accurately. It is worth examining in some detail population growth over this past quarter-century, during which Indonesia's population has grown by over 60 per cent. Table 2.2 provides a basis for so doing.

The general point made earlier about the steadily rising proportion of

TABLE 2.2

Indonesia: Population, 1961–1985; Average Annual Growth Rate, 1961–1971, 1971–1980 and 1980–1985; and Population Density by Region and Province

Region and Province	Population ('000)				Growth Rate (Per Cent)			Percentage Increase, 1961–85	Density (Persons/ sq km), 1985
	1961	1971	1980	1985	1961–71	1971–80	1980–5		
JAVA	62,993	76,102	91,270	99,502	1.9	2.0	1.7	58	735
Jakarta	2,907	4,576	6,503	7,829	4.6	3.9	3.8	169	13,270
West Java	17,615	21,633	27,454	30,733	2.1	2.7	2.3	74	664
Central Java	18,407	21,877	25,373	26,934	1.7	1.6	1.2	46	787
Yogyakarta	2,241	2,490	2,751	2,967	1.1	1.1	1.5	32	936
East Java	21,823	25,527	29,189	31,039	1.6	1.5	1.2	42	648
SUMATRA	15,739	20,812	28,016	32,667	2.8	3.3	1.2	108	69
Aceh	1,629	2,009	2,611	2,981	2.1	2.9	2.7	83	54
North Sumatra	4,965	6,623	8,361	9,444	2.9	2.6	2.5	90	133
West Sumatra	2,319	2,793	3,407	3,666	1.9	2.2	1.5	58	74
Riau	1,235	1,642	2,169	2,514	2.9	3.1	3.0	105	27
Jambi	744	1,006	1,446	1,728	3.1	4.1	4.0	132	38
South Sumatra	2,773	3,444	4,630	5,411	2.2	3.3	3.2	52	95
Bengkulu	406	519	768	936	2.5	4.4	4.0	131	44
Lampung	1,668	2,777	4,625	5,987	5.2	5.8	5.3	259	180

KALIMANTAN	*4,101*	*5,152*	*6,723*	*7,781*	*2.3*	*3.0*	*3.0*	*90*	*14*
West Kalimantan	1,581	2,020	2,486	2,815	2.5	2.3	2.5	78	19
Central Kalimantan	497	700	954	1,140	3.5	3.4	3.6	129	7
South Kalimantan	1,473	1,699	2,065	2,289	1.4	2.2	2.1	55	61
East Kalimantan	551	734	1,218	1,538	2.9	5.7	4.8	179	8
SULAWESI	*7,079*	*8,535*	*10,410*	*11,598*	*1.9*	*2.2*	*2.2*	*64*	*61*
North Sulawesi	1,310	1,718	2,115	2,375	2.8	2.3	2.3	81	125
Central Sulawesi	693	914	1,290	1,539	2.8	3.9	3.6	122	22
South Sulawesi	4,517¹	5,189	6,062	6,600	1.4	1.7	1.7	46	91
South-east Sulawesi	560	714	942	1,083	2.5	3.1	2.8	93	39
NUSA TENGGARA	*5,556*	*6,618*	*8,487*	*9,338*	*1.8*	*2.0*	*1.9*	*68*	*106*
Bali	1,783	2,120	2,470	2,638	1.8	1.7	1.3	48	474
West Nusa Tenggara	1,808	2,202	2,725	3,047	2.0	2.4	2.3	69	151
East Nusa Tenggara	1,967	2,295	2,737	3,029	1.6	2.0	2.1	54	63
East Timor	—	—	555	624	—	n.a.	2.4	—	42
MALUKU, IRIAN JAYA	*n.a.*	*2,012*	*2,585*	*2,990*	*n.a.*	*2.8*	*3.0*	*n.a.*	*6*
Maluku	848	1,089	1,411	1,633	2.5	2.9	3.0	93	22
Irian Jaya	n.a.	923	1,174	1,357	n.a.	2.9	3.0	n.a.	3
ALL INDONESIA	97,019²	119,232	147,490	163,876	2.1	2.3³	2.1	69	85

Notes:
¹ Partly guessed because of rural insecurity.
² Includes 700,000 population for Irian Jaya.
³ Excludes East Timor.
n.a. = Data not available.

the population living outside Java represents a broad generalization of trends which varied greatly at the province and sub-province level. Sumatra's population more than doubled over the past quarter-century, and Sumatra and Kalimantan have had much higher growth rates than Sulawesi and Nusa Tenggara, whose growth rates have in turn exceeded those in Java. Sumatra's rate of growth was almost double that of Java over this period.

Within Java, there has been a steady shift westward in the population's centre of gravity, due to the rapid growth of Jakarta and West Java, whose combined population has grown exactly twice as fast as that of the rest of Java. West Java's high rate of growth compared to the rest of Java has been due to three main factors: higher fertility rates, less transmigration, and more in-migration—mainly to the areas surrounding the growing metropolis of Jakarta.

West Sumatra has had rates of population growth only one-half to two-thirds the Sumatra average, whereas the growth rate in Lampung, swollen by transmigration from Java, has exceeded 5 per cent throughout the past quarter-century. Thus Lampung's population, though well below that of West Sumatra in 1961, exceeded it by over 60 per cent by 1985. Jambi, Riau and Bengkulu, all sparsely settled frontier provinces, also experienced rapid population growth during this period. The growth rate of South Kalimantan's population was less than half that of Central Kalimantan and one-third that of East Kalimantan over the same period; the growth rate of South Sulawesi's population has been only half that of South-east Sulawesi and much less than half that of Central Sulawesi.

The proximate reasons for these wide differences in population growth rates between islands and provinces have to do with differences in vital rates and in net migration. These will be elaborated in later chapters. Behind these proximate reasons, however, lie other differences in ecological, social and economic conditions which have influenced fertility and mortality levels and, in particular, the size and direction of migratory flows. It would be pointless to attempt to explain differences in population growth rates by invoking particular social or economic background factors; clearly, it is the components of the rates that have to be explained. One is tempted to generalize that, by and large, population growth over the last quarter-century has been slower in more densely settled provinces and faster in more sparsely settled ones. There is some truth in this; Java and Bali have had slower growth rates than elsewhere, due both to lower fertility and net out-migration, and growth has also been relatively slow in some of the more densely settled provinces of the other islands: West Sumatra, South Kalimantan, North and South Sulawesi, Nusa Tenggara. But the continuing high population growth rates in now densely settled Lampung and in fairly densely populated North Sumatra serve to warn us against too simplistic an invocation of high density as *the* key factor responsible for slower growth. A complex web of factors has separately influenced mortality, fertility and migration and hence the differentials in their net outcome in different provinces.

3 Interregional Variation in Indonesia

Introduction

THE wide cultural and ecological variation which exists in Indonesia has been referred to in Chapter 1. The aim of this chapter is to develop this theme further by examining the major interregional variations which exist in contemporary Indonesia, especially variations in levels of social change and economic development. It will be demonstrated in subsequent chapters that these are linked to significant differences between groups and regional populations with respect to fertility, mortality, migration and a range of other demographic parameters. Explaining such variations can further our understanding of the patterns and processes of contemporary demographic change in Indonesia. Regional differences are, of course, to a degree a function of variations in ecological conditions, but many group and regional differences are a function of socio-economic inequalities which involve, as Hinderink and Sterkenburg (1978: 6) point out, individuals and groups having unequal access to the material and non-material resources of society, resulting in an unequal development of those resources.

The Uneven Impact of Colonial Penetration

It is not possible to understand the pattern of interregional differences and spatial inequalities in contemporary Indonesia without adopting a historical perspective. In particular, the long period of colonialism had a profound influence on the shape of the Indonesian space-economy, and much of this impact is still in evidence. Colonialism led to the superimposition of a new structure of a capitalist mode of production over the pre-existing indigenous, largely subsistence, structure so that a dual system (albeit one in which the traditional sector and the modern sector were strongly linked) was developed (Missen, 1972: 148). As the level of Dutch control over the colony was strengthened and the penetration of the capitalist mode of production increased in its spatial extent and intensity, distinctive spatial inequalities began to emerge. Capital investment was concentrated on development of areas and resources which satisfied the needs of the colonial rather than the colonized populations. Hence there was an overriding concern with commodities needed by Europe rather than by the colony, and development was spatially concentrated in areas suitable for plantations, mining, and oil and timber exploitation rather than in, for example, irrigation schemes needed for subsistence food production. The location of road, railway and water transportation systems, and cities which developed was thus such that it facilitated the production and delivery of these commodities for the European market. The spatial structure that emerged under colonialism was then very different from the pre-existing indigenous structure, and inevitably the pattern of population change reflected these drastic changes in the location of investment and economic expansion.

Slater (1975: 141–2) has shown that the spatial structure of a country passes through three phases in its transformation under colonialism:

1. Pre-colonial spatial structure: characterized by local and regional trading circuits and a few long-distance trading networks based on urban centres both inland and in coastal areas.

2. Colonial penetration, initial concentration and the beginnings of internal expansion: introduction of capitalist mode of production—plantations, mines, etc.—linked to growing coastal entrepôt cities by railways and roads.

3. Colonial organization and continued extension: elaboration of the system—more rapid growth of a single, usually primate, entrepôt colonial port-city linking the colony to the metropolis, together with further development of capitalist activity in concentrated areas—further inland and in more peripheral areas than in the second phase. These are linked to the port-city by transport networks.

This pattern of development is evident in Figure 3.1 which shows the gradual extension of railways in Java during the colonial period. Prior to 1880, there were three separate rail networks which extended out from the three major entrepôt centres of Batavia (now Jakarta), Semarang and Surabaya to divest their hinterlands of their cash crops and expedite their export to Europe. These three networks were subsequently elaborated and eventually merged with the increased tempo of colonial exploitation. This led to a greater focus on Batavia which is reflected in its growth rapidly outpacing that of Surabaya and Semarang in the early twentieth century. Colonial investment and activity were concentrated along these lines of communication, creating considerable spatial inequalities which reshaped the pattern of population distribution.

Throughout the nineteenth century, most Dutch colonial activity and investment was concentrated in Java so that its share of the population of the Indies increased from 50 per cent in 1815 to over 70 per cent in 1905 (Fisher, 1964: 289–90). However, towards the end of the nineteenth century, Dutch investment turned more to the other islands, especially Sumatra, as further opportunities for expanded activity in Java dwindled. Exploitation in Sumatra had three separate foci but was especially concentrated in the northern plantation areas around Medan. The shorter history of intensive colonial development in Sumatra meant that by the beginning of World War II it was still within the second phase of Slater's

FIGURE 3.1

Development of Railways in Java during the Colonial Period

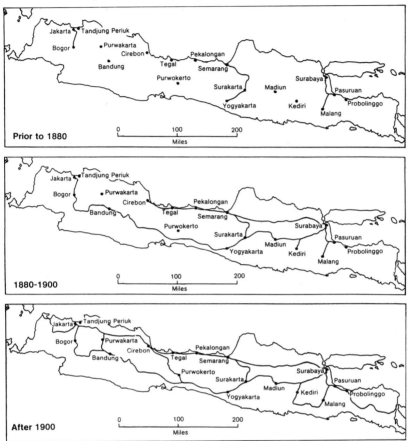

Source: Geographical Handbook Series, 1944: 415–17.

model. Hence Figure 3.2 shows that the railway network in Sumatra was 'frozen' in a pattern of three separate networks and development did not proceed to the stage where the networks merged. Fisher (1964: 287–8) concludes that the outstanding feature of production in the Indies by World War II was '... its extraordinary unevenness. Roughly at the centre of the archipelago lay the congested island of Java, full to over-flowing with people and cropped to capacity.... Outside Java, however, conditions were completely different. A few areas of intensive development ... but the greater part of the outer islands was still essentially undeveloped territory'. He shows that an important explanation of these spatial inequalities was 'great variations in the intensity and duration of European enterprise' and that these partly 'were reflected in the exceptionally wide range of population density found within the confines of the Netherlands Indies in the 1930s'.

FIGURE 3.2

Railways in Sumatra at the Close of the Colonial Period

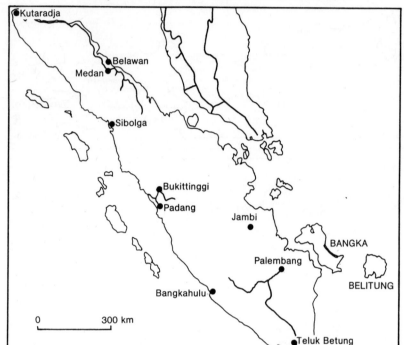

Source: Geographical Handbook Series, 1944: 415–17.

In no element of spatial structure was the impact of colonialism greater than in the development of Indonesia's urban hierarchy, in relation to both the overall level of urbanization and the spatial distribution and size of urban centres which developed. Unfortunately, it is not possible to quantify precisely these developments, since the first systematic classification of places as 'urban' or 'rural' for all Indonesia dates from the 1920 Census. Nevertheless there are some data on the size of individual cities prior to this so that some broad patterns can be discerned. Firstly, regarding the level of urbanization, there can be no doubt that colonialism dampened the growth of urbanization in Indonesia. Reid (1980) goes so far as to suggest that colonialism resulted in a decline in the level of urbanization. Using contemporary reports of the number of houses, fighting men, etc., as well as travellers' estimates of total population, he concludes that Aceh, Makassar, Surabaya and Banten all achieved populations in the range of 50,000 to 100,000 during the seventeenth century.

At the height of the colonial period, Ranneft (1929: 80) discussed why there was not a great exodus to the towns in Java as had occurred in Europe. He recognized that this situation was the direct result of a colonial policy which maintained Java as a 'country of various "subsidiary" industries'. The unprocessed and semi-processed raw materials extracted from the countryside supported secondary industry in the cities of Europe—not those of Indonesia. Cities in Indonesia were forwarding centres in which tertiary activities supporting this forwarding function increased; most employment, however, was created in rural areas, through plantation development and, later (under the Ethical Policy), through the expansion of the irrigated *sawah* area.

The size, distribution and spatial pattern of Indonesia's urban centres was fundamentally reshaped by Dutch colonial influences (Hugo, 1980; 1983). In pre-European contact times, urbanization was restricted to a number of ephemeral coastal cities (such as Sunda Kelapa near the present site of Jakarta) and a few substantial inland cities (for example, Yogyakarta and Surakarta) which were the centres of kingdoms (McGee, 1967). However, in the period from the late fourteenth to the seventeenth centuries, there was a great expansion of trade in the region and the coastal cities that served this trade came to dominate the urban pattern. As Reid (1980: 237) explains, these coastal cities 'grew into very large urban centres by the standards of the time, peopled not only by the itinerant traders and mariners but by larger numbers of indigenous dependants of the commercial aristocracy which presided over the trading towns'. Hence substantial trading cities were established throughout the archipelago. Although many were located along the Java coast (for example, Banten, Jakarta, Demak, Semarang, Tuban, Surabaya and Gresik), some were established on the other islands (for example, Aceh and Makassar).

However, in the nineteenth century, colonial exploitation demanded the growth of cities and towns in economically and politically strategic locations to expedite the efficient extraction, processing and delivery of raw materials and to maintain political and military control. The changing pattern of Indonesia's major urban centres in the last century of colonial rule is depicted in Figures 3.3 and 3.4, and the growth pattern of the twelve largest Indonesian cities is indicated in Table 3.1. The expansion of Dutch colonialism assured the supremacy of the coastal cities which functioned as transshipping points for the agricultural products from their hinterlands. By 1905, Batavia's population had increased to 138,551 (Ranneft, 1916: 84), representing an annual growth for the ninety years since 1815 of 0.74 per cent. This may seem a modest rate by contemporary standards but, in the light of Batavia's proverbial unhealthiness (Castles, 1967: 156) and high mortality rates (Haan, 1935: 685, 702), this figure indicates that substantial replenishment of the population occurred from the outside.

The period immediately preceding the 1930 Census was one of particularly rapid urban growth, with all major centres except the ancient capitals of Surakarta and Yogyakarta recording growth rates twice as large as those experienced by the population as a whole. A number of important points arise from Table 3.1 and the maps of urban centres, but the following seem especially significant:

1. Unlike many other colonies, the urban hierarchy of the Netherlands East Indies was not dominated by a single primate port city. Indeed

FIGURE 3.3

Indonesia: Location and Size of Urban Centres with Populations Exceeding
10,000 Persons in 1850 and 1905

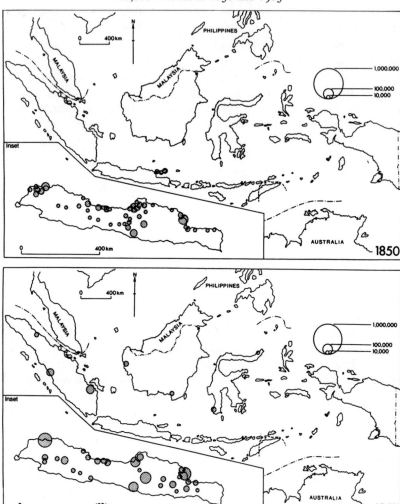

Sources: Hageman, 1852: 24–7; Encyclopedia van Nederlandsch Indie, 1907: 39.

Batavia, the colonial capital, had a smaller population than the port of
Surabaya until the early years of this century. The main reason for a 'more
balanced' urban system is Indonesia's large size and the fact that it is an
archipelago, which—given the limited transportation and communication
technology available—forced the colonial Dutch to operate through several
scattered entrepôt centres. Hence, while Batavia was the colonial capital,
the hinterland from which it collected raw materials for export was largely
restricted to West Java; Surabaya dominated the eastern part of Java;
Semarang, Central Java; and later Medan, the northern parts of Sumatra.

FIGURE 3.4

Indonesia: Location and Size of Major Urban Centres, 1920 and 1930

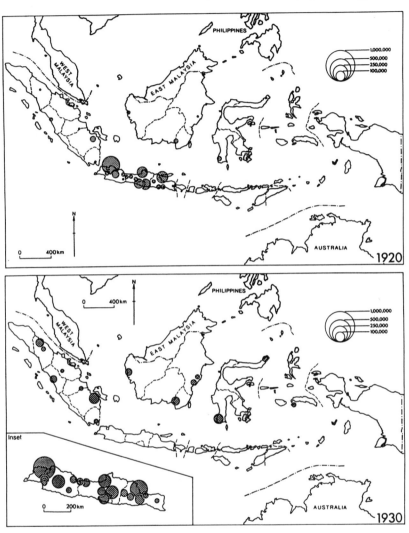

Source: Volkstelling, 1933–6.

With growing sophistication in transportation and communication, the capital's hinterland was greatly extended in both the later colonial and Independence years, and the Indonesian urban system has shown a consistent tendency to move away from the more balanced picture evident in Figure 3.2 towards a size distribution in which Jakarta dominates the urban system.

2. A second feature of the pattern of urban growth is the predominance of Java. It was not until the 1920s that an outer island city exceeded 100,000 in population, and even then there were six Javan cities with larger

TABLE 3.1

Indonesia: Population and Population Growth in Major Cities, 1855–1930

City	Island	1855	1883	1895	1905	1920	1930	Average Annual Growth	
								1855–1905	1905–1930
Batavia	Java	55,000	121,637	114,566	138,551	306,309	533,015	1.86	5.50
Surabaya	Java	88,527	121,637	124,529	150,198	192,190	341,675	1.06	3.34
Semarang	Java	n.a.	67,575	82,962	96,660	158,036	217,796	1.64	3.30
Bandung	Java	11,223*	n.a.	46,326	47,400	94,800	166,815	2.47	5.16
Surakarta	Java	n.a.	n.a.	104,589	118,378	139,285	165,484	1.25	1.35
Yogyakarta	Java	43,000	n.a.	58,299	79,569	103,711	136,649	1.24	2.19
Palembang	Sumatra	n.a.	n.a.	n.a.	61,000	73,726	108,145	n.a.	2.32
Malang	Java	n.a.	n.a.	n.a.	30,000	42,981	86,646	n.a.	4.33
Makassar	Celebes	n.a.	n.a.	n.a.	26,000	56,718	84,855	n.a.	4.85
Medan	Sumatra	n.a.	n.a.	n.a.	n.a.	45,248	76,584	n.a.	5.40
Pekalongan	Java	30,000	n.a.	n.a.	n.a.	47,852	65,982	n.a.	3.26
Banjarmasin	Borneo	n.a.	n.a.	n.a.	n.a.	46,993	65,698	n.a.	3.41

Sources: Volkstelling, 1933–6; Milone, 1966; Ranneft, 1916.

*1846 figure.

n.a. = Data not available.

populations. The dominance of Javan cities was partly attributable to the concentration of colonial activity in Java mentioned earlier.

3. There is a pattern of growing dominance of colonial cities—that is, those cities occupying key positions in the articulation of linkages between extraction of surplus in the colony and its delivery to the colonial country. Hence there is a pattern of increasing dominance of coastal entrepôt centres. In some cases, such as Jakarta, they are very much the creation of the Dutch colonial regime, while in others, such as Surabaya and Makassar, already thriving port centres were developed further. Meanwhile, the growth of the traditional inland kingdom centres was much slower. The only inland centres to grow rapidly were colonial creations such as Buitenzorg (Bogor), Bandung and Malang.

Population Distribution and Density

Many types of regional differences and inequalities can be identified within Indonesia—between urban and rural areas, between islands, between provinces, and between smaller areas. To some extent, these spatial differences are a function of intergroup differences between classes, ethnic groups, sectors of the economy etc., but adoption of a regional basis for comparison helps illuminate the extent and nature of socio-economic variation within Indonesia. Clearly, in such an analysis, there are important questions of scale. In Chapter 1, the broad 'inner–outer' Indonesia dichotomy with respect to ecological conditions was explored, but there are very significant variations within those broad regions. Figure 3.5, for example, shows population density differences within Java at the *kecamatan* (subdistrict) level at the 1930 and 1971 Censuses. Clearly, at this more detailed scale of analysis, wide differences in density of settlement are apparent. Indonesia's 'population problem' is frequently (albeit incorrectly) interpreted as being one of 'overpopulation' in Java, and an appreciation of regional differences in population density is important to an understanding of that 'problem'.

Figure 3.5 shows that there was not much change in the relative distribution pattern of population densities between 1930 and 1971, with the main changes being of areas moving up one or more categories of density. By 1930, Java had already experienced a long period of agricultural intensification, construction of irrigation facilities, and adaptation of the rural economy to changes in population growth and vice versa. There were no very dramatic developments in technology between 1930 and 1971; if anything, there was a decline in the irrigated area and the quality of the irrigation system (Booth, 1977). Thus there was nothing much to disturb the basic pattern of population density already established in 1930.

Figure 3.5 shows three major belts of high population density in Java in 1930. The first stretched along the north coastal plain from the vicinity of Indramayu and Cirebon in West Java to Semarang in Central Java; the second covered a large block of country in south Central Java and included Yogyakarta; and the third was in East Java forming a circle around the volcanoes of Gunung Arjuna and Gunung Kelud. In addition, there were

FIGURE 3.5

Java: Population Density, 1930 and 1971

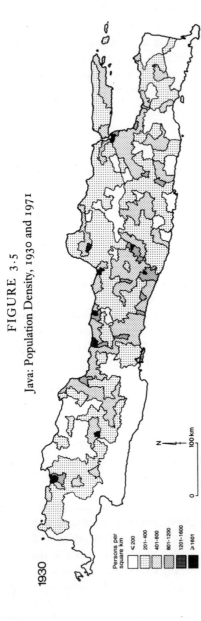

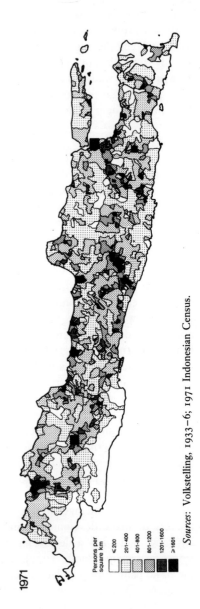

Sources: Volkstelling, 1933–6; 1971 Indonesian Census.

high-density 'outliers' in the Priangan and Jabotabek areas of West Java. The main 'low-density' areas (that is, those with less than 200 persons per square kilometre) included the entire south coastal region of West Java; the north coastal strip between Jakarta and Indramayu, and inland to the northern Priangan area; much of the eastern peninsular area of East Java; and a stretch of the middle Solo River Valley and the Kendeng mountains to its east, in Central and East Java, from Sragen and Ngawi through to the eastern end of the Kendeng range.

One obvious explanation for these patterns is the underlying differences in soils and topography. For example, several localized areas of low population density comprise major volcanic peaks such as Gunung Slamet, Gunung Merbabu and Gunung Arjuna. These tend to be surrounded by very densely settled areas, coinciding with the areas where slopes are not steep enough to prevent agriculture, and have rich volcanic soil which can be utilized for very intensive vegetable and rice growing. The main lowland areas of high density are those where good soil and suitable drainage have permitted the development of intensive irrigated agriculture, combined in many coastal areas with fish-ponds, salt-pans and offshore fishing. The major low-density areas tend to be in areas with poorer soil, especially the limestone areas of parts of south-coastal Java. Historical factors have played a role as well, including the loss of life in large areas of coastal Banten as a result of the eruption of Krakatao in 1883, and migration out of the area to escape a particularly oppressive regime, as recorded in the book *Max Havelaar*.

There is a close correspondence between areas of high population density and areas where a substantial proportion of the land was under sugar cultivation during the colonial period. One explanation for this is that sugar was only grown in areas where soil fertility was high and which therefore tended to support high population densities. Another could be that the system by which sugar was grown in Dutch times made for more rapid population increases in the sugar-growing areas. White (1973) has argued that the labour demands imposed by the Dutch 'Cultivation System' in the second half of the nineteenth century gave a strong incentive for high fertility. Thus population growth, and resulting densities in the twentieth century, tended to be greater in areas directly subject to the pressures of the Cultivation System and, by 1920, areas where sugar was grown in Java had proportionately (1) more *sawah*; (2) more population; and (3) even though more of their *sawah* is occupied by sugar, more rice than the non-sugar areas (Widjojo, 1970).

Over the course of the present century, the density of population in Java has increased tremendously. Figure 3.5 shows a reduction in the number of areas with densities below 200 persons per square kilometre between 1930 and 1971 as they moved into a higher-density category. Between 1930 and 1971, the proportion of districts (or rural *kecamatan* in the case of the 1971 data) in Java with population densities below 200 persons per square kilometre fell from 17 per cent to 6 per cent. Most of these low-density areas in 1971 were in the Banten area of West Java, certain limestone areas on the south coast, and the steep slopes of volcanoes and volcanic plateaux. At the other end of the density scale, fewer than 4 per cent of districts had densities exceeding 1,000 persons per square kilo-metre in 1930, compared with 17.5 per cent in 1971.

In Figure 3.6, the population density of the *kabupaten* of Java has been compared at five different dates—1920, 1930, 1961, 1971 and 1980. At each date, the proportion of these *kabupaten* falling into different density groups is compared. The inexorable decline in the percentage with moderate population densities, and the rise in the proportion of high densities, is clearly shown. The same trends can be shown in case studies of smaller regions or particular villages. Burger (1971) compared the village of Pekalongan in 1868 and 1928, and found that over these sixty years the average land-holding fell by half, to about half a hectare, as population growth led to the subdivision of plots and the reclaiming of fields for dwelling land. Bennett (1957) showed a similar process in East Java, and Penny and Singarimbun (1973) in Yogyakarta.

FIGURE 3.6

Java–Madura Percentage of *Kabupaten* in Different Population
Density Categories, 1920–1980

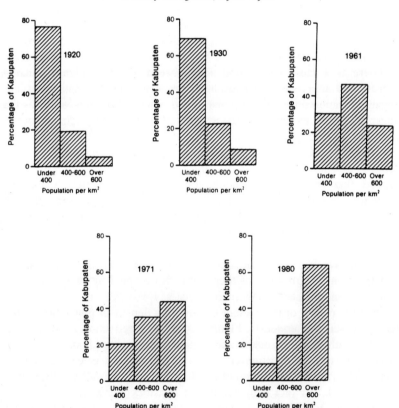

The 1971 population density map shows little change in the *patterns* of population density in rural Java since 1930. Certain areas of high density in 1930, such as southern Madura, were no longer as high relative to the rest of Java in 1971, due mainly to high out-migration but possibly also because of relatively low fertility; other areas, such as the southern Priangan region in West Java (Bandung–Garut–Tasikmalaya–Ciamis), have become major high-density belts, due to more rapid population growth since 1930 than in most other regions.

There is a clear inverse relationship between population density of *kabupaten* in 1930 and the subsequent rate of population growth from 1930 to 1971 which implies a gradual lessening of differences in population density between the various *kabupaten*, and an increase in the proportion of the island in the very high density class. This is further emphasized by simple regressions relating population growth rates of the *kabupaten* in the 1930–71 period with their population densities in 1930. Whether the regressions are calculated for Java as a whole or separately within each province, the slope of the regression is negative and the F value is significant, though the highest R^2s are measured for West Java and East Java. The results are as follows:

West Java	$y = -0.00196$	$x = +2.1016$	$R^2 = 0.54$	$F = 21.293$
Central Java	$y = -0.0007$	$x = +1.3999$	$R^2 = 0.12$	$F = 4.108$
East Java	$y = -0.00178$	$x = +1.6919$	$R^2 = 0.42$	$F = 5.851$
All Java	$y = -0.00160$	$x = +1.7729$	$R^2 = 0.28$	$F = 31.901$

It is clear that the density in 1930 bore a strong negative relationship to the growth which occurred over the 1930–71 period.

By the time of the 1973 Census of Agriculture, the average farm size in Java was only 0.66 hectares, less than half the average farm size in Sumatra or Sulawesi; moreover, 57 per cent of farms in Java were less than half a hectare in area, compared with just over a quarter of all farms in the rest of Indonesia (Booth and Sundrum, 1976). Both the total area of farm land and the average farm size declined between 1963 and 1973, partly because of the encroachment of house compounds onto agricultural land, and partly because the degree of fragmentation had increased. Although increasing population pressure on the land in Java was relieved to some extent by a combination of the following factors—the increase in irrigation, a slower natural increase in the population than elsewhere in Indonesia, out-migration, and movement into non-agricultural occupations—the growth of the agricultural labour force nevertheless outstripped the growth in the number of farms over the period, indicating that there was an increase in the proportion of landless labourers (Booth and Sundrum, 1976: 104).

A case-study of time trends in two villages in East Java (Edmundson, 1977; Edmundson and Edmundson, 1983) illustrates these trends well. In the village of Glanggang in *kabupaten* Malang, steadily increasing population on a fixed land base has lowered the land availability per person to 0.08 hectares. However, substantial increases in productivity with the new rice varieties, a well-developed set of village home-industries, and commuting to work in the nearby town of Malang have actually permitted a heightened prosperity in the face of the continued population increase. The poorer village of Pagak, on the limestone plateau further south, has fared less well despite larger farm size.

A case-study of the response to population pressure (McDonald and Sontosudarmo, 1976) in Yogyakarta showed great variety in the growth rates of *kecamatan* due to differing patterns of in-migration and out-migration. Of particular note are trends in the limestone areas of southern Gunung Kidul where the population increased from 101,000 persons in 1930 to 196,000 in 1961, indicating fairly substantial in-migration. But in the following ten years, the population increased by only 14,000, indicating a high level of out-migration. McDonald and Sontosudarmo (1976: 83) conclude that: 'Within the short span of forty years this region has switched from being an area of new settlement to an area of substantial out-migration and the ecological destruction caused by deforestation may never be repaired.'

Their study suggests that historical patterns of out-migration may play as large a role as relative poverty in leading to adjustment to population pressure through out-migration. It also highlights the increase in non-agricultural activities in areas better located in relation to transport and markets as another adjustment mechanism not requiring migration.

How serious is the increasing population pressure in rural Java? How long can it continue? Such questions have troubled observers of the Java scene for a long time. The fact that pressures have continued to build up long after the first warning notes were sounded, without evidence of serious breakdown of the social and economic system (albeit without evidence of much, if any, improvement in levels of living of poorer rural dwellers) is perhaps indicative of the resilience and adaptability of the Javanese peasant economy and a warning against further prophecies of doom based on the growing population pressure.

And yet it would be equally unwise to be sanguine about rural Java's prospects of absorbing further population increase in agriculture. Allen (1965: 76) has defined 'human carrying capacity' as 'the maximum population density which a system is capable of supporting permanently in that environment without damage to the land', and as the density level 'beyond which degeneration leading to ultimate collapse is bound to set in' He defines 'critical population density' as 'the human carrying capacity of an area in relation to a given land use system expressed in terms of population per square mile'. To determine the critical population density and whether it is being approached or indeed exceeded would require detailed information on soil types, proportion of land which can be cultivated under the prevailing technology, land use, and the area under cultivation per head of the population. These kinds of data are seriously deficient for Java, but there is enough evidence to give cause for great concern about the potential of Javanese agriculture to sustain further increases in the population dependent on it. This evidence is as follows:

1. First, there is evidence of increasing landlessness (that is, rural

household heads who do not own land), and decreasing farm size (see, for example, Table 1.4 and White, 1977).

2. There is the evidence of displacement of agricultural labour by developments stemming from, or related to, the introduction of higher-yielding rice varieties, such as the change in harvesting methods and the replacement of hand-pounding of rice by mechanical rice-hullers (White, 1977). To the extent that these developments raise total income in the economy (for example, by permitting an extra crop to be grown by shortening the harvesting period), there can be secondary effects which may in fact *raise* total employment or at least not lower it by as much as might appear at first sight. However, the income distribution effects of the green revolution appear to have been unfavourable, and there is little doubt that, whatever its effects on total employment, localized reductions in employment opportunities may be serious.

3. Although different trends are indicated by different data sources on welfare and income distribution, Sayogyo's (1977) data show that although the proportion of people below the poverty line fell very slightly in the 1970s, the proportion who are 'destitute' rose by 4 per cent of the total to 25 per cent. There does, however, appear to have been an improvement in the welfare of rural people in the early 1980s due to increased off-farm employment, much of it associated with circular migration and commuting (Collier *et al.*, 1982; Hugo, 1985).

4. Although the area of land under cultivation in Java has increased very little in recent years, what increase there has been has consisted mainly of expansion of cultivation into areas which should have been kept under forest cover (Thijsse, 1975). For example, in the upper Solo River basin, cassava has been grown on steep hillsides, resulting in severe erosion when the rains of the wet season follow the harvesting of the cassava. Continued planting of cassava on such land reduces soil fertility even without erosion. But expansion of the cultivated area is not the only reason why trees are cut down. As population pressures grow, more wood is sought for fuel and for sale in nearby urban areas. This seriously hampers efforts at reafforestation, which are now being pursued with more vigour through the government's *penghijauan* (greening) programme, but with little prospects of quick success. One result of the increasing deforestation is siltation of dams and reservoirs, thereby reducing their potential for irrigation, generation of hydro-electricity and flood control (Dick, 1980). Another result is the increasing frequency of serious floods in rivers such as the Brantas, Solo and Citarum, as well as in the smaller river systems.

These problems, together with the expansion of cities into once heavily farmed agricultural areas, are likely to lead in time to decline in the area under crops in Java, a daunting prospect in view of the continued growth of the rural population. Clearly, greatly increased double and triple cropping and yields per cultivated hectare will be required if the incomes of the rural population are to be raised through agricultural development, along with further improvements in off-farm employment opportunities.

Transmigration has long been proposed as a key solution to the problems of population pressure in Java. However, despite a notable increase in numbers moved by the transmigration programme in the early years of the 1980s, which for the first time since the programme began achieved more than a trivial impact on overall population growth in Java (see Chapter 6), the fact is that the potential of the other islands to support dense agricultural populations in areas that are now sparsely settled is very limited. Although the focus of transmigration has now shifted away from Sumatra, earlier transmigration flows and continuing spontaneous movement are likely to result in a population of 50 million in Sumatra before the year 2000, and a doubling of the 1971 population in about twenty to twenty-five years (Jones, 1978). Just how large a population Sumatra can support in primary production is a matter for sheer guesswork, due to the lack of sufficiently detailed soil surveys and other basic data. The big unanswered questions concern the possible carrying capacity of the large *pasang surut* areas, and the extent to which the enormous tracts of provinces such as South Sumatra and Jambi—at present given over to swidden agriculture which Pelzer (1946: 137–8) has calculated requires 10 hectares per farm family—are suitable for settled agriculture. But, certainly, relatively little of the land outside of Java is suitable for irrigated agriculture (Sie Kurat Soen, 1968: 71).

Regional Differences in Educational Development

The educational attainment of the Indonesian population differs very substantially by region, although the differences are narrowing over time due to the policy of post-Independence governments to greatly expand educational opportunities and to provide them at more or less the same level in all regions. Many historical factors explain the remaining differentials, among which the patterns of exposure of different ethnic groups to European and to Islamic influence, differences in colonial policies with respect to different ethnic groups, and different reactions among different ethnic groups to the challenge of European domination are of key importance (Jones, 1976).

A priori, it might be expected that Java, with its high proportion of Indonesia's population, most of its manufacturing industry, its centres of political power, its monopoly of Indonesia's most prestigious institutions of higher learning, and its old and highly refined culture, would also lead the way in educational attainment of its population. However, on the contrary, over a lengthy period, education has been more advanced in the predominantly Christian outer island areas of North Sulawesi, Maluku, and North Sumatra. These had the highest education attainment among the adult population of any provinces in 1971, and the equivalent regions had the highest literacy rates in 1930. Java lagged well behind these regions in educational development. Moreover, it was the predominantly Christian regions within the three outer island provinces (that is, Minahasa and Sangir–Talaud, Ambon, and Tapanuli, respectively) which ranked highest of all in percentages of the population that were literate or had completed a primary education.

It is not possible to draw the simplistic conclusion that all Christian areas are better educated. Not even all the areas where Christianity has long been established are educationally advanced: for example, large areas of East Nusa Tenggara are not. By the same token, not all the areas more recently converted to Christianity are backward educationally: parts of Kalimantan and Irian Jaya are, but the Tapanuli and Toraja areas are not. Comparable differentials are found with regard to education in Islamic areas. For example, the Minangkabau and the Mandailing Batak have long had a much higher proportion of the population educated than have, for example, the Banten and Pasisir areas of West Java or the Buginese–Makassarese areas of South Sulawesi.

One of the reasons for these differences is the timing and geographic allocation of missionary efforts and the timing and location of various Islamic reform movements. In the beginning, the growth of Christianity was confined largely to the areas of Eastern Indonesia (notably Minahasa, Maluku and East Nusa Tenggara) which had been little penetrated by Islam and were of special interest for Portuguese and Dutch trade. The second 'wave' of missionary activity which began in the late nineteenth century was concentrated in interior areas among ethnic groups which had remained animist—the Batak of North Sumatra, the Toraja of South Sulawesi, the Dayak of Kalimantan, and the Irianese.

The Dutch were very slow to show an interest in fostering a relatively widespread basic education in Indonesia and lagged considerably behind the British in India in this regard (Furnivall, 1956: 377). Dutch interest in education grew during the second half of the nineteenth century, but not without considerable ambivalence as to the desirability of establishing broad-based public education. Even in 1900 in Java, the budget allocation for education of Europeans was almost double that for the 'education of natives' (Day, 1966: 389) and there were only 562 schools in Java (one per 50,000 inhabitants), more than half of which had been established by private enterprise (Dahm, 1971: 15). Thus the areas which were under effective Dutch control in the nineteenth century—notably Java—did not profit thereby in terms of a more widespread basic education. Only in Ambon and Minahasa did education flourish, and this for the special reasons that mission education was firmly established there quite early, and the Dutch found educated Ambonese and Minahasans invaluable in administering their far-flung domain. By the time the Dutch interest in educating their subjects developed, most other regions were also under effective Dutch control, and in this sense they all started off on an 'equal footing' with Java.

Even had the Dutch been fairly even-handed in the provision of educational facilities, differences in educational development within the predominantly Muslim areas could have been expected as a result of the differing role accorded education by different Islamic groups, and the varying strength of these groups in different regions. Within Java, Geertz

(1960: 177) argues, the *santri* variant of Javanese Islam, 'because of its doctrinal complexity ... its lack of close integration with some of the basic social forms and fundamental attitudes of peasant society, and the hostility to it on the part of most non-*santri*', needed the reinforcement of special schools, whereas the *abangan* variant did not. Thus in areas of *santri* dominance, the *pondok* or *pesantren* (a mosque-linked religious school) developed. Since the 1920s, the modernists have succeeded both in establishing more modern forms of Islamic schools, called *madrasah*, in bringing elements of Western education into many of the *pondok*, and in opening education more widely to girls. It is therefore very difficult to generalize about the forms of Islamic education. Some *pondok* devote less than half their time to religious education; others have not compromised at all with modern educational theories. The *madrasah* emphasize general education to a greater extent than the *pondok* and in some cases differ little from public schools. There is no doubt that the *madrasah* have had a great impact on the amount of secular education available to orthodox Muslims in Indonesia. At the turn of the century there were virtually no *madrasah*; by 1954, there were about 1.5 million pupils in *madrasah* compared with nearly two million in *pesantren* (Geertz, 1960).

In line with Geertz's argument, education was more widespread by 1971 and 1980 in many of the more orthodox Islamic areas (Aceh, West Sumatra, South Sumatra, and the Priangan area of West Java, for example) than in the areas of Central and East Java where *abangan* elements were strong. Moreover, despite the clear tendency for the ratio of females to males among those receiving schooling to be lower among Muslims than among Christians, this ratio was lower in Central and East Java than in many of the areas where Islam was stronger and more orthodox.

In 1930, some of the lowest adult literacy rates in all Indonesia were recorded in the sultanates of Yogyakarta and Surakarta, and one suspects that the feudal social structure and the poverty in these regions had militated against the extension of education for any but the *bangsawan* (nobility), whereas the religious schools established in the more devout Muslim areas, for all their shortcomings, did provide basic literacy for many of their pupils. Moreover, it was precisely in the more devout Muslim areas that the reformist missionary and social action movement of Indonesian Islam, the Muhammadiyah, was most active and was therefore able to do most in the field of education.

Aside from this, special 'ethnic' factors are widely believed to be important explanatory variables. Jones (1976) has, for example, discussed the historical factors associated with the strong emphasis on education among the Minangkabau of West Sumatra and the Mandailing Batak.

In Java, 94 per cent of the adult population was still illiterate in 1930. Literacy was highest in West Java, especially in the Priangan region in and around Bandung. Outside Java, adult literacy rates on the whole were substantially higher, though there were areas of extremely low literacy such as Bali, southern Sulawesi and most of Borneo and Nusa Tenggara. Literacy was most widespread in the divisions of Lampung, Bengkulu,

Palembang, Tapanuli, and Bangka in Sumatra (all above 12 per cent), in Manado in Sulawesi (29 per cent) and in Maluku (19 per cent). In Tapanuli, Menado, and Maluku, the influence of the missions is clear, not only in the high overall literacy rates but also in the high female literacy rates relative to male and the high proportion of literates who had received formal education.

It was clear enough from the 1930 figures that literacy rates were rising and that the overwhelming predominance of males among the literates was lessening over time. By 1971, the massive broadening of the educational base due to the vigorous efforts to widen educational opportunities after Independence had removed the earlier geographical and sex differentials to some extent, though these were of course still pronounced among the population above age 40, who had received their education in the pre-Independence period. Figure 3.7 is based on data on literacy in each *kabupaten* for the population 10 years of age and above. It shows that most of the key geographic differentials in 1930 remained. Literacy rates, despite sharp increases in all regions, remained lowest in parts of Central and East Java, Bali, West Nusa Tenggara, South Sulawesi, and West Kalimantan. Within Java, the Priangan areas of West Java and the Banyumas–Yogyakarta–Salatiga area of Central Java remained far more literate than the north coastal areas of West Java and western Central Java, or Madura and peninsular East Java. Tapanuli, Minahasa and Ambon remained the most literate areas of all. Similar differentials are evident when we compare educational attainment rather than literacy in 1971 (Jones, 1976: 48–52).

Table 3.2 shows the percentage of the population in each province that had completed Lower Secondary school education in 1980. By comparing educational attainment of the younger and older age groups, it is clear that provincial differences in levels of education had narrowed considerably over time. Jakarta is becoming increasingly prominent, not only because of the heavy concentration of educational institutions there, but also because of the relatively high average educational attainment of migrants in the capital. Yogyakarta has been unique as a centre of learning in post-Independence times. Of the remaining provinces, the heritage of the historical factors noted earlier is apparent in the heavy concentration near the top of the list (especially at older ages) of provinces with a high proportion of Christians in their populations, and in the continued importance of Aceh and West Sumatra.

Sex inequality in education had also lessened dramatically over time. Census data for 1971 and 1980 show that among old people who received their elementary education in the 1920s or earlier, there were 6 to 8 males for every female among those who had completed a primary education in provinces such as East Java and North Sumatra, compared with 1 to 2 males for every female in North Sulawesi and Maluku. But for young people who had recently passed through the nation's educational system, in all provinces there were only 1 to 2 males to every female who had completed a primary education. Judging by the sharp fall in the ratio

64

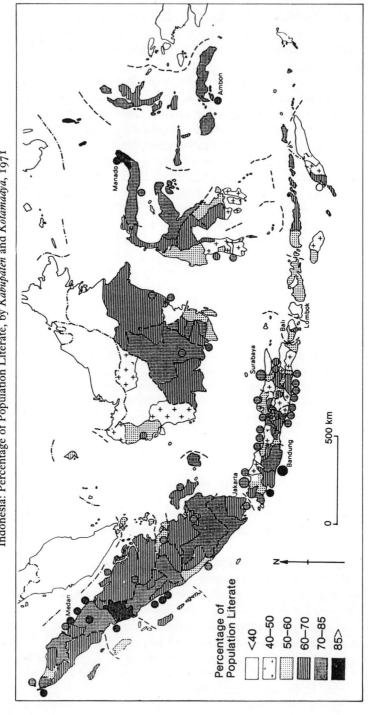

FIGURE 3.7

Indonesia: Percentage of Population Literate, by *Kabupaten* and *Kotamadya*, 1971

Percentage of
Population Literate

<40
40–50
50–60
60–70
70–85
85>

500 km

Source: Jones, 1976.

TABLE 3.2

Indonesia: Percentage of Population with Completed Lower Secondary Schooling, by Age Group, 1980

Province	Percentage of Population by Age Group						
	15–19 Years	20–24 Years	30–34 Years	40–44 Years	50–54 Years	60–64 Years	70+ Years
DKI Jakarta Raya	30.2	45.3	48.3	35.0	22.2	15.1	8.5
DI Yogyakarta	32.1	42.4	26.8	14.9	5.8	3.4	1.3
East Kalimantan	17.5	27.6	24.6	12.7	5.2	3.1	0.8
Aceh	19.2	26.9	17.8	10.4	3.6	1.5	0.9
North Sumatra	21.6	26.5	25.9	18.5	7.8	4.0	1.8
North Sulawesi	21.7	25.6	27.8	19.6	7.0	4.8	3.4
Maluku	17.2	25.2	22.7	15.1	4.9	1.8	1.2
West Sumatra	21.5	24.4	19.5	17.0	8.1	5.6	2.4
Central Kalimantan	14.1	22.8	16.6	10.4	4.1	2.1	1.7
South Sulawesi	18.1	22.5	16.5	9.8	3.3	1.6	0.5
South-east Sulawesi	16.6	21.5	16.1	7.6	2.2	0.8	0.2
Riau	15.1	20.9	20.3	12.2	4.7	3.7	1.3
Bengkulu	13.8	20.5	13.8	9.1	4.5	2.1	1.7

(continued)

TABLE 3.2 (continued)

Province	Percentage of Population by Age Group						
	15–19 Years	20–24 Years	30–34 Years	40–44 Years	50–54 Years	60–64 Years	70+ Years
South Kalimantan	15.6	20.0	15.3	9.0	4.3	1.6	0.7
South Sumatra	14.0	19.9	17.1	11.4	4.4	2.1	1.2
East Nusa Tenggara	11.4	19.3	10.3	6.8	1.9	1.4	0.8
Bali	16.8	18.8	12.9	8.9	2.8	0.6	0.5
Central Sulawesi	13.5	18.6	19.4	10.8	4.3	2.2	0.6
East Java	14.1	17.6	12.5	7.1	3.0	1.7	1.0
Central Java	14.0	17.4	13.0	7.6	3.1	1.8	1.2
West Irian	7.8	17.3	15.4	8.5	2.9	0.8	3.8
Jambi	12.9	17.3	13.5	9.9	5.1	2.8	1.3
West Java	14.0	16.8	12.2	9.2	3.9	2.2	1.3
West Nusa Tenggara	14.8	15.8	8.9	4.8	1.7	1.1	0.3
West Kalimantan	9.0	14.3	8.0	4.7	1.8	1.0	0.9
Lampung	9.5	13.5	11.1	6.7	3.0	2.2	1.2

Source: 1980 Indonesian Census, Series S, Tables 2 and 5.9.
Note: These provinces are ranked according to the percentage with completed lower secondary schooling among the age group 20–24.

TABLE 3.3

Indonesia: Percentage of Children Attending School, by Province, 1980

Province	Males (Percentage)		Females (Percentage)		Ratio Male/Female × 100	
	Age 5–12	Age 13–18	Age 5–12	Age 13–18	Age 5–12	Age 13–18
SUMATRA						
Aceh	67.9	58.0	68.1	48.3	97.1	120.1
North Sumatra	68.9	59.1	68.2	47.9	101.0	123.4
West Sumatra	68.8	59.5	69.7	55.9	98.7	106.4
Riau	62.7	53.8	60.8	41.3	103.1	130.3
Jambi	62.5	49.8	60.0	32.7	104.2	152.3
South Sumatra	65.3	51.1	65.5	39.2	99.7	130.4
Bengkulu	65.9	53.1	64.4	36.2	102.3	146.9
Lampung	62.4	45.4	63.3	34.9	98.6	130.1
JAVA						
Jakarta	76.2	71.1	76.5	51.4	99.6	138.3
West Java	64.5	34.0	64.9	33.8	99.4	100.6
Central Java	71.3	47.7	71.3	35.1	100.0	135.9
Yogyakarta	78.0	74.4	79.1	61.5	98.6	121.0
East Java	72.1	49.8	72.4	36.5	99.6	136.4
KALIMANTAN						
West Kalimantan	54.3	50.3	50.0	36.8	108.6	136.7
Central Kalimantan	63.6	53.8	66.1	44.7	96.2	120.4
South Kalimantan	69.3	51.1	69.8	37.4	99.3	136.6
East Kalimantan	62.7	56.1	63.4	43.6	98.9	128.7
SULAWESI						
North Sulawesi	73.4	52.7	77.1	53.0	95.2	99.4
Central Sulawesi	64.3	56.7	63.7	43.8	100.9	129.5
South Sulawesi	62.0	55.0	65.5	43.9	94.7	125.3
South-east Sulawesi	69.5	54.6	71.2	44.1	97.6	123.8
OTHER ISLANDS						
Bali	72.5	61.5	67.7	39.1	107.1	157.3
West Nusa Tenggara	60.8	47.0	55.7	31.3	109.2	150.2
East Nusa Tenggara	59.7	60.4	60.2	46.2	99.2	130.7
Maluku	69.1	63.4	68.3	47.8	101.2	132.6
Irian Jaya	54.5	51.9	48.4	37.2	112.6	139.5

Source: 1980 Indonesian Census.

between the 1937–41 birth cohort and the 1952–6 birth cohort in Central and East Java and in Bali, education for females in the post-Independence period would appear to have made particularly rapid strides in these provinces.

The closing of the educational gap between the regions is best demonstrated by the proportion of children attending schools or other educational institutions at the time of the 1980 Census. Because of heavy investment in rural primary schools in the 1970s under the *Inpres* programme, the proportion of school-age children attending school was much higher in 1980 than in 1971. Table 3.3 shows that the proportion of young school-age males who were in school ranged only between 54.3 per cent (West Kalimantan) and 78.0 per cent (Yogyakarta). The range for females was somewhat wider, from 48.4 per cent (Irian Jaya) to 79.1 per cent (Yogyakarta), but even this represented a very considerable narrowing of the gap which existed in 1930, as well as a very sharp rise in all provinces in the proportion of children in school. Similar sharp increases may be observed in the proportion of older school-age children (aged 13–18) in school.

What is perhaps most noteworthy in Table 3.3 is the close association between proportion of males in school and the relative development of education for girls. Provinces with high proportions of males in school tended to have a higher ratio of females to males in school, or in other words there was a tendency for provinces with low school enrolment rates for males to do especially poorly when it came to female education.

Thus, although regional educational differences are narrowing drastically, it will still be a long time before the more educationally backward provinces, such as West Nusa Tenggara and West Java, reach the educational levels of provinces such as North Sulawesi and Yogyakarta, whichever measure of educational progress is used.

Regional Income Differentials

In 1982, Indonesia's Gross Domestic Product (GDP) per capita was around US$590. There are substantial regional variations around this figure, although the quality of data on regional income differentials leaves a great deal to be desired. A regional income research group, working in the early 1970s, prepared a set of estimates of Regional Gross Domestic Product for the twenty-six provinces (Esmara, 1975). They were subject to a number of deficiencies arising from lack of basic statistical data, but they were at least consistent in the sense that similar estimates were used for the different regions, and a control was imposed that they must add up to the already calculated national total. However, these estimates do not significantly reflect differences in real levels of living between regions, because value added in a particular region might not always accrue to persons in that region (as, for example, in the case of estates which are owned by people from other provinces or outside the country, and in the case of petroleum revenues, most of which flow to the central government), and because substantial price disparities between regions make such comparisons hazardous (Arndt and Sundrum, 1975). Moreover, 'skewness' in the distribution of income may be greater in one province than in another, even if per capita income accruing to persons resident in those provinces is identical. The World Bank (1984a) has produced more recent estimates of per capita GDP for each province, presented in Table 3.4. The variation in

TABLE 3.4
Gross Domestic Product Per Capita at Current Prices, by Province, 1971, 1975 and 1979 (in '000 Rupiah)

	1971	1975	1979	Rank 1971	Rank 1979	Real Annual Growth Rate (Per Cent), 1975–1979	Increase 1971–1979 (Times)	Rank
JAVA								
DKI Jakarta*	27	78	163				5.0	
West Java	67	205	448	3	4	5.6	5.7	9
Central Java	25	79	152	19	17	5.3	5.1	14
DI Yogyakarta	22	60	127	22	22	5.8	4.8	17
East Java	19	64	119	23	23	2.7	5.3	12
	25	70	147	19	20	4.4	4.9	15
SUMATRA*+	49	166	360				6.3	
DI Aceh *+	29	101	420	15	5	18.7	13.5	3
North Sumatra*	40	102	230	6	9	5.6	4.8	17
West Sumatra	26	68	153	17	16	n.a.	4.9	15
Riau*+	178	975	1,723	1	2	3.3	8.7	4
Jambi	43	78	192	5	11	6.7	3.5	25
South Sumatra*	60	145	393	4	6	7.1	5.6	10
Bengkulu	26	57	149	17	18	8.0	4.7	19
Lampung	27	72	146	16	21	3.5	4.4	22

(continued)

TABLE 3.4 (continued)

	1971	1975	1979	Rank 1971	Rank 1979	Real Annual Growth Rate (Per Cent), 1975–1979	Increase 1971–1979 (Times)	Rank
KALIMANTAN*+	38	149	488				11.8	
West Kalimantan	30	82	168	12	13	5.7	4.6	21
Central Kalimantan*+	33	99	271	8	7	10.0	7.2	6
South Kalimantan	32	77	181	12	12	8.3	4.7	19
East Kalimantan*+	76	499	1,872	2	1	14.1	23.6	1
SULAWESI	26	70	161				5.2	
North Sulawesi	38	89	199	7	10	6.0	4.2	23
Central Sulawesi+	17	58	148	24	19	5.2	7.7	5
South Sulawesi	24	69	159	21	14	7.8	5.6	10
South-east Sulawesi	30	51	107	13	24	3.4	2.6	26
EASTERN ISLANDS+	24	78	180				6.5	
Bali	32	80	154	11	15	7.1	3.8	24
West Nusa Tenggara	16	47	99	25	25	4.3	5.2	13
East Nusa Tenggara	14	41	97	26	26	5.8	5.9	8
Maluku*	33	91	239	8	8	7.2	6.2	7
Irian Jaya*+	33	221	555	8	3	n.a.	15.8	2
ALL INDONESIA	31	97	216				6.0	

Source: World Bank, 1984a: 12.
+ Above average GDP per capita, 1979.
* Above average increase, 1971–9
n.a. = Data not available.

average income between regions is very large indeed and, in 1979, the ratio between per capita GDP in the highest province (East Kalimantan) and that in the lowest (East Nusa Tenggara) is of the order of 19 to 1. Even if we exclude the provinces of Riau and East Kalimantan (where the figures are greatly inflated by income derived from oil and timber extraction, the bulk of which accrues to the central government and foreign and indigenous companies rather than to the governments and people of the producing regions) the ratio is reduced only to 5 to 1. The World Bank (1984a: 9) reports that these spatial differentials in per capita product are quite large compared to countries like the USA, South Korea and Malaysia, but are smaller than the Philippines and Thailand (if only non-oil income is considered).

Table 3.4 indicates that the islands of Sumatra and Kalimantan had per capita product figures well above the national average, while Sulawesi was marginally poorer than Java, and the Eastern Islands region also had below-average levels. Table 3.5 shows that while Java had 62 per cent of the national population, its share of GDP was more than 10 percentage points less. Java's share of foreign investment was disproportionately low, but the other performance indicators shown in the table are more or less in proportion. Sumatra and Kalimantan present an opposite picture to that of Java.

The clear regional division that this analysis implies, however, is misleading since Table 3.4 shows quite wide interprovincial variation within these large regions. East and West Nusa Tenggara stand out as the poorest regions in per capita GDP terms. However, South-east Sulawesi and the three easternmost provinces of Java also have very low levels. It should perhaps be emphasized that these six provinces contain some 44 per cent of the total national population. At the other end of the spectrum, the two wealthiest regions are the timber-boom and oil province of East Kalimantan and the oil-producing province of Riau. However, it is apparent from Table 3.4 that, even on the islands of Kalimantan and Sumatra, there are wide differentials in GDP per capita with West and East Kalimantan, West Sumatra, Jambi, Lampung and Bengkulu having levels below the national average.

These estimates, based on money income, would accurately reflect economically meaningful differences in real per capita income among regions only if there were no interregional differences in the general level of prices. But, in fact, there are very substantial differences in prices due, among other things, to the high transport costs for shipping goods to some regions and the different extent to which fluctuations in the international price of rice affects rice prices in different regions. Esmara (1975) has adjusted money income figures by means of regional price indices, and Arndt and Sundrum (1975) have taken his adjustments one step further by using an adjusted regional price index. This analysis showed that interregional differences in per capita money income overstate the degree of disparity in per capita *real* income because regional price disparities (which are considerable) tend to be positively correlated with disparities in regional

TABLE 3.5
Regional Distribution of Key Indicators

Indicator	(Year)	Java	Sumatra	Kalimantan	Sulawesi	E. Islands	Indonesia
				Percentage Shares by Region			
Land area		6.9	24.7	28.1	9.8	30.5	100.0
Population	(1980)	61.9	19.0	4.6	7.0	7.5	100.0
GDP (constant prices)	(1971)	54.5	27.9	5.8	6.4	5.4	100.0
	(1979)	50.5	27.2	9.6	6.6	6.1	100.0
Approved investment, 1967–78							
Foreign		56.2	25.2	9.8	2.4	6.4	100.0
Domestic		65.2	18.6	7.9	4.8	3.5	100.0
Padi output	(1971)	61.5	21.0	4.5	8.1	4.9	100.0
	(1981)	62.6	18.6	5.5	7.6	5.7	100.0

Source: World Bank, 1984a: 11.

money incomes. However, this high correlation is due mainly to the few regions with relatively high per capita money incomes (East and Central Kalimantan and Riau). Aside from these provinces, price differences did not account for very many of the interregional differences in per capita income in money terms. Hence the main conclusions based on the earlier analysis—that Nusa Tenggara was on the bottom of the heap and Jakarta, East and Central Kalimantan and most of Sumatra on top—remain.

The World Bank (1984a: 11) has computed coefficients of variation for provincial per capita GDP and found that these increased from 70 per cent in 1971 to 78 per cent in 1979 when the oil sector is included and from 38 per cent to 49 per cent if it is excluded. Hence the degree of regional inequality in GDP per capita increased during the 1970s. Table 3.4 shows that, in general, the greatest rates of growth in GDP per capita during the 1970s were recorded in the richer areas. As the World Bank (1984a: 15) points out, this 'phenomenon has contributed to the widening of the provincial disparities in product per capita. The growth prospects of the lagging regions should be thoroughly investigated'.

Other Social and Economic Differences between Regions

Table 3.6 shows a range of other social and economic indicators for the provinces of Indonesia. The first six columns deal with agricultural area and production, and show that the intensively farmed areas of Java and Bali actually lost agricultural land over the 1963–73 period, whereas in Kalimantan, Sulawesi and parts of Sumatra, farmed area increased substantially. The proportion of *sawah* to total farm land ranges widely, being lowest in areas such as Riau, West and Central Kalimantan, North and Central Sulawesi, and East Nusa Tenggara where the practice of shifting cultivation is still common. *Sawah* acreage in most areas has expanded faster than total farmed acreage, or has expanded where total farmed acreage has declined, thus signifying an intensification of agricultural systems over time. By and large, there is a close correlation between wet land padi area, total padi production and population size in the different provinces, reflecting the highly labour-intensive nature of Indonesian rice farming. There is no such correlation in the case of Indonesia's second major agricultural product, rubber, which is heavily concentrated in Sumatra and West Kalimantan.

Turning to some social indicators, Table 3.6 shows that hospital beds are unevenly spread in relation to population. Jakarta is relatively over-supplied, and so, to a lesser extent, are North Sumatra, East Kalimantan, North Sulawesi and Irian Jaya. The greatest deficiencies in hospital beds are in West Java, Aceh, Jambi, Bengkulu, Lampung, Central Kalimantan, Central Sulawesi, West Nusa Tenggara and East Timor. To a small extent, the deficiency of hospital beds in some areas is counter-balanced by a higher ratio of *Puskesmas* (community health centres) to population. Thus Jakarta and North Sumatra, well-served with hospitals, have lower *Puskesmas* to population ratios than many other areas. On the whole,

TABLE 3.6
Some Economic and Social Indicators for Provinces of Indonesia

Province	Farm land as Percentage of Total Land, 1973	Average Annual Percentage Increase in Total Agricultural Land, 1963–1973	Sawah as Percentage of Farm Land, 1973	Average Annual Percentage Increase in Sawah, 1963–1973	Padi Production ('000 Tonnes), 1981	Wet Land Padi Area ('000 Ha), 1981	Rubber Area ('000 Ha), 1980	Rubber Products ('000 Tonnes), 1980	Hospital Beds/10,000 Population, 1980	Health Centres & Sub-Centres/100,000 Population, 1980	Motor Cycles/1,000 Population, 1980	Passenger Cars/1,000 Population, 1980	Average Annual Growth in Passenger Cars, 1971–1980	Attendance at Cinemas (Visits per Capita), 1980
JAVA														
Jakarta	32.6	2.54	50.2	4.14	53	16	—	—	20	4	66.0	34.0	5.5	3.5
West Java	33.0	0.18	55.1	0.62	7,287	1,835	124	53.0	4	5	12.0	4.5	10.8	0.8
Central Java	51.3	−0.38	46.2	0.28	5,761	1,372	31	26.0	5	5	17.5]	2.4]	9.7]	0.9
Yogyakarta	57.3	−0.61	23.2	−1.44	550	108	1	—	9	10				0.5
East Java	42.3	−0.45	46.0	0.37	6,879	1,448	17	16.0	5	6	16.3	3.1	6.7	0.6
SUMATRA														
Aceh	6.8	3.36	44.9	4.27	835	246	47	15.0	4	14		1.7	7.1	1.1
North Sumatra	11.4	−0.68	37.2	3.27	1,663	448	479	290.0	14	14	29.2	3.3	0.0	1.4
West Sumatra	7.0	2.19	42.1	3.88	1,030	275	47	21.0	8	15	16.4	2.5	8.2	1.2
Riau	5.4	−0.15	9.3	0.44	265	85	276	70.0	5	12	16.3	2.1	1.1	1.0
Jambi	5.4	−1.69	31.2	3.66	396	132	339	141.0	3	13				0.9
South Sumatra					944	270	473	152.0	8	11	13.3]	3.3]	6.7]	1.2
Bengkulu	9.7	−1.10	19.9	1.64	169	47	49	23.0	3	23				0.9
Lampung					784	167	35	21.0	3	6				0.4

KALIMANTAN														
West Kalimantan	7.3	3.26	16.6	4.89	612	194	442	104.0	7	16	12.2	1.1	6.7	2.0
Central Kalimantan	3.5	2.98	15.6	4.15	220	73	92	33.0	4	27	21.5]	2.2]	8.8]	1.5
South Kalimantan	7.2	2.23	54.0	3.12	786	288	70	34.0	8	19				2.1
East Kalimantan	0.5	−1.29	31.7	11.56	180	40	10	1.0	14	20	29.4	6.8	9.1	3.7
SULAWESI														
North Sulawesi	7.2	3.00	13.2	3.90	189	50	—	—	14	17	10.7]	2.7]	10.0]	0.8
Central Sulawesi					234	68	—	—	4	18				0.9
South Sulawesi	8.9	5.83	40.8	6.40	2,019	571	1	0.2	9	13				0.7
South-east Sulawesi					65	14	—	—	5	11	17.2]	1.8]	10.5]	0.6
OTHER ISLANDS														
Bali	48.0	0.59	30.6	1.05	746	167	—	—	7	17	26.9	2.6	7.7	0.5
West Nusa Tenggara	14.4	0.85	51.0	0.66	830	222	—	—	3	9	6.1	0.7	6.2	0.4
East Nusa Tenggara	13.7	4.24	9.6	6.81	247	53	—	—	5	19	3.7	0.7	9.4	0.8
Maluku					28	1	—	—	9	16	6.2	1.6	18.6	0.8
Irian Jaya					4	1	1	—	13	37	9.2	4.8	11.5	
East Timor									4	19				

Sources: 1. World Bank, *Indonesia Selected Issues in Spatial Development*, Vol. 2.
2. *Provincial Data Base*, *World Bank Resident Staff*, Jakarta, April 1983, which derive their data from a variety of official Indonesian government publications.
3. The first four columns calculated from Roger Montgomery and Toto Sugito, 'Changes in the Structure of Farming in Indonesia between Censuses 1963–1973: The Issues of Inequality and Near-landlessness', *Journal of Southeast Asian Studies*, 11(2), September 1980, p. 354.

though, the *Puskesmas* to population ratio is low in Java and high elsewhere. The extent to which this can be interpreted as reflecting a disadvantaged situation for Java would depend on whether the size and range of services provided by the *Puskesmas* are comparable in the different islands. Despite a much larger population served by each *Puskesmas* in Java, better transportation facilities there allow better physical access to *Puskesmas* in Java than in the outer islands.

As might be expected, the ratio of motor cycles and passenger cars per capita is related to per capita income levels, with the highest figures by far in Jakarta (especially for passenger cars) and relatively high figures for cars also in West Java, East Kalimantan and Irian Jaya, and for motor cycles in North Sumatra, South and East Kalimantan, and Bali (the latter no doubt partly related to the tourist trade). The growth rate of passenger cars over the 1970s was highest in West Java, Central Java–Yogyakarta, East Kalimantan, North and Central Sulawesi, East Nusa Tenggara, Maluku and Irian Jaya. In some cases (for example, East Nusa Tenggara) the high rate may be somewhat misleading as it is based on a very small number of vehicles in the base year.

The final column in Table 3.6 shows per capita attendance at cinemas. Again, the range is considerable, with East Kalimantan and Jakarta well ahead and Yogyakarta, Bali, Lampung and West Nusa Tenggara lagging. To some extent, cinema attendance appears to be correlated with income levels, but it is worth noting that two of the provinces with lowest cinema attendance—Yogyakarta and Bali—are famous for their wealth of traditional culture, including entertainment forms which might be considered competitive with the cinema.

Regional Variations in Poverty

There is considerable debate in Indonesia about income distribution and the proportions of the population living in poverty (see, for example, Arief, 1979; Esmara, 1975; King and Weldon, 1977; Booth and Sundrum, 1981; Ginneken, 1976; Perera and Budianti, 1977; World Bank, 1980; Sundrum, 1979; Sayogyo, 1978). However, there appears to be a general consensus about two things, namely:

1. The incidence of poverty is still very high in Indonesia.
2. There has been an overall reduction in this incidence over the last decade.

These conclusions are supported by an analysis (World Bank, 1984a) of per capita expenditure on food consumption from data collected in the 1980 round of the National Social and Economic Survey (*Susenas*). This analysis defined poverty in terms of a minimum expenditure per person on food (the equivalent of 1.25 times the price of 16 kilograms of rice per month). By this measure some 40 per cent of Indonesians in 1980 were living in poverty compared to 59 per cent in 1970.

Given the complex interactive nature of the relationship between poverty and population (Rodgers, 1984), it is important to establish the extent to which there are regional variations in the incidence of poverty within Indonesia. The first contrast evident in Table 3.7 is that the poverty problem is most serious in rural areas, where 85.2 per cent of those Indonesians who live in poverty are resident, numbering nearly 50 million persons. This is not to say of course that urban poverty is an insignificant problem, with a quarter of urban dwellers having expenditure on food below the poverty line. In general, regions which have a high incidence of rural poverty also show similar patterns for urban poverty, and this also applies at the province level. This implies that poverty has a definite regional dimension (World Bank, 1984a: vii).

Table 3.7 shows that both in terms of sheer numbers and rate of incidence of poverty, Java dominates the pattern. Nevertheless, especially high levels of incidence of poverty were recorded in eastern Indonesia. These broad patterns are reflected in Figure 3.8, although some significant interprovincial variations within regions should also be noted. Rural Java had 52 per cent of all Indonesians in poverty in 1980, and the map shows that there was a particular concentration in the Javanese-dominated areas of Java. West and East Nusa Tenggara also have more than half of their populations living in poverty. The World Bank (1984a: 9) argues that the high incidence of poverty as reflected in the measure used here can have two possible direct policy implications. The food consumption expenditure measure would indicate that, in areas with a high incidence of poverty, there is a need for special attention to 'measures for the enhancement of purchasing power among the poor and ensuring adequate food supplies'. Clearly, while in Java the former 'general poverty' problem is dominant, in Eastern Indonesia the 'special food cum purchasing power problem' is also of some significance. This is reflected in Figure 3.9 which shows Currey's map of the location of reported incidences of food crisis situations in Indonesia over the 1978–82 period.

The second category of poverty incidence forms a coherent geographical zone intermediate between the high incidence zone of the Eastern two-

TABLE 3.7

Indonesia: Incidence of Poverty in Urban and Rural Areas of Major Regions, 1980

Region	Incidence of Poverty					
	Urban		Rural		Total	
	Number ('000)	Percentage	Number ('000)	Percentage	Number ('000)	Percentage
Java	6,802.4	29.6	35,086.5	52.3	41,888.9	46.5
Sumatra	847.2	15.8	4,738.5	21.5	5,585.7	20.4
Kalimantan	114.3	8.1	641.9	12.4	756.2	11.5
Sulawesi	343.8	21.1	3,676.2	42.7	4,020.0	39.3
Eastern Islands	292.1	24.3	4,107.2	47.7	4,399.7	46.7
Total	8,399.8	25.8	48,250.3	43.3	56,650.5	39.3

Source: World Bank, 1984a: 87–9.

FIGURE 3.8

Indonesia: Incidence of Poverty in Provinces as Percentage of Total Population, 1980

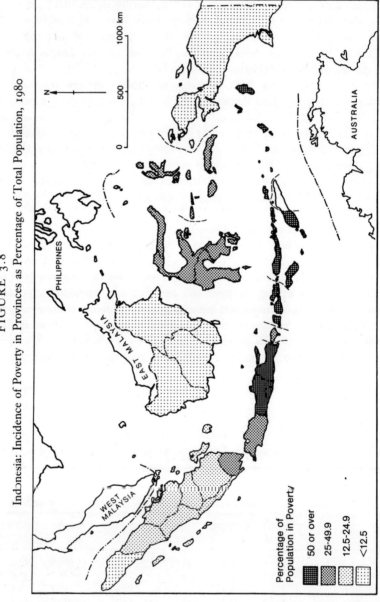

Percentage of
Population in Poverty

50 or over

25–49.9

12.5–24.9

<12.5

Source: World Bank, 1984a: 89.

FIGURE 3.9

Indonesia: Location of Food Crises Reported in National Newspapers, 1978–1982

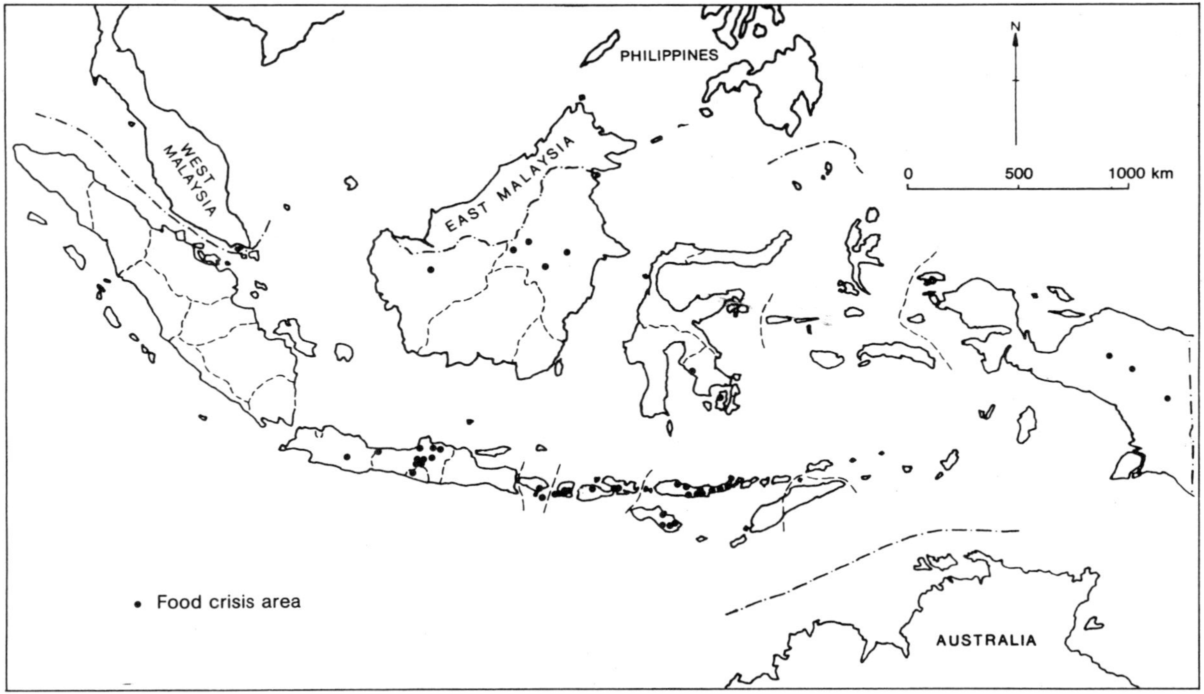

• Food crisis area

Source: Currey, 1983.

thirds of Java—East and West Nusa Tenggara and the peripheral areas with less than a quarter of their population in poverty. This comprises Lampung and West Java in the west and Bali, all of Sulawesi, and Maluku in the east. It is interesting to note Lampung's similarity to Java in this as in many other socio-economic indicators, suggesting that more than a half-century as the chief focus of the transmigration programme has made Lampung more and more like Java in its socio-economic and cultural characteristics. Indeed, Lampung has been included by the government in the same *Repelita* planning region as West Java. The lowest incidence of poverty as shown in Figure 3.8 is clearly at both the heart of Indonesia's 'core'—the metropolitan capital of Jakarta—and at the extreme periphery in Aceh, Kalimantan and Irian. There is a moderate negative correlation (Rho = −0.45) between the proportion of the population living in poverty in 1980 and the rate of population growth between 1971 and 1980.

Regional Economic Structure

The substantial interregional variations in GDP per capita in Indonesia which were outlined earlier are matched by major differences in economic structure. This is evident in Table 3.8 which shows the shares of the various economic sectors in Regional Gross Domestic Product (RGDP) for each of the major regions. All regions shared in the striking structural shift of a relative decline in importance of agriculture which occurred in Indonesia during the 1970s. The employment implications will be discussed in Chapter 8; what needs to be stressed here is that while total employment in Indonesia increased by 22.1 per cent between the 1971 and 1980 Censuses, employment in agriculture increased by only 2.5 per cent, and in ten provinces there was an overall decline in the numbers employed in agriculture. The declining relative significance of agriculture in so-called 'inner Indonesia' (Java–Bali) is readily apparent in Figure 3.10. While Java accounted for 64 per cent of all employment in 1980, it had only 57 per cent of agricultural employment. In the other islands, it is the provinces which have received large numbers of transmigrants (provinces such as Bengkulu, Lampung, Irian Jaya) or which have experienced little investment in raw material extraction (for example, West Kalimantan, East Nusa Tenggara) which have the most emphasis upon agriculture in their economies.

It was indicated earlier that one of the legacies of the colonial period was the stifling of the development of indigenous manufacturing industry such that, by 1971, it accounted for only 8.9 per cent of total employment and 8.8 per cent of RGDP. This changed dramatically in the 1970s (McCawley, 1981) although the rapid growth in manufacturing output was not equally matched by increases in employment. By 1980, 9.3 per cent of Indonesia's work-force were employed in manufacturing, with the numbers employed increasing by 60 per cent in the 1970s. Another legacy of colonialism was the spatially uneven nature of the development of manufacturing, and Figure 3.11 shows that this pattern has been maintained into the 1980s,

TABLE 3.8

Sectoral Composition of Regional Gross Domestic Product, 1971 and 1979 (at Constant Prices)

Region	Year	Percentage of RGDP from						
		Agriculture	Mining	Manufacturing	Construction	Commerce	Service	Total
Java	1971	42.7	1.7	12.2	3.5	26.8	13.1	100.0
	1979	30.3	1.6	16.3	6.4	29.6	15.8	100.0
Sumatra	1971	37.4	30.7	5.5	2.2	15.0	9.2	100.0
	1979	30.3	21.5	13.6	5.5	17.3	11.8	100.0
Kalimantan	1971	58.0	4.7	4.8	2.0	22.1	8.4	100.0
	1979	30.5	27.3	5.0	3.1	22.5	11.6	100.0
Sulawesi	1971	54.3	2.4	4.4	3.6	20.1	15.2	100.0
	1979	48.7	5.2	5.8	4.9	21.2	14.2	100.0
Eastern Islands	1971	64.4	0.9	1.5	3.5	12.7	17.0	100.0
	1979	48.0	14.2	2.6	5.2	15.0	15.0	100.0
INDONESIA	1971	44.0	9.9	8.8	3.1	22.1	12.1	100.0
	1979	32.6	10.5	13.0	5.6	24.1	14.2	100.0

Source: World Bank, 1984a: 18.

FIGURE 3.10

Indonesia: Percentage of Employed Persons in Agriculture, 1980

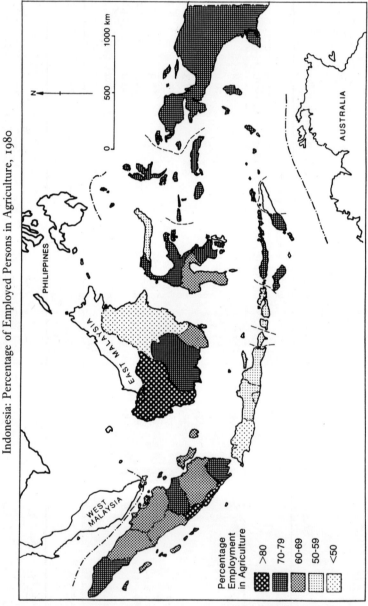

Source: World Bank, 1984b: 65.

FIGURE 3.11

Indonesia: Percentage of Employed Persons in Industry, 1980

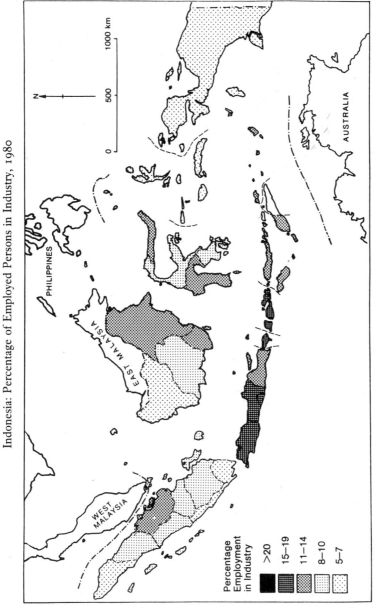

Percentage
Employment
in Industry

>20
15–19
11–14
8–10
5–7

Source: World Bank, 1984b: 65.

with the dominance of inner Indonesia clearly evident. Java had 73 per cent of the nation's manufacturing workers in 1980, and although this represented a slight fall from 1971 (75.2 per cent) there is a clear 'over-concentration' of manufacturing employment in Java. Moreover, the World Bank (1984a: 22) has shown that there was an increasing concentration of large and medium-scale manufacturing investment and employment in Java during the 1970s. The small-scale industrial sector, which is oriented much more towards regional markets, matches much more closely the spatial distribution of the total population. Table 3.8, however, shows that manufacturing is a much more significant element in the economies of Java, and to a lesser extent Sumatra, than in the more peripheral parts of the country. Mining, as expected, is also very spatially concentrated. Employment in commerce and services in Indonesia grew by 48 and 64 per cent respectively between 1971 and 1980. Again there is a disproportionate concentration of this employment in Java (74 and 69 per cent respectively). Table 3.8 indicates that this pattern is reflected in the RGDP data and that the construction sector is also 'over-represented' in Java.

The considerable interregional differences in economic structure are partly a function of variations in resource endowment, geographical location, etc., but they are also a product of the structural effects of colonialism and the uneven penetration of capitalism in that period as well as since Independence. Titus (1978) has used the centre–periphery model of Amin (1974) to categorize the provinces of Java according to not only their economic structure but also the extent to which they are incorporated into the capitalist economy. He divided Indonesia into 'core–periphery' regions by giving each province scores on the following criteria:

1. The presence of important 'modern sector' activities in mining, plantation agriculture, industry, services, etc.;

2. The presence of important commercial and transport centres functioning also as a focus for other regions;

3. The incidence of important private investment activities (foreign and domestic);

4. Disproportionate allocations of foreign exchange and development funds by the central government;

5. The presence of administrative institutions which function also for other parts of the country;

6. The extent to which a modern infrastructure has been developed outside the provincial capital;

7. The presence of big urban centres (400,000 plus) functioning on a macro-regional or national level;

8. The presence of social and cultural institutions of national importance (for example, 'centres of excellence in education').

On the basis of these scores, five types of 'centre–periphery' region were identified and these are shown in Figure 3.12. Two types of 'centre' region are noted. Firstly, eastern and western Java qualify as archetypical 'centre' regions characterized by a high level of integration into the world economy and positive scores on all or most of the criteria (designated C1 in Figure

FIGURE 3.12

Indonesia: Centre–Periphery Classification of Provinces

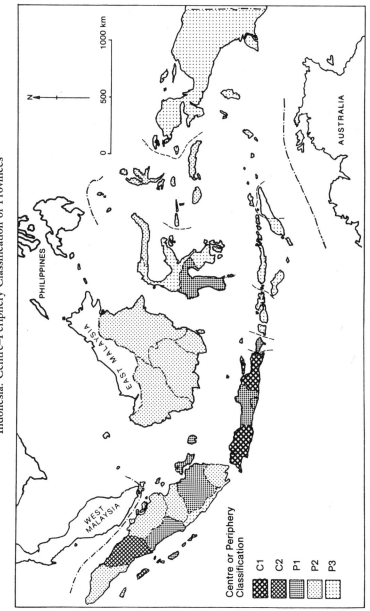

Centre or Periphery
Classification

C1
C2
P1
P2
P3

Source: After Titus, 1978.

3.12). However, there is a second category of centre (C2) identified in north-eastern Sumatra which scores positively on all but the fourth and eighth of the criteria. This region, of course, was the first major 'other island' area to be intensively exploited by the Dutch after there was some feeling in the late nineteenth century that there was little scope for extension of colonial exploitation in Java. There is also an interesting division of the remaining provinces between three types of 'periphery' classification:

   1. Category P1 represents provinces which are economically and politically tightly integrated and are the most developed sections of the periphery.

   2. Category P2 represents provinces which are also integrated to a degree but less developed and with a heavily imbalanced economy.

   3. Category P3 represents the still isolated and strongly self-sufficient peripheral regions, most of which score negatively on all of the eight criteria listed above.

There are some difficulties with the classification in that there is considerable within-province variation and it fails to differentiate 'boom' resource-exploitation peripheral provinces like East Kalimantan from more economically stagnant areas such as Maluku. Nevertheless, it does present a useful and interesting summary picture of interprovincial inequality in Indonesia. It is usual to posit a simple 'inner–outer' island dichotomy, but it is clear from Figure 3.12 that the differentiation of 'centre' and 'periphery' in Indonesia is a more complex task.

Urbanization

Indonesia has generally been considered as one of the least urbanized nations in the Asian region. The 1971 Census showed that only 17.2 per cent of Indonesians lived in towns and cities. However, it has been suggested (Hugo, 1981b: 8–12) that this underestimated the significance of urban areas in Indonesia because:

   1. The definition of 'urban' adopted at the 1971 Census excluded population and areas which were manifestly urban.

   2. There are hundreds of thousands of Indonesians who, although they have their official permanent residence in rural areas, spend much of their working lives in cities via the processes of circular migration and commuting. This 'hidden urbanization' blurs the social and economic meaning of 'rural' and 'urban' in Indonesia.

For the 1980 Census, the Central Bureau of Statistics adopted a much more meaningful, functionally based definition of what constitutes an urban area. Moreover, the Indonesian government's National Urban Development Strategy Project (NUDSP) has refined the definition even further to identify some 831 spatially distinct, functional urban areas. This has to a large extent obviated the first problem identified above, although the second remains. This is reflected in Table 3.9 which suggests that the level of urbanization in Indonesia in 1980 is still below that in other comparable countries.

TABLE 3.9

Urbanization Patterns in Indonesia and Other Selected Countries

	GNP Per Capita, 1980 (US$)	Percentage of Work-force in Secondary Industry	Annual Population Growth Rate, 1970–1980	Percentage Urban, 1980	Urban Population Annual Growth Rate, 1970–1980	Percentage Urban in	
						Largest City	Cities with More than 500,000
Indonesia	430	15	2.3	22	4.0	20	43
World Average Low-Income							
Countries	260	15	2.1	17	4.1	12	41
Bangladesh	130	n.a.	2.6	11	6.5	30	50
Burma	170	n.a.	2.4	27	4.2	23	23
India	240	13	2.1	22	3.3	6	39
Pakistan	300	20	3.1	28	4.3	21	51
World Average Middle-Income							
Countries	1,400	21	2.4	45	4.0	29	48
Thailand	670	9	2.5	25	3.4	69	69
Philippines	690	17	2.7	36	3.6	30	34
South Korea	1,520	n.a.	1.7	55	4.7	41	77
Malaysia	1,620	16	2.4	41	3.3	27	27

Sources: NUDSP, 1985: 9; World Bank, 1984b: 2.
n.a. = Data not available.

Table 3.10 shows the trajectory of urban growth and urbanization in Indonesia since 1920. After a period in the 1960s when urban growth slowed, it is apparent that there was an acceleration of growth in the 1970s. This is corroborated by careful estimation (NUDSP, 1985: 12) of changes between 1971 and 1980 in the population growth of all cities with more than 100,000 inhabitants in 1980 (which accounted for nearly two-thirds of the total urban population). Overall, the urban population in these cities showed an annual growth rate in excess of 4.2 per cent per annum. The general consensus (World Bank, 1984b; NUDSP, 1985) is that the Indonesian urban population grew by around 4 per cent per annum over the 1970s when full allowance is made for changing boundaries and definitions.

If we turn to the level of urbanization, it is apparent that gains have been more modest. While the urban population has increased more than tenfold, the percentage of the population living in urban areas quadrupled over the 1920–80 period. The table shows that the rate of increase of both the level of urbanization and the urban–rural ratio increased substantially during the 1970s over corresponding rates in the 1960s. Different urban definitions and different boundaries for many urban areas were used in the 1961, 1971 and 1980 Censuses (Hugo, 1981b; World Bank, 1984b; NUDSP, 1985); while this fact confounds precise quantification of trends, the shifts are of such magnitude that there can be no doubt there has been a substantial acceleration of urbanization in Indonesia over the last decade or so.

Figures 3.13 and 3.14 show the size and location of Indonesia's larger cities at each of the post-Independence censuses. The clear pattern is one of concentration of large urban and metropolitan centres on the island of Java and, to a lesser extent, Sumatra. In the provinces of eastern Indonesia, there is a striking lack of higher-order centres, and the urban hierarchy is dominated by the city of Ujung Pandang in South Sulawesi. The dominance of Java is also evident in Table 3.11, which shows that a quarter of the island's population was classified as urban in 1980, while all the other islands had levels of urbanization below the national average levels of urbanization. It is also apparent in the same table that Java had the largest concentration of population in large cities with fully half of its urban inhabitants living in cities with populations exceeding half a million persons. Jakarta alone accounts for a fifth of Indonesia's total urban population.

With respect to size-classes of urban areas shown in Table 3.11, it is clear that Java is 'over-represented' in the largest size-categories, having three of Indonesia's four 'million' cities. It was not until the 1970s, when Medan passed the threshold, that any outer island city had more than a million inhabitants. Partly because of the dominance of the 'million' cities of Jakarta, Bandung and Surabaya, Java is 'under-represented' (compared with the overall national figure) in the medium and smaller city size categories. Overall, one-third of Indonesian urban dwellers lived in metropolitan areas of 1 million persons or more, a tenth in cities of more than 500,000 but less than 1 million inhabitants, and a further 21 per cent in cities with populations of 100,000 to 500,000.

TABLE 3.10

Indonesia: Urban Growth and Trends in Urbanization, 1920–1980

Characteristic	Census Year					Percentage Growth Per Annum[a]			
	1920[b]	1930	1961	1971	1980	1920–1930	1930–1961	1961–1971	1971–1980
Urban population	2,881,576	4,034,149	14,358,372	20,465,377	32,846,000	+3.42	+4.18	+3.61	+5.40
Rural population	46,418,424	56,693,084	82,660,457	98,674,687	114,089,000	+2.02	+1.22	+1.79	+1.63
Urban (percentage)	5.8	6.7	14.8	17.2	22.4	+1.45	+2.59	+1.51	+2.98
Rural (percentage)	94.2	93.4	85.2	82.8	77.6	−0.09	−0.30	−0.29	−0.72
Total population	49,300,000	60,727,333	97,018,829	119,140,064	146,935,000	+2.11	+1.52	+2.08	+2.36
Urban/rural ratio	0.062	0.081	0.174	0.207	0.287	+2.71	+2.50	+1.75	+3.70

Sources: Volkstelling, 1930; Milone, 1966; Censuses of 1961 and 1971; Supas, 1976; World Bank, 1984b; Hugo, 1981a: 60.

[a] All percentage growth rates per annum are compound interest rates.

[b] Source of 1920 statistics: Milone (1966). An inaccuracy coefficient of 5 per cent has been suggested for analysis of these figures.

FIGURE 3.13

Indonesia: Location and Size of Major Urban Centres at the 1961 Census

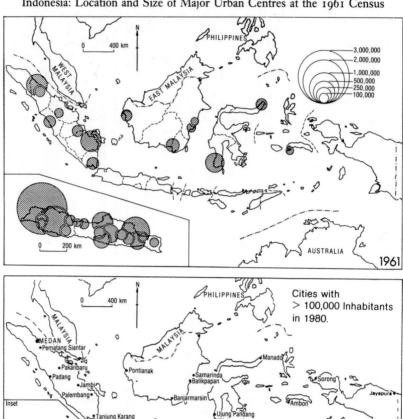

Source: Milone, 1966.

Establishing the growth rates of the urban population in the regions of Indonesia and the various size-categories of urban centres is a difficult process due to the substantial variations in the definitions adopted at the various censuses. The NUDSP (1985) estimates of growth rates for urban populations in respective provinces are shown in Table 3.12 and indicate that, while Java is the most urbanized of Indonesia's islands, its urban growth rate was below the national average while that for all other islands was above 4 per cent per annum. It is noticeable, however, that the most urbanized region in Indonesia (that is, western Java) experienced growth at above the national average while the remainder of the island experienced the lowest rates of urban population growth of all provinces (although those

FIGURE 3.14

Indonesia: Location and Size of Major Urban Centres at the 1971 and
1980 Censuses

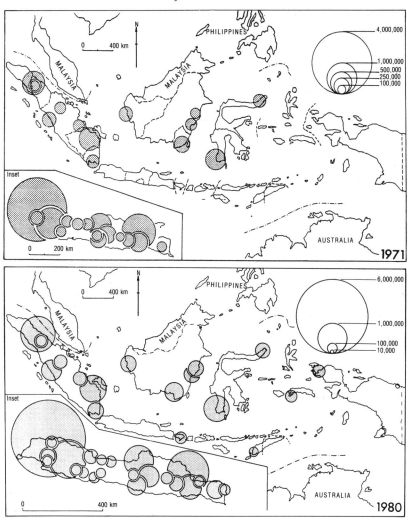

Source: Indonesian Censuses of 1971 and 1980.

rates were still substantially higher than the overall population growth rates). The most rapid rates of urban growth were in some of the peripheral, outer island provinces where there have been substantial developments in raw material extraction in the 1970s (for example, Central and East Kalimantan), and in other provinces with very small urban populations to begin with. It is important to look also at the right-hand column of Table 3.12 which puts the pattern of growth in perspective. This indicates that although Java had the slowest rate of growth, it accounted for fully 65 per cent of the growth of the urban population in the nation—38 per cent

TABLE 3.11

Indonesia: Urban Population by City-Size Class and Major Island, 1980

	Total Indonesia	Sumatra	Java	Bali/ Nusa Tenggara	Kalimantan	Sulawesi	Maluku/ Irian Jaya
URBAN POPULATION ('ooo Persons)							
1,000,000 & above	10,868	1,265	9,603	—	—	—	—
500,000–1,000,000	3,301	757	1,905	—	—	639	—
200,000–500,000	3,905	654	2,009	210	815	217	—
100,000–200,000	3,015	515	2,047	159	182	—	112
50,000–100,000	2,956	643	1,878	138	110	126	61
20,000–50,000	3,925	700	2,535	137	95	352	106
10,000–20,000	2,484	438	1,577	159	112	172	26
Subtotal	30,454	4,972	21,554	803	1,314	1,506	305
Less than 10,000	2,391	509	1,374	148	126	148	86
Total	32,845	5,481	22,928	951	1,440	1,654	391
Urban as Percentage of Total Population	22.4	19.6	25.1	12.0	21.4	15.9	15.1

PERCENTAGE OF URBAN POPULATION

1,000,000 & above	33	23	42	—	—	—	—
500,000–1,000,000	10	14	8	—	—	39	—
200,000–500,000	12	12	9	22	56	13	—
100,000–200,000	9	9	9	17	13	—	29
50,000–100,000	9	12	8	14	8	8	16
20,000–50,000	12	13	11	14	6	21	27
10,000–20,000	8	8	7	17	8	10	7
Subtotal	93	91	94	84	91	91	78
Less than 10,000	7	9	6	16	9	9	22
Total	100	100	100	100	100	100	100

Source: NUDSP, 1985: 7.

TABLE 3.12

Indonesia: Urban Population, by Province, 1971 and 1980

	Urban Population (in '000)		Percentage Urban 1980	Growth Rate, 1971–1980 (Per Cent Per Annum)	Growth Per Year, 1971–1980 (in '000)
	1971	1980			
SUMATRA	3,620	5,481	19.57	4.72	207
Aceh	143	234	8.94	5.63	10
North Sumatra	1,497	2,127	25.44	3.98	70
West Sumatra	296	433	12.71	4.32	15
Riau	407	588	27.13	4.18	20
Jambi	112	183	12.64	5.58	8
South Sumatra	846	1,267	27.37	4.59	47
Bengkulu	40	72	9.43	6.75	4
Lampung	279	577	12.47	8.39	33
JAVA	16,588	22,926	25.12	3.66	704
Jakarta/West Java	8,129	11,843	34.88	4.27	413
Central Java	3,579	4,756	18.74	3.21	131
Yogyakarta	458	607	22.07	3.18	17
East Java	4,422	5,720	19.60	2.90	144
NUSA TENGGARA	638	952	12.00	4.55	35
Bali	244	363	14.71	5.50	15
West Nusa Tenggara	278	383	14.07	3.62	12
East Nusa Tenggara	135	205	7.51	4.74	8
KALIMANTAN	859	1,441	21.44	5.92	65
West Kalimantan	280	417	16.77	4.53	15
Central Kalimantan	37	98	10.30	11.54	7
South Kalimantan	306	441	21.35	4.13	15
East Kalimantan	236	485	39.84	8.36	28
SULAWESI	1,138	1,654	15.89	4.25	57
North Sulawesi	254	355	16.77	3.80	11
Central Sulawesi	71	115	8.95	5.55	5
South Sulawesi	761	1,096	18.08	4.13	37
South-east Sulawesi	52	88	9.35	6.08	4
MALUKU/IRIAN JAYA	253	390	15.10	4.94	15
Maluku	95	153	10.84	5.37	6
Irian Jaya	157	237	20.21	4.67	9
ALL INDONESIA	23,095	32,846	22.35	4.00	1,083

Source: NUDSP, 1985: 17.

occurring in West Java alone. In Java during the 1970s, an annual net gain of 704,000 new urban residents was recorded. In West Java, the net gain was 413,000 persons—more than the combined net annual gains of urban residents in all provinces outside Java.

The NUDSP (1985) data also permit an analysis of growth trends within particular sizes of cities, and this is presented in Table 3.13. There is little variation between the various size-categories in the rates of urban popula-

TABLE 3.13

Indonesia: Urban Population Growth by City Size, 1971–1980

Size-Category	Indonesia			Java		
	Population, 1971 ('000)	Share of Urban Growth, 1971–1980	Growth Rate Per Annum, 1971–1980	Population, 1971 ('000)	Share of Urban Growth, 1971–1980	Growth Rate Per Annum, 1971–1980
More than 1,000,000	7,538	34*	4.15	6,646	47*	4.18
500,000–1,000,000	2,263	11*	4.28	1,335	9*	4.03
200,000–499,999	2,655	13*	4.38	1,490	8	3.37
100,000–199,999	2,078	10*	4.22	1,486	9	3.62
50,000–99,999	2,026	10*	4.29	1,321	9*	3.98
20,000–49,999	2,756	12	4.01	1,881	10	3.37
10,000–19,999	1,821	7	3.51	1,194	6	3.13
Subtotal	21,136	96	4.14	15,353	98	3.84
Less than 10,000	1,959	4	2.24	1,235	2	1.19
Total	23,095	100	4.00	16,588	100	3.66

Source: NUDSP, 1985: 19.
*Above categories' share of total urban population in 1980.

tion growth during the 1970s, although the largest cities did grow slightly faster than those in other categories. It was only in the very smallest cities (below 20,000 inhabitants) that annual rates of growth fell below 4 per cent. Table 3.13 also presents equivalent data for Java, and this shows a slightly greater concentration of urban growth in the largest size-categories and slower growth in the middle and small size-categories. The latter was much more marked in the 1961–71 period when Java's middle cities appeared to be stagnating (Hugo, 1981a). The other major regions have a balanced distribution of urban population growth throughout the size-categories, except for Sulawesi where urban growth is dominated by Ujung Pandang and Manado.

The fact that the 1970s in Indonesia saw an upswing in urbanization and urban growth is also reflected in trends with respect to growth in employment. Table 3.14 shows that employment in urban areas grew more than three times as fast as that in rural areas between the 1971 and 1980 Censuses. Urban employment growth was especially rapid in Java.

Turning to the question of the distribution of the sizes of cities in Indonesia, Figure 3.15 shows the rank–size distribution of Indonesia's major cities in 1980, 1930 and 1850. The diagram also shows the equivalent 'idealized' rank–size curves which represent the city distributions which would occur if the sizes of all other cities were related to the size of the largest city (Jakarta) according to the rank–size rule. The latter in its simplest form states that in any nation or region, the population of a given city tends to be equal to the population of the largest city divided by the rank of the given city (Haggett, 1975: 358). It is apparent from the diagram that, in 1980, the idealized rank–size distribution overestimates the size of all twenty-eight other cities. This of course reflects a concentration (or, in terms of the rank–size rule, an 'over-concentration') of the urban population in the nation's largest city. This is also suggested when we examine the constant 'Z', which is an index of the slope of the rank–size distribution line. If this exceeds 1, it suggests a concentration of population in the largest cities relative to the smaller. For Indonesia in 1980, this statistic was

TABLE 3.14

Indonesia: Annual Average Rural and Urban Employment Growth, 1971–1980

Region	Rural (Per Cent)	Urban (Per Cent)	Urban/Rural Growth Ratio
Java	1.1	6.2	5.6
Java, excluding Jakarta	1.1	7.0	6.4
Sumatra	3.0	4.9	1.6
Kalimantan	2.7	3.6	1.3
Sulawesi	1.5	1.9	1.3
Eastern Islands	1.6	4.7	2.9
Indonesia	1.6	5.6	3.5

Source: World Bank, 1984b.

FIGURE 3.15

Actual and Idealized Rank–Size Distributions of Indonesian Cities
in 1850, 1930 and 1980

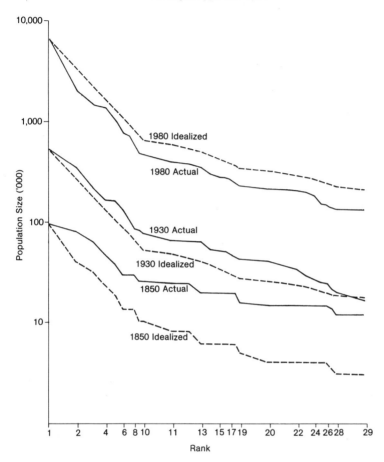

Sources: Hageman, 1852; Volkstelling, 1933–6; NUDSP, 1985.

1.15, indicating a slight tendency in this direction.

When there is a pattern of decrease in population size among the cities below the largest cities (especially those first few immediately below the largest) which is considerably greater than that predicted by the simple rank–size rule, a primate pattern is said to prevail. The pattern depicted in Figure 3.15 is one tending towards primacy, although it is not nearly as striking as that prevailing in several other South-East Asian contexts (most notably Bangkok's domination of Thailand's urban system). Milone (1966: 1008–11) stated after her analysis of the 1961 census data relating to urban areas:

Djakarta has never been a true 'primate' city in terms of being the only center for major economic political, administrative, higher education and technical functions.

Surabaya as a major port always had a substantial amount of import-export commerce and industry and was the most important naval station, while Bandung has functioned as a major transportation, communication and higher educational center as well as having industrial enterprises ... it would seem that Indonesia has more potentialities for balanced growth than many other countries of South-east Asia.

In Figure 3.15, however, there is a clear tendency for the rank–size curve to be progressively transformed from a relatively flat shape in 1930 to a 'J' shape in 1980 as the system becomes more dominated by larger metropolitan centres, especially Jakarta. The tendency for Indonesia's urban system to move away from its former 'balanced' state towards a primacy pattern is made even more apparent if we compare the 'idealized' rank–size curves for 1930 and 1980 which are shown, with the corresponding actual curves, in Figure 3.15. Whereas the 1980 idealized curve overestimated the actual populations of the largest centres, the pattern in 1930 was precisely the reverse, with the idealized rank–size curve substantially underestimating the population size of each of the twenty-eight centres largest in size after Batavia-Meester Cornelis (now called Jakarta). The 1930 pattern then is one which lacks a primate city and in which there is a much more 'balanced' distribution than in 1980.

McNicoll and Mamas (1973: 32) computed a primacy index for Indonesia which divides the population of the largest city (Jakarta) by that of the three next largest (Surabaya, Bandung and Semarang). The indices for the last century, shown in Table 3.15, progressively increase from 0.39 in 1890 to 1.34 in 1971. At the 1980 Census the index was also 1.34, perhaps indicating stabilization of the pattern.

While it is true that this level of primacy is not high when compared to many countries (Renaud, 1981), it should be pointed out that the countries with higher levels of primacy tend to be small- or medium-sized in population terms and their national space comprises a contiguous land area. The present degree of primacy in Indonesia is both historically large in the Indonesian context and substantial when compared to countries of

TABLE 3.15

Indonesia: Four City Primacy Index, 1890–1980

Year	Four City Primacy Index
1890	0.39
1905	0.59
1920	0.69
1930	0.73
1955	0.87
1961	1.17
1971	1.34
1980	1.34

Sources: Anon., 1885: 582; Abdurachim, 1970: 1; McNicoll and Mamas, 1973: 32; NUDSP, 1985: 11.

comparable population size. In the post-Independence period, notwith-standing the deep political and social change which has occurred, Indonesia's economy has retained many of the 'dependent' features of the colonial years with a stress on exporting raw materials and importing processed goods. The extremely limited development of secondary industry associated with this, and the stress on import substitution, has favoured Jakarta's further moving towards a primate situation. Moreover, there have been several new post-Independence developments which have assisted in extending Jakarta's dominance in Indonesia. Jakarta has become the focus and symbol of Indonesian national unity. The Independence period has seen a greater centralization of activities in the national capital than was the case under the Dutch. 'Not only did it maintain its function as the major intermediary with other countries but it became the major focus of national commercial, industrial, administrative and political development' (Hugo, 1975: 201). Widespread improvements in transport and communications made possible a much greater degree of centralization of administrative and commercial activity in the national capital than was the case during Dutch rule. Jakarta's growing primacy in Indonesia is reflected not only in population size but also in the fact that it has 30 per cent of all telephones in Indonesia, 25 per cent of all motor cars (Goldstein, 1975: 77) and 30 per cent of all doctors (Arndt, 1975: 21).

It is interesting to consider Jakarta's position in a regional and world context. Jakarta is now the largest city in South-East Asia, and its increasing dominance of the urban hierarchy in Indonesia is matched by an elevation in its relative position among the major metropolises of the world. During the colonial period, it could clearly not be ranked among the world's major cities. However, United Nations figures show Jakarta climbing from being the forty-second largest city in the world in 1950 to twenty-first position in 1975 (see Table 3.16). Their projections indicate that, by the year 2000, Jakarta will be the eleventh largest metropolis in a world in which 7 of the

TABLE 3.16

Ranking of Jakarta among the World's Urban Agglomerations, 1950–2000

Year	Rank	Population Size	Size of World's Largest Urban Agglomeration	Ratio to World's Largest Agglomeration
			(in millions)	
1950	42	1.6	12.3	0.13
1960	26	2.7	14.2	0.19
1970	21	4.3	16.3	0.26
1975	21	5.6	17.3	0.32
1980	20	7.2	19.7	0.37
1990	15	11.5	23.5	0.49
2000	11	16.9	31.6	0.53

Source: Hugo, 1981a: 68.

11 largest cities will be located in Asia. The table shows that the ratio of Jakarta's population size to that of the world's largest metropolis will quadruple between 1950 and 2000 as its relative importance in the world urban system increases.

Further insight into the changing size distribution within Indonesia's urban system can be gained from examining the growth of individual centres. The population growth of centres with more than 100,000 inhabitants is presented in Table 3.17. There are several striking tendencies in evidence. First, over the 1920–71 period, there is a concentration of most rapid growth in the largest cities on Java and in the cities of the outer islands. There are some minor deviations from this pattern where exceptional circumstances caused rapid growth. An example is the town of Tasikmalaya in West Java: one of the few protected centres in the Eastern Priangan when the D'arul Islam rebellion raged throughout much of that region in the 1950s, it became a haven for refugees (Hugo, 1975). In the outer islands of Sumatra, Kalimantan and Sulawesi, the period has seen the emergence of what Withington (1973: 9) calls 'second level primate centres' such as Medan, Pontianak and Ujung Pandang, and these have undergone very rapid growth. This has also been the case with towns which are the centres for major projects involved in the exploitation of raw materials (Pekanbaru, Balikpapan, Samarinda, etc.).

Turning to the 1970s, NUDSP (1985: 20) data show wide variations between centres in their rates of growth, ranging from an annual growth rate of 17.3 per cent in the growing mining centre of Soroako in the Toraja region of South Sulawesi to several small and medium-sized cities in Java (for example, Banjar, Majalengka, Jember, Purworejo) which grew at below the national population growth rate. The major patterns evident in Table 3.17 can be briefly summarized as follows:

1. There was rapid growth in major metropolitan areas and the satellite centres within commuting distance of those centres. In particular, Jakarta has overspilled its boundaries into the adjoining *kabupaten* of Bekasi, Tanggerang and Bogor. This overspill is so noticeable that a new administrative unit Jabotabek has been formed with limited powers. Hence Depok, Bekasi and Bogor all recorded very rapid growth between 1971 and 1980 as did other centres with less than 100,000 inhabitants (for example, Tanggerang and Cibinong). Similar patterns have been observed around Bandung, along the Surabaya–Malang corridor and near Medan (NUDSP, 1985: 22).

2. In Java, outside the metropolitan areas, the pattern is mixed but Table 3.17 shows that most urban areas grew faster than they did between 1961 and 1971. Clearly, though, high growth rates were more common among the major cities of the other islands than in Java. NUDSP (1985: 20) has identified a significant difference between the cities located along Java's north coast which have relatively high population growth. These are differentiated from the non-metropolitan centres of the south and east where low growth is more common.

3. In all regions outside Java, large- and medium-sized port cities grew

TABLE 3.17

Urban Centres with More than 100,000 Inhabitants in 1980, and Rate of Growth, 1920–1980

Centre	Population					Rate of Growth Per Annum		
	1920	1930	1961	1971[a]	1980[a]	1920–1971	1961–1971	1971–1980
JAVA								
Jakarta	306,309	533,015	2,973,052	4,084,950	6,071,750	5.4*	4.6*	4.5*
Surabaya	192,190	341,675	1,007,945	1,308,630	1,737,020	4.2*	4.4*	3.2
Bandung	94,800	166,815	972,566	1,310,910	1,744,520	5.1*	2.1	3.6
Semarang	158,036	217,796	503,153	566,380	820,140	2.8	2.5	4.2
Malang	42,981	86,646	341,452	365,280	491,470	4.6*	2.2	3.4
Surakarta	134,285	165,484	367,626	438,490	539,980	2.2	1.2+	2.3
Yogyakarta	103,711	136,649	312,698	347,260	460,170	2.4	0.9+	3.2
Bogor	45,595	65,431	154,092	330,160	544,790	2.9	2.4	5.7*
Kediri	43,222	48,567	158,918	130,500	176,260	2.8	1.2+	3.4
Cirebon	33,051	54,079	158,299	195,360	265,720	3.4	1.2+	3.5
Madiun	31,593	41,872	123,373	135,660	169,920	2.9	1.0+	2.5
Tasikmalaya	14,216	25,605	125,525	146,620	192,270	4.5*	0.8+	3.1
Jember	16,491	20,222	94,089	147,350	171,280	4.0*	2.7	1.7+
Pekalongan	47,852	65,982	102,380	191,590	249,170	1.7+	0.9+	3.0
Magelang	36,213	52,944	96,454	126,800	152,950	2.2	1.4+	2.1
Tegal	34,687	43,015	89,016	229,590	326,800	2.2	1.7+	4.0

(continued)

TABLE 3.17 (continued)

Centre	Population					Rate of Growth Per Annum		
	1920	1930	1961	1971ª	1980ª	1920–1971	1961–1971	1971–1980
Sukabumi	25,533	34,191	80,438	160,840	215,290	2.4	1.8+	3.3
Kudus	42,045	54,524	74,911	114,840	154,480	2.0	2.0	3.4
Garut	14,063	24,219	76,244	113,320	145,620	1.7+	3.9	2.8
Bekasi	n.a.	n.a.	32,012	61,320	144,290	n.a.	6.5*	10.0*
Purwokerto	12,584	33,266	80,556	113,160	143,790	5.2*	3.4	2.7
Cilacap	18,991	28,309	55,333	85,470	127,020	3.7	4.3*	4.5*
Depok	n.a.	n.a.	n.a.	44,640	126,690	n.a.	n.a.	12.3*
Pasuruan	n.a.	37,081	63,408	87,020	119,090	2.1	2.1	3.6
Klaten	9,373	12,039	33,400	97,550	117,560	4.5*	10.7*	2.1
Cianjur	17,955	20,812	62,546	81,430	105,660	3.8	2.6	2.9
SUMATRA								
Medan	45,248	76,584	479,098	892,130	1,265,210	5.3*	2.9	4.0
Palembang	75,726	108,145	474,971	504,340	757,490	3.1	2.1	4.6*
Tanjung Karang	14,980	25,170	133,901	166,010	357,690	5.2*	4.0*	8.9*
Padang	38,169	52,054	143,699	188,940	296,680	3.3	3.2	5.1*
Jambi	11,311	22,071	113,080	94,350	155,760	5.2*	3.4	5.7*
Pekanbaru[b]	n.a.	10,000	70,821	126,090	186,200	6.5*	7.4*	4.4*
Pematang Siantar	9,460	15,328	114,870	143,420	172,910	5.3*	1.2+	2.1

KALIMANTAN								
Banjarmasin	46,993	65,698	214,096	224,060	330,130	3.6	2.8	4.4*⁻
Pontianak	28,731	45,196	150,220	182,190	276,670	4.0*	3.8	4.8*
Samarinda	6,879	11,086	69,715	90,770	182,470	6.1*	7.0*	8.1*
Balikpapan	n.a.	29,843	91,706	97,370	208,040	2.8	4.1	8.8*
SULAWESI								
Ujung Pandang	56,718	84,855	384,159	423,560	638,800	4.1*	2.7	4.7*
Manado	17,062	27,544	129,912	151,490	217,090	4.6*	2.7	4.1
OTHER ISLANDS								
Mataram	n.a.	n.a.	n.a.	155,100	210,490	n.a.	n.a.	3.5
Ambon	11,120	17,334	56,037	64,700	111,910	3.9	3.6	6.3*
Den Pasar	8,501	16,639	56,780	72,830	159,230	4.2*	1.5*	9.1*

Sources: Hugo, 1981a: 65; NUDSP, 1985: 12–13.

* More than twice the national population growth rate.

+ Below the national growth rate.

a 1971 and 1980 figures are as defined by National Urban Development Strategy Project for boundaries of functional urban areas, and differ in some cases from administrative definitions of urban areas.

b 1930 population figure for Pekanbaru is the upper limit of the estimate made by census officials (quoted in Withington, 1963: 242). Annual growth rate for Pekanbaru is for 1930–71, not 1920–71.

n.a. = Data not available.

rapidly (NUDSP, 1985: 22) with Southern Sumatra being especially prominent. There were, however, low growth rates in inland towns in the outer islands.

National Integration

This chapter has established the enormous interregional heterogeneity which characterizes Indonesia. In concluding, it is relevant to ask what, given such huge diversity, holds Indonesia together besides geographical contiguity. One obvious answer to this question is the government which is a strong, essentially military, highly centralized one in which 'policy making is essentially a top-down process in which the central government plays a predominant role' (MacAndrews, Fisher and Sibero, 1982: 84). Moreover, through the development of satellite-based sophisticated communication systems, central control and influence can be exercised much more readily in the peripheral regions of the country. With the exception of East Timor, annexed in 1976, one of the most significant integrating factors in Indonesia is a common Dutch colonial heritage.

Successive post-Independence governments of Indonesia have recognized the significance of strong regional distinctiveness and regional interest groups and worked towards national integration. One vehicle of this integration is the national language, Indonesian or *Bahasa Indonesia*. At the 1980 Census, some 12 per cent of the population spoke Indonesian as their mother tongue while a further 49 per cent spoke it as a second language. The proportion of females unable to speak Indonesian at all (43.6 per cent) was substantially higher than was the case for males (33.6 per cent). However, there can be little doubt that the development of *Bahasa Indonesia* as a *lingua franca* in the country has greatly assisted national integration.

TABLE 3.18

Indonesia: Language Used at Home by Province or Island, 1980

Province or Island	Indonesian Used at Home	Other Language Used at Home	
		Able to Speak Indonesian	Unable to Speak Indonesian
Java	10.3	47.7	42.0
Jakarta	91.6	3.2	5.2
West Java	8.9	52.7	38.4
Central Java	1.2	50.6	48.2
Yogyakarta	4.1	55.4	40.5
East Java	2.2	48.5	49.3
Sumatra	15.8	55.8	28.4
Kalimantan	9.5	54.3	36.2
Sulawesi	15.4	48.7	36.5
Other Islands	15.2	44.3	40.5
Indonesia	12.0	49.4	38.6

Source: 1980 Indonesian Census.

FIGURE 3.16

Indonesia: Proportion of Provincial Populations with Javanese as Their Mother Tongue, 1980

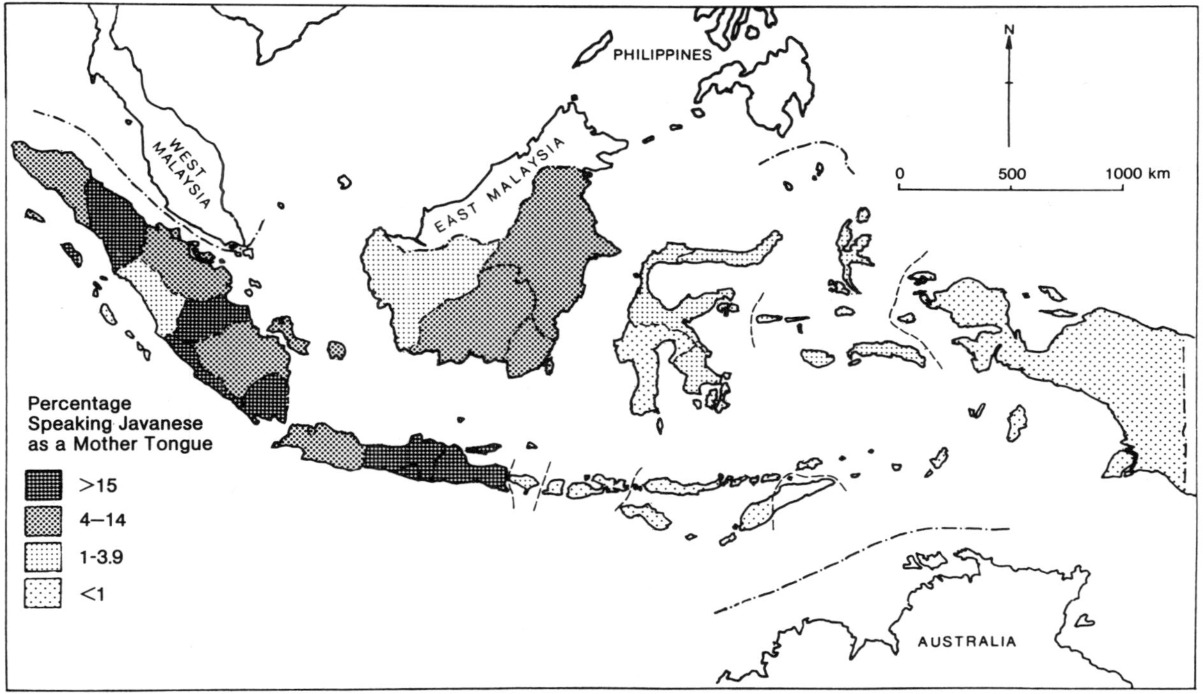

Percentage
Speaking Javanese
as a Mother Tongue

>15
4–14
1-3.9
<1

Source: Indonesian Census of 1980.

Table 3.18 shows that there is considerable variation between the different regions in the extent to which the national language is spoken. Clearly, the highest incidence is in Jakarta—which is partly a function of the fact that the language of indigenous Jakartans (the Betawi) is similar to Indonesian. More importantly, it is also because there is no single dominant ethnic group in the capital so that the city has assumed a 'melting pot' character and contains significant communities of several groups who are forced to interact, especially in employment, so there is a need for a *lingua franca*. On the other hand, the highest incidence of inability to speak Indonesian is in the Javanese-dominated areas of East and Central Java.

Interprovincial migration (considered in Chapter 6) is another integrating influence in Indonesia. The movement of the numerically dominant ethnolinguistic group (the Javanese) into other provinces, for example, is depicted in Figure 3.16 which shows the proportion of provincial populations who have the Javanese language as a mother tongue. Javanese is not only of major significance in the heartland areas of the eastern two-thirds of Java, but also in areas of Sumatra which have been the major destinations of transmigrants and contract labour working on plantations. There is also substantial Javanese representation in most other provinces.

Conclusion

This chapter has demonstrated the tremendous degree of regional diversity in Indonesia. In any discussion of the demography of the country, this heterogeneity must be borne in mind. National trends represent the average of a variety of regional tendencies which can and do vary over a wide range. This is especially important from the perspective of development. There is a growing awareness in Indonesia among policy-makers, bureaucrats and academics of the importance of regional planning. Until 1973, sectoral approaches to national development predominated (World Bank, 1984b). However, growing awareness of, and concern about widening regional inequalities has led to a number of regional planning initiatives (MacAndrews, Fisher and Sibero, 1980).

4 Mortality and Health Care

Mortality Levels and Trends to 1900

PRIOR to 1800, mortality in the Indonesian archipelago was high and subject to large fluctuations as a result of famines, wars and epidemic diseases. This is not surprising. It must be remembered that mortality rates in Europe were also high in the 1700s and 1800s, for many of the same reasons, and that for the bulk of the world's population at the time there was little that could be done to control disease, and war and hunger often went hand in hand. What is less clear is the question of whether the dramatic socio-economic changes in Indonesia, and particularly Java, between 1800 and 1900 led to a major reduction in the burden of mortality and an increase in the rate of population growth.

The nineteenth century brought industrialization to Europe, with attendant improvements in production and transportation of basic commodities. As the Dutch colonial government tightened its control on Java, it extended many of the mechanical innovations of the time to its colony, in order to better extract the raw materials needed to fuel economic transformation at home. During this period of colonial penetration, it was often argued that the changes wrought by colonial government were improving the lot of the native people, with the result that mortality rates were falling. As noted in Chapter 2, evidence for this contention tended to focus on the apparent 'results' of falling mortality and, in particular, on the rising rates of population growth in various districts and for the island as a whole. It became an article of faith among servants of the colonial power that their activities were justified because they improved the lives of people of the colony.

This belief has been called into question by many writers, most notably Widjojo Nitisastro who sifted carefully through archival evidence in preparing *Population Trends in Indonesia* (1970). Looking at the likely causes of mortality decline rather than alleged effects, he found that very little was done in the field of public health prior to 1910 with the exception of smallpox vaccination. The issue turns on the evidence of high population growth rates in Java, which, as described in Chapter 2, fails to stand up to careful scrutiny. Rather than major declines in mortality leading to rapid increases in population numbers, it seems that the population only grew at a slowly increasing rate between 1800 and 1900, and any mortality decline must have been moderate. Gardiner and Oey (1983: 1–2) have pointed out that, even at the very end of the nineteenth century, mortality experienced wide fluctuations as a result of almost completely uncontrolled epidemics which regularly swept the island. In some areas, years of 'fever' produced recorded crude death rates of 70 per thousand or more, compared to normal rates of between 20 and 30 per thousand. Under such conditions, it is hard to accept the contention that mortality had fallen in a major way in Java prior to 1900. This would imply even less change in the outer islands where positive effects of colonialism were even more limited and negative effects of warfare and introduced diseases were substantial.

Government Health Care Programmes, 1900–1980

The End of the Colonial Era: 1900–1940

During the early decades of this century, health services remained limited, in part due to the very small pool of professionally trained personnel. Two medical schools had been established (one in Jakarta in 1875, and one in Surabaya in 1913), but by 1930 there were still only a combined total of 667 doctors and native medical practitioners (*doktor djawa*) to service a population of over 60 million (Furnivall, 1948: 257). Training of local health service personnel was limited largely by the continuous insistence on the part of the colonial government that medical courses at all levels needed to be taught in Dutch and to the highest academic standards. Contemporary reformers, who called for the establishment of paramedical services using people of limited but specialized training, were largely over-ruled by the powerful interests of the medical profession whose penchant for quality care was manifest in the large hospitals built in major cities while the bulk of the population lacked even basic clinic facilities. Services were of course further limited by the general level of medical knowledge of the time, which had yet to discern the biological causes of common diseases such as malaria, plague and cholera. None the less, the basic government policy of concentrating resources was set in sharp relief by the example of a missionary hospital in Yogyakarta which established an extensive outreach programme complete with village clinics, and thus succeeded in providing services to a very large population.

The first major public health effort was a smallpox vaccination campaign which, although actually initiated in the early nineteenth century,[1] was reorganized and expanded in 1917. There were some attempts to control cholera through isolation of cases and provision of uncontaminated water to cholera areas, and some efforts at vector control for malaria. This, along with the expanded smallpox eradication campaign, may have contributed to a gradual decline in mortality prior to the influenza epidemic of 1918, when mortality rose to atypical heights (Gardiner and Oey, 1983: 12). There may also have been some impact from localized programmes, for example in the cities where there were some neighbourhood hygiene projects. It has been hypothesized that beneficial effects of the government programmes may have been felt on private estates, at least in Java, where free clinics and immunization were provided, though other disruptions brought by the colonial economy in plantation areas may have in fact operated to raise mortality (Gardiner and Oey, 1983: 25–6).

In the late 1920s, the colonial government began to give increased attention to health education (Hydrick, 1937), and emphasis began to shift to disease prevention in the rural environment. Responsibility for public health was decentralized in the hope that local health services would be more knowledgeable about local conditions (Van Thiel, 1971: 451). In the early years, the programme tended to concentrate largely on the prevention of soil and water pollution, and was associated with the Rockefeller Foundation's international efforts at hookworm control. Later, this expanded to a health propaganda campaign containing a wide variety of preventive health-care issues. In 1933, a Demonstration Unit was set up in Purwokerto, Central Java, and this served as a testing ground and training base for a full public health programme. This project, described in detail by Hydrick (1937), provides an exemplary model of community health care which would be difficult to match even today. Partially funded and with technical assistance from the Rockefeller Foundation, the project comprised an impressive array of components, including a training unit for *Hygiene Mantri* (Health Officers); health education in schools and for school teachers; a Hygiene Centre devoted to maternal and child health education; training of traditional midwives; a general or baseline survey and the collection and study of birth, morbidity, and mortality statistics; epidemiological investigations; special programmes on drinking water, the disposal of garbage and refuse, on housing and food and food suppliers; and many others. The underlying philosophy stressed teaching self-reliance and stimulating active interest on the part of the people, a philosophy which the contemporary movement to primary health care strives for. Widjojo (1970: 93) has said that 'during the 1930s, more was done in the field of health improvement than in any previous period'. All these efforts came to an abrupt end with the invasion by the Japanese in 1942.

Overall, however, the public health approach initiated in the 1930s was really 'too little, too late' in the context of evaluating the colonial government's total impact on the health of the indigenous population. Mortality declines which did take place were probably due as much to other factors such as the opening up of new agricultural land, the increase in irrigation, and tighter social control of food production, as to health interventions (Gardiner and Oey, 1983). None the less, by 1939, Indonesia had developed an elaborate public health infrastructure which was the envy of much of the rest of Asia, and had gone a long way toward eradicating plague, cholera and malaria, and controlling smallpox, tuberculosis, and nutritional deficiencies in large areas of the archipelago. With the Japanese invasion, this organization collapsed, and serious set-backs occurred in all aspects of health care. There followed eight dark years of rising death rates and institutional degradation.

Health Care in Independent Indonesia: 1950–1980

EXPANSION OF FACILITIES: 1950–1970

The health problems in Indonesia in 1950 were enormous, and the resources available to address them were very limited. Public health efforts in newly independent Indonesia were aided by public support, in turn linked to the post-Independence spread of education and, in Widjojo's terms (1970: 126), an 'increasing awareness of alternative opportunities, which led to rising demands for more and better facilities in both education and public health'. Specific public health campaigns were launched, such as the intensive malaria eradication programme which was part of the WHO global campaign. A yaws eradication campaign succeeded in ridding Java and Bali of the disease by the early 1960s, though it persists in some areas of the other islands (Mitchell, 1982: 7). Smallpox was largely controlled during the early 1950s and finally eradicated from Indonesia in the early 1970s. With UNICEF support, a network of maternal and child health centres (*Balai Kesehatan Ibu dan Anak*, or BKIA) were built during the 1950s and 1960s.

Post-war health facilities and trained personnel were still very limited, however, with only one doctor for over 100,000 people. Major developments in health infrastructure and personnel did not come until after 1960, and dramatic developments occurred from about 1970 onwards (see Table 4.1).

PRIMARY HEALTH CARE: 1970–1980

The idea of primary health care as government policy only began to receive support during the second half of the First Five-Year Development Plan (1969–74). There had been initial optimism that urban-oriented programmes and their benefits would spread to rural dwellers but, as it became clear that this hoped-for result was far from being achieved, the need to reach villages led to the development of the Community Health Centre (*Pusat Kesehatan Masyarakat* or *Puskesmas*) system, the concept of which had been developed in a Department of Health workshop in 1968 (Azwar, 1980: 10). People's acceptance of the maternal and child health centres (BKIA) further encouraged the development of a more integrated community health centre system, and the BKIA were incorporated with general out-patient clinics, family planning services, health education programmes, and other preventative and curative services. The original aim to establish a *Puskesmas* in each of Indonesia's 3,500 subdistricts (each with an average population in 1980 of 43,000) was realized during the Second Five-Year Development Plan (1974–79) (Iskandar and Rienks, 1981).

Ideally, each *Puskesmas* includes a medical team headed by a doctor. In 1980, though, about half the centres did not have a physician, even though, as Table 4.1 shows, there were more than twice the number of doctors as *Puskesmas*. As in most developing countries, the distribution of doctors is imbalanced, with concentrations in cities—and especially Jakarta. It has

TABLE 4.1

Indonesia: Selected Indicators of Health Services, 1950–1980

	Health Personnel		Hospitals, Clinics		
	Doctors	Others	Hospitals	Hospital Beds	Public Health Centres
circa 1950					
Total units	783	7,022	664	62,876	—
Population per unit	106,866	11,916	123,453	1,304	—
circa 1960					
Total units	976	18,115	832	75,819	—
Population per unit	97,601	5,259	114,494	1,156	—
circa 1970					
Total units	2,213	27,976	1,126	85,568	1,637
Population per unit	50,780	4,017	99,802	1,313	71,759
circa 1980					
Total units	11,681	68,215	1,208	98,543	4,753
Population per unit	12,627	2,162	122,103	1,497	31,033
Comparative Data (Population per doctor circa 1980)					
Bangladesh	8,780	—	—	—	—
Australia	650				

Sources: circa 1950: BPS, *Statistical Pocketbook of Indonesia* 1957, pp. 32–3.
circa 1960: BPS, *Statistical Pocketbook of Indonesia* 1963, pp. 11, 46–7.
circa 1970: BPS, *Almanak Indonesia* 1968, Djilid I, pp. 320–1.
BPS, *Statistik Indonesia* 1972/3, pp. 18, 121.
circa 1980: BPS, *Profil Statistik Anak dan Ibu di Indonesia* 1980–81, pp. 122 & 127.
BPS, *Ulasan Singkat Hasil Sensus Penduduk* 1980, p. 4.
World Bank (1983), *Indonesia: Selected Issues in Spatial Development*,
Vol. 2, p. 323.

been reported that half of Indonesia's doctors live in the four largest cities (Iskandar and Rienks, 1981: 2). The situation represents a vast change compared to the distribution a decade ago, however, when it was rare to find any medical doctor outside of a major town.

As *Puskesmas* were established, the Research Unit of the Department of Health's Community Health Care delivery section began evaluation research on coverage and utilization. They found the *Puskesmas* were used by only about 20 per cent of the target population, and the users were mainly upper and middle class rural dwellers, not the poor. It was not unusual for a centre which had a capacity for 200–300 clients per day to actually see only 20 or 30 (Iskandar and Rienks, 1981: 3–4; Mitchell, 1982: 2–3). Reasons for underutilization are complex, and probably include beliefs as to the aetiology of diseases which lead to the demand for traditional medicine, particularly for certain types of affliction; cost and travelling time to go to the clinic; attitudes of modern health personnel which discourage less-educated clients from seeking help or advice; and the irregular and inadequate supply of medicines to the centres (Iskandar and Rienks, 1981; Mitchell, 1982: 4–5; Berman, 1984).

Over time, it appears that this type of underutilization is being overcome, and some clinics are beginning to report more clients than they can effectively handle. In general, each clinic has to go through an establishment sequence: first the building and equipment, then recruitment of staff willing to spend sufficient time on a regular basis, and finally achievement of community trust. By the time of the 1980 Census, 40 per cent of people reporting an illness for the week prior to the census had sought treatment at an established source such as a *Puskesmas*, hospital or private doctor, and a further 20 per cent had received help from a health service extension worker (BPS, 1983: 140). Given that many illnesses do not require medical attention, this indicates a fairly high degree of acceptance of modern medical services.

Though it was during the decade of the 1970s that much international attention was focused on primary health care, and the Indonesian Department of Health decided that a form of this approach could help to achieve the goal of rural outreach, a number of privately sponsored programmes had been active in village areas in the 1950s and 1960s. One of the most successful of these was the YIS (*Yayasan Indonesia Sejahtera*) programme in Surakarta (Hendrata, 1981). This and other programmes introduced the concept of health cadres (*kader kesehatan*) and the idea of a community health insurance scheme (*dana sehat*), which were eventually adapted to government schemes. One of the earliest large-scale schemes was established in Banjarnegara Regency in Central Java in the early 1970s. It was initiated by *Puskesmas* doctors and local officials, and eventually gained the support of the head of the Regency Medical Service (Iskandar and Rienks, 1981: 4–5). The central government became interested in generalizing such a scheme and, in 1975, set up a project in the Regency of Karanganyar. This scheme was much less flexible and responsive to local conditions than that found in Banjarnegara.

In 1976 and 1978, two national-level programmes related to primary health care were launched. The Family Nutrition Improvement Programme (*Usaha Perbaikan Gizi Keluarga* or UPGK) trains nutrition cadres (*kader gizi*) to provide basic nutrition and health education, particularly in the field of maternal and child health, including child-weighing programmes. Although a nutrition programme already existed, the new programme aimed at achieving wider and more even coverage, and at developing nutrition in the context of primary health care linked to the local clinic. Secondly, the Village Community Health Development programme (*Pembangunan Kesehatan Masyarakat Desa*, or PKMD), is emerging as the main government primary health-care programme, training village-level health workers or *promotor kesehatan* (*prokesa*) to provide nutrition education, treat common illnesses, oversee environmental health programmes, and conduct health insurance schemes. However, as Berman (1984) and Mitchell (1982) have noted, there are also many other primary health-care projects training health and nutrition cadres—the result of, in Berman's terms, 'kader fever'—and this has often led to duplication and overlap of services. Under the Third Five-Year Development Plan, *Repelita III* (1979–84), the government's goal was to establish cadre programmes in over 20,000 villages—or about one-third of Indonesia's villages.

A recent review of available evidence indicated that cadre systems do result in better coverage, and that services seem to reach poorer groups better than does the *Puskesmas* system (Berman, 1984; 1986). However, even in the highly-regarded Banjarnegara project, it has been found that programme objectives and design were determined largely by the health centre staff and the village elite (Iskandar *et al.*, 1979, cited in Iskandar and Rienks, 1981). This situation has been illustrated poignantly in a detailed case-study of another pilot project (Williams and Satoto, 1980) which shows that, even when a group outside the official village bureaucracy attempted to initiate a programme, the ruling elite at village as well as higher levels felt threatened, and exerted a wide variety of pressures on the project leaders in order to gain control of the activity. This study also showed an unwillingness on the part of village men to allow women to participate in decision-making.

The concept of primary health care has continued to evolve in Indonesia as experience is gained with successive approaches. In the late 1970s, the 'Baby Weighing Station' with the 'Road to Health Chart' was promoted across the country, with the hope that focusing maternal attention on the baby's growth would motivate them to take steps to improve the child's nutrition and medical care. In 1984, the concept was broadened to integrate a variety of medical services such as vaccination into the weighing post. The new service was called the *Posyandu* (Integrated Service Post), and spread rapidly so that by mid-1986 there were 48,000 such posts regularly operating in villages across the country, according to press statements by the Minister for Health. In addition, it is claimed that up to 100,000 midwives had received training to improve the safety of delivery. The posts and the trained midwives are also seen as the key to tackling one of the most important health priorities in Indonesia—that of increasing the coverage of basic immunization. The Department of Health reported that the full complement of immunizations (DPT three times, polio three times, BCG once, and measles once) was received by only 6 per cent of children in 1983. By 1985, this had risen to 25 per cent, largely because of a higher proportion of children completing the full course, where previously many children had received only the first one or two DPT and polio vaccinations. The government target for coverage by the end of *Repelita IV* in 1989 was set at 65 per cent, though in the celebrations to mark the start of the Indonesian Decade of Children in July 1986, James Grant, the head of UNICEF, called on Indonesia to join in a global target to reach a coverage of 80 per cent by 1990.

Despite general support for some form of primary health care, the Indonesian health system still exhibits an urban, hospital-based orientation. It has been estimated that only one-quarter of the *Repelita III* budget allocated for health went to rural dwellers, and the scale of the health allocation in the national budget is in any case extremely small, being only 3–4 per cent of total government expenditure (Iskandar and Rienks, 1981: 2).

High-technology medicine still receives considerable priority, and the misuse and over-use of modern drugs is becoming an increasing problem. There is, among some policy-makers, a tendency to see primary health care as a type of low-cost, inferior health service provided for the poor, but quite distinct from 'real' medicine for those who can afford it. This dichotomy is also seen at the level of individual health practitioners, most of whom are government employees who work in *Puskesmas* or other government programmes during regular hours, but who conduct lucrative private practices during evening hours. A basic priority for the long-range goals of primary health care will involve medical education which stresses community health along with basic medicine. In the past, only a few medical schools have had substantial programmes of community medicine, though the government is now committed to developing programmes in all medical as well as nursing schools. Successful primary health-care programmes will depend to a large extent on developing this kind of orientation among health professionals. The more basic goal of achieving real community-based programmes, involving direct participation of citizens at all stages, will require an even more fundamental change of orientation, associated with further decentralization of power and resources. This is a formidable challenge.

Mortality Decline, 1900–1980: National Levels and Trends

The vast changes in health care which have taken place over the present century were associated not only with significant gains in medical technology and health-care policy, but also with monumental social and economic transformations which have accelerated markedly in recent decades. The task of linking these factors to changes in mortality in Indonesia is a daunting one. However, before this issue is addressed, we must examine one which is only slightly less challenging—the reconstruction of statistics on mortality levels and trends over the period.

Data Sources and Data Quality

Indonesian data on historical demographic trends are restricted in terms of reliability and also in scope, being generally limited to Java, and often to local areas. In 1910–11, largely in response to the outbreak of bubonic plague, the colonial government initiated new regulations requiring medical services in all localities to collect and report statistics on morbidity and mortality. Unfortunately, this referred primarily to the epidemic diseases, and the incidence of and mortality from significant endemic diseases such as infantile diarrhoea went unmeasured (Gardiner and Oey, 1983: 10). The high mortality period of the 1940s—a time of war, Japanese occupation, and revolution—understandably yields even scantier data than previous years. In the post-war period, data on morbidity came from household health surveys and, with increasing numbers using formal institutions, through clinic and hospital records. However, clinic data still cannot adequately represent the population and, overall, data on morbidity patterns are poor.

FIGURE 4.1

Indonesia: Changes in Mortality Levels, 1920–1980

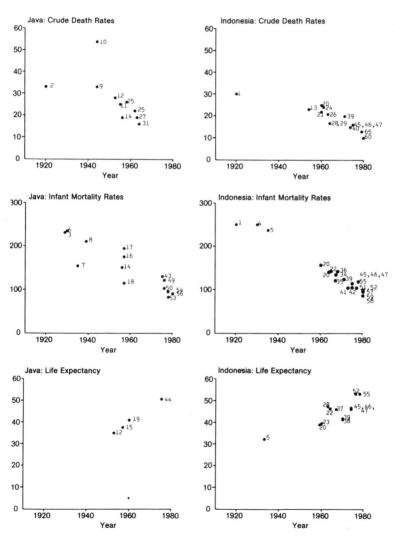

Sources: See Appendix 3.

Direct data on mortality are also of generally low reliability. The vital registration systems set up during the pre-war period were initially highly localized and, even though extended to the national level in 1955, coverage remained incomplete. Even today, except for the special project on Sample Vital Registration carried out in particular localities of Java, vital registration statistics are too flawed to be used as the primary source for estimates of mortality levels and trends. For the most part, contemporary statistics on mortality are derived using indirect techniques which convert data on numbers of children ever born and still living for mothers of given age groups into estimates of recent infant and child mortality rates. Estimates of historical mortality levels come from local studies, from extrapolations based on official records, and from 'educated guesses' of scholars, demographers and historians. Some of the estimates, to be discussed in subsequent sections, have been compiled in Figure 4.1.

Pre-1940 Mortality Levels

The official colonial records are not reliable sources of precise figures, but they can give some idea of trends in mortality. Crude death rates (CDR) for Java for the period 1916 to 1930 were reproduced by Widjojo (1970: 101–2) from these reports (Table 4.2). They show minor fluctuations over the period, except for the marked increase during 1918–19, the time of the influenza epidemic. There appears to be some slight decline in the CDR in the late 1920s which continues into the early 1930s (not shown). Breman (1971: 64–73) claims that economic improvements in the early 1920s may have resulted in slight mortality decline in Java but, he says, economic conditions in the 1930s would have been conducive to

TABLE 4.2

Officially Recorded Crude Death Rates (CDR) for Java, 1916–1930

Year	Population	Deaths	CDR
1916	32,963,861	586,757	17.8
1917	33,357,941	673,830	20.2
1918	33,629,766	1,227,121	36.5
1919	33,456,646	930,095	27.8
1920	33,087,264	764,316	23.1
1921	34,399,477	815,268	23.7
1922	34,480,630	689,613	20.0
1923	34,838,353	634,058	18.2
1924	35,070,939	655,827	18.7
1925	35,505,233	706,554	19.9
1926	35,889,883	753,688	21.0
1927	36,173,984	676,454	18.7
1928	36,439,100	717,850	19.7
1929	37,046,865	733,528	19.8
1930	40,890,244	740,113	18.1

Source: Widjojo, 1970: 102.

TABLE 4.3

Indonesia: Corrected Estimates of Crude Death Rates (CDR)
and Expectation of Life at Birth (E_0°), 1900–1960

Period	CDR	E_0°
Pre-1930	33.5	30.0
1930–1935	30.1	32.5
1935–1940	27.8	35.0
1940–1945	35.1	27.5
1945–1950	35.0	27.5
1950–1955	28.3	35.0
1955–1960	26.2	37.5

Source: Widjojo, 1970: 158.

increased mortality. Widjojo (1970: 101) notes that official records show increasing mortality in the late 1930s, and speculates that this could be due to improvements in the registration system which occurred as the Hygiene Programme spread through Java at this time. His corrected CDRs for the period 1930–60 show very small mortality declines for the 1930s (Table 4.3). What both Breman and Widjojo appear to have missed is that, while recorded death rates tended to rise as registration systems became established in specific areas, the medical observers of the time, reporting in the government's health bulletins, were careful to distinguish this statistical anomaly from the real trend. By these accounts mortality was in a state of steady decline as major infectious diseases such as smallpox, plague and to some extent malaria came under control, and sanitation programmes became more widespread, even as economic conditions worsened.

Even though there were some improvements in statistical reporting in the years prior to the War, the most reliable estimates of levels of mortality derive from local-area studies, which tended to be in urban areas. After reviewing evidence from a range of such studies, Widjojo (1970: 103–13) concluded that the expectation of life at birth during the 1930s was about 30–35 years, corresponding to an infant mortality rate of 225 to 250 per thousand. In another study, Keyfitz and Widjojo (1955: 49–50) accepted the estimates of the CDR for the pre-1940 period as ranging from 15 to 23 per thousand, though later Breman (1971) assumed the substantially higher level of 30 to 50 over the same period. The weight of evidence, from both local-area studies and later demographic evaluations, is on the side of the lower rates, though it remains disturbing that there has not been sufficient historical demographic analysis of this period to determine the degree to which the available evidence reveals or masks the true mortality trends for the country as a whole.

Mortality during the War Years, 1940–1950

Conditions of life during this period were dramatically disrupted, first by the war and the Japanese Occupation of 1942 to 1945, then by the revolution against the Dutch from 1945 to 1949. The population data available for scrutiny from these years are understandably scanty, though we have some local-area reports by the Japanese for 1944 which include crude death rates as high as 53.7 for one area of Central Java (Anderson, 1966, cited in Widjojo, 1970: 117–18). We also have an estimate, based on obscure sources, for all Java for 1944 which puts the death rate at 33 per thousand (De Vries, 1946, cited in Widjojo, 1970: 119). Widjojo claims conditions in the first half of the decade during the Japanese Occupation were worse than the second half during the revolution, because food was commandeered to feed the Japanese armies, and young men were sent away in forced labour teams (*romusha*), leading to both decreased fertility and increased mortality. During the Revolution, even though more casualties were directly related to war being fought in particular localities, food was more generally available.

Other sources of data on this period come from recent demographic surveys which included pregnancy histories of women who gave birth to children during the decade of the 1940s. The Fertility–Mortality Survey of 1973, for example, has recorded levels of child mortality for the birth cohort 1945–9 which were twice the level of those for the 1965–7 cohort (McDonald *et al.*, 1976: 69). A community study in a Yogyakarta village (Hull, 1975: 226) recorded an infant mortality rate of 271 per thousand for the years 1944–8, and 205 for 1949–53, much higher levels than those for either preceding (134 for 1939–43) or subsequent (falling to 66 in 1969–73) cohorts.

Mortality in the 1950s

During the decade following wartime disruption, mortality apparently not only declined to pre-war levels, but then continued to decline steadily, despite a return of smallpox in epidemic proportions during the decade of the 1950s (Leimena, 1953). This was the time, of the expansion of health facilities and of major public health campaigns such as malaria vector control and yaws eradication. Studies reviewed in the University of Indonesia Demographic Institute's *Demographic Factbook* have estimated CDRs of around 20 per thousand population for the 1950s, based on local-level data, though both Widjojo (1970) and Breman (1971) estimate the rate to be somewhat higher, at around 25 per thousand. The registration system had resumed after Independence, but was still inadequate overall. Some local areas were said to have particularly good systems, and one of them, Wonosobo in Central Java, recorded a CDR for this period (1958) of 21.3 (Widjojo 1970: 140).

In summarizing the probable demographic profile of 1950–60, Widjojo (1970) highlights the apparent steady decline in mortality which, in conjunction with a return to pre-war fertility levels, resulted in a rapid acceleration in the rate of population increase to historically unprecedented levels.

Mortality in the 1960s

For the 1960s there are more data on which to base demographic estimates, and information for provinces outside Java and Bali during this decade is more representative than the local studies which had been the main source of early estimates. Data sources include the 1961 Census (for Jakarta, East Java and Yogyakarta, the only provinces for which records were salvaged during the disruptive years of the mid-1960s), which can be compared to results of the 1971 Census; retrospective reports from the 1973 Fertility Mortality Survey; and the series of National Social and Economic Surveys (*Susenas*) carried out over the decade in Java and some major cities of other islands. CDR estimates from these various sources range from 22 to 16 per thousand over this period (see Table 4.2), although it has been hypothesized that, rather than a steady decline, the rates shifted with the substantial fluctuations in the economic situation over the decade. Heligman (1975) has speculated that mortality in the turbulent mid-1960s may have been higher than either the early or later part of the decade, noting that public health services deteriorated during this time, and there is also evidence of a decline in nutritional standards. Certain localities experienced excess deaths with the mass slaughter of suspected Communist sympathizers, following the abortive coup attempt of 30 September to 1 October 1965 which led to the outlawing of the Communist Party of Indonesia and the establishment of a largely military-led government in March 1966.

With the new sources of data in recent decades came the development of new techniques to estimate demographic parameters indirectly, and an unprecedented richness of estimates of mortality for different age groups. Based on the 1961 Census, the Infant Mortality Rate (IMR) for the late 1950s had been estimated at 195 per thousand for Jakarta, 175 for East Java, and 113 for Yogyakarta; Utomo (1982: 308, inferring from figures in Hull and Sunaryo, 1978: 3) estimates a rate of around 175 for Indonesia overall. A decade later, infant mortality for Indonesia was around 140 (McDonald *et al.*, 1976; and Hull and Sunaryo, 1978: 37). Relative falls in mortality rates for children under five are estimated to be even larger. For the three provinces for which we have 1961 census data, the proportion of children dying between birth and age 5 [q(5)] in the mid to late 1950s for Jakarta was 263 per thousand, declining to 199 in the mid to late 1960s; for East Java, the decline was from 245 to 184; and Yogyakarta experienced an estimated decline of 33 per cent, from 207 to 159. These estimates depend to some extent on the data source and the precise method of calculating the rate of child mortality, but all data sources and methods reach the common conclusion that child mortality was falling dramatically over the period. Heligman has estimated that a measure of adult mortality, the expectation of life at age 20, increased by an average 1–1.5 years over the decade of the 1960s, with males aged 20 in 1961 having on average 37.5 years of life remaining, compared to 38.5 years in 1971. The corresponding figures for females were 35.4 years and 36.3 years (Heligman, 1975, discussed in Utomo, 1982: 309).

Recent Mortality: Levels and Trends

SOURCES OF DATA

The major data sources on morbidity and mortality for the 1970s decade include the 1976 Intercensal Survey, the Sample Vital Registration Project carried out in ten subdistricts, the 1979 National Social and Economic Survey (*Susenas*), the 1980 Census, and the 1980 Household Health Survey. With this range of sources and with new techniques of analysis, estimates of age-specific mortality have become more plentiful and increasingly reliable.

INFANT MORTALITY

From a level of around 140 infant deaths per thousand live births at the end of the 1960s, infant mortality has fallen to just over 100 for the period 1977–8, implying an average annual decline of 3.2 per cent over the period (Kasto, 1983a; 1983b; Dasvarma, 1983; Soemantri, 1983a). An estimate for 1980 is 98 (Utomo and Iskandar, 1984). While the registered decline is assuredly a sign of progress, the fact that about 10 per cent of Indonesian infants will not survive to their first birthday, a level substantially higher than the other major countries of the region, is a matter for major concern. As Table 4.4 shows, the pace of decline in infant mortality rates has been slower for Indonesia than for many of its neighbours. Moreover, there are still important inequities in the risk of infant death in Indonesia as indicated by marked rural–urban, regional and socio-economic class differences in the mortality rates.

Soemantri (1983a: 181–7) found that the average annual decline in infant mortality during the 1970s may be composed of very different rates of decline in the early and later portions of the decade. Between the 1971 Census and the 1976 Intercensal Survey, the decline averaged 5.1 per cent per year, followed by a much lower rate of decline of only 1 per cent

TABLE 4.4

Comparison of Infant Mortality Rates (IMR) Among Countries
of South-East Asia

Country	IMR Estimates Around		Percentage Decline
	1960	*1982*	
Indonesia	150	102	32
Philippines	106	51	52
Vietnam	157	53	66
Thailand	103	51	50
Burma	158	96	39
Malaysia	72	29	60
Singapore	35	11	69

Source: World Bank Development Report, 1985: 262–3.

between 1976 and 1980. There are difficulties with the data which prevent us drawing firm conclusions.[2]

These data problems also imply that the overall average annual rate of decline of 3.2 per cent for the decade may be overstated. Soemantri (1983a) has calculated an alternative estimate of the decline, based on the time trend of mortality from the 1980 Census alone, which gives an average annual intercensal rate of decline of only 1.6 per cent. To a large extent, the difference is an indication of the margin of error involved in the application of indirect methods of calculating death rates from census and survey data. Such inconsistencies are bound to arise, and be virtually irresolvable, until the quality of registration and survey data in Indonesia improves. Meanwhile, we must be content with approximations, and the fact that all recent studies have found mortality to be declining, but at different rates depending on the method of calculation used.

CHILD MORTALITY

The probability of dying before age 2, age 3, or age 5 [q(2), q(3), and q(5) in life table symbols] were all estimated to have declined by 15 to 20 per cent between the late 1960s and 1973–4 (Hull and Sunaryo, 1978: 34), and the most common measure of child mortality, q(5), was estimated to be in the vicinity of 150 to 160, based on the 1980 Census (Munir *et al.*, 1983: 40).

There is fear among some analysts that child mortality, at least at some ages, may not have declined as rapidly as infant mortality in recent years (Adioetomo, 1984). This is difficult to verify since the indirect methods of calculating mortality rates from census data rely on model life tables to translate estimates of mortality between birth and age 2 or 3, into estimates of the IMR, that is the probability of death between birth and exact age 1. Thus if indirect methods are used, the rates of change of q(2), q(3), and q(1) will reflect the shape of the model life table mortality curves rather than any changes in the factors determining death in early childhood. By using direct measures of mortality from a pregnancy history, McDonald (n.d.) was able to show that, in the 1960s, q(5) fell faster than q(1). If there is an opposite trend today, we should track it down, but to do so we need to analyse data sources which allow the use of direct methods of estimating mortality, and these are not readily available. A change in the relative rates of decline of infant [q(1)] and child [q(5)] mortality would have important policy implications. The UNICEF publication, *An Analysis of the Situation of Children and Women in Indonesia*, argues that the slower decline of child relative to infant mortality relates to the different types of causes of death in the two groups. Infant deaths tend to occur soon after birth and are related to poor delivery practices and malnutrition of the mother, which are amenable to correction through policy interventions such as the promotion of antenatal care. Deaths between age 6 months and 5 years, on the other hand, tend to be caused by exogenous factors such as vector-borne infections, nutritional deficiencies and accidents, which are difficult to control except with major improvements to the household economy and environment.

Citing estimates of child death rates (the probability of death between ages 1 and 4 years) produced by the Bureau of Statistics, Utomo and Iskandar (1984: 9–10) note that the Indonesian level of 18 per thousand children is high by Asian standards, and in fact some three to five times higher than levels found in the Philippines, Thailand, and Sri Lanka which are 8, 4, and 4 per thousand respectively. In recognition of the serious situation faced by young children, the Indonesian government has placed high priority on programmes designed to reduce the high mortality rates. Concentrating on the *Balita*, the Indonesian acronym for 'under-fives', such programmes generally consist of a set of activities carried out at the hamlet level by health workers and local volunteers. The primary focus of the activities is a monthly meeting where children are weighed, nutrition and health lectures given, and vaccinations provided. It is too early to assess the demographic impact of such programmes, but to the extent that they focus community attention on the needs of young children, they are probably effective in bringing about behavioral changes which will be conducive to more rapid decline of child mortality.

EXPECTATION OF LIFE AT SELECTED AGES

By using model life tables, we can estimate the average life expectancy at various ages which is implied by a given level of child mortality calculated via indirect methods. Table 4.5, which presents expectation of life at birth and selected ages based on the 1971 and 1980 census data, shows a six-year increase in the average life expectancy at birth, and a three-year gap between males and females. Results from the Sample Vital Registration Project, though not necessarily representative of all Indonesia, also showed

TABLE 4.5

Indonesia: Implied Expected Average Age at Death for People at Various Ages, Based on the Mortality Levels Revealed by the 1971 and 1980 Censuses

Current Age (IMR)	1971 Census		1980 Census	
	Male	*Female*	*Male*	*Female*
	(152)	*(129)*	*(117)*	*(98)*
0 years	45.0	48.0	50.9	54.1
10 years	58.7	60.9	61.7	64.1
15 years	59.5	61.8	62.3	64.8
20 years	60.5	63.0	63.2	65.7
30 years	63.2	65.7	65.3	67.9
50 years	69.2	71.2	70.3	72.4

Source: Hull and Hull, 1984: 108.

Note: Life expectancies for given Infant Mortality Rate (IMR) (BPS data) interpolated from West model life tables.

about a three-year gap (2.7 years) between males and females for the mid-1970s (Gardiner, 1978).

The model represented in Table 4.5 implies that, given the calculated intercensal change in child mortality, changes in life expectancy at older ages would not be as great as those at birth or young ages, though results based on the model still indicate an average two-year increase in life expectancy for 30 year olds. The figures presented in the table also dispel the common misconception that a life expectancy at birth for Indonesia of just over 50 years implies that a 30 year old has on average only 20 years of life remaining. In fact, once he or she has survived the perilous infant and child mortality period, expectations of living well beyond age 60 are quite realistic.

ADULT MORTALITY

The expectations of life at various ages shown above are derived from a model life table which assumes that mortality follows a certain pattern, based on observations of behaviour in groups of countries with similar conditions. Work by McDonald (1978), as well as information from the Sample Vital Registration Project (Gardiner, 1978), indicates that compared to a General Standard Pattern, Indonesia in fact has slightly lower mortality between ages 20 and 45, and relatively higher mortality between ages 45 and 60. One explanation for this pattern is that mortality has declined at a relatively faster pace among young adults, as a result of better control and treatment of infective, parasitic, and respiratory diseases. Babies and young children remain vulnerable to diseases related to poverty, as do older people. Being weaker due to malnutrition and general body condition, both groups are more likely to succumb quickly to otherwise-minor infections of the respiratory tract. Older people also suffer from the cumulative effect of diseases experienced prior to the period of improved health measures (McDonald, 1978: 9). Nevertheless, despite the fact that McDonald's estimates showed a difference in the pattern of the expectation of life remaining compared to a General Standard Pattern, his estimate of expectation of life at age 20 is virtually the same as that shown in Table 4.5, which is based on the Coale Demeny West Model life table, thus indicating that such differences as do exist are relatively minor.

Recent Mortality: Geographic and Socio-economic Variations

REGIONAL AND RURAL—URBAN VARIATIONS

It is difficult to assess regional differences in death rates in the historical context, since such wide differences in levels of accuracy of reporting prevailed. Overall, however, in Java during the pre-1930 period, general mortality levels, and the impact of epidemics, were greatest in the north coast residencies and other residencies where there was extensive commercialization of agriculture. It is possible that reporting was better in these regions because they were under stricter colonial control, but another explanation might be the influence of the demands of the colonial economy. The commercialization process entailed disruption of subsistence farming, with consequences for nutrition; economic demands which exacerbated poverty; and the alteration of the environment, making it more vulnerable to floods and droughts. Malaria also appeared to be most common in the north coast area of Java (Gardiner and Oey, 1983).

It is even more difficult to reach firm conclusions about historical levels of mortality in areas outside Java. Virtually the only data available come from plantations on Sumatra's east coast, but the workers in these plantations were in fact from Java, and their living and health conditions differed from those of the indigenous populations. Widjojo (1970: 113) cites infant mortality rates from these sources which range from 160 to 370 per thousand in the 1930s.

During the war years, effects of Japanese occupation were more dramatic in Java than the other islands. It is thus quite likely that Java experienced a more marked increase of mortality as a result of population displacement and food shortages.

Today, fairly wide variations exist among Indonesian provinces in estimated levels of infant mortality. As Table 4.6 shows, the IMR ranges from a low of 62 per thousand in Yogyakarta to a high of 187 in the province of West Nusa Tenggara. Although both are poor provinces (Chapter 3), the difference in infant mortality recorded here implies a very large gap in life expectancy at birth of more than 20 years on average. Based on 1976 data, levels of q(2) and q(3) followed similar regional patterns, being lowest in Yogyakarta, East Java and Bali, and high in West Java and the eastern islands of East and West Nusa Tenggara (Hull and Sunaryo, 1978: 29–30). Adult mortality, as estimated from the 1976 Intercensal Survey, appears to be lowest in Yogyakarta, East Java and Bali, while the eastern islands and Sulawesi had higher mortality. Provincial differences in adult mortality, however, were not large (McDonald, n.d.: 9–10). Interprovincial variations in life expectancy at birth are depicted in Figure 4.2.

An interesting aspect of the mortality differences exhibited in Table 4.6 is that the percentage decline in infant mortality between the censuses was very high for Yogyakarta, even though it began with the lowest mortality level in the late 1960s. Some of the high-mortality provinces according to the 1971 Census also showed some of the slowest declines, with some important exceptions such as South and South-east Sulawesi, and South Sumatra and Bengkulu. One approach to quantifying such changes in simple terms is through the calculation of the index of dissimilarity. This index is derived from a comparison of two sets of percentage distributions—in this case, the distribution of live births among the provinces of Indonesia compared to the distribution of infant deaths. If the mortality rates were equal in each province, the proportions of deaths and births would be identical for each province and the index of dissimilarity would be zero. The more difference there is among provinces in terms of their mortality rates, the greater is the index. On the basis of census calculations, the index for Indonesia in 1971 was 12.0 per cent. By 1980, due to the

TABLE 4.6

Indonesia: Estimated Infant Mortality Rates (Rural, Urban and Total)
by Province, and Percentage Annual Intercensal Decline

Province	Infant Mortality Rate (1977–1978)			Percentage Annual Intercensal Decline*
	Urban	Rural	Total	
INDONESIA	86	113	107	3.2
SUMATRA				
DI Aceh	65	93	91	4.8
North Sumatra	70	94	91	3.2
West Sumatra	89	125	121	2.4
Riau	69	126	113	2.4
Jambi	79	123	118	2.9
South Sumatra	75	104	118	4.8
Bengkulu	65	110	106	5.0
Lampung	91	98	97	4.5
JAVA				
DKI Jakarta	79	92	80	4.9
West Java	105	134	129	2.7
Central Java	78	100	96	4.4
DI Yogyakarta	50	66	62	5.1
East Java	84	102	99	2.0
NUSA TENGGARA				
Bali	69	90	88	4.0
West Nusa Tenggara	142	194	187	1.7
East Nusa Tenggara	56	129	124	2.2
KALIMANTAN				
West Kalimantan	66	122	116	2.3
Central Kalimantan	72	103	100	2.7
South Kalimantan	101	124	121	3.3
East Kalimantan	75	110	99	0.7
SULAWESI				
North Sulawesi	80	96	94	2.1
Central Sulawesi	85	131	128	1.4
South Sulawesi	107	109	108	4.2
South-east Sulawesi	88	116	114	5.6
MALUKU/IRIAN JAYA				
Maluku	78	128	124	1.7
Irian Jaya	89	110	106	0.8

Sources: After Soemantri, 1983a: 188; and Utomo and Iskandar, 1984: 27.
* Refers to decline between 1968–9 and 1977–8, based on the 1971 and 1980 Censuses.

FIGURE 4.2

Indonesia: Estimated Expectation of Life at Birth, by Province, Based on 1980 Census

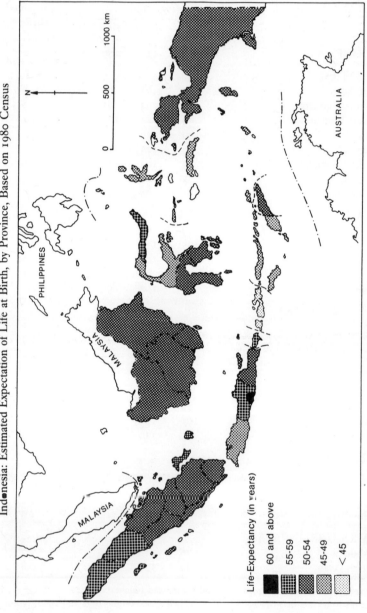

Source: Estimates from Soemantri, 1983a: 187 using Trussell method, West Model.

widening gap of mortality rates between provinces, the index had risen to 14.6 per cent: that is, 14.6 per cent of infant deaths from high-mortality areas would have to be eliminated, and an equal number of deaths added to low-mortality areas, to achieve equality of death rates across provinces.

To some degree, provincial differences can be explained by prevailing social and economic conditions, with richer provinces such as North Sumatra and better-educated areas such as North Sulawesi having lower mortality. The relationship is far from clear, however. Some of the better-off provinces have high per capita income due to the development of extractive industries such as timber and oil, 'enclave' activities which do not invariably imply improved welfare for the majority of the province's population, particularly in cases where these industries have only been developed fairly recently (Cho *et al.*, 1980: 21–2). Furthermore, the province with the lowest estimated infant mortality, Yogyakarta, in fact has one of the highest proportions of its people estimated to be living in poverty, according to a recent World Bank classification. Even within Yogyakarta, the traditionally extremely impoverished limestone region of Gunung Kidul has been estimated to have an infant mortality rate of 55 per thousand, even lower than the overall provincial average for Yogyakarta (Soemantri *et al.*, 1984: 10). While it is difficult to confirm such a figure, policy-makers have been quick to attribute this finding to the very active development efforts which were made in the regency during the 1970s. The great differences in mortality among Indonesia's different regions also reflect contrasts in history and the natural environment, and the spread of disease. Java has not had the high incidence of malaria which prevails in many of the other islands and, except for specific local areas, is generally not subject to severe seasonal food shortage.

Overall, diet and nutrition as dictated by resources and custom vary widely among the regions; there is some evidence that different infant-feeding practices in general, and breastfeeding in particular, may explain part of the variation in infant mortality rates. Breastfeeding durations among the Sundanese of West Java, for example, are shorter than is the case for the ethnic Javanese, amongst whom infant mortality is lower. Nutritional inadequacy is a problem throughout Indonesia, but is more acute in areas where cassava or sago are staples, such as the eastern islands, and parts of Sulawesi, Kalimantan and Sumatra. In Yogyakarta and Central Java, the colonial public health campaigns described earlier have also left a legacy in terms of basic practices of sanitation and hygiene, and contemporary health services are more numerous and accessible in Java and Bali in general, than is the case in the other islands. Regional differences in contemporary health facilities, and other possible explanations for differences in mortality, are discussed further as part of the section 'Factors Influencing Mortality Patterns and Trends' in this chapter.

Turning to rural–urban differences in mortality levels, we find that both the 1971 Census and the 1973 Fertility–Mortality Survey showed infant and child mortality to be some 20 per cent higher in rural areas. In an analysis using the 1976 Intercensal Survey, Kadarusman (1982: 47) found that rural infant and child mortality was about 40 per cent higher for the early 1970s, and that rural–urban differences had been somewhat less for the cohorts born before 1961. Utomo's analysis of the 1980 Census indicated that, in rural areas, infant mortality was 20 per cent higher but child mortality was 40 per cent higher than levels found in cities (Utomo, 1983). Soemantri (1983a: 187), using the same data source, concluded that the ratio of rural to urban infant mortality was 1.31 : 1. These differences demonstrate again the impact of different estimation techniques on the conclusions. The widest rural–urban differences in mortality appear to be concentrated in the eastern part of the country, particularly in East Nusa Tenggara, where the rural–urban contrast in health and welfare services is relatively significant and where the dividing line between urban and rural regions can be miles of ocean, a mountain range or a swamp. At the other extreme, Table 4.6 shows that in South Sulawesi and Lampung rural–urban mortality differences were only 2 and 7 deaths per thousand respectively (Utomo and Iskandar, 1984: 9).

A few researchers have attempted to control for the effect of educational differences in comparing rural versus urban residence. Supraptilah and Suradji (1979: 78–9), using the 1973 Fertility–Mortality Survey, found that among those with no education, the rural–urban variable made little difference to mortality except in West Java. This was also true, though to a weaker extent, for respondents with some primary schooling. However, among those with an educational attainment of having completed primary school graduate or higher, urban–rural differences were striking in most provinces. Cho *et al.* (1976) also found that residence made an increasing difference to mortality as education level rose, according to 1971 census data. McDonald (1981) reached similar conclusions, looking at child mortality and at education of both mother and father. Interestingly, however, he found that the highest mortality of all groups was amongst children of fathers with no education who lived in urban areas, even though mortality associated with people who had attained higher levels of education did not seem to be affected by residence.

SOCIO-ECONOMIC VARIATIONS

There have been several attempts to link socio-economic variables to mortality by analysing provincial-level indicators. In a regression analysis by Soemantri (1983b), one economic indicator, the proportion of households owning a radio/cassette, emerged as an important correlate. Overall, other socio-economic factors, such as illiteracy and the proportion never attending school, did not exert strong effects after controlling for health variables.

In addition to this aggregate-level analysis, there have been attempts to investigate differential mortality associated with individual social and economic characteristics. Education of mother has been a key variable for analysis. For the 1971 Census, Cho *et al.* (1976: 65–7) reported an infant mortality rate more than twice as high for infants of mothers with no schooling, as for those with at least a secondary school education. The infant mortality level for mothers who had completed secondary school was 63 per thousand, compared to 161 for those with no school; regional levels ranged around these figures. Very importantly, it was found that these differences were accentuated in urban areas. The level of infant mortality in urban Java–Madura was more than three times higher among infants of mothers with no schooling than the level for those of mothers with secondary education or higher.

Data from the 1976 Intercensal Survey for Java–Bali, analysed by both McDonald (1981) and Kadarusman (1982), show that the largest difference in child mortality occurs between the levels of primary and secondary school attainment; there is little difference in q(5) between parents (either mother or father) with no education and those with primary schooling. Figures from the 1980 Census reveal that the dramatic differentials of the earlier periods persist (see Table 4.7). Infant mortality among the group of mothers who had completed lower secondary school was less than one-half that of the group with no schooling at both the 1971 and 1980 Censuses. The most interesting result, though, is the fact that the declines of mortality in the period have been much more rapid for the children of women with little or no education than for those whose mothers had been to secondary school.

There are two considerations which should be applied to an interpretation of this table. First, it is possible that the declines in mortality over the past few decades have come about due to a particularly narrow range of interventions, or technologies, which are now yielding diminished returns in lives saved. The well-to-do and educated, having had first access to these advantages experience the decline in mortality first and are thus first to plateau at moderate levels of infant mortality while the rest of the community catches up. The corollary of this explanation is that it will be necessary to develop a new array of interventions, or technologies, or life-saving improvements in economic and social organization to break through the plateau levels and attain low rates of infant and child mortality. The

TABLE 4.7

Indonesia: Infant Mortality by Education of Mother, 1971–1980

Schooling	Infant Mortality Rate (Per 1,000 Births)		
	Census		Percentage Decline
	1971	1980	
No schooling	171	127	0.26
Some schooling	160	113	0.29
Completed primary school	113	87	0.23
Completed lower secondary school	70	63	0.10
Completed upper secondary school	—	53	—
Total weighted average	148	107	0.28

Source: Calculated from Adioetomo, 1985: 21.

second consideration is that the different rates of mortality decline between educational groups could reveal a broader set of changes in the distribution of total welfare. While there is no evidence to show that the distribution of household income (or expenditure) is becoming remarkably more egalitarian, it is obvious to even casual observers that many social services such as schools, health centres and development programmes are increasingly available in poor and remote areas. While not quantified, the increasingly egalitarian spread of basic welfare must be seen as part of the explanation of differential rates of mortality decline.

An innovative index of socio-economic status based on housing quality was constructed for 1971 census data (Suharto and Way, 1975: 18–22). Although the index has limitations due to the fact that there are great regional differences in access to various housing materials, the analysis yielded some interesting results which concur with other evidence. Within geographic regions, those with higher-quality housing had 20 to 40 per cent lower mortality, as measured by q(3), and differences in mortality across socio-economic groups appeared to be much more striking in urban than in rural areas. A similar, but more limited, examination of the 1980 census data revealed almost identical differentials (Utomo et al., 1986: 502).

The Fertility–Mortality Survey of 1973 provided more detailed household-level economic data, and an analysis of infant and child mortality differentials according to an index of ownership of consumer items showed very significant differences in all regions and, once again, that mortality differences were greater in urban than in rural areas (Supraptilah and Suradji, 1979).

One other variable, mother's occupation, has been used as an independent variable in a study of differential mortality (Kadarusman, 1982) showing the lowest mortality among infants and children with professional mothers, followed by those with mothers in the non-working category. This latter category would also tend to comprise higher socio-economic status women, at least among the Javanese, since labour force participation is more common among the poorest women who work out of necessity (Hull, 1977). There was little difference among the work categories of sales/service, manual, and agricultural, all of which had mortality rates— q(1), q(2), and q(5)—which were about twice as high as that of working mothers in professional occupations. (See also Utomo et al., 1986: 503.)

In reviewing the trends in child mortality revealed in the 1973 Fertility–Mortality Survey, McDonald (1981) found that declines were proceeding more quickly for people at the bottom of the socio-economic scale than for more well-to-do people, who had achieved improvements in mortality earlier. As a result, the differences in mortality rates among economic groups had tended to lessen somewhat, though they remained wide enough to be of continuing concern.

SOCIO-BIOLOGICAL VARIATIONS

It is not always appreciated that the risks of infant mortality in particular are sensitive to a number of maternal or familial socio-biological characteristics which should ideally be handled separately in analyses of mortality variations and their underlying causes. Very little work has been done on these variables in Indonesia, though increasing awareness of the central role played by such factors in other countries has led researchers to focus recent research on the socio-biological determinants of infant and child death.

Analyses based on World Fertility Survey data for Java and Bali (Trussell and Pebley, 1984: 271) indicate that if all births after the third were prevented and the first three births all took place between maternal age 20 to 34, infant mortality could be expected to decline by an estimated 11 per cent with further reductions if ideal birth-spacing patterns pertained as well. The reasons for this are fairly straightforward. It has long been known that children born very early or very late in a woman's reproductive age span (taken to be about ages 15 to 45) are at a much greater risk of death than those born to mothers aged around 20 to 30. This is particularly true for women suffering from poor nutrition or chronic untreated infections. Additionally, reduction in the numbers of children allows more resources—both economic and time—to be devoted to each child, with the result that survival chances are increased.

To explore this pattern, Hull and Gubhaju (1986) applied multi-variate analysis techniques to the Java–Bali Fertility Survey. They found that social factors affected infant and child mortality differently. For infants, such demographic factors as the duration of the interval between the preceding delivery and the present child, and the survival status of the preceding child are major determinants of the chance of survival of the present child. If the interval is short, the mother most likely has less time and fewer resources to devote to each child, and the risk of mortality is increased. If the preceding child had already died, that is an indication that the present child is at risk—perhaps because of poverty in the family or for other reasons—and should receive special attention. The educational levels attained by both the mother and the father are significantly related to the survival chances of the child, but these relations are overshadowed in magnitude by the demographic factors.

The situation for children who survive the first year of life is somewhat different from that of infants. The risks of mortality are then related more strongly to the education of mothers, and the social class of the family. However, again the influence of child-spacing is very important, and a one-year-old infant whose nearest older sibling is five years old has only one-third the chance of dying compared to the one-year-old whose sibling is two and a half. The implication is that pre-school children need care, and competition for resources and time puts them at risk of illness and death.

Factors Influencing Mortality Patterns and Trends

Research on the socio-economic factors affecting the level and trends of mortality in Indonesia has been very limited due to problems in data collection. The Vital Registration System, first initiated in the early decades of the century, has never achieved full coverage and, since 1939, there has been deterioration of coverage in many regions, confusion over the legal and administrative basis of a national system, and recently competition between various interests attempting to promote birth and death registration. In many other countries, the registration system allows a careful monitoring of mortality rates at the level of very small geographic zones, and according to important occupational, social and demographic characteristics of the population. This is not possible in Indonesia.

The alternative of relying on censuses and surveys for studies of mortality trends is less than satisfactory because of problems of sample size and data quality, which can only be overcome by large, expensive surveys carried out by highly skilled specialists. Unfortunately, Indonesia has neither the funds nor the trained people to undertake such elaborate research, and instead reliance is placed on small or general surveys which are feasible from the viewpoint of both finance and staffing. Such surveys can yield valuable insights into the general structure of the environment in which mortality is determined, but they do not allow definitive evaluations of, for example, changes in the age patterns of mortality in response to national health programmes, or alterations in the pattern of causes of death in different provinces.

While these problems of data availability seriously handicap detailed investigation of such phenomena, there is an additional problem which has severely limited analysis of socio-economic factors underlying mortality trends in recent years—that is, changes in the format and availability of census and survey data useful for the study of mortality levels according to educational, housing or other characteristics. As a result, researchers have found it difficult to analyse time trends in the relationship between mortality levels and socio-economic factors since the questions used to measure such factors have changed substantially from enumeration to enumeration.

Despite the limitations of data, the studies cited above indicate that mortality levels and trends are strongly influenced by a number of basic economic conditions. Differences in income and wealth are reflected in differences in mortality both between regions and among residents of particular regions. The reasons for this can be found in terms of differences in exposure to risk of illness or accident, and differences in access to effective forms of treatment, once stricken. Poor people and people living in poor communities are both more likely to fall ill and be at greater risk of dying from any case of illness. Moreover, because their poverty has many dimensions—lack of food, lack of adequate housing, lack of sanitation—individuals are exposed to a continuous series of risks, any one of which might be minor, but with cumulative effects which can be fatal.

This pattern of multiple risks and cumulative burdens of illness provides the basis for an explanation of why socio-economic differentials in mortality are strong, follow clear break-points, and drift down over time with economic development. The strength of differentials is related to the fact that any single difference in socio-economic status, such as type of housing or presence of clean water, is related to a large number of causes of illness. Thus improvement in housing quality reduces a number of risks at once. Further, because economic improvements experienced by classes of people tend to follow regular patterns or styles of consumption, the changes spread quickly among a class, and reinforce the differences between classes. Higher-income farmers use their incomes to make similar improvements to their houses, prepare similar varieties of food, and gain access to similar levels of medical care, all of which distinguish them from low-income farm labourers, and leads to a clear difference in mortality between the groups. Finally, because some changes affect the whole community, such as the provision of clean water or a mass immunization campaign, there is a tendency for everybody's health to improve with economic development, and mortality rates to drift down over time while differentials persist. These long-term declines are not captured in multivariate analysis of cross-sectional data (for example, Martin *et al.*, 1983) because they occur in a patchy way across communities and have an impact only as a synergistic amalgam of changes develops.

Estimates of Contemporary Causes of Death

Clearly, one of the key elements of this explanation of mortality differentials and trends in Indonesia is the pattern of causes of death, and the associated factors which determine the structure of risks of exposure to illness. Since data on cause of illness and death in Indonesia are very limited, attempts have been made to infer a reasonable set of estimates of cause of death indirectly, via comparison of data from countries with somewhat similar patterns of mortality and socio-economic structure (Hull and Mantra, 1981). While not an ideal procedure, and one certainly subject to a number of biases, this approach does give an approximate picture of the structure of causes of death, which can be used to guide policy discussion and highlight key areas of interest for public health planning.

The estimates in Table 4.8 show that causes of death in Indonesia in 1975 were largely those illnesses which are regarded as preventable and/or curable in developed countries. Pneumonia, tuberculosis, diarrhoea, and infectious and parasitic diseases caused nearly half of all deaths which occurred in that year and the vast bulk of deaths in childhood. The 'diseases of affluence' such as cancer and heart disease, which are regarded with great fear in developed countries, account for only one in seven deaths in Indonesia, and these cases are concentrated at the adult ages. Even among these cases, there is evidence that the underlying causes of illness in a country such as Indonesia are different from those found in the West. For example, deaths by heart attack are likely to be the consequence of

TABLE 4.8

Indonesia: Estimation of Causes of Death, by Broad Age Groups, 1975
(in Percentages)

Cause Grouping	Age Group (in Years)					
	0	1–4	5–14	15–49	50+	All Ages
Tuberculosis	0	1	2	15	4	4.7
Pneumonia[a]	20	15	12	9	13	15.4
Infectious and parasitic	8	22	25	10	3	10.2
Diarrhoea[b]	25	30	15	4	5	15.0
Infant diseases	35	0	0	0	0	10.5
Cancers	0	0	1	5	9	3.5
Heart diseases[c]	0	1	6	11	31	11.0
Degenerative diseases	0	0	2	5	6	2.8
Complications of childbirth	0	0	0	8	0	1.8
Traffic accidents	0	0	1	1	0	0.4
Other violence	1	3	8	15	3	5.4
Residual[d]	11	28	28	17	26	19.7
Total	100	100	100	100	100	100.0
Number of deaths ('000s)	549	268	116	411	474	1,818
Percentage of all deaths	30	15	6	23	26	100

Source: Hull and Mantra, 1981: 281.
[a] Includes influenza and bronchitis.
[b] Includes gastritis and enteritis.
[c] Includes vascular diseases.
[d] Includes large numbers of malnutrition-related deaths as well as unspecified causes.

rheumatic fever in childhood which scars the heart muscle, rather than of atherosclerosis resulting from a diet high in fats.

Potential for Improvements in the Expectation of Life

The implication of the pattern of causes of death is that investment in mortality prevention is likely to be most effective if directed against the preventable diseases which strike down children, rather than against the degenerative diseases that afflict adults. By this criterion, the community health system and the immunization campaigns of the Indonesian government are excellent investments, as indeed are the maternal and child health centres and the family planning programme, all of which help to reduce the incidence of both perinatal and maternal mortality. Of less certain value are the investments in high technology in urban hospitals which seem to be undertaken to provide care for the rich, or to enhance national pride in the possession of modern facilities.

However, when the current structure of expenditures is evaluated, it seems clear that Indonesia is on a path of development which will lead to the continuing reduction of preventable afflictions, and hence to lower mortality. The future is not all bright, though, since the rapid increase in smoking, consumption of fatty foods, motor vehicle ownership, and industrial and domestic pollution point to a future increase in degenerative diseases among all ages. To date, there has been little indication that the government or private groups are able to control such trends. In part, they are inhibited by the fact that some of the diseases associated with such lifestyle factors develop slowly, so the lung cancer caused by increased smoking today will be revealed through increased hospital admissions in ten or twenty years' time, and some of the cancers and heart diseases will undoubtedly kill many Indonesians without having their underlying environmental causes revealed, due to lack of information and lack of skilled epidemiologists to tract down the vital links. In such a context, it might be argued that low mortality will present Indonesia with more difficult social and economic and medical problems than has been the case with the traditional patterns of high mortality.

1. Vaccination for smallpox was introduced in Java first in 1804, and the programme was expanded several times over the century. In 1850, the division of Java into districts allowed the programme to become more systematized, the local manufacture of vaccine after 1860 increased the viability of the programme, and the development of vaccine using animal rather than human lymph led to further expansion in 1890 (Van Thiel, 1971: 443–4). Widjojo (1970: 41) argued, however, that over the last century the coverage of the programme was minimal; official reports showed levels of vaccination of about 2 to 3 per cent per annum, even as late as 1880, while Gardiner and Oey have pointed out that the vaccine used prior to 1920 was not fully effective in preventing the disease (1983: 19). On the other hand, the colonial government in its official handbook for 1930 reported that, over the preceding few decades, every *kampung* had been visited once in seven years for mass innoculation, while babies were vaccinated regularly. In 1928, only eleven smallpox deaths were reported in Java and Madura.

2. In making comparisons between the trends in infant mortality from the two censuses and the 1976 Intercensal Survey, Soemantri (1983a) has argued that comparison of 1971 and 1976 data produces an overestimate of mortality decline, whereas comparing 1976 and 1980 estimates tends to underestimate the decline compared to estimates derived from a single census. His analysis also shows that comparison of the two censuses alone also produces an overestimate of the decline. However, his time trend of mortality based on the 1980 Census may also be an underestimate, if women at older ages tend to understate the mortality experience of their children, a frequently observed phenomenon. Thus the 3.2 per cent and 1.6 per cent may be reasonably considered the upper and lower limits of the range of possible estimates of average annual decline.

5 Fertility, Marriage and Family Planning

Pre-Independence Fertility Levels

THE debate over colonial Indonesia's population growth rate (see Chapter 2) involves several different assumptions about fertility behaviour over the period from the departure of Raffles in 1819 to the institution of the 'Ethical Policy' at the turn of the century. Most observers have postulated varying degrees of adaptive fertility response, however, rather than assuming that there was completely uncontrolled or 'natural' fertility. Birth control methods such as abstinence, abortion, and perhaps traditional herbal mixtures and massage, were used to keep fertility within a range appropriate to the community and familial supports and constraints which existed and fluctuated over the years. At the same time, levels of health and nutrition presumably also contributed to the determination of fertility levels. Together, these volitional and non-volitional determinants shaped the regional patterns of fertility which are thought to have prevailed. It is commonly accepted that fertility in densely populated Java has, over a long period, been somewhat lower than that prevailing in the other islands, though in both areas the pattern was more likely one of fluctuations in response to a variety of influences rather than long-term stability of levels.

Prior to the 1930s, however, the picture is based largely on speculation. For the 1930s and 1940s, we can use evidence pieced together from the Census of 1930 and its successors in 1961, 1971, 1980, and the Intercensal Survey of 1976 to reconstruct probable patterns. Nevertheless, this evidence is still far from reliable, and demographers have had to use indirect and often ingenious approaches to produce a coherent and plausible picture (McNicoll and Singarimbun, 1982: Overview). More recent estimates of total fertility over the 1930–60 period (Cho *et al.*, 1980; McNicoll and Singarimbun, 1982: 34) do coincide, however, with the basic estimates of crude birth rates put forward by Widjojo (1970: 158), which were produced a decade earlier without the benefit of recent census and survey sources. Widjojo's estimates are reproduced in Table 5.1.

It is usually argued that fertility declined during the depression years of the 1930s, when the Indonesian economy was badly affected. Fertility behaviour had little time to respond to what was only a partial economic

TABLE 5.1
Estimates of Crude Birth Rates in Java, 1930–1960

Period	Annual Crude Birth Rate (Births/1,000 Population)
Before 1930	45.51
1930–5	45.32
1935–40	44.85
1940–5	39.03
1945–50	40.25
1950–5	47.31
1955–60	46.58

Source: Widjojo, 1970: 158.

recovery before the war and revolution intervened, and the fertility decline accelerated further. During the Japanese Occupation, food shortages, economic disruption, and generally unstable conditions produced crude birth rates estimated to have been below 40 per thousand.

The Post-War Period, 1950–1971

THE 1950S DECADE

During the 1950s, fertility appears to have risen to pre-war levels of 45 births per thousand population or a bit higher, as the extreme conditions of the Occupation and wartime period subsided. Although this was a decade of increasing political instability and inflation, childbearing underwent a period of recovery. Women who were married in the immediate post-war period achieved levels of childbearing which were unprecedented in Indonesia, and declines in mortality meant that actual family sizes were growing even more rapidly. At first, it seems counter-intuitive to find fertility reaching such high levels at a time when the economy was deteriorating and political tensions were rising. To understand this pattern, it is necessary to look behind the simple economic indicators of production and export to see how the political economy was affecting Indonesian families. Though businesses were failing and export industries were coming under pressure, the dualistic nature of the Indonesian economy implied that the greatest disruption was occurring in the commercial sector which, in any case, was dominated by European and Chinese interests. The subsistence sector, which provided for the vast bulk of the Indonesian population, was less affected by the disruption arising from political and social conflict, and the public service was burgeoning as the government rapidly expanded public-sector involvement in education, health, and public works. Overall, the bulk of Indonesian families probably benefited from the economic changes, either through increased employment, increased access to land, or increased access to public services. This would tend to support higher fertility.

In addition, cultural changes which had been spreading through Indonesia since the early part of the century began to firmly take hold in the heady era of post-Independence nationalism. The influence of films, schools and ideological rhetoric converged to promote new self-concepts among Indonesians of all ethnic backgrounds. Identity as Indonesians for one thing was new, and a major challenge to traditional notions. Part of the process of creating a new national consciousness was the denial of aspects of traditional identities; as the speech by Soekarno put it: 'The Revolution rejects yesterday'. While the overt target of this rejection was colonialism and feudalism, the impact was much wider, and young people took the call to apply to many areas of personal life such as their relations with their parents, peers, and community. A new spirit of individualism emerged which modified the ways in which marriages were arranged, households were established, and children were raised, and a new set of expectations about proper behaviour and civic responsibility altered the place of children in families. At first, in the 1950s, such changes affected the elite most strongly but, even in remote villages, the radio and the school-house brought new perspectives which changed people's view of themselves. At this early stage, the impact on fertility would most likely have been pro-natalist, with more marriages being made on the basis of love, and more families being swept along with the idea that Independence would naturally lead to a better future for children, no matter how many might be born. Of course this picture greatly over-simplifies the realities, ignoring as it does the many severe economic difficulties faced by people in chronic areas of famine such as the south coast of Java or the hills of Lombok, or even the slums of Jakarta, but it points to the fact that, for most Indonesians, the 1950s were a vast improvement on the 1940s, and held promise for an even better future.

THE 1960S DECADE

The political and economic problems of the 1950s continued to disrupt national life through the early 1960s to such an extent that people from all sectors began to suffer real declines in their standard of living. During this time, fertility did not show much change, though it may have still been rising slightly in Java (McDonald et al., 1976: Table 3.4). The bulk of the Dutch community had been expelled from Indonesia in the late 1950s, and the businesses and plantations they had run were either closing or operating at significantly reduced levels. The nation was incurring a large debt, much of which was going to the construction of heroic monuments and to the enervating campaigns against the Dutch in West New Guinea (later Irian Jaya) and against the new state of Malaysia. Agriculture was in decline as irrigation systems fell into disrepair, and the shops were chronically short of all forms of imported goods. For most Indonesian families, the rampant inflation and constant shortages put severe strains on family welfare. Interviews with people who lived through this period indicate that there was an increasing desire to prevent births, but women had no access to the technologies which would have allowed them to accomplish this safely and effectively. In any case, for the years of the 1960s, fertility estimates are on firm ground, based on results of the 1971 Census and the 1973 Fertility–Mortality Survey, and they indicate that, at the rates prevailing in 1965–70, Indonesian women would have an average of 5.5 children during their reproductive life. This rate is high, but by no means extraordinary, and is in fact quite a bit lower than the rates prevailing in Asia at that time and much of Africa today. More detailed data from the 1971 Census and subsequent surveys is presented later in this chapter as an introduction to the discussion of the onset of fertility decline.

Summary

It is difficult to determine the levels and trends of fertility for the regions of Indonesia prior to the 1960s because of the near-complete absence of census and vital statistics data which would allow the calculation of fertility rates. Nevertheless, the picture which emerges from the scanty evidence available, and from inference based on our knowledge of the social and economic conditions of the time, indicates that fertility had probably risen from low levels during the decade of war and revolution in the 1940s, to reach a peak in the 1950s, prior to the first indications of what was to become sustained fertility decline in the 1960s. These fluctuations, though due to major changes in the social and economic structure of the nation, were relatively minor, and probably in no case did the total fertility rate shift more than 20 per cent above or below a long-term average of 5.5 births per woman.

Given the declining post-war mortality levels, this fertility level implied rapid population growth for the young nation. Although both the colonial and independent governments recognized the pressures on Java and Bali, they had put their trust in efforts to shift the population of these islands to less densely settled islands. It was some time before policies were put into place for dealing directly with the issue of fertility control.

The Family Planning Programme: Development over Fifteen Years

Precursors to the National Programme

Despite the pro-natalist climate during the Soekarno period, and even earlier during colonial times, there were those both inside and outside the country who supported the dissemination of birth control methods in Indonesia (Hull and Mantra, 1981: 265). The responsibility and credit for the first practical steps toward a national birth control programme, how-ever, lay mainly with community leaders and influential women's groups who perceived a need for family planning services among individuals, regardless of the impact of birth control on the country's rate of population growth, and in the face of early sensitivity toward the topic of contraception itself. Despite local opposition, the Institute of Family Welfare was established in Yogyakarta in late 1952 to provide information on mother and child health and birth-spacing. It is reported that clients for these services were very few in number at that time (Timmer, 1961), but the fact that the service could be maintained at all given the prevailing climate of opinion is admirable. Similar groups were active in other cities in Indonesia during the 1950s, providing services for the small, mainly urban segment of the population which was knowledgeable and motivated enough to seek them out.

In 1957, these scattered groups and individuals combined to form a national voluntary association, the Indonesian Planned Parenthood Association or PKBI. The growing interest in family planning in other parts of the world was having an impact on Indonesia as numerous foreign officials and family planning advisers came to the country at the invitation of the PKBI. Although open government support was not forthcoming, the PKBI persisted and expanded its services, obtaining funds mainly through the sale of contraceptives. In 1963, it sponsored a series of seminars throughout Java and Bali to acquaint the medical community with its work. During the next three years, however, such activities were increasingly disrupted as the political and economic situation deteriorated.

Conflict between the military and Muslim parties, on the one hand, and the large Communist party, on the other, increased the difficulties of governing the nation, and President Soekarno attempted to maintain the uneasy balance of interests by providing sufficient encouragement to each faction to maintain their loyalty. Then, on the night of 30 September 1965, the balance overtipped in an attempted coup and, after substantial loss of life, the military took control.

The declaration of a 'New Order' government led by General Suharto signalled the beginning of a change in national policy on fertility control. The prevailing attitude was evolving from critical, or at best passive, neglect to one of tacit support, and the PKBI began to reopen and restock its clinics in earnest. Over the next two years, the organization was the driving force in the provision of family planning services and the sponsor of several research projects carried out to determine the future course of the programme. After nearly twenty years of disapproval by post-Independence regimes, the concept of family planning was moving towards adoption as the main government policy designed to confront the population dilemma.

The changing climate of opinion concerning birth control came amidst the period of more rational economic planning—and guarded optimism—which characterized the New Order government's first few years in power. The government role in family planning during the first two years of the New Order is perhaps described as 'benevolent encouragement and help to voluntary organizations' rather than direct commitment (Singarimbun, 1968). An early proposal for an official cabinet-level national family planning board was rejected, but an Ad Hoc Committee on Family Planning was established to advise the government on the formation of a national programme, and to represent Indonesia in dealing with foreign assistance funds for family planning. The committee drew heavily from members of the PKBI, who were both conversant with the issue and had long-established links with international aid organizations.

In 1968, the Ad Hoc Committee submitted a report recommending that the government initiate a national family planning programme, which would concentrate its efforts on the distribution of contraceptives in Java and Bali. The strategy of limiting government family planning activities to these two islands was eventually adopted; the equation of densely settled Java and Bali with Indonesia's 'population problem' was so deeply embedded in people's minds that there was little debate on the subject.

In accordance with the recommendations of the February 1968 report of the Ad Hoc Committee on Family Planning, a National Family Planning Institute, the LKBN, was established by presidential order in October of that year. The semi-official status of the LKBN was further reflection of the supportive, yet still not fully committed, stance of the government right up to 1969. In the government's First Five-Year Development Plan, family planning was mentioned in the context of maternal and child welfare rather than population control, and in a speech to an IPPF-sponsored conference on family planning held in Indonesia in 1969, President Suharto mentioned the social and religious sensitivity which surrounded the subject.

The turning point for family planning policy came later in 1969, when Indonesia invited a mission of foreign experts, sponsored by the UN, World Bank and WHO, to evaluate the country's family planning programme. The mission concluded that achievements in family planning up to that time were disappointing, primarily because of inadequate organization and administration. Their recommendation, included in a Five-Year Family Planning Programme (1971–5) for Java and Bali, contained very detailed suggestions for programme implementation and asked for a doubling of the target for new acceptors from 3 to 6 million. Included in the recommended organizational structure was not only a Central Family Planning Institute with a Chairman nominated by the President, but provincial, regency and subdistrict institutes. The report clearly advocated government involvement on a massive scale.

Development of the National Programme, 1971–1985

In 1970, the Family Planning Institute was transformed by presidential decree into the National Family Planning Co-ordinating Board (the BKKBN), with full governmental responsibility for family planning, and reporting directly to the President. In the fiscal year 1970/1, the government of Indonesia gave the equivalent of US$1.3 million to the national family planning programme, which was matched by over US$3 million from foreign donors. This commitment has increased in successive years and, although the contribution from foreign donors remains significant, an increased Indonesian government share has attested to growing commitment. In 1984, it was estimated (USAID, 1984: 15) that the relative shares were equivalent to about US$25 million from foreign donors and US$65 million from the Indonesian government, showing not only local dominance, but the magnitude of the increase over time.

THE INITIAL PROGRAMME: JAVA AND BALI

The new government programme continued its initial emphasis by concentrating efforts on Java and Bali. In the beginning, all services were operated out of existing Department of Health clinics, with the assistance of field-workers who made house-to-house visits to motivate acceptors to visit the clinics and obtain contraceptive services and supplies. For a while, incentives were offered to these workers based on the type of method accepted, but this system was phased out in 1974. Targets were set for numbers of new acceptors, attracting criticisms of 'target fever', a seasonal pattern emerging towards the end of the government fiscal year when final accounts were submitted. Periodically, the programme held 'special drives' which involved redoubled efforts and the mobilization of local leaders to recruit new acceptors. These drives were generally successful in increasing recruitment, but continuation rates of those accepting at these times were lower than those for acceptors in the regular programme. Thus not all aspects of the new programme ran smoothly during the early years, but the programme was flexible and responsive to reports from the field, and continually introduced innovations in an attempt to increase effectiveness. An outstanding feature of the Indonesian programme, which began almost with its inception, was the efficient system of reporting which allowed rapid feedback and evaluation of programme efforts.

EXPANSION AND INTENSIFICATION

The year 1974, the beginning of the Second Five-Year Development Plan, was a significant one for many programme initiatives. In this year, the programme expanded beyond Java and Bali to ten large provinces in the other islands. At the same time, the government announced that its programme objectives were unambiguously demographic: they declared a goal of a 50 per cent reduction of the 1971 birth rate, to be achieved by the year 2000.

Even while expanding the programme to new provinces, the BKKBN began a programme to intensify efforts in Java and Bali through a village family planning system. Basically, this initiative works through transferring much of the operational work to villagers, training formal and informal village leaders to manage the local programme, including contraceptive resupply. It also involves establishing groups of satisfied current users who act as motivators, and promotes group activities such as income-generating projects and nutrition education. Its overriding objective is to institutionalize family planning based on community participation.

In 1977, government family planning services were extended to all remaining provinces, and village family planning began to be extended beyond Java and Bali. Two years later in 1979, the government announced a speeding-up of its demographic target, aiming to achieve a 50 per cent birth rate decline to 22 per thousand by March 1991. This goal has been frequently mentioned in the press and government circles, but some citations speak of a target date of 1990.

THE ACHIEVEMENT OF NATIONAL COVERAGE

During the first part of the 1980s, Indonesia's family planning programme continued to develop. The islands outside Java and Bali presented special problems of logistics, being more sparsely settled and with less well-developed infrastructure. There were also problems of approach, since the new areas spanned wide cultural diversity, and many were regions of stricter religious adherence than Java. A second major area of challenge was that of Java's major cities, which surveys showed to be lagging behind in acceptance of modern contraceptive methods, thus reflecting the concentration on rural areas which had marked the programme since its inception. Additionally, urban residents were less influenced by their local government officials than were rural people, and many urban couples ignored the government's offers of free modern contraceptives in favour of traditional methods, or methods provided through private-sector physicians and pharmacists.

Training of personnel and expansion of infrastructure, particularly in Java and Bali, increased impressively. From an average women to clinic ratio of around 17,000 in Java–Bali in 1969/70, the ratio dropped to just over 4,000 per clinic in 1984/5. If we consider all 'service points' for family planning, including hospitals and clinics, village and sub-village depots, there were more than 200,000 such sources in March 1984 for Indonesia as a whole, or an average of 8 service points per 1,000 married women of reproductive age (USAID, 1984: 8).

The programme has also added new methods to its armoury, with voluntary sterilization on a small scale and injectable hormonal contraceptives on a limited, but rapidly growing, basis. The Norplant implant developed by the Population Council is currently being tested in Indonesia, and is proving to be an acceptable means of providing long-term protection from pregnancy. In addition, the BKKBN has shown an interest in developing more secure means of supplying contraceptives to meet local demand. An oral contraceptive pill factory was built so that supplies of this key method could be produced domestically. At various times, Indonesian manufacturers have explored the feasibility of producing condoms and IUDs in Indonesia, but it was not until 1986 that these plans were realized with the construction of a condom factory outside Bandung.

The BKKBN has been involved in various programmes of integrating family planning with health and nutrition, and field-workers have been trained in basic aspects of primary health care so that they may provide these services to women along with family planning messages. Generally, this training has focused on the establishment of baby-weighing programmes in villages, and emphasizes nutrition and procedures for referral of malnourished children. These programmes have received substantial support from USAID and UNICEF.

In 1983 and 1984, the BKKBN underwent a major administrative reorganization and substantial change of mandate. Until that time, the body not only co-ordinated family planning activities but was also the main focus of research, discussion, and advice on demographic and population policy issues in the government. With the formation of the new Ministry for Population and Environment (KLH), this role was shifted from the BKKBN, leaving it to concentrate more exclusively on the provision of contraceptive information, motivation, and services. The implications of this change will be discussed in Chapter 9.

Programme Results

CONTRACEPTIVE-USE RATES

The results achieved by Indonesia's family planning programme tell a story of remarkable social change and, in some provinces, of the virtual institutionalization of a modern innovation in just over a decade of work. Table 5.2 documents the recent dramatic increase in the use of modern contraception among Indonesian women. In the provinces of Java and Bali, the rise is especially striking, with current use levels above 40 per cent, thus approaching those found in the neighbouring ASEAN nations of Thailand and Malaysia, both of which have higher income levels, lower infant mortality and longer-established family planning programmes. Even the national figure of 51 per cent compares favourably with prevalence rates found in India and Korea, both of which had active family planning policies long before Indonesia's programme got under way (Nortman, 1982).

There has been some controversy about the accuracy of the family planning service statistics shown in Table 5.2. Streatfield (1985: 345) found that in 1980 the prevalence rate for all family planning methods from service statistics was 32.2 per cent compared to 27.2 per cent according to census data. Table 5.2 shows an even wider gap between 1985 service statistics and those derived from the sample census of that year. Irrespective of these differences, it remains clear that there is a high rate of acceptance of modern family planning methods in Indonesia and that the rate of acceptance has increased rapidly.

A few provinces even among the more recent stages stand out as having exceptionally high contraceptive prevalence, notably North Sulawesi, South Sulawesi, West Nusa Tenggara and Bengkulu. In contrast, provinces such as East Nusa Tenggara and Maluku have very low prevalence, and Irian Jaya and East Timor, where local statistics may be deficient and where programme facilities are not operating at optimal capacity, still show very low estimated contraceptive-use rates.

There are regional contrasts in programme effort and type of approach as well as in contraceptive use (Hull, Hull and Singarimbun, 1977), and these may account for some of the provincial differences observed in contraceptive prevalence. In Java and Bali, however, it has been shown that regional differences in rates of contraceptive use remain, even after controlling for some basic measures of programme performance such as the

TABLE 5.2

Indonesia: Estimated Proportion of Married Women of Reproductive Age Using
Contraception, by Province, in Selected Years under
Successive Development Plans

Province	1971/2 Repelita I Third Year	1974/5 Repelita II First Year	1979/80 Repelita III First Year	1984/5 Repelita IV Revised Figures July 1985	1985 Supas
INDONESIA	3	13	29	51	38
Stage I Provinces					
DKI Jakarta	4	10	20	46	44
West Java	2	11	21	54	44
Central Java	2	13	43	57	39
Yogyakarta	4	16	57	57	53
East Java	4	27	51	58	40
Bali	7	28	50	75	60
Stage II Provinces					
DI Aceh		2	7	44	22
North Sumatra		2	14	45	30
West Sumatra		1	15	41	26
South Sumatra		2	8	49	29
Lampung		1	18	41	42
West Nusa Tenggara		1	13	45	25
West Kalimantan		1	7	42	22
South Kalimantan		2	17	48	39
North Sulawesi		4	32	45	60
South Sulawesi		2	14	41	23
Stage III Provinces					
Riau			1	23	21
Jambi			4	32	38
Bengkulu			9	40	42
East Nusa Tenggara			1	20	29
Central Kalimantan			4	27	29
East Kalimantan			5	35	37
Central Sulawesi			3	34	38
South-east Sulawesi			3	31	24
Maluku			2	21	17
Irian Jaya			1	17	17
East Timor				6	10

Source: BKKBN Monthly Service Statistics, July 1985; BPS, 1986.

ratio of clinics and family planning personnel to population (Khoo, 1982).
In this latter aggregate analysis, differences in education and population
density among regions appeared to be influential factors in determining
contraceptive-use levels.

The figures in Table 5.2 are indirect estimates produced by the BKKBN. They are based on recorded numbers of contraceptives distributed or sterilization operations performed. These data are converted into estimated numbers of current users on the basis of a series of assumptions concerning the average rates of continuation of use or the average number of units of contraceptives needed to protect a couple from risk of pregnancy for a given period of time. Such figures may include a variety of biases which would tend to overestimate prevalence (Streatfield, 1985). However, there are also factors which would tend to make these figures underestimates of actual usage, including the use—often unreported in surveys—of traditional methods of varying efficacy, and of methods obtained through private channels.

The issue of the accuracy of BKKBN figures came to a head in May 1985. After years of continuous rises in the estimates of current usage and some quite spectacular apparent achievements as recorded in the statistics, the BKKBN undertook a major programme of verification, sending workers to the field to check the records of distribution of supplies and registration of acceptors. The report of this procedure was presented to a meeting of senior BKKBN officials. The result was a substantial downward revision of estimates in almost all provinces, with the recorded national estimate of contraceptive use falling from over 62 per cent of married women of reproductive ages in March 1985 to just 50 per cent in June. This decline does not imply a real change in behaviour, but simply an adjustment of statistical recording procedures. It was found that many of the local contraceptive distribution posts, which had been so important in bringing pill and condom supplies within convenient access of Indonesia's huge rural population, had built up large stocks. Because these inventories were not adequately assessed in the calculation of current users according to the formulae mentioned above, it appeared that there were many more current users than in fact existed. When the review procedures corrected the method of recording these local inventories, the result was a fall in the estimated numbers of current users. The decline was greatest in those areas where the Village Contraceptive Distribution Centres (VCDCs) had spread most widely and played an important role in distribution, namely the provinces of Java, and particularly East Java (see Table 5.3).

Readjusting service statistics might appear to be a largely innocuous matter of interest only to programme planners and demographers, and most outsiders would assume that such checks and adjustments are carried out regularly as part of routine programme operations. Both assumptions are wrong, however. From the outset of the programme, the service statistics system of the BKKBN has been both a source of pride in itself, and the source of all the good news about programme success which persuaded the government and the international community that the BKKBN was a worthy recipient of funds and praise. Statistics took on importance far beyond the value of the numbers for planning the use of resources or identifying community needs; they became a major form of political capital in the daily business of government. Signs that the statistics

TABLE 5.3
Indonesia: Impact of Rechecking Procedures in 1985 on the Recorded
Prevalence of Use of Programme Methods, by Province

Province	Prevalence Rate		Change in Recorded Prevalence (Percentage)
	March 1985	August 1985	
JAVA AND BALI			
DKI Jakarta	57.2	46.9	−18.1
West Java	65.1	55.3	−15.0
Central Java	71.9	58.8	−18.2
DI Yogyakarta	75.5	69.3	− 8.2
East Java	73.7	59.4	−19.4
Bali	74.7	74.5	− 0.3
Subtotal	69.5	57.7	−16.9
OUTER ISLANDS I			
DI Aceh	49.0	46.0	− 6.1
North Sumatra	57.6	46.7	−18.9
West Sumatra	51.1	41.8	−18.2
South Sumatra	58.6	49.6	−15.3
Lampung	54.3	46.2	−14.9
West Nusa Tenggara	58.9	48.4	−17.8
West Kalimantan	52.9	43.4	−18.0
South Kalimantan	61.6	49.5	−19.7
North Sulawesi	70.6	63.8	− 9.6
South Sulawesi	64.2	43.6	−32.1
Subtotal	57.8	47.0	−18.7
OUTER ISLANDS II			
Riau	22.6	23.2	+ 2.6
Jambi	35.0	34.8	− 0.7
Bengkulu	52.1	42.7	−18.1
East Nusa Tenggara	20.5	20.9	+ 2.0
Central Kalimantan	29.2	29.0	− 0.7
East Kalimantan	34.1	36.1	+ 5.9
Central Sulawesi	34.7	34.6	− 0.3
South-east Sulawesi	33.9	31.5	− 7.1
Maluku	21.3	21.5	+ 0.9
Irian Jaya	13.8	15.5	+12.3
East Timor	6.7	7.0	+ 4.5
Subtotal	27.1	26.9	− 0.7
INDONESIA	62.6	52.2	−16.6

Source: BKKBN Monthly Service Statistics.

were overstating success or, worse, charges that the whole system of recording data might be inherently biased, was enough to send shudders through the management of the BKKBN. As a result, when it became obvious that the data collection system had become a liability to the working of the programme, the BKKBN hesitated to take quick action for fear of the consequences of a precipitous revelation of the inadequacies. Instead, expert consultants were brought in to review the situation and suggest potential courses of action; then the initial checking operation was initiated which led to the gradual downward revision of estimates; and, finally, a regular programme of data review was designed, to be held each October, to prevent the development of a serious difference between the statistical reports and field realities in future.

CHARACTERISTICS OF ACCEPTORS AND CURRENT USERS

The evolution of the programme can also be seen in the figures on the types of couples who are becoming new acceptors, and the kinds of methods they are using. A common finding in the early stages of family planning is that women most highly motivated to accept contraception are those who have already reached, or even exceeded, their ideal family size and wish to limit childbearing through contraceptive use. As a programme evolves, however, the idea of contraceptive use becomes better institutionalized and more couples see the need for spacing children with these methods as well. Table 5.4 seems to confirm this finding for Indonesia, displaying a trend towards lower age and parity over the decade between

TABLE 5.4

Indonesia: Trends in Age and Parity of New Acceptors of Family Planning, 1971/2–1981/2

	Java and Bali	Stage II Provinces*	Stage III Provinces**
Percentage of new acceptors less than 30 years old			
1971/2	53	—	—
1976/7	67	56	—
1981/2	74	61	65
Median parity of new acceptors			
1971/2	3.48	—	—
1976/7	2.54	3.64	—
1981/2	2.31	3.04	3.13

Source: BKKBN, 1982: 101.
  * Stage II provinces are those which received the National Family Planning Programme in 1974 (Aceh, North, South and West Sumatra, Lampung, West Nusa Tenggara, West and South Kalimantan, and North and South Sulawesi).
** Stage III provinces are those which received the Programme in 1977 (Riau, Jambi, Bengkulu, East Nusa Tenggara, Central and East Kalimantan, Central and South-east Sulawesi, Maluku and Irian Jaya).

1971 and 1981 in Java and Bali, with early indications that the other provinces, where average fertility is higher, are also following this pattern. An analysis by Ross and Poedjastoeti (1983) has shown that the age pattern for current contraceptive users in 1979 for the other islands corresponded to that for Java and Bali in 1976. In 1979, the highest level of current contraceptive use occurred at ages 25 to 29 in Java–Bali, but at 30 to 34 in Kalimantan, and 35 to 39 in Sumatra and Sulawesi.[1]

According to BKKBN statistics, the proportion of new acceptors with an elementary school education or lower has remained fairly constant at around 90 per cent since the programme began (BKKBN, 1982: 129). This reflects the overall composition of the population. This is a slightly puzzling result since we would expect that recruitment of younger women over time would imply a trend towards higher education composition due to the higher educational level of the younger generation. However, current contraceptive-prevalence rates among educational attainment groups tend to increase with higher education, particularly at secondary school levels. In the 1979 *Susenas*, current users were 26 per cent of those with no schooling, 31 per cent and 36 per cent respectively of those with some primary schooling and completed primary schooling, rising to 45 per cent and 51 per cent respectively of those who had completed lower and upper secondary school (McNicoll and Singarimbun, 1982: 60). According to the 1976 Intercensal Survey, use rates display a U-shaped relation with economic status after controlling for other influences, a finding which has been explained in terms of a 'modernization' effect at the higher levels and the very different effects of poverty and social pressure at the lower levels (Freedman *et al.*, 1981).

The evolution of the 'method mix', that is, the types of contraceptive methods being selected and used by acceptors, is shown in Table 5.5. Although the pill has always been the pre-eminent method of the programme, the IUD was a very strong element in the early years in Java and Bali; it then declined in relative importance, but has since increased with recent efforts to promote the method due to its higher continuation rates and the fact that it does not require the major resupply network demanded by the oral pill. In recent years, the pill has given ground to both the IUD and the injectable. Outside Java and Bali, oral contraception remains strong in the Stage II provinces, though the IUD and also the injectable are particularly prominent in Stage III provinces with the most recent family planning programme inputs. The grouping of provinces into the three stages masks sometimes-significant contrasts among individual provinces; for example, the IUD rather than the pill has been a trade mark of the Bali programme since the early years, and condom use has been higher in Yogyakarta than elsewhere. In future, acceptance and use of the injectable may continue to increase, and female sterilization, now only a minor part of the programme, may increase if the national programme makes a commitment to this important method. The programme's information and education campaign advises concentration of childbearing between ages 20 and 30, and this implies a long period of contraception after this time which

TABLE 5.5

Methods Selected by New Acceptors, by Number of New Acceptors,
1971–1984

	Number of New Acceptors				
	Pill	IUD	Condom	Injectable	Sterilization
Java–Bali, Stage I					
1971	44	42	14	n.a.	n.a.
1972	54	41	3	n.a.	2
1973	56	35	7	n.a.	2
1974	63	21	15	n.a.	1
1975	69	11	19	n.a.	1
1976	68	13	18	n.a.	1
1977	67	18	13	n.a.	2
1978	71	17	9	n.a.	3
1979	68	20	8	n.a.	4
1980	68	20	8	n.a.	4
1981	68	19	8	n.a.	5
1982	62	23	6	n.a.	9
1983	56	30	5	6	3
1984	52	30	4	10	3
Other Islands, Stage II					
1975	66	17	14	n.a.	3
1976	69	16	11	n.a.	4
1977	69	16	11	n.a.	4
1978	73	14	7	n.a.	6
1979	75	11	8	n.a.	6
1980	75	11	8	n.a.	6
1981	73	9	12	n.a.	6
1982	72	13	5	n.a.	10
1983	72	13	8	4	3
1984	67	16	7	7	3
Other Islands, Stage III					
1980	68	15	7	n.a.	10
1981	63	21	7	n.a.	9
1982	59	21	7	n.a.	13
1983	59	23	5	10	3
1984	53	22	4	18	3

Source: USAID, 1984: 25.
n.a. = Method not available at that time.

could most safely and effectively be achieved through sterilization. Thus far, only female sterilization has been promoted widely in Indonesia, although vasectomies are available on a limited scale.

The Family Planning Programme: Strengths and Challenges

The Indonesian family planning programme has been lauded as an example of an effective government innovation in a country without the high level of economic development often considered a necessary precursor to successful family planning (Hull *et al.*, 1977; Heiby *et al.*, 1979; Freedman *et al.*, 1981; McNicoll and Singarimbun, 1982; Ross and Poedjastoeti, 1983). These observers have pointed to several ingredients of this success, citing strong government commitment as a primary factor. Another critical factor is the flexibility which characterized the programme, particularly in its early days, and which was a function of its independence from other more entrenched bureaucracies and the relative youth of its staff. The decentralization of much of the administration, and especially the efforts to base many of the services at the village level, has made a distinctive contribution to programme achievements. The high-quality service statistics system, alluded to earlier, allowed necessary feedback which also helped to promote a more efficient and responsive programme.

The programme also has a number of problems and weaknesses which will play a part in determining the future course of family planning in Indonesia. One aspect which has been commented on is the target mentality of officials which leads to irregular patterns of acceptance over the fiscal year as pressure is felt to meet end-of-year targets (Hull, 1983). Although the central administration has made several attempts to overcome this phenomenon, often the pressure is felt most keenly at lower levels as targets are transferred down the line. This approach to family planning can lead away from a service orientation to one bordering on coercion, and is an area which must continue to be monitored. A related approach, the special drives of former times and the more recent 'Family Planning Safari', in which local efforts are mobilized and intensified over a short period in order to promote the IUD in particular, also have the potential to lose sight of quality of service, including follow-up of side effects, in an effort to increase the quantity of acceptors.

Some specific provinces or local regions present ongoing challenges to the programme, and initiatives being undertaken in urban areas will remain an area of special attention. Efforts to incorporate sterilization into the programme involve consideration of potential religious opposition, but a programme responsive to the needs of the people it serves will have to address this issue, as well as the even more sensitive area of menstrual regulation, or early pregnancy termination.

Perhaps the biggest challenge facing the programme is self-imposed, and lies in the demographic goal of halving the birth rate by 1991, which was set and publicized widely in the 1970s. The achievement of a birth rate of 22 per thousand population by 1991 involves not only adequate service delivery and organization, but a substantial impact of the programme's education and motivation efforts. The challenge is greatest in many of the regions outside Java, where fertility has been higher and where birth limitation was less a part of the indigenous cultures than was the case in

Java, where modern contraception often substituted for traditional methods of birth control. The programme recognizes the challenge, and is working, in its own words, to 'institutionalize' small-family norms—but, as will be discussed in subsequent sections, fertility decline is the result of a much wider set of social and economic changes which will also contribute significantly to future levels of fertility.

Onset of Fertility Decline

RECENT TRENDS IN TOTAL FERTILITY

Recent surveys and censuses have shown that fertility is falling in Indonesia, with the greatest declines being recorded in parts of Java and Bali. Table 5.6 shows the magnitude of the decline for the major provinces and regions of Indonesia, using the total fertility rate. This measure shows the average number of children which would be born to a group of women if they maintained current age-specific fertility levels throughout their reproductive lives.

Figure 5.1 shows that there are substantial interprovincial variations in fertility. At the 1980 Census, the highest fertility rates in Indonesia were found in Sumatra while the provinces of Bengkulu, Central Sulawesi, South-east Sulawesi and West Nusa Tenggara all had total fertility rates of above 5.5. While this is very high compared to other provinces in 1980, none of these regions had a rate above that displayed by West Java in the 1960s, and all of them had experienced fertility declines in excess of 10 per cent over the preceding decade and a half.

The total fertility rates in the Yogyakarta special region, East Java and Bali were all below 3.5 in 1980. This is despite the fact that when the first fertility surveys were tabulated at the end of the 1960s, it was found that the 'ideal family size' of Indonesian women was in excess of 4 children, and in Yogyakarta the Fertility–Mortality Survey of 1973 recorded an average ideal family size of 4.6. From another viewpoint, it can be seen that provinces which had low fertility in the late 1960s achieved levels which were even lower relative to other provinces in 1980, perhaps a continuing reflection of the demand for fertility control to replace the traditional family planning common in areas of greatest population pressure.

AGE-SPECIFIC FERTILITY

Another way of viewing the decline in fertility is to look at the birth rates for each age group of women. Not only are Indonesian women having fewer children than was the case 15 or 20 years ago, but the births which have been averted were mainly among women concentrated in the young ages, thus leading to a flatter age-specific fertility rate graph (Figure 5.2). In the late 1960s, just over one-quarter of the women aged 20 to 29 gave birth in any given year, while by 1980 this proportion had fallen to one-fifth. In comparison, the older age groups have experienced proportionately greater decline in age-specific fertility rates but, because they had much

TABLE 5.6
Indonesia: Total Fertility Rates (TFR), by Province, Based on the
1971 and 1980 Censuses

Region	TFR during Reference Period		
	1967–1970	*1980*	*Percentage Decline in TFR*
INDONESIA	*5.61*	*4.27*	*24*
SUMATRA	*6.54*	*5.22*	*20*
DI Aceh	6.27	4.19	33
North Sumatra	7.20	5.40	25
West Sumatra	6.18	5.05	18
Riau	5.94	5.30	11
Jambi	6.39	5.11	20
South Sumatra	6.33	4.24	33
Bengkulu	6.72	5.76	14
Lampung	6.36	5.40	15
JAVA	*5.26*	*3.89*	*26*
DKI Jakarta	5.18	3.94	24
West Java	5.94	4.47	25
Central Java	5.33	4.08	23
DI Yogyakarta	4.76	3.25	32
East Java	4.72	3.27	31
NUSA TENGGARA			
Bali	5.96	3.50	41
West Nusa Tenggara	6.66	5.55	17
East Nusa Tenggara	5.96	5.15	14
KALIMANTAN	*5.89*	*4.61*	*22*
West Kalimantan	6.27	5.00	20
Central Kalimantan	6.83	5.20	24
South Kalimantan	5.43	3.99	26
East Kalimantan	5.41	4.51	17
SULAWESI	*6.02*	*4.52*	*25*
North Sulawesi	6.79	3.89	43
Central Sulawesi	6.53	5.76	12
South Sulawesi	5.71	4.43	22
South-east Sulawesi	6.45	5.70	12
MALUKU, IRIAN JAYA			
Maluku	6.89	6.08	12
Irian Jaya	7.20	4.11	43
EAST TIMOR	*n.a.*	*n.a.*	*n.a.*

Sources: 1967–70 rates calculated using the Own Children Method; reported in Mamas,
1983: 31–5; 1980 rates calculated by the Last Birth Method.
Notes: The figures for some provinces should be treated with caution due to problems of
sample size and data quality. The rates for Irian Jaya seem particularly suspect.
n.a. = Data not available.

154

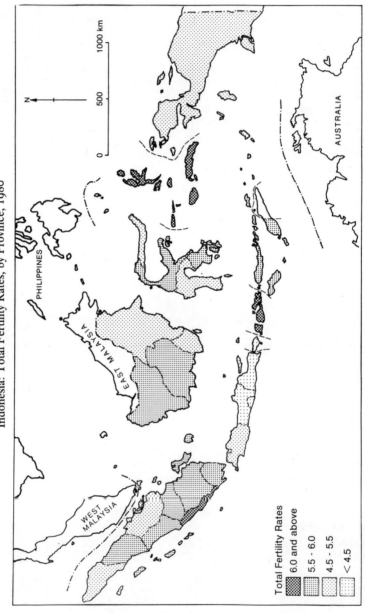

FIGURE 5.1

Indonesia: Total Fertility Rates, by Province, 1980

Total Fertility Rates

6.0 and above

5.5 - 6.0

4.5 - 5.5

< 4.5

Source: 1980 Census of Indonesia.

FIGURE 5.2
Changes in Age-specific Fertility Rates, 1967/1970–1980

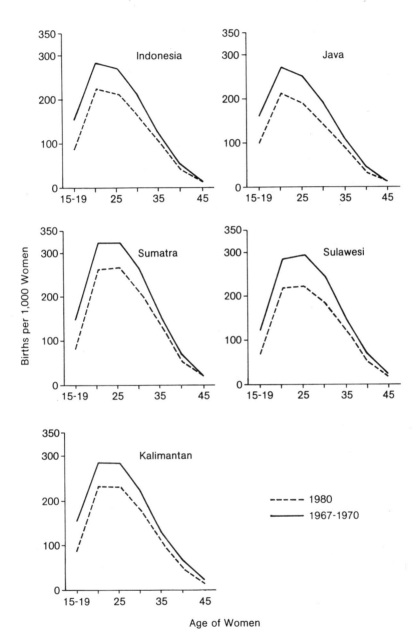

Source: Hull and Hull, 1984: 99.

lower fertility to begin with, this has had less impact on total fertility rates. Fertility decline in Indonesia has a generational component. Women currently in their twenties are responding to a set of values and perceptions different from those which motivated currently older women in their youth, and as time passes they will probably carry significantly different fertility patterns to older age groups. If this is the case, it can then be argued from a purely demographic viewpoint that fertility decline will continue in the future.

Regional Fertility Differences

The 1980 Census results confirmed some of the most important regional differences which had been noted by analysts since the early 1970s, and at the same time yielded new data on differentials which appeared to be emerging since the implementation of the family planning programme nation-wide. The long-recognized lower fertility of the ethnic Javanese of Yogyakarta and East Java continued to appear in the estimates, as did the steep fertility decline in the province of Bali. But outside Java and Bali, three provinces had moved dramatically from a fertility level of over 6 children per woman on average in the late 1960s to a total fertility rate (TFR) of under 5 in 1980: Aceh, South Sumatra, and North Sulawesi; several more (North Sumatra, Central and South Kalimantan, and South Sulawesi) had registered fertility declines of over 20 per cent (Table 5.6).

In general, these declines occurred in provinces which were also shown previously to have made impressive gains in modern contraceptive usage (see Table 5.2). North Sulawesi, for example, achieved the highest contraceptive-prevalence rates relative to other Stage II provinces during the Third Five-Year Development Plan period, and the impact on North Sulawesi's fertility of this longer-term acceptance of modern contraception is evident in its more dramatic fertility decline. The relation between the family planning data and the figures for total fertility is not without exceptions, however. Fairly early, Lampung achieved and sustained high rates of family planning use, but with only a moderate apparent fertility decline; conversely, Aceh's precipitous fertility decline is matched with a slower and somewhat less dramatic acceptance of family planning than in, for example West Nusa Tenggara. None the less, considering that there are contrasts in the method mixes and hence method effectiveness in each province, as well as the possibility of reporting inaccuracies in either family planning or fertility data, the correspondence between the two measures is quite impressive. As subsequent sections discuss, contraceptive use is not the only determinant of fertility behaviour: the changes in marriage patterns and other demographic behaviour, to the extent that these differ among the provinces, have played a role in determining current regional contrasts in fertility.

Socio-economic Fertility Differences

One of the most persistent and intriguing patterns of Indonesian fertility is the tendency for fertility to increase from lower to intermediate levels of socio-economic status. This has been noted in analyses of educational differentials in particular, where fertility is lower among mothers with no schooling than for those with some primary education. At higher levels of education, fertility declines in a more direct fashion, as has come to be expected in demographic literature. These findings have been reported for various indices of socio-economic status in addition to education—including income and economic indices created from ownership of consumer goods, landholding patterns, husband's occupation, wife's occupation, and housing quality. They have emerged in small-scale community studies in Java, and have been confirmed in national census and intercensal survey data for regions beyond Java. (See Hull and Hull, 1976 for a review of earlier evidence. More recent reports on this pattern can be found in McNicoll and Singarimbun, 1982; and Hatmadji and Achmad, 1984.)

It is all the more remarkable, then, that the analysis plan of the 1980 Census contained no effort to monitor the trends in the TFR by educational group, housing index, or any other socio-economic variable. Instead, analysis focused on the average numbers of children ever born to mothers of different groups, and this has the unfortunate problem that, being a measure of cumulative fertility, it can give misleading impressions about the trends of current fertility among women of different social groups. Moreover, the format of published tables restricted the amount of refinement which analysts could undertake to overcome these difficulties. Nevertheless, some of these data are presented in Table 5.7 and give some indications of the major fertility differentials in Indonesia. Firstly, the inverted U-shaped distribution of education differentials referred to earlier is apparent. Although the lowest fertility levels are recorded by women with tertiary education and there is the widely observed downward gradient in fertility from women with primary school education to those with tertiary education, women with no schooling had lower fertility than those with some primary education. The differences according to religion are interesting, with the high-fertility Protestant groups from North Sulawesi and North Sumatra standing out. Also, the lower-than-average fertility of the Balinese and Chinese populations are reflected in the respective figures for the Hindu and Buddhist groups. The differences according to field of economic activity show the universal pattern of women working outside the home having lower fertility than those who don't. Equally universal is the pattern of women working in agriculture having the highest fertility among those working. The relatively high fertility among trading women is interesting since most traders participate in the informal sector in which much of the organization of activity is not as incompatible with childbearing as is participation in modern-sector activities such as factory or office work.

With the crude measures available, it is not possible to answer many of the questions which planners posed in the early 1970s about who in society the family planning programme would serve, and who would be resistant to reductions in family size. Some of the sketchy evidence at hand is presented in Table 5.8 and this suggests that the fertility decline is greater among more educated women (and hence the better-off), while there may have been no change, or even some increase, in fertility among women with

TABLE 5.7

Indonesia: Average Number of Children Ever-Born to All Ever-Married Women Standardized by Age, According to Selected Background Characteristics of Mothers, 1980

Background Characteristics of Mothers	Average Number of Children Ever-Born per Ever-Married Woman
Education	
No school	3.26
Some primary school	3.44
Completed primary school	3.29
Completed lower secondary	3.13
Completed upper secondary	2.58
Completed academy/university	2.05
Religion	
Muslim	3.80
Protestant	4.02
Catholic	3.89
Hindu	3.50
Buddhist	3.57
Other	3.81
*Field of economic activity**	
Not working	3.92
Agriculture	3.78
Mining	3.55
Construction	2.87
Trade	3.57
Transportation	2.99
Other	3.15

Source: Adioetomo, 1984.
* Field of work over the year preceding the census.

no schooling. This latter trend could arise in two ways. First, the very poor and uneducated had small families in the past due to higher rates of divorces, infecundity, and the practice of long periods of abstinence. As nutrition and health improve, and abstinence practices and divorce decline, so their fertility would tend to rise unless offset by an increase in the use of contraception. The issue is thus one of the balance between the dampening effect of birth control and the countervailing effects of socio-economic change. The second possible influence lies in the fact that the proportion of women with no schooling is falling very rapidly, and the group in that category in 1980 could represent a very different background from that found among uneducated women in 1971. This process of selectivity could produce higher fertility irrespective of any changes in behaviour, especially if the remaining pockets of women with no education are increasingly located in regions of the country with higher-than-average fertility. Both explanations rely too heavily on speculation to be satisfying but, until

TABLE 5.8

Indonesia: Average Number of Children Ever-Born to All Ever-Married Women
Standardized for Current Age, According to Educational Level of
Mothers, Based on Data from 1971 and 1980

Educational Level of Mothers	Average Number of Ever-Born Children per Ever-Married Woman		Percentage Change, 1971–1980
	1971	1980	
No Schooling	3.63	3.26	−10.19
Some primary schooling	4.01	3.44	−14.21
Completed primary schooling	3.99	3.29	−17.54
Completed lower secondary schooling	3.91	3.13	−19.95
Completed upper secondary schooling	3.17	2.58	−18.61
Completed academy/ university education	2.39	2.05	−14.23

Sources: 1971: 1971 Indonesian Census, Series D, p. 137 (BPS, 1975); 1980: 1980 Indonesian Census, in Adioetomo, 1984, p. 62 (BPS, 1984).

further data from the 1980 Census are released or the results of the 1985 Intercensal Survey become available, the questions of many planners and programme officials will go unanswered.

Dimensions of the Decline

Fertility rates in any population are determined by a number of factors. Demographic factors such as the age structure of the population can influence the crude birth rate positively or negatively even when the actual pace of childbearing remains constant. This effect is minimized if we concentrate on the total fertility rates in preference to crude birth rates. However, there are other influences which are not so easily handled in analysis. Social factors regulate the formation of reproductive unions through marriage or cohabitation, and biological factors influence a couple's ability to conceive and a mother's ability to carry a pregnancy successfully to a live birth. Furthermore, ultimate family size is determined by the ability of live births to survive through childhood. For individual women, these factors tend to operate in sequence over their life cycles, with factors surrounding marriage and cohabitation being salient during adolescence and young adulthood, factors related to sexual relations being important throughout marriage, and issues of widowhood and the end of fecundity arising as the women grow older. To understand the causes of fertility decline it is necessary to analyse changes to determinants of fertility as they have operated through groups of women over time. For this purpose, we will first examine changes in the institutions of marriage, then changes in childbearing within marriage, and finally the innovations in fertility control introduced by the family planning programme.

CHANGING MARRIAGE PATTERNS

Customs and regulations related to marriage vary greatly among the hundreds of ethnic groups in Indonesia. Tribal people in Kalimantan and Irian Jaya have developed norms regarding the timing and role of marriage which differ from those found among the royal courts of Java or the Chinese settlers in port cities. Within this variety, a few general characteristics nevertheless emerge: women traditionally married during the years around menarche; they married men on average five to eight years older than themselves; and by age 30 almost no women remained unmarried. Most Indonesian women were married to men selected by their parents. The parental arrangements did not necessarily imply forced acquiescence on the part of the young girl and, in some societies, a high rate of divorce resulted from women refusing to live with the partners their parents had chosen.

Over recent decades, however, demographic and sociological studies have recorded important changes which signal a transformation in marriage patterns. The age at first marriage has increased virtually everywhere, in some cases quite substantially. By the time of the 1980 Census, the proportions of 15 to 19- and 20 to 24-year-old women who had not yet married had risen in nearly every province since the previous census. Because of the differences in traditional patterns and the impact of government initiatives, regional contrasts still persisted, with the highest proportion unmarried in the age groups 15 to 19 and 20 to 24 found in the islands of eastern Indonesia, including Sulawesi. The lowest proportions are in West Java, which has long had a reputation for child marriage. Nevertheless, overall in Indonesia in 1980, over seven out of ten girls aged 15 to 19 were not married, and nearly a quarter of those aged 20 to 24 remained single.

While the proportions unmarried give a clear idea of the changes which are taking place, it is more conventional to think in terms of the average age of women at marriage to give a summary picture of trends over time. Table 5.9 shows that the mean age had risen to 20 years by 1980. In the provinces of Java, for which we have estimates for three time periods, the increase in the mean age between 1971 and 1980 was even greater than the rise between 1964 and 1971. Again, West Java still stands out for its low average age at marriage of 18.5, and the islands of eastern Indonesia for their higher average ages at the time of first marriage.

The decrease in child marriage is related to fundamental changes in the actual arrangement of marriage, in particular the selection of partners. Marriages in more traditional times tended to be arranged by parents, often before the girl reached puberty, and even the male partner did not always have a say in the selection. This pattern of early arranged marriage, however, was sometimes associated with a delay in the actual consumma-

TABLE 5.9
Indonesia: Trends in the Singulate Mean Age at Marriage for Women,
1964–1980

Region	Mean Age of Women at Marriage			Percentage Change in Mean during Period	
	1964	1971	1980	1964–1971	1971–1980
INDONESIA	n.a.	19.3	20.0	n.a.	0.8
SUMATRA	19.9	19.9	20.6	n.a.	0.8
DI Aceh	n.a.	19.5	20.8	n.a.	1.3
North Sumatra	n.a.	20.8	21.7	n.a.	1.0
West Sumatra	n.a.	20.3	20.8	n.a.	0.5
Riau	n.a.	20.0	20.7	n.a.	0.7
Jambi	n.a.	18.4	19.2	n.a.	0.8
South Sumatra	n.a.	20.0	20.7	n.a.	0.6
Bengkulu	n.a.	19.7	19.6	n.a.	−0.1
Lampung	n.a.	18.0	18.9	n.a.	0.9
JAVA	18.1	18.7	19.5	0.6	0.8
DKI Jakarta	20.0	20.2	21.7	0.2	1.5
West Java	17.4	17.8	18.5	0.4	0.7
Central Java	18.2	19.0	19.8	0.8	0.9
DI Yogyakarta	20.7	21.8	22.5	1.1	0.7
East Java	18.1	18.7	19.4	0.6	0.7
NUSA TENGGARA	n.a.	20.8	21.6	n.a.	0.8
Bali	21.7	20.8	21.2	−1.0	0.5
West Nusa Tenggara	21.0	19.2	20.3	−1.8	1.1
East Nusa Tenggara	n.a.	22.4	23.1	n.a.	0.7
East Timor	n.a.	n.a.	n.a.	n.a.	0.0
KALIMANTAN	18.6	20.0	20.2	1.5	0.2
West Kalimantan	n.a.	20.9	20.9	n.a.	0.0
Central Kalimantan	n.a.	19.7	19.8	n.a.	0.0
South Kalimantan	n.a.	19.2	19.6	n.a.	0.4
East Kalimantan	n.a.	19.6	20.5	n.a.	0.8
SULAWESI	19.5	20.7	21.6	1.2	0.9
North Sulawesi	n.a.	21.6	21.7	n.a.	0.1
Central Sulawesi	n.a.	20.6	20.7	n.a.	0.2
South Sulawesi	n.a.	20.5	21.8	n.a.	1.3
South-east Sulawesi	n.a.	19.9	20.6	n.a.	0.7
MALUKU, IRIAN JAYA					
Maluku	n.a.	22.0	21.6	n.a.	−0.3
Irian Jaya	n.a.	20.9	19.8	n.a.	−1.1

Source: Calculations based on the results of the 1971 and 1980 Censuses of Indonesia. The mean age is calculated from data on the proportions of single women in successive five-year age groups from ages 15 to 49.
Note: The 1971 Census of Irian Jaya included urban areas only.
n.a. = Data not available.

tion of the union and husband–wife cohabitation, and some marriages were in fact dissolved following a protracted period during which the couple never cohabited. The occurrence of these delays is declining with the trend towards later marriage and marriages in which the couple has more say in the process (Hull and Hull, 1985). In terms of implications for fertility, the attenuation of the custom of delayed consummation partially offsets the trend to later marriage, so that the actual age at initiation of childbearing has not increased as dramatically as has the age at first marriage. Nevertheless, age at first childbearing has also increased, a trend with obvious demographic and health implications as will be considered below.

Also related to changing patterns of spouse selection and age at marriage is the trend towards declines in the incidence of divorce. Divorce has been generally higher in Java, especially West Java, than in the other islands, and has been higher in rural than in urban areas. Divorce tends to be most likely in cases of marriages arranged by parents and among marriages initiated at very young ages; we would expect to see a decline in its incidence as part of the overall changes being observed in the marriage relationship. Over recent decades, in fact, the proportion of women whose marriages ended in divorce—particularly within the first few years of marriage—has declined in all regions and in both rural and urban areas (Sutarsih, 1976), though the changes outside Java and Bali are less clear than those for these central islands (McNicoll and Singarimbun, 1982: 53).

CHANGING MARRIAGE PATTERNS: SOCIAL CHANGE AND
SOCIAL POLICY

To what degree have these changes in marriage, with their consequent implications for fertility, been the result of broad social change, and to what degree have they been the result of conscious policies?

In the early part of the century, the Dutch colonial government campaigned against child marriage, and instituted a series of laws and regulations designed to place marriage contracts on a legal footing while preserving the customary provisions of different major religious and ethnic groups. At the same time, the school system was beginning to cater for girls, because of a recognition of the 'significance of the improvement of the position of women in the consolidation and sanctifying of marriage and family life'. (Angelino, 1931: 227). The impact of such activities was initially greatest in areas where Dutch administration had penetrated most deeply—notably in Java, some parts of Sumatra, and North Sulawesi. With the formation of an independent republic, these policies were continued and extended, with pressure to eliminate child marriage, formalize marriage ceremonies according to procedures recognized by the state, and discourage non-marital cohabitation.

The development of a national marriage law which was acceptable to Indonesia's heterogeneous population took decades, but in 1974 a new law was passed after prolonged, and sometimes violent, public debate between modernist and traditional Islamic forces. The final version of the law made several concessions to the strict Muslims, but did provide for some fundamental changes in procedural, if not substantive, areas of marriage. In essence, the law codified a minimum legal marriage age of 16 for women and 19 for men and instituted stricter conditions for both divorce and polygyny. It is probably true to say that the new law has, in both the case of age at marriage and divorce, reinforced existing long-term trends. Indeed, legal analysts of the impact of the Marriage Law have speculated that its success is due in large measure to the very fact that it was trend-following rather than trend-setting (Katz and Katz, 1978: 318).

However, in addition to such legal changes, the picture that emerges for Indonesia, and particularly for Java, is that of a rapid evolution in the institution of marriage as a result of the social changes taking place in society. As young people increasingly take the initiative to find their own mates, the age of marriage is rising. In part, both trends reflect the increasing demand for education in a modernizing society. Further, love matches are consummated immediately, in contrast to traditional delays in cohabitation and, in an increasing proportion of cases, matches are consummated prior to formal marriage. These new patterns are consistent with new images of marriage as a union based on emotional ties. Such ties lead to declines in the incidence of divorce. Rising age at marriage and less rapid rise in the age at cohabitation have the effect of reducing fertility, while declining divorce and widowhood (with falling mortality rates) tend to exert upward pressure on fertility.

Issues for the Future Trend in Fertility

The Continuing Evolution of Traditional Restraints

The fertility decline, begun in the 1960s and quickened in the 1970s, has tended to focus attention on the increasing age at marriage and the rapid introduction of birth control. However, there have been additional changes in other behaviour affecting fertility which should be monitored. By and large, these changes are difficult to measure using large-scale surveys, or have been ignored by analysts concerned with other issues. Among the traditional restraints on fertility are prolonged breastfeeding which leads to prolonged amenorrhoea, sexual abstinence, and the use of herbs and massage to prevent conception or affect abortion. The sketchy evidence available indicates that breastfeeding may be declining in terms of the average length of time mothers breastfeed their infants, particularly in urban centres and among upper-class mothers. Sexual abstinence was an important method of spacing births in Java, but in recent years it has declined significantly in importance. Young couples who marry for love rather than through parental arrangements are more likely to ignore the old beliefs concerning the need for prolonged abstinence. While there is little evidence as to the efficacy of herbs and massage as methods of birth control, there is no doubt that they have been widely used by women in Java, Kalimantan and a number of other cultural areas. Evidence about trends in use over time is unreliable but, as examination of shops in villages and cities alike indicates, herbal treatments for preventing conception or causing abortion are readily available and very popular.

To some degree, modern contraceptives serve to substitute for some of the traditional constraints on family size which have recently waned under the influence of modernization. However, this substitution effect is minor compared to the total fall in fertility. Nevertheless, traditional methods of birth control remain important issues for study, not so much because of the effects they have had on fertility, but because of what they indicate of the changing nature of the family in Indonesia, and the motives women have traditionally had for controlling their childbearing.

Inculcation of Low Fertility

If the whole fabric of family life is changing rapidly in Indonesia, as argued above, one of the most ambitious intentions of the government is the plan to promote a new norm of a 'small, happy, healthy family', as part of the family planning programme. Over the years, the target family size described in the depiction of this new norm has declined from four children to three and recently to two, with the slogan 'boy or girl, it makes no difference' being an important message of recent advertisements. Little thought has been given to the long-term implications for Indonesian family life of a rapid transition from an average five-child to two-child family. Considering the dramatic changes occurring in the education and economic systems and in the content of mass communications, it is likely that the matter of average numbers of children in families will be less important in shaping family life than will be the rapidly changing expectations parents have for the future of each child.

Foreign Aid and the Need for Self-sufficiency

The family planning programme in Indonesia got under way with substantial financial and technical assistance from overseas, notably from the World Bank, USAID and the United Nations Fund for Population Activities (UNFPA). Over the years, these donors have increased their assistance but, because of the rapid increase in Indonesian funds devoted to this purpose, foreign contributions have steadily declined in proportionate terms. By the mid-1980s, it was becoming clear that long-term self-sufficiency is an important goal for population planners in Indonesia, as foreign donors are becoming less reliable in the family planning field. This is especially true in the case of USAID which has yielded to the pressure of anti-abortion and anti-family planning campaigners to cut off a wide variety of activities and organizations which had previously received US funding. As US support for many international family planning needs declines, so have multi-lateral agencies such as UNFPA and the IPPF been put in jeopardy through withdrawal of US funding. In order to build the groundwork for self-sufficiency, Indonesia is gradually increasing the domestic manufacture of contraceptives, and budgeting for an increasing proportion of routine expenditures.

Indonesia has experienced a remarkable change in fertility patterns over the past two decades, and all signs indicate that the decline in fertility levels is not over yet. One of the major contributing factors underlying this change is the rapid adoption of modern contraceptives provided through Indonesia's family planning programme. That programme in turn has taken full advantage of major changes in the structure of local government and the education of the population to create effective systems of contraceptive distribution and family planning information. There are still many challenges to be overcome, not the least of which is the problem of sustaining support for a family planning programme widely deemed a 'success' in a climate of rapidly rising demands for support of other worthy social and health programmes. The government's performance in meeting this challenge will do much to determine the course of fertility decline over the next few years, and the size and structure of the population until well into the next century.

1. The age composition of current users would be older than that for new acceptors, since continuation rates are higher among older women.

6 Population Mobility: Types and Patterns

Introduction

THE *immobility* of Indonesians, especially those living in Java, has been remarked upon by many commentators of the Indonesian scene (for example, Bryant, 1973; Fryer and Jackson, 1977: 18; McNicoll, 1968: 33–9; and Naim, 1974). Such pronouncements are supported by much of the available evidence on internal migration from large-scale surveys and censuses. The 1980 Census showed that only 2.4 per cent of Indonesians had migrated in the previous five years, whereas the equivalent figures for the USA and Australia were 46 and 43 per cent respectively. Such data are misleading, however, since migrations recognized by Indonesian censuses are only the tip of the iceberg of all population movement, and the vast hidden bulk of mobility that goes undetected is not only of much greater volume but is also of major social and economic significance. The overall picture which emerges from a large number of community-based studies belies the conventional stereotype of high levels of stability.

Population movement is of importance in Indonesia not only because it is the major cause of interregional variations in population growth, but also because of its influential role in social and economic change in the areas and populations on which it impinges. Indonesian governments have long sought to direct patterns of population movement through a range of explicit policies and programmes which have aimed to achieve a closer match between the spatial distributions of population and resources. Most notable is the transmigration programme which seeks to redistribute population from densely populated Java, Bali and Lombok to the other major islands of the archipelago. This is the largest agricultural 'colonization' programme of its kind in the world, and dates back to the early years of this century.

This chapter summarizes the main types of population movement which occur in contemporary Indonesia. Although our main focus is upon internal migration as reflected in data from successive Indonesian censuses, this is put in context by consideration of other types of mobility not detected by the census. Post-Independence censuses have collected information relating only to migration between provinces, whereas survey evidence suggests that

TABLE 6.1

Indonesia: A Selection of Major Census and Survey Sources of Population Movement Data

Source	Date	Type	Coverage	Migration Defining Unit	Mobility Type	Types of Analysis Possible
1961 Census	1961	Census	Nation (but complete data for only a few provinces)	Province	Permanent migration (3 months' absence or longer)	Limited analysis of stocks and flows. Very little data on characteristics of migrants
1971 Census	1971	Sample census	Nation	Province	Permanent migration (6 months' absence or longer)	Detailed analysis of stocks and flows, and demographic, social, economic and work-force characteristics of migrants and non-migrants
1980 Census	1980	Sample census	Nation	Province	Permanent migration	
1981 Census Post-Enumeration Survey	1962 1964 1965 1967	Sample survey	Java–Madura and major cities of outer islands	All changes of residence	Permanent migration	Calculation of residential mobility rates, and limited analysis of characteristics of migrants
Dept. of Labour, Labour Force Studies	1958	Sample survey	Sukabumi Kabupaten and Kotamadya, Bandung, Kotamadya Sulawesi	Kabupaten	Permanent migration	Limited analysis of labour-force characteristics of migrants
National Social and Economic Surveys (Susenas)	1964–5 1967	Sample survey	1964–5 — All nation except East Nusa Tenggara, Maluku, Irian Jaya and Jakarta 1967 — Java only	All changes of residence	Permanent migration	Mobility rates, limited interpretation of spatial patterns and characteristics of migrants

(continued)

TABLE 6.1 (*continued*)

Source	Date	Type	Coverage	Migration Defining Unit	Mobility Type	Types of Analysis Possible
1976 Intercensal Survey	1976	Sample survey	Nation except East Timor, Irian Jaya, Maluku and East Nusa Tenggara. Although accuracy of outer islands coverage is such to negate much of its usefulness	Inter-village migration	Permanent migration	Mobility rates and patterns (at least in Java), characteristics (especially work-force) of migrants
1972 *Leknas* Survey	1972	Sample survey	Jakarta	Province	Permanent migration	Mobility rates and patterns, characteristics, motivations and impacts of migration
1973–4 *Leknas* Survey	1973–4	Non-representative survey	Major cities of Sumatra, Sulawesi. Limited rural survey in these areas	All movers	Permanent migration	Characteristics, motivations and impacts of migration
1981 *Leknas* Survey	1981	Sample survey	East Java, Bali and South Sulawesi	All movers	Permanent and non-permanent migration	Mobility rates and patterns, characteristics, motivations and impacts of migration
Demographic Institute, University of Indonesia	1973 1975	Labour force sample surveys	Municipalities of Surabaya, Bandung, Palembang, and Ujung Pandang, and DKI Jakarta	Migrations from outside cities in last 5 years	Permanent migration	Migration rates among labour force, characteristics of labour-force migrants especially relating to employment and unemployment.

intraprovincial residential shifts are at least five times more numerous (Hugo, 1982a: 35). In addition, the semi-*de jure* basis on which the censuses have been conducted has meant that most persons temporarily absent from their usual place of residence have not been defined as movers, although circular, temporary migrations have been shown to be of considerable significance in Indonesia (Hugo, 1982b). The most detailed census migration information was in fact collected at the 1930 colonial *Volkstelling*, and some of this is employed here to place contemporary movements in historical context. No attempt is made to provide a comprehensive evaluation of the various sources of Indonesian population movement data.[1] They are listed in Table 6.1 along with their major characteristics and limitations. It should be noted that each successive post-Independence census has collected more information on interprovincial migration, beginning with only a birthplace question in 1961, adding a question on province of previous residence in 1971 and, in 1980, one on place of residence five years previously.

Types of Contemporary Population Movement in Indonesia

Typologies of population movement are useful in indicating the range of mobility strategies adopted by a significant proportion of the population, especially in the absence of comprehensive data relating to population mobility. Moreover they can assist in indicating which subset of total movement is actually represented in the available data. Typologies with particular purposes have been proposed by several writers on Indonesian migration (e.g. Naim, 1974; Hugo, 1983a), and that given in Table 6.2 is simply a way of indicating the great variety of movements which must be considered in examining mobility in Indonesia. The left-hand side of the table differentiates moves largely according to the extent to which movers travel beyond what is familiar to them. Movers within provinces are unlikely to travel beyond the region dominated by their *sukubangsa*, whereas movement to another province, especially if it is on a different island, is likely to involve interaction with other groups and exposure to different ways of thinking and of doing things. Movement to another country, of course, will usually involve even greater contact with different languages, peoples and customs. Moves can also be significantly differentiated according to whether they involve moving between urban and rural areas.

The question of distinguishing between permanency and non-permanency in population mobility is a complex one. Zelinsky (1971: 225–6) defines conventional migration as 'any permanent or semi-permanent change of residence', and circulation as 'a great variety of movements, usually short term, repetitive or cyclical in nature, but all having in common the lack of any declared intention of a permanent or long-lasting change in residence'. A further distinction can be made between 'commuting', defined as regular travel outside the village (usually for work or education) for between 6 to 24 hours, and 'circular migration' involving continuous but temporary absences of more than one day. These broad distinctions shown in Table 6.2

TABLE 6.2

A Simple Typology of Indonesian Population Mobility

		Commuting	Circular Migration	Migration
1. Movements within local community				
2. Movements outside the community but within the province	Rural → Rural Rural → Urban Urban → Rural Urban → Urban			
3. Interprovincial moves within an island				▒▒▒
4. Inter-island moves				▒▒▒
5. International moves				▒▒▒

▒▒▒ = Moves detected by post-Independence censuses.

have some basis in the indigenous concepts of mobility held by several major groups in Indonesia. The Javanese, for example, have several distinct concepts of types of mobility, as Mantra (1981: 166) explains:

... *nglaju* is used for those who travel to a place but return back to their home within the same day, *nginep* for people who stay in another place for several days before returning and *mondok* for those who lodge in a destination for several months a year. *Merantau* refers to those who go to the origin community. The term *pindah* is used for residents who migrate to another place.

Moves can also be differentiated in many other dimensions—especially the function of the move (to seek work, to attend an educational institution, etc.) and its underlying causes. These issues are addressed in the next chapter while our purpose here is to point out the variety of movement types, the levels of mobility, the patterns of movement, and their significance for population redistribution.

Pre-colonial and Colonial Mobility Patterns

In the traditional society of pre-colonial times, mobility was greatly constrained for most Indonesians, although some significant movements occurred—particularly those of the agricultural colonization, seasonal and trading type (see Table 6.1; and Hugo, 1980a: 97–100). The pre-colonial class structure, the rise and fall of inland kingdoms and coastal sultanates, the regular incidence of famine, the development of various trading patterns through the Indonesian archipelago, the spread of new types of agriculture and various environmental disasters, all shaped the pattern and levels of the movements which did occur. However, for the large part, movement outside the local area was prevented by lack of transport infrastructure, the obvious difficulties of moving between the regions of Indonesia's more than 200 separate ethnolinguistic groups, and in some areas the political constraints exerted by control by elite groups. This pattern was transformed, however, by the gradual penetration of capitalism via the 'step by step' growth in European control of Indonesia, culminating in the assumption of virtual total control in the nineteenth century. Several theoretical formulations have emerged to explain the relationship between colonialism and population movement—mainly by students of African population mobility (Amin, 1974; Gregory and Piche, 1978; and 1980; Binsbergen and Meilink, 1978; Gerold-Scheepers and Binsbergen, 1978). These see population movement patterns and levels as a response to broader socio-structural changes associated with the uneven penetration of capitalism during the colonial period, leading to substantial sectoral, class and spatial inequalities. Contemporary population mobility in the Third World cannot be explained without reference to the formative influence of colonialism on the country's political, economic and social systems. The argument is that the fundamentally exploitative colonial system, designed to control the local population and expedite the extraction of raw materials in the most cost-efficient way, shaped the pattern of mobility in very distinctive ways that have yet to be greatly altered.

As European influence and control increased in Indonesia during the sixteenth, seventeenth and eighteenth centuries, so did their impact on population movement (Hugo, 1980: 100–2), but it was the imposition of direct colonial rule by the Dutch (and for a short time British) government in the nineteenth century which had the most dramatic effects. Some of these effects were as follows:

1. There was probably a greater degree of peace and order which at least in part removed the physical fears associated with movement between regions;

2. The whole pattern and availability of transport underwent a revolution which greatly reduced the friction of distance;

3. The structure of the economy was changed drastically in line with the exploitative colonial aims, concentrating job opportunities in new and different types of areas from those in the past;

4. There were direct colonial-imposed laws to encourage or discourage particular types of movement;

5. There was a range of forced and semi-forced labour schemes;

6. An 'externally oriented trading system' (Riddell, 1980: 116) saw the development of urban centres in entrepôt locations and migration towards them;

7. The introduction of various schemes of taxation had effects on population movement;

8. Immigration of certain non-Indonesian foreigners was encouraged;

9. The reduction in mortality and perhaps even an increase in fertility (White, 1973) led to increasing population pressure in rural areas;

10. Primary and, to a lesser extent, secondary schools were introduced, albeit in an extremely limited way.

FIGURE 6.1

Indonesia: Major Interprovincial Lifetime Migration Streams
(Those with More than 5,000 Persons), 1930

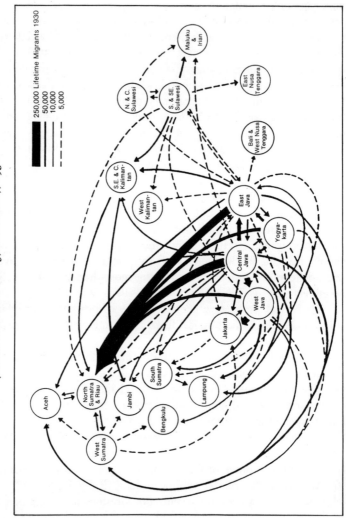

Source: Hugo, 1980a.

The impact of these changes and the patterns of population mobility which they engendered are examined in detail elsewhere (Hugo, 1980a; 1983b), and only a few of the major patterns can be mentioned here. There was a spatial reorientation of traditional movement patterns toward areas of colonial exploitation such as plantations, mining areas, and towns and cities in locations most favourable to the extraction and export of raw materials. Contract labour and agricultural colonization programmes organized by the Dutch also influenced population movement patterns. Hence the flows of interprovincial lifetime migration at the 1930 Census, shown in Figure 6.1, are dominated by the contract coolie flow from Central Java to the plantation areas of North Sumatra and, to a lesser extent, by the agricultural colonization of East and West Java, and Lampung from Central Java. A flow towards the developing colonial capital of Jakarta was in evidence, especially from nearby West Java, but it was of secondary significance to the migrations to the rural destinations mentioned earlier.

Many of the patterns and types of migration which evolved during Indonesia's colonial period have been maintained since Independence. This is largely a function of international and intranational inequalities in the distribution of resources, investments, factors of production and services, which have their roots in the colonial past. An examination of colonial migration patterns thus assists in an understanding of contemporary migration, to which we now turn.

International Migration

A significant feature of colonial migration patterns was the immigration of large numbers of Dutch, Chinese and, to a lesser extent, other foreign groups which has had a lasting impact on Indonesian society. During the Independence period, however, international movements have had only a limited impact. In the Soekarno years, there were substantial repatriations of Dutch and Chinese nationals (Hugo, 1982c: 82). In more recent years, there have been two types of international movements of importance. The first relates to refugees. Indonesia has acted as a country of first asylum for refugees from Vietnam, numbering (cumulatively) approximately 85,000 by mid-1984. Most of these have subsequently been settled in other countries. On the other hand, there has been a small outflow of refugees from East Timor and Irian Jaya (Hugo, 1983c). In the first half of 1984, for example, there was a movement of some 8,000 refugees from Irian Jaya into Papua New Guinea.

Indonesia did not share in the huge boom of contract worker movement to the Middle East and other countries which occurred in the Philippines and Thailand during the late 1970s and early 1980s. Until recently, the numbers of Indonesians engaging in this movement were small, although there has been a substantial upswing in international labour migration in recent years, which may be indicative of an even greater outmovement in the remainder of the 1980s. Part of this has been to the Middle East, but the most significant has been the movement, much of it illegal, into both

East and West Malaysia. The number of Indonesian migrant labourers working in Peninsular Malaysia is conservatively estimated to be between 100,000 and 300,000 (Lim, 1982: 3; 1985: 4), though some estimates go as high as 700,000; the Indonesian manpower ministry estimates that a further 130,000 are working in East Malaysia (Habir, 1984: 164). There have long been migration linkages between Indonesia and Malaysia (Bahrin, 1967), especially towards Peninsular Malaysia. However, temporary movement on this scale is a new phenomenon, and one which has very significant implications for both Indonesia and Malaysia.

The migrant workers in Peninsular Malaysia come predominantly from East Java (especially the island of Madura, whose inhabitants have long had a tradition of moving out from their densely populated homeland to work in all parts of the Indonesian archipelago) and from South, West and North Sumatra (which have also traditionally had high levels of outmovement). Those in East Malaysia come from Flores in East Nusa Tenggara and from South Sulawesi, again provinces whose inhabitants have a strong out-migration tradition. Those coming to Peninsular Malaysia are primarily employed in Johore, Pahang and Negri Sembilan, and work especially in the plantation and construction sectors. They usually come by boat from Tanjung Pinang across the Straits of Malacca to the west coast of Johore. The migrants to East Malaysia enter through East Kalimantan—usually the migrants from Flores and South Sulawesi arrive at Nunukan and then go to Tawau in Sabah. They work mainly in the timber and plantation sectors of Sabah.

Recent Trends in Interprovincial Migration: The 1980 Census

Introduction

Indonesia's census collects information on more or less permanent movement *between* its 27 provinces, although the bulk of mobility is not detected by the census. The patterns of migration observed at the 1971 Census have been described elsewhere (Cummings, 1975; Hugo, 1975; and 1982c;

TABLE 6.3

Interprovincial Lifetime Migration between Java and the
Other Islands, 1930, 1971 and 1980

Year	Out of Java (Millions)	Into Java (Millions)
1930	0.88	0.06
1971	1.53	0.58
1980	3.71	1.22
Percentage increase 1930–71	171	902
Percentage increase 1971–80	142	110

Sources: Volkstelling, 1933–6; Indonesian Censuses of 1971 and 1980.

FIGURE 6.2

Indonesia: Major Interprovincial Lifetime Migration Streams
(Those with More than 10,000 Persons), 1971

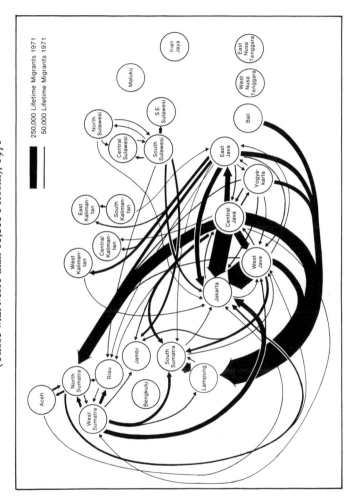

Source: Hugo, 1979a.

176

FIGURE 6.3

Indonesia: Major Interprovincial Lifetime Migration Streams, 1980

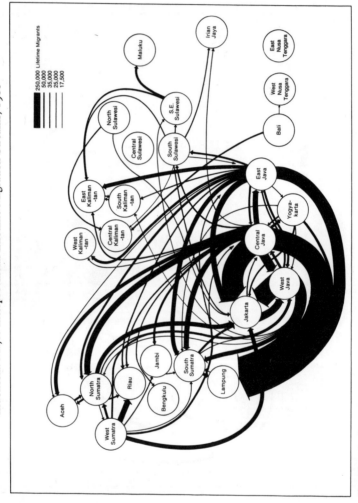

Source: 1980 Census.

TABLE 6.4

Indonesia: Proportion[a] of Provincial Populations Made up of In-migrants and Out-migrants, and Net Migration, 1971 and 1980

Province	In-migration (Percentage)		Out-migration (Percentage)		Net Migration (Percentage)	
	1971	1980	1971	1980	1971	1980
Aceh	4.5	5.9	5.9	4.0	−1.4	+1.9
North Sumatra	9.1	6.8	4.7	5.4	+4.4	+1.4
West Sumatra	9.5	7.0	11.9	14.6	−2.4	−7.6
Riau	14.5	16.4	8.8	6.7	+5.7	+9.7
Jambi	16.9	20.3	10.9	6.6	+6.0	+13.7
South Sumatra	11.1	13.4	10.1	9.1	+1.0	+4.3
Bengkulu	8.6	15.7	8.1	5.7	+0.5	+10.0
Lampung	36.8	38.2	4.2	2.3	+32.6	+35.9
Jakarta	41.1	40.1	11.0	12.1	+30.1	+28.0
West Java	3.2	4.1	6.3	5.7	−3.1	−1.6
Central Java	2.8	2.0	8.1	12.2	−5.3	−10.2
Yogyakarta	5.9	7.8	11.9	9.3	−6.0	−1.5
East Java	1.7	1.9	3.2	5.5	−1.5	−3.6
Bali	2.2	2.9	3.5	5.0	−1.3	−2.1
West Nusa Tenggara	2.1	2.2	1.1	1.8	+1.0	+0.4
East Nusa Tenggara	1.3	1.8	1.4	2.7	−0.1	−0.9
West Kalimantan	1.5	4.5	2.9	3.5	−1.4	+1.0
Central Kalimantan	8.3	15.0	3.9	3.5	+4.4	+11.5
South Kalimantan	5.8	7.4	6.6	9.4	−0.8	−2.0
East Kalimantan	6.1	23.5	8.3	5.0	−2.2	+18.5
North Sulawesi	7.1	6.2	4.2	6.1	+2.9	+0.1
Central Sulawesi	6.9	14.6	7.4	3.7	−0.5	+10.9
South Sulawesi	2.9	2.0	5.4	8.5	−2.5	−6.5
South-east Sulawesi	5.5	12.2	5.5	9.7	—	+2.5
Maluku	5.2	9.6	5.9	5.9	−0.7	+3.7
Irian Jaya	22.5[b]	8.6	3.2	3.1	—	+5.5
Indonesia[c]	6.2	7.4	6.1	6.9	—	—

Sources: Hugo, 1982c; 1980 Indonesian Census, unpublished data.
[a] In-migrants and Out-migrants expressed as percentage of total resident population in 1971 and 1980.
[b] Urban areas only.
[c] The difference between the in- and out-migration total is equivalent to the number of persons whose last residence was not stated or who were abroad.

Sundrum, 1976; Titus, 1978a and 1978b), and our focus here will be on the changes which occurred between 1971 and 1980. The pattern of lifetime migration at the 1971 Census is shown in Figure 6.2 and the contrast with the 1930 pattern is readily apparent in the large increase in the size and complexity of the streams. Although Java provinces remained the dominant origins of migrants, the major destinations were the metropolitan province of Jakarta and the major transmigration province of Lampung in southern Sumatra. The equivalent 1980 pattern of flows is shown in Figure 6.3. The differences from the 1971 pattern are more subtle than those between Figures 6.1 and 6.2, but they are significant. Of particular interest is the pattern of migration between Java and the other islands of the archipelago. Table 6.3 shows that between 1971 and 1980, the number of persons born in Java but living in the other islands at the time of the census more than doubled, as did the number of 'other island'-born persons living in Java. However, in contrast to the 1930–71 period, the increase in the number of Javans outside Java was substantially greater than the increase in other islanders in Java. It is also clear in Table 6.3 that there has been an acceleration of migration out of Java in the last decade, and an increase in the net lifetime outmovement.

Most of our analysis here will not deal with data on province of birth but with those relating to the province of previous residence of persons who had ever lived outside their present province of residence. Table 6.4 shows the levels of in, out and net migration for each province at the 1971 and 1980 Censuses, and it is clear that there are substantial regional variations. These are examined below.

Migration between Java and the Other Islands

The most striking pattern which emerges from a comparison of the 1971 and 1980 'most recent' migration data is the substantial shift in net migration of population from Java to the other islands which has occurred over the last decade. There was a 73 per cent increase in the net out-migration from Java over the 1971–80 period such that, by 1980, there were 3.57 million people who had previously lived in Java living elsewhere, representing some 6 per cent of the total population of the other islands or 4 per cent of the total Java population (Table 6.5). This pattern reflects in part a growing level of success in the government's transmigration pro-gramme in resettling significant numbers of Javans in agricultural colonies on the other islands, especially Sumatra.

TABLE 6.5

Migration into and out of Java, 1971 and 1980

Java	*1971*	*1980*	*Percentage Change, 1971–1980*
Total Out-migrants	2,062,206	3,572,560	+73
Total In-migrants	1,067,777	1,225,774	+15
Net Migration	−994,429	−2,346,786	+136

Source: Indonesian Censuses of 1971 and 1980.

The Transmigration Programme

The transmigration programme has a long history of overly ambitious and unachieved targets (Jones, 1979; Hardjono, 1977). However, during the 1970s, this changed and the target of the Third Five-Year Development Plan, which was considered by contemporary commentators to be overly optimistic (Hugo, 1982c: 144), has been achieved as Table 6.6 shows, though only by including among the transmigrants those who moved spontaneously to transmigration settlements. Hardjono (1986: 29) reports that of the 535,474 families moved during *Repelita III*, only 365,977 were named by the government transmigration agency as 'fully supported' (*umum*) transmigrants. The remaining 32 per cent were *swakarsa* transmigrants who moved with limited or no government assistance. The *umum* transmigrants also included some 22,284 local outer island families who were settled in transmigration settlements under government auspices, and 42,414 transmigrants who had to be transferred between settlement areas. Nevertheless, the performance in the Third Five-Year Development Plan represents a considerable achievement realized by dint of exponential increases in expenditure on the programme (Table 6.7); more concerted and professional attempts to overcome the logistic, administrative and socio-cultural difficulties of the programme; and more thorough preparation of the destination areas. Notwithstanding the numerical achievements of the programme, its overall impact on population growth in Java–Bali is limited, and there are increasing problems of availability of suitable land in the other islands, conflict with the established populations of those areas, and the issue of whether it is defensible to expend such a substantial proportion of the national development budget on a programme of this nature (Arndt, 1983).

The distribution of the provinces of settlement of persons who transmigrated during each of the five-year plans up to the time of writing is

TABLE 6.6

Transmigration in Indonesia's Five-Year Development Plans

Plan	Years	Target (Number of Families)	Achievement (Number of Families)
Repelita I	1969–74	40,000	45,169
Repelita II	1974–9	250,000	87,800
Repelita III	1979–84	500,000	535,474
Repelita IV	1984–9	750,000	272,520[a]

Sources: Hugo, 1982b; *Indonesia Times* XI, 21, 25 May 1984; Arndt, 1984: 30; Hardjono, 1986: 29; Directorate General of Transmigration, Jakarta.
[a] For first half of period only.

TABLE 6.7

Transmigration Development Budget Allocation and Number of
Families Settled, 1969/70–1983/4

Year	Total Development Budget Rupiah (in Billions)	Transmigration Allocation Rupiah (in Billions)	Transmigration Allocation As Percentage of Total Development Budget	Families Settled ('000)	Cost per Family Rupiah ('000)	Cost per Family US$[a]
1969/70	123	0.85	0.7	3.9	218	577
1970/1	161	1.04	0.6	4.4	236	624
1971/2	242	1.36	0.6	4.1	332	878
1972/3	314	2.32	0.7	11.3	205	522
1973/4	344	3.66	1.1	22.4	163	393
1974/5	616	6.65	1.1	13.3	500	1,204
1975/6	1,268	15.08	1.2	11.0	1,370	3,301
1976/7	1,920	27.30	1.4	11.8	2,314	5,576
1977/8	2,168	50.93	2.3	23.1	2,205	5,313
1978/9	2,455	104.50	4.3	28.8	3,628	7,344
1979/80	3,488	146.20	4.2	50.7	2,884	4,689
1980/1	5,028	272.40	5.4	79.9	3,409	5,543
1981/2	6,399	394.00	6.2	88.0	4,477	7,280
1982/3	8,605	526.70	6.1	67.4	7,815	11,663
1983/4	9,290	539.00	5.8	[125.0][b]	[4,312]	[6,436]

Source: Arndt, 1983: 66.
[a] Exchange rates used: 1969/70–71/2: US$1 = Rp 328
                      1972/3:   US$1 = Rp 393   (weighted average)
                      1973/4–77/8:   US$1 = Rp 415
                      1978/9:   US$1 = Rp 494   (weighted average)
                      1979/80–81/2:   US$1 = Rp 615
                      1982/3–83/4:   US$1 = Rp 670   (weighted average)
[b] Target; later revised to 150,000.
Note: Figures in brackets are targets.

depicted in Figure 6.4. This diagram shows clearly the acceleration in the tempo of transmigration during the last two *Repelita*, and it must be borne in mind that the data for *Repelita IV* only apply to the first half of the plan period. A number of shifts in the flows of settlers to particular provinces are in evidence in both Figure 6.4 and in Table 6.8 which shows the distribution of transmigrant destinations over a longer period. The main patterns can be summarized as follows:

1. Sumatra has always accounted for more than half of all transmigrants. However, there has been a tendency for this proportion to diminish over time. During the colonial period and the Soekarno era, nearly nine-tenths of transmigrants settled in Sumatra. However, this proportion has subsequently fallen to less than two-thirds. There was an increase in the population settled in Sumatra during *Repelita III* but, in the first few years of *Repelita IV*, this has been somewhat reduced. Indeed, the shortage of large land tracts suitable for transmigration in Sumatra has led to the announcement in 1985 that this island is expected to be closed to sponsored settlement by 1990. In the first part of *Repelita IV*, only 57 per cent of fully government-sponsored (*umum*) transmigrants settled in Sumatra, compared to 69 per cent of *swakarsa* transmigrants.

FIGURE 6.4

Distribution of Provinces of Settlement of Transmigrants in Indonesia's First Four
Five-Year Development Plans, 1969–1986*

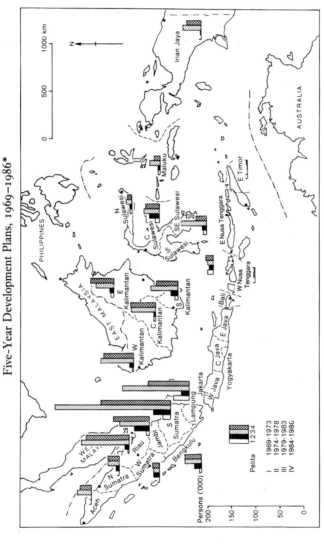

Source: Directorate General of Transmigration, Jakarta, Indonesia.

* The data for the fourth Five-Year Development Plan are from January 1984 until 12 May 1986 only, i.e. only half
of the five-year period. For the later years of the third and fourth plans, the figures include 'transmigran swakarsa'
(those who moved with little or no government assistance) and local transmigrants (Hardjono, 1986: 29–30, 41–4).

TABLE 6.8

Indonesia: Transmigration and Number of Persons Moved, by Island of Destination, 1905–1986

Year	Sumatra		Kalimantan		Sulawesi		Other		Total
	Number	Per Cent	Number	Per Cent	Number	Per Cent	Number	Per Cent	
Repelita I									
1940/1[a]	203,200	88.4	3,100	1.3	23,600	10.3	0	0.0	229,900
1951/9	197,500	89.2	12,100	5.5	5,300	2.4	1,400	0.6	221,300[b]
1960/9	116,100	76.5	23,000	15.2	10,400	6.9	2,300	1.5	151,800
1969	11,112	62.3	2,599	14.6	4,137	23.2	0	0.0	17,848
1970	8,350	41.8	2,539	12.7	8,863	44.3	233	1.2	19,985
1971	12,496	55.6	4,383	19.5	5,120	22.8	485	2.2	22,484
1972	31,757	65.1	7,027	14.4	9,538	19.5	473	1.0	48,795
1973	57,396	56.8	12,465	12.3	30,210	29.9	1,001	1.0	101,072
Total	637,911	78.9	67,213	8.3	97,168	12.0	5,892	0.7	808,184
Repelita II									
1974	29,729	65.0	5,502	12.0	9,898	21.6	595	1.3	45,724
1975	14,284	45.5	6,362	20.3	10,322	32.9	425	1.4	31,393
1976	22,652	44.7	9,869	19.5	18,152	35.8	0	0.0	50,673
1977	58,865	58.3	23,605	23.4	18,124	17.9	448	0.4	101,042
1978	73,621	65.7	18,800	16.8	17,261	15.4	2,290	2.0	111,972
Total	199,151	58.4	64,138	18.8	73,757	21.6	3,758	1.1	340,804

Repelita III									
1979	151,000	60.4	51,500	20.6	27,500	11.0	20,000	8.0	250,000
1980	210,500	56.1	82,600	22.0	62,000	16.5	20,000	5.3	375,100
1981	276,520	60.4	92,960	20.3	59,035	12.9	29,440	6.4	457,955
1982	295,595	61.6	123,250	25.7	31,685	6.6	29,440	6.1	479,970
1983	216,095	72.5	38,205	12.8	31,715	10.6	11,890	4.0	297,905
Total[c]	1,149,710	61.8	388,515	20.9	211,935	11.4	110,770	6.0	1,860,930
Repelita IV									
1984	153,695	54.1	78,320	27.6	31,430	11.1	20,820	7.3	284,265
1985	599,375	61.8	240,395	24.8	79,395	8.2	50,675	5.2	969,840
1986[d]	59,785	55.3	24,810	23.0	16,085	14.9	7,415	6.9	108,095
Total	812,855	59.7	343,525	25.2	126,910	9.3	78,910	5.8	1,362,200

Sources: Arndt, 1983: 53; Hardjono, 1977; Directorate General of Transmigration, unpublished data.

[a] The 1940/1 figures refer to the total number of migrants in colonization
settlements at that date. Hence they underestimate the total number of people
who participated in the transmigration programme during the colonial period.

[b] Including 5,032 'local transmigrants' settled in West Java.

[c] Includes a large number of *Swakarsa* transmigrants who moved without
assistance from the government (Hardjono, 1986: 42).

[d] Data to 12 May 1986.

2. Within Sumatra, the province Lampung has been the traditionally important focus of settlement, accounting for almost three-quarters of settlers during the colonial period. However, this dominance has been gradually diluted. More than a quarter of transmigrants settled in Lampung during *Repelita I*, and in subsequent plan periods the proportion fell to around one-tenth although, as Figure 6.4 shows, there was a large increase in numbers.

3. During the four five-year plans, there has been an increasingly wider diffusion of transmigration settlement into provinces other than Lampung, especially into neighbouring South Sumatra which took 23 per cent of the *Repelita III* settlers and 18 per cent of those in *Repelita IV*. Riau and Jambi now take a fifth of all settlers compared to 6 per cent in *Repelita I*, and Bengkulu, Aceh, North Sumatra and even West Sumatra have become significant recipients.

4. Sulawesi was the destination of more than 10 per cent of colonists from Java during the colonial period, and during the early five-year plans it accounted for around a quarter of all transmigrants settled in the outer islands. However, its relative significance has waned more rapidly than that of Sumatra, and it now accounts for around 10 per cent of settlers. Again it should be pointed out that, although its relative importance has decreased, there has been a substantial increase in the actual number of transmigrants settling in Sulawesi. Within Sulawesi, the focus of transmigration settlement has shifted from the southern to the south-eastern and central provinces.

5. Another major 'diffusion' trend in transmigrant settlement, evident in Figure 6.4 and Table 6.8, is the gradual eastward shifting of the focus of settlement. Kalimantan had less than 2 per cent of colonists before Independence, but subsequently each period has seen an increase in both the number of settlers and its share of all transmigrants. In *Repelita I* it received 14 per cent of settlers (29,716 persons); in *Repelita II*, 19 per cent (64,138 persons); *Repelita III*, 21 per cent (357,680 persons); and in the first half of *Repelita IV* had almost settled as many as it did in the previous entire five-year plan (343,455, 25 per cent of the total). Each of the four provinces has shared more or less equally in the expansion.

6. The eastern islands did not receive any transmigrants during the colonial period, and only around 2,000 during the Soekarno period. However, it is clear from Figure 6.4 that their significance has increased substantially. During *Repelita I*, 2,198 people were settled in Maluku and Irian Jaya (1 per cent of the total), but by *Repelita III* this had increased to 105,110 (6 per cent), and this pattern has been maintained in *Repelita IV*. The main focus is the province of Irian Jaya which is the largest and has the lowest population density of all Indonesia's provinces. Indeed, a great deal of controversy was created with the release of *Repelita IV* which gives a target of 167,739 transmigrant families for Irian Jaya. Such an intake would be equivalent to about 70 per cent of the total indigenous Melanesian population, and was interpreted in some quarters as an attempt to stifle the development of separatism in this peripheral province. However, lack of

suitable settlement areas, poor soils and logistic problems, as well as the political backlash in Irian Jaya and overseas, has meant that the transmigration target will not be approached and, in the first two and a half years, only 9,978 families were settled.

It is clear from Figure 6.4 that in *Repelita III* and *IV*, transmigration has been operating on a totally different scale than was previously the case. However, some problems are emerging which will almost certainly mean that the ambitious *Repelita IV* targets will not be met. Criticisms of the programme from outside the country have been summarized in a series of papers in the *Ecologist* (Colchester, 1986a, b, c; Otten, 1986; Secrett, 1986; Budiardjo, 1986). These criticisms have centred around the programme's role in alienating tribal groups in the outer islands from their traditional lands, sedentarizing of groups that are traditionally shifting cultivators, and the destruction of tropical rainforest. The difficulties confronting the programme from within Indonesia are several. The dramatic fall in oil prices in the mid-1980s saw the transmigration budget cut by 44 per cent in January 1986. Hence, to meet the original targets, greater reliance will have to be placed upon unassisted transmigration. A major difficulty that the programme faces is the lack of sufficient suitable land for settlement, and there have been several cases in recent years where unsuitable sites have been chosen (Hardjono, 1986) due to insufficient or inappropriate selection or preparation.

The census captured only part of the recent increase in the transmigration flow since, as Table 6.8 indicates, much of this occurred after 1980. The official transmigration flow over the five years prior to the census was 530,100 persons, substantially less than the 1,107,035 outer island residents who said they had been resident in Java in 1975. It is clear then that spontaneous migration to the outer islands is of considerable numerical significance in the redistribution of population by migration from Java to the other islands, although undoubtedly some of the spontaneous migrants were assisted and encouraged in their migration by relatives and friends who were earlier transmigrants. Table 6.6 shows that the new-found success in meeting transmigration targets encouraged the government to set an even more ambitious target for the Fourth Five-Year Development Plan.

Migration to Lampung

As in 1971, the interprovincial migration pattern in 1980 is dominated by the two provinces of Jakarta and Lampung which accounted for 39.3 per cent of all in-migrants in Indonesian provinces in 1971, and 41.2 per cent in 1980. It will be noted in Table 6.4 that Lampung had the largest percentage net migration gain of all provinces. Lampung has long been the major target of the transmigration programme, frequently accounting for more than a half of all transmigrants in the 1950s and 1960s. However, it has had to relinquish this role during the 1980s since its population to arable land area ratios are beginning to approach those of Java, to such an extent in fact that Lampung is included within the same national planning region as West Java. Moreover, at the 1980 Census, some three-quarters of the resident population of Lampung reported that the language they used at home was Javanese or Sundanese. Although government-sponsored transmigration from Java has been of major significance in Lampung's growth, spontaneous in-migrants have outnumbered those coming as part of the transmigration programme. Also, at the 1980 Census, some 253,821 residents of Lampung indicated that they were migrants who had lived in a different province in the outer islands (14 per cent of all in-migrants). The declining role of Lampung in transmigration is reflected in the decreasing significance of Sumatra as a destination of official transmigrants in Table 6.8. Indeed, although Sumatra continued to dominate the other islands in terms of the gains of migrants from Java between the 1971 and 1980 Censuses, this dominance was significantly lessened. Sumatra's proportion of Java-origin outer island migrants fell from 90 to 81 per cent, and Kalimantan's rose from 5 to 10 per cent.

Migration to and from Jakarta

While Jakarta's net migration gain when expressed as a percentage of the total resident population was less than that of Lampung (Table 6.4), the capital city still accounted for a quarter of all interprovincial in-migrants in Indonesia, although it had only 4.4 per cent of the total national population. Of its 1980 population of 6.51 million, some 2.59 million were migrants. Moreover, Jakarta also attracts a large number of non-permanent migrants whose presence in the city goes unrecorded at the census. Much of this movement is from the neighbouring province of West Java (Hugo, 1975; 1978), and the fact that circular migration and commuting has been substituted for more permanent migration to Jakarta from that province is reflected in Table 6.9, which shows that there were fewer migrants to Jakarta in the 1970s than in the 1960s, and that Central Java has become the main source of permanent migrants to the city. The scale of movement to Jakarta during the 1970s is also masked by the fact that the growth of the metropolitan area has spilled over its boundaries into the adjoining West Java *kabupaten* of Tanggerang, Bogor and Bekasi.

Another feature of Jakarta's migration pattern at the 1980 Census which differs from that of Lampung is the considerable significance of out-migration from the former, and its virtual insignificance in the latter. In fact, although Jakarta had the largest volume of interprovincial in-migration of all provinces, it also had the third largest rate of out-migration. This reflects the urban overspill pointed out earlier, the transfer of public and private sector officials by their employers from head office to provincial appointments, and a significant level of return migration of former migrants who have completed an extended stint of employment in the city. Some 58 per cent of all out-migrants from Jakarta went to West Java. Migration to Lampung is considerably more 'efficient' (United Nations, 1970: 49) than that to Jakarta in that the amount of migration required to produce a particular level of population redistribution is lower (Kartomo, 1983).

TABLE 6.9

Province of Origin of In-migrants with up to Ten Years'
Length of Residence in Jakarta, 1971 and 1980

Province of Last Residence	1961–1971		1971–1980	
	Number	Per Cent	Number	Per Cent
JAVA	786,650	76.9	859,245	75.5
West Java	382,500	37.4	317,810	28.0
Central Java	281,354	27.5	397,810	34.9
East Java	84,499	8.3	104,821	9.2
Yogyakarta	38,297	3.7	38,804	3.4
SUMATRA	153,668	15.0	194,167	17.0
North Sumatra	46,546	4.5	83,398	7.3
West Sumatra	42,134	4.1	54,862	4.8
South Sumatra	34,283	3.4	27,546	2.4
Other Sumatra	30,705	3.0	28,361	2.5
SULAWESI	34,460	3.4	36,716	3.2
South Sulawesi	20,632	2.0	23,154	2.0
Other Sulawesi	13,828	1.4	13,562	1.2
KALIMANTAN	23,627	2.3	25,568	2.2
West Kalimantan	14,438	1.4	16,525	1.4
Other Kalimantan	9,189	0.9	9,043	0.8
OTHER ISLANDS	25,041	2.4	24,965	2.2
Total	1,023,446	100.0	1,140,661	100.0

Source: Indonesian Censuses of 1971 and 1980.

At the 1971 Census, 78.7 per cent of Jakarta's migrants were born in Java while, in 1980, this had fallen slightly to 76.6 per cent. Nevertheless, it points to the numerical dominance of Sundanese and Javanese in the capital, despite a very heterogeneous ethnic profile in which all of Indonesia's major *sukubangsa* are represented by sizeable communities. Table 6.9 shows the large increases in the number of migrants from Central Java in recent years which counterbalanced the decreased significance of West Java as an origin of permanent migrants. Sumatra's share of Jakarta's in-migrants is increasing. North Sumatra passed West Sumatra as the major Sumatran province of origin during the 1970s, and the Minangkabau and various Batak communities are the largest non-Javan indigenous ethnic groups in the capital. South Sumatrans are the third largest other island group in Jakarta, and the mainly Bugis migrants from South Sulawesi are also of significance. The distribution of Jakarta's migrant origins in Table 6.9 help make it, according to Castles (1967: 153), 'the most, even the only Indonesian city ... the melting pot comes to mind—into the crucible, Sundanese, Javanese, Chinese and Batak: God is making the Indonesian'. The veracity of Castles' judgement is confirmed by 1980 census data on 'language used at home' which show that fully 92 per cent of Jakarta's inhabitants use the national language in the home. In no other province does this proportion exceed one third.

Migration to and from Other Outer Island Provinces

There is a substantial gap in rates of net migration between Lampung and Jakarta and the other provinces, but Table 6.4 shows that there were six other provinces with a net migration gain close to or more than 10 per cent of their 1980 resident population. These were all outer island 'frontier' provinces in which natural resource extraction and exploitation (especially of oil, minerals and timber) gathered pace during the 1970s, or in which there was expansion in transmigration settlements as the focus of the programme gradually moved away from Lampung. Especially striking is the pattern in East Kalimantan where nearly a quarter of the population were migrants from other provinces and the number of in-migrants reported at the census increased from 60,667 in 1971 to 285,549 in 1980. South Sulawesi and East Java provided over half of these in-migrants, who are attracted to the province under the Transmigration scheme, as well as by the job opportunities created by large-scale exploitation of timber and oil resources. In Central Kalimantan, a similar pattern applies although it is less developed than in East Kalimantan. Sumatra, Riau and Jambi have been important foci of resource exploitation for two decades, and Table 6.4 shows they recorded high rates of in-migration and net migration gains at both the 1971 and 1980 Censuses. Bengkulu has increased in significance as a destination of official transmigrants during the 1970s, as has Central Sulawesi, and this has resulted in substantial increases in their net migration gains. Other peripheral provinces which in the early 1970s had experienced only limited development but had potential for resource exploitation and for agricultural settlement by transmigrants, also increased their levels of in-migration and net migration by 1980. Hence in South Sumatra, South-east Sulawesi and Maluku, there were higher net migration gains in 1980 than 1971, while in Aceh and West Kalimantan, small net losses were transformed into net gains and, although complete data are not available for Irian Jaya in 1971, it is clear that in-migration to that province from Java has accelerated in the 1970s. The only outer island provinces to record reductions in their rates of net migration gains between 1971 and 1980 were peripheral areas which were little influenced by the overall expanded economic activity of the 1970s. These included the long-settled areas of North Sumatra and North Sulawesi, and the comparatively poor province of West Nusa Tenggara.

Although significant numbers of the in-migrants to resource-rich provinces are from Java, it is clear from Table 6.10 that a substantial part of the flow to these areas is from other islands. Indeed, in several of the more rapidly growing provinces such as Central Sulawesi, Central Kalimantan, East Kalimantan, Irian Jaya and Riau, more than half of the in-migrants are from provinces other than those in Java. It is also apparent that those other island provinces with large proportions of their in-migrants from Java

TABLE 6.10

Indonesia: Percentage of Most Recent In-migrants to Outer Island
Provinces from Java, 1980

Province	Percentage of In-migrants from Java	Province	Percentage of In-migrants from Java
Lampung	88.3	East Nusa Tenggara	39.0
West Kalimantan	78.5	West Nusa Tenggara	38.7
South Sumatra	74.9	South Sulawesi	37.6
South Kalimantan	72.7	Central Kalimantan	33.9
Bali	70.0	South-east Sulawesi	33.5
North Sumatra	65.4	West Sumatra	29.5
Bengkulu	59.4	Riau	29.2
Jambi	50.0	Irian Jaya	26.8
North Sulawesi	46.4	Maluku	26.0
East Kalimantan	44.6	Central Sulawesi	20.7
Aceh	39.7		

Source: Indonesian Census of 1980, Series S2 Publication.

are those in closest proximity—indeed, Lampung, South Sumatra, Bengkulu, West and South Kalimantan, and Bali form a northern arc around the island. As is shown below, the vast bulk of other island in-migrants to the growing resource-rich provinces are from a few regions which have long-established traditions of out-migration—North and West Sumatra, South Kalimantan and South Sulawesi.

There were four outer island provinces which reversed a pattern of net migration loss at the 1971 Census to a net gain in 1980. These included Aceh, which has been the site of several large-scale development projects such as a liquified natural gas project at Lhokseumawe, which has attracted substantial in-migration (Effendi, 1979). To some extent, the location of projects in Aceh has been a deliberate policy of the central government concerned by periodic outbreaks there of separatist activity. In West Kalimantan, the turn-about in net migration represented a return to more stable conditions after the upheavals of the 1960s (Ward and Ward, 1974). Contract coolie migration, from Java to plantations in North Sumatra, dominated interprovincial migration in Indonesia during colonial times (Hugo, 1980a). However, each post-Independence census has seen a gradual diminution of the number of in-migrants in North Sumatra and, over the five years preceding the 1980 Census, the number of out-migrants (177,289) was twice the number of in-migrants (85,889).

Migration to and from Urban Areas

It is not possible to determine the scale of rural to urban migration from Indonesian census data: firstly, because the majority of rural to urban moves are within provinces, and intraprovincial migrations are not detected by the census; secondly, because the origins of interprovincial migrants are not differentiated according to whether they were rural or urban. However, we can establish whether interprovincial migrants moved to urban or rural destinations. Table 6.11 shows the proportion of in-migrants in each province who settled in urban places. There is clearly a bias towards urban destinations, with slightly more than a half of interprovincial migrants living in urban places which contained only 22.4 per cent of the total population. Only in Lampung was the proportion of in-migrants settled in urban areas smaller than the proportion of the total population in such centres. Clearly, in that case, the predominance of transmigrants among the incoming migrants saw them move selectively to rural areas. Indeed, all of the

TABLE 6.11

Indonesia: Percentage of In-migrants to Provinces Settling in Urban Areas
Compared to Percentage of Total Population
Living in Urban Areas, 1980

Province	Percentage of In-migrants in Urban Areas	Percentage of Total Urban Population, 1980	Difference
Jakarta	96.0	93.7	+2.3
Irian Jaya	77.1	21.4	+55.7
Yogyakarta	66.7	22.1	+44.6
East Java	62.3	19.6	+42.7
Bali	57.5	14.7	+42.8
West Nusa Tenggara	57.2	14.1	+43.2
Central Java	55.9	18.7	+37.2
East Kalimantan	51.9	39.9	+12.0
West Java	51.7	21.0	+30.7
East Nusa Tenggara	51.4	7.5	+43.9
South Sulawesi	49.7	18.1	+31.6
Riau	49.2	27.2	+22.0
North Sumatra	36.6	25.5	+11.1
South Kalimantan	35.3	21.4	+13.9
West Kalimantan	34.6	16.8	+17.8
North Sulawesi	33.8	16.8	+17.0
South Sumatra	31.8	27.4	+4.4
Aceh	24.3	8.9	+15.4
Maluku	23.6	10.9	+12.7
Central Kalimantan	23.0	10.3	+12.7
West Sumatra	21.8	12.7	+9.1
Central Sulawesi	20.7	9.0	+11.7
South-east Sulawesi	20.2	9.3	+10.9
Bengkulu	17.0	9.4	+7.6
Jambi	15.8	12.7	+3.1
Lampung	10.4	12.5	−2.1
Total	50.3	22.4	+27.9

Source: Indonesian Census of 1980, Series S2 Publication.

important transmigration provinces stand out as having low proportions of in-migrants settling in urban areas and the smallest differentials between urbanized migrant and general populations. West Sumatra also tends to have a low differential, but the bulk of its in-migrants tend to be returned migrants who resettle in their villages of origin after a period of *merantau*.

Among the provinces with high proportions of their in-migrants in urban areas, only Jakarta had a low differential, and this of course is due to the province being almost totally urban. The other provinces, with more than half of their in-migrants in urban areas, tend to have wide differentials. Especially striking is Irian Jaya, where more than three-quarters of in-coming interprovincial migrants settle in urban areas. This points to the domination in Irian Jaya of both the administrative sector and the private sector (which provides goods and services) by outsiders. The former tends to be dominated by Javans while the distribution of goods and services is predominantly in the hands of in-migrants from South Sulawesi. Large differentials were also recorded in the inner Indonesian provinces of East, Central and West Java, Yogyakarta, Bali and West Nusa Tenggara, where there were gaps of more than 30 per cent between the proportion of in-migrants in urban centres and the percentage of the total population in those centres. This is of course a net migration loss region, and it appears that movement to such deficit regions is especially focused on their urban centres; it is significant that these provinces have six of Indonesia's ten largest urban centres.

Patterns of Migration between 1976 and 1980

The 1980 Indonesian Census included for the first time a question relating interprovincial migration to a finite time period—five years. This is of considerable significance because it allows us to examine recent migration trends. The major streams of five-year interprovincial migration are shown in Figure 6.5, and present a somewhat different picture to that of the lifetime and 'most recent' migration flows considered earlier. For example, Table 6.12 shows that there were five provinces which had different directions for their five-year net migration levels as compared with their total net migration figures quoted in Table 6.4. North Sumatra's long history as a net migration gain area has come to an end, with out-migrants over the last five years (half of whom went to either Jakarta or neighbouring Aceh) outnumbering in-migrants two to one. Similarly, in Java, both West Java and Yogyakarta had net gains of migrants during the late 1970s, although recording net losses over the longer period. In West Java, half of the five-year in-migrants came from Jakarta, reinforcing the earlier remarks about urban overspill from Jakarta, return migration from Jakarta, and the substitution of circulation for migration from West Java to Jakarta. A quarter of the in-migrants to West Java came from Central Java. The reversal in West Nusa Tenggara is due to the fact that much of the in-migration to that province, especially of Balinese, took place before the 1970s. On the other hand, in recent years, pressure of population on

FIGURE 6.5

Indonesia: Major Interprovincial Migration Streams, 1975–1980

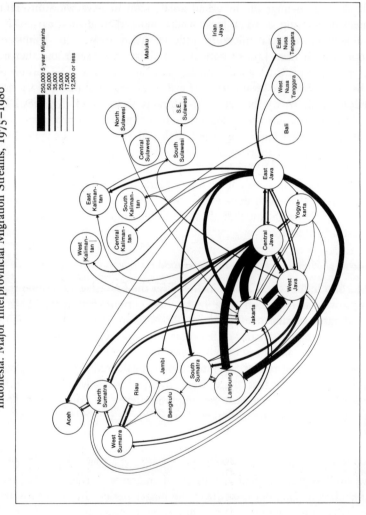

Source: Indonesian Census, 1980.

resources and frequent crop failures have led to significant out-migration. Indeed, West Nusa Tenggara has been included as an origin area in the transmigration programme.

The pattern of five-year in-migration is dominated by Jakarta and Lampung, which together received 35 per cent of the total number of in-migrants. Since they had 41 per cent of all 'most recent' in-migrants, it would appear that, in recent years, there has been a tendency for other provinces to encroach on Lampung and Jakarta's domination of the in-migration pattern. The increasing focusing of migration from Java on Kalimantan is apparent in a comparison of Figures 6.3 and 6.5, with especially large recent flows emanating from East Java. Nevertheless, Lampung and, to a lesser extent, South Sumatra remain the other island destinations of the largest numbers of Javan out-migrants. Table 6.12 shows that this migration to major other island destinations is generally efficient in demographic (or redistribution) terms, with in-migrants outnumbering out-migrants in ratios of 10 to 1 in Lampung, and 5 to 1 in

TABLE 6.12

Indonesia: Five-Year In and Out Interprovincial Migration for Provinces, 1975–1980

Province	In-migrants	Out-migrants	Net Migration	
			Number	Percentage of Resident Population
Aceh	49,857	28,248	+21,609	+0.97
North Sumatra	85,889	177,289	−91,400	−1.31
West Sumatra	91,038	153,239	−62,201	−2.16
Riau	94,209	53,757	+40,452	+2.24
Jambi	106,255	36,178	+70,077	+5.82
South Sumatra	217,242	132,011	+85,231	+2.21
Bengkulu	64,583	15,899	+48,684	+7.67
Lampung	497,246	45,594	+451,652	+11.78
Jakarta	753,121	382,326	+370,795	+6.73
West Java	508,613	468,441	+40,172	+0.17
Central Java	175,152	908,302	−733,150	−3.34
Yogyakarta	94,279	72,933	+21,346	+0.87
East Java	195,320	570,555	−375,235	−1.46
Bali	37,254	52,404	−15,150	−0.70
West Nusa Tenggara	22,659	38,987	−16,328	−0.72
East Nusa Tenggara	24,879	34,713	−9,834	−0.42
West Kalimantan	38,006	28,431	+9,575	+0.46
Central Kalimantan	47,939	15,989	+31,950	+4.04
South Kalimantan	59,835	46,061	+13,774	+0.78
East Kalimantan	109,313	20,334	+88,979	+8.70
North Sulawesi	44,475	38,259	+6,216	+0.34
Central Sulawesi	80,832	17,282	+63,550	+5.94
South Sulawesi	58,937	147,855	−88,918	−1.72
South-east Sulawesi	49,408	29,575	+19,833	+2.55
Maluku	45,909	26,995	+18,914	+1.62
Irian Jaya	31,686	16,191	+15,495	+1.68
Total	3,583,936	3,557,848		

Source: Indonesian Census of 1980.

East Kalimantan. In Jakarta, on the other hand, it is apparent from Figure 6.5 that there is a greater degree of circularity in its migration pattern, with the overall ratio being less than 2 to 1. Nevertheless, Jakarta is the focal point in the network of migration flows depicted in the diagram, and alone accounts for a fifth of all interprovincial in-migrants. This proportion is even greater if one takes into account the urban overspill into and circular migration from West Java, reflected in the fact that West Java had the second-largest number of five-year in-migrants of any province—some 14 per cent of the total.

In percentage terms, the levels of five-year net migration shown in Table 6.12 are generally low, with the exception of the major in-migration provinces. Lampung's continuing capacity to attract migrants is evident in its net migration gain over the 1975–80 period being equivalent to 11.8 per cent of its resident population, while Jambi, Bengkulu, East Kalimantan and Central Sulawesi, all had net gains of more than 5 per cent. Although 14 per cent of Jakarta's 1980 population were in-migrants arriving in the last 5 years, the net migration gain was equivalent to only 6.7 per cent because of the significant outflow from the capital.

Areas of Net Out-migration in Java and Bali

Turning to the major regions of origin of interprovincial *out-migrants*, Table 6.4 shows that the proportions comprised by out-migrants of the total population resident in those provinces increased significantly between 1971 and 1980. As with the rates of most recent in-migration, there is a tendency towards amplification of, rather than changes in direction of, trends observed in the 1971 census data. The pattern of out-migration is dominated by Central Java which was the province of origin of 30 per cent of all interprovincial out-migrants and 25 per cent of out-migrants in the 5 years prior to the census. As the Javanese heartland, Central Java has a long history of high pressure of population on available agricultural resources. There have been various responses to this pressure, of which out-migration is only one. *In-situ* adaptations have included intensification of agriculture (Geertz, 1963a; Boserup, 1963) via the configuration of social and economic arrangements known as agricultural involution; attempts to reduce fertility via abstinence, abortion, prolonged lactation and, more recently, modern forms of contraception (McNicoll and Singarimbun, 1983); as well as temporary mobility to obtain off-farm employment (Hugo, 1975; 1982b). Permanent and semi-permanent out-migration from the province has assumed much greater significance in recent years, especially to the two major destination areas of Jakarta and Lampung, where it accounts for 31 and 41 per cent of in-migrants respectively. It should be noted from Table 6.4 that there has been almost a doubling in the overall rate of net out-migration between the 1971 and 1980 Censuses for Central Java.

Table 6.13 shows the distribution of the provinces of origin of out-migrants from Java to the outer islands in 1971 and 1980. Central Java

TABLE 6.13

Indonesia, Provinces of Java: Number of In-migrants from and Out-migrants to the Outer Islands, 1971 and 1980

Province	1971			1980			Percentage Change in Net Migration, 1971–1980
	Out-migration	In-migration	Net Migration	Out-migration	In-migration	Net Migration	
Jakarta	144,321	393,850	+249,529	167,147	607,218	+440,071	+76.4
West Java	365,659	227,374	−138,285	527,205	197,564	−329,641	−138.4
Central Java	896,840	209,031	−687,809	1,593,170	157,042	−1,436,128	−108.8
Yogyakarta	126,993	37,014	−89,979	104,353	46,081	−58,272	+35.2
East Java	528,393	200,508	−327,885	1,180,685	217,869	−962,816	−193.6
Total	2,062,206	1,067,777	−994,429	3,572,560	1,225,774	−2,346,786	−136.0

Source: Indonesian Censuses of 1971 and 1980.

clearly is dominant at both censuses, although the rate of increase in net out-migration between the censuses was greater in both West and especially East Java. One of the most striking changes in the 1970s has been the increased out-migration from East Java to the outer islands. Much of this flow has been to Kalimantan (Figures 6.3 and 6.5), with which there are long-standing migration links; people from Madura have been prominent in this movement. The latter is reflected in the fact that 6 per cent of the population of West Kalimantan use Madurese language at home, as do 26 per cent of the population of Central Kalimantan. Yogyakarta was the only Javan province to record a decline in both out-migration and net migration loss to the outer islands. It is interesting to speculate on the reasons for this decline but it may be associated with a growing trend toward substituting temporary forms of mobility for permanent migration (Mantra, 1981).

In contrast to out-migration from Java, the counter-current of migrants from the other islands to Java showed only a comparatively small increase in volume, and some significant shifts in direction. In 1980, there were fewer outer island origin migrants in Central and East Java than in 1971, and there has been an increased focusing of this migration on Jakarta which had 36.8 per cent of the migrants in 1971 and 49.5 per cent in 1980. In dividing Indonesia into 'inner' and 'outer' components, Geertz (1963a) included Bali with Java and, on ecological and population pressure bases, this clearly is appropriate. Moreover, Bali has been included as a source area in the transmigration programme since 1963, when the eruption of Gunung Agung destroyed several villages and the displaced persons were offered participation in the programme. Since then, Balinese transmigration settlements have been among the most successful in the programme, especially those in Sulawesi (Davis, 1976).

Provinces of Net Out-migration in the Outer Islands

There are several Indonesian ethnic groups in the outer islands who have long established traditions of out-migration. The four remaining provinces with net out-migration in 1980—West Sumatra, East Nusa Tenggara, South Kalimantan, South Sulawesi—are the heartlands of the most important of these highly peripatetic groups. It is noticeable that, in each case, the rate of net migration loss has increased significantly between 1971 and 1980, indicating a strengthening of earlier trends. Best known among the highly mobile ethnic groups are the Minangkabau of West Sumatra (Naim, 1974) who have migrated to every city in Indonesia but are especially concentrated in other provinces of Sumatra and in the major cities of Java, particularly Jakarta. West Sumatra has the highest rates of outmovement of all Indonesia's provinces, with 18.6 per cent of all persons born in West Sumatra living outside the province in 1980, and a further 12 per cent who were living in the province reported as having previously lived in another province. The strong centrifugal forces, evident within the Minangkabau, are embodied in their concept of *merantau* which has been defined as 'leaving one's cultural territory voluntarily whether for a short or a long time, with the aim of earning a living or seeking further knowledge or experience, normally with the intention of returning home' (Naim, 1976: 150). Maude (1980) suggested, on the basis of field-work in several West Sumatran villages in the early 1970s, that the incidence of Minangkabau out-migrants settling permanently outside their heartland has increased. This finding would appear to have been borne out by census migration data which shows that the *net* out-migration rate for West Sumatra increased from 2.4 per cent in 1971 to 7.6 per cent in 1980.

The island of Sulawesi is the homeland of several of Indonesia's more mobile ethnic groups. In South Sulawesi, the three largest groups—the Bugis, Makassarese and Torajans—all have distinct patterns of mobility. The Bugis are the largest group, and have a seafaring tradition which has seen them for centuries 'roaming the archipelago in search of trade in accordance with the direction of the prevailing monsoon, returning to Sulawesi only for a few months of each year to refit and repair their *praus* (sailing boats)' (Lineton, 1975: 174). In the eighteenth century, they began establishing colonies in Kalimantan, South-east Sulawesi, Maluku, East Nusa Tenggara, and more recently in Irian Jaya, Jambi and even in Java (especially Jakarta). As in the case of West Sumatra, census data suggest that there has been a stepping up of this out-migration in the 1970s, since the net out-migration rate increased from 2.5 per cent in 1971 to 6.5 per cent in 1980.

In South Kalimantan, the Banjarese people have a long history of movement out of their home area. Rambe (1977: 22) has discussed the Banjarese concept of *madam* which traditionally has meant to leave one's natural area and cross the sea with the aim of increasing one's wealth. There are substantial Banjarese settlements in eastern Sumatra, Java (especially Surabaya), and in Malaysia and Singapore. The rate of net migration loss from South Kalimantan increased from 0.8 per cent in 1971 to 2 per cent in 1980. In East Nusa Tenggara too, there was an increase in net out-migration over the 1971–80 period from 0.1 to 0.9 per cent. There are a large number of ethnic groups within that province, with a few having high levels of mobility (Fox, 1977).

Intraprovincial Migration Patterns

The few sources of data that can be used to determine the rates at which people change their place of residence in Indonesia do not relate to recent years. One is the longitudinal follow-up surveys to the 1961 Census enumeration conducted in a sample of enumeration districts ('e.d.') within four strata (Jakarta–Surabaya–Bandung, 'other Java' urban places, Javan rural areas, and 'major outer island' urban centres) in 1962, 1964 and 1965. The numbers of persons who had moved into and out of these enumeration districts during the twelve months between surveys was noted. McNicoll (1968: 32) has questioned the utility of this information because it captures all moves which cross an 'e.d.' boundary, regardless of whether they occur within a city or village or outside it. However, because the enumeration districts are so small, the data provide insights into overall residential mobility which are not obtainable elsewhere.

In Table 6.14, the annual rates of in- and out-movement for each stratum are given. The denominator for calculation of these rates was the population at risk at the beginning of each of the migration periods. Migration turnover is more than twice as great in urban as in rural areas, and larger in non-metropolitan urban centres than in Jakarta, Bandung and Surabaya. This could be due either to 'step-migration' effects (Ravenstein, 1885: 198), or perhaps to the existence in these centres of a 'floating population' similar to that recognized in Western countries (for example, Hugo, 1974: 92), and made up of persons employed by government agencies or modern-sector private enterprises, who are transferred by their employer to a regional urban centre for a limited period. Evers (1972) recognizes both these trends in his study of migration to and from Padang in West Sumatra. Both factors would tend to inflate mobility rates in non-metropolitan urban centres. The turnover rates are somewhat lower in metropolitan centres, but do reflect the importance of return migration among migrants to cities (although movers to and from other parts of the city are also included in the rates).

Clearly, the stereotype of Indonesian immobility suggested by census interprovincial migration, examined earlier in this chapter, is a misleading one, especially since there is every indication that residential mobility has increased considerably since the data presented in Table 6.14 were collected. It is important, therefore, to realize that because Indonesian

TABLE 6.14

Indonesia: Mobility Rates, 1962, 1963 and 1964

Year		Percentage Migration in Last Twelve Months			
		Strata I Jakarta, Surabaya–Bandung	Strata II 'Other Java' Urban	Strata III Java–Rural	Strata IV Outer Islands
1962	Out-migration	13.3	16.2	6.4	14.9
	In-migration	16.6	14.7	5.0	11.9
	Turnover	29.9	30.9	11.4	26.8
	Net migration	+3.3	−1.5	−1.4	−3.0
1963	Out-migration	10.6	14.1	6.6	12.2
	In-migration	14.2	13.2	4.8	13.1
	Turnover	24.8	27.3	11.4	25.3
	Net migration	+3.6	−0.9	−1.8	+0.9
1964	Out-migration	11.5	15.4	6.3	12.6
	In-migration	11.8	16.4	5.4	13.2
	Turnover	23.3	31.8	11.7	25.8
	Net migration	+0.3	+1.0	−0.9	+0.6

Source: Hugo, 1975: 235.

census data refer only to migration between provinces, and most of those regions are large and relatively heterogeneous, a significant amount of migration occurs within their boundaries. Some indication of the scale of this undetected migration is given by data from the 1964 and 1967 *Susenas* sample surveys which included questions asking respondents their place of residence five years prior to the survey. Table 6.15 summarizes the result of these surveys and shows that, in Java, there were more than five migrants *within* provinces for each migrant *between* provinces, with rural destinations being especially dominant in intraprovincial moves. In the other islands, however, the ratio is less than half as large due partly to the smaller size of the provinces and also to the significance of 'Java–outer island' migrations, especially those associated with transmigration and job (particularly public sector) transfers. The significance of migration to transmigration settlements and natural resource exploitation sites is seen in the absence of an urban–rural differential in the ratio between inter- and intra-provincial migrations in the outer islands.

It is apparent that much intraprovincial mobility occurs over short distances, and involves little social and economic disruption or change. One village-based case study in West Java (Hugo, 1975; 1978), for example, shows the importance of marriage migration in this movement. However, a substantial amount of intraprovincial movement does occur over longer distances, and is of considerable significance for economic and social change. In this context, movement from rural to urban areas is of particular interest. For all Indonesian cities except Jakarta, the majority of in-migrants are drawn from the provinces in which those cities are located. A survey of Ujung Pandang, South Sulawesi (Jones and Supraptilah, 1975) found that 10.7 per cent of the population aged 10 and above had lived outside the city five years previously, but that 77 per cent of these migrants had lived elsewhere in South Sulawesi at that time. Similarly, Suharto *et al.* (1976: 33) found that of residents in Bandung, Semarang, Yogyakarta and Surabaya who had lived elsewhere five years previously, 71.2 per cent were intraprovincial migrants.

There have been a number of case studies of migration to and from

TABLE 6.15

Indonesia: Ratio of Intraprovincial Migrants[a] to Interprovincial Migrants, 1964–1965, and 1967

	Java, 1967[b]	*Other Islands, 1964–1965*[c]
Urban	3.43	2.35
Rural	8.11	2.21
Total	5.23	2.41

Source: Susenas, 1964–5; 1967.
[a] Migrants were persons who had moved in the five years previous to the survey.
[b] Excludes Jakarta Special Region.
[c] Excludes provinces of East Nusa Tenggara, Maluku, Irian Jaya and East Timor.

Indonesia's provincial cities (that is, excluding Jakarta), and their major findings can be summarized as follows:

1. Net migration is of little significance in most small cities and towns, the major exceptions being in those with special functions—for example, processing and service centres for rapidly expanding resource-extractive industry in the outer islands. However, there is evidence of substantial 'turnover' of migrants so that in- and out-migration rates are high.

2. The migration fields of such cities are much more restricted than those of the large metropolitan cities, as would be expected. The bulk of migrants are drawn from or to the province in which the city is located, so that such cities are usually much less heterogeneous than Jakarta and tend to be dominated by the culture of the dominant ethnolinguistic group in their hinterland. An important element in this group of migrants are students wishing to continue their education beyond the levels available in their home area. All intermediate cities have secondary schools of various types, and those that are provincial capitals have at least one university and other tertiary institutions. Some cities such as Bandung and Yogyakarta, which have a large number of tertiary institutions with good reputations, also attract students from outside the province.

3. The Chinese are a major subgroup in the population of all intermediate and small cities in Indonesia, and have an economic impact far out of proportion to their numbers. It is in some of these cities, such as Pontianak and Semarang, that the largest proportional concentration of Chinese occurs in Indonesia, and this tendency was assisted in some cases by regulations enacted in the 1950s and 1960s, forcing Chinese out of rural areas (Hugo, 1978).

4. There is usually a group of what could be called 'floating population', originating from outside the province, often Jakarta. These are persons on transfer within government departments, the army and large organizations. They have high rates of turnover and their representation and impact varies greatly from place to place.

5. The peripatetic ethnolinguistic groups referred to earlier are disproportionately concentrated in provincial cities since most are employed in some form of business enterprise. For example, Minangkabau people have established their restaurants and other small businesses in practically all major and intermediate cities in the nation. Unfortunately, little is known about the roles they play and their potential in accelerating widespread economic and social change in such cities.

6. It is clear also that much of the out-migration from intermediate and small cities is directed up the urban hierarchy. In West Java, one-third of out-migration from Bandung is to Jakarta, and two-thirds of out-migration from the next four largest centres (that is, Bogor, Cirebon, Tasikmalaya and Sukabumi) was to larger cities (Hugo, 1978). A large-scale study of migration to several cities in Indonesia (Suharso et al., 1976: 17), undertaken by the National Institute of Economic and Social Research (Leknas), indicated that a third of migrants to Jakarta came from cities, and overall around a quarter of migrants to all urban areas came from other urban

localities. Hence urban to urban migration is of considerable importance. Evers (1972: 19) notes the existence of step migration in his study of Padang, West Sumatra and speaks of this city having a 'gateway position'.

7. Another important element of out-migration from intermediate cities is the movement directed towards rural areas. The few studies available indicate that much of this is of people who have spent a considerable time in the city and returned to their village of origin; these include people who have completed their education and others who have retired from permanent occupations and who wish to spend their latter years in their *desa halaman* (village of origin).

8. The *Leknas* study (Suharso *et al.*, 1976: 56) found that the occupations of permanent migrants in intermediate cities were somewhat concentrated in what has been called the 'formal' sector, with what appear to be relatively high proportions of males in such categories as professionals (4.4 per cent), administrative and managerial staff (6.8 per cent), government servants and armed forces personnel (15.8 per cent), production workers (8.9 per cent), construction and other workers (16.1 per cent), and transportation workers, (7.9 per cent). However, the relationship between relative permanence of migration and participation in the wage and salary sector of the economy has not been fully investigated. Several authors have noted a correlation between distance of migration and occupational status (for example, Evers, 1972: 19).

Rural–Urban Migration and Urbanization

Although the fertility and mortality differentials between urban and rural areas which have been referred to in earlier chapters contribute to the differential growth of rural and urban areas in Indonesia, the major cause of the more rapid growth of the urban population outlined in Chapter 3 is net migration from rural to urban areas. As was indicated in Chapter 3, changing definitions of urban areas between the 1961, 1971 and 1980 censuses render comparative analysis very difficult. However, the World Bank (1984b) have estimated that, after making due allowance for these definitional changes, there was an increase of some 9.63 million in the urban population of Indonesia over the 1971–80 intercensal period to which net migration contributed approximately half. Their study identified four components of urban population growth:

1. natural increase of the existing urban population;
2. migration to urban areas from other provinces;
3. migration to urban areas within provinces, and the 'urbanization' of rural areas;
4. natural increase of migrants arriving within the period.

Table 6.16 presents the World Bank estimates of these components for the last two intercensal periods. While natural increase of the existing urban population contributed a similar absolute growth in the 1970s as in the 1960s, gains from net migration more than doubled. Hence, unlike the 1960s when natural increase was the dominant component of urban

TABLE 6.16

Indonesia: Components of Urbanization, 1961–1980

	1961–1971		1971–1980	
Population growth rate (percentage per annum)				
Urban	3.6		4.0	
Rural	1.8		1.7	
Total	2.1		2.3	
	Millions	*Per Cent*	*Millions*	*Per Cent*
Natural increase of existing urban population	4.59	68	4.63	48
Net migration	2.17	32	5.0	52
(From other provinces)	(n.a.)	(n.a.)	(1.6)	(17)
(From within the province)	(n.a.)	(n.a.)	(2.92)	(30)
(Natural increase of net migrants)	(n.a.)	(n.a.)	(0.42)	(5)
Total increase of urban population	6.76	100	9.63	100

Source: World Bank, 1984b: 12.
n.a. = Data not available.

population growth, net migration gains from rural areas (and the natural increase which they subsequently generated) provided 52 per cent of growth in the 1970s.

Not only have the 1970s seen a major upswing in rural to urban migration in Indonesia, but there has been a substantial change in the spatial distribution of the net migration gains recorded by the urban population. Between 1961 and 1971, Jakarta had a net migration gain of 903,000 persons (Speare, 1976b). This comprised some 41.6 per cent of all net migration gains in Indonesia's urban areas. However, in the 1970s, the capital city's dominance of the pattern of net migration was dramatically reduced with the net gain falling to 730,522 persons, or 16 per cent of the total for all urban areas (if the influence of natural increase to migrants is set aside). The documentation of net rural to urban migration gains has important implications for regional development. As was shown in Chapter 3, much of the growth in smaller and intermediate-sized cities during the 1970s was in cities outside Java, where the annual population growth rate (6.8 per cent) was more than double that of Java's urban population (3.0 per cent). It should also be noted in Table 6.16 that intraprovincial net rural to urban migration gains were nearly double the size of those derived from interprovincial migration. When it is considered that Jakarta accounts for 46 per cent of the net interprovincial gains, the dominance of intraprovincial net migration gains in the growth of provincial capitals and other intermediate cities can be readily appreciated.

Commuting and Circular Migration

A substantial and growing body of field evidence points not only to the widespread incidence, but also to the social and economic significance of circulation, seasonal migration, and commuting within Indonesia (Hugo, 1982b). The bulk of this mobility, however, goes unrecorded in large-scale demographic surveys and censuses, which routinely adopt the familiar criteria and questions designed to detect predominantly longer-distance, more-or-less permanent changes in usual place of residence. Although it is impossible to furnish accurate national provincial estimates of the extent of commuting and circular migration, the extent to which the temporal criteria adopted in the census exclude population movements of significance can be gauged from field-survey evidence. A study in fourteen West Java villages that attempted to detect all permanent and non-permanent moves associated with work and formal education found that only one-third of all such moves met the census migration–time criteria (Hugo, 1975; 1978). Moreover, in the survey villages, between 76 and 98 per cent of the movers who met the census time criteria moved within the province of West Java, and hence did not qualify as migrants as far as the census was concerned because they did not cross the boundary of a census migration-defining region.

The West Java study concentrated on population movement from villages to the major metropolitan centres of Jakarta and Bandung. Several distinct types of non-permanent mobility were identified as having major significance. These included commuting over distances of up to 50 kilometres to participate in full-time urban-based employment, or irregularly to engage in work supplementary to village-based jobs. More distinctive is circular migration, whereby movers do not change their usual place of residence in the village, but are absent at an urban destination for periods longer than a single day. Again, such movement can be associated with permanent full-time employment at the destination, but usually involves non-permanent work in the informal sector of the urban economy. Circular migrants usually maintain some village-based employment, and the frequency with which they migrate is determined by the distance involved and the costs of traversing it, their earnings at the destination, and the availability of work in the home village. Much, but by no means all, circular mobility is seasonal, occurring during the extended periods of limited job opportunity, between planting and harvesting rice during the wet season and during the dry season. There was also significant long-distance circular migration from West Java to the outer islands to work on plantations or oil or mineral development projects, often under contract and involving absences of up to two years. Rusli (1978) shows that these same types of non-permanent movement were of significance in migration between rural areas in West Java. In the fourteen study villages, three-quarters of the families were at least partly dependent on income sources outside the village, mostly in Jakarta and Bandung.

Similar findings to those for West Java have been reported in a large number of subsequent case studies. The fact that this phenomenon is not confined to a restricted geographical area is amply demonstrated in Figure 6.6, which shows the location of case studies which have demonstrated that non-permanent population movement is of importance. These studies indicate that much of this mobility is directed towards urban areas, so that urban population data greatly underestimate the number of persons working and spending significant periods in cities. Moreover, there is evidence that the scale and spatial extent of non-permanent population movements has increased substantially over the last decade (for example, see Collier *et al.*, 1982). Some indirect indications of the recent increase in the level and complexity of personal spatial mobility in Indonesia are given in Table 6.17 which shows the great increase in access to transport and mass communication during the 1970s. In particular, there has been an exponential increase in the number of motor vehicles such that the number per 1,000 population increased from around 3 in the early 1960s to 6.7 in 1970 and to 26.2 in 1980.

The World Bank (1984b: 20) has estimated that at least 25 per cent of rural households in Java have at least one family member working for part of the year in urban areas. This would imply that at least 3.75 million people are involved in this form of migration in Java, equivalent to 16.5 per cent of the measured 1980 urban population. The effect on the urban labour force is much greater, since virtually all migrants are either employed or looking for work—the figure of 3.75 million is equivalent to just over 50 per cent of the measured 1980 urban employment in Java. Of course, since

TABLE 6.17

Indonesia: Indicators of Mobility and Access to Mass
Communication Media, 1970 and 1980

Variable	Year	Numbers	Percentage
Radios	1980	12,311,307	40.75[a]
Televisions	1980	2,940,470	9.82[a]
Bicycles	1980	10,193,565	33.74[a]
Passenger cars	1980	639,464	4.32[b]
	1970	238,924	1.99[b]
Buses	1980	86,284	0.58[b]
	1970	23,541	0.20[b]
Trucks	1980	473,831	3.20[b]
	1970	102,265	0.85[b]
Motor cycles	1980	2,671,978	18.05[b]
	1970	440,005	3.66[b]
Total vehicles	1980	3,871,557	26.16[b]
	1970	804,735	6.71[b]
	1962	286,801	2.96[b]

Sources: 1980 Indonesian Census; Central Bureau of Statistics, Records on Motor Vehicle Statistics.
[a] Refers to percentage of households.
[b] Refers to number per 1,000 population.

FIGURE 6.6

Indonesia: Location of Field-Studies Demonstrating the Occurrence of
Significant Levels of Non-permanent Migration

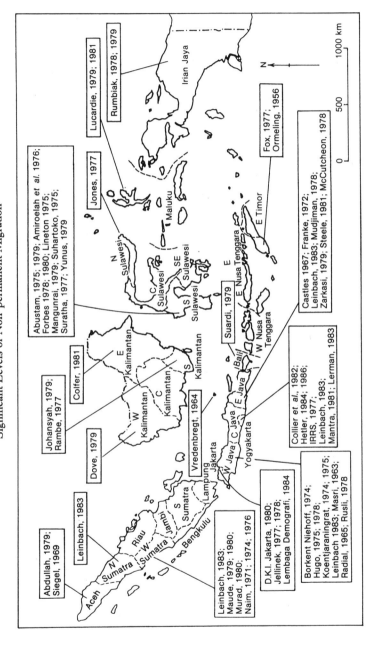

migrants are only working in the cities for part of the year, the average effect is less than this, but it is not unlikely that about one-sixth of the average urban work-force consists of temporary migrants not included in official employment figures. In sum, it is important to realize that many Indonesians work in one place but consume, spend, and invest their earnings in another place. Quite apart from the important implications of such patterns of mobility for social change, this significant phenomenon must be taken into account in planning the investment of scarce development resources. Yet, conventional census and large-scale surveys provide no detailed, nationally representative data concerning the scale, incidence, causes, and impact of this non-permanent mobility. Serious consideration must be given to including certain types of non-permanent mobility among the variables about which direct information is sought in national surveys and censuses in Indonesia.

Conclusion

In analysing contemporary patterns of migration and urbanization in Indonesia, the major difficulty which confronts the researcher is the lack of an accurate, detailed and up-to-date source of migration data. Interpretation of the data presented in this chapter requires an awareness of the limitations of those data. In particular, it should be noted that the migration questions included in the Indonesian census only detect a very selective subset of all movers, because of the time and space criteria employed in defining migration. Nevertheless, it is clear that population mobility in Indonesia has a level, scale and complexity which belies the conventional stereotyping of most Indonesians as being highly immobile, scarcely travelling beyond the 'well trodden social space' (Zelinsky, 1971) of their village and its immediate environs.

Indonesia's five-year development plans in recent years have had three overriding objectives:

1. a more even distribution of the benefits of development in order to achieve social justice for the entire population;
2. a reasonably high overall growth rate;
3. healthy and dynamic national stability.

Population redistribution obviously has a significant role in any national development strategy in that it has the potential to increase overall production via a more favourable matching of the population with the spatial distribution of productive resources. It is also argued by many that population movement has a potential role to play in the reduction of interregional and class inequality by allowing the poor and deprived to move from areas of little economic and social opportunity to localities with a greater range and number of opportunities. Whether or not the latter is occurring is a matter of considerable debate, with some arguing that existing patterns of migration are serving to reinforce existing inequalities by producing even greater spatial concentration of opportunities, and leaving deprived areas even more bereft of investment and opportunity. Forbes (1981), for example, argues that overriding structural factors in Indonesia's political economy greatly restrict the advantages to be gained by various population mobility responses to poverty, inequality, etc. Be this as it may, migration certainly does have the potential for ameliorating spatial inequality, as do the forms of mobility not captured by most censuses and surveys—that is, commuting and circular migration. Clearly, then, a thorough knowledge of existing patterns of mobility is crucial to the formulation of policies and the initiation of programmes designed to promote overall development while also improving the distribution of such benefits as accrue from that development. It is to a consideration of some of these issues that the next chapter turns.

1. For such a survey, see Hugo, 1982a.

7 Population Mobility: Causes and Effects

Introduction

POPULATION mobility is of significance not only because of its demographic role in shaping interregional differences in rates of population growth. Since it is almost always selective, population movement between regions will produce short- and long-term changes in the demographic, social and economic composition of the population at both the place of origin and place of destination. Moreover, there are complex two-way interrelationships between population movements and the processes of economic development and social change. Migration is both a response *to*, and has a formative influence *upon*, interregional and intergroup differences and inequalities within nations. This chapter explores some of these relationships in the Indonesian context. It examines the extent to which population movement is selective of particular groups, outlines some of the major explanations which have been put forward to explain this movement, discusses some of the social, demographic and economic impacts of that movement, and briefly introduces the policy interventions which have been initiated within Indonesia to reshape patterns of population mobility. Before proceeding to these issues, however, it is necessary to place the discussion of population movement in context by briefly considering some of the theoretical approaches to the study of migration and its interrelationships with economic and social development.

Population Mobility and Development: Some Theoretical Approaches

The relationships between regional development and internal migration are complex and multi-directional. Spatial differences in levels of regional development and in the distribution of the number and type of social and economic opportunities which this implies is clearly the major element causing population movement between regions. On the other hand, population mobility into and out of regions can have important implications for regional development. Our knowledge of the first set of interrelationships, in which internal migration is the dependent variable and spatial variation in levels of regional development the underlying cause, is greater than that of the consequences of migration for regional development.

Although a number of theoretical approaches have been adopted to the study of the linkages between internal migration and development, there are basically two broad perspectives which are summarized in Table 7.1. The 'neo-classical economics' equilibrium approach sees population movement as a 'natural' response to interregional differences in social and economic opportunities. People will move from areas where labour is

TABLE 7.1

Broad Theoretical Perspectives on the Relationship between
Internal Migration and Regional Development

	Neo-Classical Economic Equilibrium Perspective	Historical–Structuralist Perspective
1. Causes of internal migration	A response to spatial imbalances in the distribution of land, labour, capital and natural resources	Structural forces such as the emergence and uneven expansion of the capitalist mode of production, the nature of the development policies of government, unequal development within and between countries, the political economy of the country
2. Consequences of migration for regional development	A positive 'development-fostering' impact since the amelioration of spatial inequalities will result from redistribution of human capital from places of low to high productivity	A negative, inequality-exacerbating impact. The disproportionate concentration of talented people, resources, power and capital in particular areas (especially large cities) widens the gap between regions, contributes to major inefficiencies and social and economic problems at both origin and destination, and impedes national development
3. Policy implications	Allow market forces to operate. Interventions only to speed up or smooth flow of labour between regions by removing barriers to such movement	Intervention is favoured by most governments as part of attempt to reduce inequalities. Most fly in the face of existing population flows and are unlikely to succeed, unless underlying political economic forces are tackled

Source: Generalized from Wood, 1982; Lipton, 1980; Hugo, 1982a.

plentiful and capital is scarce to labour-deficit and capital-rich areas. Hence the level of regional development in the various regions of a country is seen as determining the magnitude and direction of migratory streams. More importantly, this approach implies that migration is beneficial to regional development. Migration is seen as an equilibrating mechanism because it 'corrects localized poverty and locally low labour productivity, because people with underprivileged living standards will vote with their feet against regional biases' (Lipton, 1980: 7). Thus, in areas of out-migration, regional development and welfare are enhanced by increased labour productivity, reduced pressure on wages and employment opportunities and, in some cases, the influx of remittances from those who have left. On the other hand, in areas of destination, the increased size of the labour force and market allows economies of scale to be achieved, and capital and resources to be more efficiently exploited. Thus, in the equilibrium approach, the gains experienced by the migrants themselves are matched by benefits which accrue to the entire society from the migration.

The opposing view is critical of the neo-classical perspective on causation of migration as placing too much emphasis on the free choice of individuals and neglecting the macro-structural forces which lie at the base of the regional disparities to which migrants respond. This perspective seeks explanation of migration in the deeper underlying forces which structure the unequal spatial distribution of opportunities between regions. As Wood (1982: 303) notes:

Explanations for the patterns of population movement draw their conceptual inspiration from numerous aspects of this general model of socio-economic and political development. Thus structural approaches to the study of internal and international migration have stressed a wide range of phenomena. These include: the emergence and expansion of the capitalist mode of production ... the style of development that is pursued ... a country's role in the international division of labour ... the unequal development between and within countries ... the articulation of capitalist and non-capitalist formations as it affects the distribution of the maintenance and reproduction costs of labour ... and the cost-lowering anticyclical functions of a migrant labour force.

From this perspective the consequences of migration for regional development are generally negative. Migration to the core regions is seen as increasing dependency and inequality by draining the periphery of its economic surplus and its most talented residents and, as a result, core-periphery disparities are increased.

Quite different policy implications for regional development flow from these two perspectives. The micro-economic 'equilibrium' theory would suggest that, in the long run at least, migration is working towards a reduction in spatial inequalities and hence is beneficial to regional development. Because market forces are working in positive developmental directions, interventions may be employed to enhance or encourage existing patterns of mobility via such initiatives as investment in transportation infrastructure, furnishing information about jobs and provision of housing (for example, barracks for single or unaccompanied men) at particular destinations, and generally removing any significant barriers to movement. The structuralist perspective, by contrast, implies the need for strategies to stop, divert or slow down existing mobility patterns. Logically, these strategies would not be solely migration policies and programmes, but would be part of an integrated regional development package which would be aimed at enhancing social and economic opportunities in peripheral regions.

Selectivity of Population Mobility in Indonesia

The structural impacts of migration, in both areas of origin and destination of migration streams, are determined by the characteristics of the migrants themselves and the scale on which the movement occurs. The most ubiquitous migration differential in both developed and less-developed contexts is that observed by Thomas a half century ago (1938: 11), that is, that 'there is an excess of adolescents and young adults among migrants'. While most Indonesian population mobility conforms to this pattern, there are variations between different types of movement which have significant implications for origin and destination populations.

One of the few sources of representative age-specific migration statistics, in which *local* areas rather than large heterogeneous provinces are the migration-defining regions, is the longitudinal follow-up survey associated with the 1961 Census. Although the source is dated, the patterns of age–sex selectivity are indicative of the contemporary situation. Figure 7.1 shows the probability that persons in five-year age cohorts at the 1961 Census would migrate into or out of sample areas within metropolitan, 'other urban' and rural strata of Java during the following year. The profiles show a consistent pattern of peak mobility occurring in the younger adult years and of female mobility peaking at a few years 'younger' than for males. The metropolitan profiles, incorporating the three largest Indonesian cities of Jakarta, Bandung and Surabaya, show higher rates of female mobility up to age 20 and over age 45, as was evident in the Jakarta interprovincial migration data. Amongst males, high mobility is less peaked than for females and spread more evenly throughout the 15 to 34 young working-age cohorts. In the 'other urban' strata, there is a greater rate of population turnover, especially in the highly mobile young adult cohorts. This is due to the combined impact of step-by-step movement to larger centres, transfer of government and other personnel, and the inmovement (and subsequent outmovement) of students to attend higher secondary and tertiary educational institutions. There are lower rates of mobility in rural areas, with males predominant in all ages except the peak marriage cohort for women (15 to 19). Marriage migration is an important phenomenon in all three strata, but it is of special importance in rural areas.

The census migration data, which include only longer distance, more or less permanent, interprovincial migration, show strong age selectivity.

FIGURE 7.1

Java: Age–Sex-specific Migration Probabilities of Metropolitan, 'Other Urban'
and Rural Population Migrating in 1961–1962

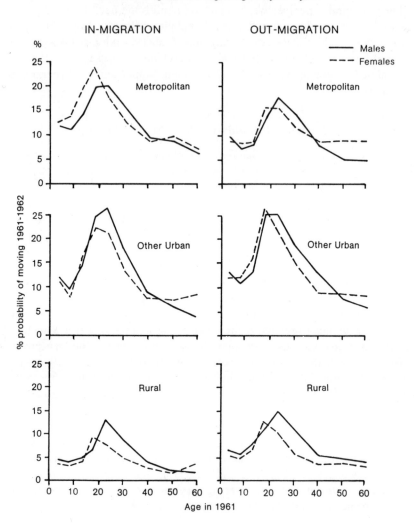

Source: Indonesia Demographic Survey, First Round.

Figure 7.2 shows the age–sex specific migration rates for the 1966–71
period expressed as probabilities that individuals in five-year age groups
would migrate across provincial boundaries during that period. Clearly, the
propensity for persons in the younger economically active cohorts to move
is substantially greater than for the rest of the population. This pattern is
mostly explained by persons in this phase of the life cycle entering the
work-force and higher education institutions, or marrying. Males predominate in this long-distance mobility, except in the 10 to 19 and 60-plus age
groups. In the teenage cohorts, the higher female mobility is probably

FIGURE 7.2

Indonesia: Age–Sex-specific Interprovincial Migration Probabilities, 1966–1971

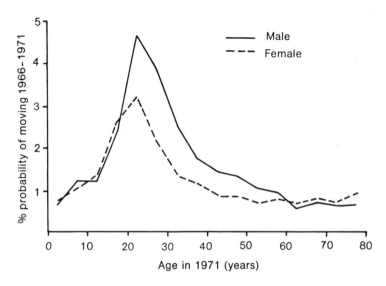

Source: Indonesian Census of 1971, Series C Tabulations.

associated with particular types of mobility such as that of house-servants to Jakarta, and of wives accompanying or joining older migrant husbands.

The 1980 census data show a similar pattern, and Figure 7.3 shows a marked over-representation of young adults among persons who moved in the five years preceding the census. The selectivity is more marked among migrants to urban areas than those moving to rural areas.

FIGURE 7.3

Indonesia: Age Distribution of Migrants (Persons who Moved in Five Years Preceding Census) and Non-migrants in Urban and Rural Areas, 1980

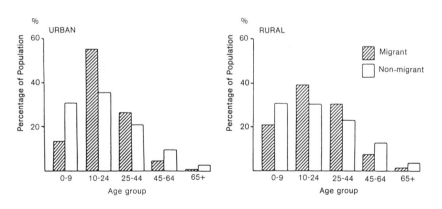

Source: Central Bureau of Statistics, 1984a: 45.

As was shown in the previous chapter, two of the major types of redistributive interprovincial migration in Indonesia are the movement to large cities and that directed from Java and Bali towards agricultural frontier regions in the outer islands. In both types of migration, field-surveys indicate the predominance of young adults. Davis (1976: 42), for example, found that half of migrants from Bali to transmigration settlements in Central Sulawesi were less than 30 years of age, while Suharso *et al.*'s (1976: 27) study of urban adult migrants indicated that nearly three-quarters were in this age category.

These patterns of selectivity are evident in the 1971 census data presented in Figure 7.4. Jakarta, the national capital, is almost entirely metropolitan and some 41.1 per cent of the total population in 1971 were migrants. Lampung in Sumatra has long been the focus of an agricultural resettlement programme, and 36.8 per cent of its population were migrants in 1971. In both areas, the non-migrant populations have a relatively

FIGURE 7.4

Indonesia, Selected Provinces: Age–Sex Structure of Migrant and Total Populations at the 1971 Census

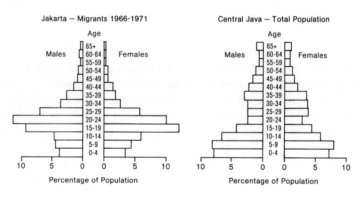

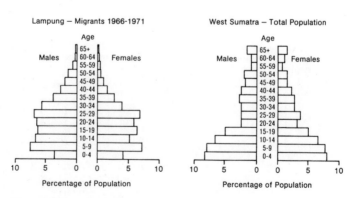

Source: Hugo, 1981a.

youthful age structure due mainly to the inclusion of children born to migrants. The age structure of migrants arriving between 1966 and 1971 shows some significant differences between Jakarta and Lampung, with the metropolitan centre having a more substantial representation of migrants in the young economically active age groups, whereas in Lampung there is a more substantial representation of dependent children. This reflects the greater importance of young families among migrants moving to the land settlement frontier area, and the dominance of married couples without children, and that of single or unaccompanied married persons in the flow to Metropolitan Jakarta. There are also some interesting sex differentials, with males outnumbering females among the total stock of migrants in the frontier area of Lampung (sex ratio of 1152) and in all economically active age cohorts. In Jakarta, females predominate overall (sex ratio of 956) and in the 5 to 19 and 45-plus age cohorts. This selectivity reflects the importance of migration of single and unaccompanied women to work as domestic servants and in other service occupations, as well as women accompanying their slightly older husbands, and the movement of widowed older women to join their children's households in Jakarta. The age structures of the provinces recording heavy net migration losses (for example, Central Java and West Sumatra where out-migrants amount to 8.1 and 11.9 per cent of their respective 1971 resident populations) show distinct notches in the economically active age cohorts. This is especially true of the young ages and of males.

Turning to non-permanent forms of mobility, there are no data sets available to indicate the patterns of age–sex selectivity over a widely representative area of Indonesia. However, the patterns observed in an intensive study of fourteen villages in West Java (Hugo, 1975; 1978) appear from later works to be indicative of patterns over much of the country (Hugo, 1982a). This study differentiated outmovers from the villages according to whether they were absent from their village of origin for more than or less than six months (designated 'migrants' and 'temporary migrants' respectively). In Figure 7.5, a comparison is made of age–sex distributions of the migrants and temporary migrants. The most striking feature is the almost complete lack of participation of females in temporary migration, a feature repeated in a study in Medan which found that 98 per cent of circular migrants were males (Leinbach and Suwarno, 1985: 40). Two comments should be made here, however. The first is that there are particular areas in Indonesia where large numbers of women engage in circular migration. This would appear to be the case in Central Java–Yogyakarta, for example. Mantra (1981: 103) found an almost equal number of males and females in his two survey villages in Yogyakarta. Hetler (1984, 1986) found in her study village in Central Java that 80 per cent of households had at least one member temporarily absent as a short-term circular migrant, and in 29 per cent of her sample households the female householder was absent, most of them selling *jamu* (traditional herbal tonics) in almost all major cities in Indonesia. Secondly, the dominance of males is much less marked in commuting than in circular

FIGURE 7.5

West Java: Age–Sex Structure of Temporary and Permanent Migrants from
Fourteen Survey Villages, 1973

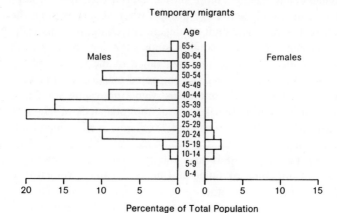

Temporary migrants

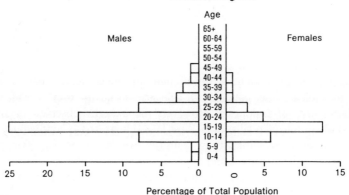

Permanent migrants

Source: Hugo, 1975.

migration. In the Medan study, 29 per cent of commuters were women,
while in a study of commuting to Jakarta from the three *kabupaten* adjoining
the city (DKI Jakarta, 1985) over 15 per cent of commuters contacted were
women.

The data from the West Java study (Figure 7.5) indicate that temporary
movers are overwhelmingly concentrated in the working ages. Thus there
was an Index of Dissimilarity of 46.5 between their age distribution and
that of resident males. If, however, attention is confined to only the
working-age population (15 to 54 years), the Index is much lower (13.7),
thereby indicating that there is little age selectivity within the work-force.
There was no strong tendency for a particular life cycle group within the
male work-force to be especially prone to circular migration and commuting. This contrasts sharply with persons migrating more or less permanently out of the villages. While working-age males are dominant among

permanent migrants, the presence of women and young children among migrants points to the significance of family migration. Despite this, the differences between the age distributions of male migrants and residents are even greater than for temporary migrants (Index of Dissimilarity = 50.6). Moreover, when only working ages are considered, the Index is only marginally reduced to 41.6. The permanent migration of work-force age groups is highly selective of those aged 15 to 19 years and, to a lesser extent, 20 to 24 years—the years that villagers are likely to enter the work-force or an institution of higher education. Moreover, less than a half of migrants were married, whereas more than three-quarters of temporary migrants were married.

The patterns of somewhat less age–sex selectivity among working-age adults with respect to circulation are also found in other studies (DKI Jakarta, 1985; Leinbach and Suwarno, 1985; Mantra, 1981). This points to a fundamental difference in selectivity between permanent and temporary out-migration in the Indonesian context. Whereas permanent migration typically involves unmarried persons or nuclear family units (although there may be some delay in spouses and children joining the initial movers), temporary migration usually involves a separation (albeit temporary) of the movers from the rest of their nuclear family and most of the wider family unit. This is important in terms of impact in both the area of origin and destination.

There are many other dimensions of selectivity in Indonesian population mobility. Among adults, recent movers are less likely to be married than non-movers. The presence of large proportions of recently born children among non-movers sometimes results in the percentage of *all* unmarried non-movers being greater than unmarried movers. However, when controlled for age, movers tend to include higher proportions who have never been married (Hugo, 1981b: 124–5) and Table 7.2 shows that this is especially the case among migrants to urban areas.

As has been explained elsewhere (Hugo, 1981b: 124), level of formal educational attainment is an important dimension differentiating migrants (especially those involved in the long-distance, more-or-less permanent migrations detected by the census) in Indonesia. In Indonesia, as in many developing countries, there is considerable inequality in the education system so that, in aggregate terms, levels of schooling are strongly correlated with socio-economic status, occupation and income. Analysis of interprovincial migration data from the 1971 Census indicated that average levels of educational attainment are higher among in-migrants than among non-migrants in all categories of urban centres and in rural areas (Hugo, 1981b: 125). Table 7.2 shows that this pattern is also evident in the 1980 census data.

Educational selectivity patterns are more complex, however, than Table 7.2 suggests. A field-survey of migrants in Jakarta (Suharso, 1976: 21–2) concluded that most migrants in Jakarta, especially those who have recently arrived, have little education, and lack capital and skills. As a result, they have difficulty getting a permanent job and are forced into marginal

TABLE 7.2

Indonesia: Selected Differentials between Interprovincial
Migrants, 1975–1980, and Others, 1980

Characteristic	Urban		Rural	
	Migrants	Non-migrants	Migrants	Non-migrants
Percentage not yet married	55.9	47.2	38.8	34.6
Percentage with secondary education and above	42.0	23.9	17.2	5.4
Percentage work-force in primary industry	2.3	11.3	60.2	66.8
Percentage work-force in secondary industry	20.8	21.2	13.1	11.4
Percentage work-force in tertiary industry	75.8	66.7	26.0	21.2

Source: Central Bureau of Statistics, 1984a.

occupations with little immediate hope for economic and social betterment. Hugo (1979: 201–2) has analysed education differentials in Jakarta using census data and observed that, while incoming migration streams from all other provinces showed a statistically significant higher level of formal educational attainment than non-migrants, there are considerable variations between the various migration streams into Jakarta according to the province of origin of the migrants. There is a general decrease in the proportion of migrants to Jakarta who have had no schooling (and a corresponding increase in the percentage of adults with higher education) with increasing distance of the province of origin from the capital. West Java was the only major donor province whose migrants included a higher proportion of men and women with no schooling as compared with the Jakarta-born. In fact, educational selectivity of migration from West Java to Jakarta tends somewhat towards a U-shaped distribution because a larger proportion of West Javan migrants had tertiary or senior secondary school experience, as compared with non-migrants. The West Java pattern suggests that caution should be exercised in the interpretation of educational differentials in census data since it is probable that much short-distance movement of the uneducated to cities, such as that from West Java to Jakarta, occurs *within* provincial boundaries (for example, from parts of Central Java to Semarang or of East Java to Surabaya) and hence does not appear in the census statistics.

The educational attainment data for lifetime migrants to Jakarta confirm the existence of a 'provincial brain-drain among the educated elite' (Smith and Carpenter, 1974: 825). Surveys of university graduates (Fischer, 1965; Smith and Carpenter, 1974) have shown that many tend not to seek employment in their native provinces (even though they may have completed their education there), but instead move to Jakarta. In 1971, 3.6 per cent of all lifetime migrants, in Jakarta, who were aged 10 years and over, reported attaining tertiary education levels compared with 0.2 per cent of the Indonesian population outside Jakarta, aged 10 years and over. Comparisons in other provinces show that the selectivity of the higher-educated groups increases with distance from Jakarta.

It is interesting to compare the educational attainment characteristics of migrants to Jakarta with those of lifetime migrants to Lampung, the other major region of heavy migration gain. Data presented by Mahmudi (1974: 12), and summarized in Table 7.3, show that the educational attainment of lifetime migrants in Jakarta is much higher than that of those in Lampung. This is primarily a function of major differences in the types of occupational opportunities available in agricultural Lampung and metropolitan Jakarta.

Little is known regarding the educational selectivity of circular migration and commuting. A study based in Botabek (DKI Jakarta, 1985: 32) found that commuting to Jakarta was extremely selective of the better educated groups, with a third of male commuters having completed post-secondary schooling. However, among the female circular migrants studied by Hetler (1984: 10), the results tended to 'discredit educational attainment as a significant explanatory variable in choices whether to migrate or stay in the village'. In the West Java study quoted earlier, educational attainment did not appear to be a major differential in circular migration, though it was for permanent migration. Moreover, its significance in circular migration tended to increase with increasing distance between origin and destination.

The issue as to whether population movement in Indonesia is selective of particular socio-economic groups has not been resolved. Table 7.4 presents some interesting results from the 1980 Census which indicate the proportions of migrant and non-migrant households in particular socio-economic categories in urban and rural areas. These data show that migrant households in urban areas are less likely to be headed by small-scale entrepreneurs than is the case for non-migrant urban households. On

TABLE 7.3

Jakarta and Lampung Provinces: Educational Attainment of
Lifetime Migrants by Percentage, 1971

Level of Educational Attainment	Jakarta		Lampung	
	Males	Females	Males	Females
	(Percentage)		(Percentage)	
No schooling	11.5	33.6	29.8	58.2
Did not finish primary school	20.7	22.0	42.6	29.2
Finished primary school	31.1	24.0	22.1	10.6
Lower secondary school	15.7	10.7	3.8	1.8
Upper secondary school	15.2	8.1	1.1	0.4
Tertiary	5.5	1.7	0.3	0.0

Source: Mahmudi, 1974: 12.

TABLE 7.4

Indonesia: Socio-economic Classification of Migrant and
Non-migrant Households, 1980

Classification of Household	Non-migrant		Migrant	
	Number	Percentage	Number	Percentage
URBAN				
Small-scale entrepreneur	8,747	35.2	1,332	28.5
Professional	4,584	18.5	1,312	28.1
Clerical and Sales	1,898	7.6	435	9.3
Unskilled labourer	5,016	20.2	921	19.7
Agriculture or no work	4,590	18.5	673	14.4
Total	24,835	100.0	4,673	100.0
RURAL				
Subsistence/Semi-subsistence Agriculture				
Own land less than 0.26 hectare	19,669	19.4	714	15.3
0.26–0.50 hectare	10,938	10.8	308	6.6
0.51–1.00 hectare	9,700	9.6	488	10.4
1.01–2.00 hectare	5,766	5.7	618	13.2
More than 2 hectare	3,006	3.0	275	5.9
Fishing	1,944	1.9	59	1.3
Other Agriculture				
Own land less than 0.26 hectare	3,381	3.3	125	2.7
More than 0.26 hectare	3,867	3.8	253	5.4
Landless agricultural labourer	9,738	9.6	273	5.8
Small-scale entrepreneur	18,129	17.9	643	13.7
Professional	4,671	4.6	331	7.1
Unskilled labourer	6,189	6.1	293	6.3
No work	4,296	4.2	297	6.4
Total	101,294	100.0	4,677	100.0

Source: Central Bureau of Statistics, 1984a: 59.

the other hand, the latter group are less likely to have heads employed in the formal or government sectors. This reflects the importance of employment transfers by the government and private sectors in interprovincial migration between cities. Much of the in-movement of informal-sector and poorer people tends to occur over shorter distances within provinces, and/or occurs on a temporary basis, and on both counts is missed in census migration data. Some interesting migration differentials for rural areas are apparent in Table 7.4. For example, it is clear that interprovincial migrant households engaged in agriculture tend on average to have larger holdings than non-migrant-headed households, and a smaller proportion are landless agricultural labourers.

Since a range of sample surveys (e.g. Suharso et al., 1976) indicate that economic motives are of prime significance in the decision to migrate in

Indonesia, it is important that attention be focused on employment-related differentials. It has been demonstrated, for example (Hugo, 1981b: 133), that for interprovincial migrants in Indonesia, economic activity rates are almost universally higher than for non-migrants. Regarding the types of activity engaged in by interprovincial migrants, Tables 7.2 and 7.4 provide some insights. The former indicates that, in urban areas, migrants are much more likely to be engaged in the tertiary sector of the economy than non-migrants, while in rural areas they are disproportionately concentrated in both the secondary and tertiary sectors. Overall census data indicate that recently-arrived interprovincial migrants have higher levels of unemployment than non-migrants, although this varies between areas; in Jakarta, for example, the migrant population tends to have lower levels of unemployment (Hugo, 1981b: 136). On average, unemployed migrants are older than unemployed non-migrants, and unemployment rates are higher among migrants with higher levels of educational attainment.

In most types of urban destination, the proportional representation of migrants in manufacturing activity is less than for non-migrants. Several elements could be involved here, including the fact that much of such activity is in the modern sector to which recently arrived migrants may have difficulty gaining access, while small-scale manufacturing in the so-called urban 'informal' sector may necessitate the operator having some capital which the recently arrived migrant may have difficulty in obtaining. There may also be a skill factor involved which would often militate against the recently arrived migrant who has on average less training than a non-migrant.

Perhaps the most striking migrant/non-migrant differentials are those relating to participation in service activities, which account for a much greater percentage of migrants than non-migrants in all destination categories. The participation rates, as well as the magnitude of the differentials, are greatest in the case of females and point again to the fact that most economically active female migrants to cities in Indonesia are employed—not in factories—but in domestic service, small-scale selling, and other service-type activities. The reasons for these differentials are probably associated in part with the greater ease of access to many service-type occupations than is the case for manufacturing (Hugo, 1978: Chapter 6). Such jobs include activities such as *becak* (pedicab) driving, small-scale selling activities, and service activities such as shoe repairing, hair-cutting etc.

The occupational structure of the employed recent migrants and non-migrants at the 1980 Census is presented in Figure 7.6. In urban areas, there is strong over-representation of recent interprovincial in-migrants in clerical, sales and service-type occupations, while in rural areas they are over-represented in all non-agricultural occupations.

There are some important contrasts in the labour force characteristics of permanent migrants and those of movers engaging in non-permanent migration. These have been discussed elsewhere (Hugo, 1978: 223–46), but can be summarized as follows:

1. The level of unemployment among temporary migrants is negligible with all such movers in the West Java study finding work within two weeks of arrival in Jakarta. On the other hand, among permanent migrants from the same survey villages, a third took longer than a fortnight to obtain their first job. This is because:

> ... permanent migrants in general come from more prosperous backgrounds than short-term movers so that their families are better able to support them through a period of unemployment ... (they) also generally had more formal education than temporary movers and hence had stronger aspirations for formal sector jobs. Thus even though entry into the informal sector may be easier, permanent migrants are more willing and able to forgo such opportunities and wait for a more desirable formal sector job (Hugo, 1978: 224).

2. Non-permanent migrants are much more likely to participate in the so-called informal sector of the economy. Table 7.5 presents results from the West Java survey on the type of employment of permanent and non-permanent migrants to urban areas, organized according to a typology developed by Hart (1973: 689). The typology distinguishes between income opportunities based on wage-earning in the formal sector, and the self-employment of the informal sector. Two-thirds of permanent migrants were in secure, permanent wage-paying jobs in the formal sector, compared to less than a fifth of temporary migrants. Some 15 per cent of the latter were day-labourers, and they should perhaps best be considered as part of the informal sector although they receive wages. This is because

FIGURE 7.6

Indonesia: Distribution of Employed Migrants (1975–1980) and Others (1980), by Occupational Categories, in Urban and Rural Areas

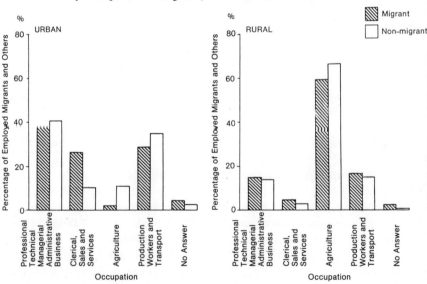

Source: Central Bureau of Statistics, 1984a: 54.

TABLE 7.5

West Java Survey Villages: Permanent and Temporary Migrants to
Urban Areas Classified According to their Participation in the Formal and
Informal Sectors of the Urban Economy, 1973

Field of Work	Temporary Migrants (Percentage)	Permanent Migrants (Percentage)
I. Formal Sector		
(a) Public sector, wages	6	22
(b) Private sector, wages (permanent)	13	42
(c) Private sector, wages (day labour)	15	1
II. Informal Sector		
(a) Primary and secondary activities	3	1
(b) Tertiary enterprises with large capital inputs	1	2
(c) Small-scale distribution	41	28
(d) Transport	16	1
(e) Other services (including illegitimate activities)	5	3
Sum of I(a), (b) and (c)	34	65
Sum of I(a) and (b)	19	64
Number of Respondents	746	399

Source: Hugo, 1978: 227.

TABLE 7.6

Percentage Distribution of Commuters and Circulators by Employment

Type of Employment	Commuters (N = 233) (Percentage)	Circulators (N = 67) (Percentage)
Government service	14.2	—
Becak driver	11.6	19.5
Driver	9.9	—
Trader	14.6	44.8
Tradesman	13.4	21.0
Factory worker	28.3	5.0
Domestic help	3.0	1.5
Salesperson	1.6	3.0
Unskilled worker	0.4	4.5
Total	100.0	100.0

Source: Generalized from Leinbach and Suwarno, 1985: 41.

they do not fit Hart's categorization of formal sector employment being 'secure, i.e. fixed, regular and relatively permanent'. Clearly, the bulk of temporary migrants are involved in informal-sector activities, especially the small-scale distribution of commodities. This participation is described elsewhere (Hugo, 1978: Chapter 6), but the flexibility in selecting which

TABLE 7.7

Indonesia: Proportions of Different Ethnic Groups Living outside their Heartland at the 1930 Census

Ethnic Group	1930 Census Total	Living outside Own Territory	
		Number	Percentage of Group Total
I. Higher Levels of Mobility			
Baweanese	45,711	16,406	35.9
Batak	919,462	140,776	15.3
Banjarese	944,235	134,393	14.2
Minangkabau	1,928,322	211,291	11.0
Buginese	1,543,035	162,701	10.5
Menadonese	281,599	26,652	9.5
Ambonese	232,573	21,166	9.1
Bengkulu	48,301	3,995	8.3
Mandarese	189,186	13,915	7.0
Total	6,132,424	730,663	(11.9)
II. Lower Levels of Mobility			
Malay	953,397	50,000	5.2
Palembanganese	770,917	37,707	4.9
Nias	202,400	7,461	3.7
Javanese	27,808,623)		
Sundanese	8,594,834)	1,364,896*	3.4
Madurese	4,305,862)		
Makassarese	642,720	12,574	2.0
Jambier	138,573	2,495	1.8
Acehnese	831,321	9,421	1.1
Timorese	1,628,864	14,126	0.9
Lampungese	181,710	1,550	0.9
Toradjan	557,590	1,000	0.2
Dayak	651,391	948	0.1
Total	49,039,338 (100.0)	1,504,478	(3.1)

Source: Generalized from Naim, 1979: 52.
* Includes Javanese migrants in Malay Peninsula (170,000), Surinam (approximately 33,000) and New Caledonia (approximately 11,000).

days and which hours of those days to work is highly compatible with circular migration.

3. The bulk of temporary migrants engaging in formal sector work are commuters or, less commonly, very short-term circular migrants. This was found in West Java but is also apparent in a Medan study, the results of which are summarized in Table 7.6.

Another dimension by which movement is differentiated is ethnicity. The analysis of this factor is complicated by the fact that an ethnicity question has not been included in post-Independence censuses. Nevertheless, Naim (1979: 52) has employed 1930 census data to categorize various ethnic groups according to their propensity to migrate. Apart from the dated statistics on which it is based, his typology is severely limited by the fact that it ignored movement *within* the heartlands of the various *sukubangsa* and is also based only upon *permanent* moves across *sukubangsa* boundaries. Nevertheless, the categorization—a generalized version of which is presented in Table 7.7—does have some validity in contemporary Indonesia. The table shows that groups like the Minangkabau, Bugis, Banjarese, Batak, Baweanese, Minahassans and Ambonese clearly have higher levels of mobility than the major Java-based groups. However, it must be stressed that much of the mobility of the latter groups occurs *within* their heartlands, so that Table 7.7 exaggerates the extent of overall mobility differentials.

Macro-determinants of Population Movement

The explanation of population mobility patterns in a country as huge and diverse as Indonesia is very complex, and all that can be attempted here is to summarize some of the major arguments that have been advanced. It is possible to divide the arguments into those which focus upon explaining broad patterns of movement, and those in which the level of analysis is the individual, family or small group.

Historical–Structuralist Arguments

These explanations are founded in the area of political economy. Basically, this argument sees population mobility as a response to broader structural changes occurring within society—in particular, those changes associated with the uneven penetration of capitalism which has created substantial sectoral, class and spatial inequalities which, in turn, have been a major determinant of the volume and direction of population movement. The seminal work here is that of Amin (1974) who has argued that labour migration in Africa can best be understood in terms of the effects of uneven capitalist expansion upon those societies. In Indonesia, elements of Amin's approach have been employed to explain population mobility. Hugo (1975: Chapter 2; 1981b) has shown that contemporary population mobility in Indonesia cannot be explained without reference to the formative influence that colonialism has had on the political, economic and social systems of the country. The argument is that the fundamentally exploitative colonial system, designed to control the local population and expedite the cost-efficient extraction of raw materials, shaped the pattern of mobility in very distinctive ways which have yet to be altered. The concentration of investment in areas of exploitative activity (plantations, mines, ports, garrisons, etc.), and its diversion from the subsistence and semi-subsistence agricultural areas where the bulk of the population lived; the extraction of surplus to the mother country stifling the development of local industrialization and a fully developed urban hierarchy; and the creation of a dependent economy, centralized political system, etc., all have had a formative and persistent influence on mobility patterns.

This perspective seeks explanation of migration in the deeper underlying forces which structure the unequal spatial distribution of opportunities between regions. Some of these issues have been taken up in the Indonesian context by Titus (1978a and b) who tested Amin's model against lifetime interprovincial migration patterns in Indonesia (i.e. a very highly selective subset of total mobility). Titus classified Indonesia's provinces on the basis of their centre–periphery characteristics (see Chapter 3) and their migration patterns were compared. On the basis of this, he concludes (Titus, 1978a: 201) that Amin's original model needed:

... some fundamental adaptations within the context of socio-economically more complex and intensively colonized regions. The densely populated centre regions on Java which are indeed the political-economic centres of gravity do not coincide with the focuses of production for the world market, and in some cases even experience net out-migration. On the other hand, strongly peripheral regions with 'boom' economies do attract migrants. Finally, there is a greater diversity of periphery types of regions in Indonesia.

It is readily apparent from the analysis of interprovincial migration in Chapter 6 that the provinces which have attracted most government investment, and are most integrated into the world economy via resource extraction, trade, etc., are the dominant net in-migration areas—that is those areas which have received disproportionately (in relation to their resident population) large shares of public and private investment, areas such as metropolitan Jakarta and the outer island provinces which are the centres of major raw material extraction enterprises or land settlement schemes. However, the major areas of net out-migration are those dominated by an economy based on food crop production, much of which does not get on to regional, let alone national or international markets. These areas have not attracted much investment, although they contain a majority of the national population. Titus has thus established the appropriateness of Amin's approach to explaining permanent interprovincial migration, but he and others are prevented from extending the promising analysis to patterns of movement more representative of the mobility of *most* Indonesians, by a complete lack of suitable representative data.

Forbes (1981) has shown that this theory can be useful in explaining circulation by examining the movement of a small group of petty commodity producers in Ujung Pandang, South Sulawesi. He argues that there is an important theoretical distinction between migration and circulation and concludes (Forbes 1981: 21) that circulation is:

... a result of the incomplete penetration of capital, and also helping to slow the rate of change in Indonesia by helping to preserve petty commodity and peasant subsistence production. If the wage labour sector should expand, or if agriculture should become increasingly capitalized, then circulation may well give way to another form of mobility.

The latter point concerning increased capitalization of agriculture has some immediacy in contemporary Indonesia because it is clear that many of Indonesia's, and especially Java's, rural areas have, in the last decade or so, experienced the impact of major modernizing and commercializing changes in agricultural technology and practice (White, 1979). The full impact of these changes on population mobility have not yet worked themselves out. However, at least at present, it would appear that the changing modes of organization in rural Java and the increased commercialization and capitalist penetration of agriculture during the period since around 1970 have led to a very rapid increase in non-permanent movements to urban areas (Hugo, 1978; 1985a). Collier *et al.* (1982: 87) reported that the most recent round of a longitudinal study of twenty-six Javan villages between 1968 and 1981 showed that 'Job opportunities for rural landless labourers and marginal farmers, and young educated villagers have expanded in off-farm activities outside the home village. Migration to large cities on an annual or monthly basis, and to nearby towns on a daily basis has become commonplace.'

Forbes' argument referred to above is that non-permanent migration is both the result and cause of inequalities in Indonesian society. It has a conservative role and is preventing the proletarianization of the population. This same argument was advanced more than half a century earlier by Ranneft (1916) in a neglected but significant paper entitled 'Movement of People in Java'. He recognized three phases in the development of Indonesia's economy, the last being a period of 'capitalistic production' which dated from around 1860. Capitalist penetration was shown not only to influence the level and direction of movement, but also whether the movement was permanent or temporary in nature. Ranneft points out the dominance of non-permanent forms of mobility during this phase in response to the distinctively different nature of capitalistic penetration (as compared with that in Europe), which was externally imposed upon the population of Java. He explicitly states that this circular migration delays the formation of a proletariat, and instead of the emergence of two social groups—an urban-based non-landowning proletariat and a small farming class—there is an undifferentiated group involving themselves in both the capitalistic and peasant modes of production.

Explanations Stressing 'Distribution of Economic Opportunities'

There can be no doubt that the main force impelling migration in Indonesian cities is the unequal distribution of the number or range of job and educational opportunities. Lipton (1980), in his review of migration literature, has suggested that the economic 'push' out of rural areas seems to operate with selective force upon two groups within rural communities, and this generalization has been shown to have applicability in Indonesia (Hugo, 1975). First, the children of well-to-do families, who seek further education and eventually high-paying, high status jobs in the civil service or the formal sector of the urban economy, have no chance to fulfil aspirations encouraged by an urban-biased education system within their home village. This group is forced out of the village and into the city by the lack of a suitable range of opportunities—rather than by other causes, since its members could survive quite comfortably in the village if they remained. The second group, however, comprises those who are forced out by a sheer lack of job opportunities. This type of movement was found to be of particular importance in a 1973 study of migrants in Indonesian cities (Suharso et al., 1976).

The Harris–Todaro migration model postulates that rural–urban migration in Third World contexts is impelled by the expectation of obtaining a higher wage in the city than is currently being received in the village. This certainly applies to the first major group of migrants discussed above. The second main group of migrants, however, tends to be motivated more by the lack, not of suitable opportunities in the village, but of any opportunities at all. It then becomes a choice not between a current and an expected job, but between no job at all in the village and a chance to obtain a job in the city. In rural Indonesia, particularly rural Java, many contemporary forces are fostering such a pattern of movement. Hugo (1975) has shown in West Java, for example, that an increase in rural population is exerting considerable pressure on the absorptive capacity of the rural sector. Traditionally, this increase has been absorbed by the process known as agricultural involution (Geertz, 1963) whereby, through a series of economic and social processes—especially the ability of wet-rice agriculture to respond to increased labour inputs with higher yields, and the complex 'shared poverty' social situation, population increase can be absorbed in situ. In Java, however, increasing commercialization of agriculture, often in conjunction with the introduction of new high-yielding varieties of rice and various types of mechanization, is acting not only to stop the creation of extra job opportunities but also in some cases to lead to a reduction in locally available opportunities. The increasing economic pressure on members of households in rural Java, who are landless or have a piece of land which is so small that it is not sufficient for the family's needs, has been documented in several studies (Temple, 1974; Hugo, 1975; 1978; White, 1979). The end result of such pressure is that many among these classes are being forced to migrate to the city.

As Lipton (1980) has argued, however, it is often not the very poorest who are forced out. This group in Java are living on the very knife-edge of existence, and have absolutely no surplus. They have no margin for experimentation and remain in the village where they eke out an existence—usually by maintaining a patron–client relationship with a landlord, which ensures that they have enough food to survive, although there is never any surplus above subsistence needs. The group who migrate tend to be those with at least a small surplus which gives them some margin for experimentation, although they are still very poor by any absolute or relative standards.

There have been very few attempts to develop structural economic models to explain migration patterns in Indonesia. One such study is that of Temple (1974) which modifies the Todaro model to take account of the specific situation in Java. In particular, he emphasizes the need to take account of the role of relatives and friends in helping migrants to get employment, as well as the fact that often the potential migrant is faced not by an earnings differential between origin and destination, but rather by a choice between *no* job and an extremely low-paying job in the informal sector.

The bulk of field studies in Indonesia, which have asked migrants why they have moved and examined the context of migration decision-making, have produced findings which confirm the dominance of the economic factors alluded to above. Such studies, of course, suffer from several limitations associated with *ex post facto* rationalization, recall difficulty, etc. While it is certainly true that some young people move to the city on a permanent or temporary basis to broaden their experience (*mencari pengalaman*), surveys have generally indicated that the 'bright lights' explanation of rural to urban population movement has little applicability in the Indonesian context. It is more often a subsidiary and secondary consideration to hard-headed economic considerations.

The two sets of explanations considered so far do not differ in explaining the pattern of migration as a function of inequalities in the distribution and availability of income-earning opportunities. But the historical–structuralist approach emphasizes the underlying causes of the inequalities in opportunities and suggests that they are the ultimate determinants of the migration pattern. Adherents of this approach criticize the neo-classical view as placing too much emphasis on the free choice of individuals, when it is the macro-structural forces underlying regional disparities to which migrants respond, which in fact give them little or no choice.

Socio-cultural Explanations

It has been suggested that migration has become institutionalized within some ethnic groups in Indonesia, such that it has become the norm for particular people within those groups to spend at least part of their life span outside their village of birth. This explanation has been particularly invoked in the case of the highly peripatetic Minangkabau people of West Sumatra. It is rare to visit an urban centre of significance within the nation which does not have a well-established Minangkabau community. Naim (1974) found that the matrilineal system within Minangkabau culture has made males marginal within the society and led to out-migration becoming the norm for young men such that, in many cases, social approbation befalls them if they do not conform to this pattern. Similarly, Abdullah (1971: 6) explains Minangkabau *merantau* in terms of an effect of the matrilineal kinship system:

The custom of going to the *rantau* can be regarded as an institutional outlet for the frustrations of unmarried young men who lack individual responsibility and rights in their own society. To a married man, going to the *rantau* means a temporary release from two families' conflicting expectations pressed upon him as a husband and a member of the maternal family.

Maude (1979) and Naim (1974: 347) both found that the majority of movers they interviewed gave economic reasons for moving, but they (together with Murad, 1980: 40) stress the significance of the fact that *merantau* has become institutionalized in the process of life of some Minangkabau people.

Similar socio-cultural influences have been observed to be a factor in causing high levels of population mobility among other ethnic groups, including the Acehnese (Siegel, 1969) and several Batak groups from the northern part of Sumatra (Bruner, 1972), the Rotinese people of East Nusa Tenggara (Fox, 1977: 56), the Banjarese of South Kalimantan (Rambe, 1977: 25), and the Bugis of South Sulawesi (Lineton, 1975: 190–1).

The institutionalization of a particular form of mobility, be it non-permanent or permanent, operates on the scale of the ethnic group but also on a regional and local scale. It is even common to find neighbouring villages with similar economic and social conditions, but with substantial circulation occurring in one while there is virtually no mobility to and from the village in the case of the other. It can be readily seen how such different traditions arise, as Lineton (1975: 190–1) shows: 'The fact that Bugis have been emigrating for centuries is in itself a factor predisposing other Bugis to leave their native land, since the Bugis colonies abroad are sources of information about more favourable economic opportunities elsewhere and often provide both financial and moral assistance to the would-be emigrant.'

The institutionalization of a pattern of mobility within a particular group often assumes an element of circularity in that mobility or outmovement from the village is encouraged, but return is equally encouraged. This certainly is the case in many of the examples quoted here, but tradition and institutionalization can also work toward encouraging stability and lack of mobility. In this latter respect, however, it is interesting to note the argument of Mantra (1981) that it is precisely because the Javanese have a very strong attachment to their natal village—which makes permanent displacement anathema to them, even in the face of bleak economic circumstances—that they have adopted commuting and other non-permanent forms of mobility with such alacrity when the newly developed road transportation systems have made such mobility possible.

Most population mobility is in response to a complex set of interacting forces, the separation of which is inevitably artificial. One cannot point to any group and say that their movement is exclusively a response to socio-cultural influences of one type or another since there are clearly many other forces at work. Some argue that the existence of a tradition of movement within a group is only a reflection of deeper underlying economic or political forces operating within the society. Yet, such arguments fail to explain interregional and intergroup variations in types and levels of mobility where economic and political considerations appear relatively homogeneous. Field-experience in Indonesia would suggest that socio-cultural elements are too frequently overlooked as an important element influencing population-movement patterns. Equally, however, that experience has pointed to the overwhelming dominance of economic considerations in shaping the volume, direction and nature of population mobility in Indonesia.

Transport Developments and Population Mobility

There can be little argument that, in Indonesia, there has been an increase in the level and complexity of personal spatial mobility during the 1970s and that this mobility can be of considerable significance in economic and social change. Table 6.17 presented data from the 1980 Census and other Central Bureau of Statistics sources regarding access to transport and mass communication sources which demonstrated that there has been an exponential increase in the number of motor vehicles and bicycles. Physical accessibility has been greatly improved such that even the most remote villages of Java now have public transport linkages to the major urban centres. Mass media penetrates a very large proportion of Indonesian households and is a much understudied and underestimated agent of social change. These changes have been instrumental in spreading information regarding the opportunities available at alternative destinations.

One of the most fundamental distinctions between non-permanent and permanent forms of population mobility is in the relative significance of the journey between the places of origin and destination. In most permanent and semi-permanent migrations, travel costs, time taken, and distance traversed between origin and destination generally constitute a minor element in a mover's overall calculations in deciding whether or not to migrate and where to migrate to. This is not the case with temporary forms of population mobility when the mover is repeatedly circulating between origin and destination. The journey itself clearly occupies a much more central position among the elements influencing movers and non-movers, and any transport costs constitute a constant and significant item in the mover's budget. It is clear that a prerequisite for long and medium-distance mass commuting and circular migration—of the types described earlier as occurring in Indonesia—is a widespread, cheap, efficient and fast transportation network.

It has been shown elsewhere that the last decade has seen a veritable revolution in the availability of public transport over most of rural Indonesia (Hugo, 1981d). Indeed, the term *revolusi colt* (literally minibus revolution) is used to describe these changes in Indonesia. The extension of roads and proliferation of vehicles of a multitude of types, especially minibuses and buses, into hitherto isolated rural areas has led to greatly increased personal spatial mobility for a wide spectrum of Indonesia's rural dwellers. The precise nature of the relationship between this striking (though, paradoxically, frequently overlooked) change in transport availability and migration has been little investigated. However, it is clear that the transport revolution has been a major *facilitating* factor in the upswing in circular migration and commuting which has been contemporaneous with it.

Micro-determinants of Population Mobility

Much of the difficulty in developing migration theory stems from our lack of success in establishing linkages between, on the one hand, the forces which operate at the individual level and influence whether or not households or individuals will move or stay and, if they move, the type and direction of that movement and, on the other hand, the structural forces which are the ultimate determinants of the overall pattern of movement. In this section, we will turn our attention to explanations of Indonesian population mobility which have focused on the movement of individuals, households and small groups.

Maximization of Family Income, and Risk Aversion or Minimization

The basic argument here is that population movement constitutes one strategy available to households or families to ensure their survival. Mobility is seen as part of the allocation of the family's labour resources to maximize their income and/or to ensure the continued existence of the family. In the past, most of this labour was deployed within the village (although sometimes in non-agricultural activities), or in nearby areas. Increased availability of transport has facilitated the extension of the area over which this job-search ranges. The reduction of local job opportunities, in the wake of the structural changes mentioned earlier, has forced families to extend the area over which their labour is deployed.

It has been suggested that this argument has some force in explaining why some individuals migrate on a temporary rather than a permanent basis. Thus it was found in West Java (Hugo, 1975; 1978), for example, that most households sending out non-permanent migrants could not earn sufficient incomes in either the city or the village to support themselves. However, circular migration or commuting provided a means whereby they could maximize their incomes by encouraging some members of the household to work in the village at times of peak labour-demand, such as planting or harvesting, but to seek work in the city or elsewhere between such times while other members of the household remained to cope with limited village-based labour demands. In addition, by leaving dependents at home in the village, the movers (mostly men) effectively reduce the costs of subsistence in the city or other destination—not only because the costs of accommodation, food and transport are usually greater at the destination (especially in the city), but also because the solitary mover can put up with cheaper and less comfortable conditions than his family would require, and thus cut personal costs to a bare minimum. Hence, by earning in the city but spending in the village, the mover maximizes the utility gained from consumption. This latter aspect (especially accommodation costs) is of basic importance to most commuters who tend to engage in village-based work to a much lesser extent than do circular migrants.

The 'spatial allocation of family labour resources' argument does appear to have considerable relevance in Java where the proportion of rural dwellers owning enough land to support themselves is small, the demands for labour in the village are highly seasonal, and where there is a complex involuted informal sector in the cities which allows relatively easy access to employment (albeit for very low income relative to time and effort invested) and which has the flexibility with respect to time commitments demanded by a non-permanent migration strategy. There can be no doubt that, in many regions, traditionally strong family and village ties and the preference for a rural-based way of life exert a strong attraction on the mover, but it is rare that non-permanent migration is an economically irrational response to this social pull of the home place. As Hugo (1978: 199) concludes: 'The fact that the movement strategy allows highly valued social benefits of village residence to be essentially maintained is thus often not the cause of villagers adopting a temporary as opposed to a permanent movement strategy but an incidental, though certainly appreciated, benefit of it.'

The explanation of circular migration outlined above often has a second element—namely, that movers consider urban employment to offer little security in old age or in times of difficulty, so that it is imperative to retain contacts with rural society. The West Java study, for example, found that a circulation strategy kept the mover's options in the village completely open, so that the risk of not being able to earn subsistence is reduced by spreading it between village and city income opportunities. Moreover, there are several village-based support systems which can be mobilized in times of economic or emotional need—namely, the nuclear and wider family, the tradition of *gotong royong* (mutual self-help) among the wider village community, and the traditionally significant *bapak/anak buah* (patron/client) relations. In many cases, such support is not available in the city, so that if a mover maintains a stake in his village he does not cut himself off from what is often the only available last-resort support in times of dire need. These risk aversion arguments have considerable applicability in Java.

Behavioural Explanations

Several of the studies concerned with migrant motivation in Indonesia have adopted an individual behaviourist perspective. This emphasizes the decision-making processes of the mover or the mover's household. This perspective is certainly productive of insights into how and why migration occurs at the individual and community levels. However, there has been a tendency to transfer uncritically the essentially Western-derived models of individual decision-making to the Indonesian context. It is assumed that the individual will migrate to a particular place if the total benefits (social, economic, emotional, etc.) which accrue to the individual from that move outweigh the costs. In Indonesia, as in much of the Third World, it has been shown that this model of the decision-making process is inappropriate

(Hugo, 1981d). The *raison d'etre* of the move is often the well-being of the family; an individual migrant may have had little or no participation in the decision-making process which was dominated by the head of the family.

One conceptual framework, which attempted to combine some of the ideas of the macro approaches outlined earlier with the decision-making processes of individuals and households, evolved out of the West Java study (Hugo, 1981c). The framework is shown diagrammatically in Figure 7.7, and is based on the simple and now very familiar theory that migration results after an individual or group decides that the perceived total benefits derived from a move outweigh its anticipated costs and total perceived benefits forgone at alternative locations. The present place of residence and potential destinations are seen as having particular perceived sets of attractive, unattractive, and neutral factors. In most Third World situations, however, the environment of social and spatial inequalities in which the decision is made greatly restricts the range of opportunities that are at all accessible to most individuals. Such inequalities have been shown to restrict greatly the choices available to potential movers in Indonesia. Papanek's (1975) study of the poor in Jakarta has shown that poor rural migrants, with little education and lacking kinship connections with power-ful established individuals in the city, have virtually no chance of obtaining permanent work with regular hours in employment and with moderate to high regular wages. The considerable constraints that unequal develop-ment imposes upon the opportunities available to individuals or groups contemplating migration greatly restrict the choices open to them.

Migration in this framework is seen as a reaction to stress exerted by the individual's or household's own physical, economic, social, and cultural environment. Potential movers will feel some stress regarding present location when they receive information about an alternative location that indicates that they may be better off in some respects—in social relations, employment, housing, access to schooling, and so forth—if they move to that place. In the West Java study, the main stresses felt in the villages tended to be related to the insufficiency of local employment opportunities.

The conceptual framework, however, draws attention to three inter-related sets of intervening variables (in addition to the structural inequalities discussed above) that influence the villager's perception of opportunities elsewhere, his evaluation of those opportunities, and the response to this evaluation. These intervening variables are:

1. First, the nature, amount, and source of information that will affect the form the stress takes and the individual's or group's evaluation of it. In West Java most of this information is of an interpersonal nature and is part of the series of important links between rural origin and urban destination that are maintained on an essentially person-to-person basis.

2. Second, the individual's or household's demographic, educational, and socio-economic characteristics, personal background, and psychosocial make-up will affect the way in which they evaluate information and will predispose them towards particular options with respect to moving or staying.

FIGURE 7.7

Schematic Representation of a Potential Mover's Decision to Stay in
or Move from a West Javan Village

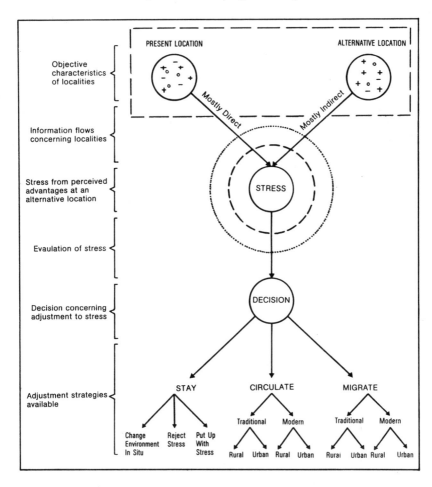

Source: Hugo, 1981c: 192.

Notes: + Favourable aspect of a particular location.
      − Unfavourable aspect of a particular location.
      o Neutral factor of a particular location.
      ___ Individual characteristics influencing the decision to move or stay.
      ...... Community norms influencing the decision to move or stay.
      Environment of social and spatial inequality which greatly restricts the choices
      open to the potential mover at both his place of origin and potential destinations.

3. Third, the whole social structure of the community of origin—its
distinctive set of standards, values, beliefs, and customary practices—will
usually colour the evaluation of information about alternative destinations
and influence the subsequent decision to move or stay. This is what
Germani (1965) refers to as 'the normative level of analysis' in studying the

causes of migration. He stresses that so-called objective influences do not operate in a vacuum but in a normative context, so that people will evaluate and perceive the attractions or repulsions of particular locations against the framework of institutionalized roles, expectations, and behaviour patterns that in a particular society regulate migration. Such norms can operate to facilitate or retard mobility.

Individual characteristics and community norms are depicted in Figure 7.7 as 'filters' through which information about the potential mover's present location and potential destinations passes and is judged, so that it affects both the nature and level of stress experienced by the potential mover. The diagram also indicates that these 'filters' will influence the evaluation of the stress and the eventual decision that is taken to relieve that stress. Normative practice may operate against mobility as Du Toit (1975: 66–7) suggests: 'When a pattern is established in a particular society it is much easier to follow a choice which receives normative sanction than to be deviant by running off to the city.' It may also operate, however, to make outmovement a normal and accepted response to particular situations (Niddrie, 1954; Hugo, 1978).

The outcome of the evaluation process depicted in Figure 7.7 is a decision that involves a person in staying or moving. Experience in West Java suggests that there is a group of people who may never have considered the possibility of moving, so that no alternatives to a staying strategy have entered their calculations. A staying strategy may also arise from a perception that the evaluation process has resulted in an excess of positive over negative factors, thereby favouring the place of origin so that the stress is rejected. Alternatively, inertia could cause some groups to recognize the existence and significance of the stress, but simply to endure it at the place of origin. For example, in Java, there is evidence that in some areas where pressure of population on resources has reached very high levels, people are putting up with it by eating less and consequently getting smaller in physical stature. A third set of stayers includes those who recognize that their evaluation has resulted in a net negative balance against their present location, but they initiate a series of *in-situ* adjustments to redress this imbalance. The literature on rural Java would suggest that this latter strategy has traditionally been the dominant one (Geertz, 1963). One of the principal mechanisms that made this strategy possible was the process called 'agricultural involution', whereby local population increases were fed and employed by increases in local agricultural productivity via labour intensification in wet-rice cultivation and a complex set of social mechanisms best summarized as 'shared poverty'. Other strategies include reduced fertility levels through traditional methods of birth control, prolonged lactation, and abstinence (Singarimbun and Manning, 1974).

Clearly, migration will result from a strongly negatively weighted evaluation of present location *vis-à-vis* an alternative location. It is often overlooked, however, that there is a third possible response to this evaluation of stress, which is in essence a compromise and involves circulating between place of origin and potential destination.

Other Micro-factors

In our discussion of the conceptual framework developed in the West Java study, several micro-level influences upon population movement in Indonesia were mentioned. We should especially stress that *chain migration* plays a very important part in population mobility in Indonesia. The bulk of movers are not pioneer migrants setting off tentatively into the great unknown. Many move along paths already blazed by other former residents of their village or family members. These prior migrants not only feed information back to the village, but usually assist new migrants in finding their way in the city, in obtaining work and housing. Hence, for many migrants, there is little uncertainty involved in deciding to spend a period of time in the city.

Forced Migrations

In Indonesia as elsewhere in South-East Asia, population movements impelled by natural disasters: religious, ethnic and political conflicts, persecutions, tyranny and war have occurred on a significant scale but have been neglected in the literature. The incidence and importance of such movements in Indonesia is discussed elsewhere (Hugo, 1983c; 1986) and only a few points will be raised here. Olson (1979: 130) identifies the following five types of external compulsions that alone or in concert create refugee movements:

1. Physical dangers (for example, floods, volcanic eruptions, etc.)
2. Economic insufficiency (for example, drought, famine)
3. Religious persecution
4. Ethnic persecution
5. Ideological persecution

There have been many examples of people being forced to migrate because of the fear or onset of a natural or physical disaster in Indonesia in recent years. For example, there are more than seventy active volcanoes which have caused calamities at an average of once every three years, resulting in 140,000 recorded deaths (Awanohara, 1982: 42). The number of people displaced by volcanic eruptions, however, has been many times greater. The 1963 eruption of Mount Agung in Bali displaced 85,000 people, while that of Mount Galunggung in West Java during 1982 has forced some 30,000 people to migrate to Indonesia's outer islands and placed some 300,000 more residents at risk of evacuation (Awanohara, 1982: 42–3). Lucardie's (1979) study of the people of Makian in Maluku province has documented the repeated abandonment of settlements after volcanic eruptions and for fear of new eruptions over the last three hundred years. His study focuses especially upon a government scheme to gradually evacuate the entire 16,000 residents of the island because vulcanologists have predicted the eventual eruption of Makian's volcano, which would lead to a disaster comparable to that of the evisceration of Krakatao in 1883.

With respect to refugee movements associated with what Olson (1979)

TABLE 7.8

Types of Conflict Initiating Refugee Movements, with Examples from South-East Asia (Mainly Indonesia)

Type of Conflict	Examples from South-East Asia (Mainly Indonesia)
1. Independence Struggles	Evacuation of virtually the entire Indonesian population (approximately half a million people) from the city of Bandung 1946–8 (Hugo, 1975: 254). In West Sumatra, a large-scale evacuation of people from Dutch-occupied coastal areas to the republican territories of the interior (Naim, 1973: 135).
2. Ethnic conflicts with autonomy/separatist dimensions	Separatist movements in Irian Jaya have at times initiated refugee flows, some of them into neighbouring New Guinea (Roosman, 1980).
3. Internal ethnic conflict not related to separatist/autonomy struggles	In 1967, some 60,000 ethnic Chinese were forced out of the interior areas of West Kalimantan due to long-standing hostility against the Chinese (Ward and Ward, 1974: 28). Similarly, displacement of Chinese occurred in West Java in the 1950s (Hugo, 1975: 245).
4. Class conflict	In the late 1970s, the Khmer Rouge drive to mobilize and reduce the urban population of Kampuchea resulted in deportation of 4 million people from Phnom Penh and other cities (Meng-Try, 1981)
5. Inter-elite power struggles	The PRRI and Permesta rebellions in Central Sumatra and North Sulawesi during the 1950s were against the authority of Jakarta and were supported mainly by the educated elite. They caused substantial movements both during the rebellions and after authority was restored (McNicoll, 1968: 44; Naim, 1973: 139).

6. State-intervention conflicts	The Indonesian annexation of East Timor in 1975 resulted in the latter's people suffering great violence and dislocation, such that its population in 1980 of 552,954 was less than that in 1970 (610,541). Perhaps up to a half of the population were displaced during the late 1970s (Rodgers, 1979; 1981).
7. International wars	The Second World War initiated many refugee flows throughout the entire region. Since then, the compounding of internal struggle by external intervention has produced huge involuntary displacements of people, as for example in Vietnam and Cambodia (Keely, 1981: 17).
8. Religious-based conflicts	In Indonesia, rebellions aimed at making Indonesia an Islamic state erupted in West Java (1948–62), South/South-east Sulawesi (1955–65), Aceh (1953–7; 1959–61), and South Kalimantan (1950–60). These initiated substantial migration flows (McNicoll, 1968: 43–8; Hugo, 1975; Harvey, 1974).
9. Colonial-based conflicts	Colonial rule tended to favour some groups over others. With decolonization, conflicts based upon these differences can initiate refugee movements. In Indonesia, several groups from Maluku were fiercely loyal to the Dutch and, after Independence, there was an attempt to set up a Republic of the South Moluccas causing refugee movements (McNicoll, 1968: 43). In fact, many South Moluccans followed their colonial masters back to the Netherlands where they settled (Kraak, 1957: 350).

Source: Hugo, 1983: 7.

calls 'economic insufficiency', there are several instances of the onset of severe food shortage or famine forcing permanent or temporary displacements of population. Again referring to the West Java region, periodic crop failures have historically initiated refugee flows. The adoption of a more reliable wet-rice cultivation system has greatly reduced the occurrence of famine, but in 1977 an infestation of brown leaf hopper (*wereng*) once again caused widespread crop failure and food shortage. As an example, in Pedes *kecamatan*, normally a fertile productive region, it was reported that 9,280 of the 22,370 residents had left to find work elsewhere (Sacerdoti, 1977: 48). Such conditions prevailed along much of the north coast of West Java and initiated substantial flows of population—especially to the metropolitan centre of Jakarta.

Suhrke (1981) has developed a model of refugee movement in which seven types of conflict are identified as producing refugees. These are listed together with specific examples mostly drawn from Indonesia in Table 7.8. Another type of forced migration which should be mentioned is that associated with large-scale development projects such as dams. Frequently such projects involve the displacement of large numbers of people, most of whom are now given the option of compensation or participation in the transmigration programme.

The Impact of Population Mobility

As was indicated earlier, the relationship between population movement and social and economic change is not a simple unidirectional one. Population movement is an influential factor in initiating change not only among movers themselves, but also in their households and communities of origin and destination. The overwhelming weight of evidence is that for most individual migrants, significant net welfare benefits result from migration. Aklilu and Harris (1978: 39–40), for example, conclude from an investigation into the employment and earnings of in-migrants in fourteen major cities in Java as follows:

This and other previous studies continue to support that at least the private, if not social, benefit of migration is positive and that migration is a rational and informed decision triggered by the differentials in expected income and opportunities. If some migrants are to continue to survive in conditions of extreme poverty even after they move to the cities, it is a further indicator of the marginal and difficult alternatives they had faced and left in the countryside.

As suggested in the above quotation, it is when the impact of population movement on areas of origin and destination is considered that there is less certainty. The two broad theoretical perspectives outlined at the beginning of this chapter imply quite different scenarios of societal (as opposed to individual) impact of population movement, as is shown in Table 7.1. The neo-classical approach implies that as an equilibrating mechanism migration is beneficial to regional and national development and will reduce inequalities. The historical–structuralist perspective, on the other hand, sees the consequences of migration for regional development as being generally negative. Migration to the core regions is seen as increasing dependency and inequality through draining the periphery of its economic surplus and its most talented residents, and as a result core-periphery disparities are increased. The disproportionate concentration of talented people, resources, power and capital in core areas, which is associated with migration, exacerbates interregional inequalities as well as contributing significantly to major inefficiencies and social and economic problems at both origin and destination.

The following changes can be initiated by migration at places of origin and destination:

1. adjustment to the permanent or temporary absence of outmovers;

2. adjustment to the permanent or temporary presence of inmovers;

3. adjustment to the reciprocal flows of money, goods, information, ideas and attitudes, initiated along the linkages established by movers between origin and destination.

These impacts are many and complex and cannot be dealt with in detail here (see Hugo, 1975; 1978; 1982; 1985b). We will simply highlight some of the findings of Indonesian studies investigating the impact of population mobility. The West Java study showed how movement had an impact upon many elements in the villages of origin of movers—including income, agricultural productivity, employment, traditional roles (especially of women), health, welfare and social change. The *raison d'etre* of most circular migration and commuting was to enhance the income of their village-based families. Hence all temporary movers remitted money and 81.1 per cent brought back goods, often in the form of gifts for their families. In West Java, as in much of Indonesia, the nuclear family is the 'unit of most decisions about consumption, savings and investment and the unit of most production'. Therefore, it is essential to consider the impact of remittances on household rather than individual incomes. Some differences in the relative importance of remittances in the total income of their households of origin were observed according to the type of mobility. First, since there was little seasonal or day-to-day fluctuation in rates of rural–urban commuting, most commuters were employed on a full-time basis in urban areas, and 60 per cent of the income of their households of origin consisted of remittances. Circular migrants were more likely to be employed in the village during part of the year, and their urban participation was thus more intermittent. Even so, their remittances still accounted on average for nearly half of the total income of their households. Among permanent migrants, 52 per cent had brought back or sent money in the year prior to survey, and 62 per cent had brought or sent goods. On average, these remittances made up 11 per cent of the incomes of migrants' households of origin.

The social implications for the village of the dominance of non-permanent movements between village and city should also not be ignored. The fact that such mobility often involves prolonged and regular separation of husbands from wives and children means that 'loss' of migrants affects not only the social organization and structure of the community, but the family during the crucial stage of the family life cycle when household heads are fertile and economically active. The findings of the village surveys concerning the role of rural–urban population mobility in bringing about social change in the village were somewhat inconclusive. However, it is clear that return-migrants themselves, and the advice they gave, were highly respected in the village, giving them a potentially important role as agents of change. Moreover, movers were generally more 'modern' than non-migrants, and there is little doubt they were important contributors to the creation of positive attitudes towards education. On the other hand, there is little evidence that movers had challenged the traditional authority structure in the village.

Lipton (1980: 7) quotes studies, many from Africa in situations with little population pressure on resources, to support the view that out-migration leads to reduced agricultural productivity and a deterioration of the agricultural system. However, in the densely settled survey villages of West Java, where the marginal productivity of labour was virtually zero except for short periods of peak labour demand such as the harvest season, there was little evidence of such a pattern. In recent years there have been some reports of labour shortage during these periods of peak demand, although Sinaga (1978: 111) suggested that these were restricted to 'occasional spots in Java ... but they can be solved (as they have always been solved in many regions) by increasing spatial mobility of labour'. For example, in the rich agricultural areas surrounding the city of Bandung, it was reported that in 1981 there was a deficit of labour during peaks of the agricultural cycle because labourers at newly constructed factories on the outskirts of Bandung were being paid at least Rp 1,400 per day, whereas agricultural labourers received only Rp 750.

Several writers have suggested that the enormous pressure placed upon services in destination areas experiencing significant in-migration is a negative impact of migration. This is particularly referred to with respect to urban areas. Competition for entrance to upper secondary schools and universities in cities like Jakarta and Yogyakarta is extremely intense. This reaches a peak in the capital of Jakarta where, in 1970, a regulation was enacted that any student wishing to enrol in an educational institution must have a certificate stating that there is no similar institution located closer to his/her place of origin. In 1975, all primary and secondary schools were closed to students whose parents were not registered citizens of Jakarta. In cities like Bandung, there are no longer enough places in primary schools for all applicant students (despite two shifts in class-rooms each day), and seven-year-olds wishing to enter school for the first time in some cities are required to sit an entrance exam. Yet urban areas are, at least in per capita terms, better provided with most services than rural areas.

The pressure on education facilities in areas of in-migration is duplicated in a range of other services and needs such as housing. Housing represents a problem of mammoth proportions in urban destination areas, with estimates of the number of new housing units required (to be constructed) in Indonesian urban areas over the period 1971–91 ranging from between 7.6 and 8.7 million units (Chatterjee, 1979: 96). This is staggering considering that, in 1970, there were only 2.9 million housing units in those urban areas. One of the factors associated with the strong selectivity of young adult males among temporary migrants is the fact that most of them, upon arrival in the city, are forced to sleep in situations highly unsuited to complete family units—such as in overcrowded and unhealthy barracks, unfinished buildings, under bridges, in the open, etc. (Hugo, 1975; 1978).

Whether the impacts of population movement are positive or negative is influenced strongly by the context in which they occur, so that it is not possible to make definitive statements about the impact of particular types of movement without reference to those contexts. Unfortunately, space restraints have enabled us to touch upon only a few of the consequences of population movements here. This is an area of migration research which has been severely neglected in Indonesia.

8 Labour Force and Labour Utilization

Introduction

OVER the past twenty-five years, the Indonesian labour force has almost doubled in size, and its structure has changed substantially. The labour force in 1985 is better educated, more urbanized, less concentrated in agriculture, less concentrated in Java, and less predominantly male than it was in 1961. There is no evidence that rates of open unemployment have risen, and average productivity and levels of remuneration have definitely risen. Nevertheless, a substantial proportion of the work-force remains in low-skill occupations yielding very low incomes. This chapter will analyse these trends in detail, based on available data sources, the limitations of which are discussed in Appendix 2.

An analysis of labour force and employment trends over the decade 1961–71 is not very revealing as the decade covers two very different periods; the first, 1961–6, was one of economic stagnation, and the second, 1966–71, a period of gradual economic reconstruction. Furthermore, the quality of data is not such as to yield very reliable indicators of changing labour force composition and productivity in the 1960s. For the 1970s, the data sources are richer and yield valuable insights into the structure of the labour force, but problems of comparability remain immense, and time series of key employment indicators are very few and must be used with caution.

A comparison of the 1961 and 1971 (Series D) Census results suggests that, between 1961 and 1971, the working-age population in Indonesia grew by 2.3 per cent and the growth of the labour force was somewhat slower (1.8 per cent). Comparison of the 1971 figures with the 1980 Census results indicates that, during the 1970s, the working-age population grew more rapidly—by 2.9 per cent—and the growth of the labour force was 2.7 per cent. The upsurge in the growth of the working-age population in the 1970s (and into the 1980s) was the result of the entry into the working ages of the large birth cohorts of the 1950s, which were eroded less by infant and child mortality than were earlier cohorts (see Keyfitz, 1965). The censuses appear to indicate that the upsurge in the labour force was mainly absorbed into employment.

How Much of the Population is Economically Active?

Perhaps the best answer to this question in a peasant setting is that virtually everybody is economically active. The household is a production unit, and the long hours the wife spends in cooking meals, carrying water from the well or river and throwing the household scraps to chickens or ducks, as well as the work of a child in caring for younger siblings and scaring birds from ripening crops are part of the household's productive effort, even if the husband's laborious hours behind the plough appear more directly productive. (For more on children's work, see White, 1976a; Hull, Meyer and Singarimbun, 1975). Moreover, not only on farms but also in family-operated shops, market stalls and handicraft industries, all family members except very young children commonly join in the work of the enterprise, at least on a part-time, seasonal, or irregular basis. For this reason, many writers have questioned the relevance of the concept of the labour force to non-industrial societies,[1] and increasing attention is at last turning to in-depth examination of actual patterns of allocation of time in households and villages to see how the macro and micro evidence fits together.[2]

And yet, even allowing for all the problems discussed above, analysis of census and survey data on labour force does tell us something. Since the same procedures are used fairly uniformly across regions, they should tell us something about regional differences, and perhaps something about time trends. But, in view of the uncritical acceptance of the data which marks a number of studies of the Indonesian labour force, this chapter will be just as concerned with noting what the labour force data do not show, or show wrongly, as with gleaning the limited amount of valid information that they contain.

Thus forewarned, we proceed to examine the rate of economic activity among the Indonesian population as indicated by the unadjusted census and *Supas* data. The crude activity rate, defined as the percentage of the total population which is economically active,[3] is dependent on two things: the age–sex structure of the population, and the percentages working in each age and sex group. Activity rates, by any definition, are low or even zero among children aged less than ten years; therefore populations with unusually high proportions of children tend to have low activity rates. It is possible to estimate the extent to which regional variations in activity rates in Indonesia are due to these different factors, and to compare the Indonesian rate with those in other countries to see whether the *internal* variation in Indonesia is particularly marked.

The methodology for such a comparison involves a procedure of standardization, in which the age–sex-specific activity rates in the different provinces are standardized on the age–sex structure of Indonesia. Specifically, we calculate the numbers of males and females who would be economically active if the provincial age-specific activity rates for each sex are applied to the numbers in each age–sex group in Indonesia as a whole. The number of active males so calculated, divided by the total Indonesian population, gives the standardized male contribution to the crude activity rate; likewise for females. These rates are denoted by 'stand'm' and 'stand'f' respectively. The sum of stand'm and stand'f, referred to as 'stand't', is the standardized activity rate of both sexes in the total population. The difference between this and the crude activity rate measures the effect of differences between the age–sex structure of each province's population and that of Indonesia as a whole. This will be called the age–sex index.[4]

It is clear that the crude activity rate in the different provinces of Indonesia is relatively little affected by differences in the standardized male participation rates: stand'm varies only between 20.3 and 24.9 (Table 8.1). In other words, measured male participation rates differ little in level or pattern. Crude activity rates are also little-affected by differences in population structure. The contribution of this factor varies only between −3.71 and +3.21, a somewhat larger range than in the case of stand'm. The population structure of Java (except West Java) is conducive to higher activity rates, no doubt due to the lower proportion of children resulting from lower fertility and to the in-migration of working-age people to Jakarta. The same holds for East and West Kalimantan, where the effects of labour in-migration are paramount. In all other areas, the age structure makes for lower activity rates when compared with Indonesia as a whole.

The major cause of differences in the crude activity rate is differences in the standardized female activity rate (stand'f). This varies from 6.14 (South Sulawesi) to 18.38 (Yogyakarta). No particular pattern can be identified to explain these large differences in terms of economic structure, religion or culture. Some of the differences may be simply an artefact of the different application of the definitions, particularly in rural areas. But some of the interprovincial differences are real, as evidenced by two important facts: namely, that such differences persist between the 1961, 1971 and 1980 Censuses, a point to which we shall return below;[5] and that some of the most striking interprovincial differentials continue to hold when the stand'f is calculated for urban areas alone (last column of Table 8.1).[6]

Differences in male activity rates and in population structure, though they are relatively unimportant in explaining regional differences in crude activity rates in Indonesia, are much more important in inter-country comparisons. The last four rows of Table 8.1 show the components of crude activity rates in four other selected countries, standardized on the Indonesian population structure. France and Australia are fairly representative of developed countries, while Thailand and Pakistan represent the wide variations found in developing countries. The crude activity rates in France and Australia are well above the rate in Indonesia, but the difference is mainly due to the higher proportion of their populations found in the working ages, and partly due to a somewhat higher stand'f than in Indonesia. Thailand's activity rate is higher still, but in this case it is not due at all to the age structure, but rather to a somewhat higher stand'm and much higher stand'f: the latter may be partly, but only partly, an artefact of census definitions and procedures.[7] Pakistan's crude activity rate, on the other hand, is well below that of Indonesia, due partly to a lower proportion

TABLE 8.1

Components of Crude Activity Rates in the Regions of Indonesia,
in 1980, and in Selected Other Countries

Province/Region of Indonesia and Other Countries	Components of Crude Activity Rates					
	Crude Activity Rates	Stand'm	Stand'f	Stand't	Population Structure (Age–Sex Index)*	Participation by Urban Females (Stand'f)
SUMATRA	34.19	24.06	12.16	36.22	−2.03	6.07
DI Aceh	32.24	23.34	9.98	33.32	−1.08	5.85
North Sumatra	35.59	23.88	15.06	38.94	−3.35	6.71
Riau	32.06	23.81	8.93	32.74	−0.68	5.61
Jambi	34.63	24.13	11.27	35.40	−0.77	4.64
West Sumatra	32.32	23.10	11.01	34.11	−1.79	6.22
Bengkulu	36.66	24.02	15.50	39.52	−2.86	5.58
South Sumatra	35.40	24.23	12.82	37.05	−1.65	5.69
Lampung	33.38	25.42	9.60	35.02	−1.64	6.49
JAVA	36.66	23.91	11.84	35.75	+0.91	9.31
DKI Jakarta	31.12	20.90	7.81	28.71	+2.41	7.99
West Java	31.36	23.04	8.81	31.85	−0.49	7.03
Central Java	39.66	24.87	14.24	39.11	+0.55	12.73
DI Yogyakarta	45.17	23.58	18.38	41.96	+3.21	12.72
East Java	39.46	24.47	12.57	37.04	+2.42	10.81
KALIMANTAN	36.95	23.94	14.03	37.97	−1.02	6.85
West Kalimantan	39.89	24.82	15.81	40.63	−0.74	4.88
Central Kalimantan	38.36	24.91	15.44	40.35	−1.99	8.18
South Kalimantan	36.24	23.59	12.64	36.23	+0.01	6.60
East Kalimantan	31.03	22.03	7.59	29.62	+1.41	5.42
SULAWESI	29.13	23.09	7.55	30.64	−1.51	6.07
North Sulawesi	31.92	23.29	9.22	32.51	−0.59	8.13
Central Sulawesi	33.42	24.35	10.33	34.68	−1.26	5.71
South Sulawesi	27.21	22.69	6.14	28.83	−1.62	5.46
South-east Sulawesi	29.26	22.99	9.98	32.97	−3.71	5.63
OTHER ISLANDS	35.00	22.97	12.73	35.70	−0.70	8.37
Bali	39.06	24.95	14.42	39.37	−0.31	12.09
West Nusa Tenggara	33.12	24.08	11.02	35.10	−1.98	9.07
East Nusa Tenggara	37.27	23.13	14.86	37.99	−0.72	6.79
Maluku	28.67	20.27	9.68	29.95	−1.28	5.32
Irian Jaya	32.89	21.43	11.28	32.71	+0.18	3.32
INDONESIA	35.53	23.81	11.72	35.53	0.00	8.77
FRANCE	43.4	20.9	14.9	35.8	+7.6	
AUSTRALIA	45.9	23.3	15.9	39.2	+6.7	
THAILAND	48.1	26.2	24.3	50.5	−2.4	
PAKISTAN	26.5	27.0	4.2	31.2	−4.7	

Source: Computed from 1980 Indonesian Census and census data from other countries.
* The numbers in this column represent the difference between the crude activity rate and
stand't. If stand't is larger than the crude activity rate, the sign (−) is used.

of population in the working ages but mainly to the very low female activity
rates, a pattern typical of many South Asian and Middle Eastern countries.

What changes have occurred in activity rates since 1961? Direct comparisons cannot be made because of the changes in definitions and the
reference period. Examining first only the census years given in Table 8.2,
measured male activity rates were lower and female rates higher in 1971,
and the 1980 rates were very close to the 1971 rates. The different trends
in male and female rates offset each other to a large extent, but on balance
the activity rate (both crude and standardized) was lower in 1971 but

TABLE 8.2

Indonesia: Measured Participation Rates in 1961, 1971,[a] 1976,[b] and 1980,[c]
Standardized on 1971 Age–Sex Structure

Year	Crude Rate	Stand'm	Stand'f	Stand't	Population Structure
1961	35.64	25.13	10.07	35.20	+0.44
1971	34.90	23.32	11.58	34.90	0.00
1976 (Supas)	43.11	25.95	16.29	42.24	+0.87
1976 (Sakernas)	37.99	24.45	12.75	37.20	+0.79
1980	35.55	22.65	11.40	34.05	+1.50

Source: Computed from 1961, 1971 and 1980 census data and 1976 Supas and Sakernas.
[a] 1971 figures relate to Series D data. Irian Jaya is omitted.
[b] 1976 Supas figures include the urban area of Kabupaten Jayapura. Aside from this, consistency is maintained as far as possible with the 1981 and 1971 data by (i) assuming that the population of East Nusa Tenggara with the exception of Kabupaten Kupang, and of Maluku with the exception of Kotamadya Ambon, grew at the same rate as that for the rest of Indonesia; (ii) assuming that age–sex-specific participation rates in these areas were unchanged from their 1971 levels.
[c] 1980 figures exclude East Timor and Irian Jaya.

regained its 1961 level in 1980. It would be unwise to jump to the conclusion that either the apparent decline in male rates or the apparent rise in female rates was real. As mentioned earlier, the 1961 definitions made for a higher estimate of male employment, and in addition there was a mysterious rise in the proportion of males recorded in the category 'other' in 1971 (see Jones, 1981: 229) and in 1980. In the case of females, different sources show widely differing estimates of female activity rates in different years, clearly reflecting different definitions and procedures rather than time trends.

There are even greater difficulties in comparing the census data and the 1976 survey data. The Supas stand'm is well above its 1971 level and higher than in 1961. The stand'f is sharply higher than in any of the census years. As a result, the standardized total participation rate is very much higher than in any of the census years. On the other hand, the Sakernas data for 1976 show a stand'm roughly equal to its 1961 level and a stand'f intermediate between the 1971 and the Supas values. The resultant stand't is higher than in either of the census years but well below its Supas value.

Though the labour force definitions in the 1980 Census were very similar to those of Supas and Sakernas, it nevertheless displayed participation rates that were fairly close to the 1971 census figures. It would seem, then, that comparisons and evaluation of time trends can more safely be made between the 1971 and 1980 census data than between either of these censuses and the 1961 and 1976 data.

Male Activity Rates

The fluctuations in recorded activity rates for males between 1961 and 1980 were necessarily accompanied by changes in the proportions recorded in various 'non-economically active' categories (those in school, home houseworkers, income recipients, and others). Changes in the proportions recorded as students were rather small over the 1961 to 1976 period, though they increased sharply in the 1976–80 period at ages 10–19, no doubt reflecting the expansion of schooling opportunities in the late 1970s which was noted in Chapter 3. There was little change in the proportion of males recorded as 'home houseworkers'.

The big change between 1961 and the two later censuses of 1971 and 1980 was in the proportion of males recorded as 'others' (see Table 8.3). This rose very sharply, particularly in Java, and especially at ages 15–24—a strange finding, because 'others' is a residual category which includes those who were neither working, looking for work, attending school, housekeeping, or receiving an independent income during the reference week.[8] One wonders what the 14 per cent of males aged 15–19 who were so classified in both 1971 and 1980 (up from 4 per cent in 1961)

TABLE 8.3

Percentage of Males and Females Classified as 'Others', in 1961, 1971 and 1980 Censuses, and Supas and Sakernas Surveys

Age Group	Population Censuses			Supas	Sakernas	Percentage by which Census Exceeds Sakernas	
	1961[a] (1)	1971[b] (2)	1980 (3)	1976 (4)	1976–1978[c] (5)	1971 (6)	1980 (7)
Males							
10–14	10.6	13.8	9.3	6.1	8.0	72	16
15–19	4.3	13.4	14.1	4.8	5.8	131	143
20–24	3.0	8.1	11.2	2.8	3.2	153	250
25–34	1.9	3.6	5.1	1.1	1.2	200	325
35–44	1.4	2.8	4.0	0.7	1.0	180	300
45–54	2.4	3.9	6.9	2.4	3.6	8	92
55+	14.7	13.4	27.8	15.0	20.6	−35	35
All ages 10+	4.8	8.1	10.4	4.3	5.2	56	100
Females							
10–14	11.5	14.5	10.9	5.8	5.8	150	88
15–19	4.0	12.0	14.3	4.1	2.4	400	496
20–24	2.1	4.9	7.3	2.4	1.1	345	564
25–34	1.9	2.4	3.3	0.8	0.6	300	450
35–44	2.7	2.6	3.1	1.0	1.1	136	182
45–54	6.1	6.4	3.1	4.2	3.7	73	−16
55+	25.5	21.7	35.5	25.7	26.8	−19	32
All ages 10+	6.1	8.3	10.7	5.4	4.5	84	138

Sources: BPS, Population Censuses of 1961, 1971 (Series C and E), 1980 (Series S, No. 2), Jakarta, various dates; *Supas* and *Sakernas* reports.
[a] Includes 'unknown'.
[b] 1971 figures based on Series D data.
[c] Average of 1976, 1977 and 1978 figures.

were doing with their time. It seems likely that many of them were at least potentially available for work, and constituted the 'discouraged unemployed' or half-hearted first-job seekers.

The 1976 *Supas* and *Sakernas* data show much the same proportions of 'others' as the 1961 Census; thus they were much lower than the 1971 or 1980 figures up to the middle working ages, for both males and females. Consequently, the overall proportion of young people shown as not economically active is well below the proportion for 1971 or 1980 (see Table 8.3).

Not surprisingly, in view of the above evidence, male participation rates measured for the young ages (15–29) in 1971 and 1980 are lower than expected on the basis of international comparisons. Rates at these ages are normally higher in the developing countries, and tend to fall over time towards Western levels (no doubt mainly because of the expansion of the

TABLE 8.4

Male Activity Rates at Ages 15–29: Indonesia Compared with Median Figures for Developing and Developed Countries, Various Years

		Male Activity Rate at Ages		
		15–19	*20–24*	*25–29*
Developing countries[a]	median 1971	54.0	86.3	94.9
	median 1980	57.4	87.6	95.7
Developed countries[a]	median 1971	47.4	83.7	95.5
	median 1980	48.7	81.4	93.9
Indonesia	1961 Census	66.7	87.2	n.a.
	1971 Series C	48.9	76.5	90.5
	1971 Series D	52.8	79.2	91.5
	1976 *Supas*	66.2	88.2	96.8
	1976 *Sakernas*	58.8	87.1	96.9
	1980 Census	47.4	79.2	92.1
Ratio of Indonesia to median of developing countries	1961 Census	1.24	1.01	n.a.
	1971 Series C	0.91	0.89	0.95
	1971 Series D	0.98	0.92	0.96
	1976 *Supas*	1.23	1.02	1.02
	1976 *Sakernas*	1.09	1.01	1.02
	1980 Census[b]	0.83	0.90	0.96

Sources: Computed from data in ILO, *Yearbook of Labour Statistics*, 1975 (Geneva, 1975) and 1982 (Geneva, 1982), Table 1. Indonesian data: as for Table 8.3.
[a] Median of all developing and developed countries with male populations exceeding 100,000. 1971 figure derived from data for years ranging between 1963 and 1973 but mostly around 1971. 1980 figure derived from data for years ranging from 1975 to 1982 but mostly around 1980.
[b] Related to median of developing countries around 1980.

education system and the tendency to stay on longer in school). But as shown in Table 8.4, Indonesia is not in its expected position. The participation rates for young Indonesian males in 1961 and 1976 are somewhat higher than the average in developing countries, but this probably reflects a lower proportion in school than in the average developing country. The really striking anomaly in Table 8.4 is the low 1971 and 1980 rates for Indonesia. Not only are they well below the average figures for developing countries: at ages 20–29, they are even well below the average figures for developed countries as well.[9] The participation rates recorded for young males in Indonesia in 1971 and 1980, then, give an unrealistically low estimate of the number of potential workers.[10] The male labour force in 1971 and 1980 is definitely underestimated relative to 1961 and 1976 unless some adjustment is made to the published data. Such an adjustment will be made later.

Female Activity Rates

The measurement of female labour force participation is even more complex than for males, because females tend to be heavily concentrated into those activities which are on the borderline between 'economic' and 'non-economic' activities, and are also more likely to work part time, erratically or seasonally in those activities. Therefore conventions about how to treat such activities can have an important bearing on the size of the female labour force measured by censuses or surveys.[11] In particular, the concept of 'housewife' as a non-economically productive role is even more suspect in peasant societies than it is in the West because 'housewifely' duties such as food gathering, raising of chickens or ducks, crude processing of food, and provision of water and fuel, are in fact productive of goods and services which are normally bought with money in a Western setting.

The effect of different definitions and procedures on the size of the female labour force is clearly illustrated by a comparison of female activity rates for Java measured by a number of different censuses and surveys. These showed the following proportions economically active among females aged 10 years and above:

1958 Labour Force Survey	–	59.5 per cent[12]
1961 Census	–	29.1 per cent
1964–5 *Susenas*	–	36.4 per cent[13]
1967 *Susenas*	–	32.8 per cent
1969 *Susenas*	–	30.3 per cent
1971 Census (Series E)	–	33.7 per cent
1976 *Supas*	–	49.1 per cent
1976 *Sakernas*	–	38.1 per cent
1977 *Sakernas*	–	37.4 per cent
1978 *Sakernas*	–	42.3 per cent
1980 Census	–	33.0 per cent

The 1958 labour force survey employed a broader definition of 'working' than that adopted in the later sources. In rural areas, the reference period was twelve months and no instructions were given as to the minimum length of time a person had to have worked or to have sought work in order to be included in the work-force. As noted earlier, the *Supas* and *Sakernas* surveys and the 1980 Census required only one hour of work in the reference week in order to qualify as 'employed'. However, they differed sharply in the percentage of women they recorded in the labour force.

It is to be expected that levels of female participation in the work force would have changed over the past two decades because of changing employment opportunities and changing conventions about women's work. The problem is that such changes may well have been small, and were probably swamped by the much greater changes due to changing definitions and procedures. The figures above give us no valid basis for detecting the direction, let alone the magnitude, of the changes which have occurred.

To set these figures in a wider context, we might note that female participation rates in Muslim countries of the Middle East tend to be around 10 or 15 per cent, and in Pakistan and Bangladesh even lower, whereas in other major South-East Asian countries they vary from 27 per cent in the Philippines and 30 per cent in Malaysia to 70 per cent in Thailand. Indonesian rates are clearly well above the rates in most Muslim countries, suggesting that, although Islam no doubt has a bearing on the Indonesian rates, it is only one of a complex web of factors. Just as women's status is very different in Indonesia from that in the Muslim countries of West Asia, it also differs widely from region to region within Indonesia.

Although the data are of very doubtful value in indicating temporal trends in female participation rates, they are of much greater value in studying regional differentials. The 1961, 1971 and 1980 Censuses and the 1976 *Supas*, while difficult to compare with each other, each provides data for the different provinces and regions based on a standard set of definitions and procedures. Even though there may be some regional variation in conventions about how to classify housewives or unmarried girls or in the application of the procedures, the centralized administration of the censuses and surveys should have held this to a minimum.

The four data sets do indeed appear to be of great value in studying regional differences in levels and patterns of female labour force participation. Tables 8.5 and 8.6 show that, although the absolute rates have changed sharply with changing definitions, there is an impressive degree of stability in the regional differentials.[14] Rates in the Javanese areas are always well above the Indonesian average; in mainly-Sundanese West Java they are much lower, and in South Sulawesi they are lower still. Kalimantan is the only region where there is no stability over time in the relationship of the rates to the Indonesian average, though there is more stability in the relationship in the urban areas. Perhaps not too much credence should be given to the rural rates for Kalimantan, especially in 1961, because of the inaccessibility of much of the island's population and the difficulty of conducting a census there.

TABLE 8.5

Indonesia: Age-standardized Labour Force Participation Rates for Females, by Region, 1961, 1971, 1976 and 1980

Province or Region	Standardized Participation Rate*				Index of Indonesian Rate[+]			
	1961	1971	1976	1980	1961	1971	1976	1980
Urban Areas								
Java	26.7	25.9	28.5	27.0	1.14	1.09	1.05	1.11
Sumatra	n.a.	19.2	28.2	17.0	n.a.	0.81	1.04	0.70
Sulawesi	n.a.	14.9	21.5	17.3	n.a.	0.63	0.79	0.71
Kalimantan	n.a.	17.4	17.5	16.2	n.a.	0.73	0.65	0.66
Other Islands	n.a.	24.2	36.2	23.5	n.a.	1.02	1.34	0.96
Urban Indonesia	23.5	23.7	27.1 (25.5)	24.5	1.00	1.00	1.00	1.00
Rural Areas								
Java	28.7	35.1	53.8	35.3	0.96	1.00	1.05	1.00
Sumatra	n.a.	40.6	48.5	38.1	n.a.	1.15	0.95	1.08
Sulawesi	n.a.	21.3	33.5	21.9	n.a.	0.61	0.65	0.62
Kalimantan	n.a.	38.9	50.8	43.1	n.a.	1.11	0.99	1.22
Other Islands	n.a.	35.8	53.3	37.3	n.a.	1.02	1.04	1.05
Rural Indonesia	29.8	35.2	51.2 (39.1)	35.4	1.00	1.00	1.00	1.00

(continued)

TABLE 8.5 (continued)

Province or Region	Standardized Participation Rate*				Index of Indonesian Rate+			
	1961	1971	1976	1980	1961	1971	1976	1980
Total								
Java	28.4	33.9	49.1	33.0	0.99	1.02	1.05	1.01
Sumatra	33.0	36.3	44.5	33.9	1.15	1.10	0.95	1.04
Sulawesi	17.6	20.3	31.2	21.1	0.61	0.61	0.67	0.65
Kalimantan	42.7	36.1	42.4	37.9	1.48	1.09	0.91	1.16
Other Islands	27.1	36.0	51.1	35.5	0.94	1.09	1.09	1.09
All Indonesia	28.8	33.1	46.7 (36.5)	32.7	1.00	1.00	1.00	1.00

Source: Computed from 1961, 1971 and 1980 census data and 1976 *Supas.*

( ) *Sakernas*

* Indonesian female age structure for 1971 used as the standard.

+ Indonesian rate for the year concerned used as the base. For urban areas, the Indonesian urban rate is used; for rural areas, the Indonesian rural rate.

TABLE 8.6

Age-standardized Labour Force Participation Rates for Females, by Selected Provinces, 1961, 1971, 1976 and 1980

Province or Region	Standardized Participation Rate*				Index of Indonesian Rate[+]			
	1961	1971	1976 (Supas)	1980	1961	1971	1976 (Supas)	1980
Urban Areas								
Jakarta	20.4	20.3	19.9	22.2	0.87	0.86	0.73	0.71
West Java	n.a.	19.8	24.2	19.6	n.a.	0.84	0.89	0.30
Central Java	n.a.	33.9	40.1	35.5	n.a.	1.43	1.48	1.45
Yogyakarta	n.a.	36.2	39.3	35.9	n.a.	1.53	1.45	1.41
East Java	n.a.	29.7	30.9	30.2	n.a.	1.25	1.14	1.23
South Sulawesi	n.a.	13.2	16.0	15.9	n.a.	0.56	0.59	0.65
Urban Indonesia	23.5	23.7	27.1	34.5	1.00	1.00	1.00	1.00
Rural Areas								
West Java	n.a.	27.9	42.2	25.9	n.a.	0.79	0.82	0.73
Central Java	n.a.	37.5	60.6	48.8	n.a.	1.07	1.18	1.35
Yogyakarta	n.a.	51.3	74.8	56.1	n.a.	1.46	1.46	1.59
East Java	n.a.	37.3	55.6	36.3	n.a.	1.06	1.09	1.03
South Sulawesi	n.a.	14.7	20.3	17.7	n.a.	0.42	0.40	0.50
Rural Indonesia	29.8	35.2	51.2	35.4	1.00	1.00	1.00	1.00

(continued)

TABLE 8.6 (continued)

Province or Region	Standardized Participation Rate*				Index of Indonesian Rate+			
	1961	1971	1976 (Supas)	1980	1961	1971	1976 (Supas)	1980
Total								
Jakarta	20.4	20.3	19.9	21.7	0.71	0.61	0.43	0.66
West Java	22.5	26.9	40.0	24.6	0.78	0.81	0.86	0.75
Central Java	27.6	37.1	58.3	39.7	0.96	1.12	1.25	1.21
Yogyakarta	44.0	48.6	68.8	51.5	1.53	1.47	1.47	1.57
East Java	32.7	36.1	52.1	35.1	1.14	1.09	1.12	1.07
South Sulawesi	n.a.	14.5	19.4	17.2	n.a.	0.44	0.42	0.53
All Indonesia	28.8	33.1	46.7	32.7	1.00	1.00	1.00	1.00

Source: As for Table 8.5.

* Indonesian female age structure for 1971 used as the standard.

+ For urban areas, Indonesian urban rate for the year concerned used as the base; for rural areas, Indonesian rural rate for the year concerned used as the base.

Figure 8.1 shows the age-specific female activity rates measured for urban and rural areas of Indonesia in 1961, 1971 and 1980; Figure 8.2, the rates for Java and Sulawesi in the same years; and Figure 8.3, the rates in both rural and urban areas of a number of more populous provinces in 1980. The 1971 and 1980 rates tend to be higher than the 1961 rates. The 1961 figures show a two-peaked pattern, with the major peak around ages 45–54 (45–64 in rural areas in 1961) and a minor peak at ages 15–24. By

FIGURE 8.1

Indonesia: Female Activity Rates, Urban and Rural Areas, 1961, 1971 and 1980

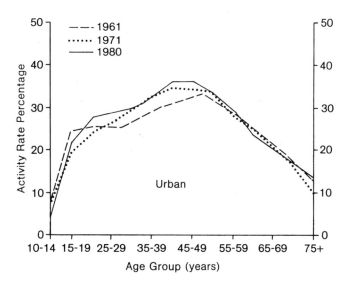

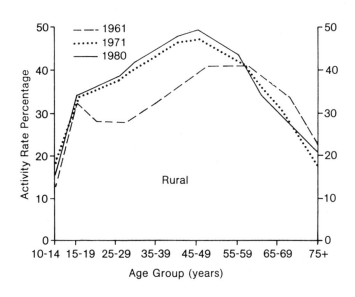

contrast, the 1971 and 1980 figures show a single peak at ages around 40–49, a pattern which conforms to that in South Asia (United Nations, 1962). Even in urban areas, there is little sign of a move towards a Western, two-peaked pattern that reflects high participation rates among young unmarried or as yet childless women.

Despite these differences in level and pattern, some consistent regional differentials are measured (see also Jones, 1986). In all years, Java has much higher rates than Sulawesi at all ages (Figure 8.2); in particular,

FIGURE 8.2

Female Activity Rates, Jaya and Sulawesi, 1961, 1971 and 1980

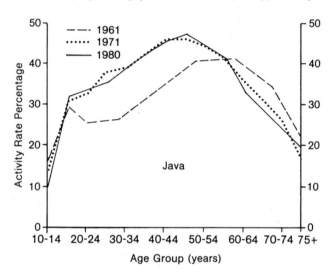

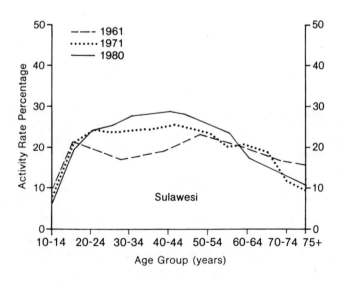

Yogyakarta and Central Java have much higher rates than South Sulawesi.[15] The tendency for many women in Yogyakarta and Central Java to be engaged in activities such as batik-making, handicraft industries, and market selling is well known, as is the tendency for women in the Bugis–Makassarese areas of South Sulawesi to be confined to the activity of housewife.

It might have been expected that cultural differences between regions in female patterns of work would have been reflected more clearly in urban than in rural participation rates. After all, the differences between work in the home and work away from the home tend to be sharper in urban areas, and the anonymity of contacts in the work-place greater, thus reducing the likelihood that women in urban areas of more conservative provinces will work. However, Figure 8.3 shows that regional differences in female work participation levels in 1980, although very wide in urban areas, are even wider in rural areas. It is tempting to interpret this as reflecting the impact of urbanization in narrowing regional differences in women's roles and status, although an alternative explanation could be that there is more scope in agricultural areas for culturally-determined differences in concepts regarding women's work to influence the rates recorded in different provinces, even when actual work patterns are much the same.

In the rural comparison, North Sumatra has the highest participation rates, even though in urban areas it does not have outstandingly high rates.[16] The contrast between Central Java and South Sulawesi is again marked. It is extraordinary that in two provinces where wet-rice cultivation is such an important rural activity and where activities such as fishing and vegetable growing are also of great importance, levels of female participation in the work-force could be so different.[17] Yet this sharp difference is not confined to the 1980 data; it is shown consistently by all data sources. West Java, though well above South Sulawesi, is also well below the rest of Java.

In urban areas, female participation rates in Central Java are much higher than those in Jakarta, West Java, or North Sumatra, which in turn are much higher than those in South Sulawesi except at ages 24–44. It might seem surprising that female activity rates in Jakarta, the metropolis and presumably the most 'modern' city of Indonesia, should be low compared with urban areas of Central and East Java. The similarity between the rates in Jakarta and urban West Java provides the clue. Although Jakarta has received migrants from all over Indonesia, including areas like Central Java where female activity rates are high, the largest source of migrants is West Java, where female activity rates are amongst the lowest in Indonesia.[18] The low participation rates among West Java-born females in Jakarta, along with even lower rates for the Jakarta-born population (the 'orang Betawi', who are known for their conservatism in matters such as female employment), are the main factors causing the low participation rates in Jakarta (see Jones, 1977).

Reasons of space preclude an adequate discussion of differences in female activity rates according to educational attainment and marital status.

260

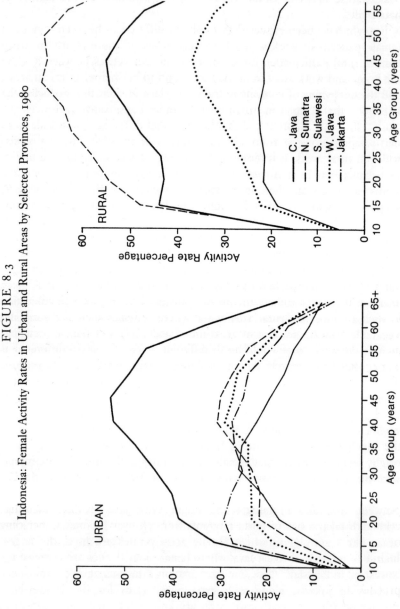

FIGURE 8.3

Indonesia: Female Activity Rates in Urban and Rural Areas by Selected Provinces, 1980

There is a U-shaped relationship between women's labour force participation and their educational attainment, which continues to hold when age and rural–urban residence are individually or simultaneously controlled for (ASEAN, 1983: Annex D; Widarti, 1984: Tables 4 and 5). Participation rates are particularly high for women with tertiary education. As in most of Asia, married women have lower rates than single women, and rates for widowed and divorced women are higher still.

Total Size of the Labour Force and its Industrial Distribution

For purposes of evaluating the success of economic policy, at least in so far as it influences economic structure and employment, there has been great interest in Indonesia in measuring the growth of the labour force and, more specifically, employment in different sectors and unemployment levels. Knowledge about the industrial distribution of the work-force and the trends in industrial composition over time can provide a basis, not only for evaluating the success of government policies, but also for forecasting labour absorption in different sectors. However, extreme care must be taken in using census data for this kind of analysis in a country at Indonesia's stage of development, because the time reference period and the definitions used can make a difference, measured in the millions, to the numbers recorded as working in agriculture and, by the same token, in other sectors. The particular problems of measuring the number of workers in agriculture, in manufacturing, and in trade and services will be discussed in the next two sections. Here we will simply examine briefly what the 1961, 1971 and 1980 Censuses appear to show about trends in employment in the different sectors, based on Tables 8.7, 8.8, and 8.9. Comparison of 1971 and 1980 data is likely to be rather more reliable than comparison of 1971 and 1961 data.[19]

In Indonesia as a whole, there appears to have been a slow increase in employment in agriculture, but a sharp decline in the proportion of the work-force in agriculture.[20] Employment in the mining sector picked up in the 1970s, but the decline in agriculture's share of employment was offset mainly by increases in the shares of manufacturing, construction, trade and services. Java has a more varied employment structure than the other islands, with the lowest percentage of persons engaged in agriculture (51 per cent in 1980) and mining, but the highest percentage in manufacturing, construction, trade, transport and services. By contrast, about 66 per cent of employment in the other islands was provided by the agricultural sector. In Indonesia as a whole, women workers are more concentrated than men in manufacturing and trade, the concentration in trade being particularly pronounced in Java.

Calculation of 'Adjusted' Labour Force

If we study a time series of total labour force measured by the census and surveys between 1961 and 1980, there are quite implausible variations in

TABLE 8.7

Distribution of Employed Persons in Indonesia According to the 1961, 1971 (Series C), and 1980 Censuses[a]

Industry	Males			Females		
	1961	1971	1980	1961	1971	1980
Absolute Numbers ('000)						
Agriculture	17,649	17,391	19,671	6,331	8,429	9,081
Mining	78	86	326	11	6	60
Manufacturing[b]	1,226	1,597	2,652	722	1,511	2,116
Construction	570	749	1,616	22	10	40
Trade	1,534	2,402	3,492	704	1,902	3,225
Transport	677	926	1,448	25	19	22
Services	2,071	3,033	5,170	1,069	1,149	2,274
Total	23,805	26,184	34,375	8,884	13,026	16,818
Percentage Distribution						
Agriculture	74.2	66.4	57.2	71.2	64.7	54.0
Mining	0.3	0.3	1.0	0.1	d	0.4
Manufacturing[b]	5.2	6.1	7.7	8.1	11.6	12.6
Construction	2.4	2.9	4.7	0.2	0.1	0.2
Trade	6.4	9.2	10.2	7.9	14.6	19.2
Transport	2.8	3.5	4.2	0.3	0.1	0.1
Services	8.7	11.6	15.0	12.2	8.8	13.5
Total	100.0	100.0	100.0	100.0	100.0	100

	Intercensal Change: Average Annual Percentage			
	Males		Females	
	1961–1971	1971–1980	1961–1971	1971–1980
Agriculture	−0.1	1.4	2.9	0.8
Mining	1.0	16.0	c	c
Manufacturing[b]	2.6	5.8	7.7	3.4
Construction	2.7	8.9	c	c
Trade	4.5	4.2	10.4	6.0
Transport	3.1	5.1	c	c
Services	3.8	6.1	0.7	7.9
Total	1.0	3.1	3.9	2.9

Source: As for Table 8.3.
[a] Data are adjusted to distribute persons with activities not adequately described and to exclude Irian Jaya and, in 1980, East Timor.
[b] Includes electricity, gas, and water.
[c] Numbers too small to be very meaningful.
[d] Less than 0.05.

TABLE 8.8

Distribution of Employed Persons in Java According to the 1961, 1971
(Series C), and 1980 Censuses[a]

Industry	Males			Females		
	1961	1971	1980	1961	1971	1980
Absolute Numbers ('000)						
Agriculture	11,075	10,636	11,591	3,782	5,070	5,127
Mining	20	32	164	9	1	30
Manufacturing[b]	994	1,264	2,025	530	1,150	1,622
Construction	423	519	1,158	14	8	24
Trade	1,096	1,809	2,522	604	1,613	2,541
Transport	481	644	1,010	19	15	16
Services	1,485	2,106	3,546	923	890	1,650
Total	15,574	17,010	22,016	5,881	8,747	11,010
Percentage Distribution						
Agriculture	71.2	62.5	52.6	64.3	58.0	46.6
Mining	0.1	0.2	0.7	0.2	d	0.3
Manufacturing[b]	6.4	7.4	9.2	9.0	13.1	14.7
Construction	2.7	3.1	5.3	0.2	0.1	0.2
Trade	7.0	10.6	11.5	10.3	18.4	23.1
Transport	3.1	3.8	4.6	0.3	0.2	0.1
Services	9.5	12.4	16.1	15.7	10.2	15.0
Total	100.0	100.0	100.0	100.0	100.0	100.0

Intercensal Change: Average Annual Percentage

Industry	Males		Females	
	1961–1971	1971–1980	1961–1971	1971–1980
Agriculture	−0.4	1.0	3.0	0.1
Mining	4.8	19.9	c	c
Manufacturing[b]	2.4	5.4	8.1	3.9
Construction	2.1	9.3	c	c
Trade	5.1	3.8	10.3	5.2
Transport	2.9	5.1	c	c
Services	3.6	6.0	−0.4	7.1
Total	0.9	2.9	4.0	2.6

Source: As for Table 8.3

[a] Data are adjusted to distribute persons with activities not adequately described and to exclude Irian Jaya and, in 1980, East Timor.

[b] Includes electricity, gas, and water.

[c] Numbers too small to be very meaningful.

[d] Less than 0.05.

TABLE 8.9

Distribution of Employed Persons in Outer Islands According to the 1961,
1971 (Series C), and 1980 Censuses[a]

Industry	Males			Females		
	1961	1971	1980	1961	1971	1980
Absolute Numbers ('000)						
Agriculture	6,575	6,755	8,080	2,549	3,359	3,954
Mining	58	54	162	2	5	30
Manufacturing[b]	232	333	627	192	361	494
Construction	146	230	458	8	2	16
Trade	439	593	970	100	289	684
Transport	196	282	438	6	4	6
Services	585	927	1,624	165	259	624
Total	8,231	9,174	12,359	3,022	4,279	5,808
Percentage Distribution						
Agriculture	79.9	73.6	65.5	84.4	78.5	68.1
Mining	0.7	0.6	1.3	d	0.1	0.5
Manufacturing[b]	2.8	3.6	5.1	6.3	8.4	8.5
Construction	1.8	2.5	3.7	0.3	d	0.3
Trade	5.4	6.5	7.8	3.3	6.7	11.8
Transport	2.3	3.1	3.5	0.2	0.1	0.1
Services	7.1	10.1	13.1	5.5	6.1	10.7
Total	100.0	100.0	100.0	100.0	100.0	100.0

	Intercensal Change: Average Annual Percentage			
	Males		Females	
	1961–1971	1971–1980	1961–1971	1971–1980
Agriculture	0.3	2.0	2.8	1.8
Mining	−0.7	13.0	c	c
Manufacturing[b]	3.7	7.3	6.5	3.5
Construction	4.6	8.0	c	c
Trade	3.1	5.6	11.2	10.0
Transport	3.7	5.0	c	c
Services	4.7	6.4	4.6	10.3
Total	1.1	3.4	3.5	3.5

Source: As for Table 8.3.
[a] Data are adjusted to distribute persons with activities not adequately described and to
exclude Irian Jaya and, in 1980, East Timor.
[b] Includes electricity, gas, and water.
[c] Numbers too small to be very meaningful.
[d] Less than 0.05.

growth rates, resulting from different definitions and procedures, seasonal timing of the enumeration, and other factors. In particular, the total labour force measured in 1971 and 1980 is too small relative to the 1961 Census, and to the *Sakernas* of 1976, 1977 and 1978, while the labour force measured by the 1976 *Supas* is too large relative to all other sources. In an earlier study (Jones, 1981: 239–45), a number of adjustments were made to the 1961 and 1971 census data to take into account the large proportion recorded in the category 'others' in 1971, the large numbers in 1971 who were outside the labour force according to the one-week reference period but who worked in agriculture in the last season, and the age misstatement and underenumeration in both censuses. These adjustments yielded more consistent estimates in the case of males than of females.

Given the complication of additional data sources and the impossibility of deriving an entirely consistent set of estimates, the present study will attempt only two straightforward adjustments of the data: one to move some of those recorded as 'others' into the labour force in 1971 and 1980; the other, to remove some of the female 'unpaid family workers' in agriculture out of the labour force in 1976. It should be stressed that these adjustments do not generate 'correct' estimates of the size of the labour force, but rather a more internally consistent time series than the unadjusted data provide.

The adjustment for the high proportion of 'others' in the 1971 and 1980 Censuses follows the procedure used by Bukit and Bakir (1983) instead of that used by Jones (1981). The proportion recorded as 'others' in each age–sex group between 10 and 55 years of age in the *Sakernas* (average of 1976–1978 rounds) was assumed to apply as well to the 1971 and 1980 Censuses; in all cases it was lower than the census figures. The difference was added to the labour force in each age–sex group. This raised the size of the 1971 labour force by 3.1 million, and that of the 1980 labour force by 4.6 million.

A major reason why *Supas* and *Sakernas* recorded a higher proportion of the population in the labour force than did the various censuses was that they included more women in the agricultural work-force as 'unpaid family workers', and they showed women as constituting a higher proportion of the agricultural work-force than did the censuses. As discussed later, the data on proportion of 'unpaid family workers' in agriculture are not easy to adjust. However, a simple adjustment that can be made is to assume that the almost identical women's share of agricultural employment recorded in 1971 and 1980 by the censuses also held in 1976. The same share can be assumed to have held in 1961, in this case resulting in an upward adjustment of the female work-force. Taking male employment in agriculture as the base then, and assuming that the ratio of male to female employment recorded in 1971 and 1980 also applied to 1976 and 1961, the adjusted 1976 and 1961 estimates of the labour force in Table 8.10 were computed.

TABLE 8.10

Size of the Indonesian Labour Force, 1961–1980,
Unadjusted and Adjusted Data

Year and Source of Data	Unadjusted Data ('000)			Adjusted Data ('000)		
	Males	Females	Total	Males	Females	Total
1961 Census	25,009	9,569	34,578	25,009	11,488	36,497
1971 Census*	27,536	13,678	41,214	28,905	15,373	44,278
1976 *Supas*	33,429	21,061	54,490	33,429	18,430	51,859
(1976 *Sakernas*)	(31,869)	(16,562)	(48,431)	(31,869)	(16,102)	(47,971)
1980 Census+	34,702	17,087	51,789	36,803	19,547	56,350
	Average Annual Rate of Increase (Percentage)					
1961–1971	1.0	3.6	1.8	1.5	3.0	2.0
1971–1976	4.0	9.0	5.7	3.0	3.7	3.2
(1971–1976)	(3.0)	(3.9)	(3.3)	(2.0)	(0.9)	(1.6)
1976–1980	0.9	−5.1	−1.3	2.4	1.5	2.1
(1976–1980)	(2.2)	(0.8)	(1.7)	(3.7)	(5.0)	(4.1)
1971–1980	2.6	2.5	2.6	2.7	2.7	2.7

Source: Computed from 1961, 1971 and 1980 census data and 1976 *Supas* and *Sakernas*.

Note: Irian Jaya has been excluded from all census figures. The *Supas* and *Sakernas* samples excluded East Nusa Tenggara except for *kabupaten* Kupang, and Maluku except for *kotamadya* Ambon; they included *kabupaten* Jayapura in Irian Jaya. The excluded areas of East Nusa Tenggara and Maluku constitute 2.5 per cent of the population of Indonesia, excluding Irian Jaya. No attempt has been made in this table to adjust for these omitted areas.

* Series D.

+ Based on the definition of 'working' consistent with the 1971 Census; that is, working at least two days in the previous week.

1976 figures in parentheses are drawn from *Sakernas*; those not in parentheses are drawn from *Supas*.

Agricultural Employment and its Seasonality

Agriculture still provides well over half of all employment in Indonesia. Trends in the size of the agricultural work-force are therefore of great importance, not least because of the somewhat misguided interpretation often placed on a decline in agriculture's share of total employment as evidence of success in 'industrialization' and 'modernization'. The fact is that, to draw any clear interpretation of the trends in agricultural employment, two items of information are needed—and these are not available, at least not in any reliable form, in Indonesia. The first of these is a measure of agricultural employment refined enough to give trends in total hours worked in the agricultural sector, not just trends in the very questionable measure of the total number of persons who reported agriculture as their main activity in response to a differing set of questions in various censuses and surveys.[21] The second is a measure of trends in labour productivity in agriculture compared to the sectors into which a section of the agricultural labour force is moving. A continuing high share of employment in agriculture does not signify economic stagnation if labour productivity in agriculture is rising, especially if it is rising in pace with that in other sectors which might be expected to absorb agricultural labour.

Table 8.11 gives estimates of the size of the agricultural labour force in Indonesia from various sources, for what they are worth. A number of writers have sought to devise more comparable estimates of the agricultural labour force (Mertens, 1978; Jones, 1981; Abey, Booth and Sundrum, 1981; World Bank, 1980: Table 2.1; Visaria, 1974).

For 1930, if the only adjustment is to prorate the large number recorded in occupations insufficiently defined across industry groups, then the proportion in agriculture comes to 74 per cent. Mertens (1978), however, made more far-reaching adjustments to improve comparability with later data sources: all those recorded in insufficiently defined occupations were placed in agriculture (a questionable procedure); the agricultural employment figure was inflated to allow for the omission of workers aged 10–14; and underrecording of female employment in agriculture (due to the exclusion of unpaid family workers from the labour force) was corrected for

TABLE 8.11

Agricultural Employment Estimates for Indonesia

Data and Source	Estimates without Major Adjustment		Estimates with Major Adjustment	
	Absolute Numbers ('000)	Percentage of Total Employment	Absolute Numbers ('000)	Percentage of Total Employment
Population Census, 1930	15,390	73.9	18,021	77.5
Population Census, 1961	23,980	73.3	25,211	74.3
Population Census, 1971, Series C	25,821	65.9	33,159	n.a.
Population Census, 1971, Series D	25,217	67.1	34,351	73.5
Agricultural Census, 1973	34,100	n.a.		
Supas, 1976	36,614	66.8	32,796	64.3
Sakernas, 1976	29,100	61.6		
Sakernas, 1977	29,700	61.5		
Sakernas, 1978	31,500	60.9		
Population Census, 1980	29,010	56.3		

Sources: Volkstelling, 1930; Indonesian Population Censuses of 1961, 1971 and 1980; Indonesian Agricultural Census of 1973; Supas, 1976; Sakernas, 1976, 1977 and 1978.
Notes: 1. For details of adjustments, see Footnote 22.
   2. Irian Jaya excluded from all estimates.
   n.a. = Data not available.

by means of an adjustment factor to make the sex composition of agri-cultural employment the same as in 1971. With these adjustments, the agricultural proportion of the 1930 labour force rose to 77.5 per cent.

For 1961, Mertens adjusted the number of female workers in agriculture upwards on the assumption that the sex ratio of agricultural employment was actually the same as in 1971. This adjustment seems reasonable, especially given that the sex ratio of agricultural employment recorded in 1980 was almost identical to that in 1971. A similar adjustment was therefore carried out to obtain the 1961 figure in the 'adjusted' column of Table 8.11.

For 1971, aside from the problem of having two alternative sets of data (Series C and Series D), there is a rather implausible slight decline in the number of males recorded in agriculture (see Table 8.8). The 1971 Census could certainly be expected to underestimate the size of the agricultural labour force relative to 1961. Compared to other sectors, relatively large numbers of those who normally worked in agriculture could be expected to be recorded as unemployed or outside the labour force by the 1971 definitions, because seasonal slackness in employment is especially pronounced in agriculture. By contrast, the longer, six-month reference period used for the second stage of determining activity status in the 1961 Census could be expected to result in the recording in agriculture of persons who, although they normally worked in agriculture, were un-employed or outside the labour force at the time of the census.[23]

Fortunately, as noted in Appendix II, the 1971 census planners added the useful question on agricultural work during the 'last season'; these data show that 35.4 million workers were recorded as having done work in agriculture, whereas the number recorded in agriculture by the one-week reference period was only 25.2 million.

The 'last season' figures undoubtedly give an unrealistically high esti-mate of the numbers working in agriculture on a fairly full-time basis, because no minimum cut-off point for time worked in the 'last season' was used. A disproportionate number of those who worked in agriculture in the 'last season' were women, and most of them were unpaid family workers. (See Jones, 1981: 235–44.) The following adjustment was used to derive the figure for 1971 in the 'adjusted' column on Table 8.11: workers who were unemployed or outside the labour force in the reference week, but who also worked in agriculture in the last season, were added to the agricultural sector. The adjusted data overstate agricultural employment in 1971 relative to 1961, because the 1971 data lack a minimum cut-off point for time spent in agriculture in the 'last season'.

Estimates of the size of the agricultural work-force in the 1970s can be derived from the 1973 Agricultural Census, the 1976 *Supas* and the 1976–8 rounds of the *Sakernas*. Unfortunately, this embarrassment of riches only serves to complicate our task. The Agricultural Census, in theory, refers only to 'regular' workers—defined as those who worked full-time in agriculture for a specified minimum period of time. In practice, though, a broader definition must have applied, since the Agricultural

Census estimates are much closer to the generous estimate of agricultural employment according to the 'last season' data for 1971 than to the unadjusted census figures. As Abey, Booth and Sundrum (1981: 41) argue, 'the specialized nature of the Agricultural Census may have meant that more households were defined as "agricultural" in the Agricultural Census than in the Population Census or labour force surveys'.

In 1976, the Intercensal Survey (*Supas*) and the Labour Force Survey (*Sakernas*) were both conducted, though their definitions and procedures for measuring the labour force differed somewhat (Appendix 2). Expectations that they would yield similar results were certainly not fulfilled. *Supas* put the agricultural labour force at 36.6 million, *Sakernas* at only 29.1 million. The later (1977 and 1978) series of *Sakernas* surveys gave figures consistent with the 1976 *Sakernas*. Why, then, the divergence between *Supas* and *Sakernas*? A small part of the explanation may be the seasonal factor, but the main reason was 'differences in the treatment of women and young workers in the agricultural sector who tended to be included as "unpaid family workers" in *Supas* but excluded from the labour force in *Sakernas*' (Arndt and Sundrum, 1980: 63). The higher figure for agricultural employment in *Supas* and *Sakernas* than in the 1971 Census might be attributed both to the nature and ordering of the questions on employment (Appendix 2) and to the one-hour-a-week minimum used in 1976 to classify respondents as employed. Even so, the indicated absolute increase of 3.3 million in agricultural employment between the 1971 and the 1976 *Sakernas* still represented a considerable decline in agriculture's share of total employment.

Finally, the 1980 Census recorded fewer people in agricultural employment than did *Sakernas*, and far fewer than did *Supas*. It showed almost identical figures for women's share of agricultural employment as did the (unadjusted) 1971 Census (Table 8.12). Interestingly, in the 1980 Census reports, employment data are presented according to both the 1971 and the 1976 definitions of 'working' and also using a one-year reference period, but the estimate of agricultural employment is almost identical in each case. This, it might be noted, throws some doubt on the explanation just offered for divergence between the 1971 and 1976 estimates of agricultural employment. What is difficult to explain in the comparison between the 1971, 1976 and 1980 figures on agricultural employment is why the 1980 data should be so low (that is, consistent with the 1971 figures), when in fact procedures followed in 1980 were closer to those followed in 1976. Seasonal factors may be part of the explanation since both the 1971 and 1980 censuses were conducted at a relatively slack time of the year, whereas *Sakernas* was spread over both slack and busy seasons; but even this is not certain, as the discussion of seasonality will reveal.

If it is accepted that the 1971 and 1980 Census figures on agricultural employment are mutually consistent, then the spatial trends in agricultural employment that they indicate are of great interest: that is, not only did agricultural employment in Java grow very slowly during the 1970s, but it actually declined in about half the *kabupaten* of Java (Jones, 1984: Fig. 3).[25]

TABLE 8.12

Women as a Percentage of Employed Population in Agriculture,
and Percentage of Women Agricultural Workers who were
'Unpaid Family Workers', 1961–1980

Year and Source of Data	Women as Percentage of those Working in Agriculture	Percentage of Women Working in Agriculture who were 'Unpaid Family Workers'	Notes
1961 Census	26.4	n.a.	
1971 Census			
(Series C)	31.9	50.8	
(Series D)	32.1	52.2	
1976 *Supas*	39.2	60.9	
1976 *Sakernas*	33.4	n.a.	
1977 *Sakernas*	32.6	58.1	'own account' were 4.9 per cent; employees, 28.5 per cent
1978 *Sakernas*	34.5	47.3	'own account' were 7.5 per cent; employees, 37.7 per cent
1980 Census	31.6	41.5	a further 26.6 per cent were 'self-employed assisted by family members/temporary help'

There were only three main belts in which agricultural employment
increased—one in the Priangan area of West Java, another along a stretch
of the north coast of Central Java from Brebes to Batang, and the third in a
wide band from the north to the south coast, straddling the Central
Java–East Java border. Elsewhere, non-agricultural employment grew
rapidly enough to absorb the entire increase in the labour force.

We receive conflicting messages from the various sources about seasonality of agricultural employment. The difference in the 1971 Census
between the 'last season' data and the data from the reference week (part
of the slack agricultural season in Java) suggests substantial seasonal
differences in agricultural employment.[26] Seasonal differences have also
been invoked by some observers (Leiserson *et al.*, 1980: 13, 22), to explain
the much higher figures for agricultural employment from the *Supas* than
from *Sakernas* 1976.[27] In the first case, agricultural employment would
appear to have declined by 25 per cent in the slack season and, in the
second case, by about 17 per cent.

Analysis of the one series of surveys designed to measure seasonality in employment—*Sakernas*—does not, however, suggest very much seasonal difference in agricultural employment in Indonesia, and what difference there is does not go in the expected direction (Table 8.13). The Differences between the May and November rounds (busy seasons in Java), the February round (moderately busy in planting), and the August round (slack season in Java)[28] show that there was no observable relationship in 1977, when indeed agricultural employment in the slack season exceeded that in the busy seasons;[29] and there was only a slight relationship in 1978, when busy-season employment in agriculture exceeded slack-season employment by about 4 per cent.

The *Supas–Sakernas* comparison does not provide a reasonable basis for the study of seasonality, and the 1971 data give an exaggerated picture of seasonal differences, for reasons elaborated earlier.[30] On balance, it appears that seasonal variation in employment in agriculture is not very great. There could be a number of reasons for this. Exacerbated problems of poverty in the 'slack' season could force people to work harder at various kinds of income-generating activities in the agricultural sector, albeit marginal in their returns (the *Sakernas* data suggests that some young people drop out of school at these times to try to supplement the family income). Alternatively, the Green Revolution and the increase in the irrigated area may have blurred seasonal effects by shortening the period between planting and harvesting and increasing the number of crops per year.

Where, then, does all this leave us on the question of trends in

TABLE 8.13

Numbers Employed in Agriculture, by Season and Hours Worked, 1977
(in Thousands)

Weekly Hours Worked	Workers Employed in Agriculture (in '000)				Change in Numbers, August to November (in '000)
	February	*May*	*August*	*November*	
0–9	2,872	3,310	4,601	4,447	−154
10–24	6,283	8,106	9,156	8,240	−916
25–34	5,960	7,427	7,972	7,674	−298
35–59	18,742	21,306	21,366	21,015	−351
60 or more	2,046	2,249	2,415	2,267	−148
Total	35,903	42,398	45,510	43,643	−1,867
Percentage of total employed working					
0–9 hours	8.0	7.8	10.1	10.2	
10–24 hours	17.5	19.1	20.1	18.9	
25–34 hours	16.6	17.5	17.5	17.6	
35–59 hours	52.2	50.3	47.0	48.2	
60 or more hours	5.7	5.3	5.3	5.2	

Source: Sakernas, 1977.

agriculture's share of total employment over the past two decades? It is quite clear that the share has fallen, although it is difficult to put a precise figure on the extent of the fall. Given that Merten's adjusted figure for 1930 is probably on the high side, there is no persuasive evidence that agriculture's share of total employment fell between 1930 and 1961. Since the adjusted figure for 1971 is too high, there *is* evidence of a decline between 1961 and 1971, though not as sharp as that shown in the column for unadjusted 'Percentage of Total Employment' of Table 8.11. The evidence of a decline during the 1970s is persuasive, though the variety of possible estimates complicates the picture. The 1980 Census figure on agricultural employment is probably too low, when compared with the *Sakernas* figures, due to its timing in the relatively slack time of the year. Between 1961 and 1980, a 'best guesstimate' might be that, had we been able to measure agricultural employment in the same way each year, the share of agriculture in total employment would have declined as follows:

1961	72 per cent
1971	68 per cent
1976	62 per cent
1980	58 per cent

If true, this represents a substantial increase in the importance of non-agricultural employment in just a nineteen-year period, and particularly during the 1970s. But before concluding that it represents an important movement toward the point where wages are driven up to herald the end of a labour-surplus economy, we need to examine the sectors where the share of employment has increased—notably, in manufacturing, and trade and services.

Trends in Employment in Manufacturing

There are two important things to note about manufacturing employment in Indonesia. Firstly, manufacturing employs a much smaller proportion of the labour force than in most of its Asian neighbours (such as Malaysia, Thailand, the Republic of Korea), and manufacturing has been relatively unimportant in providing additional employment during the 1970s: 14 per cent of the increase in total employment; 18 per cent of the increase in non-agricultural employment. Secondly, the structure of manufacturing employment is quite different from that of the more industrially advanced countries, with an extraordinarily high proportion of employment in cottage and small-scale industries and relatively little in large-scale, capital-intensive industries.

Table 8.14 provides various estimates of employment trends in manu-facturing over the course of the 1970s. It must be recognized that, since about three-quarters of all manufacturing employment is in rural areas, most of it in cottage and small-scale industries and as self-employment or unpaid family work, a high proportion of those engaged in manufacturing will also be engaged part time in agriculture and/or trade. Which industry is stated as the major industry, then, is likely to vary in a rather unsystematic

TABLE 8.14

Indonesia: Employment in Manufacturing Industry, by Various Classifications, 1971, 1976 and 1980

Classification	Numbers ('000)						Percentage Change 1971–1976[1]	Percentage Change 1976–1980[1]	Percentage Change 1971–1980[1]
	1971 (Series D)	1971 (Series C)	1976 (Supas)	1976 (Sakernas)	1978 (Sakernas)	1980 (Series S)			
Males	1,471	1,515	1,883	2,066	1,936	2,584	36	25	71
Females	1,102	1,416	1,677	1,902	1,920	2,096	34	10	48
Total	2,573[2]	2,931	3,560	3,968[3]	3,856	4,680	35	18	60
Urban	593	661	685	874	937	1,362	32	56	106
Rural	1,980	2,270	2,875	3,094	2,918	3,318	36	7	46
Jakarta	110	118	n.a.	n.a.	n.a.	285	n.a.	n.a.	142
Remainder of Java	1,894	2,168	n.a.	n.a.	n.a.	3,289	n.a.	n.a.	52
Outer Islands	569	646	n.a.	n.a.	n.a.	1,109	n.a.	n.a.	72
Employers	115	125	65	421	410	170	237	−60	36
Employees	1,432	1,545	1,601	2,183	1,935	2,239	41	3	45
Own account workers	664	788	1,089	737	997	1,733	−6	135	120
Unpaid family workers	362	473	806	627	513	537	33	−14	14
(Own account + unpaid family workers)[4]	(1,026)	(1,261)	(1,895)	(1,364)	(1,510)	(2,270)	8	66	80

Sources: 1971 Census, Series C: Table 9.3; 1971 Census, Series D: Tables 43, 43A; 1980 Census, Series S, No. 2: Tables 41 and 45; *Supas*, Tabulation Series, No. 2: Table 06; 1976 *Sakernas*: Tables 09 and 38.9; 1978 *Sakernas*: Tables XI and XXXIV.

Notes: The small numbers not classified by status in *Supas* and the 1980 Census have been distributed pro rata across industry groups in the bottom panel of the table.

[1] 1971 figures are Series C; 1976 figures are from *Sakernas*.

[2] Would rise to 2671 if we prorate 'activities not adequately defined' across industry groups.

[3] Would rise to 3970 if we prorate 'countries not adequately defined' across industry groups.

[4] Includes the category 'self-employed assisted by family member/temporary help'.

way. Too much fine-grained analysis of the data is therefore not warranted.

This is highlighted by the data on hours of work in manufacturing (Table 8.15). Among the large rural female component of the manufacturing work-force, 34 per cent worked less than 25 hours a week. Presumably, many of these were also active in many other activities, and could easily have been recorded in these other activities if the timing of the census or enumeration procedures had been different.

Overall, manufacturing employment appears to have grown steadily, though not spectacularly, over the decade. The proportion of total employment in manufacturing grew only from 7.8 per cent in 1971 to 9.1 per cent in 1980. The growth was concentrated more in urban than in rural areas, and more among men than among women. Nevertheless, rural areas still provide most manufacturing employment, and Jakarta's share of total manufacturing employment is surprisingly small compared with capital cities in other South-East Asian countries. Women's share of manufacturing employment remains at 45 per cent.

The varied trends in manufacturing employment according to work status, shown in the bottom part of Table 8.14, are clearly affected by some inconsistencies in interpretation of the different statuses. The difficulties of defining status according to the conventional four categories—'employer', 'employee', 'own account worker', and 'unpaid family worker'—were recognized in the 1980 Census by dividing the 'self-employed' into two groups—'self-employed without the assistance of other persons', and 'self-employed assisted by family members/temporary help'. Although, conceptually, both categories were included within the group 'self-employed'

TABLE 8.15

Number of Hours Worked per Week in Manufacturing, by Percentage of Urban/Rural and Male/Female Work-force, 1980

Work-force Classification	Percentage of Manufacturing Work-force, by Classification, Working:					Total Manufacturing Work-force	
	10 Hours	10–24 Hours	25–34 Hours	35–59 Hours	60+ Hours	Percentage	'000
Urban							
Male	2.4	4.0	3.7	73.1	16.8	100	907
Female	4.3	10.7	6.4	64.2	14.5	100	456
Total	3.0	6.2	4.6	70.2	16.0	100	1363
Rural							
Male	3.7	10.4	9.4	60.4	16.1	100	1677
Female	8.1	25.8	15.0	43.2	8.0	100	1640
Total	5.9	18.0	12.1	51.9	12.1	100	3317
Total	5.0	14.5	10.0	57.2	13.2	100	4680

Source: 1980 Indonesian Census, Series S, No. 2: Table 50.

in earlier censuses and surveys, the categorization appears to have resulted, in the case of manufacturing employment, in a substantial increase in the numbers recorded as 'self-employed', at the expense of 'employers' and 'unpaid family workers'. When we group 'own account' and 'unpaid family workers', the trends are less erratic.

There has been controversy about trends in employment in large and medium-scale manufacturing (L & M), compared with small-scale and cottage industry (S & C), as suggested by BPS's *Statistik Industri* series and the 1974/5 *Sensus Industri*. The *Sensus Industri* used a very generous definition of 'participant in cottage activities', which lifted its total estimate of employment in manufacturing well above that of the *Supas* or *Sakernas* conducted two years later. Nevertheless, McCawley and Tait's (1979a: 128) table prepared from these data and reproduced as Table 8.16 is immensely valuable, as 'it provides the first roughly consistent set of figures for the three subsectors of the Indonesian manufacturing sector that has ever been available'. Clearly, the cottage industry sector (of which the two most important activities are bamboo and rattan weaving and coconut sugar production) dominates employment in manufacturing, whereas the L & M sector dominates production; thus, production per worker is vastly greater in the L & M sector than in the cottage industry sector.

McCawley and Tait argue that employment in the L & M sector grew strongly over the 1970s (by 7 per cent per annum between 1970 and 1982),

TABLE 8.16

Employment in Industry and Value Added, 1974/5

Source of Data, and Type of Industry	Reference Year	Workers ('000)	Per- cent- age	Value Added at Market prices[a] (Rupiah billion)	Per cent- age	Value Added per Worker (Rupiah '000)
Statistik Industri						
Large & medium	1974	661.7	13	476.9	80	721
Small	1975	343.2	7	44.2	7	129
Cottage	1974/5	3,899.9[b]	80	75.1	13	19
Total		4,904.8[b]	100	596.2	100	122
Supas	1976	3,560.1		(890.0)[c]		

Source: McCawley and Tait, 1979a: 129.

[a] The data for value added have been adjusted to 1974 prices by deflating data for small firms by 20 per cent and for cottage firms by 10 per cent.

[b] Strictly speaking, a worker in the cottage-industry sector (defined as a 'participant' in the *Sensus Industri* data) is quantitatively different to workers in the other sectors because intensity of work (as measured in annual mandays of work per worker) in the cottage sector is low; see Footnote 4.

[c] Sectoral national income estimates, 1974. No explanation is available for the large discrepancy.

though the sector absorbed only about 4 per cent of the workers being added to the labour force each year because of its relatively small base (McCawley, 1984: 160–1; Roepstorff, 1985: 43). There may also have been 'backwash' effects in some sectors (for example, textiles), holding back the growth of S & C sector employment, though McCawley and Tait argue that employment in the S & C sector appears to have been growing quite strongly. Dapice and Snodgrass (1979) argued that McCawley and Tait's estimate of employment growth in the L & M sector was exaggerated, and that S & C sector employment had grown rapidly, but their basis for the latter argument relied too heavily on the weak reed of comparisons between 1971 Census and *Supas* data. The 1980 census data, not available to the protagonists in the debate, do not help us much, since they suffer from the same weakness as the other census and survey data. If we were to accept such data at face value, then we would be forced to argue that between 1971 and 1976, using *Sakernas* figures as being more reliable than *Supas* figures, employment increased sharply in the L & M sector, but very little in the S & C sector; however, between 1976 and 1980, this trend was reversed, and the S & C sector dominated employment growth. Such estimates would be based on employment status data in the bottom panel of Table 8.14, assuming that L & M sector workers are mainly employers and employees, whereas own account and unpaid family workers and employees were all important in the S & C sector.[31] The entire 1971–80 period trend would then be interpreted to mean that employment had grown rather more rapidly in S & C than in L & M sectors.

In actual fact, given the weaknesses of the data, all that can safely be said is: that employment in manufacturing grew by over 5 per cent per annum over the 1970s but, because of the small base, the increase was not rapid enough to soak up more than a small proportion of the annual addition to Indonesia's labour force; that growth of male employment in manufacturing has exceeded that of female, overall and in rural areas but not in urban areas (see Table 8.14 and Oey, 1985: 248–52); that, although *Sensus Industri* and *Statistik Industri* data suggest rapid growth in the L & M sectors, there is a problem in reconciling them with data on manufacturing output (see Dapice and Snodgrass, 1979); and that, clearly, employment in the S & C sector continued to increase. The estimate that L & M sector employment increased by 7 per cent per annum over the 1970s implies that S & C sector employment increased by more than 5 per cent per annum over the same period. Although we do not know whether there was much improvement in the very low productivity levels in the S & C sector, there was clearly very little shift in employment towards the much higher productivity L & M sector of manufacturing. Therefore, although the data are not inconsistent with the early stages of an industrial take-off, neither do they provide overwhelming evidence that it is taking place. Certainly, manufacturing has not been providing the dynamic growth in employment, especially for females, that it has in neighbouring countries such as Malaysia and Singapore (Jones, 1983).

Trends in Employment in Trade, Finance, and Services

If, as argued above, agriculture over the past two decades has failed to absorb a share of the increment to the labour force even approaching its share of the 1961 labour force, and if manufacturing's modest performance had a limited overall impact on employment due to its small initial employment share, then the remaining major sector—the S sector (trade, finance and public services)—must have played a major role in employment change over this period. This has indeed been the case, as data in Table 8.17 confirm. Important contrasts are revealed in two different dimensions: between the two periods 1961–71 and 1971–80, and between Indonesia as a whole and Java.

Trade and services have always been important for labour absorption in Indonesia, but their importance has increased considerably in the past two decades. In the 1960s, if the census figures are to be trusted, they provided three-quarters of all additional employment for males and one-third for females. Even in rural areas, they provided more new employment than did agriculture. In the 1970s, trade and services provided almost twice as many new jobs as agriculture even in rural areas; in Indonesia as a whole, they provided more than three times as many new jobs as manufacturing. The dominance of trade and services in providing new jobs in the 1970s was especially marked in Java and among females; among females in Java, they provided three-quarters of all new jobs.

Three problems cloud the interpretation of these trends. The first is the overlapping agriculture, manufacturing and service sector occupations for many workers (and indeed the overlapping of these occupations with household maintenance, which is not classified as an economic activity at all), so that the choice of one 'primary' occupation involves an arbitrary element and the possibility of one census overrecording employment in one sector in comparison with another census. It seems unlikely, however, that such factors could have distorted more than marginally the picture derived from Table 8.17 of steady gains in service sector employment over a twenty-year period.

The second problem is the changing definitions of 'urban' between the 1971 and 1980 Censuses, rendering comparisons of employment changes in urban and rural areas rather misleading, especially in Java. For example, the fact that agriculture's share of the 1971–80 employment increase in urban areas of Java was larger than its 1961 share had been was almost certainly due to the designation of more smaller towns as 'urban', and to boundary extensions in some of the larger ones.

The third, and most basic, problem is to interpret the developmental implications of the S sector's rising share. The designation, 'trade and services', covers an extraordinarily wide range of activities, from the 'informal sector' activities on which so much has been written in recent years (see, for example, Salih, 1982: 156–8; McGee, 1978; Sethuraman, 1976) to high finance and international banking. The service sector is represented in both the most depressingly 'make work' and low-productivity

TABLE 8.17

Indonesia and Java: Increase in Employment and its Distribution across Main Industries, by
Sex and Urban–Rural Location, 1961–1971, 1971–1980

Type of Industry	Urban			Rural			Total		
	Employment 1961	Employment Increase 1961–1971	1971–1980	Employment 1961	Employment Increase 1961–1971	1971–1980	Employment 1961	Employment Increase 1961–1971	1971–1980
ALL INDONESIA									
Male									
Absolute numbers ('000):	3,243	973	2,612	20,557	1,409	5,580	23,806	2,378	8,192
Percentage in:									
Agriculture	13	7	8	84	−24	37	74	−10	28
Manufacturing	16	−3	17	3	30	11	5	16	13
Trade, services	49	79	57	10	75	31	15	77	39
Other	22	17	18	3	19	21	6	17	20
Female									
Absolute numbers ('000):	1,050	530	1,262	7,853	3,593	2,531	8,903	4,124	3,793
Percentage in:									
Agriculture	9	8	6	79	56	24	71	51	17
Manufacturing	18	6	19	7	21	14	8	19	16
Trade, services	71	86	74	13	23	59	20	31	65
Other	2	0	1	1	0	3	1	−1	2

JAVA

Male

Absolute numbers ('000):	2,251	530	2,094	13,324	905	2,912	15,575	1,435	5,006
Percentage in:									
Agriculture	9	−1	13	82	−48	23	71	−31	19
Manufacturing	19	−13	19	4	38	12	6	19	15
Trade, services	50	96	51	11	91	37	17	93	43
Other	22	18	17	3	19	28	6	19	23

Female

Absolute numbers ('000):	847	354	1,066	5,033	2,512	1,197	5,881	2,867	2,262
Percentage in:									
Agriculture	6	2	8	74	50	−2	64	45	3
Manufacturing	18	8	21	8	24	20	9	22	21
Trade, services	74	90	69	18	27	79	26	34	75
Other	2	0	2	1	−1	3	1	−1	1

Source: 1961, 1971 and 1980 Census Reports.
Note: 'Other' industry includes construction, transport and public utilities.

end of the scale (street-vending of combs, cigarettes, kitchen utensils and clothing; cutting hair under the bridge) and in the most dynamic growth areas of banking and international trade. Although it is clear that the bulk of employment in the sector is toward the low-productivity end of the scale, it is important to determine whether the increase in employment in this sector over the 1970s merely replicated the pre-existing pattern, or whether in fact there was a shift in new employment toward modern sector and higher-productivity activities. The starting point here is the observation that employment in finance and services grew more rapidly during the 1970s than employment in trade. The following points are then relevant:

1. The average level of education is much higher for service workers than for those in trade. In 1980, 44 per cent of service workers had completed lower secondary school and above, compared with only 21 per cent in trade. Even sharper differentials prevailed in 1971: 34 per cent of service workers had completed lower secondary school and above, compared with 8 per cent of workers in trade.

2. A higher proportion of workers in finance and services are employees and work 'regular' hours than is the case with workers in agriculture, trade or transport.

3. The *Supas* tabulated monthly earnings for those whose employment status was 'employee'. Although this is not very meaningful for agriculture or trade, where most workers were not employees, we do find that in services and transportation, average monthly earnings were well above those in the manufacturing sector. For example, the proportion of employees earning more than Rp 15,000 a month was more than twice as high in transport and services (almost 37 per cent) than in manufacturing, and the difference was even more pronounced for incomes over Rp 30,000 per month.

4. The average level of education of S-sector workers, taken as a whole, is very much higher than in other sectors. In 1980, 27 per cent of S-sector workers had completed lower secondary education (SLP) or better, but only 6 per cent of workers in other sectors had reached this level. The S sector absorbed 64 per cent of the additional workers with SLP education or above in the 1971–80 period, almost exactly the same as its share of all such workers in 1971. Within the S sector, average educational levels in finance and services are much higher than those in trade.

5. Data from *Supas* (Table 8.20) indicate that almost 92 per cent of those employed in trading are in household enterprises, whereas 76 per cent of those in services are in non-household enterprises. Even in rural areas, almost 72 per cent of employment in services is in non-household enterprises, presumably much of it in government, education, health and agricultural services. Given that employment in services grew substantially faster than in trade during the 1970s, this probably means that the proportion of S-sector employment in non-household enterprises increased over the decade.

6. 'Financial services' (which has substantially higher productivity than the average of S-sector activities) showed the fastest employment growth of

S-sector components, in both urban and rural areas, no doubt reflecting the growth of banking, insurance and other financial institutions in the cities and credit-providing agencies (for example, KIK and *Candak Kulak*) in the rural areas. However, its contribution to total S-sector employment is still fairly small.

None of these points proves that the S sector has been acting as a growth-reflecting and growth-generating sector rather than as a 'soak' for unemployed or underemployed labour; however, the balance of the evidence certainly points this way. This is particularly important to note in the case of S-sector jobs in rural areas, which have provided such a large proportion of the additional employment generated in rural areas during the 1970s. In 1980, of all workers in rural areas with a lower secondary school education and above, 46 per cent were in public services alone, and 56 per cent were in the S sector as a whole. Nearly 40 per cent of the work-force in services in rural areas were professional, managerial or administrative workers, most of them presumably government employees, reflecting the large investments in education and rural health facilities. (School enrolments in rural areas rose from 14.0 million to 23.3 million, or by two-thirds, between 1971 and 1980, and the number of school teachers would have risen roughly in proportion). The growth in trade and transport employment is more likely to have been based on the growth of agricultural production and incomes, and on increased job opportunities in the towns for rural commuters or temporary migrants.

Educational Attainment of the Labour Force

In the 1961 Census, labour force data were not cross-tabulated with educational attainment. The closest we can get to a comparison of the educational attainment of the labour force in 1961 with that in later years is to compare the educational attainment of all persons aged over 15 years (Table 8.18). This should give a reasonably close approximation to the educational attainment of the labour force in the case of males, since 89 per cent of males aged over 15 were in the labour force in 1961, 82 per cent in 1971, and 89 per cent in 1976. However, the educational attainment of females aged more than 15 might not be very representative of the female labour force.

There are some problems in interpreting the data in Table 8.18, because the 1971 Census procedures led to an overstatement of the numbers with completed primary education through the inclusion in this category of some of those who had not completed their primary schooling (see Hull and Sunaryo, 1980), and the 1980 data appear to have underrecorded the numbers with academy or university education. In any event, it is clear that the educational attainment of the male labour force improved substantially over the two decades following 1961. The proportion of males over 15 years of age without schooling dropped from 56 per cent to 22 per cent, and the proportion with completed primary schooling or better rose from

TABLE 8.18

Indonesia: Population Aged 15 Years and Over, by Educational Attainment,
1961, 1971, 1976 and 1980

Sex	Year	Percentage of Population with:					
		No Schooling	Incomplete Primary Schooling	Completed Primary Schooling	Completed Lower or Upper Secondary Schooling	Academy or University Education	Total Percentage
Males	1961	55.7	22.6	16.7	4.8	0.2	100.0
	1971	32.4	29.4	27.1	10.4	0.7	100.0
	1976	26.0	38.9	22.6	10.7	1.8	100.0
	1980	21.8	35.9	25.5	15.9	0.9	100.0
Females	1961	79.6	11.2	7.3	1.9	0.0	100.0
	1971	57.0	21.2	16.5	5.1	0.2	100.0
	1976	47.5	31.3	14.8	5.8	0.7	100.0
	1980	41.4	30.4	18.8	9.1	0.3	100.0
Both sexes	1961	68.1	16.7	11.8	3.3	0.1	100.0
	1971	45.2	25.1	21.6	7.7	0.4	100.0
	1976	37.2	34.9	18.6	8.1	1.2	100.0
	1980	31.9	33.1	22.1	12.4	0.6	100.0

Sources: BPS, Population Census 1961; 1971 (Series D: Table 18); 1980 (Series S, No. 2:
Tables 02 and 09); *Supas*, 1976, Tabulation Series No. 3, Jakarta, 1977: Table 03.
Note: *Supas* figures are not adjusted for the regions not covered.

22 per cent to 42 per cent. Presumably, a similar improvement took place
in the case of the female labour force; certainly, the average educational
attainment of females over 15 rose substantially. The absolute increase in
the numbers with completed primary schooling and above was almost the
same for males and females, but the relative increase was much greater for
females because of their inferior educational status in 1961.

What was happening over time, of course, was that members of older,
poorly educated cohorts who died or retired were replaced by members of
the younger cohorts who received their education in the post-Independence
period. Thus, between 1971 and 1980, the number of workers with little or
no education grew by only 1.9 per cent per annum, and the numbers with
completed primary schooling by 2.2 per cent per annum, but those with
secondary school or tertiary education rose by 8.4 per cent per annum,
more than doubling over the nine-year period. This improvement, however, cannot disguise the remaining deficiencies in educational attainment
of the work-force. Table 8.19 shows that male workers in 1980 were
divided into three large groups, as follows: 23 per cent had no schooling at
all, another 40 per cent had incomplete primary schooling, and the
remaining 38 per cent had completed primary schooling and perhaps gone
on to secondary school. Very few had attended college or university.
Females were worse off still; almost half had no schooling at all, and only
23 per cent had completed primary school. In the case of both males and
females, the urban work-force was much better educated than the rural;

TABLE 8.19
Indonesia: Educational Attainment of the Working Population, 1980

Sex and Rural/Urban Location	Percentage of Working Population with:					
	No Schooling	Incomplete Primary Schooling	Complete Primary Schooling	Complete Lower or Upper Secondary Schooling	Academy or University Education	Total Percentage
Males						
Urban areas	9.4	25.6	28.3	32.9	3.8	100
Rural areas	25.7	43.3	23.0	7.7	0.3	100
Total males	22.5	39.7	24.1	12.7	1.0	100
Females						
Urban areas	28.8	27.7	19.6	21.7	2.2	100
Rural areas	47.3	34.3	14.6	3.7	0.1	100
Total females	44.1	33.2	15.5	6.8	0.4	100
Both sexes						
Urban areas	15.1	26.3	25.7	29.6	3.3	100
Rural areas	33.0	40.3	20.2	6.3	0.2	100
Total both sexes	29.6	37.7	21.2	10.7	0.8	100

Source: 1980 Population Census, Series S, No. 2: Table 52.

even so, almost one-third of the female work-force in urban areas had no education at all.

Urban and Rural Employment Structures

According to one popular misconception, rural areas in developing countries offer little employment outside the agricultural sector, while urban areas are largely divorced from the agricultural economy which surrounds them. In Indonesia, as elsewhere, the facts are rather different. The 1980 census data show that almost one-third of those working in rural areas (about 13.7 million people) found their livelihood outside agriculture, mainly in trade, services, and manufacturing;[32] the 1971 Census and the 1976 *Supas* (see Table 8.20) show a somewhat lower proportion—about one-quarter, a proportion very similar to that found around the same time in the Philippines, India and Peninsular Malaysia, three countries where the non-agricultural sectors of the economy are usually considered more developed than in Indonesia. Even more surprising is the fact that in 1980, 71 per cent of all manufacturing employment in Indonesia was in rural areas (down from 76 per cent in 1971, probably due partly to the altered definition of urban), including activities such as batik-making, brick-making, repair of bicycles and agricultural implements, and weaving of mats and hats. Not all rural manufacturing is small scale; in recent years many of the large plants built with foreign capital have been located in urban fringe areas outside city boundaries, for example along the Jakarta–Bogor road and the Surabaya–Sidoardjo road.

Similarly, rural areas provide more than half of all employment in

TABLE 8.20

Total, Urban and Rural Employment by Major Industry Group and Location of Activity, 1976

Major Industry Group	Total				Urban				Rural			
	Absolute Numbers ('000)			Percentage	Absolute Numbers ('000)			Percentage	Absolute Numbers ('000)			Percentage
	Household Enterprises	Non-Household	Total*		Household Enterprises	Non-Household	Total*		Household Enterprises	Non-Household	Total*	
Agriculture	32,263	2,903	35,258	66.0	771	94	915	12.7	31,492	2,814	34,343	74.3
Mining	21	23	44	0.1	7	15	22	0.3	14	8	22	0.1
Manufacturing	1,978	1,580	3,560	6.7	132	553	685	9.5	1,846	1,027	2,875	6.2
Electricity	2	32	34	0.1	1	24	24	0.3	2	9	10	negligible
Construction	165	929	1,098	2.0	53	404	459	6.4	112	525	639	1.4
Trade	5,745	500	6,253	11.7	1,576	310	1,886	26.1	4,170	190	4,367	9.4
Transportation	394	718	1,112	2.1	169	398	568	7.9	225	319	544	1.2
Financing	7	65	74	0.1	3	59	62	0.8	4	6	12	negligible
Services	1,219	3,929	5,157	9.6	441	1,943	2,387	33.1	778	1,985	2,770	6.0
Others	64	175	854	1.6	5	79	210	2.9	59	96	643	1.4
Total	41,858	10,859	53,444	100.0	3,158	3,879	7,218	100.0	38,702	6,979	46,225	100.0

Source: Supas, 1976, Tabulation Series No. 2: Table 12.
* Includes 'not stated'.

services, two-thirds of all employment in trade and construction, and half of all employment in transport. The only major industrial sectors in which a clear majority of total employment is provided in urban areas are the two relatively insignificant sectors (from an employment point of view) of public utilities and finance—including insurance, real estate, and business services. When we add to these figures the large but unknown number of rural dwellers who move to the cities to obtain work on a temporary or casual basis but are classified by the census as working in agriculture, it is clear that a substantial fraction of all work engaged in by rural dwellers is in the non-agriculture sector. This is of some importance in planning for ways to cope with the inevitable expansion of the rural labour force over the remainder of this century.

Another surprising finding is that in 1980, over 9 per cent of those employed in urban areas are employed in agriculture, and the corresponding figure in earlier years was even higher (Mertens and Alatas, 1978). The percentage rises higher in the smaller towns; if we exclude Jakarta from the urban population, agricultural employment in the remaining urban areas of Indonesia rises to about 11 per cent of total employment. Many urban dwellers also do seasonal work in agriculture at busy times of the year. Therefore, we must view the Indonesian employment structure as a continuum from large-urban to small-urban to rural, with agricultural employment penetrating into the cities and non-agricultural employment very important in rural areas, rather than as sharply dichotomized between urban and rural areas.

Some important differences emerge between urban and rural areas in the extent to which employment in different industries is divided between household and non-household enterprises (Table 8.20). Overall, the industry groups in which non-household enterprise predominates are mining, utilities, construction, transportation, finance and services. However, in urban areas, manufacturing is also dominated by the non-household sector, whereas in rural areas 64 per cent of manufacturing employment is in the household sector. In other industry groups as well, the non-household sector is relatively more prominent in urban than in rural areas.

When the figures are separated for Java and the rest of Indonesia, some noteworthy findings emerge. One is that there was a great deal more agricultural employment in the urban areas of the other islands than of Java; 21.6 per cent of total employment in these areas compared with 7 per cent in urban Java. This was no doubt partly due to the larger size of cities in Java; cities with populations above one million constituted 53 per cent of the urban population of Java, whereas there was only one such city in the other islands. The boundaries of cities outside Java also appear to encompass large rural areas more frequently than is the case in Java. Rural areas of the outer islands are also much more agricultural than those in Java, agriculture providing 84 per cent of employment on the outer islands compared with 72 per cent in Java. By the same token, manufacturing and trade employ 18 per cent of those employed in rural Java but only 8 per cent in rural areas of the outer islands. The town, in this sense, has invaded the rural areas of Java and diversified their employment structure.[33]

Unemployment and Underutilization of Labour

Unemployment is a concept that is of little relevance among Indonesian's vast rural labour force, and of only limited relevance among urban workers: low productivity and low earnings constitute a more important issue. The shaky foundations of the estimates for unemployment are shown up, in the case of the 1971 Census, by the massive increase in measured unemployment resulting from the changes in imputation procedures discussed in Appendix 2, a rise from 0.9 million in Series C to 3.7 million in Series D. The unemployment rate measured by Series C was 2.4 per cent for males and 1.8 per cent for females, compared with 7.5 per cent for males and 11.5 per cent for females in Series D. The changes were particularly large in West Java and the outer islands (Jones, 1974: 19–26; Sundrum, 1975b).

Rates of unemployment measured by *Supas* and *Sakernas* were very similar to those measured by Series C for 1971 (Table 8.21). The *Sakernas* rates tended to be slightly higher for males and lower for females than the other sources. These low rates would be viewed with envy by economic planners in any industrialized country, but as already noted, they have little real meaning. How, for example, is it possible to make sense of time trends in unemployment rates for Jakarta as erratic as those shown below?

Source and Date	Unemployment Rates (Percentage) for Jakarta	
	Males	Females
1971 Census (Series C)	5.6	4.4
1971 Census (Series D)	10.8	19.0
1972 Urban Unemployment Survey	11.9	12.1
1976 *Supas*	6.1	6.7
1980 Labour Force Survey of Jakarta	9.6	10.5
1980 Census	3.7	4.3

The data on unemployment show the usually expected relationships: higher urban than rural unemployment rates, much higher rates among the young (aged 10–24) than at older ages (Table 8.21; see also Jones, 1981: Table 8.15) and higher rates among the better educated. The educational break-point occurs at the level of completed primary school. Nevertheless, because of the low educational level prevailing among the labour force, 89 per cent of all unemployed in Java in 1971 had primary schooling or less.

The *Sakernas* surveys made available for the first time Indonesia-wide data on unemployment rates for age groups cross-tabulated by education, of which the urban rates for 1978 are presented in Table 8.22. These figures confirm that, although the lower unemployment rates among the uneducated result, in part, from their older average age, they still remain

TABLE 8.21

Indonesia: Unemployment Rates by Age and Sex, 1980,
and for All Ages, Various Years

Data Source and Date	Males			Females		
	Urban	Rural	Total	Urban	Rural	Total
All Ages	Percentage					
1971 Census, Series C	5.0	1.9	2.4	4.5	1.4	1.8
1971 Census, Series D	10.8	6.8	7.5	17.1	10.7	11.5
1976 *Supas*	5.4	1.2	1.9	5.9	1.5	2.0
1976 *Sakernas* (Sept.–Dec.)	6.9	1.9	2.7	5.1	1.1	1.6
1978 *Sakernas*	7.0	2.1	2.9	3.8	1.4	1.8
1980 Census	2.7	1.0	1.4	3.0	2.2	2.3
Age Groups, 1980 Census	Percentage					
10–14 years	6.0	2.4	2.6	4.7	3.8	3.9
15–19 years	8.3	2.7	3.5	5.7	3.8	4.1
20–24 years	6.8	1.9	3.1	6.5	3.0	3.8
25–29 years	2.3	0.9	1.3	2.6	2.1	2.2
30–34 years	1.0	0.6	0.7	1.5	1.7	1.7
35–44 years	0.8	0.5	0.6	0.9	1.5	1.4
45+ years	1.0	0.5	0.6	0.8	1.3	1.2

Sources: BPS, Population Census 1971 (Series C; Series D: Table 36; and Series E: Table 29), Jakarta, various dates; *Supas*, 1976, Tabulation Series No. 2: Table 02; BPS, *Keadaan Angkatan Kerja di Indonesia, 1961–1980*, Jakarta, 1983: Tables 1.31, 1.32; BPS, Population Census 1980, Series S, No. 2: Table 37.

well below the rates for those with completed primary education and above when we control for age.[34] Similar results were obtained from labour force surveys in some major cities of Indonesia in 1972 and 1975 (Jones, 1981: 250–3). It is noteworthy that unemployment rates reach their peak for those with upper secondary schooling, and are lower for those with academy or university education.

Half to two-thirds of Indonesia's unemployed are seeking work for the first time, and well over three-quarters of this group are under 25 years of age.[35] Data on duration of unemployment for first-time job seekers are doubtlessly unreliable because of the difficulty of establishing exactly when they started looking for work, but it is clear that many of the unemployed have been looking for work for a long time—one-third to two-thirds (depending on the source) for more than six months.[36] In the urban labour force surveys, average duration of unemployment was less for those who had worked before.

It is difficult to interpret the data on unemployment in Indonesia's cities. Clearly, the situation is serious, and the high unemployment among the young could be interpreted as meaning that the unemployment situation is

TABLE 8.22

Indonesia: Unemployment Rates, by Sex, Age Group and
Educational Attainment, in Urban Areas, 1978

Sex and Age	Unemployment Rate (Percentage) by Educational Attainment					
	No Schooling	Some Primary Schooling	Completed Primary Schooling	Lower Secondary Schooling	Upper Secondary Schooling and above	All Levels
Male						
15–19 years	18.3[+]	18.2	28.7	37.3	36.6[+]	25.0
20–24 years	4.5[+]	9.9	13.6	22.2	30.3	17.9
25–29 years	6.1[+]	4.4	6.3	6.5	8.8	6.7
30–34 years	1.4[+]	2.0	3.3	3.6	4.0	3.3
35–44 years	0.3	1.1	1.6	1.9	1.7	1.4
45+ years	0.7	1.1	1.4	1.9	1.0	1.2
All ages*	2.0	5.6	7.6	9.2	9.3	7.0
Female						
15–19 years	1.4	4.7	12.2	21.6	67.6[+]	9.5
20–24 years	2.3	4.3	6.9	15.3	20.3	10.4
25–29 years	3.1	2.1	2.9	5.3	5.5	3.9
30–34 years	0.0	0.2	3.0	0.0	2.2	1.2
35–44 years	0.8	0.4	0.2	1.7	0.4	0.6
45+ years	0.0	0.2	0.0	0.8	0.0	0.1
All ages*	0.7	2.2	5.2	8.1	10.6	3.8

Source: *Sakernas*, 1978: Tables V and XXIII.

* Includes 10–14 age group.
[+] Numbers in this group are fairly small.

worsening as a result of the growing numbers of young people entering the urban labour market at a time when job opportunities are growing only slowly. But evidence from other developing countries show that high unemployment among the young is a structural 'fact of life', inevitable when young people leave school and have to find their way in a labour-surplus economy, and the fact that unemployment rates in Indonesia are relatively low at ages above 30 suggests that there is no cause for undue alarm. Moreover, unemployment is heavily concentrated among the young people who are best able to survive lengthy periods without work—that is, those with secondary or tertiary education, who as we know, are disproportionately drawn from the middle and upper classes, and can no doubt be supported for a time by their families without undue hardship. For example, in *Sakernas* 1978, among all unemployed persons in urban areas, 84 per cent were maintained by family or friends, 10 per cent by getting an occasional job and 6 per cent by other means. There is also evidence from the urban labour force surveys that younger workers are far more likely than older workers to live in a household with at least one other working member, and this no doubt applies also to unemployed young people as well.

Open unemployment, however, is only the tip of the iceberg of labour underutilization in urban areas of Indonesia. The inability of the economy to absorb labour into minimally adequate employment manifests itself in two other ways as well—non-participation in economic activities, and extremely low returns to labour among a substantial section of the work-force.

As noted earlier, the rate of non-participation in the work-force among urban youth—even to the extent of failing to consider themselves as seeking work—is very high in Indonesia. In the age group 20–24, 39 per cent of urban males were not employed in 1980 (that is, they were either unemployed or not in the labour force). As many as 19 per cent of urban males in this age group said that they were attending educational institutions, a figure roughly consistent with official tertiary enrolment rates. However, the argument that most of the remaining 20 per cent were 'discouraged workers' is very plausible.

Underutilization of those whose family economy is too close to the margin of subsistence to afford the 'luxury' of unemployment is more likely to express itself in other ways, including engaging in marginal work with very low returns in what has come to be termed the 'informal sector'. *Sakernas* data indicate that short hours of work (less than 35 hours) and long hours of work (more than 60 hours) are almost equally common among the urban labour force: roughly one-quarter of the labour force is in each category.[37] *Sakernas* and the urban labour-force surveys show that long hours characterize particularly the following groups: the uneducated and poorly educated; employers, own-account workers and unpaid family workers; workers in the transport and trade sectors (which include *becak* drivers, hawkers, etc.); and migrants to the city. Surprisingly, in Palembang and Ujung Pandang (the only cities for which the data are available), the percentage saying that they wanted more work did not show a strong or consistent relationship with hours worked. However, the data on desire for more work made more sense if we controlled for sex and income. Weekly income itself did not show a consistent relationship with hours worked, and this means that hourly income was especially low for many of those working 60 hours or more. For a substantial proportion of workers, the struggle for what they considered a minimum income no doubt determined the length of the work-week.

The relationship between desire for more work and income has been studied, controlling for hours worked and sex (Jones and Supraptilah, 1976: Table 11). The most important finding is that desire for more work was more closely related (inversely) to income than to hours worked, the percentage wanting more work dropping sharply at incomes above Rp 5,000 per week. The 'both sexes' data to some extent obscured relationships which differed for each sex. Females constituted a substantially higher proportion of the short-working-hour, low-income groups than did males and, at any given level of income or hours worked, they were much less likely to desire more work than were males. This held down the proportions wanting more work among those working short hours in the 'both sexes' data.

Both *Supas* and the 1980 Census provide a similar picture of hours worked in different industries in Indonesia as a whole. Summarized in Table 8.23, the data for 1980 show that the number of hours worked over the entire Indonesian economy is heavily weighted by the hours worked in agriculture, where the bulk of the work-force is located. One-third of the male workers and over half the female workers in agriculture worked less than 35 hours, a partial reflection no doubt of the large numbers of unpaid family workers recorded in agriculture. In other sectors, the proportion working short hours is much less, although it is almost one-third of all workers in manufacturing, no doubt reflecting the importance of part-time work in cottage industry. The construction and transport sectors have the lowest incidence of short hours of work, and transport and trade have the highest proportions working exceptionally long hours, thus confirming the findings of the urban unemployment surveys. Females, on average, work shorter hours than males in all industries except construction, where their numbers are negligible.

TABLE 8.23

Distribution of Working Population by Hours Worked, According to Industry and Sex, 1980

Sex and Hours Worked	Percentage Distribution[a] of Working Population by Industry						
	Agricul- ture	Manufact- uring	Construc- tion	Trade	Trans- port	Services	All In- dustries[b]
Males							
<25	22.4	10.1	7.0	14.0	7.5	10.2	17.4
25–34	16.6	7.5	5.5	9.1	5.3	10.8	13.0
35–59	54.5	65.8	68.8	50.8	49.8	64.8	57.3
60+	6.5	16.6	18.7	26.1	37.4	14.2	12.3
All hours worked	100.0	100.0	100.0	100.0	100.0	100.0	100.0
Females							
<25	42.6	27.4	14.2	24.0	9.0	20.3	34.0
25–34	19.6	13.6	9.7	13.3	6.1	13.0	16.6
35–59	35.5	49.3	61.5	41.6	67.8	44.1	39.8
60+	2.3	9.7	14.6	21.1	17.1	22.6	9.6
All hours worked	100.0	100.0	100.0	100.0	100.0	100.0	100.0
Both sexes							
<25	28.7	17.7	7.0	18.7	7.5	13.3	22.7
25–34	17.5	10.1	5.6	11.1	5.4	11.4	14.2
35–59	48.7	58.6	68.7	46.4	50.0	58.4	51.7
60+	5.1	13.6	18.7	23.8	37.1	16.9	11.4
All hours worked	100.0	100.0	100.0	100.0	100.0	100.0	100.0

Source: 1980 Indonesian Census, Series S, No. 2: Table 50.

[a] The small group with hours not stated were distributed pro rata.

[b] Includes mining, electricity, finance and 'others', which are not shown in individual columns because they employ relatively few people.

Multiple Job-holding

Even though multiple job-holding is generally believed to be very wide-spread in urban areas of Indonesia, the available data on the whole do not bear out this expectation. Writing at the time of economic disorder and rampant inflation in 1964–5, Hawkins (1966) noted that official salaries of government employees were sufficient to cover about one-third of the monthly expenditures of higher-salaried officials and only one-fifth those of the lower-paid workers. He stated that 'most government employees and teachers have tried to secure multiple jobs', and noted that the opportunities to find added work seemed to be greater in the larger cities. However, another source of data for the same period—the 1964–5 *Susenas* showed only modest rates of multiple job-holding. In urban areas, 10 per cent of males had more than one economic activity, and, in rural areas, the corresponding figure was 18 per cent. Less than half as many females had a second activity—4 per cent in urban areas and 8 per cent in rural areas (Jones, 1981: Table 8.19). Care is needed in interpreting these figures because a question framed in terms of 'subsidiary activities' is more likely to record those whose secondary activity was in a completely different field than those who 'doubled up' in the same occupation—for example, by teaching in a private school as well as a government school, or by holding down two government jobs at the same time, or by working as a cook in a restaurant at midday and in a hotel in the evening. Thus second job-holding is likely to be understated for this reason alone, quite apart from respondents' unwillingness to be too open about their income-earning activities. Even so, the *Susenas* data do not show nearly as high a rate of multiple job-holding as we might have expected at a time of hyperinflation, and it appears that the percentage of second job-holders was never as large as was commonly imagined. School teachers and government employees—the groups emphasized by Hawkins—are, after all, not such a large proportion of all urban workers.[38]

The rate of multiple job-holding measured for Jakarta, Surabaya and Bandung in 1972 was only one-third to one-half as high as that shown for urban Java in 1964–5. Although the figures for both years are undoubtedly understated, the substantial drop in the 1972 figures probably does reflect a real drop in the proportion of workers with more than one job in the stabilized economic conditions of the 1970s, though it may also reflect the different coverage of the two surveys. Table 8.24, from the 1976 *Supas*, should be more directly comparable with the 1964–5 figures. It shows lower rates of multiple job-holding in urban areas than in 1964–5, but almost identical rates in rural areas. This is consistent with the argument that rates of multiple job-holding had fallen since the mid-1960s because hyperinflation cannot be expected to greatly affect patterns of economic activity in rural areas. As in 1964–5, only half as many females as males had multiple economic activities. In urban areas, the likelihood of workers engaging in multiple activities was inversely related to the number of hours worked in the primary job, but in rural areas there was no clear relationship with number of hours worked.

TABLE 8.24

Percentage of Employed Population with More than One Activity, by Hours
Worked in Primary Activity, Place of Residence and Sex, 1976

Place of Residence and Hours Worked in Primary Job	Percentage of Employed Population with More than One Job		
	Males	Females	Both Sexes
Urban			
≤34	11.6	6.1	9.3
35–59	6.7	2.7	5.8
60+	3.8	2.4	3.3
Total*	6.9	3.7	6.0
Rural			
≤34	18.1	9.5	13.5
35–59	19.8	9.2	16.6
60+	14.9	9.7	13.1
Total*	18.7	9.3	14.9

Source: *Supas*, 1976, Tabulation Series No. 2: Table 15.
* Includes 'not stated'.

One must remain sceptical about the accuracy of data on multiple
economic activities in surveys of this kind. Efforts by survey enumerators to
place workers in one industrial or occupational 'box' is likely to do most
violence to reality in the lower-income urban *kampung* (Jellinek,
1985: 51–2), and also in rural areas where occupational multiplicity is more
pronounced. To read any detailed study of work patterns in rural areas of
Java is to note the variety of ways in which people interact with each other
and with their environment to make a living (Penny and Singarimbun,
1973; White, 1976(a) and (b); Hart, 1978; White and Makali, 1979). A
telling example is the survey, carried out by the Rural Dynamics Study, on
time spent by household members in different economic activities in six
villages in West Java, ranging from relatively large landholders to the
landless and near-landless. Even though two crops of rice were generally
grown in these villages, only 30 or 40 per cent of labour time, at most, went
on rice growing, and a larger proportion of time was given to a variety of
non-agricultural activities. The one source of Indonesia-wide data which
backs up this evidence on complexity of work patterns is the 'last-season'
data from the 1971 Census, which shows that, of all those in both urban
and rural areas who worked in non-agricultural activities in the reference
week, almost exactly one-quarter were engaged in agriculture in the last
season. The 1958 Labour Force Survey also showed fairly high levels of
multiple job-holding in rural Java.

The Long-term Employment Dilemma

The economy of Indonesia, and of Java in particular, has adapted over time to a situation of excess labour. Other countries, more adequately endowed with capital, management, and skills, produce as much as Indonesia with a much smaller labour force. It can be confidently expected that even if economic development were to proceed so rapidly in Indonesia over the next decade that labour shortages were to develop, such shortages could easily be remedied by changing the industry 'mix' between the traditional and modern sectors and the technology 'mix' within industries, but this is really a rather hypothetical situation. The more likely eventuality is that changes in the technology mix, especially in agriculture, will result in labour displacement in a wide range of economic activities well before an incipient labour shortage makes itself felt. Redundant labour would then be forced in increasing numbers to find a niche in the 'informal' sector and in the kinds of marginal activities open to landless labour in rural areas.

There is evidence that changes leading to increased output per member of the utilized labour force are already taking place in a number of sectors of the Indonesian economy. Gn/Gy ratios based on census and *Susenas* data can give us little clear guidance as to what has been happening (Jones, 1978), not only because of the shaky data base but also because sectoral Gn/Gy ratios do not differentiate between trends in 'modern' and in 'marginal' enterprises within the same sector. There is conflicting evidence on whether labour redundancy is as bad as it was a decade ago. Booth and McCawley (1981: Chapter 7) conclude that there has been little decline in the absolute numbers living in poverty in Java, and no appreciable lessening of disparities in expenditure distribution. But a recent World Bank Study (1984a) estimates that, between 1970 and 1980, the incidence of poverty declined from 67 per cent to 52 per cent in rural Java, and from 56 per cent to 21 per cent in urban Java, which implies a decline of 9 million in the number living in poverty.

Given that the poor are forced to do something to make a living, trends in sectoral or overall Gn/Gy ratios give little policy guidance. A Gn/Gy ratio for the Indonesian economy as a whole of around 0.5 was used as a 'rule of thumb' for Indonesia by some authors, implying that a labour force growing by 2.5 per cent a year would require a GDP growth rate of some 5 per cent per annum to absorb all new entrants to the labour force. During the 1970s, however, faster economic growth than this was achieved, with a doubling of real GDP between 1971 and 1980. The Gn/Gy ratio appears to have been only 0.3, indicating relatively low rates of labour absorption but rising productivity among those working. Slackening output growth in the 1980s has probably led, not to increases in measured labour redundancy, but rather to a rise in the Gn/Gy ratios as more workers are forced into marginal activities with very low productivity. Thus a high Gn/Gy ratio (of 0.5 or more) only means that much new employment is in activities yielding unacceptably low levels of real income.

The problems of labour utilization, of course, differ sectorally and geographically, and these are the levels at which manpower planning really has to operate. But, in general terms, it is clear that the inexorable growth of the Indonesian labour force has greatly exacerbated the problems of providing work that yields decent levels of living.

1. See, for example, Jaffe and Stewart, 1951; Myrdal, 1968; Hauser, 1974.

2. As examples, see Nag, Peet, and White, 1977; Khuda, 1977; Cain, 1977; and Cleave, 1974.

3. The term 'activity rate' will be treated as synonymous with the term 'labour force participation rate' in this chapter.

4. The terminology follows that of Durand, 1975: 55–6, although his calculation procedure has been modified.

5. See the 1971 equivalent of Table 8.1 in Jones, 1981: Table 8.2. Only in seven provinces did the stand'f in 1980 differ by more than 2 from its value in 1971: Central Kalimantan, North Sulawesi, Bali and West Nusa Tenggara, in all of which it rose, and Central Sulawesi, South-east Sulawesi, and East Nusa Tenggara, in which it fell.

6. On the whole, there is a tendency for the more devoutly Muslim provinces to rank lower in terms of female participation rates in urban areas than they do in terms of these rates for the province as a whole. Also these provinces show a wider gap between female participation rates in urban and rural areas than do Central and East Java, Bali, and the provinces with a large proportion of Christians. But there are exceptions to these generalizations: for example, North Sumatra and East Nusa Tenggara show wide gaps between urban and rural rates.

7. See Yeh and You, 1971: 36–7. Boserup (1975: 83) wrongly claims that all farmers' wives were automatically considered to be working in the Thailand census.

8. The definition of 'others' used by the 1971 Census was 'persons who are receiving public aid or private support due to illness, age, etc.'

9. There is a surprising 'spread' in the international figures, suggesting problems with the data in a few extreme countries. In 1971, Indonesia's activity rate at ages 15 to 19 was not quite in the lowest quartile of developing countries. But its rate at ages 20 to 24 (measured by either Series C or Series D data) was in the lowest decile of developing countries, and at ages 25 to 29, in the lowest quintile.

10. The figure for ages 20 to 24 looks especially strange, given the low proportion of males still in educational institutions at this age. According to the 1971 Census (Series D), only 8.5 per cent of Indonesian males aged 20 to 24 were still attending educational institutions full-time. They were not included in the 8.1 per cent who were given a labour force categorization of 'other' (see Table 8.3).

11. For an international comparison, see Boserup (1975). One village study in Yogyakarta found that fewer than 2 per cent of women reported farm work as a primary occupation, and only 30 per cent reported farm work as a secondary occupation when questioned in an interview. Observation of this same group of women, however, revealed that at least 92 per cent took part in some harvesting activities (Stoler, 1975). See also Moir, 1980; and Peluso, 1979.

12. Actually refers to the population aged 12 years and above.

13. Excluding Jakarta.

14. When the provinces are ranked in terms of the level of their female participation rates, using three sources of data (the 1971 and 1980 Censuses and the 1978 *Sakernas*), the following values are obtained for the Spearman rank correlation coefficient:

	1971 with 1980	1971 with 1978	1978 with 1980
Rural	0.7452*	0.4478	0.8087*
Urban	0.6353*	0.7925*	0.7554*
Total	0.7938*	0.5562	0.7992*

*Significant at 1 per cent level.

15. Further support for this comes from the Indonesian Fertility–Mortality Survey of 1973, which showed that among ever-married women aged 15 to 49, the proportion 'currently working' or 'ever worked' was much higher in Java than in Sulawesi.

16. The rural participation rates for females in North Sumatra were not especially high in 1971; North Sumatra is one of the few provinces where these rates appear to have changed fairly drastically between 1971 and 1980. This requires further investigation.

17. It is possible that the differences partly reflect cultural perceptions of whether women 'really' work, rather than real differences in labour input. A study in Pakistan showed wide differences in measured female activity rates, depending on whether the husband or the wife was the respondent (Shah and Shah, 1980).

18. Of all females aged more than 10 years living in Jakarta in 1971 but born elsewhere, 45 per cent were born in West Java and 28 per cent in Central Java.

19. For reasons noted earlier, the 1971 figures used in Tables 8.7, 8.8, and 8.9 are derived from the Series C report. It might be noted that when the Series D data are used for comparison with 1961, as in Jones (1981: Table 8.6), male employment in general, and especially in the agricultural, mining, manufacturing and construction sectors, appears implausibly low in 1971.

20. The apparent decrease in male employment in agriculture in the 1960s, offset by a sharp increase in female employment, is implausible. The overall trends in agricultural employment between 1961 and 1980 are, however, plausible.

21. More basic even than this is the problem of deciding what constitutes farm work in a setting where a household is an economic unit in which all members contribute in various ways, not least important of which are activities—such as cooking and carrying food to workers in the fields, fetching water, and minding house-gardens—which release other household members for what may be defined as 'more directly productive activities'. Can a farmer's wife ever really be considered non-economically active, as is the case with more than half of them in the Indonesian censuses?

22. Sources and Notes on Table 8.11:

Data and Source	Estimates without Major Adjustment	Estimates with Major Adjustment
Population Census, 1930	'Others and unknown' distributed pro rata across industry groups.	'Others and unknown' allocated to agriculture. Agricultural share of employment adjusted upwards to make women's share equal to 1971. (See Mertens, 1978.)
Population Census, 1961	'Others and unknown' distributed pro rata across industry groups.	Adjustment applied to total male employment in agriculture on assumption that women's share of agricultural employment was the same as in 1971 (31.9 per cent). Adjusted total agricultural labour force $= \dfrac{17,169,000}{0.681}$ $= 25,211,000$
Population Census, 1971, Series C	'Others and unknown' distributed pro rata across industry groups.	Figure used is population working in agriculture in the last season.

(continued)

(continued)

Data and Source	Estimates without Major Adjustment	Estimates with Major Adjustment
Population Census, 1971, Series D	'Others and unknown' distributed pro rata across industry groups.	Persons working in the last season but unemployed or outside the labour force during the reference week are added to those working in agriculture during the reference week.
Supas, 1976	Published figure for total and for agricultural employment inflated to include estimates for the sections of East Nusa Tenggara and Maluku that were excluded from the Survey, on the assumption that agricultural employment in these areas grew by 7 per cent between 1971 and 1976.	The figure adjusted for East Nusa Tenggara and Maluku was further adjusted by lowering the estimate of female employment in agriculture on the assumption that the female share of agricultural employment was 33 per cent, the same as in the 1976 and 1977 *Sakernas*, and that those excluded from agricultural employment by the adjustment were outside the labour force.

23. Admittedly, the 1971 definitions required that farmers not working for seasonal reasons be counted as 'employed'. But it seems likely that this requirement was not always followed.

24. In particular, the leading question to determine whether those whose main activity was outside the labour force worked at least one hour during the reference week.

25. The most appropriate 1971 data on employment, for comparison with 1980, are the Series C data. For *kabupaten*-level comparisons, however, only Series E data are available. As these tend to understate employment, the *kabupaten*-level comparisons tend to exaggerate 1971–80 employment growth, though not enough to seriously distort the patterns of change revealed.

26. Among the 'last season' workers, a much higher proportion of females than of males were outside the labour force according to the one-week reference period, and of this group of seasonal agricultural workers, 71 per cent of females were unpaid family workers compared with 60 per cent of males (Jones, 1981: Table 8.8).

27. This appears rather far-fetched when we note that both *Supas* and *Sakernas* collected data on 'usual' activity for the whole year preceding the enumeration, and the difference was not much smaller. This does not entirely dispose of the argument, however, as it is commonly found in surveys which collect labour force data for both a one-week and 'previous' year reference period that the 'previous year' figures diverge very little from the one-week figures, and can therefore be assumed to be influenced by whatever seasonal factors are affecting the one-week figures.

28. 'Busy' and 'slack' periods are defined according to the area planted and harvested in Java each month over a seven-year period, 1972–8 (Strout, 1981: Table 1). There is considerable variation in seasonal patterns from year to year.

29. Although a higher proportion of agricultural workers worked short hours in the August round than in the other rounds, the total number working more than 35 hours a week was nevertheless slightly higher in August than in May or November.

30. Strout (1981: 9) also claims that September 1971 was an unusually slack month, even for September. For this reason, the 1971 data may exaggerate the degree of 'normal' seasonal change in agricultural employment.

31. One particularly striking implication of the *Sensus Industri* and 1980 census data is that, if *Sensus Industri* figures on numbers employed in the L, M and S sectors are anywhere near the mark, then more than half of the 2.2 million employees recorded in 1980 must be in the cottage industry sector.

32. This proportion would fall if we include in agriculture all those who did some work in agriculture in the last season; nevertheless, the importance of non-agricultural employment in rural areas cannot be gainsaid. For data from the Philippines and India, see ILO, 1974: 502; and India Census, 1981: Vol. 1, Pt. II-A(ii): 3–5.

33. The mechanisms by which this has happened are discussed in McDonald and Sontosudarmo, 1976: 84–5. See also Sundrum, 1975a.

34. The very low unemployment rates in Table 8.22 for females aged 15 to 19 with no education are confirmed by the 1977 *Sakernas* data.

35. The *Sakernas* data and the urban unemployment survey data of the early 1970s show almost two-thirds seeking work for the first time, in all years, whereas the 1980 Census shows 52 per cent, and the 1971 Census 46 per cent (Series C) and only 23 per cent in Series D. This latter figure can be discounted as it reflects distortions introduced by the imputation procedures. *Sakernas* data show almost 90 per cent of first-time job seekers as aged less than 25, whereas the 1980 Census and the 1971 Census (Series C) both show 77 per cent.

36. The urban unemployment surveys of the early 1970s showed about half unemployed for more than six months. The *Sakernas* findings were very varied: 60 per cent unemployed for seven months or more according to the 1976 data; only 4 per cent in 1977; and 31 per cent in 1978. The 1977 data, which show 77 per cent out of work for less than one month, appear out of line with all other sources.

37. The urban unemployment surveys in 1972 and 1975 showed more workers working long than short hours: 20 to 29 per cent of the working population compared with 10 to 20 per cent working short hours.

38. It would appear that multiple job-holding is still very common among school-teachers and lecturers in universities and IKIPs, but it is less certain that they would give accurate information on this in a general labour force survey.

39. In *Repelita II* (Vol. 1: 105), employment-output (Gn/Gy) elasticities of 0.2 are assumed to hold for agriculture, mining, and electricity, and of around 0.5 in the remaining non-agricultural sectors. The authors of the plan admit the weaknesses of these estimates, and no further estimates are provided in the *Repelita III* draft plan document.

9 The Process of Population Planning

Introduction

THERE is a long history of government intervention in population matters in Indonesia, from the early attempts to control epidemic diseases and famines, through the development of transmigration activities just after the turn of the century, to the family planning programme in the last two decades. Since the New Order government came to power in 1966, population planning has been accorded a central role in development planning, and Indonesia has achieved a degree of prominence on the world stage on account of the extent and variety of its population policies as well as the originality of some of its approaches. The importance accorded population programmes is indicated by the fact that separate ministries are responsible for transmigration, health and the work-force, and a Board (the BKKBN)—answerable directly to the President—implements family planning. Since 1983, too, the overall co-ordination of population policy, along with policy on the environment, has been made the responsibility of a separate ministry of State—the Ministry of Population and Environment.

Problems associated with previous and continuing high rates of population growth remain important and complex issues in Indonesian development planning. In particular, the huge cohorts currently working their way through the school system and presenting themselves for entry into the labour force provide a major challenge to economic planners. The consideration of alternative policies on fertility and employment is vital. Ideally, such concerns would be reflected explicitly in the various stages of the economic planning process. In this chapter we will examine the ways in which population issues are handled in Indonesian planning. The focus is on contemporary planning issues, but of necessity this is discussed in terms of the development of the economic planning process over the two decades of the New Order government.

Indonesia is placed firmly in the mainstream of Third World development planning ideology and organization. By contrast with Western non-socialist states, where government intervention is generally unsystematic and often piecemeal, the five-year plan in almost all Third World countries symbolizes government efforts to guide and direct economic and social development. The planning process typically involves, first, the definition of social objectives, then the setting of various targets, and finally the preparation, implementation and monitoring of an explicit development plan.

The rationale for this degree of interference with market processes is the belief that 'the market economy is not geared to the principal operational task of poor countries: how to mobilize resources in a way that will bring the structural change necessary to stimulate a sustained and balanced growth of the entire economy' (Todaro, 1981: 431). A development plan is often seen as a rallying point for a national campaign to unify disparate ethnic and social groups and to eliminate poverty and ignorance. The market mechanism is considered inadequate to deal with deep-seated structural rigidities which lead to misallocation of resources. Investment projects are chosen in the context of an overall development programme that takes account of external economies, indirect repercussions and long-term national objectives (Waterson, 1972).

The Political and Administrative Context of Indonesian Planning

Before specifically describing the history and present structure of population policy formulation in Indonesia, it is necessary to outline briefly the socio-political context within which development planning takes place. In comparison with Western liberal democracies, Indonesia has an authoritarian government largely dominated by the armed forces. There is a limited degree of popular representation through the House of People's Representatives (DPR) on which sit (in addition to 100 members directly appointed by the armed forces) 400 members of approved political parties elected by the adult population at large: and the People's Consultative Assembly (MPR) which consists of the DPR plus 500 others, largely a system of appointments. The decision-making process might be described as 'fiat by consensus'. The political and bureaucratic structure is very centralized. Provincial governors and regency heads are appointed by the President, and the majority of these are current or retired military personnel. One legacy of regional rebellions in the 1950s is a reluctance to allow very much regional autonomy, though there are continuing calls for more autonomy in provinces such as Irian Jaya and North Sumatra. Other reasons for this reluctance, as it relates to development planning activities, are the belief that technocratic skills are weak at the provincial and *kabupaten* level, an (expressed) suspicion that corruption will be more rampant in a decentralized system, and perhaps an (unexpressed) aim to keep centralized control on larger resources for reasons of personal/ departmental aggrandizement and/or financial gain.

In contrast with the Soekarno years prior to 1965, technocrats are given a major role in Indonesian economic management and development planning. Most of the ministers dealing with economic and social planning are professional economists, educationists or medical doctors, as are many of their key staff. Foreign aid has played a vital role in economic rehabilitation and subsequent development under the Suharto regime, and institutions such as the World Bank, the International Monetary Fund (IMF), the United Nations Development Programme (UNDP) and the United States Agency for International Development (USAID) are very influential. The National Development Planning Board (*Bappenas*) plays the key co-ordinating role in development planning, and the chairman of *Bappenas* is concurrently the state minister for development planning. During the tenure of Professor Widjojo Nitisastro as chairman of *Bappenas*, the central role of the organization was evidenced by the fact that he was also co-ordinating minister for economic, financial and industrial affairs, though since his retirement this task has been passed from *Bappenas* to Dr Ali Wardhana, the Minister of Finance. Although *Bappenas* takes the key role in preparing the *Repelita* (the Five-Year Development Plan, see below), its main function is as a budget-approval agency, and its staff resources for engaging in basic development planning activities are much thinner than those in the development planning agencies in some neighbouring countries (specifically, the National Economic and Social Development Board in Thailand, the National Economic and Development Authority in the Philippines, or the Economic Planning Unit in the Prime Minister's Department in Malaysia).

It might be noted that if the politico-planning structure in Indonesia can be summarized in three words, 'authoritarian', 'centralized', 'technocratic', so too can that in many other developing countries in Asia—for example Thailand and the Republic of Korea. There is rather less authoritarianism and more decentralization of planning and decision-making in Malaysia, and a fair degree of decentralization in the Philippines.

Interagency co-ordination remains a serious problem in development planning but in theory this is minimized by regular monthly co-ordinating meetings of ministerial groupings known as the EKUIN (ministers dealing with economic matters, industry and finance), KESRA (health and social development) and POLKAM (external and internal security), and a regular monthly meeting of the limited cabinet—that is, all ministers dealing with these three areas.

In the provinces, the provincial planning offices (*Bappeda*) are the key planning agencies, although they are allowed relatively little room for autonomous action. They vary considerably in strength from province to province, but a key feature in most provinces is the involvement of staff of regional universities in the research and evaluation work of the *Bappeda* on a part-time or contract basis.

Planning in Indonesia stresses a sectoral rather than a regional approach. There is recognition that a regional development approach is needed, symbolized by the appointment of a deputy for regional development in *Bappenas*. But there are few teeth in regional policies. One indicator of the weakness of regional planning is the fact that regional economics is no more than an embryonic field of specialization in economics faculties of Indonesian universities. Faculty and students realize that there are relatively few employment opportunities in this field compared with other planning specializations.

Setting National Goals

There is a strong emphasis in Indonesia on the ideology of development planning. In its ideal form, planning must derive from and be consistent with the Constitution (UUD) of 1945, with the official state ideology of *Pancasila*, and with the Broad Outlines of State Policy (*Garis-garis Besar Haluan Negara*, GBHN), to be described below. National ideology stresses economic growth, equity and stability. In recent years, the concept of economic 'take-off' popularized by Rostow in the 1950s has made a surprising reappearance in official pronouncements about development in Indonesia, and the Indonesian term *'tinggal landas'* has become an almost compulsory phrase in speeches by members of the government officials since 1984. *Repelita V* is supposed to prepare the way for this take-off which is to take place in *Repelita VI* (1994–9). The President has stressed that a rapid decline in fertility is a basic pre-condition for such a take-off to be achieved.

The GBHN is an innovation of the New Order government, and is an attempt, on a regular basis, to set out the principles and priorities underlying development planning. Formulation of GBHN follows a five-year cycle geared to mesh with the five-yearly election of the President and formation of the cabinet, and the preparation of the Five-Year Development Plan (*Repelita*). In formal terms, the cycle starts with the election of the People's Deliberative Assembly (the MPR) and culminates in the announcement of the *Repelita* but, historically, the first plan of the New Order, *Repelita I*, was formulated prior to the election of the first regular New Order MPR. The chronological sequence of events is shown in Table 9.1.

Successive GBHN mention population issues in a variety of ways, some of which can be regarded as ideological stances, while others are policy principles. Only the latter are reflected in the concrete plans of projects and programmes. An example of an ideological stance which appears in each reformulation of the GBHN, and contains echoes of thoughts frequently expressed by Soekarno in the heady period of 1950s' optimism, is the statement of the 'Basic Capital' of national development possessed by the Indonesian people (GBHN II: D 1). After citing 'Freedom and Unity, Geographic Position, and Natural Resources', the GBHN states that, 'A very large population, if cultivated and mobilized into an effective workforce, can be a form of development capital which is both large and greatly beneficial to development activities in all sectors'. At the same time, among the 'Dominant Factors' which influence a nation's ability to utilize the various forms of 'basic capital' for development are 'demographic and socio-cultural' factors. These are the only two mentions of population in the chapter on 'Basic Pattern of National Development'.

More specific references to a policy stance on population are contained in the chapter on the 'General Pattern of Long-Term Development' (GBHN III). The long term referred to in the chapter heading is 25 to 30 years, and is mentioned in other contexts as spanning the implementation

TABLE 9.1

Chronology of Major Political, and Administrative Events Influencing
'New Order' Population Planning

1965	September 30	'G-30-S', the attempted coup, followed by a period of social disruption which brought the New Order government of President Suharto to power.
1969	April 1	Implementation of *Repelita I*.
1971		Election of MPR and DPR.
1973		Formulation of GBHN as set out in Decision IV/MPR/1973. Election of President Suharto and Vice-President Sri Sultan Hamenkubuwono.
1974	April 1	Implementation of *Repelita II*.
1977		Election of MPR and DPR.
1978		Reformulation of GBHN as set out in Decision IV/MPR/1978. Re-election of President Suharto and election of Vice-President Adam Malik.
1979	April 1	Implementation of *Repelita III*.
1982		Election of MPR and DPR.
1983		Reformulation of GBHN as set out in Decision IV/MPR/1983. Re-election of President Suharto and election of Vice-President Umar Wirohadikusumah.
1984	April 1	Implementation of *Repelita IV*.
1987		Scheduled election of MPR and DPR.
1988		Scheduled reformulation of GBHN.
1989	April 1	Scheduled implementation of *Repelita V*.

of five successive five-year development plans. The most important paragraph (GBHN III: B 8) setting out the basis of both the family planning and transmigration programme reads as follows:

In order for economic development and the improvement in people's welfare to be implemented quickly, they must be accompanied by control of population growth through a program of family planning which obviously must be successfully implemented since failure in the implementation of family planning would lead to the results of development activities being meaningless, and could endanger future generations. The implementation of the family planning program should be carried out using voluntary means, showing respect for religion and religious beliefs. In addition, there is a need for an effort to redistribute the population more evenly through the Transmigration program, in support of initiatives to carry out development efforts more evenly throughout the entire nation.

The general sections of the GBHN contain no other statements about the role of population control or population redistribution in the development process, though there is a substantial series of statements about the need to develop a skilled labour force. It does seem incongruous that population issues are addressed so briefly in the document summarizing Indonesia's official development planning principles, and it is particularly strange to have policy statements on family planning and transmigration pressed into one densely worded paragraph. However, the general sections of the GBHN are clearly not a comprehensive statement of development goals, but rather a collation of consensus-based expressions of issues to be taken into account in planning.

Following the general sections, each successive GBHN outlines the pattern to be followed in the next development plan. In both 1978 and 1983, the GBHN reaffirmed policies on family planning and transmigration, calling on the government to intensify efforts in these areas. In 1983, the section on family planning, under the section headed 'Religion, Religious Belief, and Social-cultural Matters' (GBHN IV, 1983: D) cited six points to be included in the plan:

1. Population policies which are comprehensive and integrated should be continued, and directed toward the achievement of such development goals as improving living standards and welfare.

2. Efforts must be made to improve the implementation of population policies and population programs, including those involving the reduction of fertility, the reduction of mortality and particularly infant mortality, the extension of the expectation of life at birth, and the redistribution of population.

3. The major purpose of the family planning program is to improve the welfare of mothers and children, and to create a prosperous community through the control of childbearing and the consequent control of population growth rates.

4. The family planning program must be extensified and intensified to cover the whole nation, and all social groups, including settlers in newly opened areas.

5. The total number of family planning users needs to be increased on the basis of voluntary and fully-informed participation, taking account of religion and religious belief. To achieve this care must be taken in ensuring the continued participation of current users, the expansion of facilities for distribution of birth control, and the involvement of non-governmental organizations and community leaders.

6. Information and education concerning population issues should be improved and provided to all members of society, both female and male, and especially the younger generation. This is needed in order to develop a widespread awareness of the pressing problem of population and the importance of the small family as a proper and responsible way of life.

These statements, though still very general, provide a clearer idea of the major factors to be considered by planners in the formulation of the development plan. Again, they are largely political statements reflecting the compromise of competing views among different political parties and factions and religious groups, hence the combination of demographic and maternal welfare goals in the one sentence, and the emphasis on voluntarism, respect for religious sensibilities, and the participation of non-governmental institutions. Despite such principles, the actual family planning programme as carried out tends to emphasize demographic goals, and there have been perennial charges that coercion is used in local areas to increase numbers of acceptors. Also, the role of non-governmental institutions has declined substantially since 1970, and the government has tended to trivialize their role by restricting their service delivery activities and encouraging them to concentrate on pilot programmes and advisory roles.

Statements about transmigration and labour force are included under the rubric of 'The Economy' in the discussion of future plans. In 1983, the MPR noted in the GBHN that the expansion of employment opportunities is one of the basic issues of development, and that this must be achieved in a variety of ways, taking account of working conditions, labour relations and occupational health and safety. They also called on the government to work toward an improvement in the level and distribution of incomes. Trans-migration is proposed as a means of achieving national development through the redistribution of population and the improvement of land-use, both in densely settled Java and in other islands. This, they say, should be done both through officially sponsored programmes and the encourage-ment of spontaneous movement.

While GBHN outlines both general principles and discusses some specific issues, it is by no means a comprehensive exposition of the government's population policies. Rather, it reflects political compromises and contemporary concerns. Readers search the GBHN in vain for a systematic exposition of the government's principles guiding planning in the areas of fertility control, mortality control, urbanization, migration, and human-resource development. Instead, readers are forced to turn to the actual five-year development plans to discover what principles are revealed through the selection of projects and the distribution of funds.

Population in National Development Plans

The First Five-Year Development Plan (*Repelita I*), beginning in 1969, gave priority to the New Order's policy of economic stabilization, and aimed at raising the standard of living and setting a foundation for future development efforts by concentrating on the modernization of the agri-cultural sector. The Second Plan (1974/5 to 1978/9) gave increased emphasis to the development of industries processing raw materials, and budgeted a higher level of development expenditures for social purposes such as education, health and family planning. The Third Plan, ending on 31 March 1984, emphasized the development of industries producing manufactured goods, but also focused attention on a number of crucial areas such as regional development, transmigration, the bolstering of economically weak groups, public housing, and social welfare improvements.

The introductory statement to *Repelita IV* (1984/5 to 1988/9) reported that while the priority of this plan was still on economic development, greater emphasis was to be given to human-resource development such as education, health, manpower, water supply, nutrition, housing and human settlement. Recognizing that world economic conditions were expected to be less favourable than in previous *Repelita* periods, the Fourth Plan emphasizes efficiency, diversification, and flexibility in order to maintain growth and increase the economy's capacity to withstand unfavourable international conditions. Many of these general statements about the four

Repelita are reflected in the specific sections most relevant to population policy. These will be reviewed in turn.

Fertility Control: Family Planning

All Indonesian five-year development plans mention targets for acceptors as well as for the addition of clinics and personnel, together with the need for high quality administration, reporting and documentation, and research and evaluation. The changing approaches and emphases which have characterized the programme over the years since its inception, however, are well captured by the discussions of family planning in successive *Repelita*.

REPELITA I

The overall goals of family planning in the First Plan were: (1) to improve the health and welfare of mothers and children as well as their families and the nation as a whole; and (2) to improve living conditions by decreasing the birth rate so that population growth would not outstrip productive capacity. This apparent order of priority was repeated both in the introductory overview to the *Repelita*, as well as in the chapter devoted to health and family planning. It was clear that at this early stage the government was treading fairly lightly in terms of a fertility-control policy, an impression strengthened by a statement emphasizing the voluntary basis to the programme, and the fact that it was to be carried out 'in accordance with the morality of the Pancasila and religious beliefs' (Vol. IIc: 70). It is also revealing that the Plan stated that the programme 'would not require a large amount of financing' (Vol. I: 22) as it would largely be conducted by the people, with the protection of the government.

Repelita I outlines several specific strategies, including an initial concentration on Java and Bali and in the major cities. An urban focus was recommended in these early years because the cities had most of the existing health infrastructure and personnel, and it was also felt that there would be more acceptance of family planning in the urban environment. In practice, however, rural outreach began in the very early stages and, until very recently, the villages have been the programme's main target. It is ironic that, when the first major surveys were carried out in the 1970s, it was found that the cities of Java lagged behind the rural areas in family planning practice and, in Java, urban delivery of services and motivation has always been more difficult than in rural areas.

Specific 'targets' mentioned in the First Plan were the recruitment of 3 million new acceptors, as well as an increase in the number of clinics.

REPELITA II

The Second Plan devoted a separate chapter to family planning, rather than amalgamating the topic with health. It provided for the expansion of the programme to ten provinces outside Java and Bali, and called for further intensification of effort in Java and Bali. Recruitment of new acceptors was set at a minimum of 8 million in Java–Bali, but a more optimistic target of 12 million, if motivation and services could be optimized, was also mentioned. The Plan called for the recruitment of 1 million new acceptors in other areas. Detailed targets were also specified for the training of various personnel and the increase in numbers and opening hours of clinics. There appeared to be concern in reaching some social groups, and there was a call for increased field-worker coverage and for greater communication efforts among segments of the population who were 'most resistant' to family planning.

In the Second Plan, the concept of integration was clearly emerging. Attention was drawn to the need to emphasize other development efforts which would reinforce the aims of family planning. These efforts were to include population education, improved nutrition and health which would decrease infant mortality, higher levels of female education, old-age security, and overall equity. Specific mention was made of the necessity to eliminate pro-natalist policies of taxation, social service payments, and similar measures.

REPELITA III

In the Third Plan, where a chapter was devoted to 'Population and Family Planning' (*Kependudukan dan Keluarga Berencana* or KKB), it was announced that the family planning programme would be extended to the entire country. In Java and Bali, the aim was to recruit 10 million new acceptors, to which would be added 2.9 million in the Stage II 'other island' areas, and 0.6 million in the newest group of provinces. Transmigration areas and other newly settled areas outside Java/Bali were to receive special attention.

For the first time, there was focus on a specific contraceptive method: the IUD. It was hoped that, because of its higher continuation rates, the intra-uterine device (IUD) would make up on average 25 per cent of new acceptors.

The local manufacture of contraceptive pills had already begun, and the Plan specified greatly increased output. It also mentioned the importance of traditional methods, particularly rhythm, which had been shown by the fertility surveys of the mid-1970s to be popular choices among some groups, particularly in urban areas.

The focus on integrated programmes, introduced in the previous Plan, was strengthened in *Repelita III*. Nutrition education was to be carried out by the family planning programme, and the provinces newly opened to the programme would receive health and welfare components as part of family planning. In addition, female employment and education, as well as general employment and education opportunities, were stressed as contributing to the overall effort, and delayed marriage was also cited as an important factor. The importance of male participation in the programme was also stressed.

A subtle change in tone of the Fourth Plan is significant in that it returned to some of the caution of *Repelita I*, emphasizing the voluntary nature of family planning and the need to consider religious values. At the same time, it reiterated the goal of integration of efforts, in particular those which would achieve reduction in infant, child, and maternal mortality. Specific targets were the addition of 24.7 million new acceptors, and the IUD was again emphasized as a preferred method. The Plan envisaged increased use of IUDs and the Depo-Provera injectable contraceptives and reduced reliance on pills and condoms. Although it acknowledged that the family planning programme 'in the long term' was to assist in a 50 per cent reduction of the 1970 crude birth rate of over 40 per thousand, the stated goal for the Plan period up to 1988/9 was for a reduction in the crude birth rate from 33.46 to 31.02 per thousand. It is not clear how these goals are to be made compatible, and no mention is made of early statements that the 50 per cent reduction should be achieved by 1990.

Mortality Control: Health and Nutrition

Public health has been a priority since the time of the first development plan, but goals have become increasingly specific in both health and nutrition segments of successive plans.

At the time of the First Plan, there was concern with providing the health-care infrastructure that was needed, and targets were set for the building of various levels of health centres and the training of health personnel. Public health training in particular was a high priority. The eradication of contagious diseases, individually listed and including such relatively rare diseases as framboesia, leprosy, and plague, received significant attention in the Plan.

Nutrition and nutrition education were mentioned, but they did not receive great prominence. Nutrition in the First Plan was in fact included in the same section with mental, dental, and eye health.

The Second Plan presented health in much the same spirit as the First Plan, though it began to emphasize the integration of health with other development efforts, and to cite the need for decentralization of services. Special mention was made of the health of the young productive population, and the links between health and work-efficiency.

Nutrition was mentioned briefly under health, but received greater attention in a separate chapter entitled 'Food and Nutrition Improvement'. Specific target groups of infants and children and pregnant and lactating mothers were identified, groups which have remained the focus of nutrition programmes ever since. The need for nutrition education was stressed, as well as sanitation education. *Repelita II* envisaged the provision of education and services in nutrition through a variety of sources, including the large Nutrition Improvement (UPGK) programme; school programmes; family planning workers; *Butsi* (the Indonesian equivalent of *Vista*) volunteers; university students under the KKN (work experience) programme; and *kader gizi* or trained nutrition cadres in the villages. Specific targets for the programme were vitamin A deficiency, protein-calorie malnutrition, and endemic goitre. These have remained important through the mid-1980s.

REPELITA III

In the Third Plan, health was combined with social welfare as it had been in previous plans, although in this Plan 'Role of Women' was also included. In this Plan, there is much stronger emphasis on the poor, both urban and rural. The *Pembangunan Kesehatan Masyarakat Desa* (PKMD) programme, Indonesia's primary health care, was to be extended to all provinces by the end of the Plan period, and the *Puskesmas*, or Community Health Centre was identified as the focus of rural outreach.

Nutrition received more attention as part of the health section in *Repelita III* than it had in previous plans. In the chapter devoted to food and nutrition improvement, the government stressed the need to de-emphasize rice as a staple food by substituting other staples available in the country such as corn or tubers. Other goals were basically the same as those expressed in the previous *Repelita*.

REPELITA IV

For the first time, health had its own chapter and, although some themes were continued, overall the focus and tone of the chapter represented a significant departure from previous plans. There remained an emphasis on the relation between health and environmental sanitation, though it was more strongly expressed in this Plan. The list of diseases singled out as warranting special attention includes many of those relatively rare diseases mentioned in previous plans, but the major killers of diarrhoea, respiratory tract infection, and infectious diseases that can be prevented through immunization now headed the list. *Repelita IV* also specifically mentioned lowering fertility as a health goal, and singled out the control of dangerous drugs, foods and cosmetics (but significantly not cigarettes) as a priority.

For the first time, specific targets of mortality reduction were proposed: a decline in the crude death rate from an estimated 11.7 per thousand population at the beginning of the Plan period to 10.1 five years later; a decline in the infant mortality rate from 90.3 to 7.0 per thousand; and in child mortality from 17.8 to 14.0 per thousand. It also included specific targets for reductions in the proportion of low birth-weight babies, specific diseases, numbers of immunizations, coverage of clean water supplies, deliveries by trained midwives, and other specific conditions or activities.

The discussion on nutrition basically followed the foundations set in previous plans, with emphasis on increasing food availability to ensure proper nutritional levels for all groups in the society, and increasing variety in the diet, including the reduction of the reliance on rice. The main specific targets for nutrition programmes were vitamin A deficiency, endemic goitre and iron-deficiency anaemia. The Plan called for intensification of the school nutrition education programme, for employers to give greater attention to employee nutrition, and increased training of nutrition workers with an orientation to both health and agricultural production.

Transmigration

Although the transmigration policy extends far back into Indonesia's history, successive development plans illustrate the way in which it has become much more systematic and focused over recent years.

REPELITA I

In the First Plan, the two aspects of transmigration stipulated were (1) the redistribution of the population, and (2) the meeting of labour requirements for development of regions outside Java. The specific objectives mentioned were to increase food production by opening up new land, increase the production and export of timber, and undertake public works projects such as roads, ports, etc. outside Java.

No specific targets were set, however, and in general the discussion was limited to a short section of a short chapter on transmigration and co-operatives.

REPELITA II

In the Second Plan, transmigration was even more firmly linked to labour issues and placed in a chapter with labour force. The programme prior to *Repelita I* was criticized as not paying enough attention to regional or sectoral development. As a result, in *Repelita II*, attention was focused on the need to improve the standard of living in transmigration areas, and to support economic activities for non-farming transmigrants. Interestingly, the Plan proposed that transmigrants should contribute to development by repaying all or part of the government's contribution to moving them, once they were economically able to do so. Specific mention was made about encouraging spontaneous transmigrants through the provision of better information and improved transport. The Second Plan specified a target of moving 250,000 households over the five years of the Plan period.

REPELITA III

Although the numeric targets set for transmigration in *Repelita II* were not met, those set in the Third Plan were more ambitious yet, at 500,000 households. It was recognized that much more attention would have to be devoted to the selection and preparation of the receiving areas, and this plan gives the impression that the major issues were much more focused in the minds of the formulators than was the case in previous years. The issue of providing compensation as well as facilities to the indigenous population in particular was stated as an aim of the programme. The Third Plan stated the need for developing social institutions, such as co-operatives, in transmigration areas, as well as the need for family planning, which was also specifically mentioned in the section on family planning.

REPELITA IV

In the Fourth Plan, transmigration was discussed in a fairly substantial, separate chapter. The Plan reported that the *Repelita III* target was met, although inspection of the figures reveals that the total includes a large proportion of spontaneous transmigrants who had not previously been included in targets. As foreshadowed in the Third Plan, there was increasing emphasis on spontaneous transmigrants. At the end of *Repelita III*, a Department of Transmigration had been formed, separate from the Department of Labour, and *Repelita IV* indicated that the programme was to be larger in terms of overall totals as well as of improved quality. The new target set for the Plan period was 750,000 households. Specific targets for facilities to be built were also given in this Plan, along with minute detail on the per family allocations of rice, seeds, etc. to be distributed.

Labour Force

The subject of the labour force in successive Indonesian five-year plans is much more difficult to capture in a single section or chapter since it is so strongly interconnected with other topics. Its position in each plan, however, may well reflect a changing perception by policy makers of the relative importance of labour force problems.

REPELITA I

In the First Plan, the labour force was discussed primarily in a chapter together with education. Great emphasis was placed on the need for training and on improving school curricula so that they better reflected community needs. In this and subsequent plans, there was a call for the creation of a fair minimum wage as well as a balance between maximum and minimum wages, to achieve the so-called 'democratization of wages' (Vol. IIc: 46).

As discussed in previous references to *Repelita I*, there was appreciable concern about the uneven distribution of the labour force between rural and urban areas and between Java and the other islands. Both transmigration and the need for family planning, to reduce the rate of increase of the labour force, were mentioned in relation to labour-force issues. Two issues, the problem of labour relations and the inefficiency of the civil service, were specifically cited as negative legacies of the old regime.

REPELITA II

The Second Plan devoted a chapter to population and employment opportunities in its first volume, and another to labour force and transmigration;

many of the same issues, however, were discussed in a similar way in both chapters. Most of the issues raised in *Repelita I* were reiterated in the Second Plan, although the situation with unions and labour relations was reported as much improved—presumably because the government had instituted a series of measures to limit the right to strike and organize. Continuing the stress on rural development begun in the First Plan, the Second Plan emphasized the need for labour-intensive, appropriate technology in development projects. Specific programmes such as *Padat Karya*, *Inpres*, *Butsi*, KKN and others were to continue and be intensified. Special mention was made of the welfare of female workers, stating that family planning facilities would be made available at the work-place, and that child-care facilities should be provided, though there was no explicit policy to influence the actual rate of participation of women in the labour force.

REPELITA III

The position of the labour force as a separate topic of discussion was the same in *Repelita III* as it had been in *Repelita II*. The Third Plan was very similar in tone to *Repelita II*, with the addition of a 'Youth Programme' in which training programmes would be targeted to school dropouts and poor youth. Women in the work-force received increased mention, again in the context of ensuring that work conditions did not conflict with family roles.

REPELITA IV

The Fourth Plan included a chapter on expanding employment opportunities as well as, for the first time, a separate chapter on the labour force. As in other areas, the discussion on the labour force in the Fourth Plan appeared more complete and sophisticated than had previous efforts. It looked much more at the total picture, bringing in aspects such as exchange rates, protection of domestic industry, and pricing policy. There was, however, continuity as well: the need for appropriate technology, a fair wage, balance in the wage gap between minimum and maximum earnings, and labour-intensive development programmes. Particular measures and programmes cited, such as transmigration, *Butsi*, and women's programmes, were also basically the same as those in previous plans.

Although the Fourth Plan, as others before it, emphasized agriculture, there was recognition of the growing importance of the industrial sector, and the need for special attention to small industry. Specific points were made concerning work opportunities in small- and medium-sized cities as opposed to large cities, and the need for attention to the informal sector in urban areas.

Urbanization

Aspects of this topic were discussed under numerous headings in each plan, but the main sections addressing these urban problems in a narrow sense, were on housing, and regional, rural and urban development.

REPELITA I

The problem of rapid urbanization was stressed in the First Plan's chapter on housing and social welfare, where the need for all aspects of city planning was noted. By the end of *Repelita I*, all capital and principal cities were to have a city plan—with priority given to the biggest cities, those with harbours, and newly developing towns. Drinking water, drainage and sewerage were seen as the main priorities in city planning. The Plan clearly stated that, for the most part, financing of housing development should be borne by the private sector, although it was hoped that the provision of facilities as well as credit and tax dispensations would be able to stimulate housing development.

REPELITA II

Repelita II cited the main tasks of the proposed National Urban Development Strategy as examining the hierarchy of cities according to their functions and roles, and looking at relations between cities and their surrounding areas as part of the overall strategy of reducing income disparities among areas. In addition to repeated mention of the need for basic facilities in urban areas, the Second Plan spoke of the less tangible but nevertheless important need for improved social control among urban dwellers. It reiterated the notion of self-help; the *Kampung* Improvement Programmes were to be undertaken 'by the people' and local government, although the central government would give technical assistance and loans.

During the Second Plan period, low-cost housing was to be built in Jakarta, serving as a pilot project to be followed in other cities. The Plan stated that in general, however, areas for the poor should not be separated from better housing areas in order to avoid creating clear dividing lines between rich and poor neighbourhoods.

REPELITA III

Most of the discussion of urban development issues in the Third Plan represented a continuation of that in *Repelita II*, with expanded programmes for housing construction and *kampung* improvement. The role of small to medium-sized cities in both Java and outside Java was stressed in an effort to stem the tide of people to large cities. The Third Plan raised the issue of multi-storey housing, stating that there was a recognized need for this approach, but that it must be accompanied by efforts to ensure that there would be no social breakdown resulting from this new form of housing.

REPELITA IV

The Fourth Plan's section on urban development still expressed dissatisfaction with the lack of detailed guidelines for urban planning. Existing programmes for the informal sector in particular were criticized as being aimed only at containment and security rather than at tackling the actual problems involved. Many of the goals remained the same, although the chapter on housing provided specific targets of basic homes and flats to be built. It was announced that a programme of central-district development would begin in medium and small cities, and the need for housing for the young skilled work-force was mentioned in addition to the need to house the poor.

Evolution of the Planning Process

Over the years, the formulation of the *Repelita* has tended to be the occasion for focusing attention on the nation's population policy and targets, a process in which a co-ordinating role was played by *Bappenas* and contributions were sought from university population institutes as well as other government agencies.

The overall responsibility for population policy formulation has not been clearly defined in Indonesia, in particular with respect to the relative roles of the BKKBN as the agency responsible for the family planning pro-gramme, *Bappenas* as the agency responsible for national development planning, and the Departments of Manpower, Transmigration, and Health. Through the 1970s something of a vacuum was perceptible in the formu-lation of population policy. This was reflected in the place accorded population in successive plans. *Bappenas* was too short-staffed and too preoccupied with the processes of project approval and monitoring to devote serious attention to the broader issues of long-term population policy. The BKKBN lacked the expertise in the areas of economics and development planning needed to give it a credible voice in cabinet-level discussions of population issues, and the scope of its mandate in areas of population policy was unclear. The role of other agencies and departments was confined to the narrow fields of their particular concerns, such as transmigration, the labour force, or health, and thus they were not motivated to address the broader issues of the integration of population in the overall planning process.

This was a very unsatisfactory situation, given the need for sustained research into, and evaluation of, the options facing Indonesia in the area of population policy, an area acknowledged by the President and the MPR to be of utmost importance in overall development planning. Not only did the situation create a vacuum, it also encouraged conflict among the various agencies and departments with population interests, and set the BKKBN and *Bappenas* in opposition to one another over the issue of how responsi-bility for policy directions and co-ordination of activities should be divided.

The situation was clarified to some degree by Presidential Decision No. 38 of 1978 which gave the BKKBN responsibility for policies designed to support the National Family Planning Programme. Unfortunately, the decision left some uncertainty about the extent of the BKKBN mandate in other fields broadly associated with population policy. With the tacit agreement of *Bappenas*, the BKKBN took the wording of the presidential decision literally and made arrangements to initiate the formulation and implementation of both family planning and population policies. An office of Deputy for Population Affairs was created in the BKKBN and plans were set in motion to create a network of population officers at all levels of the bureaucracy. The National Family Planning Programme was renamed the 'Population-Family Planning Programme' (Program KKB) and the BKKBN floated the idea of renaming itself to include 'population' in its title, but this was not pursued.

In general terms, the role of the Deputy for Population Affairs was seen as one of co-ordinating policy-relevant population research and translating research findings into policy options and programmatic initiatives. Some stress was placed on the development of effective links with other agencies and departments to guide their participation in the policy process, but in practice this tended to mean the organization of numerous seminars and workshops where the Indonesian practice of *musjawarah* (mutual deliberation) and *mufakat* (consensus decision-making) was used to prevent or resolve conflicts of opinion.

In some respects, the BKKBN was in a good position to develop a strong role as co-ordinator of population policy-making. It controlled the distribution of most foreign and domestic funds for population research. Foreign assistance for the development of university and government population research establishments was channelled through the BKKBN, and the BKKBN took the lead in setting the agenda for research and training activities related to population within the Department of Education and Culture. On paper, the BKKBN appeared to be a very powerful force in policy-making.

Despite all this, the BKKBN never really established its credibility as the leader in policy-making among departments concerned with population. The university population centres resented the degree of BKKBN control over their activities, and many efforts at 'co-ordination' led to passive resistance or mere lip-service by other agencies. There were a number of problems. First, as already noted, the breadth of the BKKBN's true mandate was never entirely clear. Second, it failed to build a staff capability under the Deputy for Population Affairs that would enable it to play a dynamic role in policy discussions (for example, the expertise of the staff in the field of economics was very limited). Third, it did not succeed in building the close links with a variety of government agencies that would have been necessary for it to play its assigned roles adequately (particularly important here was the lack of close liaison with the EKUIN group of ministries dealing with economic, financial and industrial matters: links with the KESRA group of ministries dealing with social welfare matters were much better). Fourth, it did not utilize the potential of the Population Policy Research Committee effectively by holding regular meetings and focusing deliberations at such meetings on discussion papers, or at least pre-identified issues of relevance. In fact, the Committee rarely met, and never had any real influence on policy. Finally, the dispersal of effort common to all government agencies in Indonesia meant that senior staff in the office of the Deputy for Population Affairs were over-committed, both at the national and international level, to marginal tasks—such as the management of the ASEAN Population Programme, and thus could not concentrate attention and energy on the new role the BKKBN was assuming in population policy formation.

In the early 1980s, then, considerable weakness was still apparent in the integration of population concerns into the economic planning apparatus of Indonesia. The failure of *Bappenas* to build an in-house capacity to analyse population–development interactions made it much weaker in this field than its counterpart agencies in the Philippines, Thailand and Bangladesh. On the research side, Indonesia had no institution of the stature or capability of the Korean Development Institute (KDI) or the recently formed Thailand Development Research Institute (TDRI) which could be called on to conduct timely research projects needed by the planning agency. *Leknas* could not fulfil this role because of limited staff capacity and, more basically, because it was not responsible to *Bappenas*. The mandate given to BKKBN to formulate broader economic and social policies in support of the family planning programme was not being successfully carried out. Thus, the integration of population issues in development planning was less advanced in Indonesia than in other countries of South-East Asia. This was particularly paradoxical in view of the fact that the main economic planning minister (Prof. Widjojo) was the author of the definitive study of the history of Indonesian population growth, and was obviously receptive to sound ideas for innovative policies.

With the appointment of the State Minister for Population and Environment (KLH) in 1983 (Presidential Decision 25 of 1983), a clear mandate was given to one government agency to play the lead role in the formulation, management and co-ordination of population policies in Indonesia. In the same year, a decision was made to reorganize the BKKBN to narrow their responsibility specifically to family planning (Presidential Decision 64 of December 1983). Being a new agency, the KLH faced the test of providing clear and reasoned proposals for population and environmental policies to be considered by the cabinet in the lead-up to the Fifth Five-Year Development Plan, and monitoring population-related matters. For this reason it was critical for KLH to quickly produce a steady stream of high quality analyses which were clearly relevant to policy formation. By 1986, the staff of the Ministry had held a number of important workshops to direct attention to issues of importance, but no series of population policy papers had emerged.

Such policy formulation cannot be, and was not seen by KLH, as a monolithic process: many other agencies and researchers would have to make substantial inputs, not least because the KLH staff were too few to carry out extensive research activities. The ministry was seen as the point at which research results from various sources could be synthesized into policy formulations. The section of KLH responsible for this function is under the direction of an Assistant Minister for Population (ASMEN IV KLH), and includes sub-sections concerned with the following areas:

1. population growth (fertility, mortality and family planning);
2. population quality (nutrition, stature, fitness);

3. population mobility (both commuting, non-permanent and permanent movement);

4. urbanization.

The key role assigned to KLH was that of providing a forum for the discussion of population policy issues, through regular discussions and seminars to which population researchers and economic planners are invited, and through larger-scale national and regional conferences focusing on population policy themes. In the past, it was not the specific function of any single agency to organize such seminars and, as a result, there was little opportunity for systematic consideration of key population issues by the research or planning communities in Indonesia. By 1985, four technical teams had been formed consisting of ten members each, to provide specialized input for ministerial deliberations. As seen by these teams, whose members include academics, professionals and other specialists, the stages of policy formulation are as follows:

1. monitoring the effects of current policies;

2. recommending change of policy through: (a) identification of new priorities or (b) recommendations for improved implementation;

3. preparation of policy papers;

4. formulation of suggestions for the GBHN;

5. decisions of the MPR leading to the GBHN;

6. formulation of programmes and projects;

7. co-ordination of planning by *Bappenas*;

8. establishment of new Five-Year Development Plan (*Repelita*);

9. monitoring the effects of new policies, etc., through the cycle.

Clearly, this sequence is supplemented by activities aimed at population-related laws (for example, concerning marriage, migration, vital registration, etc.), *ad hoc* planning efforts, and matters of urgency, but the general task of policy formulation is seen in the context of the above cycle. During 1985, the Ministry of Population and the Environment took responsibility for promoting a draft population law which was designed to establish the basic principles of population programme implementation. This was similar in concept to the environment law which was enacted in 1982 under the name 'Act No. 4 of 1982' concerning 'Basic Provisions for the Management of the Living Environment'. The population law had been discussed in Jakarta for over a decade, but had constantly foundered on interdepartmental rivalries and concerns over key provisions linked with family planning. By the middle of 1986, there was no indication of when the draft law would be presented to the DPR, and some concern that it might become the focus of political debate, or be forgotten altogether.

Some Issues in the Integration of Population in Development Planning

In 1982–3, the United Nations carried out the fifth of a series of population enquiries, in the form of a questionnaire survey to governments. Of the 109 countries responding, 59 (including 49 developing countries) reported that they had designated a single agency to be responsible for the formulation and co-ordination of population policies. In this context, the decision of Indonesia to designate the Ministry of Population and Environment (KLH) as the single agency responsible for population policy is consistent with a growing trend to make population policy formulation overt and centralized.

Such a concentration of responsibility by no means overcomes all the problems of policy-making facing a department concerned with population. Briefly stated, the challenges fall into two groups: issues of substance, and issues of organization. On the substantive side, the role of population growth, distribution and quality in the process of economic growth is still very imperfectly understood. This is a general problem facing not only Indonesia, but the heterogeneity and size of Indonesia make these issues especially important. There is no consensus among Indonesian economists over the impact of population growth on the economy and, as a result, it is difficult to develop a consensus on the relative priority to give family planning in the constellation of government policies. Similarly, there is often quite serious—though only indirectly stated—disagreement over the need to move large numbers of people from Java to the other islands of the archipelago and, as a result, the various resettlement programmes can be regarded as an uneasy set of compromise solutions. This means that the basis for conducting cost-benefit and other analytical studies is often undermined by the lack of agreement over the nature of the returns to be expected from various population activities. Further research directed at resolving factual areas of disagreement is needed if the basis for strong population policies is to be established.

Finally, there are some issues of organizational structure concerning the co-ordination of fertility control and population mobility policies, programmes and projects. Though the government has clearly established policies to reduce fertility and to redistribute population and the labour force, it is less clear who has responsibility for making these operational and how ground rules are to be set concerning the bounds of acceptable intervention.

Institutional Problems Facing the Family Planning Programme

In the case of fertility control policies, these issues are continuously debated in a political process that has at times, pitted the BKKBN against the Department of Health, the Ministry of Population and Environment, and the Department of the Interior. There are also long-standing tensions between the BKKBN and the Central Bureau of Statistics over the issue of how the impact of programmes is to be monitored.

The debate on such issues is not necessarily a bad thing, and there are undoubtedly many legitimate issues which can only be resolved through the process of inter-agency disagreement. So far, such debates appear not to have harmed the family planning programme directly. The issue is: How broadly can the debate range, and how deep can disagreements go, before the actual policy of fertility control is endangered?

It is impossible to answer this question with any precision. One of the remarkable feats of the New Order government has been its consistent ability to identify and resolve basic conflicts before they threaten the viability of government programmes. There is a remarkable resilience to the whole structure, with the President and his ministers showing great capacity in deciding when to bend and when to stand firm on issues. For this reason, it is possible to be optimistic that the important challenges to fertility control policy will be successfully faced in future.

What are these challenges? Perhaps most important is the long term future of the BKKBN as the central co-ordinating agency for the fertility control programme. Two kinds of arguments perennially arise in this regard. First, line agencies such as the Department of Health often argue that they already carry most of the burden for implementing family planning, and thus could usefully 'absorb' the BKKBN into their existing structure, with a consequent saving of funds and simplification of operation. In response it is pointed out that the family planning programme is implemented by a large number of departments and levels of government, none of which has a particularly good track record in co-operative action. The BKKBN thus serves an essential function in focusing and co-ordinating efforts arising from disparate sources.

The second type of argument is based on the notion that a government-sponsored family planning programme is a 'temporary' measure which will fade away as community organizations and private enterprise respond to the nation's family planning needs. In following this line critics, and some influential BKKBN officials, paint a picture of a rapidly approaching stage at which the government will bow out. There are numerous hidden assumptions in this argument regarding the proper role of government in providing health and welfare services, the appropriate time scale for such a transition and the scope of the 'fading'. Is only the BKKBN to be phased out, or is the entire family planning programme, including activities in the departments of Health, Information, Internal Affairs and Religion to be shifted to voluntary or commercial agencies? The uncertainties raised by such speculations undoubtedly inhibit long term planning of bureaucratic resources. There is a long way to go yet in lowering fertility rates towards replacement, and the family planning programme, as a key government development programme, needs to be assured of continuity of support.

Institutional Problems Facing the Transmigration Programme

As for the transmigration programme, it has always required the co-operation of a number of government agencies. Over the years, the departmental focus of the transmigration programme has shifted a number of times. After the two main implementing agencies were combined in 1983 to form the Ministry of Transmigration, a new Presidential Decree was issued giving the Ministry of Transmigration responsibility for co-ordination through policy bodies and technical teams, but co-ordination has remained weak. The rather daunting task is to reach clear agreement between a number of ministries on policy objectives and their means of execution. The key ministries involved are those concerned with agriculture, forestry, population and environment, home affairs, co-operatives, public works, education and health.

The Ministry of Transmigration faces particular difficulties in the areas of planning and budgeting, and monitoring and evaluation. In planning and budgeting, the problems are due in part to the large number of agencies involved and the difficulty of programming the long sequence of activities involved in settlement. These complexities are felt even more with the government decree limiting budget carry-overs from 1986/7 onwards, meaning that accurate planning and budgeting has become essential to the success of the programme.

In monitoring and evaluation, many weaknesses are still to be overcome. In *Repelita III*, the scale of the transmigration programme stretched resources to the limit, and the drive to reach targets required a 'planning-while-doing' approach in many settlement areas. An attempt during *Repelita III* to develop an early warning system to detect and react to problems on-site failed. Steps to develop a responsive monitoring system are urgently required.

In future, the main thrust of the transmigration programme is expected to shift from movement of new settlers to maintenance and development of existing sites. This implies a shift in the weight of responsibilities from the Department of Transmigration to the line agencies which normally take over the maintenance and future development of transmigration sites after the first five years. Looking still further ahead, within twenty years, little transmigration along current lines will be taking place, but the main thrust will be to foster labour migration and promote regional development. This will require basic changes in the structure and operating style of the Department of Transmigration (if indeed it is still to exist) from one geared to a large-scale logistical operation to one focusing on policy formulation and facilitation.

Conclusion

All this raises a number of issues concerning the organization of decision-making in the population policy area. Research needs to be co-ordinated to prevent unproductive overlap and inefficiency. But to do this, KLH has to deal with a large number of actors or potential actors in the field of population–development research. Aside from institutes devoted specifically to population research, university faculties, government departments, and non-governmental organizations conduct a great deal of research relevant to population policy-making. Co-ordination of such a disparate group of institutions is not easy. In the early 1980s, the Population Policy Research Committee established by the BKKBN rarely met, but many of its members served on a competing 'co-ordinating' committee under the Ministry of Science and Technology. This group assumed control over population research as part of its mandate to deliberate on research priorities in basic human needs and socio-economic development.

Their sub-committee on population and manpower met monthly and was empowered to scrutinize all population research proposals prior to submission to *Bappenas* for funding. Against such a system, the efforts of the BKKBN seemed pale.

Since being given responsibility for population policy in Indonesia the KLH has attempted to co-ordinate policy-oriented population research. The power it has in determining the direction of research is in direct relation to the intellectual force it can muster, and the credibility it can accumulate as a source of innovative ideas. In consideration of the complex range of issues falling under the rubric of population policy and, given the limited number of KLH staff who are specialists in population issues, KLH faces a number of serious dilemmas. Time spent organizing workshops pays dividends in terms of contact with other agencies, but these returns must be balanced against the lost opportunities for serious study of research findings and preparation of policy analysis papers. Time spent travelling around the country encouraging the development of research in regional universities must be balanced against the need to study Indonesia's population issues in the context of international experience. To strike these balances is by no means easy. Another key problem is that KLH does not have the structure to implement population policy decisions. It must rely on line agencies. In particular KLH has no established presence at the provincial level, and is thus limited in its ability to formulate region-specific policies. As a result, the ministry relies on seminars and workshops in provincial capitals to get its messages across. Such meetings place a heavy burden on staff resources.

In linking population and environmental policy-making in one ministry, Indonesia is unique among ASEAN countries. Clearly, the connection between population concerns and environmental concerns is vital, and the present institutional structure fosters an awareness of such links. But it would be unhealthy if this single link was allowed to dominate the vision of the scope of population issues. True integration of population in development planning implies additional perspectives relating population to human settlement issues such as urbanization, and human resource development issues which would imply close co-operation with the departments of health and education. The biggest challenge facing KLH, like that facing most ministries in the world concerned with population, is to ensure that effective work on these substantive concerns is not inhibited by the organizational structure.

10 Future Trends in Indonesia's Population

Introduction

INDONESIA'S population of about 164 million in 1985 is growing at a rate of just over 2.0 per cent which, if continued, would lead to a doubling of the population in 35 years. However, the rate of population growth is declining and, if Indonesia's population does manage to double, it is likely that this doubling will take much longer than 35 years. Some of the crucial questions that need to be answered about future population growth in Indonesia are as follows:

1. What is a reasonable expectation about future fertility declines, bearing in mind expected economic and social trends and a continued active family planning programme? Given that growth will eventually level off, at what ultimate population size will this occur? More immediately relevant, and somewhat more easy to predict, how large will the population be in the year 2000?

2. How much will regional growth rates differ, both from each other and from their recent trends, and what will be the populations of provinces in the year 2000?

3. How rapidly will urbanization proceed?

4. Given expected trends in natural increase, interprovincial migration and urbanization, what will be the trend in population growth in rural Java?

5. What changes can be expected in the age structure over time? How rapidly will the population age? Will total dependency rates rise or fall?

6. What factors will determine the labour force in the year 2000?

In this and the next chapter we will suggest some possible answers to these and other questions using a number of different sets of population projections based on the 1980 Census.

Population projections for provinces of Indonesia have been prepared by different agencies, and the assumptions and results of these projections will be briefly compared before presenting more detailed findings of the set of projections selected as best suiting our purpose. It must be stressed at the outset that an infinite number of projections can be prepared and there is no way to say with absolute certainty that the assumptions of one will more accurately predict the future than those of another. However, we will present the results here of the projections which in our judgement employ plausible assumptions about fertility and mortality trends, as well as presenting provincial projections based on reasonable assumptions about future trends in interprovincial migration.

Table 10.1 shows the assumptions underlying recent projections for Indonesia prepared by five different agencies or individuals, and Table 10.2 shows the projected populations for the year 2000 according to these different projections. All sets of projections have their shortcomings. The BPS projection uses a conservative assumption about future fertility trends, with a much slower decline than that targeted by the BKKBN. It assumes constancy in the 1971–80 net migration rates by province, despite important shifts in the focus of the transmigration programme, which has a major influence on total migration rates. The World Bank projections also suffer from a failure to take account of changes in the transmigration programme in the most recent five-year development plan. The United Nations and Keyfitz projections are not disaggregated by province, although the latter are useful for their treatment of longer-term trends and will be used in this chapter to show the implications of different scenarios. One difficulty with both the United Nations and the Keyfitz projections is that they start with different assumptions about base-year fertility levels in their different variants.

For our purposes, the NUDSP projections prepared by Gardiner are the most useful, as they allow for planned changes in the transmigration programme to influence future rates of net migration for provinces, and they adopt not only BPS's very conservative assumption about fertility trends, but also a more optimistic assumption which nevertheless assumes that BKKBN's target of a 50 per cent reduction in 1967–80 fertility will not be reached by 1990, but only by the year 2000. The assumptions underlying these projections are presented in detail in Gardiner (1985), and they will not be discussed fully here. However, two points should be noted:

1. The assumptions of slower mortality decline and faster fertility decline in the NUDSP projection are the reasons why its projected population for the year 2000 falls short of the BPS projection by some 12 million. While trends are impossible to predict with any certainty, the NUDSP assumptions are plausible, although they do assume an even faster decline in fertility than that recorded during the 1970s. They are based on a model in which the rate of fertility decline gradually accelerates and then decelerates in subsequent periods following the introduction of the family planning programme. The acceleration is based on the assumption that there is some lag in bringing the programme to full strength, and the deceleration on the probable saturation of incipient demand as fertility rates move down to levels consistent with current preferences in much of Indonesia for a 3- to 4-child family. If these assumptions place excessive emphasis on the impact of the family planning programme, it can be argued that the alternative of modelling each province's fertility trends on the basis of trends in the complex of fertility determinants is hardly feasible at this

TABLE 10.1

Assumptions Underlying Five Sets of Population Projections for Indonesia

Projection	Base Population	Mortality Assumptions	Fertility Assumptions	Internal Migration Assumptions
Biro Pusat Statistik	Some adjustment and smoothing. Total base population 148,040,000. Similar adjustments to provincial base populations.	E_o^o for Indonesia, females, rises from 54 in 1980 to 66 in 1995–2000. Faster increases assumed in provinces with higher mortality in 1980, leading to convergence in E_o^o's.	Rate of decline of about 2 per cent per annum in TFR; some variation by provinces.	Intercensal (1971–80) net migration rates by province assumed to remain constant over projection period.
World Bank	UN smoothing procedure applied.	Steady improvement in mortality assumed; details not available.	Declines to replacement level assumed in all provinces, reaching replacement between 2015–20 (Bali) and 2025–30 (Maluku). Three different curves fitted between 1980 and replacement to project slower decline when TFR is high and faster decline at the intermediate level.	Net interprovincial migration rates by age and sex based on province of residence 5 years before 1980 Census were calculated. 'The pattern and volume of migration observed between 1975 and 1980 was held to be constant up to the year 2000.'

(continued)

TABLE 10.1 (continued)

Projection	Base Population	Mortality Assumptions	Fertility Assumptions	Internal Migration Assumptions
United Nations[a]	Not stated what adjustments made to 1980 Census population.	Life expectancy at birth, both sexes (years 1980–5 and 1995–2000): Medium projection— 52.5 to 59.7. Crude death rate (same periods): High projection— 11.2 to 9.7 Medium projection— 13.0 to 9.7 Low projection— 14.0 to 10.6	GRR, years 1980–5 and 1995–2000: High variant— 2.1 to 1.4 Medium variant— 1.9 to 1.2 Low variant— 1.8 to 1.1	No migration assumptions as subnational projections not computed.
National Urban Development Strategy	Same as Biro Pusat Statistik Projections.	Model 1 uses BPS assumptions. Model 2 assumes slower improvement, with rise in female E_0^o from 54 in 1980 to 63.4 in 1995–2000. Faster rises assumed in 1980, leading to convergence in E_0^o's.	BPS estimates of age patterns and levels of fertility for 1976–9 used as base. Age pattern assumed to remain constant. (1) BPS assumption of fertility decline: TFR falls from 4680 in 1976–9 to 3240 in 1995–2000. Some provincial variation.	Two migration matrices used, one projecting net effect of transmigration and the other, 'residual' migration outside the programme. Projection (1): adopts Repelita IV transmigration targets for 1985–90. Projection (2): Repelita III performance

		(2)	
Keyfitz	Not stated what adjustments made to 1980 Census population.	Fertility decline roughly matches earlier BKKBN target of 50 per cent decline 1967–70 to 2000. In provinces, accelerating, then decelerating, decline assumed after family planning programme introduced.	repeated in 1985–90. In both projections, 1985–90 numbers repeated in next two periods. Projection (3): assumption (2) up to 1990, then no additional transmigration. For residual migration, 1975–80 rates adjusted in future in relation to rate of natural increase in the province. Residual migration in Lampung adjusted downwards arbitrarily.
	E_0^o (both sexes) rises from 56.3 in 1980 to year 2000 figure of 66 (medium projection), 68 (high projection), 63 (low projection).	TFR, 1980 and 2000: 5.20 to 3.37 4.60 to 2.52 4.20 to 2.00	No migration assumptions as subnational projections not computed.

Sources: BPS, 1984b; Gardiner, 1985; Keyfitz, 1985b; United Nations, 1985.
[a] These projections show 'Indonesia' and 'East Timor' separately. Assumptions shown here are for 'Indonesia', but results reported in the text add the 'East Timor' figure to 'Indonesia'.

TABLE 10.2

Population Projections for Indonesia to the Year 2000

Biro Pusat Statistik	222 million
World Bank	214 million
United Nations*	223 million (high)
	205 million (medium)
	196 million (low)
NUDSP (fertility assumption 2)	210 million
Keyfitz	199 million (low)
	215 million (medium)
	239 million (high)

Sources: See Table 10.1.
*1982 assessment of world population.

stage, due both to data limitations and lack of a comprehensive quantitative model of determinants of fertility. Projected trends in fertility rates by provinces are shown in Appendix 4.

2. The migration assumptions in the NUDSP projection are complex, and the volatility of migration ensures that they will not accurately predict actual events. But they have the virtue of presenting three alternatives for transmigration (only one of them—the middle one—truly realistic). The assumptions about residual migration appear to have less logic to them. To the extent that residual migration is influenced by transmigration, they should have been linked in some way (ideally in lagged form) to transmigration flows.

Table 10.3 shows total population by five-year intervals and province for the 1980–2000 period according to the medium (Table 10.3A) and high (Table 10.3B) transmigration variants, and Table 10.4 shows growth rates of population by province over the same period. Results of the low transmigration projection are not presented because of the unlikelihood that its assumptions will be followed, though the low projection will be discussed in the context of the effect of transmigration on the growth of particular provinces. Results of the high transmigration projection are presented mainly for illustrative purposes because its assumptions, although they reflect official transmigration targets, are unrealistic.

Trends in Total Population Size

The results of the projections will be discussed in relation to the questions asked at the beginning of this chapter. The first to be considered is the ultimate size at which Indonesia's population is likely to level off. There is obviously a wide margin of error in any such projection. Since the NUDSP projection does not go beyond the year 2000, the main point to be noted is the substantial rate of population growth still expected at the time Indonesia's population reaches 210 million: 1.5 per cent per annum in the 1995–2000 period. This suggests that even with the most optimistic

TABLE 10.3A

Projected Total Population by Province, 1980–2000, Assuming
Medium Rates of Transmigration between Provinces

Region	Population ('000)				
	1980	1985	1990	1995	2000
INDONESIA	148,041	164,239	180,115	195,635	210,738
SUMATRA	28,120	33,622	39,371	45,268	51,369
DI Aceh	2,621	3,051	3,516	3,984	4,457
North Sumatra	8,392	9,556	10,704	11,813	12,896
West Sumatra	3,418	3,717	3,994	4,238	4,460
Riau	2,177	2,691	3,384	4,176	5,040
Jambi	1,452	1,833	2,326	2,899	3,531
South Sumatra	4,647	5,751	6,938	8,192	9,495
Bengkulu	771	1,016	1,307	1,646	2,017
Lampung	4,642	6,007	7,202	8,320	9,473
JAVA	91,609	98,116	102,371	105,896	108,641
DKI Jakarta	6,528	7,917	9,339	10,837	12,404
West Java	27,556	30,517	32,936	35,238	37,340
Central Java	25,467	26,549	26,660	26,318	25,565
DI Yogyakarta	2,761	2,922	2,974	3,004	3,014
East Java	29,297	30,211	30,462	30,499	30,318
NUSA TENGGARA	8,518	9,305	10,000	10,646	11,268
Bali	2,479	2,644	2,686	2,707	2,702
West Nusa Tenggara	2,735	2,991	3,256	3,514	3,793
East Nusa Tenggara	2,747	3,040	3,332	3,609	3,871
East Timor	557	630	726	816	902
KALIMANTAN	6,749	8,233	10,847	13,671	16,636
West Kalimantan	2,495	2,999	3,729	4,495	5,277
Central Kalimantan	958	1,263	2,070	2,980	3,963
South Kalimantan	2,073	2,392	2,657	2,914	3,164
East Kalimantan	1,223	1,579	2,391	3,282	4,232
SULAWESI	10,450	11,841	13,154	14,432	15,686
North Sulawesi	2,124	2,396	2,660	2,916	3,162
Central Sulawesi	1,295	1,617	1,935	2,266	2,610
South Sulawesi	6,085	6,641	7,131	7,571	7,979
South-east Sulawesi	946	1,187	1,428	1,679	1,935
MALUKU AND IRIAN JAYA	2,595	3,122	4,372	5,722	7,138
Maluku	1,416	1,672	1,966	2,268	2,577
Irian Jaya	1,179	1,450	2,406	3,454	4,561

Source: Modified from Gardiner, 1985: 70.
Note: Totals for islands and the nation may differ from the original source due to rounding
errors.

projection of continuing fertility decline, substantial population growth will
occur before population growth ceases. To find an estimate of trends
beyond the year 2000, turn to the Keyfitz (1985b) projections. His medium
projection, which yields a population 5 million larger in the year 2000 than
does the NUDSP projection, is the projection with assumptions closest to
those of the NUDSP projection. Although it assumes that replacement-
level fertility will be reached by the year 2010, it shows a 50 per cent
increase over the first half of the twenty-first century, with the population
reaching 324 million in the year 2050. This serves to emphasize the
tremendous population-growth momentum built into the age structure of

TABLE 10.3B

Projected Total Population by Province, 1980–2000, Assuming
High Rates of Transmigration between Provinces

Region	Population ('000)				
	1980	1985	1990	1995	2000
INDONESIA	148,041	164,239	180,115	195,635	210,738
SUMATRA	28,120	33,622	39,371	45,268	51,369
DI Aceh	2,621	3,051	3,516	3,984	4,457
North Sumatra	8,392	9,556	10,704	11,813	12,896
West Sumatra	3,418	3,717	3,994	4,238	4,460
Riau	2,177	2,691	3,384	4,176	5,040
Jambi	1,452	1,833	2,326	2,899	3,531
South Sumatra	4,647	5,751	6,938	8,192	9,495
Bengkulu	771	1,016	1,307	1,646	2,017
Lampung	4,642	6,007	7,202	8,320	9,473
JAVA	91,609	98,116	102,371	105,896	108,641
DKI Jakarta	6,528	7,917	9,339	10,837	12,404
West Java	27,556	30,517	32,936	35,238	37,340
Central Java	25,467	26,549	26,660	26,318	25,565
DI Yogyakarta	2,761	2,922	2,974	3,004	3,014
East Java	29,297	30,211	30,462	30,499	30,318
NUSA TENGGARA	8,518	9,305	10,000	10,646	11,268
Bali	2,479	2,644	2,686	2,707	2,702
West Nusa Tenggara	2,735	2,991	3,256	3,514	3,793
East Nusa Tenggara	2,747	3,040	3,332	3,609	3,871
East Timor	557	630	726	816	902
KALIMANTAN	6,749	8,233	10,847	13,671	16,636
West Kalimantan	2,495	2,999	3,729	4,495	5,277
Central Kalimantan	958	1,263	2,070	2,980	3,963
South Kalimantan	2,073	2,392	2,657	2,914	3,164
East Kalimantan	1,223	1,579	2,391	3,282	4,232
SULAWESI	10,450	11,841	13,154	14,432	15,686
North Sulawesi	2,124	2,396	2,660	2,916	3,162
Central Sulawesi	1,295	1,617	1,935	2,266	2,610
South Sulawesi	6,085	6,641	7,131	7,571	7,979
South-east Sulawesi	946	1,187	1,428	1,679	1,935
MALUKU AND IRIAN JAYA	2,595	3,122	4,372	5,722	7,138
Maluku	1,416	1,672	1,966	2,268	2,577
Irian Jaya	1,179	1,450	2,406	3,454	4,561

Source: Modified from Gardiner, 1985: 71.
Note: See Table 10.3A.

the Indonesian population, resulting from high birth rates in the 1950s, 1960s and early 1970s.

The more immediately relevant issue is the expected size of Indonesia's population in the year 2000. The projections in Table 10.2 range from 196 to 239 million, a wide range considering that the year 2000 is only 20 years ahead of the year to which the base data for the various projections relate. This does not mean that all figures within this range are equally likely to be reached. Keyfitz's high projection (239 million), is based on an implausibly high initial fertility level and a relatively slow rate of fertility decline. The figures 223 million and 222 million (in the United Nations and BPS projections, respectively) are based on assumptions of continuing rapid declines in mortality but only modest declines in fertility, and both these

TABLE 10.4A

Projected Population Growth Rates by Province, 1980–2000, Assuming
Medium Transmigration Rates between Provinces

Region	Projected Growth Rate (Percentage)				Factor by which 2000 Population Exceeds 1980 Population
	1980–1985	1985–1990	1990–1995	1995–2000	
INDONESIA	2.1	1.8	1.6	1.5	1.42
SUMATRA	3.6	3.2	2.8	2.5	1.83
DI Aceh	3.0	2.8	2.5	2.2	1.70
North Sumatra	2.6	2.3	2.0	1.8	1.54
West Sumatra	1.7	1.4	1.2	1.0	1.30
Riau	4.2	4.6	4.2	3.8	2.32
Jambi	4.7	4.8	4.4	3.9	2.43
South Sumatra	4.3	3.8	3.3	3.0	2.04
Bengkulu	5.5	5.0	4.6	4.1	2.62
Lampung	5.2	3.6	2.9	2.6	2.04
JAVA	1.4	1.1	1.0	0.8	1.24
DKI Jakarta	3.9	3.4	3.0	2.7	1.91
West Java	2.0	1.7	1.5	1.3	1.39
Central Java	0.8	0.5	0.2	−0.1	1.07
DI Yogyakarta	1.1	0.9	0.7	0.7	1.19
East Java	0.6	0.5	0.4	0.3	1.09
NUSA TENGGARA					
Bali	1.3	0.9	0.8	0.6	1.19
West Nusa Tenggara	1.8	1.7	1.5	1.5	1.39
East Nusa Tenggara	2.0	1.8	1.6	1.4	1.41
East Timor	2.5	2.3	1.9	1.6	1.51
KALIMANTAN	4.0	3.7	3.2	2.8	1.99
West Kalimantan	3.7	3.3	2.9	2.5	1.85
Central Kalimantan	5.5	5.5	4.7	4.0	2.68
South Kalimantan	2.9	2.1	1.9	1.6	1.53
East Kalimantan	5.1	5.1	4.3	3.7	2.50
SULAWESI	2.5	2.1	1.9	1.7	1.50
North Sulawesi	2.4	2.1	1.8	1.6	1.49
Central Sulawesi	4.4	3.6	3.2	2.8	2.02
South Sulawesi	1.8	1.4	1.2	1.0	1.31
South-east Sulawesi	4.5	3.7	3.2	2.8	2.05
MALUKU AND IRIAN JAYA					
Maluku	3.3	3.2	2.9	2.6	1.82
Irian Jaya	4.1	4.6	3.9	3.3	2.21

Source: Gardiner, 1985: 74.

assumptions can be queried. The United Nations figure of 196 million is based on an unrealistically low estimate of 1980–5 fertility rates (GRR of 1.80) and a decline to replacement-level fertility by about the year 2000. The probability of reaching a figure of around 210 million, implying fairly rapid declines in fertility—though not as rapid as the BKKBN targets imply, seems greater than the probability of reaching figures at the upper or lower end of the range given in Table 10.2.

Some of the demographic 'landmarks' which can be expected to occur between 1980 and 2000 on the basis of the projections include the following:

  1. The population of Indonesia will pass 200 million.

TABLE 10.4B

Projected Population Growth Rates by Province, 1980–2000, Assuming
High Transmigration Rates between Provinces

Region	Projected Growth Rate (Percentage)				Factor by which 2000 Population Exceeds 1980 Population
	1980–1985	1985–1990	1990–1995	1995–2000	
INDONESIA	2.1	1.8	1.7	1.5	1.42
SUMATRA	3.6	3.2	2.8	2.5	1.83
DI Aceh	3.0	2.8	2.5	2.2	1.70
North Sumatra	2.6	2.3	2.0	1.8	1.54
West Sumatra	1.7	1.4	1.2	1.0	1.30
Riau	4.2	4.6	4.2	3.8	2.32
Jambi	4.7	4.8	4.4	3.9	2.43
South Sumatra	4.3	3.8	3.3	3.0	2.04
Bengkulu	5.5	5.0	4.6	4.1	2.62
Lampung	5.2	3.6	2.9	2.6	2.04
JAVA	1.4	0.8	0.7	0.5	1.19
DKI Jakarta	3.9	3.3	3.0	1.7	1.90
West Java	2.0	1.5	1.4	1.2	1.36
Central Java	0.8	0.1	−0.3	−0.6	1.00
DI Yogyakarta	1.1	0.4	0.2	0.1	1.09
East Java	0.6	0.2	0.0	−0.1	1.03
NUSA TENGGARA					
Bali	1.3	0.3	0.2	0.0	1.09
West Nusa Tenggara	1.8	1.7	1.5	1.5	1.39
East Nusa Tenggara	2.0	1.8	1.6	1.4	1.41
East Timor	2.5	2.8	2.3	2.0	1.62
KALIMANTAN	4.0	5.5	4.6	3.9	2.47
West Kalimantan	3.7	4.4	3.7	3.2	2.11
Central Kalimantan	5.5	9.9	7.3	5.7	4.14
South Kalimantan	2.9	2.1	1.9	1.6	1.53
East Kalimantan	5.1	8.3	6.3	5.1	3.46
SULAWESI	2.5	2.1	1.9	1.7	1.50
North Sulawesi	2.4	2.1	1.8	1.6	1.49
Central Sulawesi	4.4	3.6	3.2	2.8	2.02
South Sulawesi	1.8	1.4	1.2	1.0	1.31
South-east Sulawesi	4.5	3.7	3.2	2.8	2.05
MALUKU AND IRIAN JAYA					
Maluku	3.3	3.2	2.9	2.6	1.82
Irian Jaya	4.1	10.1	7.2	5.6	3.87

Source: Gardiner, 1985: 75.

2. The population of Java will pass 100 million (actually as early as 1986 or 1987).

3. The population of Sumatra may well pass 50 million.

4. The population of Sulawesi will pass 15 million.

5. The population of Kalimantan will pass 10 million.

In 1964, the late President Soekarno, in stating why he would not introduce a birth control programme in Indonesia, said that by exploiting all the land in Indonesia, 250 million people could be fed, whereas the population at the time was only 103 million (Hull and Mantra, 1981: 264). It now appears that the 250 million figure will probably be reached by the second decade of the twenty-first century, and another demographic landmark could follow before the middle of the twenty-first century—Indonesia's population will surpass that of the United States. The main question is how far the population will grow beyond the quarter-billion figure before its growth can be halted. In Keyfitz's low projection, the answer is that growth will cease at a population only about 10 per cent above the quarter-billion figure but, in his high projection, the population would reach 400 million and still be climbing at the mid-point of the twenty-first century.

Regional Patterns of Population Growth

The next question raised at the beginning of this chapter concerned expected variation in regional rates of population growth. This is a matter of great interest because, as already noted, the aim of slowing and eventually halting population growth in Java has long appeared both important and well-nigh unattainable. Both the major instruments of population policy in Indonesia—the family planning and transmigration programmes—though they have multiple aims, started with the slowing of population growth in Java as their paramount concern. Will the long-term decline in Java's share of Indonesia's population continue, and how widely will provincial growth rates differ?

In the medium transmigration projection, the share of Indonesia's population living in Java is expected to decline from 62 per cent in 1980 to 54 per cent in the year 2000. Over the same period, Sumatra's share is projected to rise from 19 to 24 per cent and Kalimantan's from 4.6 per cent to 6.4 per cent, but the shares of Sulawesi and the other islands are not projected to alter markedly. In the high transmigration projection, Java's share is projected to decline even more sharply—from 62 to 52 per cent, Kalimantan's to rise more sharply—from 4.6 per cent to 7.9 per cent, and the other islands share to rise from 7.5 per cent to 8.7 per cent, due almost entirely to the substantial transmigration intake planned for Irian Jaya.

As far as shares of individual provinces are concerned, in the medium transmigration projection, the largest rises occur in Jakarta, Lampung, South Sumatra and Riau and the largest declines by far are in Central and East Java. In terms of relative increases, some provinces with initially small populations, such as Jambi, Bengkulu, Central Kalimantan, East Kalimantan and Irian Jaya are expected to make substantial gains, and significant relative declines will occur in Yogyakarta and Bali.

The pattern of recent decades is expected to continue, whereby not only the densely settled 'core' region of Java–Bali–Lombok will decline in its proportion of the total population, but so too will certain densely populated provinces in the other islands, notably South Sulawesi and West Sumatra, which have a long history of out-migration. Within Java, there will be a distinct westward shift in the centre of gravity of the population, as Central Java, Yogyakarta and East Java grow slowly because of low natural increase and heavy out-migration, whereas the Jakarta metropolis and its 'spill-over' areas in West Java continue to grow rapidly.

Annual rates of increase are expected to vary dramatically by province—for example, in the 1990–5 period, they are projected to range between 0.2 per cent in Central Java and 4.7 per cent in Central Kalimantan. All the key transmigration source provinces would have a rate of increase below 1 per cent in this period, and the key transmigration receiving provinces rates in excess of 3 per cent. These differences will result not only from transmigration flows, but also from expected differentials in rates of natural increase and residual migration.

In the high transmigration projection, the declines in the shares of the transmigration source provinces are naturally greater, and Jakarta, Lampung, South Sumatra and Riau are joined by Irian Jaya, Central Kalimantan and East Kalimantan as the provinces whose shares increase most in absolute terms. Central Kalimantan would actually double its share of Indonesia's population over the twenty-year period, and both it and Irian Jaya would achieve annual growth rates of close to 10 per cent over short periods. The difficulties of handling such rapid population increases in provinces with limited infrastructure and a resident population ethnically different from the newcomers raises serious questions about the advisability of pursuing the transmigration targets for these provinces—apart from which, as will be discussed in Chapter 11, it is already clear that these targets will not be reached.

A noteworthy aspect of these projections is the virtual cessation of population growth expected in Central and East Java by the 1990s. In the high transmigration projection, the population of both Central and East Java will actually decline during the 1990s, and in the more realistic medium transmigration projection, the combined population of Central Java, Yogyakarta and East Java will grow by only 2 per cent over the whole decade. In other words, the possibility of halting population growth in these extremely densely populated provinces, which for so long has appeared to be in the realm of wishful thinking, is now set to become a reality.

Trends in Urbanization

In considering the likely trends in urbanization, one of the most difficult issues is the exact definition of an 'urban' area. Many rural areas of Java now have population densities and access to facilities which would be regarded as 'urban' under current definitions. When looking at trends over time and projecting trends in the future, it is necessary to be very careful to specify the degree to which apparent changes are due to changed definitions or to real changes in the structure and function of particular geographic areas. The clarification of this distinction was one of the major contributions of the National Urban Development Strategy Project (NUDSP), organized in the early 1980s by the Indonesian Department of Public Works and the UN Centre for Human Settlements (see NUDSP, 1985: 55–78). There can be no doubt, however, that Indonesia is urbanizing at substantial rates and that there will be changes in the type of settlements many Indonesians reside in between now and the next century.

These changes will depend very much on structural economic change, differences in investment, and thus productivity between agricultural and non-agricultural activities and the extent to which higher-productivity activities are concentrated in urban areas, thereby attracting rural–urban migration through the higher wages they can pay (Jones, 1983). Urbanization will also be influenced by rural–urban differences in rates of natural increase, though these may not be very great if both fertility and mortality are lower in urban areas, thus partially offsetting each other in their effect on rates of natural increase.

As a result of this process, there seems to be little doubt that the 'formal' urban share of Indonesia's population will have risen above 30 per cent at the end of the century while the proportion of the population working in urban areas, having access to urban services and being within easy travelling distance of cities, will be well over a majority. This latter phenomenon is analogous to the 'suburbanization' process found in developed countries. Both processes could proceed at much higher rates than found at present, depending on the level and pattern of investment in infrastructure. The preferred NUDSP projection implies a figure of 36 per cent urban in the year 2000, with over 40 per cent urban in Java, but assumes to some degree a continuation of recent trends in investment, which may be overly optimistic in light of the decline in oil prices and the recession which gripped the country in the mid-1980s. To some degree, though, the process of urbanization appears inexorable. Even with reduced investments

TABLE 10.5

Indonesia: Projection of Population of the Ten Largest Cities, to Year 2000

City	Population		Ratio of Projections to 1980 Population
	1980	2000	
Jakarta	6,071,748	12,009,200	1.98
Bandung	1,794,524	3,366,653	1.88
Surabaya	1,737,019	3,227,752	1.86
Medan	1,265,208	2,555,890	2.02
Bogor	544,793	2,251,745	4.13
Palembang	757,491	1,752,024	2.31
Ujung Pandang	638,799	1,745,313	2.73
Semarang	820,142	1,587,511	1.94
Yogyakarta	492,642	967,943	1.96
Malang	491,474	947,409	1.93

Source: NUDSP Final Report, 1985, Appendix E1.

Note: 1980 Census populations for these cities have been adjusted to show populations of functional, rather than administrative, urban areas. In cases where cities were 'underbounded', this has led to an upward adjustment of the 1980 Census figure; in cases where they were 'overbounded', to a downward adjustment. See NUDSP (1985: 55–60).

in infrastructure, some people will continue to move to cities in the hope of attaining a better life for themselves and their children. Whether displaced from a crowded rural labour market or attracted by high hopes of success in the risky urban labour market, they will come. As far as these 'inevitable' migrants are concerned, the reduced investments in urban infrastructure will merely mean a less amenable life for their families and a more difficult search for work for themselves. The lack of viable alternatives will ensure that they are not deterred from the move.

The process of urbanization will lead to a transformation of Indonesian cities in both scale and function. Some idea of the former impact is found in Table 10.6, where the populations of the ten largest cities in 1980 are projected to the year 2000. Jakarta, under the NUDSP assumptions, will reach the mammoth size of over 12 million, while nearby Bogor is projected to have well over 2 million. The transformations implicit in the growth of cities by factors of 100–150 per cent in twenty years present major challenges to urban planners, and raise many important questions about the nature of social structures in Indonesia in the future.

Population Growth in Rural Java

Likely trends in urbanization, linked with expected population trends in the provinces of Java, strongly suggest that population growth in rural Java may already be coming to an end. During the decade of the 1970s, Java's rural population continued to increase, though the numbers finding employment in agriculture increased very little, and in many *kabupaten* they declined (Jones, 1984: Fig. 3). This was because of the substantial increase in non-agricultural employment in rural areas, which may have resulted from a number of factors. These include: a search for income by poor, landless and near-landless rural people whose opportunities in agriculture were becoming increasingly constricted; spillover of urban industry into surrounding rural areas; and growing work opportunities in service activities and construction. This latter factor was largely consequent on investment by the government of some of its growing oil revenues on economic and social development projects in rural areas. These developments sustained a growing population in rural areas of Java during the 1970s without much increase in agricultural employment.

Trends toward further absorption of rural workers in non-agricultural activities in rural areas could now lead to an actual decline in the numbers employed in agriculture, either full-time or on a 'full-time equivalent' basis. This would open up fascinating possibilities for technological changes in Javanese agriculture based on a new emphasis on raising labour productivity, replacing the emphasis which has perforce been required up to the present: that of raising productivity per hectare due to the need to support an ever-increasing population on a fixed land base. With the cessation of rural population growth, it will be possible to broaden the goal of agricultural development from one concentrating exclusively on increasing the productivity of land to one that places increasing emphasis on increasing unit productivity of agricultural labour. If this is indeed the case, it spells the end of the pattern of agricultural involution which has for so long gripped Java (Geertz, 1965).

Changing Age Structure

Finally, what changes can be expected in the age structure of the Indonesian population? Briefly, Table 10.6 shows the expected trends in the proportion of the population in the broad age groups 0 to 14, 15 to 64 and 65-plus in the NUDSP projections. If fertility and mortality follow the projected trends, the population will clearly age considerably over the twenty years, with a steep decline in the share of the 0 to 14 age group being offset mainly by a rise in the share of the 15 to 64 age group. This bodes well for Indonesia in that the ratio of dependents to potential workers will be declining, though the benefits of this will only be realized if the potential workers can find suitable work, and the very rapid increase in the potential working population will militate against this.

Over the longer run, population ageing will eventually result in a rise in dependency ratios, as the rise in the share of the elderly in the population will eventually more than offset the decline in the share of young dependents. However, Keyfitz's medium projection indicates that this rise will not start to occur until about 2010, and in the meantime the overall dependency ratio will decline from around 0.8 to around 0.5. Thus ageing of the Indonesian population, though it is inevitable as in all populations in which the transition to low fertility rates takes place, is not something to be feared but something which can be adjusted to gradually over time, first during a period of steadily falling overall dependency rates and finally during a period of gradually increasing dependency rates.

The very slow increase in the school-age population in the NUDSP projections (only a 23 per cent increase in the 5–19-year-old population over the twenty-year period) will facilitate the further development of the educational system. Universal primary education can be consolidated, the quality of primary schooling improved, and attention given to keeping a higher proportion of secondary-school-aged children in school. In other

TABLE 10.6

Indonesia: Proportion of Population in Broad Age Groups, 1980–2000

Age Group (Years)	Percentage of Population		
	1980	1990	2000
0–14	40.3	36.7	31.3
15–64	56.4	59.9	64.3
65+	3.3	3.5	4.5
All ages	100.0	100.0	100.0

Source: Calculated from NUDSP projections.

words, the consolidation of the impressive educational strides made in the
1970s and early 1980s should become progressively easier.

Labour Force Projections

If projections are essentially an exercise in 'what if' logic, this is nowhere
more apparent than in the case of labour force projections. In addition to
the usual assumptions about fertility, mortality and migration, the implications of which have been examined above, analysts must make assumptions
about the pattern of labour force participation by age and sex. The
projected population of each age–sex group is then multiplied by the participation rate to produce the estimated number of members of the labour
force. Further refinements are possible by making assumptions about the
proportion of the labour force who are likely to be employed in various
sectors of the economy, and even about the educational composition of the
various groups. Such calculations, though laborious when done by hand,
are essentially simple and can be carried out quickly using various readily
available computer programmes.

Most planners are hesitant to carry out such calculations in much detail
or over long projection periods because of the very substantial data
problems which arise. In the first place, the measurement of labour force
participation in the Indonesian economy is notoriously difficult (see
Chapter 8). Over time, there have been numerous changes in the definitions and reference periods used to determine exactly who should be
regarded as part of the formal labour force. In itself, the concept of a
'labour force', based as it is on notions of regular work for remuneration, is
not easily applied in an economy where much productive activity is
organized within family settings and undertaken on an irregular basis.
These problems mean that the measured labour force participation rates in
each census and survey suffer reliability problems, while changes in
definitions mean that it is unwise to make detailed comparisons of participation trends between enumerations.

These difficulties of measurement are particularly difficult with regard to
women. As noted earlier (p. 251) in a series of surveys and censuses in Java
between 1958 and 1980, the proportion of women aged 10 and over who
were said to be in the labour force varied erratically between 60 per cent
and 29 per cent. No analysts seriously contend that these figures represent
real levels, much less a real trend. At most, it might be said that, under a
very restrictive definition of participation, about a third of Indonesian
women are in the formal labour force at any time. When this definition is
loosened (as with the very broad definition used in 1958), the proportion
rises to around three-fifths or two-thirds.

From a practical viewpoint, it is important to make an attempt to project
the labour force, at least over a short period, to provide planners with
information on the flow of new entrants, the levels of skills both existing
and new workers will have, and the geographic distribution of these
workers. Both BPS and NUDSP (Table 10.1) have made projections of

the labour force, but their results are even more in conflict than are their basic population projections. Over the relatively short period up to 2000, the figures they produce for Indonesia are as follows:

	Labour Force Projections (in '000 persons)			
	1985	*1990*	*1995*	*2000*
BPS, 1983	67,043	76,952	88,496	101,626
NUDSP, 1985	60,609	68,769	77,686	86,870

The two curves diverge substantially, and their different assumptions result in radically different projections of the labour force in twenty years. The BPS estimates indicate an increase in the labour force of 52 per cent over fifteen years, while NUDSP projects an increase of only 43 per cent but, because of the very different assumptions about the initial population conditions, the difference in the absolute numbers projected are very large.

The major factor underlying these results is the two assumptions concerning the labour force participation of women. BPS examined past trends to conclude that Indonesian women will increasingly join the formal labour force from levels assumed at 39.5 per cent in 1983 to 48.2 per cent in 2000, with the result that the labour force *per se* will grow faster than the working-age population. On the other hand, Gardiner (1985)—in calculating the NUDSP projections—argues that the assumption of rising participation is based on flimsy evidence of trends and overlooks the likely impact of social changes which may well encourage women to stay out of the labour force. His argument is basically that because women with higher education and higher family incomes, in cross-sectional data, tend to participate in the labour force less than poorer less-educated women, then, as educational and income levels rise in the future, women as a group will be only equally or less likely to participate. In this scenario, the labour force will grow at the same rate or more slowly than the working-age population.

There is remarkably little evidence on which to base a critical evaluation of these conflicting assumptions. Clearly the BPS procedures are inadequate, relying as they do entirely on extrapolation of assumed trends, with no consideration of social and economic changes which will determine the role of women in future Indonesian society. At the same time, it is not satisfactory to assume that cross-sectional behaviour will accurately predict future trends, since the ability of well-to-do women to opt out of the labour force depends in part on the adequacy of their husbands' incomes to meet their needs, and the availability of relatively inexpensive services and goods produced in an economy rich in raw labour power. As overall educational and income levels rise, it is to be expected that the perceived 'needs' of families will expand, the relative costs of services and goods will rise, and hence the opportunity cost of women staying home will rise, all of which will tend to encourage increased 'formal' labour force participation among women. In addition, it should be remembered that the low participation rates are in part an illusion caused by the failure to regard many productive

TABLE 10.7

Indonesia: Projections of the Labour Force by Province to the Year 2000
(Males and Females Combined)

Region	Labour Force Projections (in '000)		Ratio of $\frac{(2)}{(1)} \times 100$
	BPS (1)	NUDSP (2)	(3)
INDONESIA	101,626	86,873	85.5
SUMATRA	20,959	20,963	100.0
DI Aceh	1,731	1,704	98.4
North Sumatra	5,509	5,493	99.7
West Sumatra	2,087	1,687	80.8
Riau	1,154	1,944	168.5
Jambi	1,093	1,446	132.3
South Sumatra	3,153	4,042	128.2
Bengkulu	885	871	98.4
Lampung	5,347	3,776	70.6
JAVA	62,860	47,772	76.0
DKI Jakarta	5,601	4,341	77.5
West Java	17,538	14,329	81.7
Central Java	18,703	12,620	67.5
DI Yogyakarta	2,003	1,746	87.2
East Java	19,015	14,736	77.5
NUSA TENGGARA	4,866	4,901	100.7
Bali	1,812	1,365	75.3
West Nusa Tenggara	1,510	1,487	98.5
East Nusa Tenggara	1,284	1,677	130.6
East Timor	260	372	143.1
KALIMANTAN	5,396	5,757	106.7
West Kalimantan	1,562	2,131	136.4
Central Kalimantan	1,215	1,166	96.0
South Kalimantan	1,261	1,364	108.2
East Kalimantan	1,358	1,096	80.7
SULAWESI	5,789	5,621	97.1
North Sulawesi	1,647	1,226	74.4
Central Sulawesi	860	1,022	118.8
South Sulawesi	2,708	2,670	98.6
South-east Sulawesi	574	703	122.5
MALUKU AND IRIAN JAYA	1,756	1,859	105.9
Maluku	924	864	93.5
Irian Jaya	832	995	119.6

Sources: BPS, 1983: 38–9; for NUDSP—Gardiner, 1985: 77.

Note: The numbers for islands and the nation as a whole differ from the original sources due to rounding errors.

activities carried out at home as part of national production. As women become more educated and apply new technologies and methods of organization to household activities, they are increasingly likely to be recognized in official enumerations, and the *reported* participation rates will rise.

In the end, we are left with a complex set of arguments but no clear resolution. It may be wise to accept the BPS assumption of rising participation, but not for the reasons offered by BPS. Instead, we would have to argue that the nature of social changes occurring in Indonesian society, and particularly the impact of schooling in instilling positive ideas about formal labour force participation, may tend to raise both the actual and reported participation of women in the national economy. On the other hand, considering the unknown impact of economic difficulties in the 1980s and the potential social impact of educational and religious changes over a longer period, it might be more prudent to accept the NUDSP assumptions as a lower limit for labour force numbers. Provincial estimates for both series are presented in Table 10.7. The differences, both overall and between provinces, are striking. In 17 provinces, the BPS projections exceed the NUDSP projections while, in 10 provinces, the reverse is the case. In Riau, Jambi, Lampung, East Nusa Tenggara and West Kalimantan, the differences are so substantial as to cast doubt on the value of the exercise for economic planning purposes. In such cases, provincial planners would have to examine the underlying assumptions about fertility, transmigration and labour force participation very carefully to make a judgement about the reasonableness of one projection compared to the other. Unfortunately it will be very difficult to make such examinations because of the paucity of basic data on trends in fertility and mortality at the provincial level, and the many open questions surrounding the determinants of future labour force participation rates.

Lack of solid data or well-formed projections will not exempt planners from the task of grappling with difficult problems of population growth. The projections presented above, even with all their limitations, effectively outline some of the important issues facing planners: the high momentum of population growth, difficulties of influencing population redistribution, and the inexorable growth of the labour force at rates which, given the elasticity of employment with respect to capital formation, dwarf the increase in productive employment likely to result from expected patterns of investment. In the end, this is the most important product of population projections in Indonesia: they are good enough to show us where the major problems are, but not yet adequate to let us devise solutions with confidence that we have the numbers right.

11 Planning for a Growing Population

The Control of Population Growth

A recurring theme in this book has been that the legacy of past demographic history is revealed in current population structure. This demographic past is always with us, dominating the present and conditioning the future. Though the familiarity of Indonesians with volcanic eruptions may suggest metaphors related to cataclysmic change, demographic processes can be better described in the metaphor of the slow, inexorable movement of the glacier. Demographic momentum—the past incorporated in the age structure and in fertility and mortality rates that change only incrementally—is a fact of life. Knowledge of this demographic momentum gives us some confidence about predicting the near future, though this confidence fades rapidly the further we look ahead.

Substantial continued growth of population in Indonesia is inevitable. The relevant issue is whether eventual population stabilization will be reached at a population only 50 per cent larger than at present, or two or three times larger. With regard to the island of Java, it is harder to say what is likely, because the options are widened by the possibility of migration to other islands. None the less, further natural increase of Java's population is inevitable, for at least the next twenty years, and because of limits on the extent of population transfer to other islands, Java's population in the year 2000 can confidently be expected to be substantially larger (by something like 15 to 20 per cent) than it is at present (see Chapter 10). The population of Javans (that is, Javanese, Sundanese and Madurese) living both on and off Java will increase even more than these figures indicate.

When we descend one level further in disaggregating the Indonesian population, and project the rural population of Java, the growth of which has caused most concern ever since the turn of the twentieth century, it is still harder to predict when growth will cease, because an additional option—in the form of movement to the cities and towns of Java—is available for absorption of natural increase of the population. We will return to this later. First, the prospects for the two components of Indonesian population increase, mortality and fertility, will be briefly reviewed.

Mortality Control

Indonesia's policy goals with regard to mortality control are simple and unambiguous: to reduce infant mortality and increase life expectancy. These goals are so simple, and interrelated, as to be virtually uncontestable. Moreover, the government has developed sensible official approaches to controlling mortality, although it must always be borne in mind that the extent to which these approaches succeed will partly depend on the extent to which levels of income and well-being among the mass of the population are improved. The means to achieve reductions in mortality have never been so clear-cut as to preclude public debate or policy analysis.

In general, modern medicine saves lives, and investment in medical care is virtually guaranteed to reduce mortality. Exceptions to this rule probably arise primarily because some medical investments are directed at health-threatening rather than life-threatening problems and, even among programmes specifically aimed at life-threatening problems, different medical interventions save the lives of very different types of people. Some save only infants, others are designed to prevent death of older people; some save more men than women, others prevent more deaths of rich people than of poor. The Department of Health thus faces crucial choices between various medical technologies, programme strategies and geographic concentrations which will influence the pattern of survival now and in the future.

In the late 1970s and early 1980s, the combined emphasis upon rural outreach, expanded immunization, growth monitoring of under-fives, oral rehydration, and infant and child nutrition represented a strong policy stance in favour of infants and children over other groups in the population. This is very reasonable in a country like Indonesia where over half of all deaths each year occur among children under five, and where infant mortality rates are four times higher than they are in neighbouring Malaysia. The planning questions which arise are twofold. First, do the present mortality-related interventions actually reflect the overt national policy of giving priority to infant and child deaths? Second, are the interventions currently being promoted sufficient to achieve the long-term policy goals?

With regard to the issue of the relevance of interventions to 'overt' policy, it is clear that Indonesia shares with most nations a concern about the quality of modern health care, and has thus invested a great deal in large hospitals, modern equipment and medical specialities, in addition to the narrower infant and childcare programmes. This investment in modern medicine is essentially a commitment to cure diseases which generally affect older people—heart disease, cancers, chronic illness—and the costs of such care and location of facilities imply that patients are primarily well-to-do urbanites. Thus the 'total' policy reflected in patterns of expenditure is less egalitarian and focused than overt expressions of policy might indicate.

But even accepting that 'total' policy is broader than the formal statements, there is some doubt that 'total' health interventions are sufficient to deal with the mortality challenges now and in future. There are a number of areas requiring appropriate policy interventions:

1. Sanitation and clean water. A high proportion of diseases continue to be water/waste-borne, and will only be prevented when effective waste-disposal and piped-water systems are developed in all regions of the country.

2. Control of 'environmental' diseases. Beyond the issues of sanitation, many diseases are increasingly caused by exposure to pollutants, either involuntarily (for example, smog) or voluntarily (for example, smoking).

3. Respiratory disease control. To date, no 'mass' campaign has addressed the common and often fatal problems of lower respiratory tract infections, particularly in children. This major cause of death requires strenuous efforts at prevention (including improved ventilation of houses and improved nutrition) and adequate curative procedures (including correct use of antibiotics and better home nursing).

4. Prevention of occupational diseases and accidents. Occupational safety is still very underdeveloped in many Indonesian factories, mines, construction sites and farms. Enforcement of current regulations and public safety education will need to be substantially increased before major progress is made. The recent successful start to the campaign to enforce the use of helmets among motor cycle riders shows the feasibility of increasing public awareness and support for needed changes.

To date, one of the constraints inhibiting the formulation of comprehensive mortality control policies is the lack of an adequate system of data collection to allow thorough epidemiological analysis. Mortality data are very crude, and seldom sufficiently detailed to inspire confidence in policy formation (see Chapter 4).

Fertility Control

The impressive decline of fertility in Indonesia over the last ten years was partly the outcome of government policy and programmes, and partly the result of changes in the nature of Indonesian family formation. As noted in Chapter 5, further advances in lowering fertility will depend on many factors, the most basic being the motivation of people to delay marriage and to control the spacing and number of children they bear after marrying. The rapid increases in education levels, the growth and increasing diversity of the economy, the need for mobility to take advantage of employment opportunities, and the rising levels of urbanization can all be expected to foster lower fertility. These forces will be particularly potent if they also serve to enhance the social and economic status of women. Beyond this, much will hinge on the success of government programmes to improve access to, and availability of, family planning services.

The appearance of continuity and success in the implementation of fertility policies would be dangerous if it tended to lull the government into a complacent attitude on the issue of family planning. The smooth fertility decline recorded thus far is unlikely to be reversed, but recent experience in the Philippines and Malaysia suggests that the rate of decline could certainly stall, leaving fertility at a plateau at rates sufficiently high to prevent the stabilization of population growth for many decades. For this reason, Indonesia needs to be increasingly vigilant in identifying potential sources of faltering in the family planning programme, and innovative in developing policies to promote declines from moderate to low fertility levels.

With current BKKBN-recorded prevalence rates over 50 per cent in the country as a whole, the Department of Health and the BKKBN have largely completed the task of informing all women about the availability of contraceptives, and providing easy access to the most common methods of birth control. Surveys and visits to villages reveal that young couples worry about the costs of child raising, and want to limit their family size to numbers well below those achieved by their parents (Darroch, Meyer and Singarimbun, 1981). Despite such favourable indicators, officials are worried. Even prevalence around 50 per cent still indicates that nearly half of Indonesia's 25 million married women of reproductive age are not using contraceptives. Moreover, many are using methods such as the condom and rhythm which are presumed by programme managers to have a low rate of effectiveness. Clearly, there is still a substantial way to go in providing motivation and adequate services to all women in need.

What are the constraints preventing universal use of contraception in Indonesia? Most important no doubt are social, economic, religious and cultural factors which sustain a fairly high desired family size among substantial sections of the population. But there is also still a widespread dissatisfaction with available methods of contraception. For while it is true that most people are familiar with the major methods of birth control, as often as not that familiarity includes fear over side-effects or concern over discomfort. The appropriateness of responses to this problem depends largely on the method concerned.

In the case of contraceptive pills, concern over side-effects is not an irrational response, and must be treated seriously by the programme. Pills in use in Indonesia are powerful drugs—more potent in fact than many of the more popular versions found in the USA and Europe. Careful research in the West has established beyond question that oral contraceptives are associated with thrombosis, especially in women over 35 years of age. Smokers are at particular risk. From the viewpoint of the programme, such risks have to be viewed in relation to the much greater dangers of pregnancy and child-bearing, but to the women reading reports in magazines such relativities are seldom clear. Their fears are quite direct, and probably dissuade a substantial proportion of potential acceptors among middle- and upper-class women from using pills.

The most relevant response to this problem is the production and dissemination of accurate information about the true relative risks and benefits of pill use. Remarkably, for a country with over 8 million women recorded as regular recipients of government-distributed pills, Indonesia has no epidemiological data on pill-related illnesses or deaths, and only the most sketchy data on the personal characteristics of pill users. This both severely handicaps information campaigns to combat fears of danger from prolonged use, and inhibits the development of procedures to minimize risks by reducing dosages and monitoring users to identify women at risk.

Lack of data also bedevils attempts to formulate policies to improve use of intra-uterine devices. Currently, the most common IUDs in use are the double S-shaped Lippes' loops, which are worn by over 4 million women. In other countries, reports of spontaneous expulsion, infections and uterine perforation have provoked doctors to adopt stringent procedures for insertions and follow-up monitoring of patients. Such controls are not rigorously carried out under the conditions of 'special drives' and other mass campaigns seen in Indonesia over recent years, and there are grounds for concern that some users—the proportion is difficult to estimate—have experienced unwarranted discomfort due to inadequate care in the provision of this contraceptive. While the number of such cases may be small relative to the number of satisfied users, they are very important both as a health problem in their own right and a source of rumours concerning dangers of the method.

In comparison with the pill and IUD, other methods provoke less medical concern, because they are inherently less dangerous, and they are used by fewer couples. The injectable Depoprovera, though lacking US Food and Drug Administration approval, has proven a popular and apparently safe contraceptive in Indonesia (Margono, 1985). Steroidal implants (Norplant) have proven successful in field trials, but are still at an experimental stage.

Condoms are a problematic method in the programme. While having no harmful side-effects, they are regarded by many men as causing an unacceptable reduction of sexual pleasure. Before 1986, the BKKBN did little to counter that attitude with advertising, since it regarded the method as 'unreliable' because of an alleged high failure rate. In fact, condoms can be a very effective method of birth control, if used regularly and properly. They also help in the prevention of sexually transmitted disease. Since they are a popular method in many countries, Japan being the foremost example, and have found favour among many Indonesian men, it was counter productive for the government to discourage the use of the method through a policy of benign neglect. In 1986, there was a reversal of attitude summed up in the policy of *kondomisasi*, in which the BKKBN launched a major series of advertising campaigns promoting condom use. The theme of the campaign was male responsibility in family planning, and the condom was cited as a particularly appropriate method to attain that goal.

Sterilization, though of increasing importance in the programme, is still classified as an 'experimental' method because of fears of Islamic opposition if it were adopted as an official programme method. Beyond the question of methods, the role of Islam in family planning in Indonesia is complex. Official support for programme goals and approaches is given by Islamic leaders, but suspicion and pro-natalism is sometimes evident among religious teachers and officials at the village level.

Some of the key tasks facing the BKKBN are to strengthen clinical and non-clinical service delivery; intensify efforts to increase the number of family planning acceptors in low-acceptance areas, mostly outside Java; strengthen the co-ordination of family-planning-related activities carried out by other government agencies; extend further the process of management decentralization and community mobilization; and develop new innovative approaches based on internal operations research and evaluation, and on the experience of non-government organizations.

The prognosis for such improvements is mixed. On the one hand, the BKKBN has shown substantial courage in the 1985 overhaul of the service statistics system and is now committed to the adoption of new management techniques to be developed with international assistance from a variety of donors. On the other, all bureaucracies develop a degree of inertia which inhibits change, and the BKKBN and government departments involved with family planning are likely to prove resistant to new measures. Moreover, there is a danger inherent in the proposed changes stressing decentralization, since targets remain firmly embedded in central office philosophy. The more rigid these targets (covering, for example, fertility, current use, method mix, etc.), the less scope lower-level central-office or provincial staff have for innovative decision-making. Decentralization may thus become a rather hollow promise leading to frustrations throughout the system. Rigid acceptance of fertility-decline targets also deflects attention from goals such as improved maternal health and consumer satisfaction.

Fertility-control policies in Indonesia are at a critical juncture. There are many difficult challenges to be faced in shaping the family planning programme into an efficient and effective organization. At the same time, political and religious sensitivities must be respected to avoid conflict on this issue. The ambiguity inherent in having major fertility policy functions in the BKKBN, the Ministry of Population and Environment, and *Bappenas*, makes the task of meeting these challenges all the more problematic.

Employment Creation and Population Redistribution

The problem of continued population growth in Indonesia is quintessentially an employment problem. Unfortunately, the factors governing the growth of the labour supply in the short and medium term are more or less independent of the labour requirements of an economy experiencing rapid growth and structural change. The crucial determinant is the underlying demographic structure, conditioned by birth and death rates decades in the past. Economic factors will, of course, influence the length of time children spend in school, female entry into the labour force, the desire (and need) for overtime work, pension and retirement arrangements, and demographic trends including fertility and migration. But these feedbacks from economic trends to the growth of the labour force are either marginal or long-term in nature. Economic planners are forced to treat labour force growth as largely exogenous to their policies and programmes over the short- to medium-term period.

Because of long delays between fertility decline and its translation into decline in the rate of growth of the labour force, the working-age population will continue to increase rapidly until the turn of the century, at a rate considerably more rapid than that for the population as a whole (see Chapter 10). To the extent that the rapid growth of the working-age population means a rise in the proportion of workers to dependants, this is a favourable development, opening the possibility for income per head of population to increase more rapidly than output per head of the work-force. But trends in output per head of the work-force will depend, in turn, on the extent to which reasonably well paying work can be found.

In pursuing this issue, we need to begin by considering the way the employment structure can be expected to change in the course of economic development in Indonesia. Employment and population redistribution need to be considered together, because shifts in the sectoral distribution of employment and in product per worker in different sectors will imply large-scale residential relocation, both between regions and between urban and rural areas.

Economic growth—the process by which output per capita increases—normally has little to do with an increase in per capita hours of work and only slightly more to do with increase in the per capita stock of material capital. Rather, it is due mainly to a high growth rate of productivity (production per unit of labour and capital), connected with the increase in the stock of knowledge and organizational skills which enter the production process in various ways—through rising average levels of education of the labour force, through introduction of new processes and products which displace other processes and products, and so forth. The scale of production can change as population grows and income levels rise, and as foreign trade possibilities are pursued. The sectoral composition of output also changes, with sharp decreases in the share of agriculture in total output and sharp increases in the shares of industry, trade and services. Similar changes, in somewhat muted form, occur in the sectoral composition of employment; as noted in Chapter 8, they have already begun in Indonesia, and they can be expected to accelerate in the coming years.

Both Kuznets (1972) and Chenery and Syrquin (1975) have analysed the structure and time trends of output and employment in a wide cross-section of countries. Their results suggest that in a 'dualistic' economy, as the structure of employment shifts from a heavy concentration in agriculture towards a higher proportion in various non-agricultural sectors, the initial large advantage in product per worker in non-agricultural sectors will eventually lessen. The theories of Lewis (1954) and Fei and Ranis (1964) suggest that the pace of this change depends on the speed with which higher-productivity sectors can absorb the growing labour force, so that a labour shortage eventually begins to emerge in agriculture, driving up wages and fostering labour-saving technological changes which enhance labour productivity in agriculture. In applying this theory to Indonesia, it is better to replace the 'agriculture–non-agriculture' dichotomy with a dichotomy between the modern sector and the 'traditional' sector, the latter including not only agriculture but low-productivity parts of other sectors as well, most of which can be considered part of the 'informal sector'. Examples are petty trade, personal services, *becak*-driving, and most cottage industries.

Because the absorptive capacity of the modern sector is limited, rapid growth of population (and labour force) hinders the shift of workers from sectors where their productivity is low to sectors where it is higher. For example, if the labour force is growing at 2.7 per cent per annum and 40 per cent are employed in non-agricultural activities (which is approximately the situation in Indonesia), employment in non-agriculture would have to increase by 6.8 per cent annually if it were to absorb all first-time job seekers (this rate is calculated as the ratio of annual labour force growth to the proportion of the labour force working in the non-agriculture sector, that is $2.7/0.4 = 6.8$, see Dovring, 1964). But the highest sustained non-agricultural employment growth rates have not exceeded 4 per cent, and this was in the rather special cases of Korea and Japan. By contrast, if the labour force is growing at only 1.5 per cent per annum, absorption of all first-time job seekers in non-agricultural activities would require that employment in these activities increase by slightly less than 4 per cent annually, a growth rate potentially attainable under very favourable conditions.

Indonesia still faces daunting problems in reaching the point where the modern sector can absorb the entire increase in the work-force. These problems include: high man to land ratios, not only in Java but in parts of the outer islands as well; a still rapidly growing labour force; a pronounced dual structure in employment, implying that the 'traditional' sector still holds a higher proportion of the work-force than the 58 per cent working in agriculture; and an international trading context which is likely to prove very resistant to rapid growth of exports of manufactures. The pessimistic prognosis for Indonesia would be a perpetuation of the present dual structure, with most of the labour force continuing to depend on agriculture and the low-income 'informal' sector in either urban or rural areas.

Rapid economic growth in Europe and its overseas offshoots was achieved with growth rates of labour supply which varied widely both temporally and across countries. But these growth rates were normally lower, and in the case of more densely settled countries much lower, than the projected growth of the labour force in Indonesia. Moreover, growth of labour supply in a particular country was often crudely adapted to economic prospects by variation in the rate of immigration or emigration. By contrast, Indonesia not only begins with a labour force far larger than necessary to produce reasonable levels of per capita income given the present economic structure and modes of production (as witnessed by the high levels of underemployment and the concentration of a substantial proportion of the work-force in very low productivity work in sectors such as agriculture, trade, transport, service, and cottage industry), but it also faces substantial additions to the labour supply. These will hinder the process of rapid structural change, dilute efforts to raise the quality of new labour force entrants by spreading thin the available educational and health services, and probably divert attention of planners from efforts to achieve rapid growth of output for the stop-gap provision of employment opportunities (though the two are not mutually exclusive).

The Regional Dimension of Employment Issues: Java

Strategies for economic growth and poverty alleviation in Indonesia must contain a strong emphasis on regional development, because poverty problems differ regionally (severe, for example, in Central Java and Nusa Tenggara), as do the prospects for rapid economic growth (good in Aceh, Jakarta, East Kalimantan). Nevertheless, the reasons for the popular obsession with the problems of rural Java are easy to understand. Java already holds 100 million people on a land area slightly smaller than that of North Carolina and little more than half as large as the smallest Australian mainland state of Victoria. Even when Java's urban populations are subtracted, rural Java contains almost half of Indonesia's entire population. Over one third of rural Java's population is landless (Jones, 1980: Table 6), and the landholdings of most of those with land are miniscule—less than 0.5 hectares (Booth and Sundrum, 1976: Table 5; Palmer, 1976: 7–8; Soemarwoto and Soemarwoto, 1984: 258). Although distribution of landholdings is fairly unequal (Sigit, 1985: 66–8), land reform would have only a slight impact on the access to land of most of the rural population, and largely for this reason has never been promoted as a major policy option in Indonesia.

Despite the rather bleak picture given by statistics such as these, it is well to keep in mind that although observers have been declaring Java to be 'overpopulated' since before the beginning of the present century, the population has grown from about 29 million at that time to 100 million today, and conditions of life appear to have improved for the bulk of Java's population (for instance, expectation of life at birth is probably twenty or so years longer than it was at the beginning of the century).[1] Can Java hope, then, to absorb a further 15 or 20 million persons in the next fifteen years? Can the much-tested resilience of the Javanese economy and ecosystem, not to mention culture and polity, hold up in the face of further increases in population?

A number of studies emphasize the tenuous situation reached in many rural areas of Java following the long history of adaptation to increasing population pressure termed 'agricultural involution' by Geertz (1963). Erosion and downstream siltation and flooding caused by cutting of forests and farming of steep slopes is becoming an increasing problem in many areas (USAID, 1984; Repetto, 1986; Soemarwoto, 1985: 202–12). Farm sizes are so small in many areas and outright landlessness so common that a large section of the rural population may be unaffected by the kinds of productivity increases made possible by improved seeds, irrigation techniques, etc. (Penny and Singarimbun, 1973; Sayogyo, 1978). Inequalities in rural areas, according to some observers, appear to be increasing for a number of reasons, including: the greater capacity of larger farmers to take advantage of the new seeds and the new technology that goes along with them (Deuster, 1971); the greater ease with which large farmers can educate their children and secure for them the more lucrative kinds of off-farm employment; and the shift in harvesting and other arrangements which have caused particular problems for hired labour, especially the landless (Papanek, 1985: 50). Altered practices in harvesting, hulling and milling of rice made large numbers of rural workers (especially women) redundant during the 1970s (Collier et al., 1973; Timmer, 1973; Hayami and Hafid, 1979). The fact that labour shortages are frequently reported at busy times of the year in parts of rural Java (Collier et al., 1982; Jones and Ward, 1981: 395–405) does not by itself indicate that labour redundancy has been overcome: it could at least equally be the result of movement away of some of the former 'pool' of available workers due to limited work opportunities in agriculture; excessive mechanization as a result of localized and short-term labour shortage and to underpricing of capital (Sinaga, 1978); to imperfect information systems; to excessive transport and other costs for the very poor to move to short-term seasonal work; and to heightened expectations among young people who have received more education than their elders. There was little evidence of any rise in real agricultural wages during the 1970s.

Yet this rather pessimistic evaluation (much of it based on studies conducted before agricultural productivity 'took off' during the later 1970s) can be countered with other evidence. Booth and Sundrum (1981) and Manning (1986) on balance find no evidence of worsening income distribution in rural areas. Booth (1985: 133) finds a narrowing of the gap in yields of rice and palawidja crops between advanced and more backward regions, apparently largely as a result of the greater expansion (or lesser contraction) of the irrigated land in low-yield areas. Many village studies (Edmundson, 1977; Keyfitz, 1985; Hetler, 1986; Kasryno (ed.), 1983; World Bank, 1985: Appendix I) show clear-cut increases in welfare of villagers across the board in recent times, partly as a result of diversification of income sources away from a near-total reliance on agriculture. Rural wages and incomes appear to have increased following the bumper harvests of the 1979–81 period (Collier et al., 1982), though by the mid-1980s they appeared to be stagnant again.

The analysis in Chapter 8 suggests that, as long ago as the beginning of the 1960s, agriculture in Java had essentially exhausted its capacity to absorb further increases in the rural work-force. In the two decades following 1961, agricultural employment in rural areas of Java increased by a bare 10 per cent (and among males by only 2 per cent). The impressive increases in output of rice (Mears, 1982; 1985) and other food crops since the early 1970s have come from increases in yields due to application of new seed-fertilizer technologies and to continuing expansion of the irrigated area.[2] These increases in production (about 60 per cent in the

1970s), along with only slow growth of the agricultural work-force, have led to substantial increases in output per worker, though the gains appear to have gone more to those who own land than to those who work as farm labourers.

The failure of agriculture to provide more work has resulted neither in increasing rural poverty nor in massive growth of Java's cities. What has happened is that, besides some migration to the cities, there have been three other adaptations: migration to the outer islands (largely through the transmigration programme), commuting and circular migration to urban jobs,[3] and growth of non-agricultural employment (especially in trade, manufacturing and services) in rural areas. The importance of the latter two trends is highlighted by the fact that non-agricultural employment for rural dwellers increased by 162 per cent between 1961 and 1980, compared with a 10 per cent increase in agricultural employment.

Fortuitously, then, the difficulty of further expanding job opportunities in agriculture despite rapidly rising agricultural production has been ameliorated by the emergence of a wide range of work opportunities (in many other sectors besides the low-productivity end of the informal sector) in both rural and urban areas. In rural areas, one reason has been the increased demand for goods and services of all kinds generated by rising real incomes based on increasing agricultural productivity and income earned in the city but spent in the village. Thus, by and large, real incomes of the rural population—both those dependent on agriculture and those relying on non-agricultural incomes—have increased, although different subgroups, defined in terms of geographic areas, educational status, land ownership status or social class, have fared differently.

However, this relatively optimistic interpretation of trends during the 1970s cannot be extrapolated to signify prospects for the rest of the century, because it is clear that the economic circumstances facing Indonesia will be less favourable than those in the 1970s. If the rate of economic growth is only 5 per cent per annum, as predicted over the period of *Repelita IV* (and even this now seems highly unlikely with the drastic fall in oil prices in 1986), then maintenance of the sectoral labour absorption capacity of the 1970s will not be enough to prevent levels of underutilization of labour from increasing (Hasibuan, 1985). Only by increasing employment elasticities in sectors such as manufacturing, construction, transport and services can this trend be avoided.

Such increases in employment elasticities will not be easy to achieve, especially in manufacturing. Oshima (1983) has shown that an emphasis on capital-intensive industrialization in countries at an early stage of their industrialization tends to inhibit the achievement of a widely based industrialization. In Indonesia, abundance of foreign exchange and an open door to foreign investment in the 1970s encouraged the use of modern technology by relatively large foreign and domestic enterprises, resulting in relatively slow absorption of unskilled labour in manufacturing. Indeed, in some cases, rapid increases in manufacturing output led to barely any increase in employment because of the displacement of workers in cottage industries or in older, more labour-intensive factories. The situation can be illustrated in microcosm in the Majalaya area south of Bandung, which has traditionally produced 40 per cent of Indonesia's output of handloom textiles, an outdated technology which cannot successfully compete with the large new textile factories being established elsewhere in the Bandung region.

Appropriate industrial development policies are therefore needed: Priority needs to be given to the promotion of export of manufactures and natural resource processing industries, and to smaller-scale industries in general (Kuyvenhoven and Poot, 1986). These goals will be furthered by a spatially

TABLE 11.1

Options for Improving Real Income in Rural Java

Strategy	Purpose	Implementation
Reduce fertility in Java	To slow rates of population growth	1. Family planning programme 2. Education, health, etc. 3. Policies for wage labour opportunities for women
Move people from Java (a) permanently	To slow rates of population growth; to raise rural Java income through remittances	1. Transmigrations 2. Other policies affecting mobility
(b) temporarily		1. International labour migration programmes 2. Other policies affecting mobility
Encourage urbanization	To slow rates of rural population growth	Industrial development policies, employment strategy, urban infrastructure development, etc.
Agricultural intensification	To raise income of the population remaining in rural areas	Irrigation, new seed varieties, fertilizer policies, etc.
Off-farm employment opportunities	To raise income of the population remaining in rural areas	Rural industrialization, expansion of government services, increased accessibility to towns (commuting, temporary migration) through improved transport etc.

Note: These strategies have other purposes as well. Here, stress is on their purpose in relation to the goal of improving real incomes in rural Java.

dispersed pattern of growth of purchasing power, especially in rural areas, and by avoiding preferential treatment for large-scale firms through credit subsidies, licensing, etc. Policies designed to increase the overall competitiveness and export orientation of Indonesian industry—for example, the elimination of excessive protection from both tariff and non-tariff barriers (Dick, 1985: 9–22)—will assist in the expansion of the small-scale sector. Moreover, the government should aim to avoid an excessively capital-intensive pattern of public expenditure. In addition, a supportive policy stance towards the informal urban sector will be needed, since this is the only sector that can be relied on to cushion any failure of work opportunities to grow rapidly enough to absorb the increasing work-force.[4]

Despite the prospect of further population growth in Java (rapid in West Java–Jakarta, slow in the rest of Java), we noted in Chapter 9 that a historically crucial point could be reached before the end of the century—that is, the point at which population growth in rural Java will cease. This will depend on trends in mortality, fertility control, out-migration from Java and urbanization within Java. It should be stressed that, unless fertility decline is very rapid indeed, stabilization of population density in rural Java can be achieved only through substantial increases in the size of the urban population in Java and further large-scale movement of Javanese to other islands, with all the costs and problems that this entails.

In planning for ways to bring rising levels of welfare to the rural areas of Java in the face of demographic realities, it is essential that simultaneous approaches be made on a number of fronts as demonstrated in very simple form in Table 11.1. We shall discuss each major strategy in turn.

Strategies for Improving Real Income in Rural Java

FERTILITY CONTROL

Prospects for fertility control were discussed at length earlier in the chapter. All that need be added here is that the projections underlying the prognosis that population growth in Central and East Java could be halted by the year 2000, assumed that fertility in Indonesia would be successfully lowered by approximately 40 per cent between 1976–9 and 1995–2000 (and in Central Java, Yogyakarta and East Java by slightly less—around 38 per cent). Although this is less than the official BKKBN target, it is roughly equivalent to the target aimed for in *Repelita IV*, and it would be a remarkable accomplishment for a country at Indonesia's stage of development. A lesser accomplishment would, of course, mean that Java's population growth would take longer to bring to a halt.

TRANSMIGRATION

It can be fairly confidently assumed that *Repelita III* represented a peak of Indonesia's transmigration efforts and that, despite even more ambitious targets in *Repelita IV*, smaller numbers will be moved. In the first one and a half years of *Repelita IV*, the numbers moved were well below target (about

81,000 households compared with a target of 185,000). In *Repelita III*, strengthening of the administrative and planning capacity of the Department of Transmigration, together with the continued availability of enough areas of arable land in the other islands to plan substantial transmigration settlement areas, enabled numbers to be moved that surprised most observers. None the less, the plan targets were only reached by dint of the inclusion of many unofficial 'spontaneous' migrants as well as official programme participants.

In *Repelita IV* and beyond, the job will be much harder. Lampung has already been closed to transmigration, and North Sulawesi is about to be closed. The need for rehabilitation of many existing transmigration projects, particularly tidal projects in Sumatra and Kalimantan[5] and projects where slopes exceed 15 per cent, will add to the burden of opening new projects. Recent surveys, using more sophisticated techniques to identify land systems and predict land suitability than those used hitherto,[6] have shown that land even reasonably suitable for agriculture is scarcer than had been believed in Central Kalimantan (and probably elsewhere) and that some of it has been classified by the Forestry Department (in some cases erroneously) as 'normal production forests' or 'limited production forests' and hence is not available for agriculture.

Therefore, large scale transmigration from here on, if it is to succeed in moving the numbers planned for, will not only have to focus on more distant areas, involving greater logistic problems, but may also have to intrude on areas needed for forestry or for water catchment protection. By developing agriculture in only marginally suitable (and often isolated) areas, it will either incur high costs or it will require a shift of strategy to concentrate more on tree-crop estates (rubber, oil palm, cocoa, timber, and so on).

The transmigration targets, on which the projections used in Chapter 10 were based, were below the Department of Transmigration's targets, but even these more modest targets may prove quite difficult to reach. Because of budgetary difficulties, in early 1986 the Ministry of Transmigration reduced its 1986/7 targets from over 100,000 fully sponsored families to 36,000 families. A World Bank transmigration sector review released in 1986 stated that the movement of about 200,000 sponsored families in the next five years was expected to be the maximum level consistent with existing implementation capacity and with adequate attention to environmental and social concerns. If official targets are not reached, this will reduce the likelihood that population growth in Java can be completely halted before the year 2000. (Transmigration targets for *Repelita IV* imply the removal of 42 per cent of Java's annual population increase, compared with 28 per cent achieved in *Repelita III*).

Even so, it will not necessarily be a bad thing if transmigration targets are not reached. Official policy on transmigration is today argued in terms of the labour needs for regional development rather than just in terms of the need to remove large numbers of workers from Java. However, this raises the question of just how great the labour needs are for regional development.[7] Although in *Repelita IV* Sumatra has been downgraded as a transmigration destination, its population is expected to reach 51 million by the year 2000. It can be argued that, while large-scale transmigration to Sumatra may have opened some regional development options, it has also closed others. Given the great differences in ecology between Sumatra and Java and the much sparser population at the time transmigration really began to build up in the early 1970s, a more mechanized, less labour-intensive pattern of agricultural development, perhaps more along the lines of Malaysia's FELDA schemes, would almost certainly have had more potential for raising rural incomes in much of Sumatra than a mere replication of Javanese patterns. In parts of Sumatra not much involved in the transmigration programme, alternative patterns of rural development are indeed proceeding. For example, in West Sumatra and Aceh, agricultural mechanization is reported to be increasing—in the case of Aceh, at least partly due to the high costs of manual cultivation.

Unfortunately, demographic realities in Indonesia have dictated that finding employment for the growing rural population of Java has been an overriding priority, resulting in replication of Javanese patterns of rural poverty in some of the areas of the other islands (notably Lampung) targeted as transmigration areas. Malaysian government investment per head in FELDA programmes, at least up to the late 1970s, was more than four times that in the transmigration projects. Thus, given the numbers that had to be moved, FELDA-type programmes were not really an option. Development of private estate agriculture, also a feature of the Malaysian scene, has been discouraged in Indonesia for similar reasons and on ideological grounds. The end-result has been that, in Lampung, high labour to land ratios after decades of transmigration raise the same problems of labour displacement by mechanization as those faced by Java; indeed, Lampung's problems have developed to the point where in 1986 it was actually declared a transmigration source province. Java's population problem thus constrained what could be achieved in Lampung, and transmigration has foreclosed the option of less labour-intensive agricultural development. In short, transmigration has not only shifted Java's poverty to Sumatra, but it has also shifted the structural constraints which have caused and are perpetuating that poverty.

URBANIZATION

Continuing urbanization in Indonesia is inevitable, and further urbanization in Java will play an important role in halting population growth in rural Java. Further urbanization is not a prospect to be feared, as the following conclusions from the National Urban Development Strategy Project report (Kingsley, Gardiner and Stolte, 1985: 28) indicate:

1. Even though Jakarta's growth rate is presently the fastest among metropolitan areas, the gap is not substantial. Primacy is not a significant problem in Indonesia compared to many developing countries. Indonesia is fortunate to have a series of competitive growth centers in the large and middle-size categories that have exhibited increasing dynamism over the past decade. They are well distributed

geographically across the archipelago. This suggests an approach of further strengthening these centers, rather than incurring the large investments needed to create new growth poles.

2. Overall, Indonesia has a reasonably balanced distribution of cities over the size-hierarchy. Changes in share among the size categories have been modest. Often publicized images of people flocking to the largest cities and leaving the middle-size cities in decline appear to be overstated.

3. This does not mean that national policy should not attempt to influence the distribution. Tempering the growth of the largest agglomerations and stimulating it in smaller and intermediate cities remain appropriate policy objectives. However, in Indonesia, there appears little need for massive adjustments to recent trends in the hierarchy.

Policies with respect to urban growth in Indonesia, as in most developing countries, have been schizophrenic, though not intentionally so: explicit policies have aimed to slow the growth of large cities and deter migration to them, whereas 'implicit policies'—those adopted for other reasons but which have important unplanned effects on urbanization—have tended to foster rapid growth of large cities (Fuchs, Jones and Pernia, 1987). Specific attempts to encourage the growth of intermediate cities as an alternative to the rapid expansion of Jakarta have been minimal (Hugo and Mantra, 1981), and the few cases attempted (for example, Batam, Cilacap) have been expensive and peripheral to the real concerns of strengthening the middle ranges of the urban hierarchy (Handoko, 1984). Meanwhile, there has been something of a revival in growth of intermediate-sized cities in parts of Java (Evans, 1984), especially along the northern coast, without specific government encouragement.

The best known of the policies adopted to slow big-city growth have been the 'closed city' policies ineffectually followed by Bandung in the late 1950s and early 1960s, and by Jakarta beginning in 1970.[8] The then-governor of Jakarta eventually admitted (Shaplan, 1974: 75) that the 'closed city' policy had failed to stem the flow of migrants to the capital, and the appointment of a new governor in the late 1970s resulted in a substantial reduction in the zeal with which the closure legislation was enforced. The reasons for the failure of the city-closure package were clearly that many people were unable to obtain sufficient employment in the village to attain a level of living they perceived as satisfactory. In such circumstances, simple city-closure policies do not in any way overcome the basic cause of rural–urban mobility so that people will try every means they can to get around them. It is clearly inequitable for large metropolitan centres to soak up a disproportionately large share of national investment and then to refuse people from other, less-favoured sections of the nation access to some of the fruits of that investment.

It should also be stressed that rural–urban distinctions in Java and Bali are not as sharp as in many countries, partly due to the high population density throughout these islands. In behavioural terms, the rural–urban dichotomy is undoubtedly becoming increasingly blurred, due to factors such as the spread of universal education, the transportation and communications revolutions, and the increasing diversity of the employment structure in rural areas.[9] Therefore, planning and policy making should emphasize city-regions rather than individual cities or cities of particular sizes.

As in most developing countries, there appears to have been a bias towards urban growth in Indonesia's industrial and trade policies; a heavy urban bias (in relation to the proportion of the population living, or the even higher proportion working, in urban areas) in government development budgets; and an even greater urban bias in routine government budgets. The pace of urbanization in future will certainly be influenced by the extent to which the government adopts a 'cost-recovery' approach to the provision of urban services such as land servicing, provision of roads, public transport, sewerage and drainage.

The locational pattern of manufacturing growth will be vital to the future patterns of urbanization in Java, even though manufacturing employment might not increase very rapidly, because manufacturing tends to be responsible for substantial additional employment through its important multiplier effects on sectors such as transport, utilities, construction, trade and services. The degree to which industrialization contributes to urbanization will depend on the extent to which industries locate in rural areas, the extent to which urban- and rural-located industries are capital intensive and not labour absorbing, the extent to which urban industries can draw on a rural-based work-force without requiring the residential relocation of the workers (and vice versa), and the multiplier effects or urban- and rural-based industry on employment in other urban- and rural-based activities.

The growth of the manufacturing sector has slowed in recent years, with output growth falling as low as 2.2. per cent in 1982–3 (Booth, 1984). Unless growth picks up, employment in this sector will be stagnant or even declining, and the implications for the rural areas could be very serious indeed, especially if there is further displacement of small-scale industry by new urban-based plants. The extent to which the slack can be made up by the continued growth of employment in the service sector in the rural areas, which was such a prominent feature of the 1970s, remains to be seen, but there is no doubt that extrapolation of past trends is unjustified in view of the much tighter government budgetary situation in the 1980s.

As mentioned in Chapter 9, projections by the National Urban Development Strategy Project (1985) suggest that, in Indonesia, the level of urbanization could rise from 22 per cent in 1980 to 36 per cent in the year 2000, and in Java from 24 per cent in 1980 to 44 per cent in the year 2000. These are trends in their preferred scenario; in other scenarios, the urbanization level for Indonesia in the year 2000 ranges between 32 and 38 per cent. In suggesting a considerable acceleration in rates of urbanization compared with the past two decades, the projections are not inconsistent with the experience of many countries once they had reached Indonesia's current stage of urbanization.

In a rough way, we can estimate the separate contribution of fertility reduction, transmigration and urbanization to the stabilization of population size in the rural areas of Java (see Table 11.2). In the unrealistic case

TABLE 11.2

Potential Contribution of Fertility Decline, Out-migration and Urbanization to
Stabilization of Population Size in Rural Java

Java: Total population, 1985—98.1 million
      Rural population, 1985—72.6 million

	Projected Population Figures for Year 2000		Potential Reduction of Rural Population Due to This Factor	
	Total Population (million)	Rural Population (million)	Absolute (million)	Percentage
1. *Basic assumption*: Unchanged fertility, migration, urbanization	132.7	100.8	—	—
2. *Modifying factors*:				
a) Reduced fertility	123.4	93.8	7.0	24.8
b) Plus medium transmigration	113.4	85.1	8.7	30.9
c) Plus urbanization raised to 36 per cent	113.4	72.6	12.5	44.3
d) Contribution of all three factors			28.2	100.0

in which fertility rates in Java remain at their 1985 levels, no net out-migration from Java occurs and urbanization levels remain constant, the population of Java would rise to 133 million in the year 2000, with the rural population rising to 101 million, a growth of 28 million in the latter. Fertility reduction along the lines envisaged in the projections used in Chapter 10 would avoid 7 million of this rural population growth, trans-migration a further 9 million, and a rise in the level of urbanization[10] a further 12.5 million, leaving rural Java's population in the year 2000 exactly the same as it was in 1985. If the level of urbanization in Java were really to rise to 44 per cent, as projected by the National Urban Development Strategy Project, then Java's rural population would actually fall by 8 million between 1985 and the year 2000.

Thus there seems to be a real prospect that rural population growth in Java is at last coming to an end. Of course, if fertility decline, transmigration performance or urbanization fail to reach the levels assumed, then rural population growth will continue beyond the end of the century and, in any case, the labour force will grow faster than the population as a whole over this period. In order to ensure that real incomes of rural dwellers continue to rise (and ideally that they rise faster than those of urban dwellers, thus narrowing the rural–urban income differential), two additional policies must be vigorously pursued—agricultural intensification and off-farm employment.

AGRICULTURAL INTENSIFICATION

Java's success in raising food-crop production in the late 1970s and early 1980s is now well known. Through a combination of expanded irrigation, improved seeds and heavier fertilization, rice production in Java increased by 40 per cent in the period. It is most unlikely that the end of the rise in productivity of Javanese agriculture is in sight: yields per hectare are still below those in Japan and Taiwan, and there is still scope for further expansion of the irrigated area. Along with the rise in agricultural productivity, labour has been drawn away from agriculture to higher-productivity sectors. The near-stagnation of agricultural employment between 1971 and 1980 noted in Chapter 8 appears to have continued in more recent times, with an actual decline in agricultural employment in rural Java between 1976 and 1982 according to a comparison of 1976 *Sakernas* and 1982 *Susenas* data (World Bank, 1985: 127). This was a positive development, as it was associated with rising wages in agriculture and rapid growth of employment opportunities outside the agricultural sector in a period when the government was investing heavily in rural development, using its rising oil revenues. However, in the more difficult economic and budgetary circumstances now being faced, it is important that excessive labour-shedding in agriculture be avoided by a cautious approach to agricultural mechanization, and by ensuring that capital investment in agriculture is not subsidized.

The extraordinary, and unexpected, situation has now been reached where Indonesia is self-sufficient in rice and has even become a modest rice exporter. Even a relatively slow increase in rice production from this point on should keep up with the demands of a growing population because the average income-elasticity of demand for rice will decline as higher income groups reach their limits of direct cereal consumption. There would be many problems involved in becoming a rice exporter (Mears, 1985: 52), and more attention needs to be given to diversification of the present livestock and cropping patterns, and to reducing the large income transfer provided to farmers by the fertilizer subsidy. While appropriate in the case of rice, however, such a reduction could 'conflict with the need to stimulate fertilizer use for corn and other long neglected crops when highly fertilizer-responsive varieties become available' (Mears, 1985: 55). Whatever the decision on these grounds, there is no doubt that, on ecological grounds, the use of chemical fertilizers and pesticides should not be overdone because of the higher energy requirements in producing them and the risk of poisoning fish in streams and estuaries.

OFF-FARM EMPLOYMENT OPPORTUNITIES

Though agricultural production has been rising rapidly, the time has long since passed when agriculture alone could meet the needs of most rural households in Java. After all, over one-third of rural households are landless, and farm employment opportunities on the tiny holdings of most of their neighbours are very limited.[11] Rural village studies conducted in West Java show that, between 1976 and 1983, a high and rising proportion of the households (62 per cent in 1976, 70 per cent in 1983) spent at least some time on non-agricultural activities (World Bank, 1985: Appendix 1), and that:

In these villages, all the economic classes appear to have participated in the process of income growth and diversification. The overall distribution remained stable and the extent of poverty was reduced. Amongst poorer households, agricultural income growth was particularly important to small farmers, while improved non-farm opportunities were central to the improved welfare of landless farm labourers. (World Bank, 1985: 134).

The range of non-agricultural activities is extraordinarily varied—and include, for example, fishing; collecting firewood; transporting passengers and goods on motor cycles; all kinds of trading activities; carpentry; the manufacture of bricks and clay tiles, footwear, baskets, mats, batik and small metal goods; blacksmithing; and bicycle repair.

Rural economic strategy should focus on the development of such activities through increased capitalization and technical assistance. Rural manufacturing and trade are based in particular on the increased rural incomes arising from the boom in rice production and the increased government expenditures in rural areas, and on reinforcing existing patterns of commuting and circular migration to make urban employment opportunities available to rural dwellers. Such patterns are already highly developed, with only a small proportion of places so isolated as to be cut off from the employment influences of the large cities. The daily commuting range, in many cases, extends up to 50 kilometres beyond city limits, and the attraction of a city such as Jakarta for circular migrants extends two-thirds of the way across Java, with villagers from the Wonogiri area regularly taking 14-hour trips on the night buses to spend a few weeks trading in Jakarta (Hetler, 1986).

It is clear, then, that a multi-faceted approach is needed to deal with the problems of continuing population growth in rural Java, with emphasis on fertility reduction, transmigration and urbanization in order to relieve the pressure of population growth, and on agricultural intensification and expansion of off-farm employment opportunities to benefit those remaining in the rural areas. From a programmatic point of view, however, the critical decision concerns the allocation of funds for such activities. Theoretically, we would need a cost-benefit analysis of expenditures on activities associated with each of these objectives (for example, the family planning programme; the transmigration programme; irrigation, rural electrification, rural credit schemes; and agricultural extension activities) in order to determine where the marginal dollar would be most effectively spent. Such studies are virtually impossible to carry out rigorously because all such programmes have multiple objectives and cannot be evaluated solely in terms of their effects on population growth and movement. In practice, the most critical choice is likely to be the balance between expenditures on family planning activities and transmigration.

Strategies for Dealing with Rapid Population Growth outside Java[12]

The strategies adopted for dealing with continued population growth in Java will strengthen the tendency for population increase in other islands to remain rapid because, on top of a rate of natural increase exceeding that in Java, these areas will continue to receive a net inflow of migrants from Java. The focus of population growth will shift in terms of absolute numbers to Sumatra, Kalimantan and Sulawesi, and in terms of growth rates to Kalimantan, Irian Jaya and Sumatra. It will be very important to ensure that this rapid growth (almost 50 per cent in the fifteen-year period 1985–2000) is absorbed in ways that do not unnecessarily destroy the environmental balance in these areas, and that ensure rising levels of living. Because the situation differs greatly from region to region, strategies for absorbing this increase will need to be regionally specific. Underlying all other strategies, however, will be the need to lower fertility rates in the outer islands. Even if, as officially argued in relation to the transmigration programme, regional development in many areas outside Java requires more labour (and this is questionable), fertility declines now will not begin to slow the growth of the labour force for more than a decade, by which time it is most unlikely that labour shortage will pose a significant constraint on development.

As noted in Chapter 6, some densely settled areas of the outer islands (for example, South Sulawesi and West Sumatra) have long experienced net migration outflows. Whether these are mainly to provinces such as East Kalimantan and Irian Jaya (in the case of migration from South Sulawesi) or to neighbouring provinces in Sumatra and to Jakarta (in the case of migration from West Sumatra), the important point is that by raising rates of population growth in these other areas they reduce the absorptive capacity of the areas to which migrants from Java are likely to move. Therefore, population policy needs to take careful account of these migration flows.

It is likely that in more densely populated outer island provinces, much the same kinds of factors are affecting labour absorption as in Java. It is noticeable, for example, that the relative increases in agricultural employment in the 1970s were lowest in the densely settled agricultural provinces—not only in Java but also in West Sumatra, West and South Kalimantan, North and South Sulawesi, Bali and Nusa Tenggara (Jones et al., 1985: 41–9). There was a net out-migration from many of these areas. The important question arising in all of these provinces, where agricultural employment was increasing by 1 per cent or less per annum, is: Has the capacity for absorbing further increases in the labour force into agriculture through mechanisms such as those stressed by Boserup (1965) been exhausted, or is the slow growth in agricultural employment simply due to better opportunities in other economic sectors or in other locations? The recent experience of both Java and densely settled regions of other islands would suggest that, even if agricultural production can continue to be increased sharply, the increase in agricultural employment will be very limited. Even in the main transmigrant receiving provinces, M- and S-sector employment grew much faster than agricultural-sector employment over the 1971–80 period.

Prospects for strengthening the industrial base in the outer islands are good, particularly if natural resource-based industrialization is stressed. However, changes in some of the policies which fostered the centralization of industrialization in the 1970s will be needed. Increasing overvaluation of the rupiah between 1971 and 1978 fostered import substitution industrialization (which tends to be highly concentrated in cities on Java), as did low tariffs on imported capital goods and high tariffs on manufactured consumer goods, import quotas, and informal barriers to imports. The government has had a major say in the pattern of industrial investment through the pattern of investment of its own resources, provision of capital at concessionary interest rates, import-licensing procedures, and control over allocation of foreign investment. The excessive volume of bureaucratic procedures engendered by the import-substitution industrialization policy has led to a highly centralized decision-making process (Paauw, 1981: 32–4). Official government encouragement of regional development fell foul of the constraints imposed by excessive centralization. In this context, the advantages of metropolitan location perceived by manufacturing entrepreneurs—their port facilities, international contacts, possibilities for interaction with key government officials, and amenities for management elites and their families—are overwhelming.

In the key transmigration receiving areas, effective planning requires the integration of a number of considerations: 'capacity' of particular areas to support agricultural settlement; the balancing of transmigration needs with the needs of forestry and mining uses and environmental protection; evaluation of the sorts of skills needed among transmigrants in order to succeed in different ecological zones; and knowledge of the potential sources of migrants with such skills from areas where a reduction in population growth rates is needed. Although it is known that security considerations sometimes transcend other elements in planning transmigration, it is doubtful whether the well-documented potential for conflict between transmigrants and local populations, especially over land tenure (Kustadi, 1984; Rahardjo, 1984; Soetrisno, 1985) is given as much consideration as it might be in modifying transmigration targets. The situation in Irian Jaya and Central Kalimantan is likely to be particularly problematic if the ambitious transmigration targets are maintained.

With the slowing of rates of natural population increase in Java, the rising costs and co-ordination problems of the transmigration programme, and with the environmental and ethnic problems to which it is giving rise, some hard questions need to be faced about the relative costs and benefits of transmigration and other programmes, and the answers could point to the need for a further modification of transmigration targets. Such questions include the following:

1. To what extent will urbanization and rural development efforts in Java enable job opportunities in Java to expand? Will urbanization bring with it greater problems than the alternative of shifting people to other islands?

2. To what extent is migration from Java–Bali–Lombok needed to increase rates of economic development in other areas?

3. To the extent that net out-migration from Java is needed both to alleviate problems in Java and to support regional development, can spontaneous movement (aided by some judicious provision of infrastructure) be expected to meet this need, or is a full-fledged transmigration pro-gramme needed?

We do not believe that the answers to any of these questions are clear, but many alternatives to present development strategies with regard to population redistribution and urbanization can be proposed, and these require careful evaluation. The context has changed since the days when government-sponsored transmigration seemed to be the only way out: for example, the 'echo' effect of the successful transmigration efforts of *Repelita III* should be drawing more spontaneous migrants; and infra-structure development such as the trans-Sumatra and trans-Sulawesi high-ways and the increased Java–Sumatra ferry services have greatly facilitated population mobility.

The Interrelationships of Population–Development Issues

We have discussed separately the issues of controlling population growth, and the employment and migration issues raised by continued population growth. There are, of course, many interlinkages and feedbacks between population and economic and social trends, and the most ambitious economic–demographic models attempt to take these into account. No such model has yet been constructed for Indonesia, and those constructed for other countries are forced to take giant 'leaps of faith' in specifying the determinants of fertility trends. Here we might just mention, for illustrative purposes, the probable mutually reinforcing linkages between three 'transi-tions' that are underway in Indonesia: the demographic transition (incor-porating a transition in the structure and functions of the family), the educational transition, and the transition in the structure of employment. The first and last of these have been discussed in detail in this and earlier chapters. The educational transition, which has proceeded quite rapidly in Indonesia over the past fifteen years, plays a key intermediate role.

In the early stages of educational development, it is generally assumed that 'supply of education creates its own demand'. This is largely true as the desire for primary education spreads throughout the population, and the much higher incomes open to those fortunate enough to reach higher levels of education are clear for all to see (Sigit, 1985: 66–8). However, Indonesia has now reached the stage where primary education is almost universal, and the decline in fertility will assist in pushing ahead in expanding the coverage of junior secondary education. At this stage, however, demand factors begin to play a major role, and the demand for education is closely linked with structural changes in the economy.

Agricultural mechanization, in the form of mechanical cultivators, transplanters, sprayers, weeders and threshers, increases the demand for education in the rural areas—as does a labour-intensive pattern of industrial development, in addition to helping develop a base of skills on which further industrialization can develop. At the same time, however, expansion of civil service and office-type job opportunities for those with secondary school and tertiary education will not be able to keep up with the pace of increase in numbers of people with these levels of education, resulting in the 'rationing device' of heightened minimum educational qualifications required for particular jobs. This will require a lowering of expectations as people learn that education can only serve as an automatic pathway to upward mobility when few are walking that pathway.

What effect will all this have on the demand for children? Introduction of mechanized processes in agriculture might be expected to lower the demand for children, both by requiring more education—and thus increasing the cost of, and delaying the returns from, children—and by eliminating the labour shortages at peak times. Labour-intensive industrialization may also tend to dampen the demand for children—firstly, by lowering the certainty of their contribution to the parents in later years (by requiring a shift of many young workers to urban areas and, even when rural-based, tending to break up the tight family-based work unit); and, secondly, by offering new work opportunities to women. The increasing competition for good jobs requiring secondary education or above will increase awareness that long periods of schooling are needed just to stay on the mobility pathway, without ensuring much progress along that pathway. This could strongly reinforce other anti-natalist tendencies.

Without elaborating further, it is clear that the pattern of economic growth and industrialization can have major implications for both the demand for education and the demand for children. Expansion of education, in turn (and to some extent irrespective of the reason why such expansion took place), tends to have manifold and powerful effects on demand for children and hence on fertility (see Jones, 1975: Chapter 10; Caldwell, 1980). Finally, declines in fertility should facilitate more rapid structural change in the economy, though to the extent to which this is due to a slowing in labour force growth, it is a lagged response. Development is, of course, a series of mutually reinforcing feedbacks, and as the historical experience of other densely populated countries such as Japan and Taiwan shows, once the process is well underway, based on appropriate agricultural mechanization and labour-intensive industrialization, it is possible for rapid economic growth to take place with only a moderate tempo of urbanization through the rapid diversification of work options available to rural dwellers. The implications for Indonesia, especially Java, are clear. In the light of the continuing rapid growth of labour force and the limited absorptive capacity of modern-sector, city-based employment in Indonesia (Hasibuan, 1985), it is crucial that overall macro-economic policy be such as to support the three crucial transitions outlined above.

Conclusion

The interrelationships of population and development issues, and the difficulty of isolating the role of population growth when it is imbedded in a matrix of interacting forces, make it very difficult to answer two key questions that have to be raised in formulating population policy: first, how serious a problem is continued population growth? and second, can efforts to halt it be left to the free choice of individuals, or is a measure of government intervention, through persuasion or even regulation, justified?

These issues are far from academic. China has taken a number of relatively draconian steps to put a stop to population growth, including pressure to adhere to the one-child family goal, implying a complete break from traditional Chinese family systems. India, for a period, permitted state governments to engage in coercive measures to accelerate declines in fertility. In many parts of Asia, family planning programmes are carried out in styles at odds with Western notions of privacy and personal freedom.

How far should the Indonesian government go in ensuring that fertility declines? Coercion has been officially eschewed, though it can certainly be argued that in the cultural and administrative context of Indonesia, considerable pressure can be, and is, exerted on people in subtle ways. However, the implementation of a forceful family planning programme, which has successfully lowered fertility rates steadily over a period of time, has obviated the need for the kinds of coercive strategies that could yet be seen as necessary in countries such as Bangladesh and Pakistan, where rapid population growth continues due to relatively weak efforts to date in the fields of family planning, female education and female employment opportunities.

Tinbergen (1974), writing on population growth and the exhaustion of natural resources, said that, 'there simply are no easy ways out of our present situation: there are only either difficult ways or no ways at all'. This sobering judgement certainly applies to population and development issues in Indonesia. We would claim, however, that these difficult ways have been followed, with great perseverance, in recent years, and we can now be more optimistic that persistence in pursuing the appropriate policies, if combined with favourable international economic conditions, will finally bring an end to the problems of rapid growth and regional imbalance of Indonesia's population.

1. Based on life-expectation of 30–35 years at the beginning of the twentieth century, and 50–55 years in 1980.

2. The changes over time in the sources of expanded agricultural production are well

summarized by Booth (1985) who shows that expansion of the cultivated area more or less kept up with population growth until at least the 1930s. After that point, by growing more *palawidja* as a second crop on *sawah* by expanding its cultivation on dry land, Javanese food-crop farmers were able to achieve a 30 per cent expansion of harvested area of food crops between the 1920s and the early 1960s with no obvious decline in per hectare yields, but this was not enough to maintain output per capita.

3. A re-study (1976–83) of eight villages in West and East Java by the Rural Dynamics Project found that the proportion of the rural labour force engaged in commuting/circular migration had increased from 22 per cent to 28 per cent, and that 52 per cent of household heads were engaged in temporary migration in 1983. More than half of these temporary migrants went to urban destinations, and more than one-third engaged in migration through-out the year rather than seasonally; more than 80 per cent were male. Of temporary migrants in non-agricultural activities, half were engaged in trade and a further 30 per cent in wage labour in transport (mainly *becak* drivers), construction or manufacturing.

4. It is encouraging that a more supportive attitude towards the role of the informal sector is at last developing in government circles, based on the findings of studies such as those of Hidayat (1979) and Ananta and Priyono (1985) and of seminars on the informal sector such as that organized by the Ministry of Population and Environment in early 1985.

5. It is now the policy to abandon projects established on peat soils more than one metre deep.

6. The techniques involve the use of aerial photography, landsat photography and SLAR (Side-looking Air-borne Radar).

7. For a more detailed discussion, see Arndt and Sundrum, 1977; and Arndt, 1983.

8. The regulations in Jakarta required in-migrants wishing to settle there to register and deposit a sum equivalent to twice the return fare to their village of origin (minimum Rp 1,000). If, after six months, the in-migrant could establish to the satisfaction of the relevant authorities that he had a permanent job and place of residence, the money was returned (minus administrative costs) and he could purchase an identity card and become a citizen of Jakarta. Alternatively, if he failed to satisfy the officials, the in-migrant was given his fare and escorted to the departure point for return public transport to his village. Periodically, checks were made by soldiers of the *team penertiban* (control team): persons found to be in Jakarta illegally were deposited on the outskirts of the city. Because this system was fraught with possibilities for administrative staff to supplement their meagre salaries, obtaining Jakarta citizenship could be very expensive. Not surprisingly, many people seeking to work in Jakarta saved themselves the expense by obtaining a 'visitor's card' (*surat keterangan lalu lintas*) from authorities in their village of origin; this allowed them to stay in Jakarta for a period of up to six months (*Jakarta Times*, 19 August 1970). On return to the village, a further card could be obtained. Such persons did not appear in official population registers in Jakarta.

9. However, in terms of wide differences in infrastructure requirements, the urban–rural distinction remains valid and it is therefore somewhat misleading to claim, as Professor Sumitro (1977) has done, that Java will be an 'urban island' by the year 2000.

10. Transmigration, it is assumed, would by itself lead to a rise in urbanization in Java, because rural areas are over-represented among transmigrants and probably among sponta-neous migrants as well: transmigration would therefore reduce their rate of population growth compared to that of urban areas. In Table 10.2, this is included in the effect attributed to migration. The reduction in rural population growth attributable to urbanization refers to urbanization over and above that caused by the loss of transmigrants from rural areas.

11. It is impossible to say how many of these landless or near-landless households are dependent mainly on agriculture for their survival, but this would appear to be a problem confined mainly to Yogyakarta and Central Java (Montgomery and Sugito, 1980: 356–8).

12. In this and subsequent discussion, 'Java' is taken to mean the transmigration source areas of Java, Bali and Lombok.

Appendices

Appendix 1
INDONESIA'S HIERARCHY OF ADMINISTRATIVE REGIONS

At several points in the text, different levels of the Indonesian administrative hierarchy are referred to. The formal administrative hierarchy is set out in the table below. The hierarchy has been well summarized by McNicoll and Singarimbun (1984: 34) as follows:

At the lowest level in rural areas is the administrative village (*kelurahan, desa*—the latter term confusing because the Javanese word *desa* means a *pedukuhan*), usually comprising a group of hamlets (perhaps 6–8 on average), sometimes clustered, in other cases strung out over a wide area. Its head, the *lurah*, is an elected official, although his term is indefinite, and in some regions the post is virtually hereditary. The higher administrative levels are headed by appointed officials (*camat, bupati,* and provincial governor). Roughly paralleling this civil administration is a military bureaucracy extending downward from the commander of each military district, the counterpart in the larger provinces to the governor.

TABLE A.1
Indonesia: Administrative Levels, *circa* 1980

Unit	Indonesia		Java	
	Number	*Average Unit Population*	*Number*	*Average Unit Population*
Province	27	5,500,000	5	18,000,000
Second-level region[a]				
Kabupaten	246	500,000	82	950,000
Kotamadya	49	300,000	19	400,000
Kecamatan[b]	3,144	40,000	1,445	60,000
Kelurahan (Desa)[c]	54,000	2,000	20,000	3,500

Source: McNicoll and Singarimbun, 1984: 35.
Note: Usual translations of names of administrative levels: *kabupaten* = regency; *kotamadya* = municipality; *kecamatan* = subdistrict; *kelurahan* = administrative village, village complex.
[a] Excluding divisions within Jakarta.
[b] Excluding *kecamatan* within municipalities.
[c] Approximate numbers, excluding *desa* within urban areas.

Two significant changes have taken place in this system since the mid-1960s: first, a considerable strengthening of its role and an increase in its effectiveness qua administrative control, and second, devolution of responsibility for many aspects of development program performance to its lower reaches—*kabupaten*, *kecamatan*, and *kelurahan*.

Appendix 2

COMPARABILITY OF DATA SOURCES ON EMPLOYMENT

The main 'bench-marks' for studying labour force and employment trends in Indonesia, listed chronologically, are the 1930, 1961 and 1971 Censuses, the 1976 Intercensal Survey (*Supas*), the 1976–8 National Labour Force Survey conducted quarterly (*Sakernas*), and the 1980 Census. Other sources include the labour force sample survey of Java and Madura in 1958, the national social and economic surveys (*Susenas*) of 1963–4, 1964–5, 1967 and 1969–70, the urban unemployment survey conducted in Jakarta, Surabaya, and Bandung in 1972, the labour force survey of Palembang and Ujung Pandang in 1975, the *Leknas* survey on labour utilization in selected areas of Java in 1976, and the *Susenas* of 1979, 1980, 1982 and 1984. The 1973 and 1983 Censuses of Agriculture can also be utilized to throw more light on aspects of agricultural employment, and the 1974/75 Industrial Census does the same for the manufacturing sector.

The data sources up to 1971 have been evaluated in a number of studies (Jones, 1966; 1974; 1981; Demographic Institute, 1974; Mertens, 1978), and comparisons of 1971 and 1980 census data in edited publications by Bakir and Manning (1983), and Manning and Papayungan (1984). All-Indonesia data in somewhat comparable form are contained only in the censuses of 1930, 1961, 1971 and 1980—although even in the case of these data the comparability is seriously limited by differences in definitions, time reference periods, and data collection procedures. The other sources—the 1958 Labour Force Survey, the *Susenas* data and, in particular, the post-1971 surveys—although covering only parts of Indonesia, nevertheless provide very useful comparative information because these surveys were able to delve more deeply than the censuses into various aspects of employment and unemployment. Even so, the more data that become available, the more apparent it becomes that there is only a very shaky basis for using them to study time trends.

Consider the census data first. There are three major problems in using the 1961 and 1971 population censuses to reconstruct changes in the Indonesian labour force. The first problem is that the two censuses, although they both used the 'labour force' rather than the 'gainful worker' approach,[1] adopted different time reference periods for their labour force questions. In order to be considered as 'employed' in 1961 a person had to be currently working (or be on leave, ill, or on strike from a regular job) or to have worked at least two months during the six months preceding the enumeration.[2] A person who was working at the time of enumeration was categorized as 'working' without any reference to the previous six-month period. If the respondent was not working at the time of enumeration, then the enumerator was instructed to ask 'Have you worked at all since last *lebaran* (or six months ago)?' If the answer was positive, the enumerator was instructed to determine whether the respondent had worked for at least two months out of the six-month period (though no minimum of hours per day or days per month was specified). If negative, the enumerator had to determine whether the respondent was currently looking for work or was in school, or engaged in housekeeping activities, etc.[3]

In 1971, the reference period was the week preceding the census, and to be counted as 'employed' the respondent must have worked for at least two days during that week.[4] This is a more precise instruction than the two-stage 'current activity' and 'past six months' approach adopted in 1961, although since it was not given on the census form itself but only in the manual of instructions to enumerators, its application in practice might be queried. The 1961 approach could be expected to overstate total employment, and also total employment in agriculture, relative to the 1971 approach, because persons who were out of work at the time of the census but who had worked two months out of the past six (amongst whom, no doubt, there would have been many seasonal workers in agriculture) would have been counted as 'employed' in 1961 but not in 1971.

The second problem in comparing the 1961 with the 1971 figures is that both censuses suffered from age mis-statement and under-reporting of young adult males.[5] If the degree of age mis-statement and under-reporting was the same in both censuses, estimates of labour force trends might not be too seriously affected, though estimates of the absolute size of the labour force certainly would be. But there is evidence that the degree of error differed in the two censuses.

The third problem in making 1961–71 comparisons is that there is a range of possible estimates of labour force which can be used for 1971. First, there are the Series C figures, based on a 10 per cent subsample[6] of the census returns giving detailed characteristics of the population (which in turn were based on a 3.8 per cent sample of the total population). Second, there are the Series D and E figures, based on the full 3.8 per cent sample of the total population. Normally, the Series D and E figures would be preferred over the Series C figures, which should differ from them only slightly due to sampling variability. However, because of a change in imputation rules after the Series C figures were published, the Series D and E figures in fact differ substantially from the Series C figures.[7] Since neither the earlier nor the later set of imputation rules is intrinsically correct or incorrect, there is justification for using both the Series C and Series D figures in examining the level of reliability of the labour force data although, for comparison with other data, there is ample evidence that Series C is to be preferred (Suharto and Sigit, 1977). This is because the Series D procedures, in giving priority to the status 'unemployed' tended to understate the actual employment in each industry and to measure much higher unemployment rates than the 1961 or 1980 census data.

Table A.2 gives a broad comparison of the Series C and Series D labour force data. The total labour force according to the Series D data is more than 1 million larger than that shown by Series C. The difference is greater still when we disaggregate it into its components. The employed population in Series D is actually 1.6 million smaller than in Series C, but the unemployed population is 2.7 million larger, resulting in the overall excess of labour force of 1.1 million in Series D. The change in imputation rules clearly had a larger relative effect on females than on males. However, the offsetting effect is about the same, with the result that the total labour force measured for both males and females is approximately 3 per cent larger in Series D than in Series C. The massive changes between Series C and Series D are not constant across provinces or regions. In Java, for example, West Java is more strongly affected by the changes than any other province, particularly where female unemployment rates are concerned.

The third set of data available from the 1971 Census is the Series C or Series D data, adjusted to allow for persons who worked in agriculture in the previous season. In recognition of the problems that would arise in comparing the 1971 figures with the 1961 figures, and in recognition also of the limited value of a one-

TABLE A.2

Labour Force in 1971 According to Series C and Series D Data[a] (Numbers in Thousands)

Province or Region	Series C			Series D			Col. (1) ÷ Col. (4)
	Total Labour Force	Unemployed		Total Labour Force	Unemployed		
		Number	Percentage		Number	Percentage	
	(1)	(2)	(3)	(4)	(5)	(6)	(7)
Males							
Jakarta	1,043	58	5.6	1,036	112	10.8	1.007
West Java	4,558	155	3.4	4,696	559	11.9	0.971
Central Java	5,172	87	1.7	5,216	215	4.1	0.992
Yogyakarta	576	12	2.1	571	19	3.4	1.009
East Java	6,092	118	1.9	6,297	361	5.7	0.968
Total Java	17,441	431	2.5	17,816	1,267	7.1	0.979
Outer Islands	9,391	218	2.3	9,720	786	8.1	0.966
Indonesia	26,832	649	2.4	27,536	2,053	7.5	0.974
Females							
Jakarta	301	13	4.4	315	60	19.0	0.955
West Java	1,791	46	2.6	1,993	415	20.8	0.898
Central Java	3,140	47	1.5	2,901	156	5.4	1.083
Yogyakarta	460	6	1.4	450	14	3.1	1.023
East Java	3,229	61	1.9	3,458	332	9.6	0.934
Total Java	8,921	174	1.9	9,116	977	10.7	0.979
Outer Islands	4,347	67	1.5	4,562	594	13.0	0.953

(continued)

TABLE A.2 (continued)

Province or Region	Series C			Series D			Col. (1) ÷ Col. (4) (7)
	Total Labour Force (1)	Unemployed Number (2)	Percentage (3)	Total Labour Force (4)	Unemployed Number (5)	Percentage (6)	
Indonesia	13,268	241	1.8	13,678	1,571	11.5	0.970
Both sexes							
Jakarta	1,344	72	5.3	1,351	172	12.8	0.995
West Java	6,349	201	3.2	6,689	974	14.6	0.949
Central Java	8,312	134	1.6	8,116	371	4.6	1.024
Yogyakarta	1,036	18	1.8	1,021	33	3.3	1.015
East Java	9,321	179	1.9	9,754	694	7.1	0.956
Total Java	26,362	605	2.3	26,932	2,244	8.3	0.979
Outer Islands	13,738	285	2.1	14,282	1,380	9.7	0.962
Indonesia	40,100	890	2.2	41,214	3,624	8.8	0.973

Source: Jones, 1981: 220–1.

a For purposes of comparison, Irian Jaya is not included in the figures for 'Outer Islands' or for Indonesia because Irian Jaya was not included in the Series C figures and only urban areas of Irian Jaya in the Series D figures. Sub-totals and totals may not add, due to rounding off.

week reference period in measuring the agricultural labour force, an additional question, 'Did you work in agriculture last season?', was added to the 1971 census schedule. The last-season figures, which raise the estimate of the agricultural labour force from 25.8 million to 35.9 million (and in Java alone, from 15.2 million to 22.9 million), undoubtedly give an unrealistically high estimate of the numbers working in agriculture on a fairly full-time basis, because no minimum cut-off point for time worked in the last season was used. Nevertheless, these data are very useful in setting an upper limit to the size of the labour force and in examining probable trends in the sectoral composition of employment between 1961 and 1971, and they will be used for this purpose below.[8]

Equally difficult problems arise in comparing the 1971 census data with *Supas* data. Although both used a one-week reference period, a different procedure was followed in determining whether the respondent was economically active in the reference week. In *Supas*, the first question established the main activity during the past week (working, studying, running the household, or 'other'), but all those whose main activity was not working were then asked, 'Besides this, did you also work at least one hour during the past week?' Those who replied 'yes' to this question were included in the labour force in the published tabulations. Therefore, not only was the time minimum for 'working' more liberal than in the 1971 Census (working at least one hour rather than working on at least two days) but, unlike the case in 1971, the format of the questionnaire ensured that the respondent was well aware of this minimum. It is hardly surprising, then, that the proportion of the population included in the labour force was higher in *Supas* than in the 1971 Census, especially in the case of women and young people.

The *Sakernas* procedures were different again (Sigit, 1977). The questionnaire was much more detailed, and respondents were asked about their activities on each day of the previous week. 'Working' was the first activity listed, followed by others, including 'in school' and 'housework'. As in the case of *Supas*, published tabulations classified respondents as working if they worked at least one hour in the reference week. In comparing the 1976 *Sakernas* with *Supas*, it must be borne in mind that there are two potentially important differences. First, *Sakernas* interviewers were not forced by the structure of the questionnaire to ask respondents whose primary activity was outside the work-force whether they did any work at all in the reference week. The extent to which they probed in practice is, of course, impossible to determine. Secondly, *Supas* was conducted in March, which is the peak agricultural season in Java and much of Indonesia, whereas *Sakernas* was conducted from September to December, which is by and large the agricultural slack season. As expected, *Supas* records a higher proportion of the population in the work-force than does the 1976 *Sakernas*; however, the magnitude of the difference is surprisingly large, fully 6 million in the case of the estimated labour force for Indonesia as a whole (54.5 million in *Supas*, 48.4 million in *Sakernas*). Comparison of the *Sakernas* data for the last week and the last year, and of the 1976 *Sakernas* with the later rounds of *Sakernas* reveals that seasonality can explain only a relatively small part of the difference.

Finally, the 1980 Census, though it employed definitions and approaches very close to those used in *Supas*, yielded labour force participation rates very close to those measured by the 1971 Census, or in other words below those indicated by *Sakernas* and well below those indicated by *Supas*.[9] Whether in fact there was little change in participation rates over the 1970s is hard to say. What seems clear is that the rates certainly did not rise sharply and then fall again sharply, as suggested by the 1971 Census–*Supas*–1980 Census comparison. Therefore, for most comparative purposes in Chapter 8, the 1971 and 1980 census data are employed, and the *Sakernas* data are used to give a more detailed picture on a number of points.

1. For a discussion of these approaches in the South-East Asian context see Hauser, 1974.

2. The enumerators were simply instructed to ask '*Apakah saudara bekerja?*' (that is, do you work, or are you working?) and if the response was 'yes' the respondent was to be classified as 'employed'. There was no instruction as to the reference period to be used for this question. The question could be taken to mean 'Do you normally work?' (that is, something very close to the 'gainful worker' approach) or 'Are you working today?' (or this week, or this month).

3. Various aspects of definitions and instructions to enumerators used in 1961, and their likely effect on measured employment, are noted in Jones, 1981: 219–22.

4. As is normal in censuses and labour force surveys, persons who work less than two days or not at all were recorded as 'employed' provided that they were temporarily absent from their usual job because of illness, strikes, or vacation, or because of temporary disorganization of work due to such reasons as bad weather or mechanical breakdown. Peasants waiting for harvest or planting time were also included in this category, as they were too in 1980. How accurately these rules were applied in practice is, of course, uncertain.

5. For a detailed analysis of these problems, see Keyfitz, 1973; and Speare, 1975.

6. With the exception of Jakarta and Yogyakarta, where the data were completely processed for the Series C report.

7. For a detailed discussion of this change in imputation rules, see Jones, 1974; and Visaria, 1974. Briefly, the editing and imputation procedures are the procedures for deciding, on the basis of answers given to other questions on the census schedule, whether to alter a response or to enter a response in a blank space in cases where schedules were not filled out correctly or were left blank, or in which the proper sequence of questions was not followed. For the Series C publication, priority was given to a person's classification as 'working', if there was conflicting evidence in responses to other questions. On the other hand, in Series D and E, the imputation rules were more complex, and there appears to have been a tendency to count people as unemployed if the enumerator had filled out information about economic activity in the past (which he was only supposed to do for persons classified as employed or for the unemployed who had worked previously), even if he had earlier classified the respondent as outside the labour force. In general, the imputation rules used for Series C had a tendency to record doubtful cases as employed or outside the labour force, whereas Series E was more likely to record them as unemployed. Both the extent of unemployment and the size of the labour force appear to have been overstated by Series E, and the estimates of Series C are closer to the intent of the census definitions. However, since Series D gives the official 'final' figures, it is used for the most part in Chapter 8.

8. The Series C and Series D figures differ, even in the case of these workers. Series D gives an estimate of 'last season' workers which is 6.6 per cent higher than that given by Series C. The differences are greater in Java than in the outer islands, especially for females. The reason for these differences is not clear, but the Series D figures are used in Chapter 8 to maintain consistency with other tables.

9. The 1980 Census report published two sets of tables on employment status. The first tabulation (Table 37) aims at consistency with the 1971 Census by classifying as employed all those who worked at least two days during the reference week. The second tabulation (Table 39) aims at consistency with *Supas* and *Sakernas* by classifying as employed all those who worked at least one hour during the reference week. Interestingly enough, the results differ very little: 51.3 million are employed according to the first measure, 51.6 million according to the second. Even more surprising is the fact that a further question on whether respondents worked during the past year yielded a lower estimate of employment—50.5 million.

Appendix 3

SOURCES OF MORTALITY ESTIMATES USED IN FIGURE 4.1

No.	Period/Year	Location	Crude Death Rate (CDR)	Infant Mortality Rate (IMR)	E_o^o	Citation
1	1900/20	Indonesia	over 30	250		LDFEUI, 1974: 94
2	1920	Java	33			Breman, 1971
3	1929	Jakarta		231		Walch-Sorgdrager, 1931, cited in Widjojo, 1970: 105
4	1930	Indonesia		250		Kartono Gunawan, 1964, in LDFEUI, 1974: 92
5	1930/9	Indonesia		225–250	30–5	Widjojo, 1970: 113
6	1930	Jakarta		176–294		Widjojo, 1970: 105
7	1935	Bandung		154		Brand, 1958, in Widjojo, 1970: 111
8	1938/40	Jakarta		211		Tesch, 1948, in Widjojo, 1970: 107
9	1944	Java	33			de Vries, in LDFEUI, 1974: 95
10	1944	Wonosobo, C. Java	53.7			Anderson, 1966, in Widjojo, 1970: 117–18
11	1950s	Java	25			Breman, 1971, in LDFEUI, 1974: 100
12	1950/5	Java	28		35.0	Widjojo, 1970: 158
13	1951/6	Indonesia	23			Sastrasuanda, 1969, in Utomo, 1982: 321
14	1954/8	Java	19	150		Wander, 1965, in LDFEUI, 1974: 98
15	1955/60	Java	26		37.5	Widjojo, 1970: 158
16	1958/9	East Java		175		Hull and Sunaryo, 1978: 3
17	1958/9	Jakarta		195		Hull and Sunaryo, 1978: 3
18	1958/9	Yogyakarta		113		Hull and Sunaryo, 1978: 3
19	1960	East Java			41.1	Iskandar, 1970: 111
20	1968	Indonesia	25	159	39	World Bank, World Development Report, 1981: 168, 174.

(continued)

Appendix 3 (*continued*)

No.	Period/Year	Location	Crude Death Rate (CDR)	Infant Mortality Rate (IMR)	E_o^o	Citation
21	1960	Indonesia	22			Iskandar, 1970: 137
22	1960/70	Indonesia		143	46	McNicoll and Mamas, 1973: 13
23	1961	Indonesia			41 M, 38 F	Heligman, 1975, in Utomo, 1982: 309
24	1961	Indonesia	24			US Bureau of Census, 1980: 99
25	1962	Java	22			Kannisto, 1963, in LDFEUI, 1974: 106
26	1963	Indonesia	21			Kannisto, 1963, in Utomo, 1982: 321
27	1963	Java	19			Ueda, 1965, in LDFEUI, 1974: 105
28	1964	Indonesia	17		46 M, 49 F	BPS, 1968, in Utomo, 1932: 321
29	1964	Indonesia	17			BPS, 1967, in LDFEUI, 1974: 109–10
30	1964	Indonesia		142		Sastrosuanda, 1971, in Hull and Sunaryo, 1978: 3
31	1964	Java	16			BPS, 1968, in LDFEUI, 1974: 105
32	1965/70	Indonesia	19			UN Demographic Yearbook, 1970, in Utomo, 1982: 321
33	1967/70	Indonesia		140		McDonald *et al.*, 1976: 68
34	1967	Indonesia		136		Kasto and Sunaryo, 1979, in Utomo, 1982: 308 (census data)
35	1967	Indonesia		121		Kasto and Sunaryo, 1979, in Utomo, 1982: 308 (*Supas* II data)
36	1968	Indonesia		143		Hull and Sunaryo, 1978: 37
37	1968	Indonesia			46	Kasto, 1983a: 5
38	1971	Indonesia			40 M, 43 F	Heligman, 1975, in Utomo, 1982: 309

39	1971	Indonesia	20	126	42	US Bureau of Census, 1978: 166
40	1971/6	Indonesia	15			McDonald, 1978: 12
41	1973	Indonesia		105		Kasto and Sunaryo, 1979, in Utomo, 1982: 308
42	1974/6	Indonesia		106–8		Soemantri, 1983, in Dasvarma, 1984: 8
43	1974/7	SVRP Regions		140 M, 121 F		Gardiner, 1978
44	1974/7	SVRP Regions			50.4 F	Gardiner, 1978, in Utomo, 1982: 311
45	1975	Indonesia	16	114	45 M, 48 F	US Bureau of Census, 1981: 66
46	1975	Indonesia	16	114	45 M, 48 F	US Bureau of Census, 1983: 222
47	1975	Indonesia	16	114	46	US Bureau of Census, 1980: 197
48	1975	Indonesia		114		Hull and Sunaryo, 1978: 37
49	1976	Java–Bali		121		World Fertility Survey, 1978, in Dasvarma, 1983: 6
50	1976	Java–Bali		103		Sullivan and Wilson, 1982, in Dasvarma, 1983: 6
51	1977	Indonesia		107		Soemantri, 1983 (1980 Census)
52	1977/8	Indonesia		107	53	Kasto, 1983b: 3
53	1978	East Java		83		BPS, 1982: 20, 22. Direct estimation techniques.
54	1978	East Java		98		BPS, 1982: 20, 22. Indirect estimation techniques.
55	1979	Indonesia	13	120	53	World Bank, World Development Report, 1981: 168, 174
56	1980	East Java		91		Dasvarma, 1983: 159
57	1980	Indonesia		100		Budiarso, 1983: 83. Conversion of Death rate under 1 year
58	1980	Indonesia		88		Budiarso, 1983: 83. Birth cohort survey
59	1980	Indonesia		97		Dasvarma, 1983: 158 [publ. conf paper]
60	1980	Indonesia	10.3			Dasvarma, 1985: 2 (RN35)

376

Appendix 4
TABLE A.3

Assumptions and Projections Regarding Total Fertility Rates (TFR), by Province, 1976–1979 to 1995–2000, for NUDSP Projections

Region and Province	BKKBN Stage	TFR Assumptions				
		1976–1979	1980–1985	1985–1990	1990–1995	1995–2000
INDONESIA		4680	4445	3550	3080	2790
SUMATRA						
DI Aceh	II	5235	4645	3945	3355	2935
North Sumatra	II	5935	5265	4475	3805	3330
West Sumatra	II	5755	5105	4340	3690	3225
Riau	III	5435	4945	4330	3680	3125
Jambi	II	5570	4940	4200	3570	3125
South Sumatra	II	5585	4955	4210	3580	3130
Bengkulu	III	6195	5635	4930	4195	3565
Lampung	II	5750	5100	4335	3685	3225
JAVA						
DKI Jakarta	I	4070	3560	3025	2650	2385
West Java	I	5070	4435	3770	3205	2725
Central Java	I	4370	3825	3250	2845	2560
DI Yogyakarta	I	3415	2990	2540	2285	2170
East Java	I	3555	3110	2645	2380	2260

NUSA TENGGARA						
Bali	I	3970	3475	2955	2585	2325
West Nusa Tenggara	II	6490	5755	4895	4160	3640
East Nusa Tenggara	III	5540	5040	4410	3750	3185
East Timor	III	5540	5040	4410	3750	3185
KALIMANTAN						
West Kalimantan	III	5520	5025	4395	3735	3175
Central Kalimantan	III	5870	5340	4675	3970	3375
South Kalimantan	II	4595	4075	3465	2945	2575
East Kalimantan	III	4985	4535	3970	3375	2870
SULAWESI						
North Sulawesi	II	4905	4350	3700	3145	2750
Central Sulawesi	III	5900	5370	4700	3995	3395
South Sulawesi	II	4875	4325	3675	3125	2735
South-east Sulawesi	III	5820	5295	4635	3940	3350
MALUKU AND IRIAN JAYA						
Maluku	III	6155	5600	4900	4165	3540
Irian Jaya	III	5350	4870	4260	3620	3080

Sources: Gardiner, 1985; based on Si Gede Made Mamas, 'Tren dan Variasi Kelahiran Indonesia, Menurut Propinsi', paper presented at the Seminar Fertilitas Indonesia, Jakarta, 30 May–1 June 1982; and on NUDSP estimates.

TABLE A.4

Percentage Projected Decline in the Total Fertility Rates (TFR), by Province,
1976–1979 to 1995–2000 (Model II)

Region and Province	Projected TFR Percentage Decline
INDONESIA	40.4
SUMATRA	
DI Aceh	43.9
North Sumatra	43.9
West Sumatra	44.0
Riau	42.5
Jambi	43.9
South Sumatra	44.0
Bengkulu	42.5
Lampung	43.9
JAVA	
DKI Jakarta	41.4
West Java	46.3
Central Java	41.4
DI Yogyakarta	36.5
East Java	36.4
NUSA TENGGARA	
Bali	41.4
West Nusa Tenggara	43.9
East Nusa Tenggara	42.5
East Timor	42.5
KALIMANTAN	
West Kalimantan	42.5
Central Kalimantan	42.5
South Kalimantan	44.0
East Kalimantan	42.4
SULAWESI	
North Sulawesi	43.9
Central Sulawesi	42.5
South Sulawesi	43.9
South-east Sulawesi	42.4
MALUKU AND IRIAN JAYA	
Maluku	42.5
Irian Jaya	42.4

Source: Calculations based on data in NUDSP, 1985b: Appendix, Table 10.1A.

Bibliography

Abdullah, A. (1979), 'Perantauan di Pidie, Aceh' (Mobility in Pidie, Aceh), paper presented at Workshop on Population Mobility, Pusat Studi dan Penelitian Kependudukan (Centre for Population Study and Research), Gadjah Mada University, Yogyakarta.

Abdullah, T. (1971), *School and Politics: The Kaum Muda Movement in West Sumatra 1927–1933*, Monograph Series, Cornell Modern Indonesia Project, New York.

Abdurachim, I. (1970), 'Migration from Rural Areas into Bandung', paper presented to Seminar on Southeast Asian Studies, IKIP, Bandung.

Abey, A., Booth, A. and Sundrum, R. M. (1981), 'Labour Absorption in Indonesian Agriculture', *Bulletin of Indonesian Economic Studies*, 17, 1: 36–65.

Abustam, M. I. (1975), *Tukang Sepatu Toraja di Ujung Pandang* (Torajan Shoe Repairers in Ujung Pandang), Pusat Latihan Penelitian Ilmu-Ilmu Sosial (Centre for Social Science Research Training), Hasanuddin University, Ujung Pandang.

—— (forthcoming), 'Gerak Penduduk pada Komunitas Padi Sawah di Sulawesi Selatan' (Population Mobility in Wet Rice Communities in South Sulawesi), Ph.D. thesis in Rural Sociology, Agricultural University, Bogor.

Adioetomo, S. M. (1984), 'Pola Fertilitas di Indonesia: Analisa Secara Umum' (Fertility Patterns in Indonesia: A General Analysis), in Hatmadji and Achmad (eds.), *Analisa Fertilitas di Indonesia Berdasarkan Data Sensus Penduduk 1980*, Biro Pusat Statistik, Jakarta.

—— (1985), 'Differensial Mortalitas Bayi dan Anak di Jakarta dan Indonesia' (Differential Infant and Child Mortality in Jakarta and Indonesia), pp. 1–52 in *Analisa Kependudukan Berdasarkan Data Sensus Penduduk 1980, Buku I (Jawa)*, Biro Pusat Statistik, Jakarta.

Adioetomo, S. M. and Dasvarma, G. (1986), *Levels and Trends of Child Mortality in Indonesia by Province Based on the 1971 and 1980 Population Censuses*, Lembaga Demografi (Demographic Institute), Faculty of Economics, University of Indonesia, Jakarta.

Aklilu, B. and Harris, J. R. (1978), *Migration, Employment and Earnings in Indonesia*, Migration and Development Study Group, Center for International Studies, Massachusetts Institute of Technology, Cambridge.

Alexander, P. (1984), 'Women, Labour and Fertility: Population Growth in Nineteenth Century Java', *Mankind*, 14, 5: 361–72.

—— (forthcoming), 'Labour Expropriation and Fertility: Population Growth in Nineteenth Century Java', in P. Handworker (ed.), *Culture and Reproduction: Reconstructing the Demographic Paradigm*, Academic Press, New York.

Allen, W. (1965), *The African Husbandman*, Oliver and Boyd, London.

Allied Geographical Section, Southwest Pacific Area (1945), *Batavia–Bandoeng*, Allied Geographical Section Terrain Study 112, London.

Amin, S. (ed.) (1984), *Modern Migrations in Western Africa*, Oxford University Press, Oxford.

Amiroelah, B. M. *et al.* (1976), *Masalah Perpindahan Penduduk Propins Sulawesi Selatan* (The Migration Problem in the Province of South Sulawesi), Hasanuddin University, Ujung Pandang.

Ananta, A. and Hatmadji, S. H. (1985), *Mutu Modal Manusia* (Quality of Human Capital), Lembaga Demografi, Faculty of Economics, University of Indonesia and Biro Pusat Statistik, Jakarta.

Ananta, A. and Priyono, T. (1985), 'Sektor Informal: Suatu Tinjauan Ekonomics' (The Informal Sector: An Economic Perspective), *Prisma*, XIX, 3: 18–26.

Anderson, B. R. O'G. (1966), 'Japan: The Light of Asia', in J. Silverstein *et al.* (eds.), *Southeast Asia in World War II: Four Essays*, Yale University Press, New Haven.

Angelino, A. D. A. de Kat (1931), *Colonial Policy Vol. 2: The Dutch East Indies* (Abridged edition from the Dutch translated by G. J. Renier in collaboration with the author), Chicago University Press, Chicago.

Anon. (1885), 'Grondgebied en Bevolking van Nedelandsch Indie' (Land Quality and Population in the Netherlands Indies), *Tidjschrift van het Nederlandsch Aardrijkskundig Genootschap*, 3, 2: 580–6.

Arief, S. (1979), *Indonesia: Pertumbuhan Ekonomi: Disparitas Pendapatan Dan Kemiskinan Massal* (Indonesia: Economic Growth: Income Disparities and Mass Poverty), Lembaga Studi Pembangunan, Jakarta.

Arndt, H. W. (1975), 'Development and Equality: The Indonesian Case', *World Development*, 3, 77–90.

—— (1983), 'Transmigration: Achievements, Problems, Prospects', *Bulletin of Indonesian Economic Studies*, 19, 3: 50–73.

—— (1984), *Transmigration in Indonesia*, Population and Labour Policies Programme, World Employment Programme Research Working Paper No. 146, International Labour Office, Geneva.

Arndt, H. W. and Sundrum, R. M. (1975), 'Regional Price Disparities', *Bulletin of Indonesian Economic Studies*, 11, 2: 30–68.

—— (1977), 'Transmigration: Land Settlement or Regional Development?', *Bulletin of Indonesian Economic Studies*, 13, 3: 72–90.

—— (1980), 'Employment, Unemployment and Underemployment', *Bulletin of Indonesian Economic Studies*, 16, 3: 61–82.

Arnold, F. and Shah, N. M. (1984), 'Asian Labour Migration to the Middle East', *International Migration Review*, 18, 2: 294–318.

ASEAN (1983), 'Institutional Development and Exchange of Personnel', Report of the Research Seminar II, Cipanas, West Java and Jakarta. Annex D, 'The Economic Activities of Women in Indonesia as Assessed in the 1980 Population Census', ASEAN/Australia Population Project.

Awanohara, S. (1982), 'In the Shadow of Death', *Far Eastern Economic Review*, 15 October: 42–3.

Azwar, A. (1980), *Puskesmas dan Usasha Kesehatan Pokok* (Community Health Centres and Basic Health Activities), C. V. Akadoma, Jakarta.

Bahrin, T. S. (1967), 'The Pattern of Indonesian Migration and Settlement in Malaya', *Asian Studies*, 5, 2: 233–57.

Bakir, Z. and Manning, C. (eds.) (1983), *Partisipasi Angkatan Kerja, Kesempatan Kerja dan Pengangguran di Indonesia* (Labour Force Participation, Employment Opportunities and Unemployment in Indonesia), *Pusat Penelitian dan Studi Kependudukan* (Center for Population Study and Research), Gadjah Mada University, Yogyakarta.

Bennett, D. (1957), 'Population Pressures in East Java', unpublished Ph.D. thesis, Syracuse University.

Berman, P. (1984), 'Village Health Workers in Java, Indonesia: Coverage and Equity', *Social Science and Medicine*, 19, 4: 411–22.

—— (1986), 'Distributional Equity in Primary Health Care: The Role of Service Organizations in Indonesia', mimeo.

Binsbergen, W. M. J. van and Meilink, H. A. (1978), 'Migration and the Transformation of Modern African Society: Introduction', *African Perspectives*, 1: 7–20.

Biro Pusat Statistik (BPS) (1982), *The 1980 Baseline Round of the East Java Population Survey: A Final Report*, Technical Report No. 1, Series SKJT 1980–82, International Programs of Laboratories for Population Statistics (POPLAB), University of North Carolina.

—— (1983a), *Keadaan Angkatan Kerja di Indonesia, 1961–1980* (The Labour Force Situation in Indonesia, 1961–1980), Biro Pusat Statistik, Jakarta.

—— (1983b), *Proyeksi Angkatan Kerja Indonesia, 1983–2001* (Indonesian Labour Force Projections, 1983–2001), Biro Pusat Statistik, Jakarta.

—— (1983c), *Penduduk Indonesia: Hasil Sensus Penduduk 1980* (Population of Indonesia: Results of the 1980 Population Census), Series S, No. 2, Biro Pusat Statistik, Jakarta.

—— (1984a), *Perpindahan Penduduk Antar Propinsi di Indonesia: Hasil Sensus Penduduk 1980* (Inter-Provincial Population Movement in Indonesia: Results of the 1980 Population Census), Biro Pusat Statistik, Jakarta.

—— (1984b), *Proyeksi Penduduk Indonesia per Propinsi 1980–2000* (Provincial Population Projections for Indonesia, 1980–2000), Biro Pusat Statistik, Jakarta.

—— *Population of Indonesia: Results of the 1980 Population Census*, Series S, No. 2, Biro Pusat Statistik, Jakarta.

—— (1986), *Penduduk Indonesia 1985 Menurut Propinsi* (Population of Indonesia in 1985 According to Province), Biro Pusat Statistik, Jakarta.

BKKBN (1982), *Basic Information on Population and Family Planning Programme*, National Family Planning Co-ordinating Board, Bureau of Population Data, Jakarta.

Boeke, J. H. (1927), 'Objective and Personal Elements in Colonial Welfare Policy', pp. 265–99 in *1966 Indonesian Economics: The Concept of Dualism in Theory and Policy*, W. van Hoeve, The Hague.

—— (1957), *Economics and Economic Policy of Dual Societies*, H. D. Tjeenk Willik, Haarlem.

Boomgaard, P. (1980), 'Bevolkingsgroei en Welvaart op Java (1800–1942)' (Population Growth and Welfare in Java), pp. 35–52 in R. N. J. Kamerling (ed.), *Indonesia Toen en Nu*, Intermediair, Amsterdam.

Booth, A. (1977a), 'Irrigation in Indonesia: Part 1', *Bulletin of Indonesian Economic Studies*, 13, 1: 33–74.

—— (1977b), 'Interprovincial Comparisons of Taxable Capacity, Tax Effort and Development Needs in Indonesia', *Malayan Economic Review*, 12, 1, 71–87.

—— (1984), 'Survey of Recent Developments', *Bulletin of Indonesian Economic Studies*, 20, 3: 1–35.

—— (1985), 'Accommodating a Growing Population in Javanese Agriculture', *Bulletin of Indonesian Economic Studies*, 19, 2: 115–45.

Booth, A. and McCawley, P. (1981), *The Indonesian Economy During the Soeharto Era*, Oxford University Press, Kuala Lumpur.

Booth, A. and Sundrum, R. M. (1976), 'The 1973 Agricultural Census', *Bulletin of Indonesian Economic Studies*, 12, 2: 90–105.

—— (1981), 'Income Distribution', pp. 181–217 in A. Booth and P. McCawley (eds.), *The Indonesian Economy During the Soeharto Era*, Oxford University Press, Kuala Lumpur.

Borkent-Niehoff, A. (1974), 'Fertility in Serpong, West Java: A Baseline Study', *Majalah Demografi Indonesia*, 1: 162–8.

Boserup, E. (1965), *The Conditions of Agricultural Growth*, Allen and Unwin, London.

―――― (1970), *Women's Role in Economic Development*, Allen and Unwin, London.

―――― (1975), 'Employment of Women in Developing Countries', in L. Tabah (ed.), *Population Growth and Economic Development in the Third World*, International Union for the Scientific Study of Population, Liege.

Bost, L., Quiggin, P. and Hull, T. (1985), 'The United Nations Population Division's Population Projections for Indonesia', Research Note No. 34, International Population Dynamics Program, Department of Demography, Australian National University, Canberra.

Breman, J. C. (1963), 'Java: Population Growth and Demographic Structure', pp. 252–308 in *Drie Geografische Studies over Java*, E. J. Brill, Leiden.

―――― (1971), *Djawa: Pertumbuhan Penduduk dan Struktur Demografis* (Java: Population Growth and Demographic Structure), Translated by Sugarda Purbakawatja, Bhratara, Jakarta.

Bruner, E. M. (1972), 'Batak Ethnic Associations in Three Indonesian Cities', mimeo.

Bryant, N. A. (1973), 'Population Pressure and Agricultural Resources in Central Java: The Dynamics of Change', unpublished Ph.D. thesis, Michigan State University.

Buchanan, K. (1967), *The Southeast Asian World: An Introductory Essay*, G. Bell and Sons, London.

Budiardjo, C. (1986), 'The Politics of Transmigration', *The Ecologist*, 16, 2/3: 111–16.

Budiarso, L. R. (1983), 'Angka dan Sebab Kematian Bayi dan Balita Berdasarkan Survei Kesehatan Rumah Tangga 1980' (Level and Causes of Infant and Child Deaths Based on the 1980 Household Health Survey), pp. 79–91 in *Seminar Tingkat Kematian Bayi di Indonesia*, 1–3 February, Biro Pusat Statistik, Jakarta.

Bukit, D. and Bakir, Z. (1983), 'Partisipasi Angkatan Kerja di Indonesia: Hasil Sensus 1971 dan 1980' (Labour Force Participation in Indonesia: Findings of the 1971 and 1980 Censuses), in Z. Bakir and C. Manning (eds.), *Partisipasi Angkatan Kerja, Kesempatan Kerja dan Pengangguran di Indonesia* (Labour Force Participation, Employment Opportunities and Unemployment in Indonesia), Pusat Penelitian dan Studi Kependudukan (Centre for Population Study and Research), Gadjah Mada University, Yogyakarta.

Burger, D. H. (1971), *Laporan Mengenai Desa Pekalongan dalam Tahun 1968 dan 1928 (Tindjauan Ekonomi)* (Report of Pekalongan Village in 1968 and 1928— Economic Observations), Bhratara, Jakarta.

Cabaton, A. (1911), *Java, Sumatra and the Other Islands of the Dutch East Indies*, Charles Sribner's Sons, New York/T. Fisher Unwin, London.

Cain, M. (1977), 'The Economic Activities of Children in a Village in Bangladesh, *Population and Development Review*, 3, 3, 201–28.

Caldwell, J. C. (1976), 'Toward a Restatement of Demographic Transition Theory', *Population and Development Review*, 2, 3–4: 321–66.

―――― (1980), 'Mass Education as a Determinant of the Timing of Fertility Decline', *Population and Development Review*, 6, 2: 225–55.

_____ (1982), *Theory of Fertility Decline*, Academic Press, London.

Cassen, Robert H. (1976), 'Population and Development: A Survey', *World Development*, 4, 10/11: 785–830.

Castles, L. (1967), 'An Ethnic Profile of Jakarta', *Indonesia*, 3: 153–204.

_____ (1972), 'The Political Life of a Sumatran Residency: Tapanuli 1915–1940', unpublished Ph.D. thesis, Monash University, Melbourne.

Chatterjee, L. (1979), *Housing in Indonesia*, Vrije Universiteit Amsterdam Geografisch en Planologisch Instituut, Bijdragen tot de Sociale Geografie 14.

Chenery, H.B. (1960), 'Patterns of Industrial Growth', *American Economic Review*, 50, 4: 624–54.

Chenery, H. and Syrquin, M. (1975), *Patterns of Development, 1950–1970*, published for the World Bank by Oxford University Press.

Cho, L.J., Suharto, S., McNicoll, G. and Mamas, S.G.M. (1976), *Estimates of Fertility and Mortality in Indonesia: Based on the 1971 Census*, Biro Pusat Statistik, Jakarta.

_____ (1980), *Population Growth of Indonesia: An Analysis of Fertility and Mortality Based on the 1971 Population Census*, Monograph No. 15, Center for Southeast Asian Studies, Kyoto University, The University Press of Hawaii, Honolulu.

Cleave, J.H. (1974), *African Farmers: Labor Use in the Development of Smallholder Agriculture*, Praeger, New York.

Coale, A.J. (1973), 'The Demographic Transition', in *International Population Conference 1973* (Vol. 1), International Union for the Scientific Study of Population, Liege, Belgium.

Colchester, M. (1986a), 'Banking on Disaster: International Support for Transmigration', *The Ecologist*, 16, 2/3: 61–70.

_____ (1986b), 'Unity and Diversity: Indonesia's Policy Towards Tribal Peoples', *The Ecologist*, 16, 2/3: 89–98.

_____ (1986c), 'The Struggle for Land: Tribal Peoples in the Face of the Transmigration Programme', *The Ecologist*, 16, 2/3: 99–110.

Colfer, C. (1981), 'On Circular Migration: From the Distaff Side', mimeo.

Collier, W.L., Gunawan, Wiradi and Soentoro (1973), 'Recent Changes in Rice Harvesting Methods', *Bulletin of Indonesian Economic Studies*, 9, 2: 36–45.

Collier, W.L., Soentoro, Wiradi, G., Pasandaran, E., Santoso, K. and Stepanek, J.F. (1982), 'Acceleration of Rural Development in Java', *Bulletin of Indonesian Economic Studies*, 18, 3: 84–101.

Coppel, C.A. (1980), 'China and the Ethnic Chinese in Indonesia', pp. 729–34 in J.J. Fox, R.G. Garnaut, P.T. McCawley and J.A.C. Mackie (eds.), *Indonesia: Australian Perspectives*, Research School of Pacific Studies, Australian National University, Canberra.

Cummings, F.G. (1975), 'Internal Migration and Regional Development Planning: Thailand, the Philippines and Indonesia', *Journal of Tropical Geography*, 41: 16–27.

Currey, B. (1983), Notes to Accompany the Map of 'Food Crises in Indonesia Reported in National Newspapers 1978–1982', mimeo.

Dahm, B. (1971), *History of Indonesia in the Twentieth Century*, Pall Mall Press, London.

Dapice, D. (1980), 'Trends in Income Distribution and Levels of Living, 1970–75', pp. 71–90 in G.F. Papanek (ed.), *The Indonesian Economy*, Praeger, New York.

Dapice, D. and Snodgrass, D. (1979), 'Employment in Manufacturing 1970–1977: A Comment', *Bulletin of Indonesian Economic Studies*, 15, 3: 127–31.

Darroch, R.K., Meyer, P.A. and Singarimbun, M. (1981), *Two Are Not Enough:*

The Value of Children to Javanese and Sundanese Parents, East–West Population Institute, Honolulu.

Dasvarma, G. L. (1983), 'Indonesian Infant Mortality Estimates for 1980 from Last Live Birth Data', pp. 140–61 in Biro Pusat Statistik, *Seminar Tingkat Kematian Bayi di Indonesia*, 1–3 February, Biro Pusat Statistik, Jakarta.

—— (1984), 'Infant and Child Deaths in Indonesia: How Many Can be Prevented?', *Majalah Demografi Indonesia* (Indonesian Journal of Demography), June: 1–14.

—— (1985), 'New Estimates of Crude Birth and Death Rates in Indonesia, 1980 by Province', Research Note No. 35, International Population Dynamics Program, Department of Demography, Australian National University, Canberra.

Davis, G. J. (1976), 'Parigi: A Social History of the Balinese Movement to Central Sulawesi 1907–1974', unpublished Ph.D. thesis, Stanford University.

Day, C. (1966), *The Dutch in Java*, Oxford University Press, Kuala Lumpur.

De Vries, E. (1946), 'Geboorte en Sterfte onder de Japansche Bezetting' (Birth and Death during the Japanese Occupation), *Economisch Weekblad voor Nederlandsch-Indie*, 7: 60–1.

Demographic Institute, Faculty of Economics, University of Indonesia (1974), Chapter VII in *Demographic Factbook of Indonesia* (2nd ed.), University of Indonesia, Jakarta.

Deuster, P. R. (1971), 'Rural Consequences of Indonesian Inflation: Case Study of the Jogjakarta Region', Ph.D. dissertation, University of Wisconsin.

Dick, H. W. (1980), 'The Oil Price Subsidy, Deforestation and Equity', *Bulletin of Indonesian Economic Studies*, 16, 3: 32–60.

—— (1985), 'Survey of Recent Developments', *Bulletin of Indonesian Economic Studies*, 21, 3: 1–29.

Directorate General of Transmigration, unpublished data, Jakarta.

DKI Jakarta (1980), *Penduduk Musiman: Penelitian Migran Sirkules di DKI Jakarta 1979* (Seasonal Population: A Study of Circular Migration in Jakarta 1979), DKI Jakarta Census and Statistical Office, Jakarta.

—— (1985), *Pola Pengendalian Mobilitas Penduduk Penglaju Botabek–Jakarta 1984–1985* (Mobility Patterns of Commuters from Bogor, Tanggerang and Bekasi to Jakarta 1984–85), Biro Bina Kependudukan dan Lingkungan Hidup Daerah Khusus Ibukota, Jakarta.

Dove, M. R. (1979), 'Shifting Cultivation in Kalimantan', paper prepared for Workshop on Population in Asian Forestry Communities Practising Shifting Cultivation (FAO/UNFPA Technical Consultation Meeting II), Yogyakarta, 8–12 October.

Dovring, F. (1964), 'The Share of Agriculture in a Growing Population', pp. 78–98 in C. Eicher and L. Witt (eds.), *Agriculture in Economic Development*, McGraw Hill, New York.

Durand, J. D. (1975), 'The Labor Force in Economic Development and Demographic Transition', in L. Tabah (ed.), *Population Growth and Economic Development in the Third World*, International Union for the Scientific Study of Population, Liege.

Du Toit, B. M. (1975), 'A Decision-Making Model for the Study of Migration', pp. 49–76 in B. M. Du Toit and H. I. Safa (eds.), *Migration and Urbanization: Models and Adaptive Strategies*, Mouton, The Hague.

Economic and Social Commission for Asia and the Pacific (ESCAP), Population Division (1981), *Migration, Urbanization and Development in Indonesia*, United Nations Economic and Social Commission for Asia and the Pacific, Bangkok.

Edmundson, W. C. (1977), 'Two Villages in Contrast, 1971–76', *Bulletin of Indonesian Economic Studies*, 13, 1: 95–110.

Edmundson, W. and Edmundson, S. (1983), 'A Decade of Village Development in East Java', *Bulletin of Indonesian Economic Studies*, 19, 2: 46–59.

Effendi, T. N. (1979), 'Pattern of Migration to an Industrial Area: A Case Study in Lhokseumawe, Aceh, Sumatra, Indonesia', *The Indonesian Journal of Geography*, 9, 37: 33–44.

Encyclopedia van Nederlandsch-Indie (1907–39), Nijhoff, The Hague and Leiden.

Esmara, H. (1975), 'Regional Income Disparities', *Bulletin of Indonesian Economic Studies*, 11, 1: 41–57.

Evans, J. (1984), 'The Growth of Urban Centres in Java since 1961', *Bulletin of Indonesian Economic Studies*, 20, 1: 44–57.

Evers, H. (1972), 'Preliminary Notes on Migration Patterns of a Sumatran Town', *Sumatra Research Bulletin*, 2, 1: 18–23.

Fei, J. C. H. and Ranis, G. (1964), *Development of the Labour Surplus Economy: Theory and Policy*, Richard C. Irwin, Homewood.

Findley, S. E. (1981), 'Rural Development Programmes: Planned Versus Actual Migration Outcomes', pp. 144–67 in United Nations, *Population Distribution Policies in Development Planning*, United Nations, New York.

Fischer, J. (1965), 'Indonesia', pp. 92–122 in J. S. Coleman (ed.), *Education and Political Development*, Princeton University Press, Princeton.

Fisher, C. A. (1964), *Southeast Asia*, Methuen, London.

——— (1967), 'Economic Myth and Geographical Reality in Indonesia', *Modern Asian Studies*, 1, 2: 155–89.

Forbes, D. (1981), 'Mobility and Uneven Development in Indonesia: A Critique of Explanations of Migration and Circular Migration', pp. 51–70 in G. W. Jones and H. V. Richter (eds.), *Population Mobility and Development: Southeast Asia and the Pacific*, Monograph No. 27, Development Studies Centre, Australian National University, Canberra.

Fox, J. J. (1977), *Harvest of the Palm: Ecological Change in Eastern Indonesia*, Harvard University Press, Cambridge.

Fox, J. J., Garnaut, R., McCawley, P. and Mackie, J. A. C. (1980), *Indonesia: Australian Perspectives*, Research School of Pacific Studies, Australian National University, Canberra.

Franke, R. (1972), 'The Green Revolution in a Javanese Village', unpublished Ph.D. thesis, Harvard University.

Freedman, R. (1979), 'Theories of Fertility Decline: A Reappraisal', in P. M. Hauser (ed.), *World Population and Development: Challenges and Prospects*, Syracuse University Press.

Freedman, R., Khoo, S. E. and Supraptilah, B. (1981), 'Modern Contraceptive Use in Indonesia: A Challenge to Conventional Wisdom', *World Fertility Survey Scientific Report* No. 20, ISI, Voorburg/WFS, London.

Friedman, J. and Douglass, M. (1978), 'Agropolitan Development: Towards a New Strategy for Regional Planning in Asia', pp. 163–92 in F. C. Lo and K. Salih (eds.), *Growth Pole Strategy and Regional Development Policy*, Pergamon, London.

Fryer, D. W. and Jackson, J. C. (1977), *Indonesia*, Ernest Benn, London.

Fuchs, R. J. and Demko, G. J. (1983), 'Rethinking Population Distribution Policies', *Population Research and Policy Review*, 2, 2: 161–87.

Fuchs, R. J., Jones, G. W. and Pernia, E. (eds.) (1987), *Urbanization and Urban Policies in the Asia-Pacific Region*, Westview Press, Boulder.

Furnivall, J. S. (1948), *Colonial Policy and Practice: A Comparative Study of Burma and*

Netherlands India, Cambridge University Press, Cambridge.

—— (1956), *Colonial Policy and Practice*, New York University Press, New York.

Gardiner, P. (1978), 'Age Patterns of Mortality in Indonesia (an Analysis of Results of the Indonesian Sample Vital Registration Project 1974–1977)', *Working Paper Series* No. 12, Pusat Penelitian dan Studi Kependudukan (Centre for Population Study and Research), Gadjah Mada University, Yogyakarta.

—— (1985), *Provincial Population Projections: Requirements, Methodology, Results*, Report T.4/C3, National Urban Development Strategy, Directorate General of Human Settlements, Department of Public Works and United Nations Centre for Human Settlements, Jakarta.

Gardiner, P. and Oey, M. (1983), 'Morbidity and Mortality in Java 1880–1940: The Evidence of the Colonial Reports', in N. G. Owen (ed.) (1987), *Death and Disease in Southeast Asia: Explorations in Social, Medical and Demographic History*, Oxford University Press, Singapore.

Geertz, C. (1960), *The Religion of Java*, The Free Press, Chicago.

—— (1963), *Agricultural Involution: The Processes of Ecological Change in Indonesia*, University of California Press, Berkeley.

—— (1973), 'Comments on Benjamin White's "Demand for Labour and Population Growth in Colonial Java"', *Human Ecology*, 1, 3: 237–9.

Geertz, H. (1983), 'Indonesian Cultures and Communities', pp. 24–96 in R. T. McVey (ed.), *Indonesia*, Human Relations Area Files, New Haven.

Geographical Handbook Series (1944), *Indonesia* (2 vols.), Admiralty Office, London.

Germani, G. (1965), 'Migration and Aculturation', in P. M. Hauser (ed.), *Handbook for Social Research in Urban Areas*, UNESCO, Paris.

Gerold-Scheepers, T. and Binsbergen, W. M. van (1978), 'Marxist and non-Marxist Approaches to Migration in Tropical Africa', *African Perspectives*, 1: 21–36.

Ginneken, W. van (1976), *Rural and Urban Income Inequalities in Indonesia, Mexico, Pakistan, Tanzania and Tunisia*, International Labour Office, Geneva.

Glassburner, B. (1986), 'Survey of Recent Developments', *Bulletin of Indonesian Economic Studies*, 22, 1: 1–33.

Goldstein, S. (1975) 'Urbanisation and Migration in Southeast Asia', pp. 69–92 in Y. Chang and P. J. Donaldson (eds.), *Population and Change in the Pacific Region*, 13th Pacific Science Congress, Vancouver.

Gregory, J. W. and Piche, V. (1978), 'African Migration and Peripheral Capitalism', *African Perspectives*, 1: 37–50.

—— (1980), *The Demographic Mechanisms of Underdevelopment, Illustrated with African Examples*, Center for Developing Areas Studies, McGill University, Montreal.

Haan, F. de (1935), *Oud Batavia* (2 vols.), G. Kolff, Batavia.

Habir, M. (1984), 'A Migration Equation', *Far Eastern Economic Review*, 26 April: 166–72.

Hageman, J. (1852), *Geschiedenis, Aardrijkskunde, Fabelleer En Tijdrekenkunde Van Java* (History, Geography, Mythology and Chronology of Java), Part II, Lange, Batavia.

Haggett, P. (1975), *Geography: A Modern Synthesis*, Harper and Row, New York.

Handoko, B. S. (1984), 'Rural–Urban Relation in a Nongrowing Growth Centre: The Cilacap Case Study', paper presented at Research Workshop on Urbanization and the Household Economy, Universiti Sains Malaysia, Penang, 15–16 August.

Hardjono, J. M. (1977), *Transmigration in Indonesia*, Oxford University Press, Kuala Lumpur.

—— (1986), 'Transmigration: Looking to the Future', *Bulletin of Indonesian Economic Studies*, 22, 2: 28–53.

Harris, J. (1979), 'Internal Migration in Indonesia', pp. 125–48 in J. W. White (ed.), *The Urban Impact of Internal Migration*, Institute for Research in Social Science, University of North Carolina, Chapel Hill.

Hart, G. (1978), 'Labour Allocation Strategies in Rural Javanese Households', unpublished Ph.D. thesis, Cornell University.

Hart, K. (1973), 'Informal Income Opportunities and Urban Employment in Ghana', *The Journal of Modern African Studies*, 2, 1: 61–89.

Harvey, B. S. (1974), 'Tradition, Islam and Rebellion: South Sulawesi 1950–1965', unpublished Ph.D. thesis, Cornell University.

Hasibuan, S. (1985), 'Pertumbuhan Ekonomi dan Kesempatan Kerja dalam Pelita IV: Beberapa Perkiraan' (Economic Growth and Employment Opportunities in Pelita IV: Some Estimates), *Ekonomi dan Keuangan Indonesia*, 33, 1: 75–104.

Hatmadji, S. H. and Achmad, S. I. (1984), *Analisa Fertilitas di Indonesia: Berdasarkan Data Sensus Penduduk 1980* (Fertility Analysis in Indonesia: Based on 1980 Population Census Data), Biro Pusat Statistik and Lembaga Demografi, Fakultas Ekonomi, Universitas Indonesia, Jakarta.

Hauser, P. M. (1974), 'The Measurement of Labour Utilisation', *Malayan Economic Review*, 19, 1: 1–15.

Hauser, P. M., Svits, D. B. and Ogawa, N. (1985), *Urbanization and Migration in Asean Development*, National Institute for Research Advancement, Tokyo.

Hawkins, E. D. (1966), 'Job Inflation in Indonesia', *Asian Survey*, 6, 5.

Hayami, Y. and Hafid, A. (1979), 'Rice Harvesting and Welfare in Rural Java', *Bulletin of Indonesian Economic Studies*, 15, 2: 94–112.

Heiby, J. R., Ness, G. D. and Pillsbury, B. (1979), *AID's Role in Indonesian Family Planning: A Case Study with General Lessons for Foreign Assistance*, AID Program Evaluation Report No. 2, USAID, Washington.

Heligman, L. (1975), *Levels and Trends of Mortality in Indonesia, 1961 to 1971*, US Bureau of the Census, Washington, DC.

Hendrata, L. (1981), 'A Model for Community Health Care in Rural Java', *Development Digest*, 19, 1: 107–14.

Hetler, C. B. (1984), 'Rural and Urban Female-Headed Households in Java: Results of a Village Study in Central Java', seminar paper presented at Department of Demography, Australian National University, December.

—— (1986), 'Female-Headed Households in a Circular Migration Village in Central Java, Indonesia', unpublished Ph.D. thesis, Department of Demography, The Australian National University.

Hidayat (1979), 'Sektor Informal dalam Struktur Ekonomi Indonesia' (The Informal Sector in the Structure of the Indonesian Economy), *Profil Indonesia*, Lembaga Studi Pembangunan (Institute of Development Studies), Jakarta.

Hinderink, J. and Sterkenburg, J. J. (1978), 'Spatial Inequality: An Attempt to Define the Concept', *Tijdschrift voor Economische en Sociale Geografie*, 69, 1–2: 5–16.

Hugo, G. J. (1974), 'Internal Migration and Urbanization in South Australia', pp. 81–98 in I. H. Burnley (ed.), *Urbanization in Australia—The Post War Experience*, Cambridge University Press, Cambridge.

—— (1975), 'Population Mobility in West Java, Indonesia', unpublished Ph.D. thesis, Department of Demography, Australian National University, Canberra.

—— (1978), *Population Mobility in West Java*, Gadjah Mada University Press, Yogyakarta.

—— (1979), 'Indonesia', chapters 14, 15 and 16 in R.J. Pryor (ed.), *Migration and Development in South-East Asia*, Oxford University Press, Kuala Lumpur.

—— (1980), 'Population Movements in Indonesia during the Colonial Period', pp. 95–135 in J.J. Fox, R.G. Garnaut, P.T. McCawley and J.A.C. Mackie (eds.), *Indonesia: Australian Perspectives*, Research School of Pacific Studies, Australian National University, Canberra.

—— (1981a), 'Levels, Trends and Patterns of Urbanization', pp. 57–80 in ESCAP, *Migration, Urbanization and Development in Indonesia*, Comparative Study on Migration, Urbanization and Development in the ESCAP Region, Country Reports III, United Nations, New York.

—— (1981b), 'Introduction', pp. 1–12 in ESCAP, *Migration, Urbanization and Development in Indonesia*, Comparative Study on Migration, Urbanization and Development in the ESCAP Region, Country Reports III, United Nations, New York.

—— (1981c), 'Patterns of Interprovincial Migration', pp. 81–110 in ESCAP, *Migration, Urbanization and Development in Indonesia*, Comparative Study on Migration, Urbanization and Development in the ESCAP Region, Country Reports III, United Nations, New York.

—— (1981d), 'Summary and Conclusions', pp. 157–62 in ESCAP, *Migration, Urbanization and Development in Indonesia*, Comparative Study on Migration, Urbanization and Development in the ESCAP Region, Country Reports III, United Nations, New York.

—— (1981e), 'Implications of the Imbalance in Age and Sex Composition of Sub Areas as a Consequence of Migration: The Case of a Rural Developing Nation—Indonesia', paper presented to International Union for the Scientific Study of Population, International Population Conference, Manila.

—— (1981f), 'Characteristics of Interprovincial Migrants', pp. 111–41 in ESCAP, *Migration, Urbanization and Development in Indonesia*, Comparative Study on Migration, Urbanization and Development in the ESCAP Region, Country Reports III, United Nations, New York.

—— (1981g), 'Village–Community Ties, Village Norms and Ethnic and Social Networks: A Review of Evidence from the Third World', pp. 186–224 in G.F. De Jong and R.W. Gardner (eds.), *Migration Decision Making*, Pergamon Press, New York.

—— (1981h), 'Road Transport, Population Mobility and Development in Indonesia', pp. 335–86 in G.W. Jones and H.V. Richter (eds.), *Population Mobility and Development: Southeast Asia and the Pacific*, Monograph No. 27, Development Studies Centre, Australian National University, Canberra.

—— (1982a), 'Sources of Internal Migration Data in Indonesia: Their Potential and Limitations', *Majalah Demografi Indonesia*, 17: 23–52.

—— (1982b), 'Circular Migration in Indonesia', *Population and Development Review*, 8, 1: 59–83.

—— (1982c), 'Evaluation of the Impact of Migration on Individuals, Households and Communities', pp. 189–215 in ESCAP, *National Migration Surveys Guidelines for Analyses*, Comparative Study on Migration, Urbanization and Development in the ESCAP Region, Survey Manuals X, United Nations, New York.

—— (1982d), 'Population Mobility, Urbanization and Development Planning Policy in Indonesia—Some Existing Data Sources and Needed Research', paper presented to meeting on Urbanization and National Development, East–West Population Institute, Honolulu, 26 January.

―――― (1983a), 'Migration and Urbanisation Trends in the 19th and Early 20th Centuries: With Particular Reference to West Java', paper prepared for Conference on Indonesian Economic History in the Dutch Colonial Period, Ursula College, Australian National University, 16–18 December.

―――― (1983b), 'New Conceptual Approaches to Migration in the Context of Urbanization: A Discussion Based on Indonesian Experience', pp. 69–114 in P. A. Morrison (ed.), *Population Movements: Their Forms and Functions in Urbanization and Development*, International Union for the Scientific Study of Population, Liege.

―――― (1983c), 'Postwar Involuntary Migrations within and between Southeast Asian Countries: A Review', paper prepared for Symposium on the Problems and Consequences of Refugee Migration in the Developing World, Population Commission of the International Geographical Union, Manitoba, Canada, 29 August–1 September.

―――― (1983d), 'Postwar Refugee Migration in Southeast Asia: Patterns, Problems and Policy Consequences', paper prepared for Symposium on the Problems and Consequences of Refugee Migration in the Developing World, IGU, Manitoba, Canada, 29 August–1 September.

―――― (1984), 'Recent Population Changes in Southeast Asia as Revealed by the 1980 Round of Censuses', paper presented to Fifth National Conference of the Asian Studies Association of Australia, Adelaide, 13–19 May.

―――― (1985), 'Structural Change and Labour Mobility in Rural Java', pp. 46–88 in G. Standing (ed.), *Labour Circulation and the Labour Process*, Croom Helm, London.

―――― (1986), 'Differences and Similarities Between Forced and Voluntary Migrations in Asia and Some Policy Implications', paper presented to International Seminar on People Affected by Uprootedness, organized by the United Nations Research Institute for Social Development, Palais des Nations, Geneva, 5–7 May.

Hugo, G. J. and Mantra, I. B. (1981), 'The Role of Small and Medium Towns and Cities in the Migration System in Indonesia', paper prepared for Fourth Pacific Science Inter-Congress Symposium on the Role of Small Towns, Singapore, 2 September.

Hull, T. H. (1975), 'Each Child Brings Its Own Fortune: An Enquiry into the Value of Children in a Javanese Village', unpublished Ph.D. thesis, Department of Demography, Australian National University, Canberra.

―――― (1978), 'Where Credit is Due: Policy Implications of the Recent Fertility Decline in Bali', paper presented at Annual Meeting of the Population Association of America, Atlanta.

―――― (1983), 'Variations of Program Outputs as an Index of Management of Effectiveness', Research Note No. 5, International Population Dynamics Program, Department of Demography, Australian National University, Canberra.

Hull, T. and Gubhaju, B. (1986), 'Multivariate Analysis of Infant and Child Mortality in Java and Bali', *Journal of Biosocial Science*, 18, 1: 109–18.

Hull, T. H. and Hull, V. J. (1984), 'Population Change in Indonesia: Findings of the 1980 Census', *Bulletin of Indonesian Economic Studies*, 20, 3: 95–119.

―――― (1985), 'Changing Marriage Behavior in Java', paper presented to the 1985 Annual Meeting of the Population Association of America, Boston, 28–30 March.

Hull, T. H., Hull, V. J. and Singarimbun, M. (1977), 'Indonesia's Family Planning Story: Success and Challenge', *Population Bulletin*, 32, 6, Population Reference Bureau, Inc., Washington, DC.

Hull, T. and Mantra, I. B. (1981), 'Indonesia's Changing Population', in A. Booth
    and P. McCawley (eds.), *The Indonesian Economy During the Soeharto Era*, Oxford
    University Press, Kuala Lumpur.
Hull, T. H. and Sunaryo (1978), 'Levels and Trends of Infant and Child Mortality
    in Indonesia', *Working Paper Series No. 15*, Population Institute, Gadjah Mada
    University, Yogyakarta.
_____ (1980), 'Difficulties of Measuring Achieved Schooling in Indonesia', *Asian
    and Pacific Census Forum*, 6, 3: 9–13.
Hull, V. (1977), 'Fertility, Women's Work and Economic Class: A Case Study from
    Southeast Asia', in S. Kupinsky (ed.), *The Fertility of Working Women: A Synthesis
    of International Research*, Praeger, New York.
Hydrick, J. (1937), *Intensive Rural Hygiene Work and Public Health Education of the
    Public Health Service of Netherlands India*, Public Health Service, Batavia.
India, Office of the Registrar General (1961), *Census of India 1961, Union Primary
    Census Abstracts*, 1, 2/a (ii), Office of the Registrar General: India.
Indonesia Times (1984), 11: 1, 12, 25 May.
Institute of Rural and Regional Studies (1977), *Seasonal Migrants and Commuters in
    Yogyakarta*, Institute of Rural and Regional Studies, Gadjah Mada University,
    Yogyakarta.
International Labour Office (ILO) (1974), *Sharing in Development: A Programme of
    Employment, Equity and Growth for the Philippines*, International Labour Office,
    Geneva.
Iskandar, N. (1970), *Some Monographic Studies on the Population in Indonesia*,
    Lembaga Demografi (Demographic Institute), Faculty of Economics, University
    of Indonesia, Jakarta.
Iskandar, P. and Rienks, A. (1981), 'Primary and Indigenous Health Care in Rural
    Central Java: A Comparison of Process and Contents', paper prepared for the
    IUAES Congress Symposium Anthropology and Primary Health Care, Amster-
    dam, 21–25 April.
Iskandar, P., Rienks, A. S., Sunarsih and Soesartono (1979), *Pengamatan Anthropol-
    ogis tentang Pembentukan dan Pelaksanaan Program Kader* (Anthropological Ob-
    servations on the Formation and Execution of Cadre Programs), HEDERA
    Report No. 2, Gadjah Mada University, Yogyakarta.
Jaffe, A. J. and Stewart, C. D. (1951), *Manpower Resources and Utilization*, John
    Wiley and Sons, New York.
Jellinek, L. (1977), 'The Pondok of Jakarta', *Bulletin of Indonesian Economic Studies*,
    13, 67–71.
_____ (1978), 'Circular Migration and the Pondok Dwelling System', in R. J.
    Rimmer *et al.* (eds.), *Food, Shelter and Transport in Southeast Asia and the Pacific*,
    Department of Human Geography, Australian National University, Canberra.
_____ (1985), 'Underview: Memories of Kebun Kacang, 1930s to 1980s', in S.
    Abeyasekere (ed.), *From Batavia to Jakarta: Indonesia's Capital 1930s to 1980s*,
    Centre for Southeast Asian Studies, Monash University, Melbourne.
Johansyah, M. (1979), 'Population Mobility in South Kalimantan', paper presented
    at Workshop on Population Mobility, Pusat Studi dan Penelitian Kependudukan
    (Centre for Population Study and Research), Gadjah Mada University, Yogya-
    karta, May.
Jones, G. W. (1966), 'The Growth and Changing Structure of the Indonesian
    Labour Force 1930–71', *Bulletin of Indonesian Economic Studies*, 4: 50–74.
_____ (1974), 'What Do We Know about the Labour Force in Indonesia?',
    Majalah Demografi Indonesia, 1, 2: 7–36.

—— (1975), *Population Growth and Educational Planning in Developing Nations*, Irvington, New York.

—— (1976), 'Religion and Education in Indonesia', *Indonesia*, 22: 36–56.

—— (1977a), *The Population of North Sulawesi*, Gadjah Mada University Press, Yogyakarta.

—— (1977b), 'Factors Affecting Labour Force Participation of Females in Jakarta', *Kajian Ekonomi Malaysia*, 14, 2: 71–93.

—— (1979), 'Indonesia: The Transmigration Programme and Development Planning', pp. 212–21 in R.J. Pryor (ed.), *Migration and Development in South-East Asia*, Oxford University Press, Kuala Lumpur.

—— (1980), 'Population Growth in Java', pp. 515–37 in R. G. Garnaut and P. T. McCawley (eds.), *Indonesia: Dualism, Growth and Poverty*, Research School of Pacific Studies, Australian National University, Canberra.

—— (1981), 'Labour Force Developments Since 1961', pp. 218–61 in A. Booth and P. McCawley (eds.), *The Indonesian Economy During the Soeharto Era*, Oxford University Press, Kuala Lumpur.

—— (1983), 'Structural Change and Prospects for Urbanization in Asian Countries', *Papers of the East–West Population Institute*, No. 88, East–West Center, Honolulu.

—— (ed.) (1984a), *Demographic Transition in Asia*, Maruzen Asia, Singapore.

—— (1984b), 'Evaluation of Population Policy in Non Socialist Southeast Asia', paper presented to Second Conference of the Australian Population Association, Sydney, December.

—— (1984c), 'Links Between Urbanization and Sectoral Shifts in Employment in Java', *Bulletin of Indonesian Economic Studies*, 20, 3: 120–57.

—— (1986), 'Differentials in Female Labour Force Participation Rates in Indonesia: Reflection of Economic Needs and Opportunities, Culture or Bad Data?', *Majalah Demografi Indonesia*, Tahun Ke XIII(26).

Jones, G.W., Nurhidayati, F.E., Simandjuntak and Prakosa, D. (1984), *Urbanization and Structural Change in Employment in Indonesia: Evidence from Province and Kabupaten—Level Analysis of 1971–1980 Census Data*, National Urban Development Strategy Report T1–4/C2, Department of Public Works, Jakarta.

Jones, G.W. and Richter, H.V. (eds.) (1982), *Population Resettlement Programs in Southeast Asia*, Monograph No. 30, Development Studies Centre, Australian National University, Canberra.

Jones, G.W. and Supraptilah, B. (1975), *Some Information on Urban Employment in Palembang and Ujung Pandang*, Lembaga Demografi (Demographic Institute), Faculty of Economics, University of Indonesia, Jakarta.

—— (1976), 'Underutilization of Labour in Palembang and Ujung Pandang', *Bulletin of Indonesian Economic Studies*, 12, 2: 30–57.

Jones, G.W. and Ward, R.G. (1981), 'Rural Labour Shortages in Southeast Asia and the Pacific: A Review of the Evidence', pp. 387–405 in G.W. Jones and H.V. Richter (eds.), *Population Mobility and Development: Southeast Asia and the Pacific*, Monograph No. 27, Development Studies Centre, Australian National University, Canberra.

Kadarusman, J. (1982), 'Infant and Childhood Mortality Differentials in Java and Bali', M.A. thesis, Department of Demography, Australian National University, Canberra.

Kamaluddin, S. (1982), 'Back to the Villages', *Far Eastern Economic Review*, 7 May: 35.

Kartomo, W. (1983), 'Patterns and Trends of Internal Migration and Urbanization in Indonesia and their Policy Implications', unpublished Ph.D. thesis, University of Indonesia, Jakarta.

Kasryno (ed.) (1983), *Prospek Pembangunan Ekonomi Pedesaan Indonesia*, Rural Dynamics Series, No. 23, Agro-Economic Survey, republished 1984, Yayasan Obor Indonesia, Jakarta.

Kasto (1983a), 'Perkiraan Tingkat Kematian Bayi di Indonesia' (Estimates of Infant Mortality Rates in Indonesia), pp. 162–72 in Biro Pusat Statistik, *Seminar on Infant Mortality Rate in Indonesia*, 1–3 February, Biro Pusat Statistik, Jakarta.

—— (1983b), 'Perkiraan Tingkat Kematian Bayi dan Faktor-Faktor Yang Mempengaruhi' (Estimates of Infant Mortality Levels and Factors Influencing Them), paper presented to the Third Congress of Ikatan Peminat dan Ahli Demografi Indonesia (*Ipadi*), Cisarua, Bogor, 4–7 October.

Katz, J. and Katz, R. (1978), 'Legislating Social Change in a Developing Country: The New Indonesian Marriage Law Revisited', *The American Journal of Comparative Law*, 26, 2: 309–20.

Keeley, C. B. (1981), 'Global Refugee Policy: The Case for a Development Oriented Strategy', The Population Council Public Issues Papers on Population, New York.

Keyfitz, N. (1953), 'The Population of Indonesia', *Ekonomi dan Keuangan Indonesia*, 6, 10: 640–55.

—— (1965), 'Age Distribution as a Challenge to Development', *American Journal of Sociology*, 70: 659–68.

—— (1972), 'Review of Widjojo Nitisastro's "Population in Indonesia"', *Economic Development and Cultural Change*, 20, 3: 606.

—— (1973), 'The Youth Cohort Revisited', in W. H. Wriggins and J. F. Guyot (eds.), *Population, Politics and the Future of Southern Asia*, Columbia University Press, New York.

—— (1985a), 'What Does Development Consist in: Observation of an East Javanese Village 1953–1985', mimeo., Jakarta.

—— (1985b), 'Indonesia's Future Population', mimeo., Jakarta.

—— (1985c), 'An East Javanese Village in 1953 and 1985: Observations on Development', *Population and Development Review*, 11, 4: 695–719.

Keyfitz, N. and Nitisastro, W. (1955), *Soal Penduduk dan Pembangunan Indonesia* (The Population Problem and Development in Indonesia), Pustaka Ekonomi, Jakarta.

Khoo, S. (1982), 'The Determinants of Modern Contraceptive Use in Indonesia: Analyses of the Effect of Program Effort', *East–West Population Institute Working Papers*, No. 23, East–West Center, Honolulu.

Khuda, B. (1977), 'Value of Children in a Bangladesh Village', in J. C. Caldwell (ed.), *The Persistence of High Fertility, Part 2*, Department of Demography, Australian National University, Canberra.

King, D. and Weldon, P. (1977), 'Income Distribution and Levels of Living in Java 1963–1970', *Economic Development and Cultural Change*, 25, 4: 699–711.

Kingsley, C. T., Gardiner, P. and Stolte, W. B. (1985), *Urban Growth and Structure in Indonesia*, National Urban Development Strategy Project, Report T1–6/C–3, Jakarta.

Knodel, J. (1977), 'Age Patterns of Fertility and the Fertility Transition: Evidence from Europe and Asia', *Population Studies*, 31, 2: 219–50.

Koentjaraningrat (1974), 'Mobilitas Penduduk sekitar Jakarta' (Population Mobility around Jakarta), *Masyarakat Indonesia*, 1, 2: 45–60.

—— (1975), 'Population Mobility in Villages around Jakarta', *Bulletin of Indonesian Economic Studies*, 11: 108–20.

Kraak, J. H. (1957), 'The Repatriation of Netherlands Citizens and Ambonese Soldiers from Indonesia', *Integration*, 4, 4: 345–55.

Kustadi (1984), 'Masalah Pertahanan di Daerah Pemukiman Transmigrasi' (Security Problems in Transmigration Receiving Areas), pp. 53–93 in R. Warsito *et al.*, *Transmigrasi: Dari Daerah Asal Sampai Benturan Budaya di Tempat Pemukiman* (Transmigration: From Area of Origin to Culture Clash in Receiving Areas), C. V. Rajawali, Jakarta.

Kuyvenhoven, Arie, and Huib Poot (1986), 'The Structure of Indonesian Manufacturing Industry: An Input–Output Approach', *Bulletin of Indonesian Economic Studies*, 22, 2: 54–79.

Kuznets, S. (1972), 'Problems in Comparing Recent Growth Rates for Developed and Less Developed Countries', *Economic Development and Cultural Change*, 20, 2: 185–209.

Lang, M. H. and Kolb, B. (1980), 'Locational Components of Urban and Regional Public Policy in Postwar Vietnam: The Case of Ho Chi Minh City (Saigon)', *Geojournal*, 4, 1: 13–18.

Leimena (1953), 'The Upbuilding of Public Health in Indonesia', in *Basic Information on Indonesia*, Ministry of Information, Jakarta.

Leinbach, T. R. (1983), 'Rural Transport and Population Mobility in Indonesia', *The Journal of Developing Areas*, 17: 349–64.

Leinbach, T. R. and Suwarno, B. (1985), 'Commuting and Circulation Characteristics in the Intermediate Sized City: The Example of Medan, Indonesia', *Singapore Journal of Tropical Geography*, 6, 1: 35–47.

Leiserson, M. *et al.* (1980), *Employment and Income Distribution in Indonesia*, The World Bank, Washington, DC.

Lembaga Demografi (1984), *Pola Pengendalan Tingkat Mobilitas Kependudukan Daerah Khusus Ibukota Jakarta 1983* (Patterns of Population Mobility in Jakarta 1983), Lembaga Demografi, Fakultas Ekonomi, Universitas Indonesia, Jakarta.

Lerman, C. (1983), 'Sex Differential Patterns of Circular Migration: A Case Study of Semarang, Indonesia', *Peasant Studies*, 10, 4: 251–69.

Lewis, W. A. (1954), 'Economic Development with Unlimited Supplies of Labour', Manchester School of Economic and Social Studies, 22 May, mimeo.

Lim Lin Lean (1982), 'Labour Shortages in the Rural Agricultural Sector of Peninsular Malaysia–A Search for Explanations and Solutions', Faculty of Economics and Administration, University of Malaya, mimeo.

–––––– (1985), 'The Impact of Immigration on the Labor Market Dynamics in Peninsular Malaysia', paper submitted for the IUSSP XXth General Conference, Session F. 12, Florence.

Lineton, J. (1975), 'Pasompe "Ugi": Bugis Migrants and Wanderers', *Archipel*, 10: 173–201.

Lipton, M. (1980), 'Migration from Rural Areas of Poor Countries: The Impact on Rural Productivity and Income Distribution', *World Development*, 8: 1–24.

–––––– (1982), 'Rural Development and the Retention of the Rural Population in the Countryside of Developing Countries', *Canadian Journal of Development Studies*, 3, 1.

Lo, F. C., Salih, K. and Douglas, M. (1978), 'Uneven Development, Rural–Urban Transformation and Regional Development Alternatives in Asia', paper presented to Seminar on Rural–Urban Transformation and Regional Development Planning, United Nations Centre for Regional Development, Nagoya, Japan.

Lucardie, G. R. E. (1979), 'The Makianese, Preliminary Remarks on the Anthropological Study of a Migration Oriented People in the Moluccas', paper presented to the Workshop on Research in Halmahera, Ternate, Indonesia, 10–20 July.

——— (1981), 'The Geographical Mobility of the Makianese: Migratory Traditions and Resettlement, mimeo.

MacAndrews, C., Fisher, H. B. and Sibero, A. (1982), 'Regional Development, Planning and Implementation in Indonesia: The Evolution of a National Policy', pp. 79–121 in C. MacAndrews and C. L. Sien (eds.), *Too Rapid Rural Development: Perceptions and Perspectives from Southeast Asia*, Ohio University Press, Athens.

Mahmudi (1974), *Beberapa Metode Penghitungan Net Migration* (Several Methods of Calculating Net Migration), Biro Pusat Statistik, Jakarta.

Mangunrai, H. (1979), *Migran Toraja di Kotamadya Ujung Pandang* (Torajan Migrants in Ujung Pandang Municipality), Universitas Hasanuddin Fakultas Ilmu-Ilmu Sosial dan Budaya, Ujung Pandang.

Manning, C. (1979), 'Wage Differentials and Labour Market Segmentation in Indonesian Manufacturing', unpublished Ph.D thesis, Australian National University, Canberra.

——— (1983), 'Labour Force and Employment in Indonesia', paper presented at the Third Congress of Ikatan Peminat dan Ahli Demografi Indonesia (Indonesian Demographic Association) (*Ipadi*), Cisarua, Bogor, 4–7 October.

——— (1986), 'The Green Revolution, Labour Displacement, Incomes and Wealth in Rural Java: A Reassessment of Trends During the Suharto Era', mimeo., The Flinders University, Adelaide.

Manning, C. and Papayungan, M. (eds.) (1984), *Analisa Ketenagakerjaan di Indonesia Berdasarkan Sensus Penduduk 1971 dan 1980* (Labour Force Analysis in Indonesia Based on the 1971 and 1980 Population Censuses), Biro Pusat Statistik, Jakarta.

Manning, C. and Soedarsono (1985), 'Employment Structure, Labour Markets and Wages in Indonesia', *ASEAN–Australia Working Paper*, No. 14, ASEAN–Australia Joint Research Project, Kuala Lumpur and Canberra.

Mantra, I. B. (1981), *Population Movement in Central Java*, Gadjah Mada University Press, Yogyakarta.

Margono, S. (1985), 'The Role of Depo Provers in the Indonesian Family Planning Program', unpublished MA thesis, Australian National University, Canberra.

Martin, L. G., Trussell, J., Salvail, F. R. and Shah, N. M. (1983), 'Covariates of Child Mortality in the Philippines, Indonesia and Pakistan: An Analysis Based on Hazard Models', *Population Studies*, 37, 3: 417–32.

Masri, M. (1963), 'Bogor sebagai Kota Forensa Kereta Api' (Bogor's Function as a Railway Based Dormitary), thesis in Geography, IKIP, Bandung.

Mather, C. (1983), 'Industrialization in the Tanggerang Regency of West Java: Women Workers and the Islamic Patriarchy', *Bulletin of Concerned Asian Scholars*, 15, 2: 2–17.

Maude, A. M. (1979), 'Intervillage Differences in Outmigration in West Sumatra', *Journal of Tropical Geography*, 49: 41–54.

——— (1980), 'How Circular is Minangkabau Migration?', *Indonesian Journal of Geography*, 9, 37: 1–12.

McCawley, P. (1981), 'The Growth of the Industrial Sector', pp. 62–101 in A. Booth and P. McCawley (eds.), *The Indonesian Economy During the Soeharto Era*, Oxford University Press, Kuala Lumpur.

McCawley, P. and Tait, M. (1979a), 'New Data on Employment in Manufacturing, 1970–1976', *Bulletin of Indonesian Economic Studies*, 15, 1: 125–36.

——— (1979b), 'Employment in Manufacturing, 1970–77: A Reply', *Bulletin of Indonesian Economic Studies*, 15, 3: 132–44.

McCutcheon, L. (1978), 'Occupation and Housing Adjustment of Migrants to Surabaya, Indonesia: The Case of a Second City', *International Migration Review*, 12, 1: 82–92.

McDonald, P. (1978), 'Adult Mortality in Indonesia: An Examination of Evidence from the 1961 and 1971 Censuses and the 1976 Intercensal Survey', paper prepared for the Indonesia Panel of the Committee on Population and Demography, National Research Council, Washington, DC.

_____ (1980), 'An Historical Perspective to Population Growth in Indonesia', in R. G. Garnaut and P. McCawley (eds.), *Indonesia: Dualism, Growth and Poverty*, Australian National University, Canberra.

_____ (1981), 'The Equality of Distribution of Child Mortality: Java–Bali, 1950–1976', *Bulletin of Indonesian Economic Studies*, 16, 3: 115–19.

_____ (n.d.), 'Mortality: An Overview of Child, Infant and Adult Mortality in Indonesia since 1960', mimeo.

McDonald, P., Yasin, M. and Jones, G. (1976), *Levels and Trends in Fertility and Childhood Mortality in Indonesia*, Indonesian Fertility–Mortality Survey 1973, Monograph No. 1, Lembaga Demografi (Demographic Institute), Faculty of Economics, University of Indonesia, Jakarta.

McDonald, P. F. and Sontosudarmo, A. (1976), *Response to Population Pressure: The Case of the Special Region of Yogyakarta*, Gadjah Mada University Press, Yogyakarta.

McGee, T. G. (1967), *The Southeast Asian City*, G. Bell and Sons, London.

_____ (1978), 'An Invitation to the "Ball"—Dress Formal or Informal?', in P. J. Rimmer, D. N. Drakakis-Smith and T. G. McGee (eds.), *Food, Shelter and Transport in Southeast Asia and the Pacific*, Department of Human Geography Publication, 6/12, Australian National University, Canberra.

McNicoll, G. (1968), 'Internal Migration in Indonesia: Descriptive Notes', *Indonesia*, 5: 29–92.

_____ (1984), 'Consequences of Rapid Population Growth: Overview and Assessment', *Population and Development Review*, 10, 2: 177–240.

McNicoll, G. and Mamas, S. G. (1973), 'The Demographic Situation in Indonesia', *East–West Population Institute Papers*, 28.

McNicoll, G. and Singarimbun, M. (1982), 'Fertility Decline in Indonesia', *Population Council Center for Policy Studies Working Papers*, No. 92 and 93 (Vols. I and II), The Population Council, New York.

_____ (1983), *Fertility Decline in Indonesia: Analysis and Interpretation*, Committee on Population and Demography, Report No. 20, National Academy Press, Washington, DC.

Mears, L. A. (1982), *The New Rice Economy of Indonesia*, Gadjah Mada University Press, Yogyakarta.

_____ (1985), 'A New Approach to Indonesian Food Crop Planning', *Ekonomi dan Keuangan Indonesia*, 33, 1: 47–57.

Meng-Try, Ea (1981), 'Kampuchea: A Country Adrift', *Population and Development Review*, 7, 2: 209–28.

Mertens, W. (1978), 'The Evaluation of the Agricultural Labor Force of Indonesia between 1930 and 1970', *Majalah Demografi Indonesia*, 9.

Mertens, W. and Alatas, S. (1978), 'Rural Urban Definition and Urban Agriculture in Indonesia', *Majalah Demografi Indonesia*, 10: 40–70.

Meyer, P. A. and MacAndrews, C. (1978), *Transmigration in Indonesia: An Annotated Bibliography*, Gadjah Mada University Press, Yogyakarta.

Milone, P. D. (1964), 'Contemporary Urbanization in Indonesia', *Asian Survey*, 4, 8: 1000–12.

——— (1966), *Urban Areas in Indonesia*, University of California Press, Berkeley.

Missen, G.J. (1972), *Viewpoint on Indonesia: A Geographical Study*, Nelson, Melbourne.

Mitchell, D. (1982), 'Primary Health Care Programs in Indonesia', paper presented to the Conference of the Australian Population Association, Canberra, November.

Moir, H. (1980), 'Economic Activities of Women in Rural Java: Are the Data Adequate?', *Occasional Paper No. 20*, Development Studies Centre, Australian National University, Canberra.

Montgomery, R. and Sugito, T. (1980), 'Changes in the Structure of Farms and Farming in Indonesia Between Censuses, 1963–1973: The Issues of Inequality and Near Landlessness', *Journal of Southeast Asian Studies*, 11, 2: 348–65.

Mudjiman, H. (1978), 'Consequences of Recurrent Movement on the Family at the Place of Origin: A Comparative Case Study of Two Villages around Surakarta', mimeographed research proposal, University of Surakarta.

Munir, R., Utomo, B., Nurdin, H. and Dasvarma, G. (1983), *Perkiraan Angka Kematian Berdasarkan Data Sensus dan Survei: Laporan Pengataran dan Lokakarya* (Estimates of Mortality Based on Census and Survey Data: Report of a Seminar and Workshop), Lembaga Demografi (Demographic Institute), Faculty of Economics, University of Indonesia and Ford Foundation, Jakarta.

Murad, A. (1980), *Merantau: Outmigration in a Matrilineal Society of West Sumatra*, Indonesian Population Monograph Series No. 3, Department of Demography, Australian National University, Canberra.

Myrdal, G. (1968), *Asian Drama*, Pantheon, New York.

Nag, M., Peet, R.C. and White, B. (1977), 'Economic Value of Children in Two Peasant Societies', *International Population Conference, Mexico 1977*, International Union for the Scientific Study of Population, Liege.

Naim, M. (1971), 'Merantau: Causes and Effects of Minangkabau Voluntary Migration', *Occasional Papers No. 5*, Institute of Southeast Asian Studies, Singapore.

——— (1973), 'Merantau: Minangkabau Voluntary Migration', unpublished Ph.D. thesis, University of Singapore.

——— (1976), 'Voluntary Migration in Indonesia', pp. 148–83 in A.H. Richmond and D. Kubat (eds.), *Internal Migration: The New World and the Third World*, Sage, London.

——— (1979), *Merantau: Pola Migrasi Suku Minangkabau* (Merantau: Migration Patterns of the Minangkabau Group), Gadjah Mada University Press, Yogyakarta.

National Research Council (1986), *Population Growth and Economic Development: Policy Questions*, National Academy Press, Washington.

National Urban Development Strategy Project (NUDSP) (1985a), *Analysis of Urban Growth and Structure*, Directorate of City and Regional Planning, Department of Public Works, Jakarta.

——— (1985b), *NUDS Final Report*, Directorate of City and Regional Planning, Department of Public Works, Jakarta.

Niddrie, D. (1954), 'The Road to Work: A Survey of the Influence of Transport on Migrant Labour in Central Africa', *Rhodes-Livingstone Journal*, 15: 31–42.

Nortman, D.L. (1982), *Population and Family Planning Programs: A Compendium of Data Through 1981*, The Population Council, New York.

Notestein, F.W. (1945), 'Population: The Long View', in T.W. Schultz (ed.), *Food for the World*, University of Chicago Press, Chicago.

Oey, M. (1985), 'The Role of Manufacturing in Labor Absorption: Indonesia During the 1970s', in P.M. Hauser, D.B. Svits and N. Ogawa, *Urbanization and*

Migration in Asean Development, National Institute for Research Advancement, Tokyo.

Oey, M. and Gardiner, P. (1983), 'Beberapa Catatan Mengenai Pertumbuhan Penduduk yang Bekerja di Indonesia 1971–1980' (Notes Concerning the Growth of the Working Population in Indonesia 1971–1980), paper presented at the Third Congress of Ikatan Peminat dan Ahli Demografi Indonesia (*Ipadi*), Cisarua, Bogor, 4–7 October.

Olson, M. E. (1979), 'Refugees as a Special Case of Population Redistribution', pp. 130–51 in L. A. P. Gosling and L. Y. C. Lim (eds.), *Population Redistribution: Patterns, Policies and Prospects*, United Nations Fund for Population Activities, New York.

Ormeling, F. J. (1956), *The Timor Problem: A Geographical Interpretation of an Underdeveloped Island*, J. B. Wolters, Jakarta and Groningen.

Oshima, H. T. (1983), 'The Industrial and Demographic Transitions in East Asia', *Population and Development Review*, 9, 4: 583–607.

Otten, M. (1986), '"Transmigrasi": From Poverty to Bare Subsistence', *The Ecologist*, 16, 2/3: 71–6.

Paauw, D. S. (1981), 'Frustrated Labour-Intensive Development: The Case of Indonesia', in E. Lee (ed.) *Export-led Industrialisation and Development*, Maruzen, Singapore.

Palmer, I. (1976), 'Rural Poverty in Indonesia with Special Reference to Java', *Working Paper*, ILO World Employment Programme Research, Geneva.

Papanek, G. F. (1975), 'The Poor of Jakarta', *Economic Development and Cultural Change*, 24, 1: 1–27.

——— (1980), 'Income Distribution and the Politics of Poverty', pp. 56–70 in G. F. Papanek (ed.), *The Indonesian Economy*, Praeger, New York.

——— (1985), 'Agricultural Income Distribution and Employment in the 1970s', *Bulletin of Indonesia Economic Studies*, 21, 2: 24–50.

Peluso, N. L. (1979), 'Putting People into Boxes, or Building Boxes around People?: Approaches to Designing Occupational Categories for Java', *Working Paper Series No. 19*, Pusat Penelitian dan Studi Kependudukan (Centre for Population Study and Research), Gadjah Mada University, Yogyakarta.

Pelzer, K. J. (1946), 'Tanah Sabrang and Java's Population Problem', *Far Eastern Quarterly*, 5, 2: 137–8.

——— (1963), 'Physical and Human Resource Patterns', pp. 1–23 in R. McVey (ed.) *Indonesia*, HRAF, New Haven.

Penny, D. H. and Singarimbun, M. (1973), *Population and Poverty in Rural Java: Some Economic Arithmetic from Sriharjo*, Cornell International Agricultural Development Mimeograph 41, Ithaca, New York.

Peper, B. (1970), 'Population Growth in Java in the 19th Century: A New Interpretation', *Population Studies*, 24, 1: 71–84.

Perera, L. N. and Budianti, S. (1977), *Economic Growth and the Distribution of Income in Indonesia 1970–1976*, United Nations Project INS/72/002, Jakarta.

Population Reference Bureau (1984), *World Population Data Sheet*, Population Reference Bureau, Washington, DC.

——— (1985), *World Population Data Sheet*, Population Reference Bureau, Washington, DC.

Radial, M. (1965), *Rencana Kota Serang* (Plan for the Town of Serang), Direktorat Perencanaan Kota Dan Daerah, Departmen Cipta Karya Dan Konstruksi, Jakarta.

Raffles, T. S. (1965), *The History of Java*, Oxford University Press, Kuala Lumpur (originally published in 1817).

Rahardjo, C.B. (1984), 'Benturan Sosial dan Budaya di Daerah Pemukiman Transmigrasi' (Social and Cultural Clashes in Transmigration Settlement Areas), pp. 143–85 in R. Warsito *et al.*, *Transmigrasi: Dari Daerah Asal Sampai Benturan Budaya di Tempat Pemukiman*, C.V. Rajawali, Jakarta.

Rambe, A. (1977), *Urbanisasi Orang Alabio di Banjarmasin* (Urbanization of People from Alabio in Banjarmasin), Faculty of Economics, Lambung Mankurat University, Banjarmasin.

Ranneft, J.M. (1916), 'Volksverplaatsing op Java' (Population Movements in Java), *Tijdschrift voor het Binnenlandsch Bestuur*, 49: 59–87, 165–84.

―――― (1929), 'The Economic Structure of Java', pp. 71–84 in B. Schrieke (ed.), *The Effect of Western Influence on Native Civilizations*, G. Kolff, The Hague.

Ravenstein, E.C. (1885), 'The Laws of Migration', *Journal of the Royal Statistical Society*, Vol. 1, 48, 2: 167–227.

Reid, A.J.S. (1980), 'The Structure of Cities in Southeast Asia, Fifteenth to Seventeenth Centuries', *Journal of Southeast Asian Studies*, 11, 2: 235–50.

―――― (ed.) (1983a), *Slavery, Bondage and Dependency in Southeast Asia*, University of Queensland Press, St. Lucia.

―――― (1983b), 'Low Population Growth and its Causes in Pre-Colonial Southeast Asia', seminar paper prepared for the Workshop on Java's Population Growth, Canberra, December.

Renaud, B. (1981), *National Urbanisation Policies in Developing Countries*, Oxford University Press, Oxford.

Repetto, Robert (1986), 'Soil Loss and Population Pressure on Java', *Ambio*, Vol. XV, No. 1, pp. 14–18.

Rhoda, R.E. (1980), 'Development Activities and Rural–Urban Migration', *Development Digest*, 18, 4: 3–21.

Riddell, J.B. (1980), 'African Migration and Regional Disparities', p. 114–34 in R.N. Thomas and J.M. Hunter (eds.), *Internal Migration Systems in the Developing World*, G.K. Hall, Boston.

Rodgers, G. (1984), *Poverty and Population: Approaches and Evidence*, International Labour Office, Geneva.

Rodgers, P. (1979), 'Where Have All the People Gone?', *Advertiser* (Adelaide), 5 November: 5.

―――― (1981), 'The Timor Debate Goes On', *Far Eastern Economic Review*, 6 February: 16–18.

Roepstorff, T.M. (1985), 'Industrial Development in Indonesia: Performance and Prospects', *Bulletin of Indonesian Economic Studies*, 21, 1: 32–61.

Roosman, R.S. (1980), 'Irian Jaya Refugees: The Problem of Shared Responsibility', *Indonesian Quarterly*, 8, 2: 83–9.

Ross, J. and Poedjastoeti, S. (1983), 'Contraceptive Use and Program Development: New Information from Indonesia', *International Family Planning Perspectives*, 9, 3: 68–77.

Rumbiak, M.C. (1978), *Urbanisasi Orang Genyem di Kota Jayapura: Suatu Studi Tentang Alasan Urbanisasi dan Kenyataan Hidup Para Inmigran* (Urbanization of the Genyem People in Jayapura: A Study of Reasons for Urbanization and the Living Situation of Inmigrants), Universitas Cenderawasih, Jayapura.

―――― (1979), 'Population Mobility in Irian Jaya', paper presented at Workshop on Population Mobility, Pusat Penelitian dan Studi Kependudukan (Centre for Population Study and Research), Gadjah Mada University, Yogyakarta, May.

―――― (1985), 'Nimboran Migration to Jayapura, Irian Jaya', in M. Chapman and

P. S. Morrison (eds.), 'Mobility and Identity in the Island Pacific', special issue of *Pacific Viewpoint*, 26, 1: 206–20.

Rusli, S. (1978), 'Inter-rural Migration and Circulation in Indonesia: The Case of West Java', unpublished MA thesis in Demography, Development Studies Centre, The Australian National University, Canberra.

Sacerdoti, G. (1977), 'Help for Java's Drought Victims', *Far Eastern Economic Review*, 98, 43: 48–9.

Salih, K. (1982), 'Urban Dilemmas in South-East Asia', *Singapore Journal of Tropical Geography*, 3, 2.

Sawit, M. H. *et al.* (1979), *Rural Dynamics Study Report 1977/1978*, Bogor.

Sayogyo (1978), 'Garis Kemiskinan dan Kebutuhan Minimum Pangan' (The Poverty Line and Minimum Food Needs), *Kompas*, 18, 11, May.

Secrett, C. (1986), 'The Environmental Impact of Transmigration', *The Ecologist*, 16, 2/3: 77–86.

Sethuraman, S. V. (1976), 'The Urban Informal Sector: Concept, Measurement and Policy', *International Labour Review*, 114, 1: 69–81.

Shah, N. M. and Shah, M. A. (1980), 'Trends and Structure of Female Labour Force Participation in Rural and Urban Pakistan', *East–West Population Institute Reprint*, No. 121.

Shaplan, T. (1974), 'Letter From Indonesia', *The New Yorker*, 1 April: 57–90.

Sie Kurat Soen (1968), *Prospects for Agricultural Development in Indonesia, with Special Reference to Java*, 2 February, Wageningen.

Siegel, J. T. (1969), *The Rope of God*, University of California Press, Berkeley.

Sigit, H. (1977), 'The Intercensal Population Survey, the National Socio-Economic Survey', *Majalah Demografi Indonesia*, No. 7.

―――― (1985), 'Income Distribution and Household Characteristics', *Bulletin of Indonesian Economic Studies*, 21, 3: 51–68.

Simmons, A. B. (1983), 'Rural Development and Population Retention: China and Cuba', paper presented at the Population Association of America meetings, Pittsburg, 14–16 May.

Sinaga, R. S. (1978), 'Implications of Agricultural Mechanization for Employment and Income Distribution: A Case Study from Indramayu, West Java', *Rural Dynamics Papers*, Series No. 2, Bogor.

Singahanetra-Renard, A. (1984), *Indonesian Overseas Contract Labour*, mimeo.

Singarimbun, M. (1968), 'Family Planning in Indonesia', *Bulletin of Indonesian Economic Studies*, 6, 3: 102–5.

―――― (1976), 'Sriharjo Revisited', *Bulletin of Indonesian Economic Studies*, 12, 2: 117–25.

Singarimbun, M. and Manning, C. (1974), *Fertility and Family Planning in Mojolama*, Gadjah Mada University, Yogyakarta.

Slater, D. (1975), 'Underdevelopment and Spatial Inequality', *Progress in Planning*, 4, 2: 139–46.

Smith, T. M. and Carpenter, H. F. (1974), 'Indonesian University Students and Their Career Aspirations', *Asian Survey*, 14, 9: 807–26.

Soedjatmoko, Ali, M., Resink, G. J. and Kahin, G. McT. (1965), *An Introduction to Indonesian Historiography*, Cornell University Press, Ithaca.

Soemantri, S. (1983a), 'Pola Perkembangan dan Perbandingan antara Daerah Angka Kematian Bayi' (Pattern of Development and Regional Comparisons of Infant Death Rates), pp. 173–92 in *Seminar Tingkat Kematian Bayi di Indonesia*, 1–3 February, Biro Pusat Statistik, Jakarta.

―――― (1983b), 'Hubungan antara Angka Kematian Bayi dan Berbagai Variabel

Upaya Kesehatan dan Sosial Ekonomi' (The Relation Between Infant Mortality and a Variety of Health and Socio-economic Variables), paper presented to the Third Congress of Ikatan Peminat dan Ahli Demografi Indonesia (Indonesian Demographic Association) (*Ipadi*), Cisarua, Bogor, 4–7 October.

Soemantri, S. and Bachroen, C. (1985), 'Tingkat Kesakitan dan Pencarian Pertolongan Pengobatan Masyarakat di Jawa Timur' (Illness Rates and Patterns of Seeking Health Care in East Java), pp. 287–327 in *Analisa Kependudukan Berdasarkan Data Sensus Penduduk 1980, Buku 1 (Jawa)*, Biro Pusat Statistik, Jakarta.

Soemantri, S., Bachroen, C. and Aisah, S. (1984), 'Variasi Angka Kematian Bayi Menurut Daerah di Pulau Jawa' (Variations in Infant Mortality by Region in Java), mimeo., Health Research and Development Board, Department of Health, Surabaya.

Soemarwoto, O. (1985), *Ekologi Lingkungan Hidup dan Pembangunan (Ecology, Environment and Development)*, Penerbit Djambatan, Jakarta.

Soemarwoto, O. and Soemarwoto, I. (1984), 'The Javanese Rural Ecosystem', in A. T. Rambo and P. E. Sajise (eds.), *An Introduction to Human Ecology Research on Agricultural Ecosystems in Southeast Asia*, University of the Philippines Press, Los Banos.

Soetrisno, L. (1985), 'Peranan Transmigrasi dalam Stabilitas Sosial Politik Daerah Perbatasan dan Problematiknya: Kasus Irian Jaya' (The Rate of Transmigration in Social and Political Stability in Border Areas and its Problems: The Case of Irian Jaya), pp. 115–27 in S. Swasono and M. Singarimbun (eds.), *Sepuluh Windu Transmigrasi di Indonesia 1905–1985*, University of Indonesia Press, Jakarta.

Speare, A. (1975), 'Quasi Stable Population Methods for Adjusting Age Distributions in Indonesia', paper presented at ESCAP Expert Working Group Meeting on Population Projections, Bangkok, September–October.

———— (1976a), 'Labour Utilization Among Recent Urban Migrants in Indonesia', paper presented at CAMS-ODA Seminar on Labour Supply, Manila, June.

———— (1976b), *Summary Report: Projections of Population and Labour Force for Regions of Indonesia 1970–2005*, LEKNAS, Jakarta.

Steele, R. (1981), 'Origin and Occupational Mobility of Lifetime Migrants to Surabaya, East Java', unpublished Ph.D. thesis in Geography, Australian National University, Canberra.

Stoler, A. (1975), 'Some Socio-economic Aspects of Rice Harvesting in a Javanese Village', *Masyarakat Indonesia*, 2, 1: 51–88.

———— (1977), 'Class Structure and Female Autonomy in Rural Java', *Signs: Journal of Women's Culture and Society*, 3, 1: 74–89.

Streatfield, P. K. (1985), 'A Comparison of Census and Family Planning Program Data on Contraceptive Prevalence, Indonesia', *Studies in Family Planning*, 16, 6, Pt. 1: 342–50.

Strout, A. M. (1981), 'Seasonal Factors and Rural Employment in Java', mimeo.

Suharso (1976), *Rural–Urban Migration in Indonesia*, LEKNAS-LIPI Monograph Series, Jakarta.

Suharso, Speare, A., Redmana, H. R. and Husin, I. (1976), *Rural–Urban Migration in Indonesia*, LEKNAS, Jakarta.

Suharto, S. and Sigit, H. (1977), 'Keadaan Kependudukan dan Ketenagakerjaan di Indonesia' (Population and Labour Force Situation in Indonesia), paper presented at Seminar Nasional Tentang Kependudukan dan Kesempatan Kerja, Jakarta, December.

Suharto, S. and Way, A. (1975), *The Effect of Household Socioeconomic Status on Fertility and Child Mortality Levels*, Biro Pusat Statistik, Jakarta.

Suhartoko (1975), *Merantau Bagi Orang Wajo* (Merantau among the Wajo People), Pusat Latihan Penelitian Ilmu-Ilmu Sosial (Centre for Social Science Research Training), Hasanuddin University, Ujung Pandang.

Suhrke, A. (1981), 'Global Refugee Movements and Strategies: An Overview', paper presented to the Wingspread Workshop on Immigration and Refugees, sponsored by the Rockefeller, Ford and Johnson Foundations.

Sumitro, D. (1977), 'Strategic Variables in Indonesia's Long Term Growth', *Ekonomi dan Keuangan Indonesia*, 25, 1: 17–33.

Sundrum, R.M. (1975a), 'Manufacturing Employment', *Bulletin of Indonesian Economic Studies*, 9, 1: 58–65.

—— (1975b), 'Unemployment in Indonesia: Analysis of Census Data', *Ekonomi dan Keuangan Indonesia*, 23, 3: 261–68.

—— (1976), 'Interprovincial Migration', *Bulletin of Indonesian Economic Studies*, 12, 1: 70–92.

—— (1979), 'Income Distribution 1970–1976', *Bulletin of Indonesian Economic Studies*, 15, 1: 137–41.

Supas (1976), 'Intercensal Population Survey, 1977', *Demography of the Indonesian Population*, Biro Pusat Statistik, Jakarta.

Supraptilah, B. and Suradji, B. (1979), 'Pengaruh Perbedaan Sosio-ekonomi Terhadap Mortalitas Masa Kanak-Kanak di Indonesia' (The Influence of Socio-economic Differences on Childhood Mortality in Indonesia), Lembaga Demografi (Demographic Institute), Faculty of Economics, University of Indonesia, Jakarta.

Suratha, I.G.W. (1977), *Tukang Mebel Toraja Ujung Pandang* (Toradjanese Furniture Makers in Ujung Pandang), Pusat Latihan Penelitian Ilmu-Ilmu Sosial (Centre for Social Science Research Training), Hasanuddin University, Ujung Pandang.

Susenas (National Social and Economic Survey) (1968), 'Perpindahan Penduduk Indonesia: Djawa–Madura, Luar Djawa Ketjuali DCI Djakarta, Nusa Tenggara Timur, Maluku, Irian Barat', *Susenas*, tahap kedua (Migration of the Population of Indonesia: Java–Madura Excluding Jakarta, East Nusa Tenggara, Maluku and West Irian: National Social and Economic Survey—Second Stage), November 1964–February 1968, Biro Pusat Statistik, Jakarta.

—— (1970), 'Perpindahan Penduduk Djawa–Madura', *Susenas*, tahap ketiga (Migration of the Population of Java–Madura, National Social and Economic Survey—Third Stage), September 1967–October 1967, Biro Pusat Statistik, Jakarta.

—— (1976), *Survey Sosial Ekonomi Tahap Ke-Lima (Januari–April 1976) Pengeluaran Untuk Konsumpsi Penduduk* (National Social and Economic Survey, Fifth Stage, January–April 1976, Peoples Expenditure on Consumption), Biro Pusat Statistik, Jakarta.

Sutarsih, M.K. (1976), *Berbagai Aspek Perbedaan Pola Perkawinan di Indonesia Dewasa Ini* (Some Aspects of Contemporary Patterns of Marriage in Indonesia), Lembaga Demografi (Demographic Institute), Faculty of Economics, University of Indonesia, Jakarta.

Temple, G.P. (1974), 'Migration to Jakarta: Empirical Search for a Theory', unpublished Ph.D. thesis, University of Wisconsin, Madison.

Thijsse, J.P. (1975), 'Perlu Tindakan Segra thd Penggundulan Hutan dan Erosi di Jawa' (Immediately Needed Measures Regarding Forest Removal and Erosion in

Java), *Sinar Harapan*, 30 October.

Thomas, D.S. (1938), *Research Memorandum on Migration Differentials*, Bulletin 43, Social Science Research Council, New York.

Timmer, C.P. (1973), 'Choice of Technique in Rice Milling in Java', *Bulletin of Indonesian Economic Studies*, 9, 2: 57–76.

Timmer, M. (1961), *Child Mortality and Population Pressure in the D.I. Jogjakarta, Java, Indonesia: A Socio-Medical Study*, Bronder-Offset, Rotterdam.

Tinbergen, J. (1974), 'Demographic Development and the Exhaustion of Natural Resources', paper delivered at Annual Meeting of the Population Association of America, New York City, April 1971.

Titus, M.J. (1978a), 'Inter-regional Migration in Indonesia as a Reflection of Social and Regional Inequalities', *Tijdschrift voor Economisch en Sociale Geografie*, 69, 4: 194–204.

———— (1978b), *Migrasi Antar Daerah di Indonesia Sebagai Cerminan Ketimpangan Regional dan Sosial* (Interregional Migration in Indonesia as a Reflection of Social and Regional Inequalities), Translation Series No. C12, Pusat Penelitian dan Studi Kependudukan (Centre for Population Research and Study), Gadjah Mada University, Yogyakarta.

Todaro, M.P. (1981), *Economic Development in the Third World* (2nd ed.), Longman, New York.

Trussell, J. and Pebley, A. (1984), 'The Potential Impact of Changes in Fertility on Infant, Child and Maternal Mortality', *Studies in Family Planning*, 15, 6, Pt. 1: 267–80.

United Nations, Department of Economic and Social Affairs (1962), 'Sex and Age Patterns of Participation in Economic Activities', *Population Studies*, No. 33, New York.

———— (1970), 'Methods of Measuring Internal Migration', *Population Studies*, No. 47, New York.

———— (1985), 'World Population Prospects, Estimates and Projections as Assessed in 1982', *Population Studies*, No. 86, New York.

USAID (1984), *Indonesia Family Planning Program Orientation Booklet*, USAID Office of Population and Health, Jakarta.

Utomo, B. (1982), 'Mortality Trends and Differentials in Indonesia 1950–1975', pp. 297–325 in L. Ruzicka (ed.), *Mortality in South and East Asia: A Review of Changing Trends and Patterns 1950–1975*, World Health Organization and ESCAP, Manila.

———— (1983a), 'Socio-economic Differentials in Morbidity and Mortality: A Study of Six Villages of Indonesia in 1980', paper prepared for Seminar on Social Policy, Health Policy and Mortality Prospects, IUSSP-INED, Paris, 28 February–4 March.

———— (1983b), 'Prospek angka Kematian Bayi dan Anak di Indonesia Menjelang Tahun 2000' (Prospects for Infant and Child Mortality Rates from Now to the Year 2000), paper presented to the Third Congress of the Ikatan Peminat dan Ahli Demografi Indonesia (Indonesian Demographic Association) (*Ipadi*), Bogor, 4–7 October.

Utomo, B., Adioetomo, S.M. and Hatmadji, S.H. (1986), 'Trends and Differentials in Infant and Child Mortality in Indonesia in the 1970s', pp. 489–507 in H. Hansluwka *et al.* (eds.), *New Developments in the Analysis of Mortality and Causes of Death*, Mahidol University and the World Health Organization, Bangkok.

Utomo, B. and Iskandar, M.B. (1984), 'Socio-economic Differentials in Infant and Child Mortality in Indonesia in the 1970s: Trends, Causes and Implications', paper presented to the IUSSP/NIRA Joint Seminar on Social and Biological Correlates of Mortality, Tokyo, Japan, 24–27 November.

Vandenbosch, A. (1944), *The Dutch East Indies*, California University Press, Berkeley.

van de Walle, E. (1966), 'Some Characteristic Features of Census Age Distributions in Illiterate Populations', *American Journal of Sociology*, 71: 549–55.

—— (1973), 'Comments on Benjamin White's "Demand for Labor and Population Growth in Colonial Java"', *Human Ecology*, 1, 3: 241–4.

van de Walle, E. and Knodel, J. (1980), 'Europe's Fertility Transition: New Evidence and Lessons for Today's Developing World', *Population Bulletin*, 34, 6.

van Setten van der Meer, N. C. (1979), *Sawah Cultivation in Ancient Java: Aspects of Development during the Indo-Javanese Period, 5th to 15th Century*, Australian National University, Canberra.

Van Thiel, P. H. (1971), 'History of Endemic Diseases in the Netherlands Overseas Territories', *Annales des Societes Belges de Medicine Tropicale*, 52, 4–5: 443–58.

Visaria, P. (1974), 'Population, Labour Force and Transmigration in Indonesia', mimeo.

Vlekke, Bernard H. M. (1943), *Nusantara: A History of Indonesia*, Harvard University Press, Cambridge, Revised edition, 1958 (reprinted 1965), W. van Hoeve, The Hague.

Volkstelling (Population Census) (1933–6), *Definitieve Uitkomsten Van de Volkstelling 1930* (8 vols.), Departement van Landbouw, Nijverheid en Handel, Batavia.

Vredenbregt, J. (1964), 'Bawean Migrations', *Bijdragen tot de Taal-Land-en Volkenkunde*, 120: 109–30.

Wander, H. (1965), *Die Beziehungen Zwischen Bevolkerungs-und-Wirtschaftsentwicklung, Dargestellt am Beispiel Indonesiens* (The Links Between Settlement and Economic Development: Illustrated by the Indonesian Case), J. C. B. Mohr, Tubingen.

Ward, M. W. and Ward, R. G. (1974), 'An Economic Survey of West Kalimantan', *Bulletin of Indonesian Economic Studies*, 10, 3: 26–53.·

Waterson, A. (1972), *Development Planning: Lessons of Experience*, Johns Hopkins University Press, Baltimore.

White, B. (1973), 'Demand for Labour and Population Growth in Colonial Java', *Human Ecology*, 1, 3: 217–36.

—— (1974), 'Reply to Geertz and van de Walle', *Human Ecology*, 2, 1: 63–5.

—— (1976a), 'Production and Reproduction in a Javanese Village', unpublished Ph.D. thesis, Department of Anthropology, Columbia University.

—— (1976b), 'Population, Involution and Employment in Rural Java', *Development and Change*, 7: 267–90.

—— (1977), 'Political Aspects of Poverty, Income Distribution and its Measurement: Some Examples from Rural Java', paper presented at Asia Society Seminar on New Measures for New Development Goals in South and Southeast Asia, Singapore, November.

—— (1979), 'Political Aspects of Poverty, Income Distribution and Their Measurement: Some Examples from Rural Java', *Development and Change*, 10: 91–114.

White, B. and Makali (1979), 'Wage Labour and Wage Relations in Javanese Agriculture: Some Preliminary Notes from the Agro-Economic Survey', mimeo., The Hague.

Widarti, D. (1984), 'Analisa Ketenagakerjaan di Indonesia Berdasarkan Data Sensus Penduduk Tahun 1971 dan 1980' (Labour Force Analysis in Indonesia

Based on Population Census Data for 1971 and 1980), in C. Manning and M. Papayungan (eds.), *Analisa Ketenagakerjaan di Indonesia Berdasarkan Sensus Penduduk 1971 dan 1980*, Biro Pusat Statistik, Jakarta.

Widjojo, N. (1970), *Population Trends in Indonesia*, Cornell University Press, New York.

Williams, G. and Satoto (1980), 'Sociopolitical Constraints on Primary Health Care: A Case Study from Indonesia', pp. 208–28 in D. Morley, J. Rohde and G. Williams (eds.), *Practising Health for All*, Oxford University Press, Oxford.

Withington, W. A. (1963), 'The Kotapradja or King Cities of Indonesia', *Pacific Viewpoint*, 4: 75–86.

———— (1973), 'Recent Growth, Change and Tradition in Sumatra's Major Urban Cities 1961–1971', *Sumatra Research Bulletin*, 3: 3–17.

Wittfogel, K. (1957), *Oriental Despotism: A Comparative Study of Total Power*, Yale University Press, New Haven.

Wolf, D. L. (1984), 'Making the Bread and Bringing it Home: Female Factory Workers and the Family Economy in Rural Java', in G. W. Jones (ed.), *Women in the Urban and Industrial Workforce: Southeast and East Asia*, Monograph No. 33, Development Studies Centre, Australian National University, Canberra.

Wood, C. H. (1982), 'Equilibrium and Historical–Structural Perspectives on Migration', *International Migration Review*, 16, 2: 298–319.

World Bank (1980), *Indonesia: Employment and Income Distribution in Indonesia*, World Bank, Washington, DC.

———— (1983), *World Development Report 1983*, Oxford University Press, Washington.

———— (1984a), *World Development Report 1984*, Oxford University Press, New York.

———— (1984b), 'Economic and Social Development: An Overview of Regional Differentials and Related Processes', main report from *Indonesia: Selected Aspects of Spatial Development*, Report No. 4776–IND, Country Programs Department, East Asia and Pacific Regional Office, World Bank.

———— (1984c), *Indonesia: Policies and Prospects for Economic Growth and Transformation*, Report No. 5066–IND, World Bank, Washington, DC.

———— (1984d), *Indonesia: Selected Aspects of Spatial Development; Annex 2, Demographic Patterns and Population Projections*, World Bank, Washington, DC.

———— (1985), *Indonesia: Policies for Growth and Employment*, Report No. 5597–IND, World Bank, Washington, DC.

Yeh, S. and You, P. S. (1971), 'Labour Force Supply in Southeast Asia', *Malayan Economic Review*, 16, 2: 25–54.

Yunus, D. (1979), '"Pagaden" Suplaier Terbesar Kebutuhan Kota' (Pagaden: Major Supplier of Urban Needs), *Pedoman Rakhyat*, 33, 30: 1–2.

Zarkasi (1979), 'Population Mobility in Central Java', paper presented at Workshop on Population Mobility, Pusat Penelitian dan Studi Kependudukan (Centre for Population Research and Study), Gadjah Mada University, Yogyakarta, May.

Zelinsky, W. (1971), 'The Hypothesis of the Mobility Transition', *Geographical Review*, 41, 2: 219–49.

Index

ABORTION, *see* Fertility control
Abstinence, *see* Fertility control
Accidents, 121, 134, 342
Aceh, 36, 38, 49; and agriculture, 74, 354; economy, 69, 348; education, 62–7; fertility, 145–7, 152–6, 376, 378; health, 73–4; labour force, 247, 338; marriage, 161; migration, 177, 188–91, 193; mortality, 125; population density, 30, 42; population growth, 42, 48, 327–30; religious rebellion, 239; socio-economic, 80; urban/rural, 94
Acehnese, 184, 224, 230
Activity rate (labour force), 245–61; and changes in, 247–61; crude, 245–8; effect of Islam, 252; female, 246–8, 250–61; international comparisons, 245–7, 250, 294n; male, 245–8, 250–2; regional differences, 245–6; rural, 253, 255, 257, 259–60; standardized, 245–8, 250–6; urban, 246–7, 253, 255, 257, 258–60; youth, 249–50
Ad Hoc Committee on Family Planning, 140–1
Adat, 18
Administrative regions, 366
Africa: fertility, 139; population movement, 224–6
Age–sex: index, 246; distribution, 2
Age structure, 2–4, 9, 11, 33, 159, 245, 321; projections, 335–6
Agriculture, 73–5, 80–1, 138; Agricultural Census, 1973 and 1983, 57, 267–9, 367; agricultural colonization, 166, 170, 172 (*see also* Transmigration); 'agricultural involution', 28, 35–6, 194, 228, 236, 335, 348; capitalization, 227; development, 109, 214, 311, 318, 364–5; extension, 359; intensification, 53, 59, 73, 194, 351, 358–9; mechanization, 59, 228, 348, 354, 358, 363; modernization, 227, 304, 334, 349; policy, 226 (*see also* Labour force)

Agung, Sultan, 30
Ambon, Ambonese, 103, 224–5; education, 60–3
Arabs, 18, 20
Army, 201, 299; garrisons, 226
ASEAN Population Programme, 315
Asia, fertility, 139, 364
Australia, 111, 348; activity rates, 246–7; internal migration, 166

BABY-WEIGHING, 112–13, 122, 143, 341
Bahasa Indonesia, 20, 21, 104
Bali, 17, 20, 36, 38; agriculture, 28, 73, 75, 80–2; economy, 70; education, 62–7; fertility, 140–56, 306, 377–8; health, 75, 127; labour force, 247, 294n, 338, 360; marriage, 161–2; migration, 14, 20, 166, 168, 177, 179, 189–91, 193–6, 214, 362, 365n; mortality, 124–5, 129, 131, 375; population density, 11, 29, 30, 43, 139, 355; population growth, 31, 43–4, 179, 327–31; socio-economic, 8, 80; urban/rural, 92–4, 294n, 355
Balikpapan, 100, 103
Balinese, 20, 21, 191, 196
Balita, 122
Bandung: evacuation, 238; growth, 52, 53, 57, 100–1, 355, labour force, 242, 291; literacy, 62; manufacturing, 143, 351; mobility, 167–8, 197–200, 203, 211, 242; mortality, 373; size, 88, 98, 333
Bangka, 63
Bangkok, 97
Bangladesh, 111, 364; labour force, 252; population–development analysis, 315
Bangsawan, 62
Banjar, Banjarese, 21–2, 100, 197, 224–5, 230
Banjarmasin, 52, 103
Banjarnegara Regency, 112–13
Banten, 48–9, 55, 61
Banyumas, 63

'adjusted', 261–8; age structure, 245, 249–51, 253–4, 257–8, 260, 271, 286–9, 290, 292; agricultural, 7, 9, 10, 49, 57, 80–2, 261–4, 265–72, 277–9, 283–5, 290, 295n, 297n, 334, 346, 349; by industry, 275; child, 245; colonial schemes, 35, 49; in construction, 261–4, 284–5, 290, 295n, 334, 350; contract, 173, 189, 203 (*see also* Coolies); crude activity rate, 245–8; data sources, 244–5, 261, 367–72; definitions, 246–50, 252, 259, 261, 265–7, 269, 277, 294n, 296n, 336, 367–8, 371–2; educational attainment, *see* Education; female, 245–8, 250–61, 266, 273–4, 276–9, 281–3, 288, 290–2, 294n, 295n, 297n, 306, 311, 336–7, 349, 363; forced labour, 171; formal sector, 201, 222–3, 228, 337, 339; Gn/Gy ratio, 293, 297n; growth, 7, 244, 261, 293, 296n, 298, 321, 336–9, 345–8, 360, 363; industrial distribution, 80–1, 82, 261; informal sector, 203, 221, 222–3, 229, 233, 245, 277, 289, 293, 311, 346, 365n; male, 244–8, 250–2, 266, 273–4, 276–9, 281–3, 288–92, 294n, 295n; in manufacturing, 84, 261–4, 272–9, 295n, 350; in mining, 261–4, 284, 295n, 297n; non-agricultural, 39, 57–9, 194, 227, 292, 297n, 334, 346–7, 350, 358–60, 365n; multiple job-holding, 291–2, 297n; participation rate, *see* Activity rate; part-time, 245, 250; productivity, 275–8, 280, 286, 293, 333–5, 346, 349, 358; projections, 336–9; in public utilities, 284–5; reference period used in measuring, 247, 252, 261, 268–9, 336, 367–8, 371–2; regional differences, 309, 317; rural, 252–3, 255, 273–4, 276–9, 281–6, 291–2, 294n, 295n, 310, 333–4, 365n; seasonality, 203, 245, 250, 266–72, 349; size, 244, 261–6; structure, 244, 362; survey, 1958, 167, 251, 292; Survey of Jakarta, 1980, 286; in trade, finance and services, 221, 261–4, 277–81, 283, 284–5, 289–90, 334, 346, 350, 365n; in transport, 262–4, 284–5, 289–90, 350; trends in employment, 248–9; unpaid family workers, 265, 267–70, 272–6, 289–90; urban, 204, 206, 253, 255, 273–4, 276–9, 281–6, 288–9, 291, 294n, 297n, 310, 333–4, 350, 363
Labour relations, 310–11
Ladang farmers, 35
Lampung, Lampungese: agriculture, 28, 74, 80; economy, 69, 71; education, 62, 64–7; fertility, 145–7, 153–6, 376, 378; health, 74; labour force, 247, 338–9; marriage,

161; migration, 44, 80, 173, 174, 177, 184–6, 188–90, 193–4, 214–15, 219, 353; mortality, 125, 128; population density, 42; population growth, 42, 44, 327–32; socio-economic, 80, 354; urban/rural, 94
Land: cultivated, 36; rent, 36; servicing, 356; tenure, 9, 10, 36; use, 304, 353
Landlessness, 9, 10, 58–9, 334, 348, 359, 365n
Language: linguistic differences, 5, 18, 21, 104, 106; national, 104, 106
Leknas, 315, 367; surveys, 168, 200–1
Lesser Sundas, 31
Lhokseumawe, 189
Life expectancy, 3, 115–16, 119, 122, 124, 126, 134–5, 303, 341, 348, 364n, 373–5
Literacy, 7, 9, 60–3, 128 (*see also* Education)
LKBN, 141, 313
Lombok, 17, 20, 28; migration, 166, 362, 365n; population growth, 331; socio-economic, 138
Lurah, 366

MADAM, 197
Madiun, 101
Madrasah, 62
Madura, 30, 56–7, 63, 129, 167, 174, 196
Madurese, 20, 21, 35, 196, 224, 340
Magelang, 101
Majalaya, 351
Majalengka, 100
Majapahit Kingdom, 29
Makassar, 48, 49, 52, 53, (*see also* Ujung Pandang)
Makassarese, 22, 61, 197, 224, 259
Makian, 237
Malang, 52, 53, 57–8, 100–1, 333
Malays, 22, 224
Malaysia, 138; Economic Planning Unit, 300; FELDA schemes, 354; fertility control, 144; fertility decline, 343; GDP, 71; infant mortality rate, 120, 341; labour force, 252, 272, 276, 283; labour migration to, 173–4, 197; population density, 39
Malik, Adam, 302
Maluku, 61; agriculture, 75; economy, 70; education, 60, 63–7; fertility, 144–7, 153–5, 377–8; health, 75; labour force, 247, 296n, 338; loyalty to Dutch, 239; marriage, 161; migration, 178, 184, 188–90, 193, 197, 237; mortality, 125; population density, 11, 42; population growth, 15, 42, 327–30; socio-economic, 8; urban/rural, 92–4

density, 43, 44; population growth, 43, 44, 327–30; rebellion, 238; urban/rural, 94, 294n

North Sumatra, 14, 299; agriculture, 36, 74; Bataks, 22, 61; economy, 69; education, 60, 63–7; fertility, 145–7, 153–6, 376, 378; health, 73–4; labour force, 174, 247, 259, 295n, 338; marriage, 161, 172; migration, 177, 184, 187–91, 193; mortality, 125, 127; population density, 42, 44; population growth, 42, 44, 327–30; urban/rural, 94, 259, 295n

NUDSP, 312, 322, 324–7, 332–9, 354–7

Nunukan, 174

Nusa Tenggara, 14, 17, 62; economy, 70–3, 75, 81; education, 64–7; fertility, 377–8; labour force, 96, 338, 360; marriage, 161; mortality, 125; population density, 42, 44; population growth, 42, 44, 327–30; socio-economic, 8, 77, 348; urban/rural, 92–4, 103; (see also East Nusa Tenggara; West Nusa Tenggara)

Nutrition, 7, 32, 136, 143, 153–5, 158, 304, 307–9, 315; anaemia, 309; breastfeeding, 36, 127, 307; cadres, see Kader gizi; deficiencies, 36, 109, 119, 121, 123, 127; education, 112–13, 142, 306–7, 309; goitre, 308–9; of infants and children, 306–7, 341; protein calorie malnutrition, 308; UPGK, 308; Vitamin A deficiency, 308–9 (see also PKMD; Promotor kesehatan)

OCCUPATION, see Labour force

Oil, 6, 26, 46, 71, 73, 127, 185, 188, 203, 334, 350

Oral contraceptives, see Fertility control

Oral rehydration, 341

'Orang Betawi', 259

Outer Islands or 'other islands', 21–3; agriculture, 36, 38; education, 64–7; fertility, 15, 142–3, 360; labour force, 247, 253–4, 261, 273, 285, 369–70; migration, 15, 20, 39, 177–9, 185–6, 188–9, 194–9, 203, 226, 237, 317, 352; mortality, 38; population density, 11, 304, 360; population growth, 15, 31, 36, 38, 39

PADANG, 102, 198, 201

Padat Karya, 311

Pagak, 58

Pahang, 174

Pakistan: activity rate, 246–7, 252, 295n; population growth, 364

Palawidja, 41, 349, 365n

Palembang, Palembangese, 30, 52, 62, 102, 168, 224, 333, 367

Pancasila, 301, 305

Papua New Guinea, Papuans, 22, 172

Pasang surut, 60

Pasisir, 61

Pasuruan, 102

Pax Neerlandica, 32, 34

Pekalongan, 52, 56

Pekanbaru, 100, 102

Pematang Siantar, 102

'Penghijauan' programme, 59

Permesta Rebellion, 238

Pesantren, 62

Philippines: agriculture, 41; fertility decline, 343; GDP, 71; labour force, 252, 283, 297n; migration to Middle East, 172; mortality, 120, 122; National Economic and Development Authority, 300; population–development analysis, 315

Pill, see Oral contraception

Pindah, 170

Piracy, 38

PKBI, 140, 164

PKMD, 112, 308

Plantations, 28, 46, 49, 84, 173, 203, 226

POLKAM, 300

Pollution, 135, 342

Polygamy, 30, 163

Pondok, 62

Pontianak, 100, 103, 200

Population: change, 4, 6, 11; decline, 29, 30; density, 11, 13–15, 17, 28, 43, 44, 47, 53–60; distribution, 2, 3, 11, 25, 46, 53–60, 317 (see also Migration); economically active, 245 (see also Labour force); growth, 2–4, 9, 15, 24, 28, 29, 32–6, 41–3, 101, 107–8, 136, 139, 201–2, 244, 295, 302–3, 305, 315, 317, 321–65; international comparisons, 331, 348; mobility 166–207, 316 (see also Migration); natural increase, 201–2; 'non-economically active', 249–50 (see also Labour force); policy, 2, 26, 298–320; pressure, 28, 57–8, 139, 171, 191, 194, 196, 236, 348, 357; quality, 315, 317; redistribution, 36, 39, 44, 206, 302–4, 309, 346; size, 3, 14, 28–34, 321, 326–31; urban/rural, 89 (see also Projections)

Population and the Environment, Ministry of (KLH), 144, 298, 315–20, 345, 365n

Population Council, 143

Population counts, 1815, 32–3

Population Policy Research Committee, 314, 319

Ports, 35, 100–4, 226, 309, 361

Portuguese, 61

Posyandu, 113

75; economy, 70; education, 61, 63–7; fertility, 144–7, 153–6, 377–8; health, 75; labour force, 246–7, 252, 255–6, 338, 360; marriage, 161; migration, 168, 174, 177, 184, 187–91, 193, 196–7, 199, 230, 360; mortality, 124–5, 128; population density, 29, 30, 43; population growth, 43–4, 327–31; religious rebellion, 239; urban/rural, 94, 100

South Sumatra, 20; agriculture, 60, 74; economy, 69; education, 62, 64–7; fertility, 145–7, 153–6, 376, 378; health, 74; labour force, 174, 247, 338; marriage, 161; migration, 60, 177, 184, 187–90, 193; mortality, 124–5; population density, 30, 42; population growth, 42, 327–32; urban/rural, 94

South-East Asia, 1, 28, 29, 97–9, 238–9, 252, 274, 315, 372

South-east Sulawesi: agriculture, 75; economy, 70–1; education, 64–7; fertility, 145–7, 152–5, 377–8; health, 75; labour force, 247, 259, 294n, 338; marriage, 161; migration, 178, 184, 188–90, 193; mortality, 124–5; population density, 43; population growth, 43, 44, 327–30; religious rebellion, 239; urban/rural, 94

Sragen, 55

Sri Lanka, mortality, 122

Sriwijaya Empire, 30

Standard of living, 304

Statistik Industri, 275–6

Sterilization, *see* Fertility control

Suharto, 25–6, 140–1, 299, 302

Sukabumi, 102, 167, 200

Sukubangsa, 169, 187, 223–4

Sulawesi, 17–22, 36; agriculture, 57, 73, 75; economy, 70–1, 81, 362; education, 62–7; fertility, 15, 149, 153–5, 377–8; labour force, 96, 247, 253–4, 258, 295n, 338; marriage, 160–1; migration, 167–8, 182–4, 187, 190, 193, 196–7; mortality, 15; population density, 11, 43; population growth, 15, 31, 43, 44, 327–31, 360; socio-economic, 8, 72–3, 75, 77–8, 80, 104–5; urban/rural, 92–4, 96, 100, 103, 247, 253–4 (*see also* Central Sulawesi; North Sulawesi; South Sulawesi; South-east Sulawesi)

Sumatra, 17–22; agriculture, 57, 73–4; coolies, 18, 20; economy, 69, 71, 73, 81; education, 63–7; fertility, 15, 149, 152–5, 376, 378; investment, 46, 71–2, 362; labour force, 84, 96, 247, 253–4, 338; marriage, 161–2; migration, 20, 60, 104–5, 168, 174, 177, 180, 182–4,

186–8, 190, 193, 196–7, 230, 353–4, 360; mortality, 15; population density, 11, 30, 36, 39, 42; population growth, 14, 15, 31, 60, 327–30, 331, 360; rebellion, 238; socio-economic, 8, 72–3, 75, 77, 104–5; urban/rural, 88, 92–4, 100, 102, 247, 253–4 (*see also* Aceh; Bengkulu; Jambi; Lampung; North Sumatra; Riau; South Sumatra; West Sumatra)

Sunda Kelapa, 49

Sundanese, 20, 21, 127, 186–7, 225, 252, 340

Supas, 120, 127, 129, 136, 149, 168, 245, 248–52, 265–71, 276, 280–3, 286–7, 290–1, 296n, 367

Surabaya, 30, 46, 48, 49, 50, 52, 53, 88, 98, 100–1, 169, 197–8, 199, 211, 218, 283, 291, 333

Surakarta, 49, 52, 62, 101, 112

Surat keterangan lalu lintas, 365n

Susenas, 7, 76, 119, 120, 149, 167, 199, 251, 291, 293, 358, 367

Swakarsa transmigrants, 179, 180

Swidden, 14, 30, 33, 36, (*see also* Shifting cultivation)

TAIWAN, 358

Tanggerang, 100, 186

Tanjung Karang, 102

Tanjung Pinang, 174

Tapanuli, education, 60–3

Tasikmalaya, 57, 100–1, 200

Tawau, 174

Tax, 36, 171

Team penertiban, 365n

Technology, 311

Tegal, 41

Tegal, 101

Television, 26, 204

Textiles, 351

Thailand, 97; activity rate, 246–7, 252; agriculture, 41; fertility control, 144; GDP, 71; labour force, 272, 294n; migration to Middle East, 172; mortality, 120, 122; National Economic and Social Development Board, 300; population density, 39; population–development analysis, 315; Thailand Development Research Institute, 315

Threshold hypothesis, 5

Timber, 46, 127, 188, 309, 353 (*see also* Forest products)

Time, allocation of, 245

Timorese, 22, 225

Tinggal landas, 301

Toba Batak, 31